R-4

PRESIDENTIAL POLITICS

PRESIDENTIAL POLITICS

Lyn Ragsdale
University of Arizona

Houghton Mifflin Company   Boston   Toronto

Dallas   Geneva, Illinois   Palo Alto   Princeton, New Jersey

To Jerry
Tir Na Nog

Sponsoring Editor: Margaret H. Seawell
Senior Development Editor: Lance Wickens
Project Editor: Christina M. Horn
Senior Production/Design Coordinator: Karen Rappaport
Senior Manufacturing Coordinator: Marie Barnes
Marketing Manager: Karen Natale

Cover photograph: View of the South Lawn and the Washington Monument from the Blue Room of the White House. The Image Bank/Melchior Degiac
Cover design: Perennial Design

Printed in the U.S.A.

Library of Congress Catalog Card Number: 91-72685

ISBN: 0-395-51554-8

123456789–AH–96 95 94 93 92

CONTENTS

PREFACE

I began writing this book in London. Although it may seem odd to write a book about the American presidency abroad, the location offered a fresh perspective on a familiar subject. The English know a good deal about the American presidency, but they do not view it with the cycles of elation and frustration that Americans do. I finished writing the book in Washington, D.C., while working for a member of the House of Representatives. Not possessing the objectivity of the English, many members of Congress have a raw fixation about the presidency—they know what they want from the White House, they know what they can get, and they know that the two are rarely identical. These two perspectives lent appropriate balance to studying the politics of the presidency.

Presidential Politics explores how presidents use two central features of the modern presidency—the single executive image and the plural presidency—to influence political outcomes. The single executive image depicts the president as the one person in charge of the government, who solves national problems, upholds national values, and sets the direction of the country. This is a flamboyant image that makes the president the single most powerful, visible, unique, and important official in the nation. The plural presidency is the large, diverse, decentralized institution of offices and people that carries out the president's work. This plural institution exists so presidents may try to live up to the responsibilities created by the single executive image. Presidents rely on the image and the institution to outline policy initiatives, put together political deals, and persuade the public that presidential efforts are the right efforts. Presidents' use of the image and the institution is the essence of presidential politics. This book, intended as a core text for the presidency course, analyzes that essence.

Presidential Politics is divided into four sections. Part I examines the single executive image and its foundation in presidents' interpretations of the Constitution, presidential election campaigns, public perceptions, and media attention. In this part, an analysis of the historical development of the presidency since Washington clarifies how the single executive image emerged. Parts II and III analyze the plural presidency. Part II focuses on the way decisions are made in the White House—how a decentralized organization makes numerous decisions for presidents without necessarily full-fledged presidential involvement and how ambiguous goals, methods, and participants beset presidential decisions. Part III considers the substance of presidential decisions—the complexity of presidential policymaking and policies in foreign, economic, and domestic affairs. Part IV discusses how presidents use both the single executive image and the plural presidency to influence other institutions of government—Congress, the bureaucracy, and the courts. Although recent books on the presidency have tended to treat presidential relations with other institutions before considering presidential policymaking, I think it is important to study the decisions presidents make before analyzing how presidents attempt to sell those decisions to the other branches of government.

Throughout the book, case studies elicit the features of the single executive image and the plural presidency. These include the Truman administration's efforts in the Korean War, the Eisenhower and Johnson administrations' decisions in the Vietnam War, the Kennedy administration's actions during the coup against President Diem of South Vietnam, the Nixon administration's debacle in Watergate and its use of wage-price controls, the Carter administration's trade policy on shoes, the Reagan administration's Iran-contra imbroglio, the Bush administration's efforts in the Persian Gulf War and its environmental policies, and a comparison of the 1988 and 1992 presidential election campaigns. Lastly, the outcome of the 1992 presidential election is assessed.

Among the many books on the American presidency, none of them adopts the perspective of presidential politics. We know a great deal about presidential power, presidential leadership, presidents' personalities, and presidents' individual achievements and failures in office. We have not adequately examined the resources and constraints the office gives presidents to influence national politicians, organized interests, the public, and world leaders. The book is as much an extended thematic essay on the nature of presidential politics as it is a comprehensive text on the institution and workings of the office.

My thanks go to the people at Houghton Mifflin for their enthusiasm about the project and their respect for my view of the project. I appreciate Greg Tobin's original interest in the book and Margaret Seawell's continued commitment to it. Thanks, too, to Lance Wickens for his editorial acumen and political insights, to Christina Horn for her careful, well-organized, and timely production of the book, and to Patricia Herbst, whose copyediting skills invariably improved the prose. I am also grateful to

Theodore S. Arrington, University of North Carolina at Charlotte
Paul Brace, University of Illinois
John P. Burke, University of Vermont
Florence Heffron, University of Idaho

John R. Johannes, Marquette University
Kevin V. Mulcahy, Louisiana State University
David L. Paletz, Duke University
Joseph A. Pika, University of Delaware
William D. Richardson, Georgia State University
Richard K. Scher, University of Florida
L. Earl Shaw, Northern Arizona University

whose painstaking critiques of the book helped the final draft immeasurably. I also would like to thank Sue Bate, Julie Bridwell, Adnan Hayajneh, Gwen Torges, and Richard Witmer for help in gathering data for the book. Finally, and most especially, I wish to thank my husband, Jerry Rusk, who quietly kept asking, "When's the book going to be done?" I dedicate the book to him for his encouragement and understanding, and at last I can say "It's done."

Lyn Ragsdale

PRESIDENTIAL
POLITICS

CHAPTER 1

Image and Institution

T his look at presidential politics begins with the description of a photograph that hangs on a wall among several hundred photographs in Henry Ford's museum, Greenfield Village, in Dearborn, Michigan. Taken in the summer of 1921, the picture shows four men standing together on a rolling lawn—Henry Ford, Thomas Edison, Harvey Firestone, and Warren Harding. All are dressed in crisp white trousers, and three of them are wearing straw hats. If the photo reflects its times in America, one may well ask which of the four men was viewed as most important, most powerful, most visible, and most revered. Ford had changed American life with the assembly line production of affordable automobiles. His good friend Edison had invented a long-burning electric light bulb. Firestone had pioneered research on the production of rubber and was a leading manufacturer of tires. Warren Harding was then president of the United States.

THE SINGLE EXECUTIVE IMAGE

The question might give a casual observer pause. But students of the presidency who understand the prominence of chief executives as central political actors and legendary figures in American life would focus immediately on Harding. This prominence is part of a *single executive image* of the American presidency. The single executive image portrays the president, speaking with a clear lone voice, as the one person in charge of the government. In this view, the president is the nation's principal problem solver, who identifies the nation's most pressing issues and offers solutions. In times of crisis, the president single-handedly protects the nation. As the only person elected by the entire country, the president is the representative of the people. The single executive image involves four components: importance, power, visibility, and uniqueness. It typecasts presidents as the single most important, powerful, visible, and unique figures in American politics.

The idea is simple. The single executive image reflects people's tendency to focus on the president as an individual. This personalizes the office of the presidency by embodying all its units, staff, and decisions in one person—the president. In the mind's eye of the nation, the president is the person who matters most in the political life of the country. American politics is presidential politics. American government is presidential government. People's impressions of American politics are likely to be the day Kennedy was shot, the day Nixon resigned, the day after day that Carter could not free the hostages in Iran. This does not mean that they forget about the rest of the government: Congress gives the president a hard time; the Supreme Court tells both what to do; the bureaucracy does whatever it wants. There *are* limits to the single executive image. Yet people often simplify their views of both the presidency and American politics by focusing on the exploits of one man.

Images are simplifications. An image is one's mental picture of an object, a product, a situation, or, in this case, a political office. The image usually magnifies certain features, while glossing over other relevant details. The single executive image highlights the president and overshadows both the institution of the presidency and the political environment that surrounds it. The image suits most Americans, who do not want to spend time worrying about what the Office of Management and Budget, the National Security Council, the Office of Special Trade Representative, and other major offices in the presidency do on a given day. They pay little attention to how these offices act and react to the prospects for industrial production, to Pakistan's plans for nuclear weapons, to Colombian coffee prices, or to anything else. Instead, they concentrate on the more colorful and entertaining adventures of the president himself, as he asks Congress to declare war, flies to Moscow for a summit, or takes the afternoon off to play golf.

To get a better sense of the single executive image, consider its four elements of importance, power, visibility, and uniqueness with the following questions. First, "Who is the most important person in the country today?" Most people reply almost by reflex: "the president." If asked their reasons, they point to the ways in which the president is at the center of government. Policy proposals to solve national problems, such as budget deficits, relations with Russia, and the soaring costs of health care, are often expected from 1600 Pennsylvania Avenue. Presidents represent the United States to other countries. They approve military strategies that lead to war and peace.

Second, "Who is the most powerful person in America today?" Again, most people are likely to answer rather emphatically: "the president." They indicate that the president, and no one else, can press "the button" to launch nuclear missiles and that he, and he alone, can order troops to any place in the world. Although Congress as a body has considerable power to challenge what a president wants done, no one member of Congress has the authority the president has to make such global decisions on behalf of the country.

Third, "What are the names of the following people: the member of Congress from your district, the chief justice of the United States, the attorney general of your state, and the president of the United States?" Most Americans instantly know who the last person is but have some difficulty coming up with the names of the others. There is little doubt that the president is the most widely known—the most highly visible—person in the country. The media of newspapers, magazines, and especially television cover the president more than they cover any other politician. Every public move the president makes is captured on videotape in case he is involved in something amusing, embarrassing, or tragic. In a poll conducted by the University of Michigan before the 1988 election, people were asked to name the president and 98 percent correctly named Ronald Reagan.

Finally, consider the unique position the president holds. "Which of these two statements comes closer to your view? (1) In general, the job of the president is not much more difficult than the job of the president of a large corporation such as Ford or General Motors. (2) The president has perhaps the most difficult job in the country." The second statement matches many Americans' views of the presidency.[1] There is a perception that presidents endure the toughest, loneliest, most wearisome job in the world. Even the labors of Henry Ford III, the current president of Ford Motor Company, or Lee Iacocca, the head of Chrysler Corporation, do not quite measure up.

People talk in superlatives about presidents. Truman's motto "The Buck Stops Here," engraved on a plaque that adorned his Oval Office desk, sums up this uniqueness. Presidents are expected to make the really difficult decisions of the nation and accept the responsibility for what happens. If the job is tough, it also inspires. People often say that the president is the only person elected by all the people, that he is the representative of no one group but of everyone. Americans are often awed by presidents; they make them larger than life. They are captivated by presidents' personal lives and are also quite willing to judge their foibles. One last question summarizes this uniqueness: "What other politician, movie star, sports figure, or rock singer do most Americans treat quite in this way?"

Reconsidering the photograph at Greenfield Village, even though Harding is often thought of as a lackluster president, we see that importance, power, visibility, and uniqueness nevertheless surrounded him in 1921. The answers to the questions back then would have been no different from the answers now. Not even Ford, Edison, or Firestone generated the exceptional fascination associated with American presidents. One of the ironies of the single executive image is that even weak and ineffective presidents are considered important, powerful, visible, and unique.

The single executive, while an image, is a very real element of the presidency. It is one of presidents' chief political assets. In the political world of an independent legislature, an unmanageable bureaucracy, and unpredictable foreign governments, the image provides presidents with one of their few opportunities to assert their goals unilaterally. By carefully conveying the image, presidents may be able to convince Congress, the press, and the public that presidential priorities are national priorities. Although the single executive image offers presidents advantages in games of political influence, it also poses difficulties for them. The image prompts people to expect more and more of presidents. The more control presidents assert, the more control the public and politicians expect presidents to have; and when they do not live up to the image and appear to lack control, their political standing suffers. Thus, the single executive image is both a resource and a constraint for presidential action.

THE PLURAL PRESIDENCY

The story of the Iran-contra affair, described later in this chapter, illustrates a different aspect of the presidency: the *plural presidency*, an institution in which the president is but one player among many. The plural presidency flips the single executive image on its head. Rather than viewing the presidency and the government through the deeds of one person, the plural presidency confines the president within the institution of the presidency.

An institution is an organization of people established to carry out some set of official functions. There are many such entities in modern society, including schools, churches, corporations, police departments, labor unions, government offices, legislatures, and courts. A peculiar characteristic of an institution is that it acts independently of the people within it. An institution establishes regular patterns of behavior for members to follow.[2] Typically, an institution is arranged according to a division of labor. Within the institution, offices are set up in which people specialize in one task and know little about the rest. The institution also establishes standard operating procedures—rules according to which things are done. People within the institution follow these pre-established routines, which endure as members come and go. People behave in these ways when they are within the institution even though they might not be so inclined when they are outside it. People can modify institutions, but often an institution's capacity to change people surpasses people's ability to change the organization.

The modern presidency is an institution. It is an organization of people who carry out an array of policy, public, and political functions for which the president has acquired responsibility. The White House institution—the plural presidency—is no small family business. It is a complex organization of forty-two separate offices and over sixteen hundred people. It operates with a division of labor. Offices within the White House institution specialize in foreign, domestic, military, and economic policy, press relations, public appearances, congressional affairs, and group interests. Over the years, the institution has developed standard operating procedures to develop budgets, legislation, and vetoes, to name only a few. These procedures continue with only modest changes from president to president. In fact, many presidential decisions are made with little personal involvement by the president. The White House institution issues decisions in the president's name, but the president may know little, if anything, about many of them. The institution enjoys a life of its own.

Nonetheless, the White House institution, like the single executive image, offers presidents a valuable resource. Presidents recognize that they cannot (nor do they want to) do all the work alone or even with the aid of a group of close advisers. Presidents employ the institution to develop their policy proposals; devise appropriate strategies to see the proposals through Congress, the executive branch, and the courts; plan public relations efforts; fight wars and negotiate with foreign countries; and meet the demands of the press, organized interests, and state and city politicians. Yet the plural presidency, like the single executive image, limits presidents. Presidents have difficulty gaining firm control over the activities of the institution's many offices and people. As political scientist Alfred de Grazia wrote, "The President is a Congress with a skin thrown over him. . . . [He] operates under all the fictions of a single person . . . , [but this] defies the truth of the normalcy of the typical President and *the collectivity of his behavior.*"[3] The plural presidency too is both a resource and a constraint for presidential action.

The White House institution is *not* the executive branch of government, also known as the bureaucracy. Although it is commonplace to talk of the president as the head of the executive branch, this designation is inaccurate. Except at the very highest levels, the president has little, if any, say over the more than 3 million people who work in executive departments and agencies. The president may talk regularly with the secretary of state, but the chief executive is not the head of the State Department. The State Department, Treasury Department, Commerce Department, Federal Communications Commission, and the National Aeronautics and Space Administration, as examples, are institutions in their own right and are not run by the White House.

There are four dimensions to the presidency as an institution: (1) decentralized organization, (2) ambiguous decision making, (3) policy complexity, and (4) political fragmentation. Their interplay creates the plural presidency—a conglomerate of semi-feudal, loosely allied offices, with considerable independence from each other. The plural presidency is not a coherent, smoothly run operation. Many hands go off in many directions to take care of everything. Rather than one presidency, there are several presidencies, often distinct from one another. Thus, presidential behavior can be understood less as the deliberate choices of the president and his top advisers and more as the outputs of a large, complex organization.

Decentralized Organization

The presidency is a large *decentralized organization* that houses a variety of specialized offices that are relatively autonomous. Decentralization is evident in the proliferation of units, the roughly equal status of many of the units, and the ability of the various units to direct presidential decisions. Specialization in the White House affects policy matters, political interests, and daily tasks.

First, offices in the White House focus on specific policies: for example, the Office of Policy Development (domestic policy), the National Security Council (foreign and defense policy), the Council of Economic Advisers (economic policy), and the Office of Special Trade Representative (trade). Second, specific units entertain the demands of various public and political interests and court their support: the White House Press Office (the press), the Public Liaison Office (organized groups), the Office of Intergovernmental Relations (local and state officials), and the Office of Legislative Affairs (members of Congress). Finally, still other offices are task specialists that run the daily operation of the White House. The Office of Administration keeps track of White House job openings and finds candidates to fill them. The Office of Management and Budget reviews legislative proposals from the executive branch, makes recommendations to the president on whether to sign or veto legislation passed by Congress, develops the presidential budget, and evaluates executive branch regulations.

Ambiguous Decision Making

Because of the size and complexity of institutions such as the presidency, decision making often is difficult. *Institutional ambiguity* characterizes decision making: decision makers often are unclear about what is going on, what they want, how they will attain it, and who will be involved, *yet they make decisions nonetheless*. White House officials lack complete information about unfolding events and the actions of other politicians. They are often hazy about what problems to tackle and how to tackle them. They also are unclear about the full operation of the presidency. For example, in late December 1990, a lone attorney in the Education Department announced a policy against minority scholarships, reportedly without the approval of anyone at the White House. Public cries of racism taunted several White House offices, which openly disagreed with each other about whether the policy was appropriate. Bush officials then spent several days feverishly backing away from the position. The large, decentralized organization of the presidency exacerbates the ambiguity. Many right hands often do not know what many left hands are doing. Nonetheless, thousands of decisions are made and policies announced amid this ambiguity.

Policy Complexity

One function of the presidency is to make policy proposals and policies in a dizzying array of issue areas. *Policy complexity* refers to the sheer numbers of policies the presidency develops and to the inconsistencies and overlaps that arise among them. The institution has expanded to take positions and make decisions in *all* major issue areas and most minor ones. The institution acts on agriculture, foreign aid, health care, defense, the budget, drugs, business regulations, safety, social security, nuclear power, natural resources, clean air, and civil rights. It also takes positions on commemorative stamps, the length of government reports, and the shape of the national Christmas tree. Although the lists may look long, they catalog only a few of the policy areas in which the presidency is involved today.

The policy arenas in which the presidency operates are often incompatible, and the policy proposals that emerge may be inconsistent. The Reagan administration quickly encountered this problem when it simultaneously advocated a luxurious defense build-up and a thrifty balanced budget. The two policies were contradictory, and the result was not a balanced budget but the largest budget deficit in American history. Policy inconsistency may be acute even within a single policy area. In 1969, the newly inaugurated Nixon administration publicly pledged a policy to withdraw American troops from Vietnam, yet felt compelled to conduct American bombing missions over Cambodia, thus enlarging the theater of war. Fearing that a public outcry would ensue if the Cambodian mission were disclosed, the administration initially tried to cope with the incongruity between getting out and appearing to get in deeper by conducting the Cambodian missions in secrecy.

Perhaps the most fundamental result of policy complexity is that the president as an individual finds it difficult to keep up with what is going on. President Kennedy ordered the removal of U.S. missiles from bases in Turkey three times. During the Cuban missile crisis, in October 1962, the Soviets informed him that the missiles were still there. Because there are so many different, potentially conflicting policy areas for the presidency, presidents themselves have limited ability to supervise directly the decisions of the institution. Political scientist Graham Allison writes, "The overriding fact about large organizations is that their size prevents any single central authority from making all important decisions or directing all important activities."[4]

Political Fragmentation

The American political system is renowned for its divisions of power across several branches of government and for the pressure exerted on these branches by organized groups, corporations, and attentive individuals. The result of the divisions and pressure is known as *political fragmentation*. The presidency must take into account the wide range of political interests (or fragments) represented by organized groups and by other government institutions. The political fragmentation arises in two forms: group fragmentation and government fragmentation.

Group fragmentation involves the attention the White House pays to a plethora of social, economic, and political groups and the conflicts among them. The institution works to meet the demands of large corporations, small businesses, workers, consumers, farmers, the media, conservationists, the poor, the homeless, the elderly, gun owners, gunshot victims, health care providers, the handicapped, civil rights advocates, abortion opponents, abortion supporters, students, teachers, immigrants, and others. Efforts to deal with group fragmentation are made by the Office of Public Liaison, which handles the policy requests of organized group interests. Group fragmentation also affects the president's public appearances, legislative proposals, and presidential appointments.

The Bush administration faced clashes among multiple interests over the Civil Rights Act of 1990, which the Congress passed and Bush vetoed. Civil rights organizations, such as the National Association for the Advancement of Colored People (NAACP), the Urban League, and the Rainbow Coalition, as well as labor unions, American clergy, and many governors, lined up in favor of the legislation. Conservative groups, some large corporations, and many small businesses opposed it as a perceived step toward quotas in the workplace.

The constitutional scheme of separation of powers and checks and balances creates government fragmentation. Each branch is responsible for a separate set of functions, even though its power may be checked by another branch. Because of government fragmentation, the institutions of the government may proceed independently of each other. Sometimes the White House has little, if any, say in a policy decision. For example, in 1977 the Food and Drug Administration (FDA) proposed to ban saccharin, an artificial sweetener, after a study showed that high doses of the substance led to cancer in laboratory rats. The Calorie Control Council, an organization representing the diet food and soft drink industries, fought the proposed ban with a huge advertising campaign directed at Congress. Congress eventually capitulated to the diet industries and wrote legislation postponing the ban and requiring warning labels instead. Although President Carter signed the bill, the battle among the FDA, Congress, and the industry took place as though the Carter administration did not exist.

Sometimes, fragmented politics allows the presidency to act independently of other institutions. When the Bush administration ordered the U.S. invasion of Panama in December 1989, it did so without seeking congressional approval. Fragmentation also may lead to situations in which the jurisdictions of several institutions overlap, prompting one to be at odds with another. In May 1975, without consulting members of Congress, President Ford ordered marines to rescue the U.S. merchant ship *Mayaguez* captured by Cambodia. Congress protested that it had not been informed under the War Powers Resolution of 1973, which expressly directs presidents to announce to Congress when they have engaged troops in hostilities. Ford retorted that Congress was encroaching "greatly on the capability of the president to carry out his functions as the chief of the Executive Branch."[5] Fragmentation pits the presidential powers of commander in chief and chief executive against the congressional powers to declare war and appropriate funds for the armed forces. One task of the plural presidency is to try to win such tugs of war.

The story below of the Iran-contra affair provides an example of how the plural presidency operates. During 1985 and 1986, the Reagan administration conducted two secret policies. The first was to fund a guerrilla resistance movement in Nicaragua. Known as the contras, the guerrillas were attempting to overthrow Nicaragua's Marxist government. The second policy was to sell arms to Iran in exchange for Iran's help in securing the release of hostages held by Middle Eastern terrorists. The two policies were linked when profits from the Iranian arms sales were diverted to the contras. Consider what happened to the importance, power, uniqueness, and even the visibility of the president in this episode. Instead, elements of complexity, fragmentation, decentralization, and ambiguity emerged. Within the plural presidency, the president often looks smaller than life.

WANT TO KNOW A SECRET?

Dressed in camouflage fatigues with swirls of olive, brown, and black, three men with dirt-smudged faces stood watch on a rise that dropped off into a deep gorge. Each hugged a new Polish-made AK-

47 automatic rifle and occasionally swung at the mosquitoes lurking in the darkness. The insects' buzzing was the only sound that broke the night's silence. The guns had arrived at the men's camp the previous afternoon. The camp was too remote for cargo planes and even if landing had been possible, the available planes were likely to be broken and lacking parts. Instead, a mule train traveling across bone-jarring muddy roads that snaked up steep ridges deep in the Nicaraguan jungle had taken nearly three weeks to bring in the goods.

Some nine hundred miles to the northeast, two businessmen awaited the arrival of a third in the lobby of the Miami Airport Hilton on the hot night of June 28, 1985. One man in his mid-fifties had closely cropped silver hair and wore an expensive, hand-tailored tan suit. He was Adolfo Calero, one of the leaders of the contras camped in the rugged southern part of Nicaragua. The other man, more plainly dressed and slightly heavier than his associate, was retired U.S. Air Force Major General Richard Secord—well known to William Casey, director of the Central Intelligence Agency (CIA), and Oliver North, a member of the National Security Council (NSC) staff, for his experience in covert air operations inside enemy lines. At Casey's request, North had asked Secord to buy guns for the contras. It was nearly 10 P.M. when Oliver North arrived at the Miami Hilton from Washington.

North sat down and in his staccato bass voice announced: "Gentlemen, we've got a problem." The forty-two-year-old marine lieutenant colonel worried that some of the $32 million he had helped transfer to the contra rebels under Calero was being wasted or pilfered.

The contras, or "freedom fighters" as President Reagan often referred to them, were attempting to overthrow the Cuban-backed Sandinista government of Nicaragua. But the U.S. Congress had refused to fund the contras and had passed the Boland Amendment to the 1982 Department of Defense Appropriations Act, expressly prohibiting the Central Intelligence Agency and the Defense Department from engaging in any efforts to overthrow the Nicaraguan government. So White House officials, including Casey, North, and North's immediate superior, National Security Adviser Robert "Bud" McFarlane, had devised a plan to get around what they saw as congressional meddling. They solicited private money from other nations and from wealthy conservative Americans to help the contras. The largest sums flowed in a cash pipeline set up in May 1984 from King Fahd of Saudi Arabia. The king gave the contras an allowance of $1 million a month. In exchange, President Reagan secretly sent the king four hundred brand-new Stinger missiles without congressional knowledge or approval.[6]

North was playing the president's game as North saw it and was taking charge of projects that brought him closer and closer to the president and Casey. North kept the money in the form of cash and traveler's checks in a small safe in his office on the third floor of the Executive Office Building. North often used (and then replaced) some of the cash earmarked for the contras to pick up groceries or the dry cleaning on his way home or buy leotards for his two daughters. He gave his secretary, Fawn Hall, spending money for the weekend. But, talking to Calero and Secord in Miami, he worried about what happened to the cash once it was in contra hands.[7]

Upon hearing that North wanted greater U.S. control of the funds, Calero stormed out of the meeting. North asked Secord to take over the contra supply system and administer the money. Several days later Secord agreed. On July 19, 1985, in Geneva, Secord's Swiss financial agent opened a Crédit Suisse bank account, number 386430-221, for a dummy company—Lake Resources—through which aid for the contras would be funneled as part of North's secret plan, dubbed "Project Democracy."[8]

The Iranian Shopping List

Project Democracy was not the only mission on which Oliver North worked. Less than one week after his meeting with Secord and Calero, Operation Recovery was set in motion. On July 3, 1985, Israeli Foreign Minister David Kimche talked to National Security Adviser Bud McFarlane about funneling arms through Israel to moderate elements in Iran to help free American hostages being held in Lebanon. The most glamorous items on the Iranian shopping list were five hundred TOW (tube-launched, optically tracked, wire-guided) anti-tank missiles, which Iran wanted to use in its debilitating war with Iraq. Kimche proposed that Israel deliver the American-made weapons from its own inventories to Iran, so long as the United States formally approved the transfer and agreed to replenish Israeli stock. McFarlane liked the idea.

In a meeting on August 6, 1985, McFarlane outlined the plan to President Reagan, Vice President George Bush, Secretary of Defense Caspar Weinberger, Secretary of State George Shultz, and General John Vessey, chairman of the Joint Chiefs of Staff. Weinberger and Shultz vociferously spoke out against the proposal, saying it violated the president's expressed policy of not dealing with terrorists. McFarlane undertook a vigorous rebuttal. Reagan expressed no approval or disapproval of the mission at the meeting. It was typical of Reagan, when his aides were in dispute, to postpone his own decision on a matter. McFarlane later contended that a day or so later Reagan called him at home from the presidential mountain retreat, Camp David, to give his approval. Yet Reagan was never at Camp David during the time McFarlane said the conversation took place and was not in the habit of calling his aides, especially at home.[9] In any case, there was no written approval of the mission from the president, at least not then.

With or without presidential approval, Israeli soldiers delivered the first planeload of 100 TOWs to Iran on August 20, 1985. The remaining 408 TOWs were delivered on September 14. Israel received two checks, one in August for $1 million and one in September for $4 million, drawn from an Iranian Swiss bank account, both of which were turned over to the United States. The day after the second TOW shipment, one hostage, Presbyterian minister Benjamin Weir, was released outside the eerie, charred remains of the U.S. Embassy in Teheran. It was the first, and by far the easiest, swap of arms for a hostage.

Winter Sales

In November 1985, Ronald Reagan and Soviet leader Mikhail Gorbachev met in Geneva, Switzerland, at their first summit. In the midst of the summit's hectic agenda, McFarlane informed Reagan and Chief of Staff Donald Regan that a third shipment of arms to Iran was scheduled for delivery even though the first two shipments had netted only one "live American," in McFarlane's words. McFarlane, preoccupied at the summit, left the conduct of the arms delivery to Oliver North, his chief aide. North asked the Israelis to again deliver Iran's purchases. The Israeli aircraft was scheduled to stop in Lisbon to refuel, but Portugal's new socialist government refused to grant landing clearance. Rather than abort the mission, North had the goods flown aboard an airplane from St. Lucia Airways, a small, little-known carrier operated by the Central Intelligence Agency. Richard Secord supplied the crew for the flight. North arranged to pay Secord $1 million for his several hours of work out of the original $5 million received from the Iranians for the first two arms shipments in September. A short distance from the site where the American president and the Soviet leader talked of world peace and strategic arms reductions, Secord had the money deposited into Crédit Suisse bank account number 386430-221.[10]

Secord had spent only $150,000 on the mission. Since the funds were already in the Lake Resources account, North and Secord decided to use the remaining $850,000 from the Iranian escapade to fund the contras in Nicaragua. Secord later laughed about this "contra-bution."[11] That was the first diversion of funds. The third Iranian arms shipment freed no hostages. Yet it was critically important because the personnel from Project Democracy became the personnel for Operation Recovery and the money from Operation Recovery became the money for Project Democracy.

The use of the CIA plane enraged its deputy director, John McMahon, and chief counsel, Stanley Sporkin. Using the plane directly violated the Hughes-Ryan Amendment, the principal law on CIA operations. The law required that the agency obtain a presidential determination, or "finding," before it engaged in covert operations without notifying Congress. The two long-time agents hastily wrote an after-the-fact finding to cover the CIA's involvement in the November 1985 mission. They delivered the single sheet of paper to Vice Admiral John Poindexter, who had just become the new national security adviser. Robert McFarlane, taunted by Chief of Staff Regan, had emotionally resigned his post. On November 26, 1985, Poindexter sent a copy of the finding to CIA Director William Casey, who said it "should go to the president for his signature." Reagan apparently did not sign this draft.[12]

North next proposed to Poindexter that the United States deal directly with Iran. The Israeli smoke screen would be disassembled, and the CIA would purchase and replace four thousand TOWs from Defense Department stock. Richard Secord would be the private delivery man. This plan required a new presidential finding that covered not only the Central Intelligence Agency but also "third parties"—namely Secord. On January 6, 1986, Reagan signed a rough draft of this second finding.[13] He signed without reading the final draft of the finding on Friday morning, January 17, 1986.[14] That evening Reagan wrote in this personal diary: "I agreed to sell TOWs to Iran."[15]

As Table 1.1 shows, during the eleven months between January and November 1986, arms sales to Iran continued. The Defense Department sold 2,008 TOWs and a variety of HAWK missile spare parts to the CIA, which, in turn, shipped them to Iran. The Israeli smoke screen was never fully dismantled. For three of the four shipments, Israel again made the deliveries, although, unlike the early shipments, the weapons came directly from American supplies. Two hostages were released during this period: Father Lawrence Jenco was freed on July 26 after the Americans threatened to cut off all arms shipments unless Iran secured the release of at least one prisoner. On November 2, two days before the American congressional elections, David Jacobson was spirited out of Lebanon. Meanwhile, extremists took three new hostages in September and October.

The United States sold the TOWs to the Iranians at a hefty profit. Over the little more than a year in which the arms deals went on, Iran paid some $50 million for the missiles and spare parts. Their actual cost was little more than $12 million. The middlemen, Secord and an associate, skimmed off $5–10 million, leaving around $30 million in sheer profit. North used those proceeds, as well as the private funds from King Fahd and conservative Americans, to buy equipment and ammunition for Project Democracy.[16] With help from the Iranian arms sale profits, during a three-month period Project Democracy delivered eighty tons of guns, ammunition, and other materials to the contras. Project Democracy owned an airstrip in Costa Rica, four new cargo planes, and a sea freighter to facilitate the deliveries.[17]

Table 1.1 Chronology of Events in the Iran-Contra Affair

May 5, 1984	King Fahd of Saudi Arabia agrees to fund the contras.
May 22, 1984	President Reagan agrees to send Fahd Stinger missiles.
June 28, 1985	North transfers control of contra money from contra leader Calero to Secord.
July 3, 1985	McFarlane and Israeli Foreign Minister Kimche discuss funneling arms through Israel to Iran to free American hostages in Lebanon.
July 19, 1985	Secord's Swiss bank account is set up to receive contra aid money.
August 6, 1985	McFarlane outlines arms-for-hostages idea to Reagan.
August 8, 1985	McFarlane claims Reagan gives approval to an arms shipment to Iran.
August 20, 1985	100 TOW missiles are shipped to Iran through Israel.
September 14, 1985	408 TOW missiles are shipped.
September 15, 1985	Hostage Benjamin Weir is released.
November 25, 1985	18 HAWK missiles are delivered to Iran aboard a CIA plane.
November, 22–25, 1985	$850,000 of Iran arms-sale money is diverted to contras.
December 5, 1985	Reagan signs an "after the fact" finding to cover the use of the CIA plane.
January 17, 1986	Reagan signs a second finding to sell TOWs directly to Iran without Israel as intermediary.
January–October, 1986	2,008 TOWs and HAWK missile spare parts are shipped to Iran; $30 million of Iran arms-sale money is diverted to contras.
July 26, 1986	Hostage Lawrence Jenco is released.
October 31, 1986	Lebanese newspaper breaks arms-for-hostages story.
November 2, 1986	Hostage David Jacobson is released.
November 25, 1986	Poindexter and North resign.
December 1, 1986	Reagan appoints Tower Commission.

Cowboys and Shoe Clerks

Within the Central Intelligence Agency, agents who desired unfettered covert operations were known as "cowboys," and those who were more cautious and worked within the guidelines set by Congress were called "shoe clerks."[18] Within the White House, cowboys and shoe clerks also feuded with one another. No one, not even the former cowboy actor Ronald Reagan, was as much of a cowboy as Oliver North. North, Casey, and Poindexter firmly supported the use of covert actions. They saw nothing wrong in running the contra military supply mission out of North's office and thus under the official auspices of the National Security Council. North argued that the NSC was not covered by the Boland Amendment, passed by Congress in December 1982 and made tougher in 1983 with new language that required that "no funds available to the Central Intelligence Agency, the Department of Defense, *or any other agency or entity of the United States involved in intelligence activities* may be . . . expended [to] support, directly or indirectly, military or paramilitary operations in Nicaragua."[19]

The shoe clerks irritated the cowboys. They were too cautious and, the cowboys felt, did not represent the president's true desires about either the hostages or the contras. Secretary of State Shultz, Defense Secretary Weinberger, and former National Security Adviser McFarlane, who continued to work on the operation from the outside, raised questions about the propriety of running the contra mission out of North's desk drawer. They felt the new words in the Boland Amendment were pretty clear and also doubted the propriety, if not the legality, of the Iranian mission. Shultz objected that the negotiations were straight arms-for-hostages deals that violated President Reagan's policy against dealing with terrorists. The State Department's legal adviser remarked that the shipments made by Israel on behalf of the United States before the presidential finding of January 17, 1986, were illegal. The diversion of funds to the contras had the most blatant problems of legality and constitutionality. Financing covert operations by selling government property at a profit directly usurped constitutional provisions for congressional control of appropriations. The cowboys decided that the easiest way to avoid the shoe clerks' complaints was simply not to tell them about the diversion. Although McFarlane knew, Shultz and possibly Weinberger were not told about the diversion of funds from the Iranian to the Nicaraguan operation.

Covering Tracks

An obscure Lebanese newspaper, not the shoe clerks, first exposed the Iran effort in October 1986. Official comment from the Iranian government followed. As the American press began to uncover more details of the Iranian mission, North shredded reams of documents about both the Iranian and the Nicaraguan assignments, including a ledger in which he had neatly recorded all the purchases and assets of Project Democracy. He tampered with other documents and destroyed computer files.[20] During the ensuing weeks, North, Poindexter, McFarlane, and Casey spent endless hours creating a chronology of the events that had taken place over the past year. In a fifteen-day period, from November 5 to November 20, 1986, they wrote and rewrote at least a dozen versions of the chronology; the later ones were called "Maximum Versions."[21]

To hide the initial U.S. involvement, McFarlane insisted that the chronology portray Israel as acting unilaterally in the first arms shipments to Iran in August and September 1985. Casey pressed to erase the CIA's involvement in the November 1985 mission (the one North had handled while McFarlane was at Geneva). Poindexter obliged:

he destroyed what he thought was the only copy of the December 1985 presidential finding that authorized the CIA to deliver arms (another copy was later found). With the finding gone, at least for the moment, the story could read as though the November effort had never occurred. The initial disclosures from the White House made no mention of the November venture. When the November shipment was uncovered, the story, with the ink barely dry, had to be rewritten. According to the new version, the November cargo was oil-drilling parts, not missiles.[22]

As for the contra diversion, North concocted the idea that Israel should again play the instigator. Israel refused to grant the favor, but the White House proceeded with the story anyway.[23] When Justice Department investigators spotted a memo that acknowledged American, not Israeli, involvement in the diversion, North told McFarlane, "I missed one," and the story had to be revised to include people in the Reagan administration.[24]

The word went out that Poindexter knew, but not too much. Casey told congressional investigators that McFarlane also knew. When it became clear from press reports that North also knew about the diversion, Poindexter and North resigned their posts. Federal grand juries indicted them on obstruction of justice and other charges. North was convicted on several minor charges. Robert McFarlane, after an unsuccessful suicide attempt, pleaded guilty to charges of withholding information from Congress. William Casey died of a brain tumor before his full role in the Iran-contra affair was ascertained. Ronald Reagan denied any knowledge of the diversion and also claimed ignorance of the first three arms shipments to Iran by way of Israel. Reagan dismissed Donald Regan as chief of staff. George Shultz and Caspar Weinberger remained in their posts, and the State Department gained control of a new Iran policy that ended the arms deals.[25] The shoe clerks finally won a small victory.

EXPLORING THE PLURAL PRESIDENCY

The madcap story of Iranian arms sales, American hostages, Israeli diplomacy with Islam, and Nicaraguan contra rebels highlights the four dimensions of the plural presidency. First, the Tower Commission, a panel appointed by President Reagan to investigate the series of policy blunders, expressed alarm about *policy complexity* in the White House. The commission concluded that the arms sales to Iran occurred because of inconsistencies and contradictions among three policies: the president's stated policy against terrorism, the administration's desire to develop more stable relations with Iran, and the actual arms-for-hostages deals. The result of these contradictions, the panel concluded, was that the Reagan policymakers never considered that selling arms could actually increase terrorism.

Second, the commission observed *political fragmentation*. The Reagan administration took advantage of government fragmentation to disregard congressional prohibitions. Yet, the commission concluded, this tactic harmed the very Nicaraguan interests the administration sought to help. According to the *Tower Commission Report*, "the appearance of the president's personal staff doing what Congress had forbade, once disclosed, only touched off a firestorm in Congress and threatened the Administration's whole policy on the Contras."[26]

Third, the *decentralized organization* of the presidency was in evidence. The commission commented that the National Security Council staff operated with virtual autonomy from other agencies of the government and from the president. The Central Intelligence Agency acted as a willing accomplice, but the NSC called the shots. As one of Chief of Staff Donald Regan's aides warned in a memorandum, the "NSC is out of control."[27] The decentralized organization of the presidency made it all very easy—too easy.

Finally, the episode involved *ambiguous decision making*. The decision to link the contra and Iranian missions occurred more by accident than by planning, amid the complexity of each policy. Many key White House officials did not know about key decisions or about how they were made. Only a few members of the National Security Council staff knew of North's plans. The secretaries of state and defense and the White House chief of staff were shut out of one or more important details about Project Democracy, Operation Recovery, and their ominous union. President Reagan himself drifted in and out of the decision making. Poindexter testified that he deliberately withheld information on the diversion of funds from Reagan. "I made a very deliberate decision not to ask the president, so that I could insulate him from the decision and provide some future deniability for the president if it ever leaked out. . . . On this whole issue, you know, the buck stops here with me. I made the decision. I felt that I had the authority to do it; I thought it was a good idea; I was convinced that the president would, in the end, think it was a good idea."[28]

Poindexter's logic, no matter how faulty, points to two elements of ambiguous decision making in the plural presidency. First, people make decisions for a president without necessarily having the president's approval. Poindexter inferred what Reagan wanted and did not bother to ask him. Poindexter was not alone in this habit. North invoked the name and the office of the president to advance the initial TOW sales to Iran when it was unclear what Reagan himself had done or said. In the labyrinth of the plural presidency, it becomes hard to tell if the president has expressed an opinion, ordered something, or not ordered something.

The second characteristic of ambiguous decision making is that a president can deny responsibility for decisions made within the institution. The buck stops with an aide, if it stops at all, and not with the president. Whether Reagan knew of the Iran-contra diversion scheme is open to question. Two scenarios are possible. One takes Reagan at his word and says he did not know. The complexity and disparateness of the plural presidency, its motto of everyone for himself, would suggest that something like the diversion could have taken place without the president's knowledge. Reagan was preoccupied with other things. He was convalescing slowly from cancer surgery and preparing for a major U.S.-Soviet summit. The other scenario says the president did know. But even if he did, the buck still need not stop with the president. The plural presidency provides presidents with "plausible deniability," in Poindexter's words. They can hide out within the institution and claim they got lost in its maze of offices and officers. To prove otherwise is impossible.

There is a third element of ambiguous decision making in the plural presidency that Poindexter's efforts to insulate the president do not reveal. Within the collective institution no one need take responsibility for decisions. This situation is summed up by a plaque that was on the top of Donald Regan's White House desk: "The buck doesn't even pause here." As the Iran and contra missions began to fall apart under the spotlight of public scrutiny, everyone tried to deny responsibility for everything. No one knew anything, except North and Poindexter, the appointed fall guys, who initially denied knowing as much as they did. The plural presidency allows all participants, not just the president, to cover their tracks, at least for a while.

Some might argue that the Iran-contra decisions were unique to the Reagan presidency, rather than examples of more general patterns of the plural presidency. In this view, Reagan's hands-off style made it easy for advisers to take charge; his friendliness made it difficult for him to make tough decisions that pitted one adviser against another. Many people suggest that the episode was the peculiar product of a president dozing at his watch. The plural presidency does not eliminate presidents' styles and personalities. But concentrating on only these factors discounts the very office in which presidents serve.

Ronald Reagan was neither the first nor the last president to work within the plural presidency. As we will explore throughout the rest of this book, the number and variety of participants, their free hand in taking actions within complex policy areas surrounded by diverse political interests, and the ambiguity of their decision processes are anything but unique. The plural presidency was a critical factor in Truman's decision to invade North Korea, in Kennedy's decision to back a coup against South Vietnamese president Diem, in Johnson's decision to escalate American involvement in Vietnam, in Carter's decision to oppose shoe import quotas. Each president had a unique personality and style, yet they all worked within the plural presidency. The presidents' decisions were only partly their own. People in the institution handled the details of the creation and the execution of these policies. These details, as we will see, made all the difference.

THE PRESIDENTIAL IRONY

The single executive image and the plural presidency are two inter-connected but contradictory parts of a whole. The single executive image displays the president as the one official uniquely in charge of government. Successful use of the single executive image may allow a president to get things done. A president who matches his skills to the single executive image may persuade the public, the Congress, and the press that presidential goals are the right goals. When Ronald Reagan's aides nicknamed him the "Big Cannon," they were refer-ring to his ability to communicate loudly and effectively that, backed by the people, he was in charge. Although the Iran-contra deals all but stalled the Reagan presidency, they did not bring down Reagan the president because he had mastered the single executive image so well. His robustness, self-confidence, assertive public presence, and genial manner conveyed that he was still the single most important, powerful, visible, and unique politician in the land.

Yet a president can meet the responsibilities of the single execu-tive image—problem solving, crisis management, and even public leadership—only by assigning them to the presidential institution. The image places demands on a president to be the most influential public leader, who solves national problems, upholds national val-ues, courts public opinion, and sets the direction for the country. The demands are so great that a president alone or with his immediate advisers cannot meet the test. To match the image, a president re-quires an elaborate, diverse, plural institution. Myriad White House offices are responsible for developing policy positions, gathering in-formation on international predicaments, and creating the very media events that display a president as the lone person in charge of govern-ment. The central irony of the presidency is this: the plural presi-dency exists so presidents may live up to the single executive image. Without the White House institution, the image would fade. Yet the institution blurs the image. At times when presidents attempt to sug-gest that they are in charge of the nation, they face difficulties taking charge of their own institution.

The irony of the single executive image and the plural presidency has serious consequences for the viability of the presidency as a dem-ocratic office. The single executive image portrays the president as the representative of the entire nation. The plural presidency says that the representative is bound to an institution that may deny the people the ability to retain control over their representative. Presi-dents proclaim themselves as the people's officers and shoulder greater and greater responsibility for more and more aspects of Amer-ican life. Although the singular imagery suggests that a democratic leader wields effective power in the system, the plural institution dissipates the president's power and accentuates the power of others. The president loses considerable control of the institution but also can deny his own accountability for its efforts. The executive office may make presidents much less democratic leaders than is commonly believed. It is tempting to see modern presidential politics as the actions and antics of individual presidents. Yet how they accommodate the irony between image and institution determines their very actions.

OUTLINE OF THE BOOK

The book is divided into four sections. Part I analyzes the single executive image. The single executive image portrays the president as the one person in charge of the government and the nation. This is a flashy picture that makes the president the single most important, unique, visible, and powerful official in the land. The image rests on an elegant, if erroneous, democratic rationale that the president is the only individual who acts on behalf of all the people. The question of whether any person or group can act in a meaningful way on behalf of all the people disturbs neither presidents nor the imagery. There are four foundations to this democratic rationale and, hence, to the single executive image: presidents' interpretations of the Constitution, election mandates, public perceptions, and media attention.

Chapters 2 and 3 describe the constitutional development of the presidency. Chapter 2 outlines the decisions of the constitutional framers and the restricted theory of power that most presidents subscribed to during the nineteenth century. This presidency of restraint precluded any hint of a single executive image. Chapter 3 considers how twentieth-century presidents have adopted a far more expansive approach to power. Modern presidents assert that they have power beyond the specific words of the Constitution to carry out the public good. They define what that "good" is and actively pursue it, unless there are prohibitions in the Constitution to the contrary. They couple this theory of presidential activism to a theory of governmental activism—the government's expansive involvement in all aspects of society. Presidents thereby lead the government's comprehensive efforts to deal with societal problems. Presidents truly look in charge of the whole show.

Chapter 4 explores how presidential activism derives partly from the election mandates that presidents assert. They can act on behalf of all the people because they claim they are elected by all the people. Moreover, in their campaigns, they present images of candidates who will do everything right—who have answers to all problems, who will make none of the mistakes of past presidents or current opponents, and who live by the moral values of the nation. Presidential election campaigns have a great deal to say about the importance, visibility, uniqueness, and power that presidents assume once the election results are in.

Chapter 5 highlights the public's perceptions of presidents. It explores the cultural assumptions, symbolism, and expectations upon which people base their opinions of presidents. The American people treat presidents as symbols of the nation. They rely on presidents as convenient cognitive aids to understand politics. Presidents also serve as sources of emotional reassurance. Their presence assures the public that crises will be managed and major problems will be tackled, if not solved. The symbolism reinforces the democratic rationale and helps create the importance and uniqueness of the single executive image.

As discussed in Chapter 6, the media readily reinforce this symbolism, importance, and uniqueness. Television, newspapers, and magazines devote so much coverage to presidents that one might think that the chief executive alone does indeed run the government. Presidents, acting as their own medium, frequently assert the democratic rationale in their public rhetoric. They use the tiny word "we" to tie the public to their actions and goals.

Part II and Part III examine the four dimensions of the plural presidency: decentralized organization, ambiguous decision making, policy complexity, and political fragmentation. Part II focuses on the way decisions are made in the White House. Chapter 7 offers an overview of the impact of the White House environment, the White House institution, presidents' immediate advisers, and presidents themselves on presidential decisions. Chapter 8 examines the effects of decentralization in the White House organization on presidential decisions. Chapter 9 describes the ambiguity that besets presidential decisions. When problems and policies are linked, players in the institution do so through political bargaining, not through an analysis of the best solution for a given problem.

Part III highlights the substance of presidential decisions. As part of the single executive image, executive activism, coupled with governmental activism, places presidents in the thick of a complex policy environment. The more they say they will do in the name of activism, the more complexity the plural presidency encounters in its decisions. Chapter 10 covers the complexity of presidential policymaking in foreign affairs. Presidents rely on four policy tools: nuclear deterrence, covert action, diplomacy, and, mainly, conventional military actions. Chapter 11 analyzes presidents' principal economic policies of budget decisions and tax cuts. Chapter 12 discusses the policy complexity and political fragmentation of domestic affairs. Presidents offer social welfare, civil rights, and regulatory policies to satisfy competing political interests. The chapters in Part III make clear that it is impossible for presidents to face the intricacies of these policy areas alone or with a small network of advisers.

Part IV explores how presidents use both the single executive image and the plural presidency to influence other institutions of the government. Conflict and cooperation result. Chapter 13 examines relations between the presidency and Congress. Invoking the single executive image, presidents offer comprehensive legislative programs to Congress. In so doing, they suggest that they are the individuals who can best solve the problems of the nation. Presidents employ the plural presidency to sell their programs in Congress. Congress, however, decides what it is willing to buy.

Chapter 14 explores relations between the presidency and the executive bureaucracy. Presidents use the single executive image to present major reorganization plans for the bureaucracy and to convey the impression that they are in control of the executive branch, whether in fact they are. Presidents employ the plural presidency to centralize decisions of the executive branch in the White House. Such efforts increase the size and complexity of the White House organization and leave most of the bureaucracy untouched.

In Chapter 15, presidents' relations with the courts, especially the Supreme Court, are analyzed. Supreme Court decisions have facilitated the expansion of presidential power and presidents' claim to be the single most powerful politicians in the nation. The plural presidency has influenced the courts, especially in its handling of judicial appointments.

The final chapter discusses how presidents can succeed in office by balancing the single executive image and the plural presidency. Most writers view presidential power as the key to this success. They fail to consider the two prime sources of presidential power: image and institution. The book concludes with an examination of presidential politics—the strategies that modern presidents undertake to balance the image and the institution. ■

FURTHER READING

On image in the presidency, see: Alfred de Grazia, "The Myth of the President," in *The Presidency*, ed. A. Wildavsky (Boston: Little, Brown, 1969), 49–73. On the institution of the presidency, see: Graham Allison, *The Essence of Decision: Explaining the Cuban Missile Crisis* (Boston: Little, Brown, 1971). On the Iran-contra affair, see: Jane Mayer and Doyle McManus, *Landslide: The Unmaking of the President, 1984–1988* (Boston: Houghton Mifflin, 1988); *The Tower Commission Report* (New York: Times Books, 1987).

NOTES

1. Roberta Sigel, "Image of the American Presidency: Part II of An Exploration into Popular Views of Presidential Power," *Midwest Journal of Political Science* 10 (February 1966): 123–137. Similar results were found in Jack Dennis, "Public Support for Presidents," *Political Behavior* 3 (1981): 319–350.

2. James March and Johan Olsen, *Rediscovering Institutions* (New York: Free Press, 1989), 16–18.

3. Alfred de Grazia, "The Myth of the President," in *The Presidency*, ed. A. Wildavsky (Boston: Little, Brown, 1969), 51–52, emphasis added.

4. Graham T. Allison, *The Essence of Decision: Explaining the Cuban Missile Crisis* (Boston: Little, Brown, 1971), 80.

5. Gerald Ford, "The President and Political Leadership," in *The Virginia Papers on the Presidency*, ed. K. Thompson, 2 vols. (Lanham, Md.: University Press of America, 1980), 2:21–40.

6. This account of the meeting among North, Calero, and Secord is taken principally from Jane Mayer and Doyle McManus, *Landslide: The Unmaking of the President, 1984–1988* (Boston: Houghton Mifflin, 1988), 78–79, 141–147; and from *The Tower Commission Report* (New York: Times Books, 1987).

7. Mayer and McManus, 153.

8. Ibid., 147.

9. Ibid., 129.

10. Ibid., 167–169.

11. Ibid., 169.

12. *Tower Commission Report*, 177.

13. Ibid., 213–219.

14. Ibid., 228.

15. Ibid., 38.

16. Figures calculated ibid., 438–449.

17. U.S. Congress, House of Representatives Select Committee to Investigate Covert Arms Transactions with Iran and Senate Select Committee on Secret Military Assistance to Iran and the Nicaraguan Opposition, *Select Committees Report* (Washington, D.C.: U.S. Government Printing Office, 1987), 79–81.

18. Mayer and McManus, 74.

19. *Tower Commission Report*, 450–452, emphasis added.

20. Mayer and McManus, 326–327.

21. *Tower Commission Report*, 480.

22. Mayer and McManus, 337.

23. *Tower Commission Report*, 466.

24. McFarlane testimony before the House and Senate Select Committees, as quoted in Mayer and McManus, 352.

25. In May 1992 Caspar Weinberger was indicted on federal obstruction of justice charges for allegedly having lied to prosecutors and congressional investigators about his knowledge of the shipments of arms to Iran. Weinberger pleaded not guilty.

26. *Tower Commission Report*, 66.

27. As quoted in Mayer and McManus, 206–207.

28. Poindexter testimony, July 15, 1987, before the House and Senate Select Committee, in *Select Committee Reports* (Washington, D.C.: U.S. Government Printing Office, 1987).

THE SINGLE EXECUTIVE IMAGE

The single executive image presents the president as the one person, backed by the people, who is in charge of governing the country. The image makes the president the single most powerful, important, unique, and visible politician in the nation, if not the world. No other public official is thought of in quite this way. The president must strive for world freedom and peace, ensure a sound economy, and cure domestic ills from poverty to the post office. Part I explores the four foundations of the single executive image: presidents' interpretations of constitutional power, electoral strategies, public perceptions, and media coverage.

The American Constitution does not provide for the president to be the most powerful figure in the government. As described in Chapter 2, it offers a short list of presidential powers limited by a strong legislative branch. Nineteenth-century presidents followed the framers' wishes. They were modest players in an equally modest government enterprise. Yet, as spelled out in Chapter 3, twentieth-century presidents expanded the scope of presidential power within an ever-expanding government. Today this presidential activism extends into five areas: diplomacy, military efforts, executive action, agenda-setting in legislation and budgeting, and public leadership. In each area, presidents overshadow Congress and the intentions of the framers and become the single most powerful officials in the government.

The single executive image also rests on presidents' claims, discussed in Chapter 4, that they are the only officials elected by the entire country. Presidential elections help define the uniqueness and importance of the single executive image. Candidates spend much of their time on the campaign trail suggesting how they will live up to this image. They indicate that they will solve all the major ills of the nation even though no other politician has succeeded in doing so. They profess compassion for the average American and passion in the American dream. Once elected, a president can assert that he has a mandate to govern.

As examined in Chapter 5, presidents serve as symbols of the nation. They stand for, or embody, all Americans—their problems, desires, and values. People establish expectations based on the symbolism. Presidents are supposed to live up to the qualifications laid out by the single executive image: exemplary personal behavior, adept problem solving, and leadership skills that ensure a vision for America's future. Americans judge real live presidents on the basis of these expectations. When the expectations come close to being met, presidents' public approval ratings are high; when the expectations go unfulfilled, public approval drops.

Finally, Chapter 6 highlights how the national media promote presidents as the single most visible figures in the country. The national media are of two sorts: (1) television, newspapers, and magazines that cover all presidential activities; and (2) the White House press organization itself, which feeds presidential news to the other news organizations. The result is that presidential news—whether it's the spunk of the president's dog or the success of the president's foreign policy—dominates the national news. Presidents are the most visible public celebrities in the nation.

Together these foundations and the single executive image that results provide presidents with a key resource. The president can use the image to proclaim that he should direct the government and provide solutions to complex national problems. The image provides the president with the ability to persuade others to do what the president desires. If the president fails to make such proclamations, then questions of leadership, resolve, and progress will abound, and the president, not the single executive image, will fade. ■

CHAPTER 2

The Presidency
of Restraint

F ifty-five people cram into a narrow room roughly thirty feet wide by fifty feet long. Some people work at small wooden desks. Others stand for hours and constantly shift the weight of their bodies from one leg to the other. Despite the unseasonably hot and humid weather, the door and the windows of the room are shut. Sentries prevent anyone from entering who has not been invited. No passers-by or zealous news reporters are privy to the group's secret work. There is no air conditioning, fans, or electric lights. Several of the people smoke, creating a gray haze that dances through the room. The chamber seems smaller and hotter each time a pipe or cigar is lit. Except for Sundays, these people meet every day from ten o'clock in the morning until three in the afternoon for nearly four months. On several occasions the sessions drag on until dark. Like children waiting for the school bell to ring, the group can think of nothing else but finishing the work and setting off for home.

The scene is Philadelphia in late May 1787. The group's charge is to create a new government for the United States. Although many of the decisions made by the framers of the American Constitution were based on philosophical debates and practical concerns about government, some were made because people were hot, uncomfortable, increasingly impatient, and longing to be anywhere but Philadelphia. Dr. William Samuel Johnson, a delegate from Connecticut, wrote in his diary that there were only five cool days during the entire convention, and two of them were Sundays.[1] Crabbiness and frustration were particularly evident as the framers intermittently directed their attention to the presidency in June and July and then again in late August and early September. By far the greatest part of the convention's business was devoted to discussions about Congress. Nonetheless, people came to Philadelphia armed with ideas about the executive, even though it was not their primary concern.

This and the next chapter examine how constitutional power developed as one of the pivotal ingredients of the single executive image. Little did the framers know that presidents, especially those of the twentieth century, would embellish the Constitution's descriptions of presidential powers and limitations to assert that they are the most powerful figures in the country. This assertion of superlative executive power has two ingredients: a powerful president and a powerful government. To be powerful, presidents must broadly interpret their constitutional powers. They must act where the framers may have intended their idleness. They act first even when the framers may have intended them to play a subordinate role. They must act unilaterally on measures that the framers may have intended them to act on jointly with Congress. Alone, however, such assertions of will are insufficient to permit claims of superlative executive power. The government too must be powerful. In order for the presidential claims to work, the government must be comprehensive in its scope. It must be fully integrated into society, affecting the lives of all citizens by its rule, benefits, and programs. A president's declaration of superlative executive power would ring hollow if he were in charge of a government that was small and incidental.

This chapter explains why the image of a single powerful executive *could not have developed* in the eighteenth and nineteenth centuries. Throughout these years, a powerful executive and a powerful government were present, but never at the same time. Indeed, they worked at odds with one another. Chapter 3 considers how the two came to coexist during the twentieth century, thus permitting presidents to make the claim of superlative executive power and providing one foundation of the single executive image.

THE FRAMERS' CHOICE

The Philadelphia debates centered on two issues. First, would there be a single (one-person) executive or a plural (multi-person) executive? Second, what mode of selection would be adopted—would the executive be selected by the legislature, as in a parliamentary system of government, or through some independent means? Mixing and matching these two matters gave the convention a variety of options to consider. They can be arranged along a continuum from the strongest to the weakest possible executive:

1. A monarch

2. A single executive elected by some mechanism other than the legislature

3. A single executive chosen by the legislature

4. A plural executive chosen by the legislature

5. No executive

The framers swiftly rejected the first and the last options. As colonists of Great Britain, they had had enough of monarchy. Many of the rallying cries of the American Revolution were against King George III. Even though George was going insane and had no real control of decisions made against the colonies, the Americans liked to place the blame at the top. In the Declaration of Independence, Thomas Jefferson vehemently accused the king of, among other things, having "sent hither swarms of officers to harass our people and eat out their substance." So when Alexander Hamilton proposed to the convention that there be a monarch and a legislature elected for life, the body quickly shunned the idea.[2]

With equal speed the convention disposed of the last option, that there be no executive. In fact, the idea never came up. The framers were well aware of the problems created by the absence of an executive. For nearly six years, from 1781 to 1787, they had lived unjoyously with the Articles of Confederation, under which the legislature was the only government body and the only executive was a presiding officer with no real powers. The absence of an executive under the Articles of Confederation was one of the reasons they suffered through the heat and humidity of Philadelphia.

One or More Executives?

The framers knew what they did *not* want. They did not wish to repeat their experience with too strong an executive. Nor did they want the vacuum created in the absence of any executive at all. The framers were less certain about what they did want. Debate at the convention on the remaining three options reflected a genuine ambivalence toward executive power. The framers knew an executive was necessary but also felt it could easily get out of hand.

On the issue of whether there would be a single or a plural executive, James Wilson of Pennsylvania introduced a motion early Friday morning, June 1, that the executive consist of a single person. Stony silence met his proposal. It was a radical idea—a single executive. Many at the convention agreed with Edmund Randolph, governor of Virginia, who feared "that a single executive is the fetus of monarchy." Randolph preferred a plan that called for an executive council of at least three people selected from different regions of the country. Wilson and others responded that a plural executive would result in "uncontrolled, continued, and violent animosities" among its members. Wilson's motion for a single executive carried three days later— seven states in favor, three opposed. The convention thus resolved one of the two issues regarding the executive: there would be one person. Three heads were not better than one.[3]

The Problem of Selection

The issue of selection proved to be a much tougher matter. No other question of the convention was so often raised, settled, reconsidered, settled again, and raised again. On June 2, the convention initially approved the selection of the executive by Congress. Yet over the course of the next three months, off and on, sometimes three and four times in one day, members introduced motions about the selection of the executive. Eight times the convention agreed to have Congress select the executive. Ten times they rejected the use of an electoral college chosen by the states. Twice they rejected direct election by the people. Several times they moved to reconsider their motion on legislative selection, postponed decision on it once or twice, and by the last day of August still had not made up their minds.

On that day, the convention reported all unfinished business, including the selection of the executive, to a committee of one delegate from each state. On September 5, the Committee on Unfinished Business made the eleventh proposal, that the executive be chosen by a college of electors designated in a manner directed by state legislatures. The next day the convention approved the committee's recommendation by a vote of nine states to two. It was the last vote taken on the matter, just eleven days before the convention signed the Constitution and adjourned.[4] In Madison's words, the "tedious and reiterated discussions" of this "peculiarly embarrassing" aspect of the convention were now over.[5] The convention selected Option 2—a single executive elected independently of the Congress.

Energy and Safety

In that decision the framers created the strongest, most independent executive they could have, given their remaining three choices. Nonetheless, they viewed the executive as subordinate to a stronger, more well-developed Congress. They imbued the executive with two features. First, the executive had the proper "energy" to act. The framers made a crucial decision that there would be one individual, no more, in charge of the executive. They made the person independent of the legislature. They assigned to this individual a list of nine enumerated, but relatively general, constitutional powers:

1. Make treaties with advice and consent of Senate

2. Receive ambassadors from other countries

3. Serve as commander in chief of the armed forces

4. Appoint executive officers, judicial officers, and ambassadors with advice and consent of Senate

5. Ask the opinions of officers of the executive departments

6. Take care that the laws be faithfully executed

7. Sign and veto legislation

8. Give information on the state of the union

9. Grant pardons and reprieves

Second, however, the executive was made "safe." Safety resulted from the sharing of these powers with other parts of the government. The framers designed the Congress as the first—the pre-eminent—branch. They placed the legislature in charge of the very stuff of government, giving it the sole authority to raise, borrow, make, and spend money. They granted it the power to regulate the nation's business in interstate and foreign commerce. The framers also let Congress oversee the executive. Congress held the power to declare war and raise and support the army and navy, even though presidents were given the title "commander in chief." Congress could impeach executive officers. It could override presidential vetoes of legislation, although only with a stringent two-thirds vote. Presidents had to seek Senate approval of their appointments and treaties. The framers anticipated that the executive would be secondary to, albeit independent from, the legislature. Congress would restrain any executive tendencies toward domination. Besides Congress, the framers offered the electoral college scheme of indirect control by the people as another safety measure.

Energy and safety are contradictory requirements. The former works to increase the executive's constitutional power while the latter restricts it. Yet such a contradiction was exactly what the framers sought. Hamilton summarized the convention's accomplishment in *The Federalist*, No. 70:

The ingredients which constitute energy in the executive are unity; duration; an adequate provision for its support; and competent powers. The ingredients which constitute safety in the republican sense are a due dependence on the people, and a due responsibility. . . . That unity is conducive to energy will not be disputed. Decision, activity, secrecy, and dispatch will generally characterize the proceedings of one man in a much more eminent degree than the proceedings of any greater number.[6]

Their fears of a tyrant king seemed to fade. Washington, who it was understood would be the first president, felt that a fitting title for the newly created executive would be "His High Mightiness, the President of the United States and Protector of their Liberties."[7] No one hinted that this might sound a bit too regal.

THEORIES OF PRESIDENTIAL POWER

Two theories of presidential power have guided presidents in their exercise of constitutional powers: (1) a theory of presidential restraint and (2) a theory of presidential activism. The differences between the two approaches are seen in alternate views of the first sentence of Article II of the Constitution: "The executive power shall be vested in a President of the United States." These are either the most innocuous thirteen words or the most tempting, untamed words in the entire document. Do the words mean only that there will be a single executive called "president," instead of "chancellor," "premier," or some other title? Or is the emphasis in the sentence on the words "executive power," thus providing an inherent, unspecified grant of authority? The first interpretation takes steps away from the image of one powerful executive; the other hastens toward it.

The Theory of Presidential Restraint

The presidential restraint doctrine envisions a presidency that follows most closely the intent of the framers. Presidents, according to James Madison, principal author of the Constitution, would serve merely as executors of legislative wishes. He argued that only "foreigners and degenerate citizens among us, who hate our republican government," would believe that an inherent executive power existed.[8] William Howard Taft echoed Madison more than a century later:

The true view of the Executive function is, as I conceive it, that the President can exercise no power which cannot be fairly and reasonably traced to some specific grant of power or justly implied and included within such expressed grant as proper and necessary to its exercise. Such specific grant must be either in the Federal Constitution or in an Act of Congress passed in pursuance thereof. There is no undefined residuum of power which he can exercise because it seems to him to be in the public interest.[9]

Presidential restraint rests on two premises. First, presidents possess no inherent grant of executive power. They have the authority to act only so long as there is a specific grant of power in either the Constitution or federal law. An unstated second premise also exists: presidents draw no power from the people to sanction their decisions. They do not act in some special way on behalf of the public. The notion of presidential restraint makes presidents the short noontime shadows of Congress, which takes the lead in the government. Under this logic, presidents cannot claim, nor do they wish to claim, that they are singularly powerful. Instead, they prefer to paint an image of cool restraint and polite deference to Congress.

The Theory of Presidential Activism

The presidential activism doctrine sets forth a justification for discretionary presidential power. Alexander Hamilton, Madison's opponent in a series of newspaper debates in 1793, claimed that the first sentence of Article II was a pronouncement of inherent executive authority.[10] Hamilton wrote that presidents held an executive power of their own definition "subject only to the exceptions and qualifications which are expressed in the Constitution."[11]

Theodore Roosevelt also advocated a theory of presidential activism, one that he was sure his handpicked successor Taft would uphold. In his *Autobiography*, written in 1913, Roosevelt laid out the claims against which Taft rebelled. He insisted

upon the theory that the executive power was limited only by specific restrictions and prohibition appearing in the Constitution or imposed by Congress under its constitutional powers. My view was that every Executive officer and above all every Executive officer in high position was a steward of the people bound actively and affirmatively to do all he could for the people. . . . I declined to adopt this view that what was imperatively necessary for the Nation could not be done by the President, unless he could find some specific authorization to do it. My belief was that it was not only his right but his duty to do anything that the needs of the nation demanded unless such action was forbidden by the Constitution or by the laws. . . . I did not usurp power but I did greatly broaden the use of executive power. In other words, I acted for the common well being of all our people whenever and in whatever measure was necessary, unless prevented by direct constitutional or legislative prohibition.[12]

Presidential activism rests on two points. First, the opening sentence of Article II supplies an inherent grant of executive power. Thus, presidents have the power to act so long as there is no expressed constitutional or congressional prohibition. Hamilton and Roosevelt believed that presidents can do more or less whatever they want unless there is an expressed prohibition in the Constitution or the laws. Second, presidents use the inherent grant to provide for the well-being of the people—to act as the people's stewards.[13] This is perhaps the most important element of presidential activism. By fusing the presidency to the public, the approach transforms presidents from the executors of congressional will, under the specified powers approach, to the executors of the people's will, the people's representatives. Democracy replaces safety as the principal public foundation of the office. The public is not the check on presidential power that the framers envisioned. Instead, it is the source of presidential power. Under the logic of activism, presidents can claim they are singularly powerful. To fully project the single executive image, however, an omnipresent government also must be in place.

THEORIES OF GOVERNMENT

Theories of the presidency (or any institution) meet broader theories of national government. These theories establish the scope of the national government—how deeply intertwined it will be with society and the economy, which issues the government will handle, and which it will shun. A *theory of governmental restraint*, and a *theory of governmental activism* have preoccupied American politics.

The theory of governmental restraint has two tenets. First, there should be only a limited link between the national government and society. The national government acts as a watchdog to prevent the excesses of people's behavior, principally by establishing criminal laws. The theory pre-empts an active role of the national government in providing such benefits as education, social welfare, or health care. The theory permits the states and localities in the federal system to undertake these tasks, notably education, yet even their involvement in society is decidedly limited. At the national, state, and local levels, government's involvement in the economy is restricted. It provides for only those services that are difficult for private companies to supply, such as roads and post offices. It furnishes no central communication services, such as telegraph or later telephone, radio, or television. Nor does it protect people from economic downturns or personal financial hardships due to illness, age, or disability. Government at any level is small in budget and scope.

Second, the nation's involvement in foreign affairs should be limited. This means that the size of the armed forces is kept small. It also means that diplomatic ventures are limited to protecting America's position on the North American continent rather than developing international liaisons. The United States stays out of the rest of the world's business so long as the rest of the world stays out of North America.

A competing theory of governmental activism rests on two premises. First, government should actively intervene in society. It is impractical to draw a line that artificially distinguishes government from society, since one reflects the other. Government provides services and assistance to people who are unable to meet their basic needs for income, food, housing, and education. Government also intervenes in the economy. It helps industries, protects workers, and provides transportation systems. It is large in budget and scope.

Second, the United States should play an active role in foreign affairs. The U.S. is protector of the world. Its diplomatic and military ventures are not confined to North America, but extend around the globe. The world protectorate requires a large armed force. At the very least, the military will secure international stability. At the very most, it will attempt to maintain or create freedom and democracy.

THE MIX AND MATCH OF THEORIES

Theories of power often are concerned about means and ends. Means pertain to the ability of a government or its institutions to act; ends involve what government or its institutions should accomplish through action. The theories of *presidential* power are about *means*— the ability of the executive to make government decisions. The theory of presidential restraint says that presidents' role should be limited to executing the actions of Congress. The theory of presidential activism says that as the people's representatives, presidents should act independently of Congress to pursue policy. The theories of *governmental* power are about *ends*—the goals of government. The theory of governmental restraint states the old adage that the government that governs least governs best. This view stands behind the Constitution. The framers advocated limited government and felt that government should adhere narrowly to the precepts of the Constitution. The activist theory reverses the adage: the government that governs most governs best. The national government should not rigidly adhere to the language of the Constitution but should interpret it to meet changing conditions and exigencies. The four theories mix means and ends in four ways.

1. *Presidential restraint/Governmental restraint:* Logically, the theory of presidential restraint complements the theory of governmental restraint: a president closely adhering to the prescriptions of the Constitution works within a government that also construes its powers narrowly. Presidents do little in a government that does little.

2. *Presidential restraint/Governmental activism:* Yet it is not mandatory that the two theories of restraint be combined. Presidents could engage in restricted efforts while Congress pursues a course of governmental activism. Presidents do little in a government run by Congress, which does a lot.

3. *Presidential activism/Governmental activism:* The two theories of activism also appear congruous: presidents who vigorously pursue courses of action on behalf of the people lead a government that provides a wide band of public benefits. Presidents do a lot to help the government do a lot.

4. *Presidential activism/Governmental restraint:* Again, there is no necessary reason that presidential activism should be joined to governmental activism. It is possible that presidential activism could be directed toward restricting government's domestic and international activities. Presidents do a lot to keep the government little.

Of the four combinations of theories, only the third brings into focus the single executive image. Presidential activism and governmental activism together foster the superlative power of the single executive image. Presidents are *the* source of governmental activism—social progress and change internally and peace and stability internationally. Presidents expand the responsibilities of the national government as they expand their own responsibilities. They legitimize the union of presidential activism with governmental activism on the grounds that they are the only individuals who act on behalf of all the people. This democratic rationale becomes one of the key elements of the single executive image. It is not merely that one powerful person leads the government's efforts to secure the nation's domestic and international welfare. This person is the people's representative. In this way, presidents offer both the means and the ends of government.

THE PRACTICE OF THEORIES: BEGINNINGS UNDER WASHINGTON

Practice inevitably differed from these theories as presidents began to make decisions and set precedents in five areas: diplomacy, war, executive action, agenda setting, and public leadership.

> *Diplomacy:* Washington and subsequent presidents in the nineteenth century gained relatively free rein in the negotiation of treaties and in establishing relations with other nations.
>
> *War:* Presidents' assertions of power in wartime were more consistent with the doctrine of presidential restraint than was their diplomacy. For the most part, presidents believed they could act unilaterally only to defend the United States. Offensive action, they assumed, required a declaration of war or some other form of authorization from Congress. Lincoln alone did not follow the general custom.
>
> *Executive Action:* Congress during much of the nineteenth century dictated presidential restraint on the appointment and the removal of executive officials. Not until late in the century did presidents finally establish their unilateral authority to remove appointees without congressional approval.
>
> *Agenda Setting:* Most nineteenth-century presidents were hesitant to sponsor a national policy agenda. They did not intervene actively in the legislative process to identify major national problems or offer their solutions. This was Congress's domain.
>
> *Public Leadership:* Presidents' greatest restraint was reserved for public leadership. Presidents typically were private figures who rarely appealed for public support to gain a political edge with Congress.

George Washington set precedents for both presidential activism and presidential restraint in four of the five areas: diplomacy, executive action, agenda setting, and public leadership. It would remain for Jefferson to define early presidential restraint in war.

Diplomacy

In foreign relations, Washington provided the earliest assertion of the theory of presidential activism. The Constitution grants presidents power to negotiate treaties and to appoint and receive ambassadors. Although the framers saw foreign relations as a joint presidential-senatorial venture, Washington moved the Senate to a subordinate role. The president was, according to Congressman John Marshall, later the chief justice of the United States, "the sole organ of the nation in its external relations, and its sole representative with foreign nations."[14] Future presidents eagerly embraced this idea.

Washington offered three elements of what subsequently became known as the "sole organ doctrine." First, on a general level, he established a role for the executive in making foreign policy. In 1793 he proclaimed the neutrality of the U.S. in a war between Britain and France. Washington adopted Hamilton's argument that, in the absence of a declaration of war from Congress, the executive had full authority to proclaim and enforce U.S. neutrality. After cries of usurpation of legislative power, Washington demurred to "the wisdom of Congress to correct, improve or enforce" the neutrality policy.[15] In the following year, Congress passed a Neutrality Act. Both the Congress and the president won victories. Neutrality has been considered a congressional prerogative since 1794. Yet Washington's position asserted policymaking powers of the president, constitutionally free of direction by Congress, though capable of being checked by it.[16]

Second, on a more specific level, Washington asserted that the negotiation of treaties was under the exclusive purview of the executive. Early in his term, Washington interpreted the constitutional requirement of "advice and consent of the Senate" in treaty making to mean that presidents should consult with the chamber before treaty negotiations commenced. He met with the Senate in 1789 to discuss a pending treaty with the Indians in western Georgia. The Senate referred Washington's inquiry to committee. Washington was furious, saying, "This defeats every purpose of my coming here."[17] He later agreed to return in three days to receive the Senate's answers. Upon his departure, he swore, "I would be damned if I ever go back there again."[18] Washington was the first and the last president to consult personally with the Senate in the treaty-making process. In 1795, without prior consultation, Washington presented to the Senate for ratification the controversial Jay Treaty with Great Britain, officially ending the Revolutionary War. He denied the House's request for documents related to the treaty's negotiation. Thereafter, the constitutional provision that the president "shall have the power, by and with the advice and consent of the Senate to make treaties" meant that the Senate would ratify the actions of the president, not help initiate them.

Finally, Washington claimed a presidential monopoly on the right to communicate with foreign governments. He refused to accept the credentials of two diplomats desired by the French minister to the United States, Edmond Genêt. Genêt, so incensed at Washington's rebuke, sought their recognition from Congress despite Secretary of State Thomas Jefferson's warnings that Congress had no authority. Only the president could act (under his constitutional power to receive ambassadors). This Washington did; he asked the French government to recall Genêt after his dubious visit to Congress. In these actions and those involving treaty making, Washington developed a strategy of unilateral action. He presented Congress with faits accomplis that the body could accept or reject, but not alter. This strategy provided one of the firmest foundations for transforming the presidential activism theory into practice.

Executive Action

Washington asserted a broad definition of "chief executive." In 1794, he claimed the authority of presidents to "faithfully execute the laws" by resolutely quashing the Whiskey Rebellion of western Pennsylvania farmers who opposed a federal excise tax on the whiskey they made from their grain crops. The action not only asserted the executive's responsibility to see the laws obeyed but also helped establish the supremacy of federal law and the authority of the federal government to lay and collect taxes.

Washington further claimed a unilateral power of presidents to remove executive appointees from their jobs. The Constitution provides for presidents to appoint executive officials with the advice and consent of the Senate. It is silent on their removal. Congress narrowly defeated a bill opposed by Washington that would have made removal subject to Senate consent.[19] Washington and Madison as his ally argued that senatorial consent would weaken presidents' control over executive officers.[20]

Agenda Setting

By contrast, the presidential restraint doctrine more nearly directed Washington's actions on agenda setting. Washington felt that the president's role was to faithfully carry out the laws of Congress, not actively initiate legislation. He made sparing recommendations to Congress and mounted no special effort to see his programs enacted. He vetoed legislation only twice in his eight years in office, once on constitutional grounds, once on political grounds.[21]

Washington, however, did acquiesce to the policy agenda of his secretary of the treasury, Alexander Hamilton. In reports to Congress in 1790 and 1791, Hamilton proposed a plan to fund the national debt, assume the war debts of the states, create a national bank, maintain an excise tax on liquor distillers, and enact a tariff system to protect fledgling American industries.[22] Congress passed the proposals, except for the tariff. By modern standards, Hamilton's plan may not appear especially path breaking, yet for the time his approach was one of governmental activism. Jefferson and Madison, by contrast, favored a much narrower role for the national government, preferring that the states act as the central decision-making bodies. The debate over Hamilton's agenda and the controversies surrounding the Jay Treaty led to the emergence of a two-party conflict between the Hamiltonian Federalists and the Jeffersonian Democratic-Republicans. Despite Washington's admonitions against the evils of political parties, they arose to house different economic interests (commercial and business interests of the Federalists, agrarian interests of the Democrats) and to espouse opposing philosophies of government (an activist government for the Federalists, a restrained government for the Democrats).

Public Leadership

Washington did not conceive of himself as a popular leader who would take appeals directly to the people. He believed that presidential power emerged from the Constitution, not from public mandates. Nonetheless, he felt that the presidency should secure the respect and support of the public. Washington asked the advice of Hamilton, Vice President John Adams, and Chief Justice John Jay about

whether it would tend to prompt impertinent applications and involve disagreeable consequences to have it known, that the President will, every Morning at eight O'clock, be at leisure to give Audience to persons who may have business with him?

Whether it would be satisfactory to the public for the President to make about four great entertainments in a year on such great occasions as . . . , The Anniversary of the Declaration of Independence . . . , The Alliance with France . . . , The Peace with Great Britain . . . , The Organization of the general Government: and whether arrangements of these . . . kinds could be in danger of diverting too much of the President's time from business, or of producing the evils which it was intended to avoid by his living more reclusive than the Presidts. of Congress have heretofore lived.

Whether, during the recess of Congress, it would not be advantageous to the interests of the Union for the President to make the tour of the United States, in order to become better acquainted with their principal Characters and internal Circumstances, as well as to be more accessible to numbers of well-informed persons, who might give him useful information and advice on political subjects?[23]

Washington established two types of weekly meetings with "common people" who had no real business with the president and who needed no formal invitations. One was the "President's levee" for men every Tuesday from three to four o'clock in the afternoon;

the other was "Martha's tea party" held every Friday afternoon for men and women.[24] Washington also went on two "grand tours"—one to New England and the other, a 1,877-mile, two-month journey through the South. During his travels, he avoided any policy remarks and confined his words to short greetings upon his arrival in a city.[25] Thus, public ties were a significant but *limited* part of Washington's view of the office, well within the bounds of presidential restraint.

JEFFERSON: A STEWARD OF RESTRAINT

Washington's tenure offered an amalgam of presidential activism, presidential restraint, and, through Hamilton's economic plans, governmental activism. After Washington's farewell, the "Arch-Federalists," allied with Hamilton, continued to back notions of strong government. They advocated a large standing military and tax increases to pay for it. Washington's successor John Adams (1797–1801), more moderate than his extreme Federalist colleagues, nonetheless concurred with the need for a strong government. This view provided the Jeffersonians with the perfect platform on which to stand in the election of 1800. Their program was largely negative, aimed at undoing Federalist policies and Federalist activist government philosophy. In his first inaugural address in 1801, Jefferson stated his preference for a "wise and frugal government" that would allow people to "regulate their own pursuits of industry."[26] Yet Jefferson's actions in office exhibited a duality. He sought smaller government but at the same time adopted the Federalist concept of presidential activism in order to do so. As Hamilton observed, Jefferson was "no enemy to the power of the executive."[27]

Diplomacy

Jefferson's most significant use of presidential activism was at once reluctant and sweeping when in 1802 the United States arranged the purchase of the Louisiana Territory from France. The deal gave the U.S. a region that stretched from present-day Montana to the Gulf of Mexico for $15 million. Happy to have obtained such a "noble bargain," Jefferson was chagrined that, in his oft-stated view, the United States lacked the constitutional power to accept the deal. Since the Constitution did not provide for the acquisition of new territory, Jefferson believed that an amendment was required to make the purchase. Others convinced him that the executive's treaty-making power could be construed to permit the purchase, which the Senate swiftly approved. Later Jefferson wrote that the purchase presented a national emergency that justified action beyond the Constitution. He likened himself to a guardian looking out for the well-being of a ward: "I did this for your good; you may disavow me . . . [but] I thought it was my duty to risk myself for you."[28]

Jefferson's presidential activism continued with an effort to maintain U.S. neutrality in the ongoing Napoleonic Wars between Britain and France. In 1807 he secured from Congress a total embargo on all foreign trade—imports and exports. The enforcement of the embargo expanded presidential power and broadened the regulatory powers of the national government. The theory of governmental restraint and practice slipped apart under Jefferson.

War

In war, Jefferson was a more reluctant activist. He believed that the president's unilateral war powers were only defensive in scope. He wrote that the president was "unauthorized by the Constitution without the sanction of Congress to go beyond the line of defense."[29] Jefferson stated that to act offensively the commander in chief required an official declaration of war from Congress. In 1801 when Tripoli declared war on the U.S. and again in 1805 when Spain made incursions from Florida into newly purchased Louisiana, Jefferson requested action of Congress rather than proceeding unilaterally: "Considering that Congress alone is constitutionally invested with the power of changing our condition from peace to war, I have thought it my duty to await their authority for using force. . . . The course to be pursued will require the command of means which it belongs to Congress exclusively to yield or to deny."[30] Congress denied both requests, and Jefferson yielded to Congress.[31] Jefferson's belief that an offensive war required an official congressional declaration set the standard for American military exercises before and after the Civil War. Although Lincoln did not concur, all other presidents acted as commanders in chief under the theory of presidential restraint.

Agenda Setting

Washington had been hesitant to enter the tumult of agenda setting in Congress, but Jefferson relished it. He developed a disciplined party organization in Congress with the president as its leader. He did so mindful of the precedent set by Washington that presidents should not directly guide the congressional course of events. So as not to appear "to register the edicts of a sovereign," Jefferson formulated legislation and privately funneled proposals to Democratic-Republican members of Congress.[32] He relied on Democratic-Republican floor leaders in the House and Senate to advance his agenda. Jefferson also used another device of party unity: the Democratic-Republican party caucus. The caucus was made up of party members in Congress and executive department secretaries who gathered frequently to formulate policy, plan strategy, and nominate the party's presidential candidates from 1808 to 1824. Jefferson presided over the meetings from time to time and had a strong influence on their discussion even when he was not in attendance.[33] The Democratic-Republicans passed a broad agenda of legislation to retrieve the government from what they perceived as the clutches of Hamilton's activist national plan. They set about reducing the size of the military and drastically cutting army and navy appropriations. Congress also abolished most internal taxes, including the detested whiskey tax and direct property taxes.[34]

Public Leadership

Activism marked Jefferson's presidency in its relation to the people. "In a government like ours," he observed, "it is the duty of the Chief Magistrate, in order to enable himself to do all the good which his station requires, . . . to unite in himself the confidence of the whole people. This alone, in any case, where the energy of the nation is required, can produce a union of the powers of the whole, and point them in a single direction, as if all constituted by one body and one mind."[35] Jefferson made the connection between the executive and the public through his party, not directly. He repeated none of Washington's bids to meet the people. He made only three short public statements (all of them to Native American tribes) during his tenure.[36] Nor did he attempt to inform the public about the unpopular foreign trade embargo. His response was "an imperturbable, almost sphinxlike silence to the nation."[37] Acting for the people did not extend to direct appeals to them.

The Party Seesaw

Jefferson's combination of presidential activism and governmental restraint built a philosophical seesaw within the party system throughout the nineteenth century. Even as party names and memberships changed, the parties continued to take obverse positions on the mix of means and ends. Although the Hamiltonian lesson had been to combine presidential and governmental activism, the Federalists did not return to this view. They took the position opposite Jefferson's: presidential restraint and governmental activism. Jefferson's successors, Madison and Monroe, did return to Democratic-Republican orthodoxy: presidential restraint and governmental restraint. But the Jacksonian Democrats renewed Jefferson's stance.

The Whigs (who emerged after the Federalists' collapse) countered again with presidential restraint and governmental activism, a view that dominated American politics until the Civil War. Neither side on the seesaw had room for the single executive image: on the one side, presidents were of secondary importance; on the other, presidents kept the government of secondary importance.

Viewed through a late-twentieth-century looking glass, Jefferson's most prominent legacy is the activism he brought to the presidency. At the time, however, the more significant result was the development of the party machinery that tied together the executive and the legislature. With Jefferson in office, the party apparatus, and thus the Congress, were executive directed. When Jefferson left office, the party apparatus, and thus the presidency, became legislative directed. With the Federalist party in decline, politicians from all regions and with all viewpoints found themselves within the Democratic-Republican party. The rise of this dominant party shifted attention to Congress, within which the various factions bargained. Legislative power also increased with the rise of the Speaker of the House as a powerful post and the expansion of congressional committees. Both developments placed obstacles in the way of continued presidential direction of legislation. Speaker Henry Clay, a tall, magnetic Kentuckian, gained the upper hand against Presidents Madison (1809–1817), Monroe (1817–1825), and John Quincy Adams (1825–1829). Clay, not the president, was arguably the most powerful figure in American politics during his tenure as Speaker from 1811 to 1825.[38]

Thus, during the twenty years after Jefferson left office, the party apparatus he had founded permitted Congress, not the president, to invoke its own activism. During these two decades, presidents broke little new ground in their commander-in-chief duties, lawmaking endeavors, and public leadership. Only in the area of diplomacy did President Monroe enhance the precepts of presidential activism. Forty-one years after the framers had met in Philadelphia, their plan that Congress, not the executive, be at the center of the government held firm. People would have bet no money on the proposition that in the future the president would be looked on, through the single executive image, as the one person in charge of the country.

War

The presidency after Jefferson shrank. The House of Representatives became the focus of decision making in the government. Although today it is difficult to think of Congress as the initiator of war, it was difficult then to think of presidents as unilaterally ordering military action. When the new session of Congress opened in 1811, Speaker Clay and John C. Calhoun of South Carolina led a faction of Democratic-Republicans from the South and West, known as the War Hawks, who pressured Madison for war against Britain. They used as rallying points Britain's supplying weapons to Native American tribes who were fighting settlers in search of cheap land and Britain's seizure of American ships and the impressment (forced service) of American crews. In May, the War Hawks led the Democratic-

Republican caucus to secure Madison's renomination for a second term. On June 1, Madison sent his message to Congress asking for a declaration of war. Two weeks later Congress passed the resolution that commenced the War of 1812.

At war, Madison found himself trapped in the theory of governmental restraint that he had staunchly advocated at Jefferson's side. Having dismantled much of the army and navy under Jefferson, Madison faced a nation ill prepared for war. Having repealed a series of taxes under Jefferson, Congress was hesitant to raise taxes sufficient to fight the war. On several occasions, Madison turned to state governors to call out their militias. Yet when the governors of Massachusetts and Connecticut, among the few remaining Federalists, refused, Madison, a strong advocate of states' rights, backed down. Madison not only held to the theory of governmental restraint, but, unlike his friend Jefferson, he also practiced presidential restraint. He took no steps during the war, which ended two years later, that would have been considered emergency measures outside the bounds of the Constitution.

Agenda Setting

Congress not only dictated the War of 1812 but dominated the policy agenda after it. The war had led to chaos in shipping and banking, stimulated the growth of manufactures, accelerated western migration, and exposed the inadequacy of the existing transportation system. Congressional leaders Clay and Calhoun, the former War Hawks and sectional champions, offered a national postwar program called the "American system." Harking back to Hamilton, the Congress re-established a national bank (the Second Bank of the United States), placed a high tariff on textile imports to protect new industries, and tried to gain federal money for internal improvements—roads, bridges, and canals—to move the country westward. Madison did not take an active role in passing these measures, although on his last day in office he vetoed the improvements measure. He believed that a constitutional amendment was needed to establish that Congress, rather than the states, had the authority to provide for such construction. James Monroe vetoed a similar measure, also subscribing to the philosophy of governmental restraint.

Monroe's restraint on the national policy agenda made him all but invisible during major congressional debate on the admission of Missouri as a slave state. The compromise eventually worked out in 1820 was to admit Missouri as a slave state, Maine as a free state, and prohibit slavery in the northern portion of the Louisiana Territory. Slavery and western expansion ultimately were congressional issues, resting, as they did, on geographic representation. Their increasing prominence augmented presidential restraint.

Public Leadership

Presidents were unwilling to make direct appeals to the people to protect the bonds of the Union. Although Monroe re-established Washington's grand tour, he designed the "swings around the circle," one to New England in 1817 and another to the South and West in 1819, to dampen party factions and not to discuss issues.[39] Lawmakers ignored Monroe's successor, John Quincy Adams, who tried but failed to establish a more activist presidency and government. They watched as Andrew Jackson, who had lost to Adams in 1824, mounted a three-year presidential campaign beginning in 1826 to wrest the office from the second President Adams. Supreme Court Justice Joseph Story summarized the passivity of the post-Jefferson presidency: "the Executive has no longer a commanding influence. The House of Representatives has absorbed all the popular feeling and all the effective power of the country."[40]

Diplomacy

Despite presidents' adherence to the doctrine of presidential restraint in war, in legislation, and in public leadership, activism firmly anchored their diplomatic initiatives. Monroe demonstrated this when he announced that the North American continent was "free and independent" and "henceforth not to be considered as subjects for future colonization by any European powers." The Monroe Doctrine, as it became known only in 1853, pledged that America would not "interfere in the internal concerns of any [European] powers" so long as Europeans upheld the integrity of North America."[41] On its face, the Monroe Doctrine removed the United States from Europe, yet left unsaid was U.S. willingness to intercede in the affairs of Latin American states. Monroe's announcement did not shake Europeans who knew that after the War of 1812 the United States did not have the capacity to halt European ventures in the Western hemisphere. Rivalries among Britain, France, and Russia, not Monroe's words, kept Europe out of North America. The message, however, did reinforce the unilateral presidential direction of foreign policy established by Washington.

THE JACKSONIAN TENSION

Andrew Jackson (1829–1837), running as a member of the Democrats, a faction of the Democratic-Republican party, convincingly defeated John Quincy Adams in 1828 and returned the Jeffersonian profiles of the presidency and the government. Jackson favored an active presidency in a restrained national government that would leave most work to the states. The National Republicans (a new party formed from a faction of the Democratic-Republican party) opposed Jackson's view. They coupled the old Democratic-Republican means of presidential restraint with a Hamiltonian construction of ends—governmental activism that continued to include banking, tariffs, and internal improvements.

Executive Action

Jackson practiced presidential activism that showed the executive as an independent policymaker, not simply an administrator of congressional will. In 1832 Jackson firmly asserted the presidential power to faithfully execute the laws when South Carolina attempted to declare a tariff harmful to cotton growers unconstitutional—that is, null and void within its borders. John C. Calhoun, a nationalist just a few years before and, inconveniently, Jackson's vice president, led the charge for nullification. South Carolinians also proclaimed that any attempt to enforce the tariff would lead the state to separate from the Union. Jackson, though a proponent of states' rights, was devoted to the sovereignty of the Union. He announced that nullification would be met with force. Calhoun resigned as vice president and Jackson threatened to hang him as a traitor. In February 1833, Jackson declared, "I consider, then, the power to annul a law of the United States, assumed by one State, incompatible with the existence of the Union, contradicted expressly by the letter of the Constitution, unauthorized by its spirit, inconsistent with every principle on which it is founded, and destructive of the great object for which it was formed."[42] South Carolina suspended its nullification ordinance, and Congress passed a new, less harsh tariff.

Agenda Setting

As further evidence of presidential activism, Jackson expanded the president's veto power in both its frequency and its importance to enhance presidential agenda-setting efforts. In setting the national agenda, presidents not only would propose policy ideas that they did want but they would reject those ideas that they did not want. Earlier presidents had vetoed legislation sparingly—only ten times in forty-three years, citing both constitutional and policy grounds. Jackson vetoed twelve bills, the most important of which was his rejection of a bill to recharter the national bank in 1832. The bank veto expanded both the constitutional and the policy rationales of his predecessors.

First, although the Supreme Court had established in *McCulloch v. Maryland* (1819) that the Congress could charter a bank, Jackson challenged the Court's authority as final arbiter of the Constitution. He argued that "The Congress, the Executive, and the Court must each for itself be guided by its own opinion of the Constitution."[43]

Jackson's interpretation of the executive's ability to act as an arbiter of the Constitution did not prevail. The courts maintained their role as final arbiter. Yet at the time Jackson's pronouncement was a loud statement of executive power, louder than that heard from past presidents.

Second, Jackson, more firmly than any of his predecessors, argued for "the undoubted right of the Executive to withhold his assent from bills on grounds other than their constitutionality."[44] To Jackson, the national bank hurt southern and western interests and took too much power away from the states. Congress failed to override, and Jackson's veto stood. Many presidents followed suit, vetoing legislation they did not like on policy or political grounds. The leading authority on the subject at the end of the nineteenth century wrote: "From Jackson's administration to the Civil War vetoes on grounds of expediency became more frequent, but they were still in a decided minority. Since the [Civil] War constitutional arguments in a veto message have been almost unknown."[45]

After his re-election victory in 1832, Jackson requested of Congress the authority to remove federal funds from the bank and destroy what he called the "monster" once and for all. Congress refused, leaving the authority to remove the funds with the secretary of the treasury. Jackson ordered two treasury secretaries to transfer the funds to state banks, but both of them refused. Not until Jackson selected Roger Taney as his third treasury secretary in six months was he able to dictate the removal of the funds.

Jackson's clear statement of presidential agenda setting in his bank veto and its aftermath was met with an equally clear response. The National Republicans now assumed the name Whig, chosen expressly to taunt Jackson. The term denoted the party in England that opposed the power of the monarch and supported the supremacy of Parliament. Newspapers printed cartoons of King Andrew I. The Whigs defended Congress as the principal instrument of government against what they saw as executive aggrandizement. Although not the majority party in either house of Congress, in the Senate the Whigs formed a coalition with southern Democrats, who resented Jackson's stance on the South Carolina nullification crisis, to pass a censure resolution against Jackson on the bank veto. The resolution chastised the president for assuming "authority and power not conferred by the Constitution and laws." Jackson replied in a vehement protest that the Senate's own act of censure exceeded the Constitution.

Thus, Jackson's broad definition of presidential power galvanized congressional opposition. Future sessions of Congress confined the actions of all but two of Jackson's nineteenth-century successors—Polk and Lincoln—within the doctrine of presidential restraint. Jackson won his battle with the bank but lost the war for future presidents with Congress.

Public Leadership

The most novel and long-lasting aspect of Jackson's activism was his claim that the president was the representative of the American people. During the Jacksonian period, a series of electoral reforms increased citizen participation. New states entering the Union granted suffrage to all white men; older states followed suit, dropping property and religious requirements. By 1832, the parties introduced national nominating conventions to replace the broken-down congressional caucus system.[46] Popular election of electors to the Electoral College also was adopted. Some of the changes the Jacksonians pushed for; others they capitalized on. In the elections of 1828 and 1832, the reforms allowed Jackson to be painted as a symbol of the common man, the tribune of the people. The new symbolism carried Jackson's presidential activism beyond Jefferson's. Like Jefferson, Jackson worked as the people's representative through his party. The bank war, for instance, was waged through the Democratic party press and not carried directly to the people. Jackson spoke publicly little more than had Jefferson. Yet Jackson also consciously separated himself from the Democratic party and Congress. With the support of the newly enlarged electorate, Jackson could afford to untether the presidency from congressional dominance in a way that early presidents including Jefferson could not. Jackson implied that because the executive was the branch closest to the public he had a duty to uphold the "wishes and interests of the people."[47]

THE WHIG PRESIDENCY

From a modern perspective, Jackson's presidency had some of the ingredients of the single executive image. Jackson was portrayed as a heroic man of the people who enlivened the presidency with representative ideals and emboldened it by claims of new powers and the expansion of existing ones. His doctrine of governmental restraint, however, pre-empted the image from emerging more fully. It left a powerful president in charge of a circumscribed government. Too, perhaps because Jackson moved so quickly toward the view that the president was in charge, Congress responded to restrain future presidents.

After Jackson's retirement and the single term of Jackson's handpicked successor Martin Van Buren (1837–1841), the party seesaw once again tipped in the opposite direction: Jackson's activist president within a restrained government returned to a restrained president within an activist government. The Whig party controlled the White House for just eight years during the pre–Civil War period, and in four of those years Whig control was questionable. Yet the Whigs thoroughly controlled the philosophy of both the government and the presidency. In the election of 1840, Whigs in Congress campaigned on a familiar set of issues: reincorporation of the national bank, a protective tariff for growing industries, government bonds to cover the national debt, and the sale of public lands to continue westward expansion. The Whigs' presidential candidate in the election, aging military hero William Henry Harrison, also offered a blueprint for the restrained presidency: a single term, no authority to control the public treasury, a restricted use of the veto, no participation in the preparation of legislation, and the submission of reasons for the removal of all executive officers to the Senate. Harrison pledged to do nothing that Jackson had done and do everything that Jackson had not done.

Yet logical integrity often suffers at the hands of politicians. Although Harrison offered his plan to "restore the Administration to its original simplicity and purity," his campaign for president in 1840 out-Jacksoned Jackson.[48] The Whigs conducted a popular canvass, depicting Harrison as a simple man of the people who loved log cabins and hard cider (even though Harrison was well-off and lived in a large brick home). The campaign set a new course for American politics. It established the importance of symbols—the log cabin and cider, which voters identified with the Whig party. It inaugurated the circus-carnival atmosphere of many campaigns to come—vast meetings, songs, parades, party badges, and signs.[49] Harrison's campaign broadened the claim of Jefferson and Jackson that presidents were the representatives of the people. The representatives now became accessible popular figures at election time (even though candidates still did not campaign in person).

Harrison died after only thirty-two days in office and for the first time a vice president succeeded to the presidency in the middle of a term. John Tyler (1841–1845), a one-time Virginia Democrat and only nominally a Whig, disavowed Harrison's plan for a "simple and pure" presidency. Following Jackson, Tyler vetoed two bills to recharter the national bank. Because rechartering the bank was a major Whig project, every member of Tyler's cabinet except Secretary of State Daniel Webster resigned in protest, and Whigs in Congress voted to expel Tyler from the party. In 1842, when Tyler vetoed a tariff measure, the Whigs attempted but failed to push through an impeachment bill and a constitutional amendment to strip the presidency of its veto power.[50] Tyler teetered on the edge of political limbo for the remainder of his term. Except during the wartime administrations of Polk and Lincoln, Whig principles of presidential restraint and governmental activism through Congress reigned during the remaining sixty years of the nineteenth century.

Polk's Activism

Polk (1845–1849), a Democrat, attempted to revive Jackson's presidential activism. He argued that "the President represents in the executive department the whole people of the United States, as each member of the legislative department represents portions of them."[51] He pushed through Congress a program of domestic legislation that included standard Democratic measures of limited government and vetoed, as unconstitutional, bills for internal improvements such as roads and canals.

Polk's chief interest as a policy activist was territorial expansion. He acquired the Oregon Territory and was determined to add land in California and New Mexico following John Tyler's annexation of Texas. Tensions with Mexico mounted as Texas pressed for statehood, and Polk, unable to negotiate a purchase, determined to take California and New Mexico by force. Polk asked Congress to declare war, which it did on May 13, 1846. Unlike Madison, Polk exercised unilateral executive authority during the Mexican-American War. He maintained firm civilian control over the military, personally making some of the battlefield decisions. He reviewed and coordinated the budgets of all executive departments in order to limit expenditures. Yet after the war, sectionalism and the issue of slavery dominated politics and stalled the continuation of an activist presidency.

The Presidency and Sectionalism

Political life before sectionalism and slavery appeared to be remarkably simple. The two parties took opposite sides on issues of banking, tariff, internal improvements, and the military. The Whigs and Democrats, however, did not immediately oppose each other on sectional concerns. Instead, they sought to avoid the economic, cultural, social, and political issues that divided the regions and to strike compromises that would, if nothing else, buy time. This strategy made sectionalism, first and last, a congressional issue—geographic in origin and prone to negotiation in solution. It left little room for presidents to behave as party leaders or as national leaders. Two Whig presidents, Zachary Taylor (1849–1850) and Millard Fillmore (1850–1853), and two Democratic presidents, Franklin Pierce (1853–1857) and James Buchanan (1857–1861) participated in a series of sectional compromises on slavery as the newly settled western territories sought statehood. Yet, under the Whig theory of a restrained presidency, they lacked a claim to steer the direction of legislation, regardless of the topic. They also lacked the wherewithal to appeal directly to the people for national unity.

By Buchanan's term, the two parties began to disintegrate as Congress became increasingly unable to devise new compromises on the issue of slavery. Southern Whigs drifted toward the southern Democrats. Northern Whigs joined northern Democrats to form a new party, known as the Republicans, who sought to prevent the expansion of slavery into the territories. As the sectional split widened and compromises quickly fell apart, presidents acting under the presidential restraint doctrine could do little in response. The political party was their principal vehicle for influence in Congress, the states, and the territories. Yet as the parties crumbled so too did any presidential attempts at intervention. With the unity of the country itself in doubt, the president could hardly claim to be the one person in charge of the country.

LINCOLN

In a four-way race in November 1860, Abraham Lincoln (1861–1865) was elected the nation's first Republican president. During the campaign, southerners protested that they would secede from the Union if the Republicans were elected. Northerners took this threat as a bluff. But by the time of Lincoln's inauguration in March 1861, seven of the deep South states had formed the Confederacy.

In sharp contrast to his four predecessors, Lincoln invoked the theory of presidential activism to meet the national emergency. He combined two clauses from Article II of the Constitution—the commander-in-chief power and the provision that the president "shall take care that the laws be faithfully executed"—to justify a set of extraordinary executive actions taken from April 1861, when southern guns first fired on Fort Sumter, to June 1861, when Congress convened in special session. During those busy three months, Lincoln called out state militias, expanded the army and navy, spent $2 million from the treasury without congressional appropriation, blockaded southern ports, closed post offices to "treasonable correspondences," suspended the writ of habeas corpus in several locations, and ordered the arrest and military detention of suspected traitors.[52] Under his authority as commander in chief, he issued the first Emancipation Proclamation on New Year's Day 1863. He thereby freed the slaves in southern states and ordered the military to protect the new freedom.

To do all this, Lincoln ignored one constitutional provision after another; he broke an assortment of laws. He extended presidential power well beyond military matters to cut deeply into the routine operations of government and the prevailing liberties of the citizenry. Congress authorized none of these matters at the time, although it approved some of them after the fact. The Supreme Court later approved most of Lincoln's actions. The Court stated that the question of whether the South was a belligerent against the nation was "a question to be decided by him and this Court must be governed by the decisions and acts." The Court sternly checked Lincoln's use of military tribunals to try suspected southern saboteurs in areas of the country remote from actual warfare.[53] Yet only after Appomattox and Lincoln's death did the Court say that the president had gone too far.

Lincoln's actions established presidential activism in military affairs. First, he not only claimed sweeping constitutional power but asserted power beyond the Constitution. "Was it possible," he observed, "to lose the nation and yet preserve the Constitution? . . . I felt that measures otherwise unconstitutional might become lawful by becoming indispensable to the preservation of the Constitution through the preservation of the nation."[54] Political scientist Edward Corwin wrote that Lincoln asserted "for the President, for the first time in our history, an initiative of indefinite scope and legislative effect in meeting . . . a war emergency."[55] Second, like Washington in foreign relations, Lincoln followed a strategy of unilateral action. For the most part, Congress and the courts either said yes or did not say no to Lincoln's actions. Third, Lincoln justified his efforts as a representative of the people to determine when the emergency existed and to take all measures necessary to quell it. Still missing, though, to achieve the single executive image was a strong government to complement the extraordinary presidential powers. The government during the Civil War was preoccupied with survival, not with the bold expansion of authority.

THE PRESIDENCY IN DISARRAY

After Lincoln's assassination, executive-legislative relations picked up where they had left off before southern guns fired on Fort Sumter. Before the war, Congress had largely succeeded in imposing presidential restraint. After the war, a large faction of the Republican party, known as the Radical Republicans, again vigorously enforced presidential restraint. They maintained that Congress, not the executive, should be responsible for a tough national policy of Reconstruction that would fully reintegrate the South into the Union and establish rights for southern blacks. They also sought congressional involvement in the appointment and removal of executive officers. Like the Whigs before the war, they favored an activist government that would energetically sponsor legislation to promote the interests of businesses, industries, and railroads.

Agenda Setting

Lincoln's vice president and successor, Democrat Andrew Johnson (1865–1869) attempted to resist the radicals' plans, partly because he favored a more flexible Reconstruction, and partly because he opposed a return to presidential restraint. While Congress was out of session, Johnson issued a series of Reconstruction proclamations of his own. He vetoed the Civil Rights Act of 1866, which granted blacks citizenship, and he urged southern states to oppose ratification of the Fourteenth Amendment.[56] Congress swiftly overrode Johnson's veto of the civil rights bill. The Republicans made the midterm elections of 1866 a referendum on whether the legislature or the executive should control the national agenda. The voters answered in favor of the Radical Republicans. In his assertion of presidential activism, Johnson seemed to plot recklessly his political suicide.

Unlike Andrew Johnson, presidents from Ulysses Grant (1869–1877) through William McKinley (1897–1901) endorsed presidential restraint. They offered few agenda items and did not vigorously pursue their passage in Congress. The main agenda issue of the day was the tariff. Grover Cleveland (1885–1889, 1893–1897), a Democrat, proposed lowering the tariff, but when the measure stalled in the Republican Senate, he did little to rescue it. Cleveland's successor, Benjamin Harrison (1889–1893), supported the highest tariff of the century in 1890 as a good Republican, but he stayed on the sidelines during its passage. Reforms such as the Interstate Commerce Act of 1887, which regulated railroads, and the Sherman Anti-Trust Act of 1890 also were congressional initiatives. War proponents in Congress and the press pressured McKinley to ask for a declaration of war against Spain in 1898, in spite of information he had of a last-minute Spanish decision to suspend hostilities in Cuba. For Grant, Rutherford B. Hayes (1877–1881), Benjamin Harrison, and especially Cleveland, the primary measure of influence over Congress was negative—the veto. Cleveland vetoed 584 bills, more than double the vetoes of all other presidents since Washington combined. Of those, Congress overrode only seven. Yet the veto alone was insufficient to achieve presidential activism.

Executive Action

The post–Civil War presidents spent much of their time making appointments to executive posts. Jefferson and Jackson had begun the practice of patronage, named the "spoils system" during Jackson's tenure. Presidents gave government jobs (the spoils) to loyal party members, replacing officeholders from the losing party. To maintain party unity, presidents accepted the names of job applicants from members of Congress and from state party officials. As the number of government employees grew, patronage grew as a device to control the parties and the executive branch. Presidents made some 619 patronage appointments during the 1820s and 1830s. Lincoln undertook the most thoroughgoing rotation of people from office; he removed 1,457 of the 1,639 officials he inherited from Democrat Buchanan and replaced them with "loyal" Republicans.[57] This number did not include another 8,000 deputy postmasters whom the president also appointed. The number of appointments continued to increase after the war. The question that arose, however, was who would control patronage: the president or those congressional and party officials who gave him the increasingly lengthy lists of names.

Congress stridently answered the question in March 1867 when it overrode President Johnson's veto of the Tenure of Office Act. The act required Senate consent for the president's removal of any executive official previously confirmed by the Senate. To test its dubious constitutionality, Johnson purposely violated the act by removing his nemesis, Secretary of War Edwin M. Stanton. Radical Republicans in the House presented to the Senate eleven charges of impeachment against Johnson, ten of which pertained to violations of the Tenure of Office Act. Johnson, the first and only president to be impeached, was saved from Senate conviction by one vote.[58] The impeachment proceedings marked the nadir of presidential power. Never before or since has Congress so enfeebled a president.

Congress continued to strictly enforce presidential restraint on Johnson's successors. As the issue of Reconstruction began to fade, a new faction in the Republican party, known as the Stalwarts, arose. They were hard-core political professionals committed to building the Republican party organization and heavily dependent on patronage for their political future. On entering office, Republican Ulysses S. Grant, hero of the Civil War, requested the repeal of the Tenure of Office Act. When Senate Stalwart Republicans refused, Grant acquiesced. Grant set up a civil service commission to establish new competitive rules for hiring but the Stalwarts refused to appropriate funds for the commission. Grant abandoned the reform plan, believing that the Congress, not the president, represented the true will of the American people.[59]

Rutherford Hayes and James Garfield fought against the Stalwart's attempts to block presidential nominations. Hayes succeeded in making his cabinet nominations without consulting key Republican senators. After an eighteen-month battle with a leading Stalwart, Senator Roscoe Conkling of New York, Hayes also replaced three top officials of the New York federal customhouse, Conkling's key political base and known to be the most corrupt customhouse in the nation. "The end I have chiefly aimed at," wrote Hayes, "has been to break down congressional patronage. The contest has been a bitter one. It has exposed me to attack, opposition, misconstruction, and the actual hatred of powerful men. But I have had great success. No member of either house now attempts even to dictate appointments. My sole right to make appointments is now tacitly conceded."[60]

Hayes was only partly right. Stalwarts succeeded in forcing his successor and fellow Republican, Garfield, to appoint their choice as secretary of the treasury. To retaliate, Garfield nominated a long-time enemy of Stalwart Conkling, William Robertson, to serve as the collector of the port of New York, one of Conkling's most important patronage positions. "This brings on the contest at once and will settle the question whether the President is registering clerk of the Senate or the Executive of the United States," Garfield wrote.[61] Vice President Chester Arthur, who had been one of the three customhouse bosses fired by Hayes, entered the contest on the side of his close friend Conkling and urged Garfield to capitulate. Attempting to outsmart Garfield, Conkling announced that he would confirm all other appointments except Robertson's. But Garfield responded by withdrawing all New York appointments save Robertson's. The *Baltimore American* proclaimed, "President Garfield has answered the question 'Who is president?'"[62] The Senate confirmed the Robertson nomination on May 16, 1881, and Conkling resigned.

Garfield's victory was fleeting; less than a month later on July 2, 1881, he was shot by a disappointed Stalwart office-seeker. "I am a Stalwart," deranged Charles Guiteau yelled as he shot the president in the back. "Now Arthur is President." Although many expected Arthur (1881–1885) to live up to his reputation as customhouse boss, he supported civil service reform in the Pendleton Act. The act called for removing various positions from patronage and requiring government employees to pass a test of competence. The act's initial application was limited and presidents were still bothered by, in Grover Cleveland's words, "this dreadful damnable office-seeking [that] hangs over me and surrounds me—and makes me feel like resigning."[63] Senators continued to block executive appointments. The Republican Senate lethargically examined the nominations of Democrat Cleveland and attempted to invoke the Tenure of Office Act on many occasions. Finally, however, Congress repealed the act in 1887. After a struggle of two decades, presidents regained their control over executive appointments and removals. Yet the victory did little more than recapture old ground. It did not embolden late-nineteenth-century presidents to advocate executive activism. Presidents recaptured control of the executive domain, but the domain itself was decidedly restricted.

Public Leadership

Finally, the post–Civil War presidents did little to assert themselves as representatives of the people. They did adopt Jackson's rhetoric joining presidents and the public. Hayes wrote in his diary that he was "content to abide the judgment—the sober second thought—of the people." Cleveland had "an idea that the Presidency is preeminently the people's office." McKinley announced that "I can no longer be called the President of a party; I am now the President of the whole people."[64] Yet, they did not act upon the rhetoric. Nor did they offer programs in the people's name or make public appeals on national issues. Johnson, Hayes, and Benjamin Harrison revitalized various forms of the "grand tour" once made by Monroe. Johnson, however, was the only post-war president to speak about policy in any depth. He toured the country to explain his opposition to the Tenure of Office Act. The eleventh impeachment charge against Johnson was about these policy speeches, which people viewed as inflammatory and improper presidential behavior.[65] Thereafter, Hayes made six tours by train, but uttered no policy remarks. Harrison only offered a few very cautious comments on pending legislation. McKinley made no mention of the Spanish-American War or other issues in his speeches. Although presidents claimed a special connection with the public, they resolutely practiced restraint in maintaining it.

CONCLUSION

The presidents immediately before and after the Civil War are often depicted as prosaic, unhappy men unable to champion the office in which they served. In this view, they were too shy, too lazy, too inept, or too stupid to live up to the office's potential. They are blamed as individuals for the shortcomings of their administrations. Yet personality and talent hardly seem to explain why twenty of the twenty-five presidents during the nineteenth century were lords of passivity. Only Washington, Jefferson, Jackson, Polk, and Lincoln are clear exceptions to the nineteenth-century rule of presidential restraint. Nor does it seem possible that the restraint resulted from the charisma, energy, cunning, and intelligence of members of Congress. What stood in the way of nineteenth-century presidents were ideas—those that the framers had fashioned years before. The framers offered a congressionally dominant scheme of government. They proposed a theory of presidential restraint. For the most part, the nineteenth-century presidency followed the framers' philosophy. Woodrow Wilson declared in 1885 that "unquestionably, the predominant and controlling force, the center and source of all motive and of all regulative power, is Congress."[66]

Some of the nineteenth-century presidents had other ideas, each of which moved the office away from the intent of the framers and toward presidential activism. In these views, some elements of the single executive image can be spotted. Jackson mostly firmly asserted that presidents, as the only officials elected by the nation, were the representatives of the people. This assertion is a key element of the single executive image because it says that presidents' powers are derived from a unique, democratic source that no other elected official can claim. William Henry Harrison bolstered this dimension of public leadership by running the first fully popular campaign for office, thereby digging deeper the democratic foundation of the office and the corresponding justification for presidents' use of power. Washington led the way in establishing presidents as the sole organ of foreign relations. Congress never severely questioned this ingredient of presidential activism. Jackson and other presidents vetoed legislation because they disliked it, not necessarily bcause it was unconstitutional. This brought presidents into the legislative process as agenda setters. Congress would have to consider presidents' views on legislation *before* passage or risk a veto. Polk and especially Lincoln established the unilateral authority of presidents as commanders in chief. Decades, however, separated these precedents and they were not incorporated together. As a result, presidential power at the close of the century was confined within the Constitution, as the framers wished.

Moreover, the other ingredient of the single executive image—an activist government—was less evident at the century's end than it had been earlier. Although governmental activism may have inspired socioeconomic changes in the early part of the century under Alexander Hamilton's and Henry Clay's directions, it did not fully keep pace with those changes at the century's close. The activism was narrow and designed to aid businesses and industries. It did little to alleviate the growing problems of farmers, immigrants, laborers, city dwellers, or consumers. By then, government attention to the rights of blacks also had dimmed. The century ended with a presidency of restraint and a national government active within a limited sphere defined by Congress. The framers continued to run the government more than one hundred years after they met in the crowded and comfortless room in Philadelphia. ■

FURTHER READING

On the Constitutional Convention, see: Alexander Hamilton, James Madison, and John Jay, *The Federalist Papers* (New York: Mentor, 1961); Max Farrand, *The Framing of the Constitution of the United States* (New Haven: Yale University Press, 1913); Max Farrand, *The Records of the Federal Convention of 1787*, 4 vols. (New Haven: Yale University Press, 1966). On presidential power, see: William Howard Taft, *The Chief Magistrate and His Powers* (New York: Columbia University Press, 1916); Theodore Roosevelt, *Theodore Roosevelt: An Autobiography* (New York: Macmillan, 1913); Edward Corwin, *The President: Office and Powers*, 4th ed. (New York: New York University Press, 1957). On the nineteenth-century presidency, see: William Goldsmith, *The Growth of Presidential Power: A Documented History*, 3 vols. (New York: Chelsea House, 1974); Jeffrey Tulis, *The Rhetorical Presidency* (Princeton, N.J.: Princeton University Press, 1987); Arthur Schlesinger, Jr., *The Imperial Presidency* (Boston: Houghton Mifflin, 1973); Ralph Ketcham, *Presidents Above Party: The First American Presidency, 1789–1829* (Chapel Hill: University of North Carolina Press, 1984). Sidney Milkis and Michael Nelson, *The American Presidency: Origins and Development, 1776–1990* (Washington, D.C.: CQ Press, 1990); Arthur Tourtellot, *The Presidents on the Presidency* (New York: Doubleday, 1964); James D. Richardson, ed., *Messages and Papers of the Presidents*, 20 vols. (New York: Bureau of National Literature, 1897).

NOTES

1. Max Farrand, *The Framing of the Constitution of the United States* (New Haven: Yale University Press, 1913), 134.

2. Max Farrand, *The Records of the Federal Convention of 1787*, 4 vols. (New Haven: Yale University Press, 1966), 1:289–293.

3. Ibid., 1:65–66, 96–97.

4. Ibid., 2:516–517.

5. Ibid., 3:132.

6. Alexander Hamilton, James Madison, and John Jay, *The Federalist Papers* (New York: Mentor, 1961), 424.

7. Farrand, *Framing*, 163.

8. Reprinted in Robert Hirschfield, *Power of the Presidency* (New York: Aldine, 1982), 53–65. Madison wrote this in the *Gazette of the United States*, Philadelphia, January 29, 1793, August 24, 1793.

9. William Howard Taft, *The Chief Magistrate and His Powers* (New York: Columbia University Press, 1916), 138–145.

10. The immediate topic of their debate was President Washington's Neutrality Proclamation, which claimed U.S. impartiality in a dispute between Britain and France. Hamilton wrote under the pseudonym "Pacificus"; Madison responded as "Helvidius." Their exchange more broadly concerned the proper role of the executive in foreign affairs and the loose versus strict interpretation of executive power in the Constitution.

11. Hirschfield, 53–65.

12. Theodore Roosevelt, *Theodore Roosevelt: An Autobiography* (New York: Macmillan, 1913), 389.

13. Hamilton did not subscribe to this public foundation, although all nineteenth-century presidential advocates (Jefferson, Jackson, Polk, Lincoln) did. Hamilton believed that presidents should energetically direct government, not on behalf of the people but as a curb on the people.

14. Quoted in Edward Corwin, *The President: Office and Powers*, 4th ed. (New York: New York University Press, 1957), 177.

15. James D. Richardson, ed., *Messages and Papers of the Presidents*, 20 vols. (New York: Bureau of National Literature, 1897), 1:131.

16. Corwin, 181.

17. "Account by William Maclay of President George Washington's First Attempt to Obtain the Advice and Consent of the Senate to a Treaty," August 22, 1789, in William Goldsmith, *The Growth of Presidential Power: A Documented History*, 3 vols. (New York: Chelsea House, 1974), 1:392–396.

18. As told by William Crawford of Georgia to John Quincy Adams, who recorded the remark in his memoirs. Quoted in Corwin, 442.

19. In the Senate, Vice President Adams broke a tie vote in favor of Washington's position.

20. Corwin, 87.

21. Ibid., 279.

22. T. Harry Williams, Richard Current, and Frank Freidel, *A History of the United States to 1876* (New York: Knopf, 1959), 187–188.

23. John Fitzpatrick, ed., *Writings of George Washington* (Washington, D.C.: U.S. Government Printing Office, 1940), 30:310–311.

24. Thomas Jefferson to Elbridge Gerry, May 13, 1797, in Merrill Peterson, ed., *The Portable Thomas Jefferson* (New York: Viking Press, 1975), 471–474.

25. Jeffrey Tulis, *The Rhetorical Presidency* (Princeton, N.J.: Princeton University Press, 1987), 65.

26. First Inaugural Address, March 4, 1801, in Peterson, 290–295.

27. Quoted in Leonard White, *The Jeffersonians: A Study in Administrative History, 1801–1829* (New York: Macmillan, 1951), 551.

28. Quoted in Benjamin Page and Mark Petracca, *The American Presidency* (New York: McGraw-Hill, 1983), 44.

29. Quoted in Arthur Schlesinger, Jr., *The Imperial Presidency* (Boston: Houghton Mifflin, 1973), 22.

30. James D. Richardson, ed., *A Compilation of the Messages and Papers of the Presidents, 1789–1897*, 10 vols. (Washington, D.C.: U.S. Government Printing Office, 1896–1899), 1:377–378.

31. In the Tripoli instance, Congress passed a law authorizing the U.S. Navy to conduct a limited war.

32. Quoted in Ralph Ketcham, *Presidents Above Party: The First American Presidency, 1789–1829* (Chapel Hill: University of North Carolina Press, 1984), 109.

33. White, 48–59.

34. Forest McDonald, *The Presidency of Thomas Jefferson* (Lawrence: University of Kansas Press, 1976), 41.

35. Paul Ford, ed., *The Writings of Thomas Jefferson* (New York: Putnam, 1892–1899), 8:26.

36. Tulis, 70–71.

37. Leonard Levy, *Jefferson and Civil Liberties: The Darker Side* (Cambridge, Mass.: Harvard University Press, 1963), 94.

38. White, 55.

39. Stuart Brown, *The American Presidency: Leadership, Partisanship, and Popularity* (New York: Macmillan, 1966), 11–12.

40. White, 39.

41. State of the Union Address of James Monroe, December 2, 1823, in Richardson, *Messages and Papers*, 2:778.

42. Ibid., 3:1206.

43. Veto Message, July 10, 1832, ibid., 2:582.

44. Ibid.

45. Edward C. Mason, quoted in Corwin, 279.

46. Fewer than a third of the Democratic-Republicans in Congress met in caucus to select a candidate, William Crawford of Georgia, in the 1824 election. Three other candidates—John Quincy Adams, Henry Clay, and Andrew Jackson—ran without the caucus's nod. See the discussion in Chapter 4.

47. Second Annual Message, December 6, 1830, Richardson, *Messages and Papers*, 2:512.

48. Goldsmith, 2:637.

49. Stefan Lorant, *The Presidency: A Pictorial History of Presidential Elections from Washington to Truman* (New York: Macmillan, 1951), 143–162.

50. Goldsmith, 2:681.

51. Richardson, *Messages and Papers*, 6:2514–2515.

52. The writ of habeas corpus requires that the government explain why it is holding an individual.

53. *Prize* Cases, 67 U.S. 635 (1863); *Ex Parte Milligan* 71 U.S. 2 (1866).

54. Letter to A. G. Hodgers, April 4, 1864, reprinted in Harry Bailey, Jr., and Jay Shafritz, eds., *The American Presidency: Historical and Contemporary Perspectives* (Chicago: Dorsey Press, 1988), 33.

55. Corwin, 232.

56. The amendment grants blacks citizenship, prohibits any state from denying any person life, liberty, or property without due process of law, and calls for the equal protection of the laws for all people.

57. Goldsmith, 2:981–983.

58. Richard Nixon resigned before the House voted on impeachment articles against him stemming from Watergate.

59. Wilfred Binkley, *The Powers of the President: Problems of American Democracy* (Garden City, N.J.: Doubleday, 1937), 159.

60. Diary entry, July 14, 1880, in Williams, 3:612–613.

61. Theodore Clarke Smith, *James Abram Garfield: Life and Letters* (New Haven: Yale University Press, 1925), 2:1109.

62. Quoted in Sidney Milkis and Michael Nelson, *The American Presidency: Origins and Development, 1776–1990* (Washington, D.C.: CQ Press, 1990), 174.

63. Quoted in Arthur Tourtellot, *The Presidents on the Presidency* (New York: Doubleday, 1964), 166.

64. Ibid.

65. Tulis, 83–93.

66. Woodrow Wilson, *Congressional Government* (Cleveland: World, 1973), 31; first published in 1885.

CHAPTER 3

The Presidency of Activism

L illian Hellman, a twentieth-century American writer and political activist, reflected on the layers of the past in her memoirs *Pentimento*:

Old paint on canvas, as it ages, sometimes becomes transparent. When that happens it is possible, in some pictures, to see the original lines: a tree will show through a woman's dress, a child makes way for a dog, a large boat is no longer on an open sea. That is called pentimento because the painter "repented," changed his mind. Perhaps it would be as well to say that the old conception replaced by a later choice, is a way of seeing and then seeing again.[1]

Around the turn of the twentieth century, Americans gradually replaced their old conceptions of the presidency and government with new ideas. Americans saw once, and then saw again, slowly changing their minds. The previous chapter discussed the power criterion of the single executive image, which states that the president is the single most powerful person in the United States, if not in the world. The chapter defined two ingredients needed to bring about this power criterion: a theory of presidential activism mixed with a theory of governmental activism. During the nineteenth century, the government and the executive were confined for the most part within a theory of restraint espoused by the framers of the Constitution. The government itself, while growing in size, did not grow significantly in tasks. The presidency witnessed a restrained exercise of power by its incumbents. Although Washington, Jefferson, Jackson, Polk, and Lincoln pursued some elements of activism, even they did so in the name of limited government or during war.

In the early years of the new century, governmental activism and presidential activism combined for the first time. As the century moved on, the union of these two kinds of activism, although pulled by remnants of the past, stood. The combined activism grew faster in some areas than in others. The old thoughts were not erased, but many became hidden and forgotten, like layers of oil on canvas. The image of the single executive in charge of the government began to rival and conceal the once vivid scene of a dominant Congress. This chapter explores why the single executive image is a creation of the twentieth century and why the plural presidency is a creation of that image.

GOVERNMENTAL ACTIVISM

The growth of the United States—in international involvement, territory, population, and industry—placed demands on the government to grow. As a result of the Spanish-American War in 1898, the United States gained possession of the Philippines (for $20 million), Puerto Rico, and Guam, and annexed the Hawaiian Islands. By 1900, America was also a growing military power with a standing army of 125,000 men compared to just 42,000 five years before. Too, the United States was a growing world economic power as the value of exports tripled and the value of imports doubled from 1870 to 1900, totaling more than $2 billion in trade.[2] The population of the United States doubled between 1870 and 1900, in part because of the arrival of hundreds of thousands of European immigrants. Industrialization grew in steel, automobiles, and oil. In 1860, $1 billion had been invested in American industry, which produced goods valued at $1.8 billion. By 1890, American industrial investment topped $6.5 billion and the annual value of production neared $10 billion. By 1910, in spite of the depression of the mid-1890s, these figures doubled. The transformation also was evident in the work force. From 1860 to 1890, nonagricultural employment soared 300 percent while those engaged in agriculture grew by only 50 percent. Only three in ten people worked as farmers in what was once Jefferson's pastoral nation.[3]

To accommodate these changes, governmental activism was spurred in three directions. First, the government did more of everything it was already doing. In 1880, the government's internal revenue collections amounted to $123 million; by 1900, this figure more than doubled to $295 million.[4] Second, the government did more things. During the nineteenth century, government activity could be placed neatly in one of five categories: postal services, tariffs and customs, diplomacy, territorial expansion, and Indian affairs. In the early twentieth century, government policies spread to railroads, drugs, food, banks, and national parks. Third, as political scientist Hugh Heclo observes, "more government means not merely more things done more extensively; it implies a larger cumulative presence of the governmental sector vis à vis the rest of society."[5] The government entered society in ways not envisioned before. Government regulation of the market, heretofore unknown, became accepted practice. Government became a major employer. Government expenditures and the number of federal government employees roughly doubled in the two decades between 1881 and 1901.[6] Government redistribution of income, by means of a national income tax and various tax cuts, added to government's omnipresence.

The expansion of government was not merely the inescapable result of a changing society. Changing ideas about the role of government accompanied these societal developments. A disparate group of urban and middle-class reformers known as the Progressives attracted elements of both the Democratic and the Republican parties from 1900 onward. The Progressives urged social responsibility through government. They worried, as had the earlier, less successful, agrarian Populists, that the nation was on the verge of moral, political, and material ruin. Their principal solution was government regulation—the direct intervention of government in the market to end unfair practices. The Progressives wanted the government to slow the nation's wild laissez-faire ride and end an array of repugnant conditions: unsafe factories, wide disparities in income, shaky farm prices, corporate dominance, political corruption, banking chaos, and urban poverty. Thus, not only societal change but new social thinking expanded the raison d'être of government, redefining it as an active participant in society rather than a passive creature of society.

PRESIDENTIAL ACTIVISM

Theodore Roosevelt (1901–1909) and Woodrow Wilson (1913–1921) were the first two presidents to join presidential activism with governmental activism. Both were Progressives and they believed, as other Progressives did, that one central force should direct government's reforms and that the president was that central force. In their enthusiasm for reform, Roosevelt and Wilson offered a new view of an active executive leading an active government. The first hint of the single executive image appeared.

Roosevelt's definition of presidential activism was twofold. First, in the absence of any specific prohibitions in the Constitution or in law, presidents had an inherent grant of executive power to do whatever they felt was necessary to bring about reform. Presidents should take charge of the government by dominating foreign policy, controlling the executive branch, and pursuing a domestic policy agenda. Second, presidents could make such claims because they were representatives of the people. Presidents took charge by attaining and claiming public support. Roosevelt harked back to the views of Lincoln and Jackson but gave them bolder form. Lincoln had acted during crisis; Jackson had proclaimed stewardship to limit the scope of government. "Men who understand and practice the deep underlying philosophy of the Lincoln school of American political thought," wrote Roosevelt, "are necessarily Hamiltonian in their belief in a strong and efficient National Government and Jeffersonian in their belief in the people as the ultimate authority, and in the welfare of the people as the end of government."[7]

Wilson intensified Roosevelt's claims of public leadership. Roosevelt had felt that public leadership was a significant aspect of the presidency, but Wilson maintained that the link between the president and the public was the most significant feature of the office. He wrote that the president "is the only national voice in affairs. Let him once win the admiration and confidence of the country, and no other single force can withstand him, no combination of forces will easily overpower him. His position takes the imagination of the country."[8]

Presidential activism coupled with governmental activism entered five areas of influence at different times during the twentieth century:

Public leadership: Presidents became visible public leaders through their public appearances, radio addresses, and television performances.

Agenda setting: Presidents defined the public agenda in legislation and budgeting.

Executive action: Presidents prepared unilateral executive actions that carried the same weight as laws, but did not require congressional approval.

Diplomacy: Presidents gained tight control over diplomacy in making treaties and other international agreements.

Military efforts: Presidents engaged in military actions without congressional permission.

The five areas did not come together and stay together with Roosevelt and Wilson. Other presidents during the early quarter century—Harding (1921–1923), Coolidge (1923–1929), Hoover (1929–1933), and especially Taft (1909–1913)—did not much like Roosevelt's and Wilson's ideas. Yet the combination of further societal changes, technology advances, and political strategies tugged along the more reticent executives. The single executive image, its foundation laid, emerged slowly, but permanently.

PUBLIC LEADERSHIP

Of the five areas, presidents' efforts as leaders of public opinion were perhaps the most significant transformation from the nineteenth century.[9] Although there were precedents in the nineteenth century in each of the other four areas, precedents for public leadership were sparse and went in directions opposite those taken by Wilson and Roosevelt. To be sure, many presidents of the nineteenth century pointed out that they were the lone representatives of the public, yet they made the observation in private—in their diaries and to friends. They did little to shape the public debate in the name of the public.[10] In three stages, twentieth-century presidents embraced the symbolically powerful, if impossible, claim that they were the only officials who represented all the people: through direct public appeals, on radio, and on television.

Presidential Appeals

Roosevelt and Wilson made numerous public appearances, and with these direct appeals the single executive image came more sharply into view in four ways. First, Roosevelt and Wilson showed how presidents could become well-known public figures. "Roosevelt has the knack of doing things, and doing them noisily, clamorously," remarked a critic; "while he is in the neighborhood the public can no more look the other way than the small boy can turn his head away from a circus parade followed by a steam calliope."[11] Not to be outdone, Wilson personally delivered his first State of the Union message to a special session of Congress—a practice last employed by John Adams. Surprised that Roosevelt had missed such an opportunity for publicity, Wilson remarked to his wife, "Yes, I think I put one over on Teddy."[12]

Roosevelt also recognized that the tools were in place to make presidential newspaper headlines. During the early years of the twentieth century, newspaper stories were increasingly nonpolitical, but Roosevelt took a very short step to blur the distinction between nonpolitical, human interest stories and human interest stories about political figures.[13] He captured the attention and the enthusiasm of the American public for his personal exploits as a safari hunter, nature lover, and cavalryman and for the energy of his political stands. The new attention on presidents centralized political news in Washington and at the White House. It also raised the visibility element of the single executive image—the president began to be recognized as the single most visible politician in the nation.

Second, Roosevelt and Wilson used their public remarks to reaffirm the moral principles of the nation. This in itself was not new. Nineteenth-century presidents frequently articulated these ideals in their inaugural addresses but would never have dreamed of personalizing these principles. Roosevelt and Wilson, however, tied the moral focus expressly to the executive. This was the essence of Roosevelt's "bully pulpit." Wilson went further, delivering "visionary speeches" that, in the Progressive mode, set out new creeds rather than merely reinforcing well-established ones.[14] The two presidents' didactic lessons provided an even stronger base for the single executive image. The president was not only the public's representative, but he was also the moral leader of the nation.

Third, Roosevelt and Wilson advocated policy stands and attempted to mold public opinion in favor of those stands. Unlike their nineteenth-century counterparts who shunned talking policy, both presidents not only announced where they stood on specific issues but offered their own initiatives for public debate. To capture public attention, Roosevelt gave his plan to moderate the excesses of business the catchy title the "Square Deal." Wilson followed with his reform program, the "New Freedom." The enunciation of these programs was a significant step toward the single executive image. The programs highlighted the presidents' preferences for change, not the preferences of party or Congress.

Fourth, the two presidents sought public support for presidential policy positions before Congress. Roosevelt spelled out the new strategy: "I achieved results only by appealing over the heads of the Senate and House leaders to the people, who were the masters of both of us."[15] The mobilization of public support also extended the single executive image: presidents' self-proclaimed special link to the people became a bargaining chip with Congress. As one might imagine, not only was the claim of public support far-reaching, but its success was problematic. Presidents had to line up numerous tactical devices such as talking to the public at the right time with the right message and conveying public support to Congress at the right time in the right way. In 1906, Roosevelt strongly directed public attention to the passage of the Hepburn Act to regulate railroad rates. Before congressional debate opened, he rallied public support in two national trips; but once debate began, he fell silent. He worried about "Old Guard" Republicans, especially in the Senate, who eschewed Progressive reforms and who had to be courted carefully and quietly under nineteenth-century rules.

Wilson expanded Roosevelt's practice by making direct appeals to the public even as congressional debate went on. Wilson's biggest personal campaign, arguably the most elaborate of any president, involved his attempt to secure Senate ratification of the Versailles Treaty, which ended World War I. In the treaty were provisions for the League of Nations, Wilson's impassioned vision of an international peacekeeping organization. Wilson embarked on a 22-day, 8,000-mile journey during which he made 37 major speeches and numerous shorter ones and rode in a dozen parades. The trip ruined his health and came too late in the deliberations of the Republican Senate, which turned down the League. Yet Wilson's defeat did not claim presidential persuasion as a victim. Later presidents saw political advantages in public relations, and the public fancied the show even if it did not always buy the message.

Sandwiched between Roosevelt and Wilson was William Howard Taft. "After T. R. came Taft," Gifford Pinchot, head of the Forest Service, reminisced. "It was as though a sharp sword had been succeeded by a roll of paper, legal size."[16] Taft strictly adhered to the theory of presidential restraint and shunned public leadership. He believed that presidents were granted only the powers stated in the Constitution or in federal laws and that there was no inherent executive power to act on behalf of the people. Yet, much to Taft's dismay, people expected such public leadership because of Roosevelt. According to his biographer, Taft suffered from an "inability to popularize or make exciting his accomplishments."[17] The three Republican presidents after Wilson—Harding, Coolidge, and Hoover—who followed the general guidelines of presidential restraint, nonetheless played by Roosevelt's and Wilson's new rules on public leadership. Indeed, Harding and Coolidge were quite good at it. Clinton Gilbert, a commentator of the times, summed up the outlook at the outset of Warren Harding's term:

We magnified the office of President and satisfied that primitive instinct in us which must see the public welfare and the public safety personified in a single individual, something visible, tangible, palpable. The President speaks and you read about him in the daily press; the President poses and you see him in the movies and feel assured, as in smaller realms under simpler conditions people were able to see their monarch dressed and equipaged in ways that connected him with all the permanence of the past, a symbol of stability, wisdom, and the divine favor.[18]

The outlines of the single executive image were becoming ever more distinct.

Radio Politics

Although Harding and Coolidge rejected Roosevelt's and Wilson's practice of influencing Congress through public opinion, they were not bashful. These two Republicans recognized that they could easily make news as policy advocates, moral leaders, and public celebrities. On several occasions they publicly expressed their policy preferences about topics ranging from coal mines to farms.[19] Harding and Coolidge also sought to exalt the moral principles of the nation. Harding spoke of the "temple of democracy."[20] Coolidge called for "idealism in its most practical form."[21] But they most ably demonstrated the significance of personal news about a national figure. They benefited immeasurably from two technological advances: motion pictures and radio. The two presidents were popular subjects of newsreels, which captivated audiences in the growing number of movie theaters across America.

Wilson's defeat on the League of Nations highlighted the gap between technology and presidential efforts to rally public opinion in the first two decades of the century. Presidents' chief means of reaching the public were the same as they had been since Washington's day: the printed word and speeches before live audiences.[22] The national scope of Wilson's campaign for the League was best suited to a national, direct medium such as radio, but Wilson had to undertake a tiring and time-consuming cross-country trip, which allowed him to reach only a fraction of the populace. Radio, only a few years away, was too many years away to help Wilson. Radio greatly enlarged presidents' leadership of public opinion. It offered a direct, immediate link between the chief executive and the entire nation. Radio's effect on the public's perception of presidents as representatives of the people and on the development of the single executive image can hardly be overstated.

Coolidge was the first mass media president. Although nicknamed "Silent Cal," Coolidge was anything but mute in front of a radio microphone. "I am very fortunate that I came in with the radio," he remarked. "I can't make an engaging, rousing, or oratorical speech to a crowd . . . but I have a good radio voice, and now I can get my messages across to them without acquainting them with my lack of oratorical ability."[23] Coolidge's State of the Union message was the first presidential address broadcast to major cities across the nation. Garrulous Coolidge continued each month with broadcasts during which avid radio listeners tuned in to platitudinous speeches about the Daughters of the American Revolution, Washington's Birthday, and Armistice Day. Elmer Cornwell writes, "Here was the first President in history whom more than a tiny fraction of the populace could actually listen to, and whose voice they could come to know at first hand. Small wonder that the man developed a tangible meaning for millions—more so perhaps than any of his predecessors."[24] Radio enlivened a human dimension in the single executive image.

Hoover continued Coolidge's practices of making ceremonial talks over the radio but avoiding public explanations of policy measures. Despite his efforts to implement policies to restore the nation's confidence after the stock market crash of 1929 and the growing depression, Hoover did little to explain his plans to the public and did not make effective use of radio. In an era of prosperity, Coolidge's broadcasts made the use of radio look foolproof. In darker times, Hoover's broadcasts were insufficient to the task. Hoover failed to recognize that the power of the presidency was now tied to public leadership and that the president needed to perform as a public spokesman in order for presidential policy plans to have any chance for success.

By the time Franklin Roosevelt (1933–1945) made his first fireside chat to the nation in 1933, the main innovations in presidents' mass leadership were well in place. Roosevelt's contributions were refinements of past presidents' efforts. His radio broadcasts no longer supplemented public speeches; they *were* public speeches, and Roosevelt made many more of them than had even Coolidge. This practice fit well with the growing popularity of radio. By 1933, between 50 and 60 million listeners tuned in to radio programs broadcast by two networks, CBS and NBC.[25] Too, Roosevelt, by means of radio, rejuvenated the practice of seeking public support for presidential policy measures before Congress. All future presidents followed his lead. This permanently tied public leadership to claims of presidential power as part of the single executive image. Presidents would seek policy initiatives in the name of the people and use radio, and eventually television, to win public backing.

Presidential Television

Modernity often tricks people. They assume that the most recent events are the most important. In an era of global television coverage by satellites and cable hookups in living color, it is easy to think that the biggest change in presidential public leadership occurred with the introduction of television. Yet there was perhaps less change from radio to television in the 1950s and 1960s than from newspapers to radio in the 1920s and 1930s. Radio already provided presidents with direct, unmediated, instantaneous, and mass contact with the entire nation.

Television's principal contribution was to create a "mediated intimacy" between the president and the public. Gone was the disembodied voice; in its place was a walking, talking figure whom people could observe as they would a family member or a friend. Television offered more diverse formats and techniques than radio. Videotape and live coverage conveyed action and drama—including historic meetings with other heads of state, public appearances, family events, and even presidential assassinations—in ways that radio and newsreels could not capture. Television heightened the personal dimension of the single executive image that Coolidge had cultivated so fastidiously. In a few short years, the medium captured Truman (1945–1953), who spoke stiffly in front of a podium and only occasionally looked to the camera; Eisenhower (1953–1961), who hired actor Robert Montgomery as a television coach to make him more comfortable with the new medium; and Kennedy (1961–1963), who needed no coaching.

The early television presidents relied heavily on the spoken word, as had their radio predecessors. Eisenhower made major national addresses to provide regular updates on legislation, cabinet activity, and his foreign travels. Kennedy instituted nationally televised news conferences. More recently, however, presidents have heightened the importance of "photo opportunities." These events generate vivid pictures of a president engaging in a colorful ceremony or conducting presidential business in an especially photogenic setting. The powerful visual image takes the place of the spoken word. Ronald Reagan's advisers carefully sought positive pictures and were less concerned about what was said—whether positive or negative. George Bush took part in a classic photo opportunity when he flew to the Grand Canyon to herald the signing of an agreement to clean up smog from a nearby power plant and to pose, talking to park rangers, with the canyon's majesty as his backdrop. A single picture provided Bush the chance to promote himself as the "environmental president."

Over the last three decades, the visual message, the positive picture with the president prominently displayed, has become an integral part of presidential leadership. Yet it has not added another dimension to presidential public leadership. From Franklin Roosevelt onward, presidents have regularly appeared as public celebrities, moral leaders, policy advocates, and congressional persuaders. Today television allows them to carry out these tasks. Had television not been invented, they would have continued to meet the tasks on radio.

SETTING THE NATIONAL AGENDA

As policy advocates and congressional persuaders, presidents in the twentieth century began to set national policy agendas. Agenda setting involves the identification of major national problems and the formulation of plans for their solution. Presidents, once reticent about taking any policy positions, began to assert the directions the government should take in solving social and economic problems. This assertiveness simultaneously deepened the connection between presidential activism and governmental activism and illuminated the single executive image. Presidents began to appear as the one official in charge of the government's plans for action—and these plans were more ambitious and sweeping than ever before. Presidents sought to identify national agenda items in two arenas: legislation and budgeting.

Presidents as Lawmakers

The old adage about legislation, "The president proposes; the Congress disposes," is not that old. Indeed, the nineteenth-century maxim, following the Constitution, was the reverse: "Congress proposes; the president disposes." The Constitution provides for a limited role of presidents in legislative affairs. They sign and veto bills and from time to time inform Congress about the state of the Union. The constitutional framers and nineteenth-century practitioners did not view these powers as vehicles by which presidents would propose national policy plans. Not until the Progressives championed the view that innovative reform could be expected from a single official did a new presidential power of agenda setting in legislative affairs emerge.

Progressive Programs. Theodore Roosevelt sent to Congress moderate Progressive initiatives designed to "subordinate the big corporations to the public welfare."[26] His Square Deal included antitrust action, railroad regulation, consumer protection, civil service reform, and conservation. Wilson's New Freedom crafted Progressivism to the traditions of the Democratic party: lower tariffs, an overhaul of the banking system, agricultural reform, and the adoption of a federal income tax. Although many of the topics of the legislation were those that Democrats had brought up time and again since the generation of Jackson, the scope of government action anticipated by the legislation was something Jackson, who favored governmental restraint, would have disliked.

Normalcy. The end of World War I in 1919 signified the dénouement of the Progressive era. Warren Harding, campaigning for president in 1920, asserted a new vision: "America's present need is not heroics, but healing; not nostrums but normalcy."[27] The term "normalcy," which had not existed in the English language before Harding's speech, became a household word and a watchword for government action from 1920 to 1929. "What we want in America," Harding said, "is less government in business and more business in government."[28] This policy platform was at once simple yet comprehensive. It required government to cease efforts to control, limit, and regulate the activities of business. Harding wished to return to the economic prudence at the core of conservative Republican philosophy through a series of tax cuts and tariff hikes.

Presidential normalcy of the 1920s had three features. First, Harding's and Coolidge's efforts to reinvigorate business did not dismantle the government's regulatory structure. The various agencies created during Theodore Roosevelt's and Wilson's terms remained: the Federal Reserve Board, the Federal Trade Commission, the Food and Drug Administration, the Forest Service. Second, as discussed below, Republicans felt that prudence in government required a coordinated budget. This was a tacit recognition of both the growth of government and the need for a brand-new executive power, one not envisioned in the Constitution. Finally, both Harding and Coolidge eschewed the legislative silence of their nineteenth-century Republican ancestors Grant, Harrison, and Hayes and their twentieth-century compatriot Taft. Although Harding and Coolidge were in no measure as active as Wilson and Roosevelt, they publicly urged Congress to cut taxes on several occasions. The barrier against presidents making public statements on policy measures tumbled when presidents who believed in the general policy of restraint spoke out on legislation nonetheless. Harding's and Coolidge's faithful, albeit cautious, following of the new activism of Roosevelt and Wilson drafted the single executive image in indelible ink. The image would not fade away.

Political Choice in the Depression. Hoover believed in a more activist presidency than did Coolidge or Harding, especially once the Great Depression struck. Although Hoover often is blamed for the depression, which began with the stock market panic in 1929, he did more than any former president faced with a similar economic collapse had done. Hoover gave strong support to an agricultural program to improve farm credit, a $2.5 billion public construction plan to ease unemployment, and government loans to state governments and businesses to prevent bankruptcies. Yet Hoover, bound to a conservative philosophy, would go only so far. He battled Congress over the key issue of direct relief to the unemployed and drought-stricken farmers in the Southwest. He felt that public welfare assistance, known then as the "dole," was unconstitutional and would bankrupt the treasury. Hoover instead believed that private relief agencies should ease the situation.

Hoover was both an emblem and a victim of the single executive image. His several initiatives designed to ease the economic calamity revealed how accepted the union of presidential and governmental activism had become. Yet, the limits to those actions revealed how much farther people expected the president and the government to go. People turned to the president, as the popular focus of politics, to alleviate the situation. The worse the situation became, the more people blamed Hoover for not acting boldly enough. An entire language of unfulfilled expectations arose: "Hoovervilles" (makeshift encampments of the homeless and unemployed), "Hoover blankets" (newspapers used for warmth), and "Hoover flags" (empty pockets turned inside out).[29] Hoover could not run or hide from public expectations of presidential and governmental activism.

The New Deal. In the election of 1932, voters did more than defeat Herbert Hoover and elect Franklin Roosevelt. Although they did not know it at the time, Roosevelt's election immeasurably and irrevocably widened the activism of the presidency and the government. Roosevelt's view of executive power was bold and expansive. He believed, as had his cousin Theodore, in an inherent executive power, especially in times of economic or military emergency. In his inaugural address, Roosevelt declared, "This Nation asks for action and action now." He promised to seek from Congress "broad executive powers to wage a war against the emergency, as great as the power that would be given to me if we were in fact invaded by a foreign foe."[30]

Franklin Roosevelt raised the legislative agenda-setting power of Theodore Roosevelt and Woodrow Wilson to two new levels. First, the sheer quantity of his initiatives surpassed earlier presidential activism. New Deal legislation was adopted on a wide range of topics, including banking, securities, direct relief to states and localities, industrial codes, labor practices, and farm relief. Second, much of the legislation contained a delegation of power from the Congress to the president to implement the programs. The president not only asserted power to propose programs but gained from Congress discretionary power to implement the programs. In 1935 the Supreme Court did tell Congress and Roosevelt that there were limits to this discretion. It struck down key New Deal legislation in agriculture and industry.[31] Yet, given the full sweep of legislation in which the president received delegated powers, the Court's decision did not severely impede Roosevelt's approach to presidential activism.

The New Deal measures also advanced governmental activism. The government grew in size and expenditures. In the decade from 1931 to 1941, expenditures quadrupled and 800,000 people were added to the government payroll. The New Deal's boldest measure of governmental activism was the Social Security Act of 1935. It added an entire dimension of policy action that the government heretofore had shunned: direct social welfare assistance. Although today the term "social security" colloquially refers to government benefits given retired workers, the Social Security Act also provided for other forms of assistance to the jobless, the disabled, widows, and poor families with dependent children. The idea of social insurance, well known in Europe, was a drastic departure from normally accepted U.S. policy. It argued for the government doing what Americans had always insisted the states or private groups should do. Yet Roosevelt insisted that the government's duty was to provide individuals with financial security during hard times. The president, by implication, was the provider of this new security.

Roosevelt's initiatives thus strengthened the single executive image. As a legislative agenda setter, the president could assert that he, more than any other official, was the one person in charge of the government. Moreover, with the president depicted as a guarantor of newly established government services, the substance of the image grew. The president was not just the representative of the public but was a representative who looked out for citizens' personal well-being.

Postwar Programs. Although most of Roosevelt's actions were taken under the guise of emergency—first economic and then international—his lengthy tenure and the enlarged scope of government left precedents for all future presidents regardless of whether an emergency was present. Presidents since Truman have actively asserted the legislative agenda-setting power. Truman announced the "Fair Deal," Kennedy heralded the "New Frontier," Johnson (1963–1969) called for the "Great Society," and Richard Nixon (1969–1974) announced the "New Federalism." The Reagan (1981–1989) initiatives were never officially titled because the nickname "Reaganomics" stuck so well. Contemporary presidents not only announce policy packages, they busily submit annual legislative programs to Congress. The expansion of governmental activism has also continued into space, medical care, civil rights, housing, education, occupational safety, and the environment. The government intervenes in virtually all areas of the economy and society in at least some small way and often in much bigger ways. The union of presidential activism and governmental activism is now a permanent feature of government.

Presidents' legislative agenda-setting power adds to their images as the single most powerful figure in charge of the government. In their State of the Union messages, presidents annually suggest that they are in charge of the government by the set of legislative priorities they send to Capitol Hill. Yet presidents' efforts at agenda setting also show limits to the single executive image. Government activism spurs congressional activism too. Congress ultimately decides what issues will be dealt with in what ways. For instance, in 1977, Jimmy Carter (1977–1981) presented to Congress a comprehensive package of energy legislation that contained ten major programs. Two years later, Congress had rejected four of the ten proposals, significantly modified three, and enacted three into law. Carter's win-loss record is not atypical. Presidents set agendas, but Congress settles them.

Budget Control

Presidents also attempt to set the national agenda through budgeting. They establish priorities about how much or how little money should be spent on government programs. During the early twentieth century, agencies submitted individual requests throughout the year to various congressional committees. Congress found it difficult to sift through all the proposals and determine how much money to raise and spend. In 1921, Harding backed legislation that instituted a central comprehensive budget under presidential control. All departments and agencies would submit their money requests to a Bureau of the Budget, located in the Treasury Department, which would coordinate the requests as part of "The President's Budget." Ironically, Harding favored the virtues of government frugality more than he resisted presidential activism. He spiritedly invoked the new authority, trimming $2 billion from the 1923 budget. The presidential budget process was reinforced in 1946 when Congress passed the Full Employment Act, which held presidents responsible for developing a plan to maintain full national employment. Presidents use both the budget and employment devices to promote priorities for government spending within the economy. The measures considerably strengthen the president's hand with Congress and the bureaucracy, giving the executive a much greater say in the government agenda. They also enliven the single executive image as the president appears at the center of the budget process.

Nonetheless, as in legislation, Congress limits presidents' claims of power and control in budgeting. The Budget and Impoundment Control Act of 1974 placed restrictions on presidents' abilities to impound—that is, refuse to spend congressionally appropriated money. It also brought Congress into the budget process on equal footing with the executive, creating the Congressional Budget Office and a congressional budget process to parallel that of the president. Congressional activism in budgeting now matches presidential activism in budgeting.

Presidents as active budgeteers and lawmakers add to the single executive image. Both tasks allow presidents considerable visibility in proposing national priorities—whether a budget proposal for an increase in defense spending or a legislative proposal to clean up the environment. The single executive image thus carries with it the notion that presidents serve as chief problem solvers. Yet there may be incongruities among the presidentially proposed solutions, the final solutions mandated in Congress, and the results of those final choices. These disparities create a raw edge for the single executive image. People come to expect presidents to actively solve problems, and presidents happily oblige by establishing a set of agenda items; but presidents face grave difficulties in solving the problems in the manner they prefer or in solving them at all.

EXECUTIVE ACTION

In grade school, Americans are taught that Congress passes the laws, the courts interpret the laws, and the president executes the laws. But the execution—or putting the laws into effect—always seems vague. In this regard, the Constitution itself is of little help. Ironically, the document is least clear on the very core of what executives are supposed to do—execute. Presidents are supposed to "take care that the laws be faithfully executed."

With the help of Congress, presidents have created a unilateral "presidential lawmaking power" under the guise of faithful execution of the laws. Congress sets down general policy in a piece of legislation and then delegates to the president the authority to execute the laws. To carry out these general mandates, presidents have principally employed "executive orders," as shown in Table 3.1, which carry the weight of law, but which do not require the approval of Congress. Executive orders technically constitute execution of the law, but most often they amount to its creation.

During the early twentieth century, presidents issued executive orders primarily for two administrative purposes: to dispose of public lands and to issue rules for government employees. Franklin Roosevelt extended the use of executive orders beyond administrative matters to presidential policy initiatives. As a notable example, on taking office, he signed an executive order temporarily closing all banks in the nation until a plan could be worked out to put them on a stable footing. Presidents have issued executive orders on civil rights as a way around legislative inaction. Roosevelt established the Fair Employment Practices Commission in 1943 to prevent discrimination in

Table 3.1 Executive Orders Since Franklin Roosevelt

President	Total	Average Per Year
Roosevelt, I	1663	416
Roosevelt, II	1057	264
Roosevelt, III/IV	802	187
Truman, I	499	136
Truman, II	398	100
Eisenhower, I	272	68
Eisenhower, II	206	52
Kennedy	228	76
Johnson	316	63
Nixon, I	251	63
Nixon, II	104	66
Ford	152	63
Carter	311	78
Reagan, I	237	59
Reagan, II	165	41
Bush[1]	125	42

1. 1989–1991.
Source: Calculated by the author from *Code of Federal Regulations* (Washington, D.C.: U.S. Government Printing Office) successive volumes 1936–1991.

hiring by government agencies and military suppliers. Truman ended segregation in the armed services by executive order. Eisenhower and Kennedy issued executive orders to enforce desegregation of schools in Arkansas, Mississippi, and Alabama. In 1965, Johnson signed an executive order that required affirmative action (affirmatively seeking qualified minority applicants) in hiring by the federal government and government contractors. Reagan, who opposed affirmative action, sought to "repeal" Johnson's order, but public controversy swelled and he dropped the idea.

The courts usually have upheld executive orders as having the same force in law as statutes. Recently, a fervent controversy about U.S. abortion policy has centered on an executive order signed by Reagan and continued by Bush that prohibits family planning clinics that receive federal funds from informing their clients about abortion. The Supreme Court upheld the order in *Rust* v. *Sullivan* (1991). Although Congress tried several times to pass legislation that would negate the executive order, Bush vetoed one such attempt and threatened to veto others. Congress was unable to rally the two-thirds votes from both houses needed to override a Bush veto. The law would have taken precedence over (and therefore voided) the executive order. Constitutionally, a law is superior to an executive order when the two are in conflict. Executive orders allow presidents to act as substitute legislators and thus reinforce the image of a single executive who can issue laws without becoming entangled in the tedium of the congressional lawmaking process.

PRESIDENTIAL DIPLOMACY

Throughout the nineteenth century, presidential activism in diplomacy was well established (see Chapter 2). The central change in the twentieth century has been the increasingly global nature of American foreign policy. Theodore Roosevelt and Woodrow Wilson embraced the Progressive belief that America should spread its version of peace and justice throughout the globe. World War I and World War II assured the permanent global posture of the United States. The Supreme Court ratified the doctrine that presidents are the "sole organ of foreign relations" for the United States in *U.S.* v. *Curtiss-Wright Export Corporation* (1936). The Court stated that the president is "the sole organ of the federal government in the field of international relations—a power which does not require as a basis for its exercise an act of Congress, but which, of course, like every other governmental power, must be exercised in subordination to the applicable provisions of the Constitution."[32]

Presidents have expanded their foreign policy role still further by the use of what are known as "executive agreements." These are international agreements entered into by presidents, but, unlike treaties, they do not require Senate consent. Executive agreements often are used on relatively routine matters such as the exchange of postal services between the United States and other countries or the tax status of Americans living abroad. But presidents also have signed executive agreements that significantly shape foreign policy. The practice was begun in 1817 by James Monroe, who arranged with Great Britain to limit naval forces on the Great Lakes. By executive agreement, John Tyler annexed Texas and William McKinley ended the war with Spain. Twentieth-century presidents have been more active. By executive agreement, Franklin Roosevelt exchanged American destroyers for the lease of British military bases and finalized the postwar agreement at Yalta, Harry Truman both started and ended U.S. involvement in the Korean War, and Lyndon Johnson and Richard Nixon made key decisions to escalate the Vietnam War.[33]

Today, the executive agreement is the principal instrument of American foreign policy. Most agreements with other nations are consummated by executive agreements rather than by treaties.[34] Presidents since Truman have entered into roughly seven times more executive agreements than treaties, as Table 3.2 shows. Presidents keenly prefer executive agreements as foreign policy devices for three reasons. First, they need not fuss with the Senate, as the Constitution requires with the ratification of a treaty. Second, presidents prefer executive agreements as a matter of practicality to handle the nation's burgeoning diplomatic workload. If all agreements entered into by the U.S. took the form of treaties, the president and Senate would have time to do little else other than work on their ratification. Finally, the Supreme Court has consistently maintained that executive

Table 3.2 International Agreements Since Franklin Roosevelt

President	Executive Agreements	Treaties	Total
Roosevelt, I	87	59	146
Roosevelt, II	120	45	105
Roosevelt, III/IV	402	15	417
Truman, I	605	63	668
Truman, II	766	82	848
Eisenhower, I	857	105	962
Eisenhower, II	848	110	958
Kennedy	763	68	831
Johnson	1008	104	1112
Nixon, I	797	118	915
Nixon, II	319	62	381
Ford	677	99	776
Carter	1021	148	1169
Reagan, I	775	125	900
Reagan, II	1224	47	1271

Source: Calculated by the author from U.S. Department of State, *Treaties and Other International Agreements* (1950–1980), for 1981–1983 *Current Treaty Index* (1987); from *Treaties in Force* (1989), for 1984–1988.

agreements have the same legal effect as treaties.[35] The Court has argued that the presidential power to make executive agreements is "a modest implied power of the President who is the 'sole organ of the Federal Government in the field of international relations.'"[36]

Treaties, however, have not been abandoned as a form of diplomatic exchange. In some instances, the importance of the diplomatic effort mandates a treaty, as did the creation of the North Atlantic Treaty Organization (NATO) after World War II and several Strategic Arms Limitation Talks (SALT) beginning in the Nixon administration. Presidents see political advantages in having the Senate on board. In other cases, tradition dictates that a treaty, rather than an executive agreement, be adopted. Even with treaties, there are few difficulties for presidents. To be sure, presidents must keep an eye on Congress, especially the Senate, in negotiating them. Provisions of important treaties frequently evolve through informal consultation with senators. Senate ratification, however, is usually pro forma. Since 1949, presidents have won approval of all but two treaties submitted to the Senate.[37] If a treaty is in trouble, a president is more likely to withdraw it rather than face its defeat. In addition, the Supreme Court has held that presidents may unilaterally break treaties.[38]

The sole organ doctrine espoused by presidents and approved by the Supreme Court gives presidents a broad, inherent claim of constitutional power and plenty of room for unilateral action. Part of the sole organ doctrine states that presidents know best what the interests of the nation are. Presidents thus take action in foreign affairs as representatives of the people, looking out for the best interests of the nation. The single executive image is easily observed.

MAKING WAR WITHOUT
DECLARING WAR

The President shall be Commander in Chief of the Army and Navy of the United States, and of the Militia of the several States, when called into the actual Service of the United States.

Presidents' greatest activism and that of the nation is in military affairs. The framers felt that the designation "commander in chief" merely established that a civilian head would be in charge of the military. The commander would have the power to respond to surprise attacks but do little more without congressional authorization. Congress was expressly given the power to declare war. Presidents, however, have never accepted such a cramped view of their commander-in-chief power. Instead, they have created their own "war-making" power. Although Congress is supposed to declare war, presidents have effectively devised a preemptory executive power to declare de facto states of war. Thus, the constitutional power of Congress to declare war is a virtual nullity. As Madison sardonically observed to Jefferson in 1798 "the History of all Govts demonstrates, that the Ex. is the branch of power most interested in war, & most prone to it."[39]

At its most basic, this presidential war-making power involves presidents' ability to unilaterally commit American troops anywhere on the globe. Americans are often confused about whether a war must be officially declared by Congress in order for it to be a right and proper war. There have been just five declared wars in American history: the War of 1812 with Great Britain, the Mexican-American War in 1846, the Spanish-American War in 1898, World War I, and World War II. American politicians add to this confusion by their language about wars. Wars become "police actions," "conflicts," "protective reactions," and "peacekeeping missions." Wars need not be declared, and they need not be very long in order to be wars. "The ceremony of a formal denunciation of war has of late fallen into disuse," Hamilton wrote in 1788.[40]

Presidents' powers in the two declared total wars of the twentieth century—World War I and World War II—were vast, extending over the American economy and social order. For instance, Congress gave Wilson the power to take over factories, fix prices in certain industries, declare certain exports unlawful, censor foreign communications, and operate the telephone and telegraph systems. Similarly, Congress gave Roosevelt the authority to establish and staff numerous emergency boards, to negotiate with other countries the sale, lease, or exchange of various defense-related items, and to evacuate and confine seventy thousand American citizens of Japanese descent from the West Coast. The types of actions Lincoln took during the Civil War were enlarged by twentieth-century delegations of power from Congress.

Twentieth-century presidents have most frequently exercised the commander-in-chief authority unilaterally in two types of restricted military interventions: (1) limited wars, limited as to persons, places, and things, and (2) emergency interventions, in which a few American troops are committed for a short duration to protect American lives (see Chapter 8 for a complete discussion).

Limited War

Limited wars are limited in resources and goals. They involve specific initial commitments of troops, although the numbers typically increase incrementally as the war goes on. The goal of the war is often short of all-out victory. The U.S. objective has been to prevent communism in a vulnerable nation or to stop the aggression of a dictator, not necessarily to bring the enemy to its knees. Often, the logic of a limited war is that stopping aggression in one region will prevent global instability. Limited wars are defensive military efforts confined to one country or one region. Today, however, because the United States is a world military and economic power, the necessities of "defense" are open to extravagant interpretation. A president can determine that almost any nation at any moment in some way impinges on the security of the United States. Presidents have conducted three limited wars in the twentieth century: the Korean War, the Vietnam War, and the Persian Gulf War.

Harry Truman took the most expansive view of the president's power to conduct limited war. In six days during June 1950, Truman committed air, sea, and ground forces to aid South Korea, which was under attack by communist forces from the north. When a senator asked Truman to seek a congressional resolution to authorize the American intervention, Truman replied that he did not need one but instead could use his constitutional powers as commander in chief. As the war went on over the remainder of his term, Truman consistently relied on the commander-in-chief power to add more men, expand the theater of war into North Korea, and threaten the use of nuclear weapons.

Unlike Truman, Lyndon Johnson sought a resolution from Congress to support his decision to commit major ground troops in Vietnam after a reported attack on two American destroyers by North Vietnamese gunboats in the Gulf of Tonkin. Eight days later, on August 7, 1964, Congress passed what became known as the Gulf of Tonkin Resolution, which read, "The Congress approves and supports the determination of the President, as Commander in Chief, to take all necessary measures to repeal any armed attack against the forces of the United States and to prevent further aggression." The resolution, passed unanimously in the House and with only two dissenting votes in the Senate, stated further that "The United States regards as vital to its national interests and to world peace the maintenance of international peace and security in Southeast Asia."[41]

Johnson sought the resolution as a matter of political expedience, not constitutional principle. He agreed with Truman that the president already had full constitutional authority to send troops. In 1967, Johnson remarked, "We did not think the resolution was necessary to what we did and what we're doing."[42] Johnson saw the resolution as political insurance. Having congressional permission placed the president in an enviable position: Congress gave him full power to direct the war but shared responsibility for it in case something went wrong. When the Vietnam War turned ugly and Congress repealed the Tonkin Gulf Resolution in January 1971, Nixon returned to Truman's exclusive reliance on the commander-in-chief power.

Congress attempted to reassert its own role in war making with the War Powers Resolution of 1973. Passed over President Nixon's veto, the act was designed to prevent protracted and costly wars like Vietnam. The act requires that the president "in every possible instance shall consult with Congress before introducing United States Armed Forces into hostilities or into situations where imminent involvement in hostilities is clearly indicated." The president must submit a report to Congress within forty-eight hours after committing U.S. troops into actual or "imminent" hostilities, describing the reasons and the constitutional authority for the action. Once the notification has been given, a clock starts ticking. The president has sixty days to complete the military action, although he may request a thirty-day extension. The operation, however, must be completed in the ninety-day period unless Congress declares war or supplies specific authorization for the use of American armed forces.[43] The War Powers Resolution looks good on paper as a device by which Congress reclaims some control over American military efforts. Yet Presidents Ford, Carter, Reagan, and Bush have brushed aside its requirements.

After Iraq invaded Kuwait in August 1990, Bush asserted that he had the sole authority to send first 120,000, then 200,000, and ultimately 560,000 men and women from all branches of the armed forces to fight Iraq. The buildup began for America's first limited war since Vietnam. Bush, like Johnson, asked Congress to pass a resolution sanctioning the use of force. The resolution was consistent with a United Nations declaration that requested member nations to use "all necessary means" to force Iraq out of Kuwait unless it ended its occupation by January 15, 1991. Several days before the deadline, a sharply divided Congress passed Bush's resolution. With the resolution in hand, Bush saw no need to follow the requirements of the War Powers Resolution.

It is unclear what precedents Bush and Congress set. Although asking for the resolution, Bush insisted that he had the authority to deploy troops without a vote. "I don't think I need it," he said.[44] Although granting the resolution, many members of Congress denied they were giving Bush a declaration of war without saying it in so many words. Given the doctrine of presidential war, Bush was factually correct though constitutionally in error. Had Bush, like Truman, ordered the war commenced without congressional approval, Congress could have done little. Yet the Constitution is on Congress's side. The framers believed that presidents, as commanders in chief, should be able *only* to repel sudden attack against Americans without consulting Congress. For this reason, most presidents have jealously guarded the impression that they are acting defensively rather than offensively. The framers also believed that the president and the Congress would act together in *all* offensive situations. Although Bush's plans at the time of congressional debate were not crystal clear, it seemed likely that he would engage in an offensive war and not wait for an Iraqi ploy as a justification for a defensive riposte. A day after the U.N. deadline expired, Bush ordered the war to begin. This marked the first time since James K. Polk sent American troops after Mexican dictator Santa Anna that a president had ordered an offensive military action that was unprovoked by a direct attack on the United States or American troops.

Although factually correct, congressional members who denied that they had declared war probably misconstrued the constitutional import of their resolution. The sweeping language of the resolution certainly made it easy for Bush to maintain that he had congressional consent. The language was even more open-ended than had been the Tonkin Gulf Resolution.

In commencing limited war, the president can use the single executive image as a resource to rally the country behind the cause. But, if the war drags on and the enemy claims victories, as Truman and Johnson found out, the president's ability to use the single executive image as a resource diminishes. Unable to conclude the wars, both presidents' public and congressional support tumbled.

Emergency Intervention

Since the Vietnam War, presidents have favored the use of emergency interventions—the engagement of a small number of troops for a short period of time in situations that purportedly involve threats to American lives. Emergency interventions are often symbolic flexings of American military muscle that do not risk the large-scale entanglements of limited wars.

Presidents have consistently circumvented the requirements of the War Powers Resolution in entering emergency interventions. They are loath to have their hands tied by fiddling with the consultation and report procedures specified in the act. When Gerald Ford ordered the marines and navy to rescue a U.S. merchant ship, the *Mayaguez,* seized by Cambodia in May 1975, he did not report to Congress. A White House spokesman announced that "Mr. Ford acted under his constitutional war powers to protect the lives and property of Americans."[45] Ford himself called the War Powers Resolution a "very serious intrusion on the responsibilities of the President as Commander-in-Chief and the person who formulates and ought to execute foreign policy."[46] Similarly, Carter did not tell Congress beforehand of the secret, ultimately unsuccessful, helicopter mission in March 1980 to free the Americans held hostage in Iran. In October 1985, Ronald Reagan did inform congressional leaders that he was sending nineteen hundred troops to Grenada to protect the lives of American students on the island. But he expressly refused to comply with the notification requirements of the War Powers Resolution. George Bush followed Reagan's lead when he ordered the invasion of Panama in December 1990. Harry Truman summed up the presidential logic long before the War Powers Resolution was passed. When asked whether he should consult Congress in his decision to send four more divisions to reinforce the U.S. Army in Europe, Truman replied that, "I do not have to unless I want to. But of course I am polite and I usually always consult them."[47] Yet Truman did not consult Congress, nor have most presidents, with or without the War Powers Resolution.

Only once has a president come close to being bound by the provisions of the War Powers Resolution. In 1983, President Reagan ordered U.S. marines to Lebanon as part of an international peacekeeping force. Thus began a battle between Reagan and Congress over whether the troops were in actual or imminent hostilities and whether the War Powers Resolution was operative. On August 29, 1983, two marines were killed. The adminstration played down the idea that the marines were targets of extremist groups in Lebanon. In a congressional hearing, Secretary of State George Shultz contended that the attacks were really against the Lebanese Army. The marines, said Shultz, were not facing imminent hostilities; they had, unfortunately, gotten in the way. On September 1, the Pentagon announced that two thousand marines would join a U.S. Navy task force off the Lebanese coast. The administration again argued that the marines were not in imminent hostilities, because they were going to be aboard ships. But on September 5 two more marines were killed and three days later an American warship fired on a Muslim artillery position. Senator Charles Percy of Illinois remarked, "We have people up in helicopters, we're shooting rockets and artillery—if that isn't imminent hostilities, I don't know what is."[48]

A complex compromise was worked out. Congress passed and Reagan signed a joint resolution with two key provisions. First, the imminent hostilities provision of the War Powers Resolution was invoked and the clock started ticking retroactively, as of August 29, 1983, the day the first marines were killed. Second, the president was given up to eighteen months (rather than the ninety-day maximum called for in the War Powers Resolution) to keep the marines in Lebanon. In turn, President Reagan declared in writing that he did not recognize the constitutionality of the War Powers Resolution and that he retained constitutional authority as commander in chief to deploy American armed forces whenever and wherever he wanted.[49]

It is unclear who, if anyone, won this battle between the president and Congress. By allowing the president eighteen months to complete U.S. involvement in Lebanon, Congress was indirectly acknowledging that the ninety-day requirement of the War Powers Resolution was too restrictive. By talking out of both sides of his mouth, acknowledging that the marines were indeed facing imminent hostilities but denying the constitutionality of the War Powers Resolution, Reagan cleverly muddled the presidential side of the compromise. American troops left Lebanon before the eighteen-month deadline. On October 23, 1983, a truck operated by a suicidal driver carrying more than 10,000 pounds of explosives rammed into a building at the Beirut airport, killing 241 American marines asleep inside. By the end of the year, after a direct military clash between U.S. and Syrian military forces in Lebanon, Reagan came under increasing pressure from Congress and the American public to withdraw the "peacekeeping force" from Lebanon. By early 1984, Reagan quietly removed the remaining marines and sailors.

War at Pleasure

Restricted military action, whether in the form of limited wars or emergency interventions, provides presidents unique opportunities to expand their war-making power. Presidents have moved from wars directly affecting the United States to wars affecting the "security of the United States," as Lyndon Johnson did in Vietnam. Presidents once asked congressional permission in advance of troop commitments, as James Madison did during a war against Algeria in 1815. But now they ask Congress for a blank check in advance, as Johnson and Bush did. Or they maintain that they need no congressional permission at all, as Truman and Nixon asserted. They have treated the requirements of the War Powers Resolution as optional rather than mandatory, as Ford, Carter, Reagan, and Bush did.

The dangers of this expansion are captured in the sentiments of Congressman Abraham Lincoln, who wrote in 1848 about President Polk's actions against Mexico. Congressman Lincoln stated his objections to the president being "the sole judge" of the necessity to invade another country. "Allow the President to invade a neighboring nation, whenever he shall deem it necessary to repel an invasion" said Lincoln, ". . . and you allow him to make war at pleasure."

Suppose, Lincoln argued, a president says that "he thinks it necessary to invade Canada, to prevent the British from invading us, how could you stop him?" How could Congress force him to change his mind? "You may say to him, 'I see no probability of the British invading us' but he will say to you 'be silent; I see it, if you don't.'"[50]

Congress today, weary after Vietnam, plainly sees these perils. As the debates before the Persian Gulf War attested, Congress is no longer likely to be the silent partner of military affairs that presidents prefer. For the foreseeable future Congress will act as a watchdog. Its best weapon is not the War Powers Resolution but its appropriations power—its ability to give money to presidents and take money from presidents. But congressional efforts are almost always reactive and inevitably sporadic. Congress finds it difficult to keep in tow presidents who have a penchant for military solutions to international problems. Political scientist Michael Rubner has observed that especially in the numerous emergency interventions—the "low-intensity and low-risk conflict situations that produce quick and seemingly favorable military outcomes, the political power of Congress to limit the chief executive . . . is very feeble."[51] As a result, the power criterion of the single executive image—the president as the single most powerful official of the government—despite some constraints, is very bold in military affairs.

ACTIVISM, THE SINGLE EXECUTIVE IMAGE, AND THE PLURAL PRESIDENCY

Of the sixteen American presidents of the twentieth century, only one—William Howard Taft—vigorously fought presidential activism. All other presidents of this century advanced, or at least did not oppose activism in one, if not more, of the five areas of newly found presidential power: public leadership, agenda setting in legislation and budgeting, executive action, diplomacy, and military efforts. Power in each of these areas not only fosters presidential activism but enlarges the scope of governmental activism. Too, each new power adds form and substance to the power criterion of the single executive image—the president as the single most powerful official in the government. To be sure, the image of one bold, powerful figure is less vibrant in some areas than in others. Presidents are more in charge of the government in its dealings in foreign and military affairs than they are in setting legislative and budget agendas. Nevertheless, the single executive image is always a part of presidential reality. It is a resource for presidents to use in their dealings with Congress, bureaucrats, the courts, other nations, and the public.

The activism of presidents not only reinforces the single executive image but creates demands for a diverse, plural institution equipped to handle the workload. The plural presidency comprises four central components: (1) a decentralized organization, (2) ambiguous decision making, (3) policy complexity, and (4) political fragmentation. The more responsibilities presidents and the government claim, the more presidents require institutional help to meet their obligations. The activism of presidents is the activity of the presidency as an institution. As presidents do more of any single thing, the presidency as an institution handles it. Andrew Johnson signed 79 executive orders. Lyndon Johnson recorded 316, roughly 60 each year. Yet Lyndon Johnson issued these orders only in the most technical sense. Most were requested by and drafted in departments and agencies of the executive branch and screened in the Bureau of the Budget (which was reorganized as the Office of Management and Budget in 1970).

As presidents do more things, policy complexity and political fragmentation grow. Whereas presidents now announce urban policies, 150 years ago the nation had fewer than twenty cities with populations over 100,000. Today presidents have highway programs when 150 years ago there were no cars. Today presidents have nuclear waste policies, air traffic control policies, global warming policies, trade policies, offshore oil policies, and endangered species policies. Political fragmentation also affects these policies. The presidency must accommodate the policy views of Congress, the courts, state governments, and organized groups on these issues.

The combination of decentralized organization, policy complexity, and political fragmentation pulls the presidency in many directions and pushes the organization toward ambiguous decision making. In the confluence of complex policy areas, group and governmental pressures, and disparate organizational units, the presidency makes up the president's mind. Presidents are public leaders, but they have a team of press and speech writers to bring their leadership to life. Presidents deliver policy programs and budgets, but they rely on domestic policy analysts, legislative liaison experts, and a large contingent in the Office of Management and Budget, which checks the various proposals as they come from departments and agencies. Presidents neither see nor sign many executive agreements. Because there are so many, they are often drawn up and signed on behalf of the president by the American chargé d'affaires in the country involved. Presidents go to war, but the National Security Council, the Joint Chiefs of Staff, the national security adviser, the secretaries of defense and state, and assorted generals and admirals go, too. Within and across the various units of the plural presidency, ambiguity mounts. Many advisers do not know what others involved in their policy area are doing, and they know even less about what others working on different projects are accomplishing. Presidents convey the single executive image, but the presidency moves as a plural body.

CONCLUSION

The framers of the Constitution did not conceive of the president as the single most powerful figure in the country. Indeed, they would have shuddered at such a suggestion. Yet they nonetheless set the wheels in motion for the single executive image coming to fruition in the twentieth century at the hands of presidents, aided and abetted at times by Congress and the courts. The framers wrote a broad and loosely worded grant of constitutional power to a single individual as president. Presidents have capitalized on the fact that there is only one executive. The exclusivity almost by definition gives people the impression that one person is in charge of the whole show. The electoral autonomy and the general grant of constitutional authority give presidents the opportunity to assert claims of indefinite, expandable power to be exercised on behalf of the people.

According to Jeffrey Tulis, modern presidential activism has created a "second Constitution" that is at odds with the framers' "first Constitution."[52] The "second Constitution" establishes powers for the president far beyond what the framers intended. It grants the president authority as representative of all the people. It gives the chief executive vast power as the sole organ of the nation in foreign affairs. It provides for a presidential war-making power created by presidents and a presidential lawmaking power delegated by Congress. It adds an agenda-setting role for the president in the legislative and the budget processes. As the scope of government has expanded in the twentieth century, so has the scope of presidential power. Presidents have taken or have been given almost every constitutional power imaginable in the "second Constitution." The single executive image fits best in foreign and military affairs, where the "second Constitution" is most clear. Presidents can create the image of a bold, decisive executive who single-handedly represents the United States to the world and fends off its enemies.

Still, the core of the framers' work—separate institutions sharing power—remains. The "first Constitution" unmistakably places limits on presidents' abilities to effectively use the single executive image. Although modern presidents like to assert an ambitious role in legislation, ambition does not presage success. Because of the very nature of the legislative process, it is impossible for presidents to assert the kind of unilateral action in legislation and budgeting that they assert in diplomacy and war. What members of Congress do to presidents' programs once they get their hands on them is usually not a pretty sight. The same is true when presidents attempt to direct the budget. In the areas of legislation and budgeting, the lines of the single executive image are less distinct than those in the areas of foreign and military affairs, but presidents nonetheless enjoy considerable ability to darken the lines.

Presidents must contend with both the "first Constitution" and the "second Constitution." They must be activists within a system that constrains their unilateral actions and rarely gets them what they want in many policy matters. The framers have not had the last laugh. But they are still smiling. ∎

FURTHER READING

On presidential public leadership, see: Woodrow Wilson, *Constitutional Government in the United States* (New York: Columbia University Press, 1908); Jeffrey Tulis, *The Rhetorical Presidency* (Princeton, N.J.: Princeton University Press, 1987); Elmer Cornwell, *Presidential Leadership of Public Opinion* (Bloomington: Indiana University Press, 1965); Richard Rubin, *Press, Party, and Presidency* (New York: Norton, 1981). On agenda setting, see: Sidney Milkis and Michael Nelson, *The American Presidency: Origins and Development, 1776–1990* (Washington, D.C.: CQ Press, 1990). On executive action, see: Gary King and Lyn Ragsdale, *The Elusive Executive* (Washington, D.C.: CQ Press, 1988). On diplomacy, see: Lawrence Margolis, *Executive Agreements and Presidential Power in Foreign Policy* (New York: Praeger, 1986); Loch Johnson, *The Making of International Agreements: Congress Confronts the Executive* (New York: New York University Press, 1984). On war, see: Arthur Schlesinger, Jr., *The Imperial Presidency* (Boston: Houghton Mifflin, 1973); Cecil Crabb and Kevin Mulcahy, *American National Security: A Presidential Perspective* (Pacific Grove, CA.: Brooks/Cole, 1991).

NOTES

1. Lillian Hellman, *Pentimento: A Book of Portraits* (Boston: Little, Brown, 1973), 3.
2. Richard Hofstadter, William Miller, and Daniel Aaron, *The American Republic*, 2 vols. (Englewood Cliffs, N.J.: Prentice-Hall, 1959), 2:339.
3. Ibid., 2:162–189, 194.
4. U.S. Department of Commerce, *Historical Statistics of the United States: Colonial Times to the Present*, 2 vols. (Washington, D.C.: U.S. Government Printing Office, 1975), 2:1108.
5. The argument is taken from Hugh Heclo, "Introduction: The Presidential Illusion," in H. Heclo and L. Salamon, *The Illusion of Presidential Government* (Boulder, Colo.: Westview, 1981), 3–4.
6. *Historical Statistics*, 1:224, 2:1114.
7. Theodore Roosevelt, *The Works of Theodore Roosevelt* (New York: Scribner, 1926), 20:414.
8. Woodrow Wilson, *Constitutional Government in the United States* (New York: Columbia University Press, 1908), 68.

9. Jeffrey Tulis, *The Rhetorical Presidency* (Princeton, N.J.: Princeton University Press, 1987).

10. The one exception was Andrew Jackson, who toured the country to lambast Congress's passage of the Tenure of Office Act, which required presidents to submit their removals of executive officials to the Senate for confirmation (see Chapter 2).

11. Quoted in Elmer Cornwell, *Presidential Leadership of Public Opinion* (Bloomington: Indiana University Press, 1965), 15.

12. Quoted ibid., 46.

13. Richard Rubin reports that in a sample of front-page stories, only 20 percent were political during the 1880s and 1890s, and this continued through the 1940s. See Rubin, *Press, Party, and Presidency* (New York: Norton, 1981), 58, 119.

14. Tulis, 135.

15. T. Roosevelt, 20:342.

16. Quoted in Sidney Milkis and Michael Nelson, *The American Presidency: Origins and Development, 1776–1990* (Washington, D.C.: CQ Press, 1990), 211.

17. Henry Pringle, *The Life and Times of William Howard Taft*, 2 vols. (New York: Farrar and Rinehart, 1939), 2:603.

18. Clinton Gilbert, *Behind the Mirrors* (New York: Putnam, 1921), 61.

19. Barbara Hinckley, *The Symbolic Presidency* (New York: Routledge, 1990), 112–113.

20. Quoted ibid., 117–118.

21. Calvin Coolidge, Inaugural Address, March 4, 1925. *Inaugural Addresses of the Presidents* (Washington, D.C.: U.S. Government Printing Office, 1982); and Calvin Coolidge, "The Destiny of America," in *The Price of Freedom: Speeches and Addresses* (New York: Scribner, 1924), 342.

22. Cornwell, 254.

23. Quoted ibid., 90.

24. Ibid., 92, 96.

25. Rubin, 132.

26. T. Roosevelt, 20:416.

27. Quoted in Robert Murray, *The Harding Era: Warren G. Harding and His Administration* (Minneapolis: University of Minnesota Press, 1969), 70.

28. Quoted in Hofstadter, Miller, and Aaron, 442.

29. James David Barber, *The Presidential Character* (Englewood Cliffs, N.J.: Prentice-Hall, 1985), 20.

30. *Inaugural Addresses of the United States* (Washington, D.C.: U.S. Government Printing Office, 1982).

31. *Schechter Poultry Corp.* v. *U.S.*, 295 U.S. 495 (1935); and *Panama Refining Co.* v. *Ryan*, 293 U.S. 388 (1935).

32. *U.S.* v. *Curtiss-Wright Export Corporation*, 299 U.S. 304 (1936).

33. Lawrence Margolis, *Executive Agreements and Presidential Power in Foreign Policy* (New York: Praeger, 1986).

34. Loch Johnson, *The Making of International Agreements: Congress Confronts the Executive* (New York: New York University Press, 1984), 12; and Johnny Killian, ed., *The Constitution of the United States of America: Analysis and Interpretation* (Washington, D.C.: U.S. Government Printing Office, 1987), 531.

35. *U.S.* v. *Belmont,* 301 U.S. 324 (1937); *U.S.* v. *Pink,* 315 U.S. 203 (1942); *Dames and Moore* v. *Regan,* 453 U.S. 654 (1981).

36. *U.S.* v. *Pink,* 315 U.S. 203 (1942), at 229.

37. Gary King and Lyn Ragsdale, *The Elusive Executive* (Washington, D.C.: CQ Press, 1988), 144–145, Table 3.4.

38. *Goldwater* v. *Carter,* 444 U.S. 996 (1979), involved Senator Barry Goldwater's challenge to President Carter's decision to establish diplomatic relations with the People's Republic of China by breaking the 1955 Mutual Defense Treaty with Taiwan. The Court supported Carter's claim that he could break the treaty without obtaining Senate approval.

39. Madison to Jefferson, April 2, 1798, in James Madison, *Writings,* ed. Galliard Hunt (New York: 1906), 6:312–313.

40. Alexander Hamilton, James Madison, and John Jay, *The Federalist,* No. 25 in *The Federalist Papers* (New York: Mentor Books, 1961), 165.

41. Public Law 88–408.

42. Quoted in Arthur Schlesinger, Jr., *The Imperial Presidency* (Boston: Houghton Mifflin, 1973), 180–181.

43. Public Law 93–148, 87 Stat. 555 (1973).

44. Joan Biskupic, "Constitutional Questions Remain," *Congressional Quarterly Weekly Report,* January 12, 1991, 70.

45. Quoted in Larry Berman, *The New American Presidency* (Boston: Little, Brown, 1987), 75.

46. Gerald Ford, "The President and Political Leadership," in *The Virginia Papers on the Presidency,* ed. K. Thompson, 2 vols. (Lanham, Md.: University Press of America, 1980), 2:21–40.

47. *Public Papers of the Presidents: Harry S Truman, 1951.* (Washington, D.C.: U.S. Government Printing Office, 1952), 19.

48. *Congressional Quarterly Almanac, 1983* (Washington, D.C.: CQ Press, 1984), 114–117.

49. Ibid., 113–118 and E-36–E-38.

50. Letter to W. H. Herdon, February 15, 1848, in Abraham Lincoln, *Collected Works of Abraham Lincoln,* ed. R. P. Basler, 8 vols. (New Brunswick, N.J.: Rutgers University Press, 1953), 1:451–452.

51. Michael Rubner, "Antiterrorism and the Withering of the 1973 War Powers Resolution," *Political Science Quarterly* 102 (Summer, 1987): 210.

52. Tulis, 17–18.

CHAPTER 4

Running for President

E lection 1: The campaign starts three weeks before election day. By law, the campaign period can last only twenty-one days. The two candidates for chief executive are well known to the public. One has twenty-six years of experience in the legislature; the other has thirteen. Both also have served in the executive. There are no primaries or regional caucuses. No paid campaigning on television is allowed. Each candidate is allocated a set number of ten-minute broadcasts aired free by each of the television networks. The candidates speak on issues advanced by their parties; their personal images have relatively little to do with the outcome of the campaign. Turnout for the election is 75 percent.

Election 2: The campaign starts more than a year before election day. Of the two candidates for chief executive, one is well known to the public, and one has gained visibility only in the last six months of the campaign. The first candidate has five years of experience in the legislature and eleven years of experience in the executive. The other candidate has never held an elected post in the national government. Both go through months of primaries and their parties' conventions. Paid television commercials dominate the campaign, which turns on the images of the candidates, notably the darker side of their images. Turnout for the election is just below 50 percent.

Americans reading the account of Election 1 would be hard pressed to believe that such a national election exists. They undoubtedly would shake their heads and mutter about the luxuries of utopia. Yet the passage describes a typical general election in Great Britain (specifically, in 1992). British observers pondering Election 2 would have a similarly hard time figuring out why so much fuss and bother is spent on a fairly typical American presidential election (in 1988).[1]

Explaining American presidential elections to someone from another country is a task often fraught with embarrassment and confusion. Presidential elections, from the preparations for the New

90

Hampshire primary to the final tallies in the electoral college, are among the oddest in the modern world. Americans begrudgingly take for granted what foreigners find difficult to comprehend: that today's presidential elections are all-consuming processes that place inordinate amounts of attention, time, and money into a single elected office. There are some 529,000 elected offices in America, but only one of them is a national industry.

Each feature of the single executive image—uniqueness, importance, power, visibility—is found in modern presidential elections. The fact that presidents are the only officials elected by the entire country immediately defines their *uniqueness* and *importance*. In Great Britain (and other parliamentary countries) there are no executive elections per se. The British prime minister actually is elected only within his or her own constituency (legislative district). The parties, not the prime ministerial candidates, are the central focus of the campaign. Each party names a member of Parliament as its leader, and those party leaders become candidates for prime minister at election time. The leaders run in safe seats that their parties always win, so they will be re-elected to Parliament even though only one will serve as prime minister. Normally, the party winning the most seats in Parliament is entitled to form a government and name the prime minister. The losing party forms a "shadow cabinet," and its candidate becomes the opposition leader. Imagine in the 1992 race, George Bush and Bill Clinton holding seats in Congress; Bush is designated as opposition leader for the Republicans and confronts Clinton on all major issues rather than disappearing from the media spotlight after the election.

Separate executive and legislative elections in the United States create an uncommon electoral prize that makes presidential candidates and presidents a unique focus of national politics. Prime ministers, as the title implies, are the head of a team of ministers who are all members of Parliament. The overlap between the executive and the legislature and the presence of the opposition leader diffuse some attention away from the prime minister.

Presidents since Jefferson have claimed *power* from their election victories. The framers of the American Constitution felt that popular consent would act as a constraint against errant executives. But presidents have claimed their election victories as a source of power, not a restriction on power. Indeed, their claims of presidential activism are based on their election by the entire nation. The bigger their victories, the more presidents assert that they have a "mandate" to exercise power on behalf of the people. British prime ministers also claim mandates to carry out campaign promises, but the mandates are for the party as a unit rather than for the prime minister as an individual.

Unceasing media coverage of the presidential race skews public attention toward presidents. It is the lead story for months on end.

Little about congressional races is mentioned in either the national or the local media. As a result, the *visibility* of presidential candidates and of the president is heightened. Although media coverage of British elections is plentiful, the coverage takes place during a compressed period, and the coverage describes the parties' efforts, not simply the efforts of the prime ministerial candidates.

RULES OF THE GAME

The single executive image arises from the rules of the presidential election game. These rules are not necessarily official state laws or party regulations, although some are. Many are informal practices, developed slowly over time, that have become accepted routines. People who wish to enter the game understand that they must play by these rules even if they are not written down. Both written and unwritten rules determine who will run, the types of campaigns they will wage, and, often, who will win. When the rules change, the candidates who surface will change and the types of campaigns they wage will too. Although election rules often appear arbitrary and capricious, they are neither. They typically reflect the interests and fears of a nation. Two prominent characteristics of the American polity have been written into its election rules.

First, American elections have always been influenced by the rhetoric, if not the practice, of democracy. Americans believe in principles of openness, popular control, and mass participation. Elections have been restructured through several stages of greater democratization—moves toward broader suffrage (barriers of wealth, race, and sex fell during the nineteenth and early twentieth centuries) and wider participation in nominations (especially with the advent of the party primary, discussed below). Formally, Americans have the opportunity to participate at numerous levels of the presidential election process, even if many do not take the opportunity. Presidential candidates also convey democratic themes in their campaigns. Since Andrew Jackson, many have portrayed themselves as candidates of the common people. They jockey to uphold the single executive image and demonstrate that they are very aware of and sympathetic to the plight of average citizens. Over time, the openness and democratic themes in presidential elections have fostered greater connections between candidates and voters and have dimished party as a conduit between them. In the United States, parties win elections through their candidates; in Britain (and other European countries), candidates win elections through their parties.

Second, Americans have long seen political parties as barriers against democracy rather than as vehicles for democracy. The Constitution's requirement of separate elections for the executive and the legislature was expressly designed to subdue the "mischiefs of factions" ("factions" was an early term applied to parties). Even when parties inevitably formed during Washington's first term, there were strong feelings of antipathy toward them. In his Farewell Address, Washington spoke of "the baneful effects of the spirit of party generally," which serve "always to distract the public councils and enfeeble the public administration." It is "a spirit not to be encouraged."[2] And it was not. Even in the parties' heyday in the nineteenth century, many looked on parties as a necessary evil at best. As a consequence, parties serve narrowly as devices to select candidates rather than as they do in Britain (and in the rest of Europe) as political unions of like interests that stand for certain ideas but shun others. American parties are vast "umbrellas" that try to shelter as many different interests under one covering as possible. This inclusiveness makes it difficult for voters to figure out what, if anything, the parties stand for.

As added evidence of Americans' ambivalence toward political parties, five presidential candidates in the twentieth century have attempted to by-pass the two major parties altogether. Theodore Roosevelt in 1912 and Robert La Follette in 1924 ran on the Progressive party ticket. The Progressives hoped, but failed, to replace one of the two main parties. George Wallace in 1968, John Anderson in 1980, and Ross Perot in 1992 took on the two main parties as lone candidates without any significant third-party affiliation.[3] The antiparty spirit of America has allowed presidential races to become personal battles among candidates with less emphasis on political parties.

The single executive image looms ever larger as these characteristics define presidential campaigns. "Antiparty democracy" leads toward greater personalization of the campaigns. Candidates do not run on a party platform but make personal appeals as the "people's candidate." They seek to embody a kind of "ideal president": a composite image of past great presidents that lingers in Americans' minds.[4] The imaginary figure has never campaigned for office nor served in office. He therefore has never made a mistake. He combines the wisdom of Washington, the strength of Lincoln, and energy of Theodore Roosevelt, the inventiveness of Franklin Roosevelt, and the charisma of Kennedy. He has none of the reticence of Millard Fillmore, the shyness of Calvin Coolidge, or the dishonesty of Richard Nixon. The ideal president is a problem solver, one who aggressively addresses the ills of the nation. He is a compassionate man of the people yet a tough negotiator with world foes. He is a moral man—someone of heroic proportions.

Presidential candidates reinforce the ideal when they announce that they will accomplish things that have eluded others—peace with honor, a balanced budget, no new taxes. They assert that they will match the ideal phantom who trails real live presidential candidates and presidents wherever they go. People do not merely judge a presidential candidate on his own merits or compare him with his competitors. Voters often say that they like none of the candidates for president. This remark may be a comment on the field of mortals seeking office, but it also may be a judgment based on visions of the ideal that voters expect candidates to match. The ideal reinforces the single executive image. The ideal says that a single individual, acting on behalf of the people, can successfully run the government. The impact of formal and informal rules on the personalization of presidential campaigns and on the search for the ideal can be examined in the three main stages of presidential elections: nomination, general election, and voting by the electoral college.

THE NOMINATION

William Marcy "Boss" Tweed, the political baron of New York City in the nineteenth century, remarked, "I don't care who does the electing just so I can do the nominating."[5] This observation underscores the basic political fact of life that the nomination is the most important step in the election of a president. The rules of the selection process have changed in successive decades from limited public participation to broad participation and from party control to party isolation. There have been four distinct phases to presidential nominations: (1) the congressional caucus system, (2) brokered conventions,[6] (3) emergent primaries, and (4) the media primary. Each has had its own set of rules.

The Congressional Caucus, 1800–1824

The congressional caucuses emerged in the election of 1800. Members of Congress from the two principal parties—the Federalists and the Democratic-Republicans (later known as the Democrats)—met to recommend candidates. Forty-three of the fifty-five Democratic-Republican members of Congress met as a caucus in Marache's boarding house in Philadelphia and in secret selected Thomas Jefferson as their candidate for president and Aaron Burr as their choice for vice president. Meanwhile, the Federalists pursued the same practice; but to rally party support to the caucus decision, they met in public and announced the selection of John Adams and Charles Cotesworth Pinckney.

The first nomination system was the simplest and the most party-dominant. The congressional caucus placed the nomination in the hands of the party elite. Members of Congress, as leaders of the national parties, knew whom they were getting as presidential candidates. It was no accident that members of Congress chose former members of Congress—Jefferson, Madison, Monroe—as nominees. The system came close to a European style of nomination—controlled from the top. (The Conservative party in Great Britain, for example, selects its leader, the individual who will run for prime minister, by ballot from among all Conservative members of Parliament.) The selection process did not readily take into acount the preferences of rank and file party members. It was no accident that the congressional caucus system did not nominate an outside candidate such as Andrew Jackson, who enjoyed popular support but whom party leaders disdained. The caucus system also established an informal tie between the president and the Congress, the Constitution's separation of powers notwithstanding. Had the caucus system continued, the American political system would have moved toward a parliamentary form of government.

The congressional caucus system, however, soon broke down. With the demise of the Federalist party and the rise of factions among the dominant Democratic-Republicans, the congressional caucus in 1824 nominated William Crawford of Georgia with only 20 percent of the members of Congress voting. The system, disparagingly called "King Caucus," was criticized as an undemocratic device that thwarted popular wishes. Benjamin Austin wrote: "Do we send members to Congress to *cabal* once in four years for President?"[7] State legislatures, disregarding the caucus, gave support to three regional candidates: John Quincy Adams from the East, Henry Clay from the South, and Andrew Jackson from the West.

Brokered Conventions, 1828–1912

The caucus born in a boarding house was replaced by a national convention housed in a large, two-story saloon in Baltimore. An upstart party, the Anti-Masons, unhappy with the Democratic-Republicans but having no seats in Congress, met as a large, rowdy group to nominate a presidential candidate. The two major parties, the Democrats and the newly emerging Whigs, soon followed suit. Delegates were nominated in a first round to state conventions, where, in turn, a second round nominated state delegates to the national conventions. Although enjoying the appearance of greater representativeness than "King Caucus," the state and national conventions were controlled by party bosses. The rules of the game had state party leaders, wielding large blocs of delegates, compete with each other over the candidates. Candidates were forced to make promises about cabinet positions, other patronage, and issues facing certain regions of the country before being given a state leader's support. Numerous ballots were taken while deals were cut in smoke-filled rooms. From out of the heavy blue haze emerged nominees and eventual presidents, including Franklin Pierce after 49 ballots, James Garfield after 36 ballots, and James Buchanan after 17 rounds.[8]

Emergent Primaries, 1912–1968

The national convention, born in a saloon, was recast during a Wisconsin winter. In 1902 Robert La Follette, governor and then senator of Wisconsin, advocated the adoption of a new device: the party primary. "Put aside the caucus and convention," La Follette urged. "They answer no purpose further than to give respectable form to political robbery."[9]

The primary allows voters who are affiliated with a party to cast their ballots directly to nominate that party's candidates for office. Early primaries were aimed at reforming city and state politics. Presidential primaries were something of an afterthought. Yet, by 1912, a dozen states had adopted presidential primaries.[10] By 1916, the number more than doubled. Then the primary movement stalled. After World War I, eight states moved to repeal their presidential primary laws. At no time from 1912 to 1968 was a majority of delegates to either party's convention chosen in the primaries.

During this period, states adopted rules that made primaries "beauty contests" or "advisory." Elected delegates were not pledged to a specific candidate, and the presidential-preference ballots cast by party voters usually were not binding on the state delegation. State party leaders continued to control campaigns. Nonetheless, in a few instances, candidates began to use the primaries to test their popularity and demonstrate to party bosses their electability. Herbert Hoover and Al Smith did not "campaign" but won commanding victories in their party primaries in 1928. Their names appeared on the ballots, but, not wishing to evade the bosses, neither Hoover nor Smith set foot in any of the states whose primaries they had entered.[11]

In the 1940s and 1950s the symbolic, if not strategic, importance of primaries grew. Candidates began to personally barnstorm primary states in search of votes. Eisenhower used the primaries to throw off stride Robert Taft, who enjoyed broad support among Republican regulars in 1952. In May 1960, Senator John F. Kennedy of Massachusetts upset Minnesota senator Hubert Humphrey in a full-throttle effort to win the West Virginia primary. Never before had two candidates placed so much effort into winning a single state. In the hills of West Virginia, Kennedy, a Roman Catholic, demonstrated that he could win in an overwhelmingly Protestant state (only 6 percent of the voters were listed as Catholic). The victory established Kennedy as the popular favorite and opened the door for an outsider to capture the Democratic presidential nomination.

Yet despite the greater use of the primaries, brokered party politics continued. The high and the low point for primaries during this period occurred in 1968. Throughout the early primaries, Senator Eugene McCarthy of Minnesota and Senator Robert F. Kennedy of New York attacked President Johnson on the Vietnam War. Then, in late March, Johnson announced that he would not seek re-election. Vice President Hubert Humphrey entered the contest in Johnson's place but entered *no* primaries. Humphrey concentrated on the majority of delegates who had been selected in party caucuses and conventions in 1967—a full year before the convention and before Humphrey had announced his candidacy. These delegates, uncommitted to any candidate at the time of the convention, were held by state party leaders whom the Humphrey forces assiduously wooed. The juxtaposition between Humphrey, the inside candidate, and the primaries, the outside forum, could not have been sharper. Robert Kennedy's assassination left Humphrey without credible opposition, and he won the Democratic nomination on the first ballot.

In sum, two rules characterized the period of emergent primaries: (1) state party leaders had power to deliver delegates, regardless of party voters' choices, and (2) the primaries were a wild card. Success in the primaries was, under the right conditions, of some strategic importance in the fight for the nomination. The primaries forced party leaders to pay attention to particular candidates. In so doing, the contests placed greater demands on candidates to adopt new styles of campaigning through personal contact with state party voters and with mediated messages on radio and television. But even though primary victories were sometimes a necessary condition to arouse party leaders, they were never a sufficient condition to secure the nomination.[12]

Media Primary, 1972 to the Present

Since 1972, primaries have been *the* road to the White House. The nomination is typified by one long, continuous primary covered passionately by the media, especially television. This giant "media primary" starts long before the election year as candidates test the waters, sometimes two or more years earlier. It continues through the official schedule of state party primaries and conventions that begin with the Iowa caucuses and the New Hampshire primary in February. It closes at the party conventions held in July by the Democrats and in August by the Republicans.

The camera is on at each step. Journalists monitor public opinion polls, state primary victories, state caucus and convention results, delegate counts, endorsements, and the candidates' cash flow. The media primary is a survival-of-the-fittest obstacle course among an increasing variety of candidates who are not necessarily taken seriously by party leaders but who hope to be taken seriously by party voters in key states. The hallmarks of the latest nomination system are (1) the predominance of state primaries, (2) the impact of television, (3) the importance of money, (4) the significance of public opinion polls, and (5) the waning influence of party.

Primaries. The bloody battles in the streets of Chicago in 1968 outside the Democrats' convention hall and the fervor inside the hall over charges that Humphrey's nomination was bossed—closed to party workers and voters—led to Democratic party reforms. The reforms, put in place in 1972, were based on recommendations of the McGovern-Fraser Commission. Although the commission itself took no position on delegate selection, many states moved away from two predominant methods used during the emergent primary period and toward two new methods of delegate selection. Because in most cases the changes involved new laws passed by state legislatures, state Republican parties also followed suit:

The Old Methods:

1. *Party-controlled caucus/convention:* A hierarchy of meetings, known as either caucuses or conventions, begins at the precinct or county level (the terms "caucus" and "convention" typically refer to different parts of the same approach; sometimes the two terms are used interchangeably). The caucuses (conventions) are made up of elected party committee people who select delegates to a state convention. At the state conventions, delegates are chosen for the national convention.

2. *Uncommitted delegate primary:* Primaries are beauty contests. Delegates' names appear on the ballots; candidates' names do not. Delegates arrive at the national convention formally uncommitted but informally in the pockets of state party leaders.

The New Methods:

1. *Grass-roots caucus/convention:* A move in a number of states, notably Iowa, opened the initial caucus (convention) rounds to any party supporter rather than to people holding elected party positions. Caucuses (conventions) are the local meetings that start the process. The local caucuses (conventions) send representatives to state conventions. State conventions nominate delegates to the national conventions.

2. *Candidate primary:* The name of the presidential candidate appears on the ballot either alone or along with the delegates' names. Delegates are pledged to a specific candidate and must vote according to state voters' wishes at the national convention.

As seen in Table 4.1, between 1968 and 1972, the percentage of delegates chosen by primary nearly doubled. By 1980, nearly three-fourths of the delegates to both parties' conventions were selected through primaries. In 1992, the eleven largest states—California, New York, Texas, Pennsylvania, Illinois, Ohio, Florida, Michigan, New Jersey, North Carolina, Georgia—held presidential primaries.[13] The proliferation of primaries and the binding of delegates to a candidate have led to states jockeying for the best possible time slot for their races. Because early primaries receive the greatest media coverage and have a decisive impact on the outcome of subsequent primaries, several states have moved their primary or caucus and convention dates to the first six weeks of the season. This move is known

Table 4.1 The Rise of Presidential Primaries

	Democrats		Republicans	
Year	Number of primaries	Percentage of delegates	Number of primaries	Percentage of delegates
1912	12	32.9	13	41.7
1916	20	53.5	20	58.9
1920	16	44.6	20	57.8
1924	14	35.5	17	45.3
1928	17	42.2	16	44.9
1932	16	40.0	14	37.7
1936	14	36.5	12	37.5
1940	13	35.8	13	38.8
1944	14	36.7	13	38.7
1948	14	36.3	12	36.0
1952	15	38.7	13	39.0
1956	19	42.7	19	44.8
1960	16	38.3	15	38.6
1964	17	45.7	17	45.6
1968	17	37.5	16	34.3
1972	23	60.5	22	52.7
1976	29	72.6	28	67.9
1980	31	71.8	35	76.0
1984	26	62.1	30	71.0
1988	34	66.6	35	76.9
1992	36	77.1	29	67.8

Source: James Davis, *The American Presidency: A New Pespective* (New York: Harper and Row, 1987), 49. Used by permission. Updated by the author.

as "frontloading." Some twenty states, many from the South, now conduct their delegate selections in various caucuses and primaries on "Super Tuesday," the first Tuesday in March. In 1992, 33 percent of the delegates for both parties' conventions were chosen on Super Tuesday.

The early primaries, including those on Super Tuesday, have replaced party bosses as the key mechanism for picking the parties' nominees. Frontloading *opens* the nomination to a wider range of candidates, all of whom hope they can do well in at least one early contest. Frontloading also *closes* the nomination more quickly than before, because an aspirant who does not do well in the early going is not considered a serious contender for later rounds.

Television. The large number of primaries and frontloading have elevated the importance of television coverage of the campaign and increased the candidates' use of television. The media match the frontloading of primaries with the frontloading of primary coverage. Of the 616 news stories about some 50 state primaries in 1976, 250 stories were about the New Hampshire primary (41 percent of the total). In 1980, 14 percent of CBS News's coverage of the preconvention period went to the Iowa caucuses' selection of 87 delegates (1.6 percent of the combined Democrat and Republican delegates), and another 14 percent of CBS News's coverage went to New Hampshire's 41 delegates (0.7 percent of the total delegates).[14] Frontloading also draws attention to the preprimary campaign. Because there is no official procedure (other than the formal announcement of candidacy) during this phase, the media establish early benchmarks for candidates' credibility, success, and failure. Political scientist Richard Rubin observes that "the press has assumed much of the recruitment and evaluative role that was once reserved for practicing politicians."[15]

The candidates themselves rely heavily on television to build name recognition and convey positive images. Television has the same effects as the primaries. It *opens* the nomination to a broader pool of hopeful candidates. Television exposure provides lesser-known or unknown candidates the chance to gain quick recognition among the party's electorate. But it *closes* the nomination quickly to candidates who cannot afford the high price of television campaigning.

Money. Running for office is not cheap. Running for the presidency is the most expensive campaign in the world. Much of a campaign's effectiveness depends on the amount of money available and the gap between a candidate's war chest and the money spent by rival candidates. The key to success on the media primary road is to raise money early and thus build sufficient momentum to raise money later and participate in primaries later on.

Candidates solicit money from several sources. The bulk of pre-nomination money comes from individual contributors, who are limited to $1,000 contributions by the Federal Election Campaign Act of 1974 and amendments passed in 1976. Political action committees, which are the campaign spending arms of organized interest groups, also give money to presidential primary candidates. They are limited to $5,000 contributions per election (that is, $5,000 in the primaries and $5,000 in the general election). Candidates may supply some of their own money. Before declaring their candidacies, candidates may spend as much of their own money as they like. After the candidacy is formally declared, the ceiling on personal funds is $50,000. The 1974 campaign act somewhat eased the burden of fund raising by providing federal matching funds for primary candidates who raise $5,000 in twenty states in contributions of $250 or less—a total of $100,000. Candidates who accept federal funds are limited in the amount of money they can spend in their quest for the nomination. The ceiling was $31.2 million in 1992. Despite the variety of sources of funds, when candidates win a primary, money, from whatever source, comes in, and when they lose a primary, money, from whatever source, typically dries up.

Public Opinion Polls. Media coverage of numerous primaries heightens the significance of public opinion polls. Television news, especially, relies on poll results as measures of candidates' chances. Yet the numbers to not speak for themselves, and journalists typically do the talking. Journalists and other observers set well-publicized but arbitrary standards for candidates' strengths: 5 percent support nationwide at a minimum, 15 percent to be considered a serious contender. Poll results before a primary become convenient assessments of how well a candidate is "expected" to do. As Nelson Polsby comments:

In some primary elections, "Expected" becomes a phantom candidate who does not always obey the laws of logic or mathematics: Johnson did not do as well as "Expected" in New Hampshire in 1968; McCarthy did better than "Expected." The fact that Johnson outpolled McCarthy was not given anywhere near the coverage as was their success against the phantom candidate.[16]

Party Decline. The importance of television, the cost of campaigning, and the attention paid to public opinion polls point to the weakening of political parties as partners in the current nomination process. Increasingly, self-sufficient candidate organizations direct candidates' schedules, plan fund raising, gather volunteers, and staff campaign offices in as many states as possible. Candidates make their most critical appeals to party voters in the growing list of primaries and grass-roots caucuses. They circumvent the party and get their messages across through the media. Journalists follow individual candidates around, keeping their ears to the ground and their eyes on the polls, and decide how well the candidates are doing.

As party vehicles, the national conventions can no longer be considered the deliberative, bargaining bodies they once were. Only once since 1936 has the Democratic convention taken more than one ballot to select a nominee. Adlai Stevenson was nominated on the third ballot in the Chicago convention of 1952. Similarly, the last time the Republicans took more than one ballot was in 1948, when Thomas Dewey was chosen on the third ballot.

The role of party leaders, however, has not completely vanished. In 1983 the Democrats attempted to bring back into the nomination process elected and party officials who largely had been excluded in the post–McGovern-Fraser period. Of the total Democratic delegates, 14 percent were designated as unpledged "superdelegates" in 1984, 15 percent in 1988. In 1992, the 771 superdelegate seats were occupied by members of the Democratic National Committee, Democratic governors, and Democratic members of Congress. The Republicans always have allowed party officials a central role in their conventions. In order to win the nomination in either party, a candidate must rally the support of politicos along the way. The era of the media primary restricts, although it does not remove, the role of party from the nomination process.

The Media Primary and the Single Executive Image. In the media primary system, "presidential campaigning has become a year-in, year-out activity with no off season."[17] Nominations are mass popularity contests in which candidates attempt to demonstrate to the public, the media, other candidates, and even themselves that they are the top party choice. The transformation from a closed "insider" system to a popular "outsider" selection process fosters the image of a single executive. During the nomination races, all eyes are on individual candidates and their styles. Primaries and television heighten the need for candidates to develop images distinct from their opponents'. Party, never as strong a vehicle in the American selection process as in European systems, is infirm, leaving candidates largely on their own. Each candidate attempts to show that he or she, better than anyone else, will live up to "the ideal president"—a heroic moral leader who solves all major national ills.

THE GENERAL ELECTION

For most Americans, Labor Day weekend represents the last gasp of summer—the final family picnic or one more trip to the beach before schools reopen and fall sets in. For two Americans every four years, Labor Day weekend begins a grueling season of traveling, smiling, waving, and eating their way across the country. For the Republican and Democratic candidates for president, Labor Day marks the official kickoff of the general election campaign.

Today's general election campaign is an extension of the media primary nomination process. Its heaviest emphasis is on the images of the candidates—images created through the media, especially television. Often the contest is as much between the image of a candidate and the single executive image as it is between the images of the two candidates. The press spotlights the ways in which candidates do and do not fit preconceived notions about what a president should be. Just as the phantom candidate "Expected" pesters candidates during the nomination process, the spirit of the ideal president nags them during the general election campaign.

Elements of the Campaign

The success of the candidates' campaigns depends on money, organization, and strategies.

Money. In 1860, Abraham Lincoln spent $100,000 in his successful bid for the presidency. His Democratic opponent, Stephen A. Douglas, spent only half that amount. Presidential campaign costs exceeded $1 million for the first time in 1880, when James Garfield outspent his rival by 3 to 1. Campaign costs skyrocketed in the 1960s as television became the preferred medium for reaching voters. High costs made campaigns increasingly dependent on large donors. In 1964, only $2 million was raised in contributions of $10,000 or more. By 1972, $51 million was collected from donations of that size or larger, especially for the re-election campaign of President Nixon, which spent $61.4 million, more than twice the amount spent by George McGovern's campaign ($30 million).[18]

These inequalities, the rising costs of campaigns, and the increasing reliance on "fat cat" contributors ended when Congress passed the Federal Election Campaign Act of 1974. It and its 1976 amendments introduced public financing of presidential elections, for both primaries and general elections. The law as originally written limited candidates who accepted public funds to $20 million in the general election, plus a cost-of-living adjustment. In 1992, the adjustment boosted the totals received by each of the major candidates to $55.2 million.

Organization.   The money goes partly toward building an organization. A presidential candidate's organization spends millions of dollars to coordinate a variety of activities: advance work, scheduling, press relations, speech writing, volunteers, fund raising, advertising, polling, and party and group efforts.

All recent campaigns have had organizations with similar features. A director stays in close contact with the candidate and with party officials. A manager supervises the daily campaign efforts. There are chiefs for public relations, finance, direct mail, issues, media, groups, and other areas. The national organization is on top of an array of state and local organizations. Today, campaigns rely heavily on professional media consultants, pollsters, and advertising agencies to design the candidate's appeal.[19] The Carter campaign spent nearly 60 percent of its entire budget on the media, with about 85 percent of this for television airtime, the production of commercials, and consulting firm fees.[20] The Bush and Clinton campaigns in 1992 developed campaign themes based on the results of a series of nationwide and group-specific polls.

Strategies.   Many campaign organizations run from a comprehensive game plan; others adopt a "plan as you go" approach. Either strategy reflects attempts to build a winning coalition from among various demographic groups. For recent Democratic candidates, the main strategy has been to rally groups traditionally associated with the Democratic party: ethnic and religious minorities, blue-collar workers, middle- and low-income families, and the very poor. Many analysts have argued that one of the reasons why the Democrats have captured the White House only once in twenty years is that they have not moved beyond these New Deal and Great Society groupings to capture new regions and new socioeconomic groups. Republicans, as a more homogeneous party, know they must make a more general appeal to both Democrats and Independents to win. The 1992 Clinton campaign consciously adopted the Republicans' approach. Clinton and his running mate, Senator Al Gore of Tennessee, were moderate Democrats, and they made strong appeals to middle America.

Voters' Perceptions of Campaigns

Whether campaigns make a difference depends on the answers to three questions. The first is, When do voters make up their minds? If they make up their minds early, at the time of the conventions, then the campaign's biggest effect is likely to be a reinforcing one. It will confirm for people that they made the right choice, if they pay attention at all. As shown in Table 4.2, roughly two-thirds of the voters make up their minds before the campaign begins. These early decision makers are a variety of people. Some strongly identify with a particular party and regularly vote for its candidates, no matter who they are. Others, satisfied with the performance of the current government, vote for the incumbent or the incumbent's party. Still others know early that they strongly like or dislike one of the candidates and vote accordingly.

The second question is, Whom do the undecided voters choose? That so many people decide early should not lead to the conclusion that the campaign has no effect. The undecided voters who make up their minds after the conventions can make a crucial difference to the outcome. Evidence indicates that they do not split their votes evenly between the two candidates. Instead, most of these unsure voters decide in favor of the one candidate who has gained momentum near the campaign's end. In 1968, momentum at the end of the campaign shifted from Richard Nixon to Hubert Humphrey. Those who decided late voted disproportionately for Humphrey. Analysts suggested that if the election had been held a few days later, Humphrey would have won.

Table 4.2 Time of Voters' Decisions for President, 1960–1988

	1960	1964	1968	1972	1976	1980	1984	1988
Knew all along, always vote same party, preconvention	31%	41%	35%	44%	33%	41%	52%	43%
At time of conventions	31	25	24	18	21	18	18	18
After conventions	26	21	19	22	22	15	17	22
Within two weeks of election, on election day	12	13	21	13	24	26	13	17

Note: The responses are in answer to a question from the American National Election Studies conducted by the University of Michigan: "How long before the election did you decide that you were going to vote the way you did?"

The third question is, On what basis do people make up their minds? Five factors have the greatest impact on voters' decisions: party identification, candidates' positions on the issues, the performance of the incumbent, candidates' images, and the horse race. Voters' decisions typically reflect several of these factors.

Party Identification. Party identification is the attachment voters feel to a party. It is generally based on family influence (for instance, people whose parents are Democrats are most likely to be Democrats), but it can also be affected by peers, political figures, and the performance of the parties on issues and events throughout a person's lifetime.[21] There are two elements involved in the importance of party identification. Do people indeed "identify" with the Democratic or Republican parties, or do they see themselves as independent of either party? Over the past thirty years, there has been a decline in the percentage of the electorate identifying with either of the two main parties, as noted in Table 4.3. Does someone who has a party identification actually vote for the party's candidate or "defect" to the other party? As Figure 4.1 reveals, over the same thirty-year period, defections, especially among Democrats, have become increasingly common.

Candidates encourage defection in their campaign strategies. Republican presidential candidates, who know only too well that Democrats outnumber Republicans, build strategies to court Democratic identifiers. In 1980, Reagan captured disaffected Democrats, primarily union members and Catholics, who subsequently became known as "Reagan Democrats." In 1984, he continued to hold their support by concentrating on nonpartisan themes such as "America's back" and a strong economy. In 1988, Bush and Dukakis both developed strategies to attract the Reagan Democrats. The results were mixed. Some Reagan Democrats voted for Bush, but others returned to the Democratic camp. The erosion of both party identification and party

Table 4.3 Distribution of Party Identification, 1952–1988

Year	Democrats	Independents	Republicans
1952	47%	22%	27%
1956	44	24	29
1960	46	23	27
1964	51	23	25
1968	45	31	24
1972	40	35	23
1976	40	36	23
1980	41	34	23
1984	38	35	28
1988	33	34	30

Source: Calculated by the author from results of the American National Election Studies.

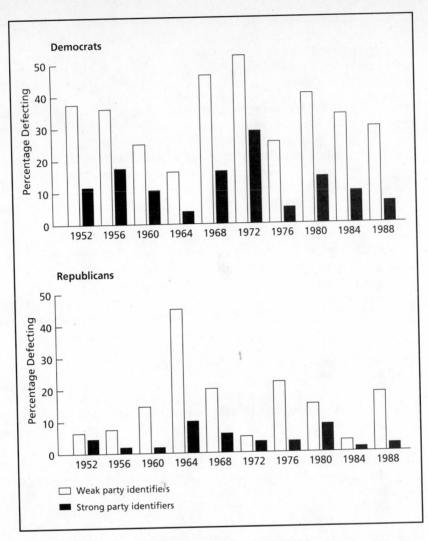

Figure 4.1 Defections Among Party Identifiers, 1952–1988

Democrats are more likely to vote for a Republican presidential candidate than Republicans are to vote for a Democratic candidate. [*Source:* Stephen Wayne, *The Road to the White House, 1992*, 3d ed. (New York: St. Martin's Press, 1992), 70; updated by the author. Used by permission.]

voting further weakens party organizations during the nomination phase of the campaign. Images of the candidates as individuals become salient, and the more important these images are, the greater is the role played by the single executive image in the campaign.

Issues.   Although all candidates say they fight their campaigns "on the issues," they rarely do. Nor do voters vote on the basis of issues as often as they say. Three ingredients are necessary for people to vote on the issues:

1. The voter must have a position on an issue. In the course of a campaign, many issues about which a voter has thought little arise. The complexities of world trade talks, for example, often leave voters with nothing to say.

2. The voter must find an issue salient. A voter may have a position on an issue but not see the issue as crucial to her vote. For instance, a voter may be in favor of gun control but may not evaluate candidates in terms of their position on that issue.

3. The voter must be able to perceive a difference between the two candidates on an issue. This criterion is very difficult to meet. Candidates are notorious for taking ambiguous or similar policy stands so as not to antagonize unnecessarily any voters.

A classic example of the difficulty of issue voting occurred in 1968. Voters had opinions on the Vietnam War. The country was split between hawks, who wanted to win the war, and doves, who wanted it wound down. It was without question the most salient issue of the campaign: 60 percent of the electorate saw it as the most important problem facing the nation. The next most important problem was inflation, named by 7 percent of the electorate. The first two criteria for issue voting were met, but the third criterion was missing.

Candidate Nixon emphasized that new leadership was needed; he stressed peace; and he said he had a secret plan to end the war. Because the plan was secret, however, he could not discuss it other than to hint that if he were elected there would be less American involvement and a negotiated settlement. Candidate Humphrey chose not to discuss the war in his speeches, saying that any comment would upset the peace negotiations. He too called for the lessening of American involvement, conditioned on North Vietnamese negotiation. Not surprisingly, 57 percent of the voters in 1968 saw no difference between the two candidates on Vietnam.

The pervasiveness of issue ambiguity in presidential elections draws attention toward candidates as individuals. Each candidate attempts to convince the electorate that he is the best person to "take charge" of the pressing issues of the day. Taking charge supplants taking positions. The issues the candidates will be in charge of are blurred in the fog of campaign rhetoric. As candidates attempt to confidently convey their abilities to take charge, the single executive image emerges.

Incumbent's Performance. Often, evaluations of the incumbent's performance on such matters as the economy and national defense substitute for issue voting. Is the voter satisfied with the way things have been going and are likely to continue? The answer given in

1980 was no when challenger Reagan asked voters about incumbent Carter's term: "Are you better off now than you were four years ago?" The answer given in 1984 was yes when incumbent Reagan asked the same question about his own record. Although presidents and presidential candidates do not have a great deal of control over the economy, they make loud noises to the contrary during the campaign. The elections are quadrennial appraisals of the major problems that the nation must solve. Consistent with the single executive image, candidates campaign as the chief problem solvers for these latest national dilemmas.

Image.   Candidates spend much of their efforts in the campaign developing images to which voters will be attracted—impressionistic accounts of who the candidate is, his personal qualities and background. Voters find images much easier than issues to get a handle on. They either like an image or they do not. Today's imagery is part of a "new politics" that emphasizes personal appeals through the impersonal medium of television and supplants the "old politics" with its somewhat more programmatic appeals through party.

The watershed year for the "new politics" was 1960, when the Kennedy campaign used television to its advantage. The efforts were especially telling in the Nixon-Kennedy debates broadcast live on radio and television. In the crucial first debate, those who were listening to the debate on radio concluded that there was no real winner or gave Nixon a slight edge. Those who saw the debate on television named Kennedy the victor. Nixon had been campaigning with such intensity that he had developed a knee problem, leaving him in pain throughout the debate. He looked pale. When he crossed his leg, he winced. The painkiller he was on made his voice sound groggy. Perspiration on his upper lip, visible under the bright camera lights, gave the impression that he was feeling great pressure. His five-o'clock shadow, evident on the black and white TV picture, made him look surly.

Kennedy, by contrast, appeared poised and in control. He seemed well versed, rapidly citing many facts and statistics. He exhibited ideal president qualities of decisiveness and conviction. Although the three other debates were judged to be virtual stand-offs, the die was cast after the first debate. Momentum shifted to Kennedy, who went on to win the election by one of the narrowest margins in American electoral history. Kennedy campaigners convinced Americans that their candidate was not only young, vigorous, and good-looking but also *qualified* to be president.

The Nixon camp prepared to do battle in the 1968 campaign, having learned the hard way. People recognized Nixon's experience and strength, but many did not find him warm or trustworthy. The campaign set out to change these negative impressions while highlighting his good points. Talk of a "new Nixon" ensued. The idea was to sell Nixon to America as one would sell a bar of soap. With the right box, size, and price, the contents were less important. Raymond Price, one of the key image makers on the Nixon team, wrote an internal campaign memo recommending

saturation with film, in which the candidate can be shown better than he can be shown in person because it can be edited, so only the best moments are shown; then a quick parading of the candidate in the flesh so that the guy they've gotten intimately acquainted with in the screen takes on a living presence—not saying anything just being seen. . . .

[Nixon] has to come across as a person larger than life, the stuff of legend. People are stirred by the legend, including the living legend, not by the man himself. It's the aura that surrounds the charismatic figure, more than it is the figure itself, that draws the followers. Our task is to build that aura. . . .

So let's not be afraid of television gimmicks . . . get the voters to like the guy and the battle's two-thirds won.[22]

Another memo outlined how the aura was created in Nixon's preparation for a campaign commercial. Roger Ailes, in his first effort as a media consultant (followed by successful fights for Reagan in 1984 and Bush in 1988), assured that the candidate "will never look bad":

A. He looks good on his feet. . . .
B. Standing adds to his "feel" of confidence and the viewers "feel" his confidence.
C. He still uses his arms a little too "predictably" and a little too often, but at this point it is better not to inhibit him. . . .
F. We are still working on lighting up his eyes a bit. . . .
   1. I may lower the front two key spots a bit.
   2. I may try slightly whiter makeup on upper eyelids.
   3. I may lower the riser he stands on a couple of inches. . . .
H. Color lights are hot and he has a tendency to perspire, especially along the upper lip.
   1. Whenever he is going to tape a show, the studio air conditioner should be turned up full at least four hours prior to broadcast, and camera rehearsal should be limited as much as possible in this time period to keep the lights off and the heat down. If camera rehearsal is necessary, the air conditioner should be turned on sooner and the studio sealed off. Keep all studio doors (especially the large leading doors) closed.
I. An effort should be made to keep him in the sun occasionally to maintain a fairly constant level of tan.

J. Generally, he has a very "Presidential" look and style—he he smiles easily (and looks good doing it).[23]

When Mrs. Nixon and a friend arrived at the television studio during rehearsal one day, Nixon was livid when they opened the studio door and momentarily disrupted the temperature of the studio—and the image of the candidate.[24]

Hyperimagery. There is evidence that the imagery of presidential campaigns is moving into a new "hyperimage" phase, in which the image sells the candidate. Although the aim of the "new politics" is to display the best qualities of the candidate and try to downplay less favorable qualities, it is still the candidate who shapes the image. But consider the opposite possibility as hyperimagery: the image seeks a candidate. Using this hyperimage approach, political strategists rely on results of public opinion polls to come up with the image of a perfect candidate—just what Americans want. The trick, then, is to go out and find a real live politician who fits or can be made to fit the image.

In a 150-page memo, Democratic pollster Pat Caddell extrapolated from 1983 poll data the profile of the perfect Democratic candidate. He was a moderately liberal senator in his forties, compassionate but clear-eyed about liberal programs that had failed, bold enough to break with party tradition, and able to appeal to young and ethnic voters in the Kennedy style. Caddell nicknamed the candidate "Senator Smith." After the birth of Senator Smith, Caddell went shopping for a candidate in 1984 who fit the profile. He approached three Democratic senators, including Joseph Biden of Delaware, but none wanted to run. Then Gary Hart, his campaign in trouble, called Caddell for help.

Ironically, Hart did not fit the Senator Smith image well enough to be among Caddell's first choices, but Hart could be made to fit the profile. After three hours of meetings with Caddell, Hart emerged as the candidate of a new generation with new ideas. Kathy Buskin, a Hart spokeswoman in the 1984 campaign, felt that Hart was "stretching it" in his political biography crafted under Caddell's watchful eye: "He [Hart] made more of incidents than they were . . . in an effort, I think, to connect this Mr. Smith thing to himself."[25] Hart would run as Senator Smith, not as Senator Hart.

Although Hart lost to Mondale in 1984, Caddell was undeterred. In 1988, he returned to Biden, who was now receptive. The 1988 Biden campaign soon floundered over charges of plagiarism. The candidate had gotten caught in the gap between Senator Smith and himself.[26]

Image Building. As the foregoing discussion of Kennedy, Nixon, and Senator Smith makes clear, the image of a candidate is only loosely related to the "real" candidate. Image-building efforts not only include keeping Richard Nixon looking tan but trying to convince Walter Mondale to give up wearing a heavy, slick hair tonic, giving George Bush voice lessons, and training Dwight Eisenhower to look natural in front of television cameras. Image builders conduct public opinion polls in order to assess the concerns about which voters are most sensitive and the candidate characteristics for which they are looking.

In drawing on these polls, the campaign often works as hard to ruin the opponent's positive image as it does to build a favorable image for its own candidate. "Attack politics," recently in vogue, has been a staple of American presidential campaigns since the first competitive election, in 1796. Thomas Jefferson's Republicans accused John Adams of being a tyrannical demigod, and John Adams's Federalists accused Thomas Jefferson of being an atheist radical. A staunch Federalist and president of Yale College, Timothy Dwight, wrote of a Jefferson victory: "The Bible would be cast into a bonfire, our holy worship changed into a dance of Jacobin phrensy, our wives and daughters dishonored, and our sons converted into disciples of Voltaire and the dragoons of Marat."[27]

In the campaign of 1828, the National Republicans accused Andrew Jackson of being an adulterer and a murderer, while the Democrats charged that John Quincy Adams had purchased gambling devices with public funds and procured a prostitute for the czar of Russia. None of the charges on either side was true. In the campaign of 1884, Republicans gleefully publicized the fact that bachelor Grover Cleveland had acknowledged being the father of an illegitimate child. Not to be outdone, the Democrats discovered that Republican candidate James Blaine, while Speaker of the House, had used his influence on behalf of certain railroads.

Perhaps the most infamous negative advertising was a commercial sponsored by Lyndon Johnson's campaign in 1964. It portrayed Barry Goldwater as a trigger-happy wildman who would use nuclear weapons at a moment's notice. The commercial opened with a little girl quietly sitting in a field ablaze with yellow daisies. As she plucked the petals of one of the flowers, she softly counted to herself: "Nine-ten-eleven . . ." The little girl stopped, and a grave male voice began counting down to zero. Then came the sound of an atomic explosion, and a mushroom cloud rose into the air. The little girl disappeared. President Johnson's voice intoned: "These are the stakes, to make a world in which all of God's children can live or go into the dark. . . . The stakes are too high for you to stay at home." "Vote Johnson" then flashed on the screen in bold white letters. The commercial ran only once. Goldwater supporters were so incensed that the Johnson campaign feared a backlash. But the commercial had made its point. Although attack politics is not new, today it dovetails with a candidate's efforts to convince voters that only he can live up to the single executive image. The attacks allow one candidate to show that the other candidate could not possibly be an acceptable, let alone a remarkable, president.[28]

The Horse Race.   Who will win? Presidential elections are supposed to involve choices about national leadership and policy, but they are also contests between winners and losers. Toward the campaign's end, the horse race may influence voters who remain undecided. Voters may jump on the expected winner's bandwagon for no other reason than that the candidate is ahead. Although a campaign for any office is a horse race to a certain extent, the horse race often dominates presidential campaigns because of television and the ritual of the debates.

   Media Coverage. Because the campaign is so long, most of the attention given to presidential candidates' issue positions, performance accomplishments, and images is given in the nomination part of the election year. Once reported, this material is no longer "news." Television news, in particular, is not structured to analyze such matters in depth. Television has difficulty covering complex and tedious issues in quick and lively formats. Studies conclude that most election issues are mentioned so infrequently and vaguely in newscasts that voters learn little about them. "Television news adds little to the average voter's understanding of election issues."[29] Voters actually get more information from candidates' television advertisements than they do from the evening news. The ads are concise and repeated often. Reporters also shy away from too much coverage of candidates' images because they fear they might be accused of indulging in subjective judgments about the candidates' personalities.

   To keep coverage of the campaign engaging, novel, and "objective," journalists concentrate on up-to-the-minute measures of the candidates' momentum as indicated by the most recent public opinion polls. A study of the CBS Evening News during the 1980 campaign found that five out of six stories emphasized the horse race. Only 90 seconds per program, approximately 20 to 25 percent of total campaign coverage, were spent on policy issues.[30] In the last week of the 1984 election, the *New York Times* ran fifteen stories—nearly one-third of its total election coverage—based wholly or largely on public opinion polls it had conducted with CBS News. Another 25 percent of its election stories that week made at least some mention of poll results.[31] Thomas Patterson and Richard Davis state: "Most election coverage is devoted to the campaign contest itself rather than to what the choice of one candidate or the other may mean to the nation."[32]

   Candidates gear their campaigns with the media's preoccupation on the horse race in mind. *Media events* are carefully planned—rallies downtown at noontime, factory visits, farmland tours—to show not only the color and excitement of the candidate's campaign but also how well the campaign is doing in the horse race. Reporters can rate the size of the crowds, their enthusiasm, and the candidate's oratorical ability. Candidates also speak in *sound bites*—short, catchy lines that sound good and can be said in seconds—for the electronic media. Candidates know that their discussion of issues must be made simple yet dramatic in order to be covered. Recent campaigns have been sprinkled with such pithy policy pronouncements as "Are you better off now than you were four years ago?" "Where's the beef?" "It's morning in America," "Read my lips: no new taxes." Reading some of these slogans out of context, one might guess that they were the names of new fall television shows.

The Debates. Televised presidential debates should be considered an extension of television coverage of the horse race. Many people say they watch the debates to hear the candidates air their views on important national issues and then make up their minds about who is better. But the debates demonstrate less about the candidates' issue stands than about how they stand at all—how well they handle themselves under pressure, whether they make some sort of political gaffe. President Ford lost points in his second debate with Jimmy Carter when he made the statement that Poland was not under Soviet domination. Ford refused to retract his remark for several days, making matters worse. Many observers felt that it was not the comment itself but the perception that the president had made a mistake that stalled Ford's uphill battle against Carter. The media sharpen their focus on the horse race during the debates because they offer the last (and therefore biggest) opportunity to judge how the two candidates are doing and often the only opportunity to evaluate them together. Thus, calling the winner of the debates—especially the first debate, which more people tend to watch—becomes critical.

Debates, featured in every election since 1976, are a strange but apparently indispensable democratic ritual. The debates make it seem as though the candidates are seriously vying for votes and dealing with the most important issues of the day. They allow voters to forgive (or forget) the rest of the campaign and tune in at the end. Candidates can hide in the Rose Garden, avoid the issues, and call each other names, so long as they come out swinging in the debates. But ultimately what candidates display during the debates and what voters judge are the styles of the candidates, not their specific arguments. Whether the candidates properly display key qualities of the ideal president—strength, decisiveness, confidence—is far more important than their plans to end the budget deficit, improve education, or deal with terrorism. The debates resolve which candidate looks most presidential, not necessarily which candidate would make the best president.

The Feel of the Campaign

In the end, American presidential elections are not about parties or issues or performance or images or the horse race. They are about the combination of all five. Candidates must demonstrate that they can be trusted to lead the nation. Pat Caddell remarked: "Voters don't remember specific issues, they remember the 'feel' of the candidate—his values, his passions, his competence, his persona—and they are most influenced by the continual consistent drumbeat of the larger messages, i.e., themes, by the candidate."[33] The importance of this overall "feel" of the candidates—a mix of image, themes, values, and partisanship—dominates American elections. A comparison of the 1988 and 1992 presidential races demonstrates the candidates' search for the right feel through public opinion polls, campaign events, themes designed to appeal to specific partisan voters, and advertising that pits the good guys against the bad guys.

1988: Guts and Compassion. In 1988, both the Bush and the Dukakis campaigns developed their candidates' "feel" early. During the New Hampshire primary, public opinion polls conducted for the Bush campaign showed that voters felt Bush was honest and sincere but lacked both the guts and the compassion necessary to be president. To develop a gutsy, tough-guy profile, Bush's campaign manager, Lee Atwater, told the candidate, "You gotta go negative." This strategy, aides felt, would divert attention from Bush himself, from his lackluster and sometimes incoherent speaking style, and overcome what had become known as the "wimp factor" (Bush as an indecisive minion for Reagan). Bush would be his own hit man.

Public opinion polls foretold not only where Bush was vulnerable but how the campaign would go negative. Robert Teeter, the Bush campaign's chief pollster, identified the "hot button issues" of the campaign—those to which Americans, especially the Reagan Democrats, gave the most visceral responses: patriotism, crime (prisons, guns, and the death penalty), and defense. Teeter's polls also showed that people had tired of the aggressiveness of the Reagan years. So a kindler, gentler Bush was also developed. Bush's big, happy family was highlighted; his commitment to education and to the environment was announced. The basic incongruity of a kind, gentle "dirty Harry" did not stop the image meisters once they had identified the feel they wanted for Bush. This image of the candidate was designed to match the single executive image. As someone who was both kind and tough, Bush could be presidential.

The Dukakis campaign chose to highlight two aspects of Dukakis's "feel" to counter the tough but gentle Bush. First, to gather votes from Republicans and bring the Reagan Democrats back to the Democratic camp, Dukakis wished to portray himself as a moderate, even a conservative, Democrat. He was shown to be a budget balancer in Massachusetts, a fiscal cop who would not let the acceleration of the national deficit during the "Reagan-Bush years" continue. The effort worked well early in the campaign against Jesse Jackson, but it worked much less well once Dukakis was on his own against Bush. Columnist George Will wrote, "The premise of the Bush campaign is that many people west of the Berkshires think that only two things come from Massachusetts, liberals and lobsters, and pretty soon they're going to wake up and say, 'That's not a lobster.' "[34]

Second, Dukakis highlighted his credentials as a competent manager. He wished to convey the idea that he was a careful, intelligent man who was thoroughly familiar with the specifics of government programs. But this effort left Dukakis's audiences feeling that he was aloof, unemotional, cerebral, and bland. *Newsweek* writers nicknamed Dukakis "the Mr. Spock of politics, a totally rational alien bemused by the passions around him."[35]

In an effort to negate Dukakis's image as a competent manager with the very emotional values they wished to highlight, the Bush campaign told the story of Willie Horton. Horton, a black man serving a life sentence for child murder, was released briefly under a Massachusetts furlough program designed to readjust long-serving prisoners to society. (The law creating the program had been passed by the Massachusetts legislature and actually signed by Dukakis's Republican predecessor as governor.) Horton, on his tenth weekend pass, ran off to Maryland, kidnapped a white couple, stabbed the husband, and repeatedly raped the wife. Atwater boasted to Bush that Willie Horton would be a household name by the end of the campaign. He was right. Advertisements from the Bush camp appeared in Illinois proclaiming: "All the Murderers and Rapists and Drug Pushers and Child Molesters in Massachusetts Vote for Michael Dukakis." A television ad featured prisoners walking through a revolving door. The voice-over intoned: "Dukakis's revolving-door prison policy gave weekend furloughs to first-degree murderers not eligible for parole. While out, many committed other crimes like kidnap and rape, and many are still at large. What Dukakis did for Massachusetts, he now wants to do for America. America can't afford that risk."[36] Unlike the Johnson "daisy girl" ad, which ran only once, Willy Horton ran for weeks on prime-time television.

The Dukakis campaign was incredulous that Americans would fall for such gimmickry. Instead of hitting back, they largely ignored these and other charges about Dukakis's views on the Pledge of Allegiance, gun control, and abortion. In doing so, the Dukakis people let their chance to claim the single executive image slip away. Dukakis failed to realize the importance of emotional, symbolic themes that resonate among many voters and that connect the people to the one government official who claims to be the leader of all the people. Political scientist Marjorie Hershey summed up the 1988 race:

One reason the [Bush] campaign stayed with these negative appeals was that even after many months of work, George Bush was still not considered a strong enough candidate to win on his own, with positive messages. Another, quite simply, was that the negative campaigning kept working. By late October, even Jesse Jackson's approval ratings were higher than Dukakis's. Even more significantly, the proportion of respondents saying that George Bush was "tough enough" on crime and criminals rose from 23 percent in July to a full 61 percent in late October, while the proportion saying Dukakis was not tough enough rose from 36 to 49 percent. It would be hard to find more convincing proof of the efficacy of attack politics. The campaign did make a difference.[37]

Bush won the election with 54 percent of the popular vote.

1992: A Bad Economy and a New Covenant. The "feel" that works once does not necessarily work again. For months during 1992 the Bush re-election campaign struggled to define their candidate. They knew the feel they wanted. They wished to highlight the president as leader of the world presiding over prosperity at home. This approach would readily reinforce the single executive image. The difficulty was that Bush's four years in office marked the slowest period of economic growth since Herbert Hoover's presidency. A stubborn recession that began in 1990 refused to improve; the budget deficit continued to soar; and Bush had abandoned his no-new-tax pledge. With prosperity elusive, polls showed that Americans were not much interested in foreign policy. Nevertheless, the Republican National Convention was turned into a tribute to the Persian Gulf War. It was also a showcase for Republican-defined "family values," including support of religion and opposition to abortion and homosexuality.

The Bush camp, however, remained skeptical that this tactic would be enough to win. Heading into the general election, Bush's popularity had dropped from its Gulf War peak of 90 percent to hover in the 30 percent range. Bush strategists also worried that Bush had little to show for himself in economic and domestic policy. He had accomplished few of his education reforms and had a mixed record on the environment, leaving both slogans from 1988—"the education president" and "the environmental president"—to ring hollow. The Bush campaign, feeling vulnerable on Bush's record, turned again to attack politics. Bush mostly took the high road, except in deriding the disrespectful Democratic Congress, and Vice President Quayle led the charge against Democratic candidate Governor Bill Clinton of Arkansas. If, as in 1988, the Republicans could not sell their own candidate, they could try to destroy the other candidate.

The Clinton campaign was prepared to do everything the Dukakis campaign had not done. They lay in wait for negative commercials and other messages to come from the Bush camp. The Clinton campaign would not allow the Bush camp to destroy the feel of the Clinton candidacy as they had done with Dukakis four years before.

The Clinton campaign wished to convey that their candidate was a man from a humble background who had a firm grasp on policy proposals needed to correct the major problems of the country. Clinton spoke of a "New Covenant" between people who would take on greater responsibilities and government, which would work more effectively. Clinton wished to portray himself as a candidate for change as Bush campaigned on the grounds that things were fundamentally sound and prosperity was just around the corner.

The Bush campaign attacked this approach on two fronts. First, they charged that Clinton and his running mate, Senator Al Gore of Tennessee, were "tax and spend liberals." The two southern moderates, however, did not seem to be either New England liberals or lobsters, and Bush himself was open to a "tax and spend" charge because of his decision to increase taxes. Second, the Bush campaign assailed Clinton on trustworthiness, probing questions of marital infidelity, draft status, and marijuana use. But the charges had first been brought up months before during the primaries by several Arkansas Republicans, and many people had already made up their minds about these matters before the Republicans resurrected them during the general election campaign.

The campaign took another turn in September when billionaire Ross Perot, who had run an unofficial campaign for several months and dropped out of the race during the summer, re-entered as an independent candidate. Spending $60 million of his own money and gaining attention during a series of three-way presidential debates, Perot campaigned primarily via television to discuss his plan to end the federal deficit and his desire to end government gridlock. Clinton won with 43 percent of the vote, Bush received 38 percent, and Perot garnered 19 percent—the largest vote for a third candidate since 1912. Clinton was the candidate who apparently best demonstrated his understanding of the attributes of the ideal president and the claims of the single executive image.

THE ELECTORAL COLLEGE

Some Americans think that the electoral college is a small liberal arts institution of higher learning in the Northeast. Others wish that it were. No one fully understands the electoral college, the device that the framers of the Constitution created, after much haranguing, to elect the president. When Americans finally go to the polls after the multiyear campaign, they do not actually elect the president. They select electors to the electoral college. In December those electors gather in state capitols to officially elect the president. A candidate must win a majority of the electoral college votes to be elected president. To understand the electoral college, it is helpful to examine this final phase of American presidential elections step by step.

Step 1: Calculation of the Number of Electors

The Constitution stipulates that the number of electors must equal "the whole number of Senators and Representatives to which the State may be entitled in the Congress." Thus, the formula for calculating a state's total number of electors is

Number of Senators (2) + Number of Representatives (which varies depending on the population of the state).

Alaska, for example, with 2 senators and 1 member of the House of Representatives, has 3 electoral votes. This is the fewest electoral votes a state can have. Five other states plus the District of Columbia have only 3 electoral college votes. California, with 52 members of the House and 2 senators, has the highest number of electoral votes, 54. The formula clearly favors the large states. Currently there is a total of 538 electoral votes, because there are 100 senators, 435 House members, and 3 electors designated for the District of Columbia by the Twenty-third Amendment.

Step 2: Selection of Electors

The Constitution allows state legislatures to decide how to select electors, although it expressly prohibits members of the U.S. House or Senate from serving as electors. Originally, most of the legislatures chose electors from among leading state politicians and state legislators. States dominated by the Democratic party would nominate Democratic electors; likewise, states dominated by the National Republicans would nominate members of that party. But by 1824, some state legislatures had rewritten laws to allow electors to be chosen by popular vote. All states except South Carolina followed suit by 1832.

A "winner-take-all" approach was adopted to determine the victor. The candidate who wins a plurality of the state's popular votes (that is, wins more votes than any of the other candidates) wins *all* the electoral college votes for that state. For instance, in 1988 Illinois voters decided in favor of George Bush by a margin of 51.3 percent to Dukakis's 48.7 percent. Although Dukakis received almost half of the votes in Illinois, the winner-take-all system gave Bush all 23 of Illinois's electoral college votes. In neighboring Wisconsin, Dukakis tallied 51.8 percent of the popular vote to Bush's 48.2 percent. Bush did well in Wisconsin, but under winner-take-all rules, Dukakis captured all 11 of Wisconsin's electoral college votes.

Step 3: Determining a Winner

The Constitution says that the person who receives a majority of the electoral college votes wins the election. Today, 270 of the 538 total electoral college votes are needed to win. A candidate who receives a majority of the popular votes but does not receive a majority of electoral votes (because of the winner-take-all system) will not be declared president. This has happened three times—in 1824, 1876, and 1888. In 1888, Grover Cleveland won a plurality (48.6 percent) of some 95,000 votes against Benjamin Harrison, but Harrison gained 233 electoral votes to Cleveland's 168. Harrison, not Cleveland, was elected president. Cleveland won his revenge in a rematch in 1892, when he won a plurality of the popular vote and a majority of the electoral votes.

Dozens of "what ifs" can be recounted in studying the relationship between electoral college and popular votes. Harry Truman always relished his upset victory over Thomas Dewey in 1948, but if Dewey had captured 12,487 more votes in California, Truman would have been very unhappy. In 1960, a shift of 9,000 votes in Illinois and Missouri would have given Nixon an electoral college majority. In 1976, only 5,559 more votes in Ohio and 3,687 more votes in Hawaii would have returned Gerald Ford to the White House.

Step 4: No Winner

What happens if no candidate wins a majority of electoral college votes? The Constitution provides that the race is then decided by the House of Representatives, voting not as individual members, as representatives do every day on legislation, but as state delegations. To win, a candidate must receive a majority of the states' votes (26) in the House. The House selected John Quincy Adams as President in 1824 after an indecisive four-way race among Adams, Andrew Jackson, Henry Clay, and William Crawford. In the election, Jackson had received a plurality, but not a majority, of the electoral votes. He received 99 electoral votes to 84 for Adams, 41 for Crawford, and 37 for Clay. Speaker of the House Clay threw his support to Adams, who won the House vote. The House has not been called on since, although people worried in 1968 that third-party candidate George Wallace of Alabama might win sufficient electoral college votes to deny either Nixon or Humphrey a majority. Wallace won five southern states and 45 electoral college votes. Nixon, however, won 301 electoral college votes.

Outlook

The electoral college system may seem foreign to the rest of the presidential election process, but in fact it is an integral part. The mathematics of the electoral college directs presidential candidates' campaign strategies in three key ways.

First, campaigns take for granted those states that they know they can win without much effort. Throughout American history there have been regions of the country within which a party does very well—or at least consistently does better than the other party. For the Democrats from the Civil War through the 1960s the region

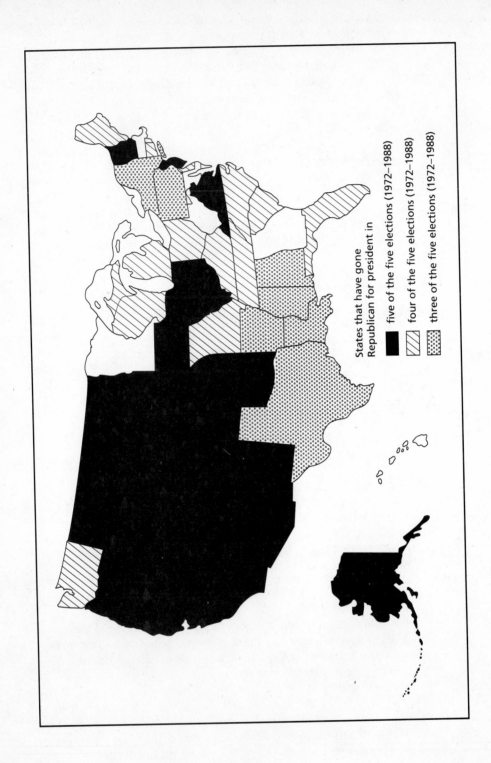

States that have gone
Republican for president in

■ five of the five elections (1972–1988)

▨ four of the five elections (1972–1988)

▨ three of the five elections (1972–1988)

was the "Solid South." For the Republicans the region was the "Solid West" from 1972 to 1988. This Republican stronghold, which Bush did *not* dominate in 1992, is depicted in Figure 4.2.

Second, campaigns spend little time in small states with few electoral college votes. Covering each state saps the candidates' time and energy. In 1960, Richard Nixon made a campaign pledge that he would visit all fifty states, because Alaska and Hawaii recently had been admitted to the Union. The pace of the trek crisscrossing the country left Nixon exhausted by the end of the campaign and the debates. After the race, Nixon acknowledged the promise was a stupid one, and in 1968 he vowed not to repeat it.

Third, campaigns lavish as much time and attention as they can on states with large numbers of electoral college votes. Every would-be president knows by heart that in 1992 twelve states—California, New York, Texas, Pennsylvania, Illinois, Ohio, Florida, Michigan, New Jersey, North Carolina, Georgia, and Virginia—totaled 283 electoral votes, more than enough to elect a candidate who loses all of the remaining thirty-eight states.

The electoral college system not only steers the strategies of the two major party candidates but also inhibits third-party candidacy. The winner-take-all system in the states combined with the majority needed to win in the electoral college makes it difficult for small parties or independent candidates to mount a national race. Only candidates with heavy regional support are likely to do well enough to gain any electoral college votes, as George Wallace did in 1968.

The electoral college system is integral to the presidency in one final way. Because of the winner-take-all system, winning presidential candidates often rack up very impressive, lopsided victories in the electoral college. In 1992, Bill Clinton won 370 electoral votes (69 percent) and George Bush won 168 (31 percent), yet the popular vote split was only 43 to 38 percent (with Ross Perot taking 19 percent). Even more dramatically, in 1984 President Reagan won re-election by taking every state but Minnesota and the District of Columbia in the electoral college. He received 525 electoral college votes (98 percent of the total), and Walter Mondale received only 13 (2 percent). The national popular vote difference was not quite as wide: 58.8 percent to 40.6 percent. The news media, in highlighting the electoral college vote, exaggerates the victor's win. John Kennedy won his race in 1960 against Richard Nixon by 0.1 percent, less than 100,000 votes. But he claimed a mandate to "get the country moving again" from his electoral college win of 57 percent to Nixon's 43 percent.

◀ **Figure 4.2 The Republicans' Solid West, 1972–1988**

Over the five presidential elections from 1972 to 1988, most western states voted for the Republican ticket. [*Source:* Gerald Pomper, *The Election of 1988* (Chatham, N.J.: Chatham House, 1989). Copyright © 1989 Chatham House Publishers. Used by permission.]

Proposals to reform or abolish the electoral college have been discussed off and on throughout American history. Four Presidents—Johnson, Nixon, Ford, and Carter—endorsed a constitutional amendment that would abolish the electoral college and provide for direct election by the voters. Others have advocated retaining the electoral college but dropping the winner-take-all approach in favor of a proportional system that would calculate the number of electors given a candidate from the proportion of the popular vote the candidate received in a state.

Each reform creates its own problems. Proponents of direct election and proponents of the proportional system must grapple with the issue of whether the winning candidate needs to receive a majority or only a plurality of the popular vote. If a majority is required and no candidate receives it, what mechanism would decide the winner? A national runoff of the top two candidates is typically proposed. But many groan at the idea of another costly, time-consuming election after an already arduous campaign season. If only a plurality is required, the field is open to more candidates and it is possible that the top vote getter could receive a very small percentage (25 to 30 percent) of the vote but still win. Many people argue that this would be too frail a mandate from which to lead the country.

None of these concerns is likely to be resolved until the electoral college elects, as it last did 100 years ago, a president who is not the popular vote winner or until the race is decided in the House of Representatives, as last happened well over 150 years ago. Only then will calls for reform be taken seriously. For now, the quaint, antiquated system of the electoral college will continue to elect American presidents.

CONCLUSION

Medieval chroniclers tell of fair princesses who sent Christian knights to wander for many days and nights in heathen forests in search of dragons and bits of the True Cross. Modern-day candidates for the American presidency travel through similar forests. They go thousands of miles, often in a single day, wander for months and years through decaying downtowns, suburban shopping malls, and ballrooms of bland hotels. On their journey they come up with sound bites, smile steadfastly into a camera that never sleeps, and always proclaim that victory, the True Cross, is within their grasp.

The victor in the last six races for president—since 1972—has been the candidate who has best survived the glare and intensity of the camera and lights. The attributes that become known in the campaign through two-second sound bites and photo opportunities that freeze candidates in time and space detract from all the other attributes that remain unknown but fundamentally important. What the candidates stand for, other than the vaguest generalities, and how they will govern the country go unexplored.

What goes unexplored during the election has profound effects on presidential governance. The imagery of the campaign becomes the imagery of governing. The media values of the campaign become the values of governing. In this way the campaign lends content to the single executive image. Visibility drawn from the campaign arranges the substance of each of the other three criteria of the single executive image: uniqueness, importance, and power. Presidents are unique and important in part because so much broadcast attention and time is paid to electing them. Their uniqueness and importance are defined in terms of media values: appear decisive even if wrong; be popular even if wrong. The horse race continues after a candidate is elected, only then the president runs against himself and the ideal president in public opinion polls. How well the president does in the polls depends on how well he can mimic the ideal. Looking presidential—having those qualities the media deem to be the qualities of the ideal president (confidence and strength, warmth and likableness)—becomes a necessary ingredient of being both a successful presidential candidate and a successful president. Power can be drawn as much from this presidential look as from the Constitution. The single executive image thus draws many of its characteristics from the election campaign.

But the image is also missing something as a result of the campaign. Tough discussions of the problems facing the government are as absent after the election as they are during it. The incentives of modern campaigns push candidates to create emotional, symbolic themes, oversimplify problems and solutions, and plot strategies guided by the latest public opinion polls. These incentives are identical for the president once in office. In 1988, candidate George Bush adopted the snappy slogan "No New Taxes" as the theme of his campaign. President George Bush made the slogan the central policy of a country facing a multibillion-dollar deficit. Only after a year in office did Bush begrudgingly acknowledge that the slogan could no longer be policy. The campaign suggests that the president is the one person in charge. But what he will take charge of—the problems and processes of government—remains a mystery to both the new president and the country. ∎

FURTHER READING

On presidential primaries, see: James Davis, *Presidential Primaries: Road to the White House*, 2d ed. (Westport, Conn.: Greenwood Press, 1980); William Crotty and John Jackson, *Presidential Primaries and Nominations* (Washington,

D.C.: CQ Press, 1985); Thomas Marshall, *Presidential Nominations in a Reform Age* (New York: Praeger, 1981). On general election campaigns for president, see: Steven Wayne, *The Road to the White House*, 4th ed. (New York: St. Martin's Press, 1992); Gerald Pomper, ed., *The Election of 1988* (Chatham, N.J.: Chatham House, 1989). On imagery and the media in presidential campaigns, see: Joe McGinniss, *The Selling of the President* (New York: Pocket Books, 1969); Thomas Patterson and Robert McClure, *The Unseeing Eye* (New York: Putnam, 1976); Michael Robinson and Margaret Sheehan, *Over the Wire and on TV: CBS and UPI in Campaign '80* (New York: Russell Sage Foundation, 1983).

N O T E S

1. The *1992* U.S. election was less than typical with the presence of a third candidate—Texas billionaire H. Ross Perot—in the race. Although Perot campaigned for several months as an undeclared candidate, he dropped out of the race in July 1992 before officially getting in. The general election campaign then became a traditional two-candidate race, between incumbent George Bush and Bill Clinton, the governor of Arkansas, until Perot re-entered the race in September.

2. Quoted in William Chambers, *Political Parties in a New Nation: The American Experience, 1776–1809* (New York: Oxford University Press, 1963), 6–7.

3. Wallace did run under the banner of the "American Independent Party," but this was nothing more than a label attached to the Wallace campaign.

4. For an empirical study of this composite image, see Joseph Tannenhaus and Mary Ann Foley, "Separating Objects of Specific and Diffuse Support: Experiments on Presidents and the Presidency," *Micropolitics* 1 (December 1981): 345–367.

5. Quoted in James Davis, *Presidential Primaries: Road to the White House*, 2d ed. (Westport, Conn.: Greenwood Press, 1980), 28.

6. This category name is adapted from Thomas Marshall, who refers to the entire period from 1832–1968 as the Brokered Convention period. See Thomas Marshall, *Presidential Nominations in a Reform Age* (New York: Praeger, 1981).

7. Quoted in Noble Cunningham, Jr., *The Jeffersonian Republicans: The Formation of Party Organization, 1789–1801* (Chapel Hill: University of North Carolina Press, 1957), 166, original emphasis.

8. For a good discussion of this period, see James Davis, *National Conventions in an Age of Party Reform* (New York: Greenwood Press, 1983), 30–32.

9. Robert M. La Follette, *La Follette's Autobiography* (Madison, Wis.: R. La Follette, 1913), 197–198.

10. It should be noted that parties themselves do not adopt primaries. States must pass laws requiring such election changes. Consequently, when a state adopts a primary law, the law is typically in place for both parties whether both want it or not.

11. Davis, *Presidential Primaries*, 45.

12. See William Crotty and John Jackson, *Presidential Primaries and Nominations* (Washington, D.C.: Congressional Quarterly Press, 1985), 17.

13. New York Republicans employed the caucus/convention method in 1988.

14. Crotty and Jackson, 76.

15. Richard Rubin, *Press, Party, and Presidency* (New York: Norton, 1981), 209.

16. Nelson Polsby, *Consequences of Party Reform* (New York: Oxford University Press, 1983), 144.

17. Davis, *Presidential Primaries*, 7.

18. Stephen Wayne, *The Road to the White House*, 3d ed. (New York: St. Martin's Press, 1988), 29.

19. Ibid., Chap. 6.

20. Stephen Wayne, *The Road to the White House* (New York: St. Martin's Press, 1980), 31.

21. There are two predominant schools of thought about how people develop party identification. One school maintains that it is a long-term predisposition toward a party based primarily on family socialization. See Angus Campbell et al., *The American Voter* (New York: Wiley, 1960). The other school sees party identification as a short-term response to the records of the two parties in office. In this view, voters make "retrospective evaluations" of party performance. See Morris Fiorina, *Retrospective Voting in American National Elections* (New Haven: Yale University Press, 1981). Although researchers hotly debate which view is correct, party identification is most likely a combination of long- and short-term judgments.

22. Quoted in Joe McGinniss, *The Selling of the President* (New York: Pocket Books, 1969), 32–33.

23. Quoted ibid., 70–71.

24. Fawn Brodie, *Richard Nixon: The Shaping of His Character* (New York: Norton, 1981), 145.

25. Quoted in Tom Fielder and Carl Cannon, "Biden's Exit Is Second Setback for the 'Senator Smith' Image-Maker," *Arizona Daily Star*, September 27, 1987, A15.

26. Ibid.

27. Quoted in T. Harry Williams, Richard Current, and Frank Freidel, *A History of the United States to 1876* (New York: Knopf, 1959), 213.

28. Wayne (1980), 206.

29. Thomas Patterson and Robert McClure, *The Unseeing Eye* (New York: Putnam, 1976), 54.

30. Michael Robinson and Margaret Sheehan, *Over the Wire and on TV: CBS and UPI in Campaign '80* (New York: Russell Sage Foundation, 1983), 146–148.

31. Thomas Patterson and Richard Davis, "The Media Campaign: Struggle for the Agenda," in *The Election of 1984*, ed. M. Nelson (Washington, D.C.: CQ Press, 1985), 124.

32. Ibid., 122.

33. Patrick Caddell memorandum of September 30, 1984, quoted in Peter Goldman and Tony Fuller, *The Quest for the Presidency, 1984* (Toronto: Bantam Books, 1985), 432.

34. Quoted in Maureen Dowd, "Dukakis and Bush Spar on Conservatism," *New York Times,* June 8, 1988, 14.

35. Larry Martz et al., "Dukakis by the People Who Know Him Best," *Newsweek,* July 25, 1988, 25.

36. Quoted in John Cassidy, "From Wimp to Winner," *London Sunday Times,* November 6, 1988, B1, B4.

37. Quoted in Marjorie Hershey, "The Campaign and the Media," in *The Election of 1988,* ed. Gerald Pomper (Chatham, N.J.: Chatham House, 1989), 95–96.

Public Perceptions

I magine that you are actually living a version of Plato's cave allegory. For as long as you can remember, you have been held captive in a cave. You are strapped to a chair and can only look straight ahead. Your captor provides you with food, drink, and entertainment. Everyday you stare at the cave wall in front of you as flickering shadows of rabbits, cats, trees, and people float by. From behind, your captor projects these images on the wall with a lantern and hand puppets. You cannot see this apparatus. One afternoon while your captor sleeps, you escape from the cave into a world of harsh light and burning color. You stumble across "real" rabbits, cats, and trees but find them strange and frightening. What do you do? Do you return to the cave? Or do you stay out in the new, foreign world?

Most people would probably beat a hasty retreat to the cave because living there is the only life they have known. It is familiar and not uncomfortable. To them, the shadows on the cave wall are "real" "live" objects. What they *perceive* to be real *is* real.

People perceive politics, including presidential politics, like shadows on the cave wall. At the heart of politics are people's perceptions of what they take to be real. This chapter explores how Americans' perceptions of the president are drawn from four shadows on the wall of the American cave: the political culture, symbolism, public expectations, and presidential popularity. *The political culture of a society is a set of assumptions by which people perceive politics.* The most perplexing aspect of cultural assumptions is that they are not necessarily factually true but they are real. Their truth or falsity is rarely tested because people usually remain in the cave. If the French assume that France is the best nation on Earth, then this assumption is real to the French. Other cultures, however, are unlikely to share it. They have their own assumptions that they do not question either. Americans are happy in another cave: they assume that the United States is the best nation on Earth. The American culture also colors people's perceptions of presidents. Americans look to presidents as the chief representatives of the best nation on Earth.

Culture alone does not shape people's perceptions of politics. Cultural assumptions are slippery phenomena that cannot be seen or touched. This elusiveness gives rise to the use of symbols. A symbol is something—an object, a person, or an event—that stands for or represents an idea, quality, condition, or other abstraction. The symbol is socially based. An object, person, or event becomes a symbol when people give it meaning beyond the literal description of the item itself.[1]

Symbols are mechanisms by which people come to know cultural assumptions. *Political symbols are translation devices that allow people to employ cultural assumptions in everyday politics.* The American flag is a symbol of the nation—of its past glories and future promise. Behind the symbolism is the cultural assumption that America is the best nation on Earth. Yet for someone who has never set foot in the American cave, the flag is simply a piece of red, white, and blue cloth with a lot of stars stuck in the upper-left corner. For this individual, the flag has no meaning beyond its literal meaning, because the connection between the object and the cultural assumption is absent.[2] There are many other political symbols. The British monarchy is a symbol of the tradition and greatness of the British Empire. Bastille Day symbolizes France's values of independence, freedom, and democracy, just as Independence Day symbolizes similar values in the United States. To the rest of the world, July 14 and July 4 are just like any other days. The president too is seen as an American symbol. Americans want the chief executive to stand for the nation's power and mission in the world.

Symbols stand as models by which real-world objects, individuals, and events are judged. *Symbols thus create political expectations— individuals' best guess at what they think will happen in a given political situation.* For instance, most Americans saw the Soviet Union, prior to its collapse, as a symbol of wickedness. Terms such as "evil empire" and "red menace" typified the symbolism. This symbolism established a set of expectations in Americans' minds about the actions of the USSR—destructive domestic and foreign policies. Americans thus viewed Soviet President Mikhail Gorbachev's early attempts at glasnost and perestroika with suspicion because the policies of improved foreign relations and internal reforms did not conform to expectations. Indeed, many Americans thought Gorbachev's endeavors were a crafty ploy to catch the United States off guard. Since the collapse of the communist system, the symbolism has changed. Americans now are more likely to see the new Commonwealth of Independent States as a symbol of raw uncertainty—struggling against long odds to set up free market democracies. Expectations have changed accordingly. Symbolism provides a base line for people's expectations of the president. As a symbol of the nation, the president is expected to be a singular heroic leader: a man-on-horseback in time of war and a steadfast guardian of the nation's economic and domestic well-being.

The expectations people hold of the president influence the president's popularity. There is a temptation to simplify public opinion about the president to a chain of poll results. Is a president's popularity up or down? Yet people's opinions of presidents are much more complicated than merely answering yes or no to the question "Do you approve or disapprove of the way the president is handling his job in office?" When a president meets the expectations the public holds—the chief executive undaunted by a crisis and unbending against a foe—his popularity will likely rise. But when he fails to meet such public expectations, his popularity will fall. Each of the four shadows—the political culture, symbolism, expectations, and opinions—help define uniqueness and importance in the single executive image. Americans perceive the president to be a figure who is unique and alone in a pivotally important position. And what they perceive to be real is real.

THE POLITICAL CULTURE

The political culture of the United States intertwines four basic assumptions that color Americans' perceptions of politics: (1) individualism, (2) pragmatism, (3) the chosen people, and (4) antiparty democracy.[3] They are the red-white-and-blue lenses through which Americans watch political events and political figures, including presidents.

Individualism

Individualism focuses citizens' attention on the president as a single person. Individualism is a belief in the importance of the solitary effort of one person. Americans emphasize qualities of self-reliance, independence, hard work, and personal success. They believe that a person can achieve whatever she wants without help from anyone. Conversely, if she fails, the failure is her fault. She is not a victim of circumstance, nor has she been cast off by others. Individualism creates idealized notions of people who have accomplished things by themselves, who are "self-made" or who have "pulled themselves up by their own bootstraps." This American preoccupation with individual accomplishment is in contrast to other cultures that place greater emphasis on community, collective spirit, and society's protection of individuals.

Individualism accentuates heroes, political and otherwise. Americans are attracted to images of the cowboy on the range, the frontiersman in the wilderness, the soldier who saves the whole squad, the astronaut in outer space, or some other individual who tames a vast unknown territory. An Italian interviewer asked Henry Kissinger how, as secretary of state under Richard Nixon, he had attained such an "incredible movie-star status." Kissinger replied that it came from "the fact" that he had always "acted alone." Kissinger continued:

Americans like that immensely. Americans like the cowboy who leads the wagon train by riding ahead alone on his horse, the cowboy who rides all alone into the town . . . with his horse and nothing else. Maybe even without a pistol. . . . This cowboy doesn't have to be courageous. All he needs is to be alone, to show others that he rides into the town and does everything by himself.[4]

American presidents are political cowboys. Some of them have played cowboy, like Theodore Roosevelt and Lyndon Johnson, and one of them, Ronald Reagan, performed as a cowboy in the movies. But the picture fits all presidents. Americans see them as single individuals who act alone—fighting Congress, boldly meeting crises, or failing to control danger—all by themselves. Americans celebrate the birthdays of Washington and Lincoln, who embody the virtues and talents for which the nation strives. Presidential candidates often reminisce about their humble backgrounds and tout how they single-handedly struggled against long odds to succeed. According to historian James Robertson, the president ties together "All the logic and mythology of individualism—of independence, of the loner, of community service, of legitimate fame, of popularity and the approval of one's equals, and of the effectiveness of one sturdy, adaptive jack-of-all-trades set down in the midst of a savage, chaotic wilderness."[5]

Individualism has another familiar strand applied to presidents. As small children, Americans often are told that "Anyone can grow up to be president." This slogan has three aspects that reveal a great deal about how individualism shapes Americans' perceptions of presidents. First, it implies that the presidency is a pinnacle in American society. It is the highest achievement or among the highest achievements a person can realize. Parents do not tell their children that "Anyone can grow up to be a cashier." Second, it is a very egalitarian notion, which says that any person, no matter what her or his background, can succeed in America. The president holds the most special political position in the land, but everyone has an equal chance to attain it. Third, this expression of individualism is utterly false. Not everyone can grow up to be president. It is unlikely that a person born a woman, a black, a Jew, or a Native American will become president soon. Yet despite the slogan's falsehood, Americans are continually inspired by it: "If a peanut farmer can become president, why not me?"

The individualism assumption says not only that presidents act alone but that they have attained a pre-eminent position in America—an accomplishment of personal success to which anyone can aspire. In these ways, the individualism assumption helps establish the importance and the uniqueness of the single executive image.

Pragmatism

The second assumption—pragmatism—states that the purpose of politics is to construct simple, quick, concrete solutions to complex problems. American politics is well known for its practicality, give-and-take, compromise, and consensus-seeking. Policymaking in the United States rests not so much on determining the right or wrong approach but rather on adopting an approach on which a majority can agree. Politically practical—that is, electorally popular—policies are proposed that offer something for everyone. These policies are not necessarily workable, well-crafted, long-range plans; instead, they are likely to be quick fixes that will show some results, any results, before the next election.

Under the assumption of pragmatism, one convenient technique of policymaking has been to spend money to solve a problem. According to the "logic of money," the larger the problem, the more money that should be spent, and the more money spent, the faster the problem will go away. America's response to a growing drug crisis, to the AIDS epidemic, and to the Soviet collapse, to name only a few, has been to spend money. Means matter more than ends in pragmatic politics. This approach usually does not alleviate the problem, but it may create the impression that something is being done.

Out of the logic of pragmatism grows a president's role as chief problem solver. If pragmatic politics demands quick, easy solutions to complex problems, then one of the quickest, easiest ways to solve problems is to place one person in charge—someone who will do most of the work and take most of the responsibility. The larger a problem, the more pragmatism assumes that a president should be the one policymaker who solves it. This cultural assumption reinforces presidential activism, discussed in Chapters 2 and 3. The president uses and enlarges his constitutional power to act as the chief problem solver.

A president, given the responsibility to deal with major national problems, often relies on the logic of money for solutions. The Johnson administration applied this reasoning to the Vietnam War: the more money allocated to the war effort, the faster it would be won. It also applied a parallel principle that the more men sent to fight the war, the greater the victory would be. Both applications of pragmatic politics disregarded Pentagon reports that stated that in guerrilla warfare more is not necessarily better.

One might suspect that the logic of money has become an illogical approach for presidents to take in the face of a $400 billion budget deficit.[6] Yet George Bush's 1992 State of the Union message provided prime evidence of the president's role as chief problem solver and the temptations of the logic of money. After more than two months of anticipation, Bush unveiled before Congress his plan to revive a faltering economy and respond to criticisms that he had no domestic agenda. The result was a speech that contained something for almost everyone: lower withholding tax rates for workers, a $5,000 tax credit for first-time home buyers, income tax exemptions of $500 for every child a family has, tax breaks for student loans, an end to the capital gains tax, a ninety-day moratorium on new government regulations, health care reforms, and defense cuts. Economists argued that the defense cuts were insufficient to match the price tags of the other items. They complained that Bush's proposals were quick fixes that would add significantly to the deficit and cause the economy long-term harm.[7] In an election year, the Democratic-controlled Congress did not act on any of Bush's proposals.

The assumption of pragmatic politics is no more factually true than the assumption of individualism, but its consequences for a president are just as real. Complex problems often require complex, long-term solutions, but people's political careers are long over before the effects of such solutions can be judged. Such solutions are not likely even to be proposed. Nor is it true that a president alone can cope with major national problems. William Howard Taft lamented the effects of the pragmatism assumption on the presidency:

There is a class of people that . . . visit the President with responsibility for everything that is done and that is not done. If poverty prevails where, in their judgment, it should not prevail, then the President is responsible. If other people are richer than they ought to be, the President is responsible. While the President's powers are broad, he cannot do everything. . . . This would be ludicrous if it did not sometimes take serious results. The President cannot make clouds to rain, he cannot make the corn to grow, he cannot make business to be good.[8]

One of Taft's successors, Herbert Hoover, was even more blunt when he said, "Once upon a time my political opponents honored me as possessing the fabulous intellectual and economic power by which I created a world-wide depression all by myself."[9] According to the pragmatism assumption, the president, as chief problem solver, does whatever it takes to alleviate major national problems. The individualism assumption adds to this: the president must come up with solutions by himself; if he fails, as Hoover was perceived to have done, then he fails all by himself. This again underscores the uniqueness and importance of a president as a single executive. No other politician shoulders such demands.

The Chosen People

A third assumption says that Americans are "the chosen people." As noted at the outset of his chapter, Americans assume that the United

States is the best nation on Earth. Americans see their country as a special democratic society that has a better understanding of world history, world problems, and the way things should be done than any other nation. Americans have a mission in the world to protect freedom and the "American way of life." Herman Melville wrote that "we Americans are the peculiar chosen people . . . the Israel of our time."[10] America is a city set upon a hill, a colony that bears the responsibility to set a pattern for all the world to follow.

Based on this assumption, a president is the leader of the chosen people. He must uphold the ideals of liberty, justice, freedom, and equality that Americans often feel are exclusively or especially their own. A president must command America's moral and spiritual energy to protect and spread these values across the world. George Bush accepted the mantle of leader of the chosen people at his inauguration:

We meet on democracy's front porch, a good place to talk as neighbors and as friends. . . . We know what works: Freedom works. We know what's right: Freedom is right. We know how to secure a more just and prosperous life for man on Earth: through free markets, free speech, free elections, and the exercise of free will unhampered by the state. . . . America is never wholly herself unless she is engaged in high moral principle. We as a people have such a purpose today. It is to make kinder the face of the nation and gentler the face of the world.[11]

The chief executive must behave as a moral leader in his personal life, setting examples for the rest of the chosen people to follow. His leadership is judged on how well it embodies and conveys America's image of itself: decisive yet compassionate, orderly yet flexible, congenial yet private.

A president also is anointed as leader of the chosen people from his role as chief of state. The president is the ceremonial head of the nation who greets foreign visitors, lights the national Christmas tree, places wreaths on the tombs of war dead, throws out the first baseball, makes proclamations of thanksgiving, bestows medals on shy heroes, and shakes hands with long processions of smiling schoolchildren. In performing these tasks, a president reflects the values of America. Other nations, like Great Britain and the Netherlands, divide the tasks of chief of state and chief executive between the monarch, who handles the work of the former, and the prime minister, who acts as the latter. But an American president does both jobs, and this arrangement too heightens presidential importance and uniqueness.

Antiparty Democracy

According to the fourth assumption, America is a democracy for the people and against party. Americans hail democracy in the country, despite the nuisance of parties. They highlight their personal freedoms. Young children caught doing something wrong snap back, "It's a free country." Americans applaud majority rule and universal suffrage. Many, though a declining number, feel they have a personal stake in the decisions of government. In contrast, Americans have long held a spirited distrust of parties. They feel that these organizations taint politics, making it more prone to corruption. They also consider parties as the chief obstacle to progress in the nation. Disagreements between the parties turn good solutions into watered-down compromises.

The antiparty democracy assumption places presidents above party and as surrogates for the public.[12] Andrew Jackson, the first self-proclaimed tribune of the people, maintained that ordinary citizens were incapable of undertaking collective action. He pointed out that they were preoccupied with daily chores of work and family and thus relied on their advocate in the White House to best protect their interests.[13] Presidents since Jackson have invoked a familiar chant that they are the only officials elected by the entire nation. This status automatically ensures presidential uniqueness and importance. A president is not just leader of the chosen people; he is their democratic leader. While the president charges that other politicians represent self-seeking "special" or partisan interests, the president often portrays himself as the champion of the public interest. He characterizes himself as standing above the fray of organized interests and party.

Yet what presidents say and what they do are often distant relatives. Like the other assumptions, the perception of presidents as democratic champions is real but not necessarily completely true. Presidents often stand firmly in favor of special interests, especially those that have helped to elect them. President Bush's opposition to gun control, although couched in the language of the national interest, also reflected the National Rifle Association's weighty support of the 1988 Bush campaign. Presidents love to implore Congress to set aside partisan differences and pass or quash legislation for the good of the nation. All the while, though, presidents are party spokesmen. President Kennedy's hesitancy on civil rights reflected the need to keep southern Democrats happy.

PRESIDENTIAL SYMBOLS

Because of the assumptions of the political culture, Americans often perceive the president as a symbol of the nation. There is a symbolic equivalence between the president and "the people." The individualism assumption portrays each president as a heroic figure who is larger than life but also says that any one of the people can become president. According to the logic of pragmatism, the president is expected to solve the acute economic, domestic, and foreign problems of the nation; the people's problems are the president's problems. As leader of the chosen people, the president stands for, or embodies, America, its unity, values, and special mission in the world. As the nation's democratic leader, he alone looks out for the "little guy."

Political symbols have two essential functions: as cognitive devices, they simplify; as emotional ones, they evoke feelings rather than reason.

Simplification

People simplify the operation of government by concentrating on the actions of presidents. Many Americans pay little attention to politics. They are usually only dimly aware of who government officials are, what they do, and what programs they develop. The one person people may know something about is the president. This attention to the president not only simplifies the operation of American government but, perhaps of greater importance, personalizes it. Political scientist Fred Greenstein observes, "Our own lack of interest in the details of how the nation is governed becomes more acceptable if we feel that *someone* is attending to such matters. The assumption is that events are being controlled, that life is not whimsical and dangerous."[14] Consequently, there is a greater emphasis on this single individual than there would be otherwise. Each of the cultural assumptions is found behind the simplification. Individualism focuses on a lone figure. Practical politics promotes the president as chief problem solver. The chosen people have but one leader. Antiparty democracy says that this leader is the only truly democratic figure in the nation. In each way, politics is condensed to the activities of the president and how others respond to him, rather than what these other politicians do on their own. A president draws uniqueness and importance from the simplification and personalization.

Emotions

People respond to symbols emotionally rather than rationally. A person reacts rationally toward politicians when she calculates the material benefits and costs of the politicians' decisions. She supports those decisions for which the material benefits outweigh the costs— decisions that improve her personal life or better society. She rejects those decisions for which the material costs outweigh the benefits. But people also may seek feelings of emotional satisfaction in politics, quite apart from any material benefits they may desire. This emotional satisfaction or reassurance is known as "quiescence."[15] It is difficult for ordinary citizens who are inattentive and unorganized to get something tangible from politics, unlike a major corporation receiving a tax break or an interest group securing favorable legislation. Instead, ordinary citizens often supplant material satisfaction with quiescence. For instance, in 1989 the constitutional amendment proposed to prohibit flag burning aroused quiescence. Feelings of patriotism and nationalism, not the monetary costs of buying or burning a flag, were at stake.

People seek quiescence from presidents—emotional reassurance that everything is all right or at least that someone is in charge—in three ways. The symbolism arises from presidents as objects, from the activities of presidents, and from presidential decisions. Emotions of concern and anxiety are evident in the extreme when a president becomes sick, is shot, or is killed. The president serves as a symbolic object. The events create a sense of instability, unpredictability, danger, and disorder. After President Kennedy was assassinated, a study showed that people felt physically ill over the news and had a hard time sleeping. Even citizens who were not supportive of Kennedy in office, notably southern whites, were severely distressed by his assassination.[16] The emotion was partly for Kennedy as a person, but it also was for Kennedy *as president*, symbolizing the goals, values, and identity of the nation. There was a symbolic equivalence between the president and the people, with the two blurring together as one: grief by the nation for Kennedy was ultimately grief by the nation for itself.

Symbolism also intertwines the daily activities of a president. Jimmy Carter began his presidency by stepping from his bulletproof limousine during his inaugural parade and walking, hand in hand with his wife, down Pennsylvania Avenue from the Capitol to the White House. Carter was acutely aware of the symbolism he was trying to highlight as the "people's president," thus reinforcing the assumption of antiparty democracy:

I began to realize that the symbolism of our leaving the armored car would be much more far-reaching than simply to promote exercise. I remembered the angry demonstrators who had habitually confronted recent Presidents and Vice Presidents, furious over the Vietnam war and later the revelations of Watergate. I wanted to provide a vivid demonstration of my confidence in the people as security was concerned, and I felt a simple walk would be a tangible indication of some reduction in the imperial status of the President and his family.[17]

Symbolism also can be part of major presidential policy decisions. People may achieve quiescence from an action or event that gains them no material benefit or actually materially harms them. In the spring of 1965, Lyndon Johnson sent first 500, then another 1,500, and eventually a total of 22,000 troops to quell civil unrest in the Dominican Republic. Acting on information from the U.S. ambassador in Santo Domingo that American lives were in danger, Johnson announced to the nation the initial troop commitment, saying:

There was no longer any choice for the man who is your President. I know that no American serviceman wants to kill anyone. I know that no American

President wants to give an order which brings shooting and casualties and death. But I want you to know and I want the world to know that as long as I am President of this country, we are going to defend ourselves. We will defend our soldiers against attackers. We will honor our treaties. We will keep our commitments. We will defend our nation against all those who seek to destroy not only the United States but every free country in this hemisphere. We do not want to bury anyone as I have said so many times before. But we do not intend to be buried.[18]

Johnson's words display the way in which a president may use symbolism to manipulate public opinion in favor of his policy decisions. The president attempts to create an emotional consensus about his actions. The four cultural assumptions are evident in Johnson's remarks. Johnson portrays himself as a heroic figure bravely defending America. He takes on the role of chief problem solver and conveys the impression that he knows what must be done. In the process, he uses the pragmatic answer that the more men sent, the faster the problem will be solved. As leader of the chosen people, he suggests that the United States will not bury anyone, but neither will it be buried. Johnson speaks of the American people and "their President," thereby establishing a democratic bond between himself and the public.

It is not surprising that 76 percent of the American public supported Johnson's decision even though few knew exactly where the Dominican Republic was and most were unclear about why the troops were sent. Was there a communist threat? Was the deployment a show of American force? The support arose not because of any rational explanation that was given or sought. People did not stop to evaluate whether the benefits of U.S. intervention outweighed the costs. The support was given quite simply because *the president* had sent the troops. The symbolism has the effect of legitimizing the decision. Reagan's air raids against Libya in 1986 gained the United States no concrete advantage at the time and had high costs afterward from Libya's retaliatory bombing of a German nightclub frequented by American soldiers. Nonetheless, people received considerable emotional satisfaction, or quiescence, from Reagan's action.

PUBLIC EXPECTATIONS

Public expectations follow a president as symbol of the nation. The symbolism helps create the imaginary figure of the ideal president discussed in Chapter 4.[19] The ideal is like a ghost that trails real live presidents wherever they go. It becomes the model or standard on which public expectations of presidents are based. The ideal president is exuberant about life, solves major national problems, and has a vision to lead the country into the future. People do not merely judge George Bush on his own merits or compare him to his immediate predecessors. Instead, he is expected to live up to the popular notion of the ideal president. When the expectations are met, a president gains considerable advantages in his relations with other politicians and the public. He can revel in the uniqueness and importance of the single executive image. When the expectations are not met, the image will likely overwhelm him.

Upon entering office, Jimmy Carter tried to downplay the ideal. He insisted that presidents could not be all things to all people, nor could they cure the ills of the country overnight. Carter's tampering with the ideal backfired. Instead of recognizing that expectations drawn from the ideal were unrealistic, people judged Carter a failure for not living up to them. In 1979, Carter went on national television to lament a "malaise" of the American spirit. Many people felt the crisis was at least partly of Carter's own making, stemming from his diminution of presidential uniqueness and importance. Ronald Reagan was careful to reassert and capitalize on these two elements of the single executive image.

Many of the expectations are drawn from the election campaign, when presidential candidates tout their unique ability to live up to the ideal. The expectations also are learned during childhood. Studies of political socialization—the process by which people learn politics—indicate that the first image American children have of government is of the president. White, middle-class children most often see the president as powerful and benevolent. Black and poor children emphasize power and fear. Watergate had a negative, though not permanent, effect on all children's attitudes. Scholars agree that children (and adults) distinguish between the person temporarily occupying the office and the office itself—between a president and *the president*. Researchers assume that children's expectations of power and benevolence serve as a basis of support for the office as they grow into late adolescence and adulthood.[20]

Three sets of expectations are especially relevant: (1) personal behavior, (2) policy performance, and (3) leadership. Each set contributes to the ideal and creates standards for presidents. Presidents will find it difficult if they accommodate one type of expectation but let the others lapse.

Personal Behavior

People are fascinated with the personal lives of a president and his family. This interest results partly from the cultural assumption of individualism. It is also a product of the news media watching a president every hour of every day. Much of the attention is on exceptionally trivial matters that nonetheless become part of people's evaluations of how well a president governs. Think about all the actions you take in any five-minute period of any given day. Suppose you are late for work and you gulp down a large cup of coffee. Your dog gets underfoot as you rush around and you yell at it to get out of the way. You frown and hurry out the door. Imagine that Barbara Walters and a film crew have recorded those five minutes. She asks you why you yelled at your dog. Do you have a hot temper and might you therefore make rash decisions? Should you cut back on your coffee consumption so that you are less jittery and irritable? Do you dash about because you are disorganized?

This scenario seems ludicrous when applied to normal, daily actions, but it is very serious when applied to an American president's daily actions, which are closely scrutinized. Lyndon Johnson loved to play with his two beagles, Him and Her, pulling them up by their long floppy ears. One day, photographers recorded Johnson's play session on the White House lawn. The next morning, pictures in newspapers across the country showed Johnson with a broad smile and one of the dogs, with a queasy look, suspended by his or her ears in midair. Dog owners were enraged. The White House swiftly announced that the president would abandon the practice. Other presidents have received more favorable publicity about the "first pet," including George Bush, whose dog Millie was the "author" of a best-selling book.

Attempting to convey that he was a common man assuming the presidency, Gerald Ford invited reporters to his suburban Washington home to observe him making his own breakfast. (Ford took several weeks before actually moving into the White House.) Dozens of camera people and reporters squeezed into the Fords' kitchen and watched the president eagerly select a single English muffin from a wrapper in the refrigerator, slice it, and place it in the toaster. He chatted amiably with the reporters as they all waited for the muffin to pop up. Joe McGinniss took note of the nonsense that accompanies all presidents:

At this stage of Gerald Ford's Presidency there is only one impression we are capable of receiving, and, unfortunately—both for him and for us—it is unrealistic.

Consider what we know of him: he dances, he prays, he walks onto his front lawn in his bathrobe to get his morning paper. He makes his own breakfast, he swims, he holds meetings, he sleeps in the same bed as his wife. Hardly the stuff of which legends are made. Yet, since his elevation, each of these acts has been perceived as a source of hope and inspiration for the nation.[21]

Later, on the golf course, Ford sent a ball flying toward another player. Shortly thereafter he slipped on an icy White House sidewalk. An image of Ford as a bumbling klutz, not merely as a person but as the president, began to emerge. Ford himself observed that every time I stumbled or bumped my head or fell in the snow, reporters zeroed in on that to the exclusion of almost everything else. The news coverage was harmful, but even more damaging was the fact that Johnny Carson and Chevy Chase used my "missteps" for their jokes. Their antics—and I'll admit that I laughed at them myself—helped create the public perception of me as a stumbler. And that wasn't funny.[22]

The standards that Americans establish for a president's behavior are a mix of realism and idealism. A survey of Americans inquired whether they would "strongly object" if a president engaged in certain types of behavior: if he smoked marijuana occasionally, told ethnic or racial jokes in private, were not a church member, used tranquilizers occasionally, used profane language in private, had seen a psychiatrist, wore jeans in the Oval Office, were divorced, had a cocktail before dinner each night. As Table 5.1 shows, people are relatively tolerant of a president doing some of the things they themselves do, but at the same time they want a president to set examples for the nation.

Policy Performance

People also hold policy expectations of the president—expectations about what he should accomplish in office. These expectations are drawn from the assumption of pragmatism, which depicts a president as the nation's chief problem solver. They also are drawn from the presidential campaign, in which candidates eagerly promise that they, unlike anyone before them, will cure major national ills. As a result, the public's performance expectations are quite high and cover a broad range of policy areas, including the economy, the size of government, and national defense. Table 5.2 shows the results of polls taken in December 1976 and December 1980 before the inaugurations of Presidents Carter and Reagan. People held lavishly optimistic views of what the new presidents would accomplish. The ideal

Table 5.1 Public Standards of Presidents' Personal Behavior

Behavior	Percentage Who Strongly Object
Smoked marijuana occasionally	70%
Told ethnic or racial jokes in private	43
Were not a member of a church	38
Used tranquilizers occasionally	36
Used profane language in private	33
Had seen a psychiatrist	30
Wore blue jeans occasionally in the Oval Office	21
Were divorced	17
Had a cocktail before dinner each night	14

Source: Gallup Survey, Fall 1979, in Stephen Wayne, "Expectations of Presidents," in *Presidents and Publics*, ed. D. Graber (Philadelphia: Institute for the Study of Human Issues, 1982), 31. Used by permission.

Table 5.2 Early Expectations of Policy Performance

Policy	Those who feel the president can ...	
	Carter	Reagan
Reduce unemployment	72%	69%
Reduce inflation	—	66
Reduce cost of government	59	70
Increase government efficiency	81	89
Deal effectively with foreign policy	79	77
Strengthen national defense	81	66

Source: "Early Expectations: Comparing Chief Executives," *Public Opinion,* February–March 1981, 39. Reprinted by permission of The American Enterprise Institute for Public Policy Research, Washington, D.C.

president can do anything, and not-yet-installed presidents can do almost as well. As Carter later observed, "When things go bad you [the president] get entirely too much blame. And I have to admit that when things go good [sic], you get entirely too much credit."[23]

A president perhaps receives the greatest credit for efforts in foreign and military affairs. Because a president has the ability to act unilaterally in foreign and military affairs, expectations are exceedingly high but the president can often meet them. At Carter's midterm in 1978, 56 percent of the American public approved of his handling of foreign affairs. At the midpoint in Reagan's first term, 53 percent registered similar support. By comparison, numerous people other than the president are involved in economic decisions, including the independent Federal Reserve Board, Congress, American consumers, corporations, and a multitude of foreign investors and trading partners. Although the cultural assumption of pragmatism says that the president is in charge and therefore responsible for curing economic ills, this expectation is likely to be very difficult to meet. By mid-1978 as inflation worsened, only 16 percent of the American public supported President Carter's handling of the economy. After two years in office with rising unemployment, only 38 percent of the public approved of Reagan's handling of the ecomony.[24]

Leadership

People have a set of expectations about how a president should behave as a leader. As Table 5.3 shows, many of the leadership qualities that Americans desire are contradictory or at least difficult to manage together. A president is supposed to be compassionate yet forceful; place the country's interests ahead of politics yet be politically savvy; be willing to compromise yet take consistent policy positions. The president's central dilemma is to balance leadership with democratic responsiveness: he must attempt to lead while also following public opinion. As a leader, the president is expected to show vision about the way the nation must face the future that may be obscure to the

Table 5.3 Presidents' Leadership Qualities

	Those who feel it is important
Placing country's interest ahead of politics	83%
Intelligence	82
Sound judgment in a crisis	81
Taking firm stand on issues	75
Competence, ability to get job done	74
Compassion, concern for little man/average citizen	70
Ability to anticipate the nation's needs	68
High ethical standards	66
Saying what one believes, even if unpopular	64
Ability to inspire confidence	63
Forcefulness, decisiveness	59
Having consistent positions on issues	52
Flexibility, willingness to compromise	52
Political savvy, know-how	51
Having modern, up-to-date ideas and solutions	51
Sense of humor	50
Imagination	42
Personal charm, style, charisma	33
Loyalty to one's party	30

Source: Gallup Survey, Fall 1979, in George Edwards, *The Public Presidency* (New York: St. Martin's Press, 1983), 190, 196. Used by permission.

average citizen, and he must present new initiatives not currently on the public agenda. George Bush was criticized early in his term for lacking what he, sounding like an awkward teenager, termed "the vision thing." But as the sole representative of the people, a president cannot achieve "the vision thing" without the immediate support of the public. Theodore Roosevelt resolved the tension in this manner: "People used to say of me that I . . . divined what the people were going to think. I did not 'divine.' I simply made up my mind what they ought to think, and then did my best to get them to think it."[25]

Presidents have attempted to use Roosevelt's logic by creating rather than following public opinion. But success is not always guaranteed. In 1970, before Richard Nixon announced his decision to send U.S. troops to Cambodia, only 7 percent of the public favored the policy. After Nixon's announcement, 50 percent of the public supported the troop commitment. In contrast, prior to Jimmy Carter's many appeals on the energy crisis, 41 percent of the public believed the situation was "very serious." After a year of speeches, programs, and publicity about the "crisis," the same percentage of the public, 41 percent, saw the situation as critical.[26] Carter had been unable to convince the public and Congress of the desirability of his energy program.

Personal, policy, and leadership expectations provide a vivid picture of the ideal president. He is a warm individual who, despite his high office, continues to act like an ordinary citizen. He drinks occasionally and cusses every once in a while. He makes tough decisions on policies and meets unexpected crises with courage. He leads the nation with vision but keeps a careful eye on the latest public opinion polls.

Which presidents lived up to these expectations? Figure 5.1 presents a look at how scholars rate the personal character, policy accomplishments and appointments, and leadership and political skills of Presidents Washington to Carter. Only seven presidents—Lincoln, the two Roosevelts, Washington, Jefferson, Jackson, and Wilson—did especially well. The scholars are probably not much tougher than other Americans rating the presidents; indeed, they may not be as tough. The expectations attached to the ideal president are unrealistic yet very real. Presidents must attempt to satisfy them, and they have a difficult time dismantling them. No other political figure is viewed in this symbolic light.

PRESIDENTS' POPULARITY

Expectations bear on Americans' opinions about a president's performance in office, or presidential popularity.[27] Just as symbolism creates expectations about how a president should act, expectations, in turn, are convenient barometers to judge a president's actual performance. When expectations are met, a president's popularity is likely to remain stable or rise. When expectations go unmet, a president's popularity is likely to decline.

The most common way to assess presidential popularity is to look at national public opinion polls. Since 1938, the Gallup Poll has asked a sample of Americans whether they "approve or disapprove of the way [the incumbent president] is handling his job in office." Approval ratings are plotted in Figure 5.2 for presidents from Truman to Bush. As can be seen, presidents enjoy something of a roller coaster ride in their relations with the American public. The course of presidential popularity proceeds up and down, in varying sequences of intensity and duration, yet always moves inevitably downward. The one obvious difference between the presidential ride and the amusement park ride is that presidents do not finish where they began. Instead, they start higher, finish lower, and presumably have less fun. There are two basic features to the presidential popularity ride. First, with the exception of Eisenhower, whose popularity remained fairly stable, the trend for most presidents is from high popularity to low popularity. Second, there are immediate shifts up and down during the presidents' terms.

Three Phases of Popularity

Presidents' popularity goes through three phases during their terms: the honeymoon, disillusionment, and forgiveness.

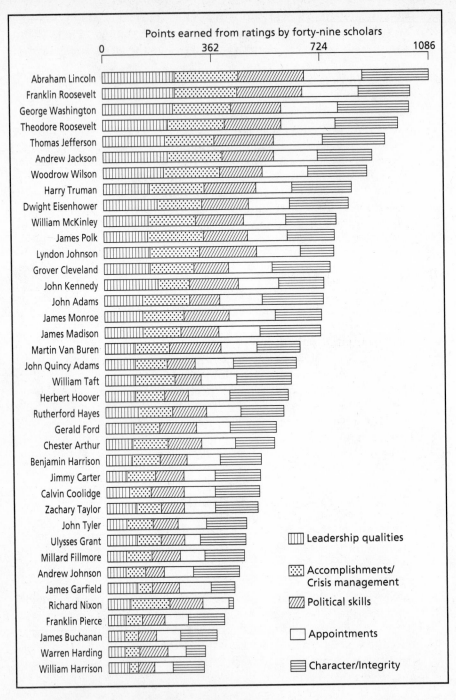

Figure 5.1   Scholar's Ratings of the Presidents

At the request of the *Chicago Tribune,* in 1982 forty-nine historians and political scientists rated all presidents (through Jimmy Carter) on a scale from 5 (best) to 0 (worst) in five categories. The scholars judged that only a few presidents possessed all five characteristics. [*Source:* Copyright 1988, Chicago Tribune Company. All rights re-served. Used by permission.]

The Honeymoon. A president arrives at the White House with a very high level of support. Presidents Truman, Eisenhower, Johnson, and Ford received the highest level of support for their entire terms during their first month in office. Presidents Kennedy, Nixon, Carter, and Reagan all found their high point within the first four months in office. During these early months, the president comes as close as possible to matching the ideal president. He has not yet done anything to stir controversy or disappoint expectations. Presidents must find this a nasty realization: there is little they can do in office or little that can happen to them that will be better than having done nothing. President Bush proved an exception and enjoyed an unusually long honeymoon. He began his term with 75 percent approval, but this number was topped by the 89 percent approval rating he received at the end of the Persian Gulf War in March 1991—the highest figure ever recorded for an American president.

Reflective of individualism, citizens concentrate on the personal habits and the likes and dislikes of the new "first family." In the first months of the Bush term, stories abounded in the press about the president's grandchildren's stay at the White House, the president's fishing skills, and Mrs. Bush's clothes (compared to those of former first lady Mrs. Reagan). Meeting the demands of pragmatic politics, a president may announce policy initiatives during this period. The White House will portray them as bold, new ideas that will solve major unmanageable problems and fulfill various campaign promises. This activity, too, is typically received warmly by the public. The president demonstrates that he is on top of the situation, as demanded by the assumption of pragmatic politics. The trick that remains is to convince Congress of the proposals' merits and turn proposals into programs rather than into more promises. Citizens also celebrate the peaceful transfer of power as one leader of the chosen people replaces another.

Honeymoons are of varying duration. They end sometimes with a whimper and at other times after a big row. The shortest and most abruptly ended honeymoon was Gerald Ford's. Sworn into office in August 1974 with a public approval rating of 71 percent, Ford watched his popularity plummet twenty-one points in October when he pardoned Richard Nixon. Other honeymoons end more gradually, as evidence that all is not well begins to accumulate. Johnson's popularity eroded slowly as pessimism about Vietnam grew. His popularity averaged 63 percent during 1965, but by May 1966 approval dipped to the 50 percent mark.[28]

Disillusionment. The disillusionment phase begins when a president is judged on how well he has lived up to expectations associated with the ideal and to the promises that he made during the election campaign. A president cannot possibly deliver on all of the promises spoken during the campaign or on all of the unspoken promises

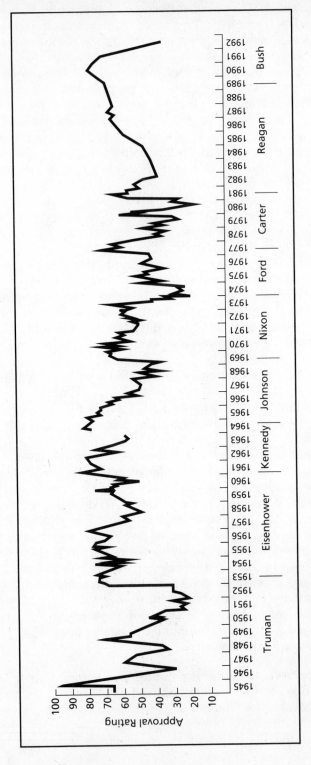

Figure 5.2 President's Popularity from Truman Through Bush

The general pattern for presidential popularity is that the longer a president is in office, the lower is his popularity. This pattern is especially clear when looking at popularity ratings for Presidents Truman, Johnson, Nixon, and Carter. [*Source:* Adapted from *The Gallup Opinion Index*, Report 182, October–November 1980, pp. 13–59; updated by the author. Used by permission of The Gallup Poll.]

that derive from the American political culture and its symbolism. Disillusionment arises as the gap between public expectations and presidential performance grows. When people discover, as Taft observed, that a president cannot make rain, they are disheartened. Often the disillusionment centers on the president's efforts to push his proposals through Congress. Although people are relatively uninformed about the details of specific proposals, they can keep a scorecard of the president's congressional wins and losses. Disillusionment may also emerge over a president's attempts to tackle major national problems, notably in the economy. Here too a scorecard can be kept: "How well is the president doing what he is expected to do?"

A president generally encounters disillusionment during the second and third years of his term. Just at the time when he has settled into his job, he finds the public growing tired. Although this middle period of the term should be a time when a president can get a great deal done, he typically can get less done than he would like as public support weakens. This pattern is recreated for president after president. The cultural assumptions and the symbols remain intact, but successive presidents' popular images are tarnished. People, it seems, do not recognize over time that their expectations of presidents' efforts are unreasonable. Rather, they are convinced that the efforts of the chief executives are inadequate.

Many people have the impression that Ronald Reagan was able to satisfy public expectations that other presidents failed to meet. The press dubbed him the "Teflon President." Problems encountered by his administration never seemed to stick to Reagan, and his honeymoon never completely ended. Yet, as Figure 5.3 shows, even Reagan did not escape the disillusionment phase. The level of public support that he received during his first three years in office was nearly identical to that received by his predecessor, Carter. Both Carter and Reagan saw their honeymoons fade toward the end of their first year in office; both faced disillusionment over deepening economic woe—Carter's primarily inflation, Reagan's primarily unemployment. Neither president seemed effective as the nation's chief problem solver in halting the deterioration of the economy, and both were left promising that good times were to come. Although Reagan may have projected a more comfortable image than Carter, he was no more a "Teflon President" than was his predecessor.

Forgiveness. In the fourth year of the term, a president may enjoy slight increases in popularity.[29] Carter and Reagan saw upturns in support at the beginning of their fourth year—Carter after the Soviet invasion of Afghanistan and Reagan in the aftermath of the U.S. invasion of Grenada. Good fortune continued for Reagan as the economy slowly improved, but Carter suffered from inflationary pressures and from being unable to free the American hostages held in

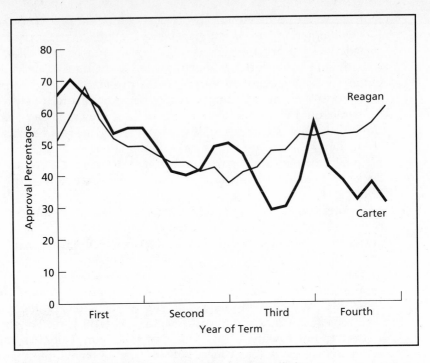

Figure 5.3 Comparison of Carter's and Reagan's Popularity

Because of economic woes, Carter and Reagan experienced similar declines in their popularity during their first two years in office. Carter lost more ground by the end of the term because of the Iran hostage crisis; in the last half of his first term, Reagan regained popularity as the economy improved. [*Source:* Data from Gary King and Lyn Ragsdale, *The Elusive Executive* (Washington, D.C.: CQ Press), 305–307.]

Iran. The public tends to be somewhat forgiving as a president leaves office or heads into a re-election campaign. Many people in 1984 felt that, regardless of his foibles, Ronald Reagan was a better bet than Walter Mondale. A president may not perfectly match the ideal, but when compared to his opponent, he may look like Zeus.

The Ups and Downs of Popularity

Several factors account for short-term increases and decreases in approval: (1) world events, (2) wars, (3) the economy, (4) political scandals, and (5) presidential initiatives.[30] Many of the ups and downs reflect the way the media, especially television news, report on the five factors. In general, bad news—or, more accurately, what is perceived to be bad news—diminishes presidents' approval ratings, and perceived good news enhances them, even when a president may have little to do with either the good or the bad news.[31]

Rallying Around the President. A president benefits strongly from two types of circumstances that show the world that he is the symbolic leader of the nation: diplomatic achievements and international crises. Diplomatic forays offer a president opportunities to be seen as a statesman and peacemaker. During the cold war, presidents almost always received at least a small boost in popularity after summits with the Soviet Union. Indeed, the summits were often more important to a president's standing at home than they were as major events in superpower relations. Kennedy's popularity rose slightly after his meeting with Soviet leader Khrushchev in Vienna in 1961. Nixon's approval increased after his historic trip to China and the Moscow summit of 1972. Nixon staged a second Soviet summit two months before his resignation in 1974, when his popularity had reached its lowest point. But his approval actually dropped again during the month as more Watergate revelations unfolded. In the past a president also benefited from peace initiatives unrelated to U.S.-Soviet affairs. Carter's support rose after the signing of the Camp David agreement, an Israeli-Egyptian peace treaty that he helped negotiate.

International crises even more than diplomatic achievements boost a president's public support. The chief executive, however, has limited ability to control when they occur and what they are. Franklin Roosevelt's approval soared 12 points to an 84 percent approval rating after the Japanese bombing of Pearl Harbor. Truman's popularity shot up 9 points after his decision to send American troops to South Korea in 1950. Carter enjoyed a huge 14-point increase in approval after the Iranian seizure of American hostages and a more modest 4-point increase when the Soviets invaded Afghanistan.

Even presidential blunders receive public support. The Bay of Pigs fiasco raised serious questions about the foreign policy savvy of the Kennedy administration and bruised U.S. relations with the Soviet Union, but Kennedy's popularity rose 10 points. Carter gained a 3-point boost after the failed Iranian hostage rescue attempt. Instances of presidential failure underscore Americans' emotional reactions to presidents. A rational response, based on the costs and the benefits of such clear-cut failures as the Bay of Pigs invasion or the Iran hostage rescue, would be to disapprove of the president's performance. Instead, the president actually benefits from his mistakes. Citizens "rally around the flag" and rally around the president during crises that in some way threaten the nation.[32] People seek quiescence, or symbolic reassurance, that the challenge is being met, no matter what the actual outcome of the challenge is.

Waging War. Marching off to war, unlike rally events, does not automatically improve a president's approval ratings. When a war is being won or must be won to ensure the survival of the country, a president's approval likely benefits. Franklin Roosevelt's popularity was high during critical years of World War II. Bush's popularity soared during the Persian Gulf War. Yet, as some commentators observed, Bush's support was like a Texas river—"a mile wide and an inch deep." As the euphoria of victory wore off, so too did Bush's invincibility, and his approval ratings dropped from an all-time presidential high (89 percent) to 55 percent one year later. Too, people worry when a war looks intractable or unwinnable. Truman found himself in trouble as the Korean War dragged on. The controversy surrounding his firing of General Douglas MacArthur, commander of the United Nations forces in Korea, added to public discontent. With the economy also slowing down, Truman's popularity plummeted to 23 percent. Johnson's popularity suffered a similar fate with the war in Vietnam. He once said that he would be remembered for two things, "What I did for the Negro and seeing it through in Vietnam for all of Asia. The Negro cost me 15 points in the polls and Vietnam cost me 20."[33] One study estimates that Johnson's guess was a little high: his popularity declined by 12 points from the war. Nixon, by contrast, gained nearly 13 points in approval as the conflict wound down.[34]

The Economy. No patriotic rally occurs when internal economic troubles, rather than an outside foe, threaten the nation. High inflation, sharp rises in unemployment, and their combination negatively influence presidential approval ratings. Conversely, robust prosperity or significant improvement in the economy improves presidents' standings with the public. The effects vary from one president to the next. Kennedy's popularity was neither harmed nor helped much by economic performance. Johnson suffered approval losses from inflation but gained some momentum from low unemployment.[35] Severe unemployment initially plagued Reagan's popularity, but after 1983 the economy's improvement boosted Reagan's approval throughout the remainder of his two terms.[36] The influence of economic problems on people's attitudes depends on their incomes. Reagan, for instance, lost support from middle-income and, especially, lower-income people over unemployment. People with high incomes were not as bothered by it.[37]

Scandal. A president is assumed to be honest, so honesty itself is not likely to enhance popularity. But questions about integrity are likely to detract from popular support. Nixon's and Reagan's approval ratings dropped during the Watergate and Iran-contra scandals, respectively. Reagan was able to recover from his scandal, but Nixon's term in office ended because of Watergate. Nixon had the dubious distinction of tying with Truman for the lowest approval rating reached by any modern president: 23 percent of the public approved of Nixon's performance in office shortly before he resigned.

Presidents' Initiatives. With the exception of honesty and some diplomatic overtures, the ups and downs of presidential popularity seem to be out of a president's hands. But a president does have two opportunities to improve his own popularity. First, a president's major addresses to the nation delivered during prime-time television hours boost popularity by an average of three to four percentage points.[38] Regular programming is pre-empted, and a large national audience of some 30 to 40 million people watches the presidential address. Second, a president's success in Congress on legislation he favors will boost public support.[39] The public expects legislative effectiveness from the president. When such achievement is in evidence, popularity rises. However, a president who decides to submit a grocery list of proposals to satisfy campaign promises may find that this decision will actually harm rather than help his public support. Too many pieces of legislation brought forward means too many pieces of legislation on which the president may lose.[40] When a president takes positions on a few major pieces of legislation and wins on most of them, he happily accommodates the single executive image. He looks to be in charge.

CONCLUSION

"Public sentiment is everything," observed Abraham Lincoln. "With public sentiment nothing can fail, without it nothing can succeed."[41] As the single most important, unique figure in American politics, a president receives public support that he can use to persuade other politicians. A president realizes that even if he has the categorical constitutional power to do something, rarely is he in a position to dictate what should be done. Instead, as Richard Neustadt argues, the president must rely on persuasion.[42] Although Lincoln may overstate the case, few would doubt that public support facilitates the president's ability to persuade others—members of Congress, foreign heads of state, bureaucrats, lobbyists, governors, members of the press. But public support does not rest on people's cold, hard-nosed, precise evaluations of what a president is doing at a particular moment. Instead, how a president is *perceived* to be doing at a particular moment depends on how well he reflects the cultural assumptions, symbolism, and expectations woven into the fabric of the presidency. A White House aide during the Johnson administration observed, "What a President does may matter less than what the people think he is doing."[43] The president's use of public opinion as a source of influence can be very powerful, but it must be exercised within the constraints of the American political culture and its symbols. The president, too, remains in the cave. ■

F U R T H E R   R E A D I N G

On political culture, see: Donald Divine, *The Political Culture of the United States* (Boston: Little, Brown, 1972); James Robertson, *American Myth, Ameri-*

can *Reality* (New York: Hill and Wang, 1980). On symbolism, see: Murray Edelman, *The Symbolic Uses of Politics* (Urbana: University of Illinois Press, 1964); Fred Greenstein, "What the President Means to Americans," in *Choosing the President*, ed. J. Barber (Englewood Cliffs, N.J.: Prentice-Hall, 1974), 121–148; Godfrey Hodgson, *All Things to All Men: The False Promise of the Modern American Presidency* (New York: Simon and Schuster, 1980). On public expectations, see: Lee Sigelman and Kathleen Knight, "Why Does Presidential Popularity Decline? A Test of the Expectation/Disillusion Theory," *Public Opinion Quarterly* 47 (Fall 1983): 310–324; James Stimson, "Public Support for American Presidents: A Cyclical Model," *Public Opinion Quarterly* 40 (Spring 1976): 1–21. On presidential popularity, see: John Mueller, *War, Presidents, and Public Opinion* (New York: Wiley, 1973); Lyn Ragsdale, "The Politics of Presidential Speechmaking," *American Political Science Review* 78 (December 1984): 971–984; Charles Ostrom and Dennis Simon, "Promise and Performance: A Dynamic Model of Presidential Popularity," *American Political Science Review* 79 (June 1985): 334–358.

N O T E S

1. Charles Elder and Roger Cobb, *The Political Use of Symbols* (New York: Longman, 1983), 29.

2. For a good discussion of symbols, see Barbara Hinckley, *The Symbolic Presidency* (New York: Routledge, 1990), 4–5.

3. The chapter highlights those assumptions that are most relevant to the presidency. It does not say that there are only four assumptions. Research has discussed such matters as tolerance and racism as parts of the American political culture. See Donald Devine, *The Political Culture of the United States* (Boston: Little, Brown, 1972), and Gabriel Almond and Sidney Verba, *The Civic Culture* (Princeton, N.J.: Princeton University Press, 1963), for two other perspectives on culture.

4. Henry Kissinger, quoted in James Robertson, *American Myth, American Reality* (New York: Hill and Wang, 1980), 6.

5. Robertson, 310.

6. This is the Office of Management and Budget's estimate for the fiscal year 1992 deficit as stated in the 1993 *Budget of the United States.*

7. "A Wimp of a Budget," *The Economist*, February 1, 1992, 23–24.

8. William Howard Taft, *The Presidency* (New York: Scribner, 1916), 47–50.

9. Quoted in Gary King and Lyn Ragsdale, *The Elusive Executive* (Washington, D.C.: CQ Press, 1988), 488.

10. Quoted in Thomas Cronin, *The State of the Presidency* (Boston: Little, Brown, 1980), 161.

11. *Weekly Compilation of Presidential Documents*, January 1989 (Washington, D.C.: U.S. Government Printing Office, 1989), 1.

12. See Bruce Miroff, "Monopolizing the Public Space: The President as a Problem for Democratic Politics," in *Rethinking the Presidency*, ed. T. Cronin (Boston: Little, Brown, 1982), 218–232.

13. Andrew Jackson, Farewell Address in *Social Theories of Jacksonian Democracy*, ed. Joseph Blau (Indianapolis: Bobbs-Merrill, 1954), 17.

14. Fred Greenstein, "What the President Means to Americans," in *Choosing the President*, ed. J. Barber (Englewood Cliffs, N.J.: Prentice-Hall, 1974), 145, original emphasis.

15. Murray Edelman, *The Symbolic Uses of Politics* (Urbana: University of Illinois Press, 1964), 22–43.

16. Paul Sheatsley and Jacob Feldman, "The Assassination of President Kennedy: A Preliminary Report on Public Reactions and Behavior," *Public Opinion Quarterly* 28 (Summer 1964): 189–215.

17. Jimmy Carter, *Keeping Faith* (New York: Bantam Books, 1982), 17–18.

18. *Public Papers of the Presidents: Lyndon Johnson, 1965* (Washington, D.C.: U.S. Government Printing Office, 1966), 469–476.

19. Joseph Tannenhaus and Mary Ann Foley, "Separating Objects of Specific and Diffuse Support: Experiments on Presidents and the Presidency," *Micropolitics* 1 (December 1981): 345–367.

20. See David Easton and Jack Dennis, *Children in the Political System* (New York: McGraw-Hill, 1969), on children's positive personal views of presidents. For a study of poor Appalachian children's views of presidents, see Dean Jaros, Herbert Hirsh, and Frederick Fleron, Jr., "The Malevolent Leader: Political Socialization in an American Subculture," *American Political Science Review* 62 (June 1968): 564–575. Racial differences are discussed in Greenstein, 132–133. The impact of Watergate is discussed in Jack Dennis and Carol Webster, "Children's Images of the President and Government in 1962 and 1974," *American Politics Quarterly* 3 (October 1975): 386–405.

21. Joe McGinniss, *New York Times*, September 8, 1974, p. E19.

22. Gerald Ford, *A Time to Heal: An Autobiography of Gerald R. Ford* (New York: Harper and Row, 1979), 289.

23. Quoted in Godfrey Hodgson, *All Things to All Men: The False Promise of the Modern American Presidency* (New York: Simon and Schuster, 1980), 25.

24. King and Ragsdale, 356–357.

25. Quoted in George Edwards, *The Public Presidency* (New York: St. Martin's Press, 1983), 38.

26. Ibid., 42–43.

27. Lee Sigelman and Kathleen Knight, "Why Does Presidential Popularity Decline? A Test of the Expectation/Disillusion Theory," *Public Opinion Quarterly* 47 (Fall 1983): 310–324.

28. King and Ragsdale, Table 6.2, 299–300.

29. James Stimson, "Public Support for American Presidents: A Cyclical Model," *Public Opinion Quarterly* 40 (Spring 1976): 1–21.

30. John Mueller, *War, Presidents, and Public Opinion* (New York: Wiley, 1973).

31. Richard Brody, *Assessing the President* (Stanford, Calif.: Stanford University Press, 1991).

32. John Mueller, "Presidential Popularity from Truman to Johnson," *American Political Science Review* 64 (March 1970): 18–34.

33. Quoted ibid., 18.

34. Helmut Norpoth, "Economics, Politics, and the Cycle of Presidential Popularity," *Political Behavior* 6 (1984): 267.

35. Results from Kennedy to Carter are found ibid., 266.

36. Charles Ostrom, Jr., and Dennis Simon, "The Man in the Teflon Suit," *Public Opinion Quarterly* 53 (Fall 1989): 379.

37. Lyn Ragsdale, "Presidential Speechmaking and the Public Audience: Individual Presidents and Group Attitudes," *Journal of Politics* 49 (1987): 726–727.

38. Lyn Ragsdale, "The Politics of Presidential Speechmaking," *American Political Science Review* 78 (December 1984): 971–984.

39. Charles Ostrom and Dennis Simon, "Promise and Performance: A Dynamic Model of Presidential Popularity," *American Political Science Review* 79 (June 1985): 334–358.

40. Paul Light, *The President's Agenda* (Baltimore: Johns Hopkins University Press, 1982).

41. Quoted in Edwards, 1.

42. Richard Neustadt, *Presidential Power* (New York: Wiley, 1960).

43. Quoted in Michael Grossman and Martha Kumar, *Portraying the President* (Baltimore: Johns Hopkins University Press, 1981), 3.

CHAPTER 6

Presidential Media

F rom the Constitution, presidents assert power through the theory of presidential activism. From the election campaign, presidents draw the importance, uniqueness, power, and visibility of being the only officials elected by the entire nation. From the American political culture, presidents derive uniqueness and importance as solitary individuals who act as national heroes, problem solvers, and moral leaders. These three foundations of the single executive image are reinforced by a fourth: the national media, which heighten the visibility of presidents.

Presidents are the most visible politicians in the country. Yet, ironically, most Americans have never actually seen a president. They have never met one personally. Nor have many crowded along a sidewalk to catch a glimpse of one in a motorcade. Most people do not really know firsthand that Bill Clinton exists. He could be the creation of organizations that define what is important to know and distill what is deemed important into a few words and pictures. Indeed, in key ways, President Clinton, or any other modern president, is such a creation. Most of what people know about American presidents they draw from coverage provided by news organizations.

These organizations are of two sorts. The first is typically labeled "the media" and includes the television networks, major newspapers, the wire services, radio, and national news magazines. These organizations receive many of their stories from a second, very different sort of news organization: the White House. The White House is, in effect, a medium to "the media." The White House is often in the enviable position of filtering what it wants the other news organizations to convey to their audiences. Americans are then in the unenviable position of relying almost completely on twice-mediated stories: mediated once from the White House to the other news organizations and mediated a second time from newspapers, magazines, television, and radio to the public.

The White House and the other news organizations control what Americans "know" about Bill Clinton. But the knowledge is a product of visibility, not of experience. "Visibility" is a term in modern political parlance that should immediately raise suspicions. Visibility is reserved for mediated images of people (not the people themselves), for filtered accounts of their actions (not the actions themselves), and for the vicarious experience of events (not participation in the events themselves). Visibility is the opposite of intimacy and firsthand knowledge. Visibility has no everyday anchor. One does not say, "My best friend is very visible to me." One says, "I know my friend well." In an environment where visibility is important, words like "credibility," "accessibility," and "deniability" crop up in order to judge if the visible image has a basis in reality.

PRESIDENTIAL-PRESS SYMBIOSIS

Presidential visibility is the product of a *symbiosis* between the press and presidents. In this context, the word describes a close living together, or an association, of two dissimilar organizations in a mutually beneficial relationship. Reporters and White House officials feed off each other and create a normal work routine in which one group does not act without the other. Richard Cheney, White House chief of staff for President Ford, commented on the symbiosis: "There is no way to do this job as president if you are not willing to think about the media as part of the process."[1] Bob Schieffer of CBS News gave the press perspective: "They want to talk to you. The sources need the reporters, just like the reporter needs the sources."[2] The symbiotic relationship has two dimensions: dependency and antagonism. The news organizations and the White House are dependent on one another but often act as antagonists or adversaries. Former CBS News anchor Walter Cronkite summed up the inherent tension: "Politics and the media are inseparable. It is only the politicians and the media that are incompatible."[3] The dependence and antagonism can be examined in turn.

Dependence

The dependence exists because claiming the president as the single most visible politician in America is to the mutual advantage of both the press and the White House. Presidential visibility is advantageous for the press because it satisfies the press's desire to have something seemingly important to report about on a continuous basis. The press finds presidents to be conspicuous and convenient stories. The president's position places him at the center of numerous conflicts, nationwide and worldwide. White House officials, if not always the president, are easily accessible to reporters. Since the 1960s, presidential press secretaries have held daily briefings with reporters. The press secretary's office also centralizes the release of material from various

White House offices and often from some executive departments. In short, reporters must get a story, and the White House is a good place to go.

The visibility is beneficial for presidents who wish to get their stories out to the public. Presidents find the press to be a conspicuous and convenient storyteller of interrelated policy messages and symbolic messages. The media are free channels for presidents to convey *policy messages* to the public and to political elites. In the modern White House it is assumed that if the media can be managed, public opinion can be influenced and the political agenda controlled. In particular, White House aides view television as a major resource for gaining public support for the president and his decision. "These people [White House staffers]," observed Walter Rodgers of Associated Press Radio, "are all members of the Howdy Doody generation. It's hard to get them to think about the importance of any other medium."[4] White House officials also believe that if press coverage is good, victories in Congress and in other parts of the government will flourish. Lawrence O'Brien, chief congressional liaison for Kennedy and Johnson, said, "If the press backs the White House position and the congressman believes that what he reads reflects public support, he may be won over."[5]

The media also allow modern presidents to convey *symbolic messages*. Presidents make numerous public appearances in Washington and throughout the country every month, captured on nightly news broadcasts and in the morning papers. Television allows presidents to create a "mediated intimacy" between themselves and both their physical and their electronic audiences. As Murray Edelman observes, an appearance "presenting a live performance, creates not close contact, but a semblance of close contact. . . . The president [although] remote" is nevertheless in one's own living room.[6] Presidents attempt to convey that they share much in common with their audience and understand an audience's needs and desires. In addition, the appearances give the audience a glance at the "human president"—his personality, warmth, and skills. Symbolism also is invoked in the setting chosen. President Reagan, on a trip to Montana, rode into a rodeo pavilion aboard an old stagecoach, dressed in cowboy gear, waving his hat at the crowd, and looking thoroughly relaxed. The symbolism fit the audience without Reagan uttering a word.

The presidential-press dependence yields more news about the president than about any other person or group in the world. Michael Grossman and Martha Kumar, who have conducted the most complete study of White House–press relations, found in a sample of 615 issues of the *New York Times* and 656 issues of *Time* magazine (from 1953 to 1978) and 236 programs of the CBS Evening News (from 1968 to 1978) that there were no White House articles in only 8 *New York Times* issues, 10 *Time* issues, and 8 CBS news broadcasts.[7] Another

Table 6.1 Evening Network News Coverage of the Three Branches of Government, July 1986–June 1987

Month	President N[1]	President Time[2]	Congress N	Congress Time	Supreme Court N	Supreme Court Time
1986						
July	158	5:53	26	0:47	29	0:56
August	183	5:44	13	0:28	21	0:39
September	159	6:46	17	0:28	12	0:23
October	204	9:29	15	0:31	12	0:24
November	167	9:28	27	2:18	13	0:14
December	166	9:58	21	1:40	4	0:10
1987						
January	181	7:16	24	0:59	12	0:16
February	190	8:31	30	1:24	9	0:14
March	178	6:37	30	1:07	17	0:35
April	129	5:22	29	0:57	16	0:29
May	166	8:14	30	1:42	11	0:22
June	184	7:16	22	0:46	41	1:17
Total	2,065	90:34	284	13:07	197	5:59
Average	172	7:33	24	1:05	16	0:30

1. N = total number of stories for the month by the three networks.
2. *Time* = average minutes of coverage across the three networks

Note: Stories are from ABC, CBS, and NBC nightly news broadcasts, calculated from the Vanderbilt Television News Archives Indexes.

Source: Doris Graber, *Mass Media and American Politics* 3d ed. (Washington, D.C.: CQ Press, 1989), 237. Used by permission.

study comparing television news coverage of the president, Congress, and the Supreme Court found the greatest attention given to the president, as shown in Table 6.1.[8] As a result, the media over-cover the president and undercover Congress. The sheer quantity of stories about the president helps mold the image of a single executive in charge of the nation. Stories are told with the president as the pivotal figure. Even when other politicians are mentioned—members of Congress, executive branch officials, governors, heads of state—they are depicted as supporting characters to the president in the lead role. Moreover, the president's free hand in telling many of the stories—in policy matters and national symbolism—reinforces the impression that one executive dominates the government and the country.

Antagonism

Antagonism complicates the dependence between the press and presidents. The interests of the press and presidents, though inter-twined, are fundamentally different. Like all public figures, presidents want their actions placed in the best possible light. Yet, given historic notions of a free press rooted in the First Amendment, the press asserts a responsibility to report the negative as well as the positive side of a story. Thomas Jefferson, an ardent proponent of a free press, nonetheless vehemently charged that "nothing in a newspaper is to be believed [since it] presents only a caricature of dissaffected minds."[9] Modern presidents no doubt would add television as a target of Jefferson's vitriol. The adversarial side of the symbiosis is encapsulated in a tense encounter between President Nixon and Dan Rather, who was then chief White House correspondent for CBS News. In a news conference, Rather asked a question that Nixon found impertinent. Nixon shot back, "Are you running for office, Mr. Rather?" Rather replied stingingly, "No, Mr. President, are you?" This antagonism also can arise in press relations with presidential candidates. Attempting to overcome his "wimp" image, presidential candidate George Bush provoked a heated exchange with Dan Rather during an interview, reminiscent of the Nixon-Rather clash.

Reporters are often upset about the extent to which the White House controls the news. The Reagan administration imposed a news blackout in the early days of the invasion of Grenada in 1983. The White House defended the blackout, saying it was imposed out of concern for the safety of the journalists and the military success of the operation. Secretary of State George Shultz was more blunt about the ban: "Reporters are always against us, and so they're always seeking to report something that's going to screw things up."[10] During the Persian Gulf War, the Bush administration drafted a set of twelve rules for reporters. They included a ban on reporting troop strength, locations, types and amounts of weapons, and future operations. Reporters' access to and mobility in combat zones was tightly restricted. The administration wanted to prevent reporters from wandering freely as they had during the Vietnam War.[11]

The White House does not merely attempt to control the news; it also goes to great lengths to create the news. It schedules "media events"—cannily crafted occasions at which presidents do things for the sole purpose of being covered by the press. President Carter, for instance, timed his departure for the Middle East in March 1979 not only so the television networks could cover it live but so they could cover it live on their evening news broadcasts. Although White House correspondent Lesley Stahl objected to what she saw as a White House manipulation of television news, her superiors at CBS News had her faithfully cover Carter's farewell.[12] As a Ford administration press official observed, "Whenever possible, everything was done to take into account the need for coverage. After all, most of the events are done for coverage. Why else are you doing them?"[13]

For their part, reporters bedevil presidents by exposing gaps between what the White House discloses and what is happening behind the scenes. Nixon administration officials were perturbed about several journalists' stories on the Vietnam War that were based on secret information leaked from the National Security Council. To trace the leaks, the FBI was ordered to wiretap the telephones of three reporters.[14] Other presidents have adopted various forms of "punishment" to deal with unfriendly reporters—denying them access to key officials, refusing to answer their questions at news conferences, or giving exclusive stories to other reporters. The Reagan administration systematized efforts to escape press distortion of its side of a story. Reagan officials demanded and received unequal airtime in their appearances on news-talk shows. The press also was barred from asking Reagan questions during photo opportunities in the Oval Office. The White House team feared Reagan's off-the-cuff answers, which often proved embarrassing.[15] John Kennedy summed up presidents' perspective on the antagonism within the symbiosis: about his daily morning newspaper reading he commented, "I am reading more and enjoying it less."[16]

To understand the symbiosis between the press and presidents, it is important to consider the two partners separately. The next section discusses the press and the process of news making. The chapter then outlines White House news management and presidents' public appearances. The final section traces the phases of the symbiosis in the course of a president's term.

MAKING THE NEWS

Three aspects of journalism contribute to the visibility of the single executive: (1) news production, (2) news sources, and (3) news content. Readers and viewers are exposed only to the finished product of political journalism: the headline story with accompanying photo or film and a reporter's commentary. They may be vaguely aware that editors assign story ideas to reporters, sometimes along with a camera crew, who go out to track down sources, leads, and ultimately, a story. They also may know that editors arrange the stories and place them in easily digestible formats. Yet for most people, the central aspects of political journalism—what pieces of the world become stories, why some pieces do not become stories, and how the relative importance of each story is determined—are as clear as milk in a glass.

News Production

Making news involves a routine. The two most crucial ingredients to the routine are deadlines and brevity. Deadlines are ever present. Decisions are compressed into narrow time frames of days for news magazines and hours and minutes for television and newspapers.

Brevity is also essential. The nightly television news broadcast is allotted only 22 or 23 minutes of airtime; the average story length is 30 seconds; a long story runs 2 minutes. Newspapers and magazines have somewhat greater luxury, but they too face demands for brevity. Editors must satisfy and balance all sections of publication—from sports and entertainment to foreign news. They must also avoid problems of reader boredom and confusion. Stories must be short to keep readers interested, and they must be simple to attract as many readers as possible.

Deadlines and brevity push the news toward being descriptive. News stories do not contain in-depth analysis of the causes or consequences of a particular situation. Most frequently, the descriptions are of individuals, rather than the more complex social, economic, or political processes of which the individuals may be only small parts. Individuals are the focus of the news for two reasons. First, they are easy to cover, chiefly because they talk. It is difficult to interview a budget deficit. Many people want to be in the news and carefully plan their activities for maximum exposure. Second, audiences find stories about individuals easy to understand and interesting. People may identify or sympathize with the individuals. Thus, individuals' actions or remarks become "the peg" on which journalists hang many of their stories. Presidents are handy news pegs. Among all political individuals, presidents are perhaps the easiest to cover because the White House, as part of the symbiotic relationship, is so willing to help. Viewers and readers also easily understand stories about presidents. Presidents are remote from everyday life, but news creates much of their significance based on qualities and experiences of everyday life—how diligently they work, how they get along with other people, how assertive or passive they are. This presidential news adds to the single executive image. Without such sustained coverage, a president would look merely like *a* political participant rather than *the* political participant.

A small group of "gatekeepers"—newspaper and magazine editors and television program executives—determines story selection and hence what makes the news.[17] These individuals open the gates for some stories and decide how much coverage they receive; they close the gate to others, so that the public knows little if anything about certain events. On an average newspaper, the gatekeepers number fewer than twenty-five people. At the networks, the editorial personnel number fewer than fifty people.

A profile of one network illustrates that television news gatekeepers work in a two-tiered hierarchy. On the top level are three people. A vice president in charge of news establishes general news policy. An executive producer (sometimes the anchor person) selects the news, sets the sequence and length of the stories, and decides the amount of film and voice coverage for each. An associate executive producer assists the executive producer. People in the second tier follow up on the decisions from above. These individuals are a Washington bureau chief, a news editor who monitors the progress of stories and edits films and reports, an assignment editor who apportions reporters and camera crews to various stories, and several writers and copy editors.[18]

Most network personnel are totally unknown to the public, but when Tom Brokaw, Peter Jennings, or Dan Rather declares something is news, the work of the faceless network editors can have extraordinary impact. By targeting events for positive or negative news coverage, the anchors and their editors may influence public and official attitudes. A study of network news coverage of the January 1968 North Vietnamese Tet offensive concluded that poor story selection and improper interpretations created the impression among the public and government officials that the North Vietnamese had won the battle, though they actually had lost it. The portrayal of North Vietnamese victory fueled antiwar sentiment and may have contributed to Lyndon Johnson's decision several months later not to run for a second term.[19] Such coverage also can have an impact on the White House itself. Lloyd Cutler, President Carter's chief counsel, observed that the networks' relentless 444-day count of "America Held Hostage" in Iran created so much pressure that Carter and his advisers handled other issues badly, including an embargo of grain to the Soviet Union after its invasion of Afghanistan.[20]

The primary criteria by which the gatekeepers select news are conflict, familiarity, and novelty.[21] Presidential stories satisfy each criterion. The gatekeepers invoke these measures, anticipating the reactions of their audiences as the ultimate judges—the final gatekeepers. According to political scientist Doris Graber, "What they [the audiences] accept, thrives. What they reject languishes or dies."[22]

Conflict—crimes, wars, confrontations involving prominent people—excites audiences. Presidents frequently face conflict—with Congress, foreign nations, members of their own administrations, and sometimes the press itself. In the midst of a CBS evening news broadcast, President Reagan called anchor Dan Rather and asked him to clarify on the air Rather's characterization of the administration's plan to sell arms to Taiwan as a "reversal of policy."[23]

Familiarity lends vividness to stories. Such familiarity can involve a car accident that happens down the block. Or it can involve events that are far away but about which the audience nevertheless feels it knows a lot. People feel they know presidents, and they often identify with them. When President Bush was diagnosed with Graves' disease, which can cause an irregular heartbeat, people avidly watched the medical bulletins. Familiarity of this sort bridges the gap between individuals' private lives and the public world. People value the feeling of personal intimacy that comes from knowing details of a famous person's life.

Last, *novelty* absorbs audiences. Events that have just occurred or are out of the ordinary make good stories. President Nixon's trip to the People's Republic of China in 1972 marked the first time an American president had ever set foot on Chinese soil. Live satellite coverage captured the unusual event.

News Sources

What becomes news is determined partly by who reporters' sources are. Who the sources are depends on who is considered important and legitimate in society. Lacking any firm empirical data about what readers and viewers find important, journalists construct their own loose measures based on the enduring structure of society. Access to sources, according to Herbert Gans, "reflects the social structure outside the newsroom; and because that structure is hierarchical, the extent to which information about various parts of America is available to journalists is hierarchical and differentially distributed."[24] "The news deals mostly with those who hold power within various national or societal strata; with the most powerful officials in the most powerful agencies; with the coalition of upper-class and upper middle class people which dominates the socioeconomic hierarchy."[25] News organizations have much less tendency to consider the plight of the downtrodden, disenchanted, or disorganized as news. Stories about the homeless, mothers struggling to get off welfare, and families losing their farms are done. But the space and time allotted to them is far less than that given to "official news." They are not deemed as important as the actions of elected and unelected government officials, especially presidents.

Presidential news dominates official news. Such abundant coverage reinforces the notion of the single executive image. When so much time is spent on what presidents do, one can only believe that they are in charge of or responsible for a large part of what is going on. Also, because the media tend not to cover groups and social processes, news watchers gain little understanding of other power bases in America—in business, in government, and even in the media.

News Content

People who say they watch or read the news to stay informed would be surprised to learn that they actually gain little information from the content of a news broadcast or even a high-quality newspaper or magazine. Although information almost always makes the news, news is not always information. *Information* is new and unforeseen. It challenges previous ideas. It stabs normal patterns of behavior, and its meaning is not immediately clear. *News* is most often the routine, orderly activities of public officials.[26] News translates information into an easily understood story that has a beginning, an ending, and entertainment value. English writer Evelyn Waugh observed: "News is what the chap who does not care about much of anything wants to read."

The following short list of polar opposites highlights the tension between information and news:

Information	News
Disorder	Order
Confusing	Intelligible
Unpredictable	Predictable
Novel	Banal
Original	Redundant
Complex	Simple

The key question that distinguishes information from news is "Do I really need to know this?" *News is often something about which one does not need to know anything.* A newsworthy item is not necessarily an important item. Human interest stories—the lady who has two hundred cats, the man who plays a banjo behind his back—may be entertaining, but they are surely nothing one needs to know about. Similarly, people did not really need to know about Jimmy Carter and George Bush as fishermen or Gerald Ford as a golfer. Nonetheless, their sports activities were "news." *Information is something about which one does need to know.* It fundamentally affects the well-being of society or individuals. Some news stories do contain information and do educate the audience, but not all do.

For decades people needed information about the global warming caused by the deterioration of the ozone layer as more and more pollutants enter the atmosphere. But global warming was not news because it was a complex process avoided by politicians and not fully understood even by scientists. Finding a peg for the story was difficult until researchers observed that carbon dioxide gases emitted by automobiles contribute to the problem. The problem could then be discussed in terms of everyday things that ordinary people own. The information could be translated into news.

A good example of the difference between information and news occurred during the attempted assassination of President Reagan in 1981. Journalists often comment that a presidential assassination is the most important story that they will ever cover. One executive producer observed in a macabre fashion, "We cover the president expecting he will die."[27] Plainly, this story *is* information. It is unforeseen, jarring, something everyone needs to know. As the story broke, Reagan was initially reported to be unharmed. Then it was confirmed that he had been shot. Reports then turned to Press Secretary James Brady, who also was hit. A rumor that Brady had died circulated on Capitol Hill, where it was passed on to reporters. All three networks announced Brady's death. CBS anchor Dan Rather and ABC anchor Frank Reynolds solemnly delivered obituaries. A half-hour later,

Reynolds was informed through his earpiece that the report of Brady's death was in error. Reynolds exploded over the air: "Let's get it nailed down, somebody!" Brady lived. The incident lays bare the difficulty the media, especially television, have in handling information. News reporters have a great deal of trouble covering sudden, fast-breaking events that have no predictable course and do not happen on schedule well before deadline—the very kinds of things their audiences need to know most about.

Presidents make good news. Their schedules are announced in advance and are tailored to reporters' deadlines. When they are at the White House, they are very easy to find. When they leave town, there is plenty of advance warning. Many events at which presidents will appear are planned to such a degree that minute-by-minute scripts are given to reporters so they know what is going to happen next. Covering presidents becomes routine and fits well with the production of the news. The White House likes to disseminate *news*. It does not like *information*. It loathes instances when information that it does not control is leaked, uncovered by eager reporters, or disclosed by employees elsewhere in the government. For example, the Nixon administration took the *New York Times* to court to stop publication of leaked documents about the Vietnam War that became known as the *Pentagon Papers*. The Supreme Court allowed the newspaper to print the accounts, saying they did not endanger national security.

PRESIDENTIAL MANAGEMENT OF THE NEWS

In its direct relations with the press, the White House has four key techniques to attempt control: (1) story coordination, (2) press conferences, (3) background information, and (4) leaks. The White House also has at its disposal other devices (discussed later in the chapter) that permit presidents more direct access to the American public. Each allows the White House to manage the visibility and positive coverage of the president, thereby reinforcing the single executive image.

Story Coordination

A growing part of the White House staff handles story coordination. A lone presidential press secretary evolved into the White House Press Office of ten employees during Eisenhower's administration, and eleven today. The Press Office also is bolstered by a larger media team of twenty-five other people in the Office of Communication, which coordinates all of the administration's communication, and a Media Liaison Office, which handles non-Washington and ethnic journalists. Coordination of the White House story involves presidential press secretaries' daily relations with reporters and presidents' long-range, comprehensive communication strategy.

The Daily News. Presidents' press secretaries hold daily press briefings, which numbered nearly ten thousand between the Kennedy and Reagan administrations.[28] During the briefings, press secretaries provide the official White House response to an event or announce the president's position on a policy or political matter. William Greener, deputy press secretary to Ford, observed that his morning routine began at 7:30 A.M. to "check out the press room, in particular the wire service reporters, find out what's hot, what's bothering them, the three networks. Get the answers and then . . . find out what the president knows about this." At 10:15, the press secretary, his deputy, senior advisers, and President Ford would meet to discuss what the president's position would be on assorted topics. Members of the press team then returned to their office around 10:45 to perfect the final answers that would be used at the 11:30 briefing.[29] The briefing itself and the sheer volume of briefings give the White House tremendous control over what is deemed to be news. A White House correspondent, Dom Bonafede, observed during the Ford administration that "every day when Nessen [Ford's press secretary] gets out there he determines, with his opening statement, what the news is going to be for that day."[30]

Communication Strategy. Presidents, their chief policy advisers, and White House communication experts also develop long-range communication strategies. The strategies identify a White House priority, coordinate who says what, and plan presidents' schedules of public activities to highlight the White House position. The term "long-range" is a bit misleading. Long-range media planning involves a day rather than hours or a few weeks rather than a day. But it is clearly planning, because the strategies are geared toward tomorrow's reactions to today's stories.

Such planning originated with President Nixon, who established the Office of Communication, distinct from the Press Office. Nixon, who could barely conceal his contempt for the press, wanted to keep on top of long-range publicity efforts to avoid embarrassing coverage. "The purpose of the [office]," explained William Safire, a White House speechwriter, "was to plan the public activities of the president and to see that Administration figures were lined up to make news in an orderly fashion—that is, no two major stories purposely broken on the same day, or if a bad story was due, to try and smother it with other news."[31]

The Reagan White House developed the "line of the day" as part of its long-range planning. This was a standardized message emphasized by all participants in the White House publicity apparatus during a single news day. One day, when reporters tried to distract Reagan from the appointed line of the day, he replied, "If I answer that question, none of you will say anything about what we're here for today. I'm not going to give you a different lead."[32] One barometer of the success of White House story coordination was the way other officials in Washington followed the White House line rather than leading off with their own. There was a fear among others in Washington, especially in Congress, that if they attempted to compete directly with the White House story, their story would be buried. The press secretary to Speaker of the House Thomas P. "Tip" O'Neill acknowledged that the Speaker chose to respond to the ever abundant Reagan news rather than create news of his own.[33] The communication strategies plan presidential visibility to match the single executive image of a competent, effective leader. The strategies permit presidents to control both the message and the messengers, thus portraying presidential leadership in the best possible light.

Access and Control. Recently, White House efforts at story coordination have become easier. One main reason is the astronomical growth in the number of reporters assigned to the White House. In the 1970s, some 120 reporters regularly covered the White House. In the 1990s, the number more than doubled. Bush's press secretary Marlin Fitzwater estimated that there were 2,000 reporters with White House credentials (although not all are present at any one time). The length of the presidential motorcade is now so long—more than twenty vehicles—that a president is inside his destination before the last press vans at the rear roll up.

The sheer increase in numbers has three effects on the ability of the White House to control its own story. First, the burgeoning press corps minimizes individual reporters' regular access to the president. On most indoor locations, including the Oval Office, a rotating press pool represents the correspondents because as a group they are simply too big to fit in the interior spaces. The pool consists of seven reporters—four from the wire services and one each representing television, radio, and newspapers. Consequently, many White House reporters rely on news briefings and written announcements distilled from the Press Office. Second, size encumbers individual reporters' efforts to cultivate White House staff members as reliable sources. "There are so many reporters clamoring for the attention of relatively few staffers who know anything that it is a constant battle for meaningful access," says Tom DeFrank, *Newsweek*'s White House correspondent since 1974. Third, size creates a pecking order among reporters, the top echelon of whom set the agenda for the rest of the group. This makes the White House's job still easier. It courts the correspondents of the networks, wire services, and the "big 3" newspapers—the *New York Times,* the *Washington Post,* and the *Wall Street*

Journal. The stories they air and write become the topics of the next day's press briefing, and their slants become the slants of other reporters.[34]

As an example, Cable News Network (CNN) has dramatically risen in the pecking order in the past decade. It has become an indispensable tool for the White House because of its live, comprehensive coverage of key White House events. The White House can get its story out by means of CNN without any pesky editing or analysis. Indeed, the roles of the White House and CNN have become blurred on occasion. Shortly after Iraq's invasion of Kuwait in 1990, Iraqi president Saddam Hussein suggested he would withdraw his troops if Israel ended its occupation of Arab territories. CNN reporter Frank Sesno rushed on the air with a White House reaction that he had not had time to get. He ad-libbed, saying that the White House would no doubt reject Hussein's offer. Marlin Fitzwater, watching the live report, said, "It sounds good to me," and publicly backed CNN's creation of the White House's position. Reporters also rely on CNN. On overseas trips, reporters too low on the pecking order to cover some of the events on the president's itinerary watch the events on CNN from their hotel rooms.[35]

The large number of White House reporters accentuates pressures toward "pack journalism": reporters follow a story in similar ways, and the sources, stories, and interpretations given by top reporters are followed by other reporters.[36] Pack journalism increases news homogeneity and reliance on the "official story." As a result of it, the White House Press Office gains greater control over the content of press coverage, and the single executive image of one dominant figure in American politics carefully saying the right thing looms larger.

Press Conferences

Theodore Roosevelt initiated the management of the news by means of the presidential press conference.[37] Roosevelt, who enjoyed personally conducting meetings with the press, held press conferences on an informal and irregular basis. He also was the first president to bring the press into the White House—by setting up a White House press room.[38] Woodrow Wilson transformed the sporadic press conference of Roosevelt into a formal, twice-weekly event. In response to Wilson's initiative, Washington reporters formed the White House Correspondents Association (which still exists) to become a more professional body. Roosevelt's and Wilson's actions institutionalized a presidential-press relation. The press conference provided an official forum from which presidents could disseminate their stories, in addition to the briefings of the press secretary.[39]

Presidents Harding, Coolidge, and Hoover continued to use the press conference as a way to manage news stories about the White

House. All required reporters' questions in writing in advance. Franklin Roosevelt relaxed this requirement, holding formal "spontaneous" news conferences and informal sessions in the Oval Office. President Truman moved the conferences out of the Oval Office and into an auditorium. The Eisenhower administration invited the networks to film the news conferences after Eisenhower was convinced of press bias. "Pres upset at press reaction," wrote Press Secretary James Hagerty in his diary. "[S]traight New Deal in thinking and in writing. . . . Real reaction will be favorable. That's why I'm glad we released tape of statement to radio, TV and news reels . . . we'll go directly to the people."[40] Since the Kennedy administration, press conferences have been covered live.

The dependence and antagonism of presidential-press relations are keenly evident at presidential news conferences. Although press conferences would seem to put presidents and reporters on equal footing, presidents typically have the upper hand. For modern presidents, the press conference is a stylized sparring match. Presidents are drilled beforehand by staff members who take on the roles of reporters. Although presidents often come to press conferences armed like commandos, evidence indicates a dearth of hostile questions from reporters. A study of press conferences from 1961 to 1975 found that the number of questions that could be considered hostile never exceeded 3 out of an average of 16 to 20 questions.[41] The presidential-press dependence holds nasty questions in check. To the extent that the press advances an antagonist role, it does so by asking questions related to presidents' policy initiatives. Roughly 25 percent of the questions asked at press conferences between 1961 and 1975 were classified as related to presidents' agendas.

But presidents often respond to both the hostile and the agenda-related questions with evasive or indirect answers. President Eisenhower deliberately conveyed ambiguous answers to questions he preferred the press not to ask. Risking looking unprepared, Eisenhower quoted favorably "an old proverb . . . 'Keep silent and appear stupid; open your mouth and remove all doubt.' " In a pre–press conference briefing, Eisenhower, peeved that his secretary of state had made remarks about American missiles in Europe, told aides he would "be evasive" when the question came up.[42]

As can be seen in Figure 6.1, the number of evasive answers that presidents give tracks the number of policy-related questions that reporters ask. Presidents' counterattacks leave the public little news from "news" conferences. As John Ehrlichman, Nixon's domestic policy chief, once said, there are "a lot of flabby and fairly dumb questions" asked during press conferences.[43] Given presidential evasiveness, there are similar numbers of flabby answers.

Another tactic that presidents may use to diminish the adversarial potential of press conferences is to refrain from calling them. As shown in Table 6.2, presidents Nixon and Reagan held fewer news

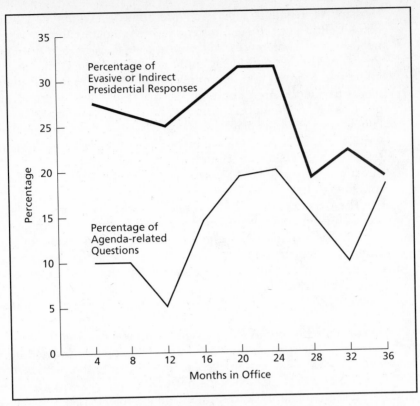

Figure 6.1 Agenda Control at Presidential News Conferences, 1961–1975

The more often reporters ask presidents questions related to their policy agenda, the more often presidents will respond with evasive or indirect answers. [*Source:* Jarol Manheim, "The Honeymoon's Over: The News Conference and the Development of Presidential Style," *Journal of Politics* 41 (February 1979): 66. Used by permission of the author and the University of Texas Press.]

conferences than other presidents. The combination of dependence and antagonism makes press conferences opportunities for presidents to control their visibility and highlight the single executive image with minimal costs in terms of tricky or nasty questions.

Background Information

In addition to the public story, the White House also disseminates material for reporters' private use. Four types of private briefings have been devised. Some briefings are held *off the record*. Franklin Roosevelt started this practice of giving reporters information that was for their own edification but that, it was agreed, they would never report. Some briefings are done *on deep background*. This means that reporters can use the material in a story but cannot attribute it to anyone. There are also briefings *on background*. The source of the

Table 6.2 Presidential News Conferences, 1949–1988

President	Total conferences	Yearly average	Monthly average
Truman	160	40	3.3
Eisenhower, I	99	25	2.1
Eisenhower, II	94	24	2.0
Kennedy	65	22	1.9
Johnson[1]	132	26	2.1
Nixon, I	30	8	0.6
Nixon, II	9	5	0.5
Ford	41	19	1.4
Carter	59	15	1.2
Reagan I	23	6	0.5
Reagan II	18	5	0.4

1. Includes full term from November 1963 to January 1969.

Note: News conferences are defined as formal exchanges with reporters. Excludes interviews and informal remarks at arrivals and departures.

Source: Gary King and Lyn Ragsdale, *The Elusive Executive* (Washington, D.C.: 1988), 268; updated by the author. Used by permission of CQ Press.

information can be identified, but the source's position can be referenced in a general way, as "a high-ranking White House official" or "a source close to the president." People in Washington knew all too well that the "high-ranking White House official" who was responsible for several stories about the last days of the Nixon presidency, including Nixon's heavy drinking, was Henry Kissinger.[44] Briefings are also held *on the record*. In this case the source of the material is identified.

White House rules regarding attribution and quotation result in White House control of the press's portrayal of presidents. A reporter who violates one of the rules is unlikely to be given information in the future. As one Ford official remarked, "What we are trying to do is give them no choice on what they will use."[45]

Leaks

Leaks are the unofficial, clandestine disclosure of material by a White House official who makes anonymity a condition for the story. Unlike deep background or off the record briefings, which are official in nature and are attended by members of the White House press corps, a leak is secretly given to one or two select reporters. The majority of leaks are deliberately planted by presidents or their aides to build policy support, improve the presidential image, or attack the opposition. Henry Kissinger consistently leaked information to favored reporters and columnists to help gain support for the Nixon administration's policy on Vietnam. A Kissinger aide said, "We called it 'feeding the animals.' "[46] Although presidents themselves use leaks, they are also irritated by leaks made behind their backs. Lyndon Johnson remarked, "I have enough trouble with myself. I ought not to have to put up with everybody else too."[47]

Although it is unclear that any method can stop leaks, several presidents have tried. Lyndon Johnson, for a time, had White House officials log all visits by reporters. Reagan added modern technology to Johnson's idea by having the visits recorded on computer. In November 1985, Reagan got tougher still. He signed a secret directive that included periodic lie detector tests for all those with access to highly secret information. The directive itself was promptly leaked. Reagan eventually backed away from the plan after the firm dissent of Secretary of State George Schultz.[48] Schulz said he would undergo a lie detector test "once." Perhaps the most infamous attempt to stop leaks occurred in 1971, when former Defense Department employee Daniel Ellsberg disclosed the *Pentagon Papers*, a secret documentary history about American involvement in the Vietnam War. The narrative contained nothing about the Nixon administration's handling of the war, but Nixon and his staff felt that many other leaks were coming out of National Security Council staff. Under John Ehrlichman's supervision, a group called the Plumbers was charged with finding the sources of the leaks. Ironically, most of the leaks were coming out of the Office of National Security Adviser Henry Kissinger, who strongly backed the Plumbers' wild-goose chase.[49]

Results of News Management

The White House uses news management to control presidents' visibility. Because people see presidents so often on news broadcasts and read about them so many times in the newspapers, the White House motto seems to be "The more visibility, the better." But the real key to news management by the White House is "The more control of the visibility, the better." The White House hopes that news management will enable presidents to dictate the national policy agenda, achieve national public support, and gain the upper hand over Congress.

Presidents can be conspicuous by their absence from the airwaves if it serves their purpose. During the early days of President Bush's term, the press grew upset that the White House media apparatus was generating much less news than had that of President Reagan. Bush fell off the front page for days at a time. Barely a word was heard from him on nightly newscasts. Even though Reagan was known to be heavy-handed in his efforts to control press access, the reporters felt his efforts were preferable to no news at all. Bush confused the reporters still more by inviting them to lunch at the White House, giving some of the daily White House news briefings himself, and opening his office to numerous background briefings for reporters. Reporters felt they had little to do but report that there was nothing to report. The White House held the cards and decided when to play them. This tactic was to Bush's advantage as he planned various policy reviews and developed priorities for the administration that were not clearly spelled out during the campaign. Visibility control bought Bush time. His disappearance was brief. He returned to center stage armed with proposals on the environment, drugs, education, and space exploration, using his visibility, as had his predecessor, to dominate the national policy agenda by dominating the national news. Once again, out of the White House came a strong image of one highly visible person in charge.

PRESIDENTIAL DRAMA

A president adopts news management strategies in the hopes of minimizing the amount of the presidential message that gets lost in press translation. A president also employs a strategy of "going public" in the hopes that even less will be lost. He "promotes himself and his policies in Washington by appealing [directly] to the American public for support."[50] Although the press remains a mediator and an interpreter, presidents make public appearances that will place them in the best possible light. By one estimate, American chief executives spend a third of their time in office making public appearances.[51] This amounted to over ten thousand appearances between 1945 to 1992.[52] Presidents make major nationwide addresses, pre-empting prime-time programs to reach over 50 million viewers. They deliver minor speeches that outline specific policy proposals before smaller audiences at university commencements, labor conventions, and business meetings. They make many ceremonial appearances in Washington and elsewhere in the country—signing bills, greeting White House visitors, issuing proclamations, and dedicating buildings. Figure 6.2 displays the yearly averages of several types of appearances from Truman through Reagan's first term.[53] These appearances offer presidents their own opportunities to convey the single executive image. In effectively using the appearances, presidents and their aides hope they can convince other politicians that the White House has the support of the American people to do what the White House wants.

A Choice of Words

The exact words that presidents speak during their many appearances are less important than the impressions they impart. A study of presidents since Eisenhower finds five themes that appear and reappear in their speeches.[54] First, presidents join themselves to the

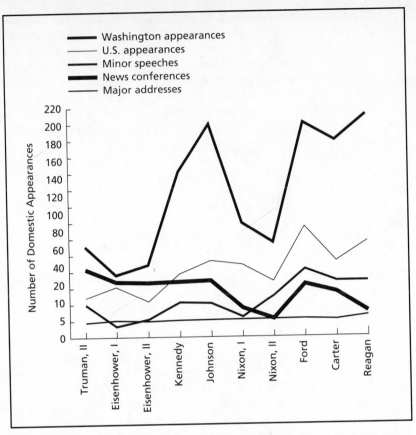

Figure 6.2 Domestic Public Appearances by the President 1949–1984 (yearly averages)

Presidents since Truman have sharply increased the number of ceremonial appearances in Washington, D.C. ("Washington appearances"), and throughout the rest of the country ("U.S. appearances"). [*Source:* Gary King and Lyn Ragsdale, *The Elusive Executive* (Washington, D.C.: CQ Press, 1988), 276. Used by permission of CQ Press.]

American people by constantly using the pronoun "we."[55] In this way, presidents simultaneously justify their actions on behalf of the nation and ask for the nation's support for those actions.

Second, presidents portray themselves as working alone in the government. They defy separation of powers. Congress, executive officials, and foreign leaders are often invisible. Only 3 percent of the presidents' statements refer to the executive branch, and only 2 percent make reference to Congress.[56] Even presidents who were long-time former members of Congress tend to be dismissive of Congress. In foreign policy speeches, presidents make little mention of the Joint Chiefs of Staff, secretaries of state, or ambassadors. Presidents also portray themselves as acting without their advisers and as unaffected by the legacies of their predecessors (with the exception of a few great presidents).

Third, presidents present themselves as the moral and religious leaders of the nation. They speak of the values of the nation—freedom, hope, patriotism, prosperity, the American dream. They also invoke God, read from the Bible, and ask for the prayers of the American people. President Carter remarked, "The president is the only person who can speak with a clear voice to the American people and set a standard of ethics and morality, excellence and greatness."[57] Presidents reinforce the cultural assumption of "the chosen people." Johnson said at his inaugural that America has been "allowed by God to seek greatness through its own work and spiritual strength."[58] Truman, announcing American involvement in Korea, commented, "We are a tolerant and restrained people, deeply aware of our moral responsibilities."[59]

Fourth, presidents downplay the importance of elections and parties. Presidents, by their own accounts, do not engage in political or electoral activity. They remain high above party. Nixon referred to his "good friends in the field of politics."[60] Kennedy said that his inauguration marked "not a victory of party but a celebration of freedom."[61]

Finally, presidents disavow the idea that interest groups reflect any disagreements or different perspectives in politics. Instead, interests groups are simply combined under the rubric "the American people." "Our concern must be for a special interest group that has been too long neglected," proclaimed Ronald Reagan in his inaugural address. He continued:

It knows no sectional boundaries or ethnic and racial divisions, and it crosses party lines. It is made of men and women who raise our food, patrol our streets, man our mines and factories, teach our children, keep our homes and heal us when we're sick—professionals, industrialists, shopkeepers, clerks, cabbies, and truck drivers. They are, in short, "We the people," this breed called Americans.[62]

In articulating these five themes, presidents offer the country the single executive image in their own words. They become its chief sponsor. They alone are linked to the American people, above politics, beyond party, and next to God. Each theme underscores presidential uniqueness and importance. In any one presidential appearance, something may be lost in the translation—for example, if the media report only part of the event or do not present the words accurately. Nevertheless, because of the large number of appearances that presidents make and because of the small variations among presidents, the five themes—and, with them, the single executive image—become embedded in the public's beliefs about presidents.

The Impact of Presidents' Speeches

Presidents are able to momentarily influence their audiences with their speeches. Research indicates that when presidents make a major address to the nation, delivered live and pre-empting regular broadcasts, their popularity rises by three to four percentage points.[63] Similarly, these addresses also improve presidents' chances of success in Congress.[64] After the addresses, presidents are able to get more bills they favor through the legislative process. The effects undoubtedly do not last long. Moreover, other types of appearances—minor speeches, news conferences, and ceremonial appearances in Washington and elsewhere—do not have these positive effects. Yet according to communications expert Roderick Hart, politicians know, or think they know, that a well-received speech can create momentum and that several well-received speeches can create an avalanche of it."[65] Although the latter assumption is overly optimistic, the former is appropriate for presidents making major addresses. Presidents gain immediate, direct access to the public. In pre-empting regular broadcasting, they receive the all-but-undivided attention of millions of radio listeners and television viewers. The audience is not just ordinary citizens but also attentive politicians. The forum presents presidents as sole speakers, uninterrupted by the queries of news reporters and challenged only afterward by the rebuttals of partisan foes or the interpretation of political commentators.[66] Through their major national addresses, the single executive image becomes a key resource for presidents in their attempts to influence the public, other politicians, and the media.

THE STORY UNFOLDS

The symbiosis between the White House and the press generates a daily collaborative product: the White House story. Scholars Michael Grossman and Martha Kumar write that "the White House story is the president: who he is, what he does, and what his programs, actions, and goals are."[67] The coverage of *Time* magazine, the *New York Times*, and CBS News, as shown in Table 6.3 reveals three broad categories of stories that are most consistently reported: programs and policies, activities (such as speeches, news conferences, and ceremonies), and personal matters (daily routines, health, and family). A recent study finds press coverage of Reagan's role in the 1981 tax cut and his 1984 European trip in a local newspaper, in the *New York Times*, and by CBS to be relatively similar and most often capturing policies and activities.[68]

The latter two categories—activities and personal matters—form an important version of the White House story known as the "body watch." As one might guess, reporters on the body watch cover

Table 6.3 Topics of White House Stories

	Time magazine (1953–1978)	*New York Times* (1953–1978)	CBS News (1968–1978)
Programs and policies	30.4%	24.7%	32.3%
Activities	20.2	30.5	18.4
Personal	20.4	12.2	9.9
Vice president	6.9	6.1	5.6
Congress	8.8	10.9	10.5
Election	4.2	6.7	8.1
Staff	3.6	2.7	1.8
President and press	1.8	1.4	1.1
Watergate	3.6	4.7	12.2

Note: Entries are percentages of the total number of stories.

Source: Michael Baruch Grossman and Martha Joynt Kumar. *Portraying the President* (Baltimore/London: The Johns Hopkins University Press, 1981), 269. Used by permission.

every move presidents make in case something shocking happens—whether it be an international crisis or an assassination, what Ronald Reagan referred to as "the awful, awful." The White House uses the body watch to its own advantage, offering the press numerous opportunities to watch presidents do all kinds of things, knowing the cameras will be on. According to Elmer Cornwell, an expert on presidential-press relations, "Unlike the other branches of government, the President is 'news' as a person, as well as in his official role. Congress or the Supreme Court rarely make news save in their corporate capacity."[69]

The body watch carries with it a distinct irony. Especially since John Kennedy, the press assumes, probably rightly, that people want to know if a president falls ill, is injured, or is killed. But on most days, nothing dramatic happens. The body watch then captures the routine, often trivial, aspects of the lives of presidents and their families: Harry Truman's morning walks, Amy Carter's first day of school, and Nancy Reagan's china. CBS News correspondent Ed Bradley complained, "This is the sort of thing that eats up our time. Most of it doesn't mean a damn thing, but the White House grinds it out and we eat it up. The network wants everything we can give them on the president."[70] Americans end up knowing more and more about less and less important aspects of presidents' lives.

Whereas press coverage, especially the body watch, is consistently favorable, stories on programs and policies are somewhat less so.[71] Grossman and Kumar's study indicates that during the twenty-five-year period, from 1953 through 1978, *Time*, the *New York Times*, and CBS News had more positive than negative stories about each of six presidents across the policy, activity, and personal categories (see Figure 6.3). Across the three categories, 40 percent of the stories in the *New York Times* were positive, 23 percent negative, and the

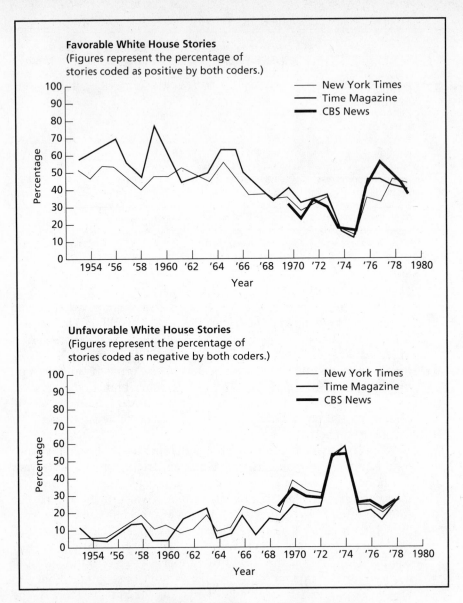

Favorable White House Stories
(Figures represent the percentage of stories coded as positive by both coders.)

New York Times
Time Magazine
CBS News

Unfavorable White House Stories
(Figures represent the percentage of stories coded as negative by both coders.)

New York Times
Time Magazine
CBS News

Figure 6.3 Favorable and Unfavorable White House Stories

During the period of 1953–1978, the percentage of favorable stories about the president exceeded the percentage of unfavorable stories, except during the Watergate era. [*Source:* Michael Baruch Grossman and Martha Joynt Kumar, *Portraying the President* (Baltimore/London: The Johns Hopkins University Press, 1981), 257. Used by permission.]

remainder neutral. *Time* was also mostly favorable, with 45 percent of its stories positive and 31 percent negative. Although CBS had sharply unfavorable stories during Watergate, in the post-Watergate period from 1974 to 1978, when Ford and Carter were president, 45 percent of the network's stories were positive, 24 percent negative. Despite presidents' complaints of unfair press treatment, the symbiosis produces a generally favorable White House story.

The symbiotic relationship passes through three phases during presidents' terms: (1) alliance, (2) competition, and (3) detachment. The timing of the phases is similar to the timing of the three phases of presidential popularity—the honeymoon (highly favorable public opinion), disillusionment (disappointment over presidents' failure to meet expectations), and forgiveness (some realization that expectations may be too high). Indeed, the press phases may shape the public phases. Across the three press phases the shifts between dependence and antagonism in the symbiotic relationship gave rise to four different types of White House story: in the alliance phase, a personal story and a policy planning story; in the competition phase, a policy performance story; in the detachment phase, an administration infighting story. As the stories change, the public is exposed to greater realism in presidential news, and public opinion may respond accordingly.

Alliance

During the alliance phase dependence overshadows antagonism. News organizations and the White House emphasize cooperation. The alliance phase rarely lasts longer than a year. The greatest number of stories and the greatest number of favorable stories occur in the first year of presidents' terms. This favorable coverage helps define the honeymoon between presidents and the public. Access to White House officials is also generous. During this phase, reporters rely on White House–sponsored press arrangements, such as briefings and press releases. Later they acquire other informal sources or receive on background information from White House officials. Grossman and Kumar state: "During this period both sides have more to gain by cooperation. They both want to obtain maximum media exposure for the new administration, its people, and its proposed policies. As long as they hold the same definition of news, it makes sense for them to cooperate."[72]

The White House story during this phase is of two types. One focuses on presidents' personalities, what they and their families are like. A Ford White House official predicted that the press would be very interested in "personality" stories in the early days of the new Carter administration. "Who is Jimmy Carter? What is his personality? Does he get mad? Does he golf? Does he fish in a pond? How do you find out who somebody is? You look at his friends, his habits, his manner, his character, his personality."[73]

The "second story" according to the same Ford official "is what is he doing as president?" The answer is that he is developing policy. Policy planning stories tend to be favorable because the work presidents are doing has not yet engendered controversy. The Ford staffer continued, "When you develop policy and consult, it is almost universally attractive. That's why there is a honeymoon. It is attractive because you are not making that many decisions. . . . Nothing is as attractive to the country and the press as dealing—or appearing to deal—with problems."[74]

Competition

The alliance phase is characterized by an open presidency in which reporters' phone calls are returned, their requests for interviews are granted, and information is forthcoming. In contrast, suspicion characterizes the presidency in the competition phase. Certain reporters are excluded from inside information, and the president may have fewer news conferences. This phase lasts during the second and third years of presidents' terms. "Both sides," in the words of Grossman and Kumar, use manipulative tactics to present a story "their way."[75] Reporters shift attention to conflicts among individuals in and out of the administration and to controversies over policies.

During this phase, the White House story centers on the success or failure of presidents' decisions. Expectations drawn from the campaign and from the political culture suggest that presidents should do more than just plan and consult. They eventually must act. Once presidents enter the policy fray, there is no turning back. People outside the administration will criticize their proposals, both on and off the record. People inside the administration will leak information to push particular policy directions. More critical news stories result. Presidential popularity tends to erode as negative policy performance stories appear. The White House responds to them with greater manipulation of access and news management.

Detachment

The final phase is characterized by fewer encounters between presidents and the press, and the encounters that do occur are more formal and structured than before. Detachment usually emerges in the last year of the term. There is not an all-out war between the press and the White House because dependence tempers antagonism. But the White House dictum during this final phase is "Get the most coverage with the least risk." Presidents appear more often in favorable settings that the White House controls. News conferences become few and far between. Stories about administration infighting emerge. Reporters concentrate on controversies among administration officials to reveal the strains and infighting within the administration.

During each successive phase, reporters become more and more willing to point out that the image of the single executive is just that—an image. They point out the extent to which numerous people, other than presidents themselves, dictate presidential decisions. Stories appear about the complexities of the White House office and the clashes of personalities within it. Presidents may begin to appear as prisoners in the White House, held captive by increasingly rambunctious staffers. For presidents who win re-election, the alliance phase may return briefly at the beginning of the second term, but the competition and detachment phases quickly resume. Presidents and the press adopt overall approaches to each other that do not drastically change in the second term. In short, the longer presidents are in office, the more the image of the single executive is likely to erode.

CONCLUSION

In the symbiotic relationship between the White House and the press, the stakes for the American public are high. The symbiosis allows presidents to communicate with the public, and it gives the public its only mechanism by which to assess presidents' conduct and decisions. But the symbiosis also clouds these assessments as people take the media and the news they provide for granted. It is easy to forget Marshall McLuhan's famous statement that the medium does not convey the message; instead, "the medium is the message." People often are unaware that journalists define the news in particular ways. They also are unaware of the extent to which the White House is its own news medium. News is not a dispassionate account of events; it is not a mirror held up to the world. True, journalists do not make up the news. They instead begin with what they deem to be an external reality that they must make readily understandable to their audience. But this real world of politics is ultimately a world of realistic images offered by politicians. The news becomes simple, personal, and dramatic. It varies little from network to network, from paper to paper. The images are less likely to inform than to entertain.

The press does not simply cover "what is out there." If it did, there would be much less presidential news. The belief that the president is the number-one story for the national media is hauntingly self-fulfilling. Reporters comment that they like to be assigned to the White House because they are almost guaranteed that their stories will be aired or printed. But what a president does on a given day is not necessarily important for the well-being of society, the government, or even the executive branch. As Jody Powell, President Carter's press secretary, asserted, "There is clearly not something that is newsworthy [at the White House] every day."[76] But because presidents are defined as newsworthy, their decisions and personal actions take on importance. And because their actions are defined as important, they are automatically newsworthy. The press is not really covering the president but instead is covering the image of a single executive at the head of the government. ∎

FURTHER READING

On presidential-press relations, see: Michael Grossman and Martha Kumar, *Portraying the President* (Baltimore: Johns Hopkins University Press, 1981); George Edwards, *The Public Presidency* (New York: St. Martin's Press, 1983); James Pollard, *Presidents and the Press* (New York: Macmillan, 1974). On news production, see: Doris Graber, *Mass Media and American Politics,* 3d ed. (Washington, D.C.: CQ Press, 1989); Herbert Gans, *Deciding What's News* (New York: Pantheon, 1979). On presidential news management, see: Steven Weisman, "The President and the Press: The Art of Controlled Access," *New York Times Magazine,* October 14, 1984, 34–37, 71–73, 80; Mark Hertsgaard, *On Bended Knee* (New York: Farrar Straus Giroux, 1988). On news conferences, see: Elmer Cornwell, *Presidential Leadership of Public Opinion* (Bloomington: Indiana University Press, 1965); Jarol Manheim, "The Honeymoon's Over: The News Conference and the Development of Presidential Style," *Journal of Politics* 41 (November 1979): 55–74. On presidential speeches, see: Roderick Hart, *The Sound of Leadership* (Chicago: University of Chicago Press, 1987); Samuel Kernell, *Going Public* (Washington, D.C.: CQ Press, 1986); Gary King and Lyn Ragsdale, *The Elusive Executive* (Washington, D.C.: CQ Press, 1988); Barbara Hinckley, *The Symbolic Presidency* (New York: Routledge, 1990).

NOTES

1. Interviewed by Michael Grossman and Martha Kumar, *Portraying the President* (Baltimore: Johns Hopkins University Press, 1981), 4.
2. Ibid., 202.
3. James Fixx, ed., *The Mass Media and Politics* (New York: New York Times, Arno Press, 1971), ix.
4. Interviewed by Grossman and Kumar, 28.
5. Lawrence O'Brien, "Larry O'Brien Discusses White House Contacts with Capitol Hill," in *The Presidency,* ed. A. Wildavsky (Boston: Little, Brown, 1969), 484.
6. Murray Edelman, *The Symbolic Uses of Politics* (Urbana: University of Illinois Press, 1964), 101.
7. Grossman and Kumar, 265.

8. Doris Graber, *Mass Media and American Politics,* 3d ed. (Washington, D.C.: CQ Press, 1989) 235–237.

9. Quoted in George Edwards, *The Public Presidency* (New York: St. Martin's Press, 1983), 106.

10. Hedrick Smith, *The Power Game* (New York: Random House, 1988), 435.

11. Bob Woodward, *The Commanders* (New York: Simon and Schuster, 1991), 368.

12. Interviewed by Grossman and Kumar, 28.

13. William Greener, Jr., Ford's deputy press secretary, interviewed ibid., 29.

14. Seymour Hersh, *The Price of Power: Kissinger in the Nixon White House* (New York: Summit Books, 1983), 92–96.

15. Smith, 430, 434.

16. David Wise, *The Politics of Lying* (New York: Vintage, 1973), 460, 479–480.

17. Doris Graber, *Mass Media and American Politics,* 2d ed. (Washington, D.C.: CQ Press, 1984), 72.

18. Malcolm Warner, "Decision-Making in Network News," in *Media Sociology,* ed. Jeremy Tunstall (Urbana: University of Illinois Press, 1970) 158–167.

19. Peter Braestrup, *Big Story* (Garden City, N.Y.: Anchor Books, 1978).

20. Smith, 403.

21. Graber, 1984, 78–79.

22. Ibid., 71–79.

23. Barbara Matusow, *The Evening Stars: The Rise of the Network News Anchors* (Boston: Houghton Mifflin, 1983), 1.

24. Herbert Gans, *Deciding What's News* (New York: Pantheon, 1979), 81.

25. Ibid., 62.

26. Graber, 1984, 80.

27. Gans, 145.

28. Bradley Patterson, Jr., *The Ring of Power* (New York: Basic Books, 1988), 170.

29. Grossman and Kumar, 139–140.

30. Interviewed ibid., 33.

31. William Safire, *Before the Fall: An Inside View of the Pre-Watergate White House* (Garden City, N.Y.: Doubleday, 1975), 361.

32. Steven Weisman, "The President and the Press: The Art of Controlled Access," *New York Times Magazine,* October 14, 1984, 34–37, 71–73, 80; see also Mark Hertsgaard, *On Bended Knee* (New York: Farrar Straus Giroux, 1988).

33. Comments at the annual meeting of the American Political Science Association, Washington, D.C., 1986.

34. Owen Ullmann, "Inside the White House," *The Washingtonian* 26 (January 1991): 56–60.

35. Ibid., 60.

36. Dan Nimmo and James Combs, *Mediated Political Realities* (New York: Longman, 1983), Chap. 8.

37. For a detailed account of the development of the press conference see Elmer Cornwell, *Presidential Leadership of Public Opinion* (Bloomington: Indiana University Press, 1966).

38. James Pollard, *Presidents and the Press* (New York: Macmillan, 1974), 574.

39. Richard Rubin, *Press, Party, and Presidency* (New York: Norton, 1981), 87.

40. Grossman and Kumar, 243.

41. Jarol Manheim, "The Honeymoon's Over: The News Conference and the Development of Presidential Style," *Journal of Politics* 41 (November 1979): 55–74.

42. Fred Greenstein, *The Hidden Hand Presidency* (New York: Basic Books, 1982), 66–72.

43. John Ehrlichman, *Witness to Power: The Nixon Years* (New York: Simon and Schuster, 1982), 285–287.

44. Bob Woodward and Carl Bernstein, *The Final Days* (New York: Avon, 1976), 470–472.

45. Quoted in Grossman and Kumar, 227.

46. Hersh, 93.

47. Quoted in George Christian, *The President Steps Down: A Personal Memoir of the Transfer of Power* (New York: Macmillan, 1970), 203.

48. Jane Mayer and Doyle McManus, *Landslide: The Unmaking of the President, 1984–1988* (Boston: Houghton Mifflin, 1988), 187.

49. Hersh, 397.

50. Samuel Kernell, *Going Public* (Washington, D.C.: CQ Press, 1986), 1.

51. Samuel Kernell, "The Presidency and the People: The Modern Paradox," in *The Presidency and the Political System*, ed. M. Nelson (Washington, D.C.: CQ Press), 1984, 243.

52. Roderick Hart, *The Sound of Leadership* (Chicago: University of Chicago Press, 1987), 9.

53. Gary King and Lyn Ragsdale, *The Elusive Executive* (Washington, D.C.: CQ Press, 1988), Chap. 5.

54. Barbara Hinckley, *The Symbolic Presidency* (New York: Routledge, 1990).

55. Ibid., 39.

56. Ibid., 52.

57. Quoted ibid., 79.

58. Inaugural Address, January 20, 1965, *Public Papers of the Presidents: Lyndon Johnson, 1965* (Washington, D.C.: U.S. Government Printing Office, 1966).

59. "Declaring a National Emergency About the Conflict in Korea," December 15, 1950, *Public Papers of the Presidents: Harry S Truman, 1950* (Washington, D.C.: U.S. Government Printing Office, 1951).

60. "Address to the Nation on Economic Stabilization," October 9, 1971, *Public Papers of the Presidents: Richard Nixon, 1971* (Washington, D.C.: U.S. Government Printing Office, 1972).

61. Inaugural Address, January 20, 1961, *Public Papers of the Presidents: John Kennedy, 1961* (Washington, D.C.: U.S. Government Printing Office, 1962).

62. Inaugural Address, January 20, 1981, *Public Papers of the Presidents: Ronald Reagan, 1981* (Washington, D.C.: U.S. Government Printing Office, 1982), 2.

63. Lyn Ragsdale, "The Politics of Presidential Speechmaking," *American Political Science Review* 78 (December 1980): 971–984.

64. Lyn Ragsdale, "Presidents' Perpetual Campaigns: Public Appearances from Truman to Reagan," mimeo, University of Arizona, Tucson, 1992.

65. Hart, 88.

66. Research is mixed on the impact of news commentators' instant analyses of presidential addresses. Dwight Davis, Lynda Kaid, and Donald Singleton, "Information Effects of Political Commentary," *Experimental Study of Politics* 6 (June 1977): 45–68, find no effects. David Paletz and Richard Vinegar, "Presidents on Television: The Effects of Instant Analysis," *Public Opinion Quarterly* 41 (Winter 1977–1978): 488–497, conclude that a shift in attitudes does occur.

67. Grossman and Kumar, 263.

68. David Paletz and K. Kendall Guthrie, "The Three Faces of Ronald Reagan," *Journal of Communication* 37 (Autumn 1987): 7–23.

69. Cornwell, 5.

70. Anthony Lukas, "The White House Press 'Club,' " *New York Times Magazine*, May 15, 1977, 68.

71. Grossman and Kumar, 271.

72. Ibid., 275.

73. Ibid., 276.

74. Interview ibid., 276.

75. Ibid., 274.

76. Interview ibid., 32.

PART II

THE PLURAL PRESIDENCY: MAKING DECISIONS

T he single executive image gives presidents considerable advantages. They claim to be the single most powerful person not only in the government but in the world. Presidents have cleverly created an array of unilateral powers that are nowhere to be found in the Constitution. They have concocted a legislative agenda-setting power to take the lead in submitting programs to Congress. They have fiscal power to draw up an executive budget. They act as substitute lawmakers, issuing executive orders. They have exclusive control over diplomacy and virtually unlimited power to fight limited wars. They combine this presidential power with a government that intervenes on all matters domestic, economic, and foreign. Presidents claim that they are in charge, not of a shop with dusty shelves and little stock but of a gargantuan warehouse, its inventory spilling out the doors.

Presidents justify their overflowing warehouse with a claim of unique importance: they are the sole representative of all the people. This democratic rationale derives from presidents' electoral status as the lone official elected nationally. Although the election is indirect, by means of the electoral college, this detail does not derail presidents' logic.

Not only do presidential elections provide presidents with an ingenious democratic rationale for power, they also focus public attention on personal leadership, as distinct from institutional dynamics. The images the candidates convey and the promises they make as individuals order people's view of politics. The campaign imagery is reinforced by symbolism that magnifies the importance of the office and personifies the public welfare in a single, visible individual. Using the constitutional powers and the democratic rationale, presidents suggest that they are national problem solvers and moral leaders. Media visibility enables presidents to make these claims of uniqueness and importance and allows them to dominate the attention of the public and of other politicians more than any other public figure.

Yet the image of a single executive in charge of the government and leading the public confronts presidents with a dilemma. The powers available, the promises made, and the leadership offered create expectations in the minds of private citizens and public officials about how the president will run the country. Presidents must contend with an all-but-infinite array of policy issues. They receive requests for actions from a variety of organized and unorganized groups. To meet any of these requests or devise plans in any of these policy areas, they must work with a host of officials in and out of government. Presidents thus devise an institution the contours of which are shaped around multiple policy and political demands. Part II explores how presidents make decisions within the institution of the presidency (Chapter 7) and the internal plurality of the institution: its decentralized organization (Chapter 8) and ambiguous decision-making processes (Chapter 9). The ironic result of presidents' claims of singular power, unique importance, and visibility is a plural institution of diverse offices that employ ambiguous decision processes in numerous policy areas among a panoply of political pressures. ■

Decisions in the Plural Presidency

The essence of what presidents do in office is the decisions they make, yet presidential decisions often seem inscrutable. The mystery is partly the result of the single executive image, which sustains the illusion of a lonely, overworked president who makes decisions all by himself. Theodore Sorensen, a top Kennedy adviser, affirmed the image: "In the 'valley of decision,' there can be only one lonely man—the President of the United States."[1] The single executive image also portrays presidential decisions as full of action, intrigue, and crisis. People remember the decisions as though they were newspaper headlines and often know as much about them as the headlines convey: "Kennedy Orders Blockade of Cuba." "Johnson Bombs Hanoi and Haiphong." "Carter Attempts Hostage Rescue." "Reagan Invades Grenada." "Bush Sends Troops Against Iraq." The single executive image thus colors people's views about presidential decision making. Presidents' power, visibility, uniqueness, and importance loom. Presidents are at the center of the decisions. They make them alone or with the help of only a few advisers. The decisions are bold; they shape the fate of the world.

Many presidential decisions, however, are mundane and ordinary. Indeed, the single executive image assures that they are. It places demands on presidents to make decisions about everything: "Johnson Orders Limits on Whisk Broom Imports." "Carter Reduces Federal Paper Work." "Eisenhower Pushes for Savings Bond Program." Because of the range of issues—both routine and extraordinary—on which the single executive image requires action, the institution of the plural presidency has grown to help presidents make their decisions.

The presidency has institutional and plural features. It is an institution—that is, an organization consisting of specialized units whose officials deal with a complicated set of responsibilities. The presidential institution comprises 42 offices and over 1,600 people who gather information, develop policy proposals, political strategies, and public explanations, and make recommendations to the president. The institution's work is ongoing and self-perpetuating. It follows routines that continue from president to president. Many decisions are made with only minimal involvement of the president. People, including the president, who work in the plural presidency come and go, but the institution persists.

The presidency may be characterized as "plural" because many hands go off in many directions to meet all the responsibilities. Within the bureaucracy, influence and interests are diffused rather than concentrated. Even though the president holds the top position, the diversity and size of the institution make it difficult for the president to have either firsthand or secondhand knowledge of much of what goes on. The plural presidency is thus distinct from monolithic, hierarchical organizations in which all orders come down from the top and all information moves up from the bottom.

This chapter examines how the plural presidency—an organization of many autonomous offices, not fully coordinated from the top—makes presidential decisions. Because of the sheer number of decisions that must be made, the tediousness of many of them, and the numerous players helping to make them, presidents are less pivotal to the decision process than many people might think. Consider the plural presidency at work on a typical presidential decision— about shoes.

ROUTINE DECISIONS

On January 21, 1977, one day after his inauguration, President Jimmy Carter received Presidential Review Memorandum No. 7 from the National Security Council. The report outlined for Carter the foreign policy implications of shoe import quotas—limits on the number of shoes that foreign countries could ship to the United States. Carter had campaigned for free trade and federal aid to industries hurt by imports. The American Footwear Industries Association, a group organized to represent American shoe manufacturers, was upset that imports accounted for nearly one-half of the American shoe market. The association cried of three hundred closed shoe factories and seventy thousand lost jobs. The International Trade Commission (ITC), established by Congress to handle trade complaints, had twice recommended shoe import quotas to President Ford. Rejecting the first ITC call for quotas, Ford received its second report just fourteen days before departing office. Busy packing, attending farewell dinners, and not wishing to reopen the issue, Ford left the matter on his successor's desk.

On February 4, the Office of Special Trade Representative—a White House unit that advises presidents on trade—sent a memo to

Carter's Economic Policy Group. The group was a circle of twelve, chaired by Secretary of the Treasury Michael Blumenthal, which included Vice President Mondale, five cabinet secretaries, and five key White House aides. Designated to coordinate economic policy, it met on February 7 to discuss the several options outlined by the Office of Special Trade Representative: (1) some kind of quota, (2) free trade, or (3) orderly marketing agreements (OMAs)—contracts negotiated between the United States and another country that specified the number of products for importation. The OMAs were less restrictive than quotas but still regulated the number of shoes entering the country. The Economic Policy Group also had before it a State Department memo attacking the International Trade Commission's quota recommendation.

During February and March, forces lined up for and against quotas. The pro-quota group enlisted George Meany, the irascible president of the country's largest labor union, the AFL-CIO. Thirty-six governors signed a petition calling for quotas to protect American jobs and American industry from "the current tidal wave of footwear imports."[2] Members of the House and Senate shared the state executives' fears. Among the free trade supporters were consumer groups; the Volume Retailers Association of America, which represented discount merchandisers; National Security Adviser Zbigniew Brzezinski; and Arthur Burns, chair of the Federal Reserve Board.

The Economic Policy Group met again on March 21 to make its recommendation to Carter. The group, like those pressuring from the outside, was split. The secretaries of state, treasury, and housing and urban development and the chair of the Council of Economic Advisers opposed quotas. The secretaries of labor, commerce, and agriculture, the director of the Office of Management and Budget, and the special trade representative supported quotas. Carter's domestic policy chief, Stuart Eizenstadt, briefly raised orderly marketing agreements as a compromise position, but they received little notice. At the close of the meeting, Special Trade Representative Robert Strauss delivered a memo to President Carter that outlined the views of the two camps. Strauss mentioned nothing about OMAs.

One week later, on March 28, 1977, President Carter joined the Economic Policy Group to discuss shoe imports for the first time. During the meeting, the group turned to orderly marketing agreements as the best way to break the deadlock between pro-quota and free trade forces. Carter liked the idea but was frustrated by the policy group's failure to discuss the option at its previous meeting. He ordered Strauss to write a brief outlining the OMAs. Strauss sent the report to Carter two days later. The Domestic Policy Staff also sent Carter a memo backing OMAs. Others pressed Carter to reject them. The State Department feared that OMAs were too restrictive; the Labor Department felt that OMAs were not restrictive enough. A short time later, Carter approved the use of orderly marketing agreements and loan relief to the shoe industry.

If one were to elicit people's impression of this story, the comment that might be uttered loudest is "How boring!" Yet most presidential decisions are about shoes or something equally exciting, and they are handled in similar ways.[3] The institutional and plural features of the presidency are in evidence.

The institution did not miss a beat between President Ford and President Carter. White House work on shoe imports was ongoing while one administration was leaving and the other was moving in. The National Security Council busily crafted a memo in January 1977, before Carter's inauguration but after Ford's decision not to make a decision. Presidential decision making was under way for two months before Carter met with the Economic Policy Group. The plurality of the institution is evident from the complex of units handling the issue: the Economic Policy Group, Office of Special Trade Representative, Domestic Policy Staff, and relevant departments. They determined Carter's final decision as much as Carter's own preferences about free trade or flagging American industries. Moreover, the parts did not always function as a whole. The plural presidency acted on the shoe decision. Carter "made up his mind" only in the most general sense.

OUT-OF-THE-ORDINARY DECISIONS

Skeptics might protest that routine decisions are not at the heart of presidential decision making, that "important" decisions on such matters as naval blockades, invasion plans, and domestic unrest are the true prototypes. In these instances, so the argument goes, presidents do make up their own minds, the significance of the plural institution fades, and the image of a singularly powerful figure meets reality as the president wrestles with the crisis. As a contrast to the Carter shoe import decision, ponder President Kennedy's approval of plans for the overthrow of President Ngo Dinh Diem of South Vietnam.

Predawn View

At 1:30 P.M. on November 1, 1963, South Vietnamese generals launched a coup against President Diem. Opposition to Diem had mounted over several years after he suppressed Buddhist protests against the government; allowed his brother, Nhu, to run his own private army; and tolerated several public power plays by his brother's wife, Madame Nhu. The generals felt that if the Diem regime did not go, the war with North Vietnam would be lost. Within three hours, the military crushed all of Diem's forces within Saigon except at the presidential palace, where Diem hurriedly called the U.S. ambassador to South Vietnam, Henry Cabot Lodge:

DIEM: Some units have made a rebellion, and I want to know what is the attitude of the U.S.

LODGE: I do not feel well enough informed to be able to tell you. I have heard the shooting, but am not acquainted with all the facts. Also it is 4:30 A.M. in Washington and the U.S. Government cannot possibly have a view.

DIEM: But you must have general ideas. After all, I am a chief of state. I have tried to do my duty. I want to do now what duty and good sense require. I believe in duty above all.

LODGE: You have certainly done your duty. As I told you only this morning, I admire your courage and your great contributions to your country. No one can take away from you the credit for all you have done. Now I am worried about your physical safety. I have a report that those in charge of the current activity offer you and your brother safe conduct out of the country if you resign. Have you heard this?

DIEM: No. [*pause*] You have my telephone number.

LODGE: Yes. If I can do anything for your physical safety, please call me.

DIEM: I am trying to reestablish order.[4]

Although the generals offered Diem and his brother safe passage, insurgents shot them to death. In the months and years after the coup, Ambassador Lodge and other Kennedy administration officials denied U.S. complicity.[5]

Yet Washington did have "a view" at 4:30 that morning, and Lodge was well informed. Less than forty-eight hours after his arrival in Saigon on August 21, 1963, as the newly appointed ambassador, Lodge, a Republican and vice presidential running mate for Richard Nixon in the 1960 election, reported to the State Department that several generals in the South Vietnamese army were planning a coup. U.S. officials saw the replacement of Diem as an attractive possibility. Washington especially wanted to end the family government Diem had styled by eliminating the influence of Diem's brother, Nhu, and Nhu's wife. At the State Department, Roger Hilsman, assistant secretary of state, Averell Harriman, under secretary of state for political affairs, Michael Forrestal, White House specialist on Vietnam from the National Security Council (NSC) staff, and George Ball, under secretary of state for economic affairs, met to draft a cable to Lodge. President Kennedy, spending the weekend in Hyannis Port, Massachusetts, approved by telephone the final draft, which sanctioned plans for a coup:

You may also tell appropriate military commanders we will give them direct support in any period of breakdown central government mechanism. . . . Ambassador and country team should urgently examine all possible alternative leadership and make detailed plans as to how we might bring about Diem's replacement if this should become necessary. . . . You will understand that we cannot from Washington give you detailed instructions as to how this operation should proceed, but you will also know we will back you to the hilt on actions you take to achieve our objective.[6]

Two days after the cable was sent, an acrimonious National Security Council meeting was held. Senior State Department officials, including Secretary of State Dean Rusk, favored the coup. General Maxwell Taylor, Secretary of Defense Robert McNamara, and CIA Director John McCone opposed it.[7] Kennedy, dismayed by the split, personally cabled the top two Americans "in country" (that is, in Vietnam) for their advice: General Paul Harkins, chief of the American command in Vietnam, and Ambassador Lodge. Harkins defended Diem and saw no reason for "crash approval" of the coup.[8] Lodge wrote back to Rusk on August 29, 1963:

We are launched on a course from which there is no respectable turning back: the overthrow of the Diem government. There is no turning back in part because U.S. prestige is already publicly committed to this end in large measure and will become more so as the facts leak out. In a more fundamental sense, there is no turning back because there is no possibility, in my view, that the war can be won under a Diem administration.[9]

Kennedy sided with the State Department and approved a cable from Rusk to Lodge saying that the United States "will support a coup which has a good chance of succeeding . . . but will not engage directly in joint coup planning."[10] Kennedy then sent his own private message to Lodge, giving his full support to the Rusk cable and promising that Washington would do everything possible "to help you conclude this operation successfully."[11] The fighting within the Kennedy administration turned out to be pointless; Lodge informed Washington on August 31, 1963, that the generals, fearing they could not take Saigon, had called off the coup.

Policy Stumbles

U.S. relations with Diem continued to deteriorate. The National Security Council met twice, on August 31 and September 4, without the president in attendance. It explored options but reached no conclusions about whether to re-establish relations with Diem.[12] Secretary of Defense McNamara suggested a temporary way out of the standstill: a fact-finding mission. After the first mission failed to clarify the situation, Kennedy sent McNamara himself and General Taylor.

In their report of October 2, McNamara and Taylor found the political problems for Diem "seething" and likely to erupt at any time. Still, they concluded that for the moment Diem was the only game in town, so "we should work with the Diem regime but not support it."[13] In the period between the two trips, the Kennedy administration stepped up pressure on Diem. It deferred a State Department program to finance imports to South Vietnam. In televised remarks, Kennedy himself asserted that a change in personnel might be needed. This was a veiled threat against Diem's brother, Nhu. Direct contact with Diem, cut off before the failed coup attempt, still was not renewed.[14] The Vietnamese generals, buoyed by the administration's signals against Diem, decided to try again.

The Second Coup

On October 2, Lieutenant Colonel Lucien Conein, a long-time CIA operative in Vietnam, learned from General Tran Van Don that the coup was back on track. The White House sent Lodge a cablegram drawn up from a National Security Council meeting on October 5, 1963:

President today approved recommendation that no initiative should now be taken to give any active covert encouragement to a coup. There should, however, be urgent covert effort with closest security, under broad guidance of Ambassador, to identify and build contacts with possible alternative leadership as and when it appears. Essential that this effort be totally secure and fully deniable and separated entirely from normal political analysis and reporting and other activities of country team. We repeat that this effort is not, repeat, not to be aimed at active promotion of coup but only at surveillance and readiness. In order to provide plausibility to denial suggest you and no one else in Embassy issue these instructions orally to Action Station Chief and hold him responsible to you alone for making appropriate contacts and reporting to you alone.[15]

Fear and suspicion mounted in Washington. CIA Director John McCone and National Security Adviser McGeorge Bundy worried in a cable to Lodge that General Don was a double agent from the Diem regime trying to trap the United States. Bundy suggested that Conein was too close to Don and should be replaced. Lodge defended Conein and discounted the possibility that Don was a provocateur. The ambassador argued that the United States should not "pour cold water" on the plot. "It seems at least an even bet," wrote Lodge, "that the next government would not bungle and stumble as much as the present one has."[16] At a Saigon airport on October 28, Diem and Lodge waited to depart for a ceremony dedicating a power plant. General Don came up to the two and pluckily took Lodge aside. Don asked whether Conein was still authorized to speak for the ambassador. Lodge said yes. Lodge asked about the timing of the coup. Don replied that the generals were not ready. Diem stood nearby looking like a bejeweled dowager in a dark alleyway.

The following day, Lodge told Washington that the United States was committed to the coup and it was too late to turn back. On October 30, General Harkins, irate about Lodge's stance, wired General Taylor: "I would suggest we try not to change horses too quickly. . . . The U.S. has been his [Diem's] mother superior and father confessor since he's been in office and he has leaned on us heavily."[17] McNamara and the Joint Chiefs of Staff worried about the diametrically opposed views of Lodge and Harkins. National Security Adviser Bundy, in an anxious cable to Lodge the same day, indicated that the United States could and should stop a coup if it looked as though the coup would fail. Lodge reiterated his position that the U.S. did not "have the power to delay or discourage a coup."[18] Bundy sternly disagreed but left it up to Lodge to judge the prospects for the coup's success.[19]

Lodge's gamble did not pay off. The next government, indeed the next succession of governments, bungled and stumbled as badly as had Diem. Within three months, Major General Nguyen Khanh deposed General Doung Van "Big" Minh, who had taken charge immediately after Diem's death. With the Diem regime gone, the Kennedy administration could have reconsidered the entire U.S. commitment to South Vietnam. But just twenty-one days after Diem's murder, Kennedy himself was killed in Dallas. The new Johnson administration pledged its support to the new South Vietnamese government and attempted to prop up the successive regimes. As each new South Vietnamese government came and went, with it went the opportunity for U.S. disengagement.[20]

Institutional Decisions

The plural presidency, not the president, made Kennedy's decision to involve the United States in the overthrow of Diem. Institutional dynamics allowed one person on the scene, Ambassador Lodge, to direct the presidential decision more than Kennedy himself did. Although Washington wanted to back a coup only if it would succeed, Lodge pushed the White House to support the coup that unfolded without firm calculations of success. The plural nature of the institution was evident in the network of individuals and offices that also participated: the national security adviser, the staff of the National Security Council, the secretary of state and other State Department officials, the secretary of defense, the Joint Chiefs of Staff, and the director of the CIA. Early in his term, Kennedy had let it be known that the State Department was too inert and the National Security Council too large to make foreign policy, even after Kennedy had whittled down the size of the NSC staff that had existed under Eisenhower. Yet both played major roles because of their ongoing institutional significance. The National Security Council was a well-established intersection for the other units. The White House also had a well-worn institutional bridge to the State Department, which drafted the early policy in support of the coup before contacting Kennedy at Hyannis Port.

The Carter shoe import decision makes clear that a president is not always crucial to a presidential decision. The Kennedy decision reveals that a president may be heavily involved but may be moved along by circumstances and advisers. Presidents do not necessarily have great control over matters just because the decisions affect important secret missions.

PRESIDENTIAL DECISION MAKING

Instead of taking the institutional perspective offered here, most people choose between two other approaches to presidential decision making. According to one, presidents' personalities are the key to their decision making; their personal habits, likes, and dislikes are the most important determinants of decisions. This perspective comes as close to matching the single executive image as possible. If the president is the single most powerful, unique, important, and visible national figure, then surely who he is must have a great deal to say about how he makes decisions. There is one lonely man.

According to an alternative approach, the salient factors are interpersonal relations among presidents and their key advisers. This perspective too meshes well with the single executive image. It often characterizes the president and his advisers as being isolated from the rest of the government. In this view, the president is only slightly less lonely.

Both approaches, however, are too simplistic. They do not adequately explain either the Carter or the Kennedy decision. Neither decision rested on the dealings of the presidents' immediate advisers alone. Each expanded well beyond those groups. Moreover, because so many people contributed to the decisions, the importance of the presidents' personalities appears muffled. The two approaches neglect the fact that twentieth-century presidents are part of a large institution specifically established to help them make decisions. Alfred de Grazia commented on the gap between the image of a single executive making tough decisions and modern presidents' actions:

Apart from the fact that the President *need* take no decision himself, there is the question of how many presidents have made up their minds alone how many times, and whether when such occurred a feeling of loneliness was imparted. . . . With a million-dollar income, in cash and kind, and a huge staff and retinue, the President need be neither lonely nor hardworking. If he wishes to drive himself into a state of fatigue and desperation from working, he may of course do so. But he has less excuse for so doing than, let us say, the small businessman, the writer, the newspaper editor.[21]

The remainder of the chapter provides an answer to de Grazia's not-so-rhetorical question about how lonely presidents truly are when they make decisions. Four ingredients in presidential decision

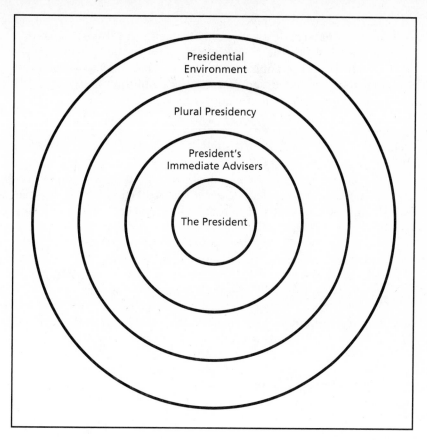

Figure 7.1 Circles of Decision Making

making are analyzed: the presidential environment, the plural presidency, presidents' immediate advisers, and presidents themselves. The concentric circles shown in Figure 7.1 depict their interrelationship. The outermost circle is the environment within which the presidency operates: the economy, the world situation, public expectations, group demands, congressional, bureaucratic, and judicial actions, and the like. The second circle is the plural presidency: the diverse and relatively autonomous offices and officers of the presidential institution. The third circle is the group dynamics among presidents and their immediate advisers: how they relate to one another. The innermost circle represents presidents as individuals: their personalities, abilities to deal with other people, and outlooks on the world. Each circle influences presidential decisions. Influence also radiates from one circle to another. Although the inner two circles may look most central, they cannot be detached from the institution or the environment. As Hugh Heclo observes, "What that familiar face ponders in the Oval Office is likely to be a series of conversations with advisers or a few pages of paper containing several options. These represent the last distillates produced by immense rivers of information flowing from sources—and condensed in ways—about which the president knows little."[22] The embedding of presidents and their immediate advisers in the institution makes it difficult for one person, even the president, to make up his mind alone.

THE PRESIDENTIAL ENVIRONMENT

The environment is the social, economic, cultural, and political times within which presidential decisions are made. The single executive image assures that presidents make decisions in at least three environments: (1) the policy environment, (2) the interinstitutional environment, and (3) the group environment. As singularly powerful officials, presidents are actively engaged in making decisions on foreign, military, domestic, and economic policy (to name the broadest categories). The public expects presidents to solve numerous problems within and across each one of those areas in the *policy* environment. In attempting to take charge of the government, presidents face a variety of institutions in the *interinstitutional* environment: the Congress, the executive branch, the courts, and state and local governments. In attempting to set a national agenda, presidents step into the *group* environment, where they encounter the desires and the demands of organized interest groups, businesses, and attentive citizens.

The need to operate in multiple environments traps presidents in the central irony of the presidency: the single executive image creates a need for the plural presidency. Because of the standards set by the single executive image, the environments present circumstances that are impossible for presidents to avoid. The image demands that presidents be fast dancers. They must be everywhere at once, be all things to all people, and have plans to solve all pressing and not-so-pressing national problems. The demands are so great, however, that the president alone or with his immediate advisers cannot do the dance with grace and surefootedness. The plural presidency rescues presidents. Built into the institution are offices and procedures to take account of the three environments.

The plural presidency filters policy information and goals for presidents. The National Security Council, the Office of Special Trade Representative, and the Economic Policy Group served to frame Carter's trade options. Moreover, the plural presidency has long-standing relations with other institutions. The well-established institutional connection between the State Department and the presidency provided the origins of several sweeping presidential policies—the Marshall Plan, NATO, and the Truman Doctrine—as well as the Diem coup, a coup against the premier of Iran in 1953, and a coup against the president of Guatemala in 1954. The plural presidency also adjusts to group demands. Factions among industry, labor, and consumer groups in the White House precipitated the Economic Policy Group's initial failure to discuss the orderly marketing agreements. Consequently, features of the environment become features of the plural presidency. The chaos on the outside finds its way inside.

THE PLURAL PRESIDENCY

Presidents, burdened with the requirements of the single executive image, use the plural presidency as their primary decision-making apparatus. Presidential decision making raises four separate but related questions:

1. Who makes the decisions? This question addresses how many people and units are involved, and their specialties and jurisdictions.

2. How are decisions made? This question pertains to the information the decision makers gather, the goals they set, and how they go about achieving their goals.

3. What is the substance of the decision? This question asks about the specific policy issue at stake, the complexity of the issue, and its relationship to other issues. It also asks about the specific policy solution offered, its complexity, and its relationship to other solutions.

4. Will the decision work? This question focuses on whether other political institutions, organized groups, and the public at large are likely to support the decision, their stake in the issue, and the degree of their involvement.

The plural nature, or plurality, of the presidency arises in its answers to these questions. Plurality, of course, is equated with such terms as *many, numerous,* and *multitude.* The plurality of the presidency involves the many people in and out of the White House who make presidential decisions in numerous ad hoc ways. The plurality also encompasses the multiple policy problems and various institutional and group demands confronting presidential decision makers. The plurality, then, is found both in the internal workings of the institution (as numerous people pursue numerous options) and in its relations with the external environment (in the numbers of policy issues, government institutions, and organized groups).

Internal Plurality

Two manifestations of internal plurality are decentralized organization and ambiguous decision processes, which affect how the many offices and officers within the institution interact to make decisions. Internal plurality results from decentralization because many people influence any given decision (the "who" question). Internal plurality emerges from ambiguous decision processes when decision makers have few agreed-upon ways of making a decision (the "how" question).

Decentralized Organization.   Internal plurality originates in the decentralized structure of the presidency. In a decentralized organization there is a horizontal dispersion of power, rather than a vertical accumulation of power. Some hierarchy does exist in the presidency (the president is in the top position), but the hierarchy is challenged by the presence of numerous, relatively independent, and equally powerful offices that compete for the president's attention. The diffusion of power is heightened by the fact that the institution does not merely encompass offices in the White House. It also includes offices and individuals that are close satellites to the White House, such as top department officials, the Joint Chiefs of Staff, and the Central Intelligence Agency.

Rival baronies among offices in the Carter White House and in the departments outside the White House fought over the shoes. Although Kennedy's decision about the Diem coup was secret, it involved no fewer than six units or representatives of units either within the White House or closely connected to it: the national security adviser, the National Security Council, the secretary of state, the secretary of defense, the director of the Central Intelligence Agency, and the Joint Chiefs of Staff. The Kennedy administration also firmly relied on a division of labor between its "in country" and "at home" teams, the latter dependent on the knowledge of the former. Even the fact-finding missions by "at home" team members did not tether the free hand given Ambassador Lodge "in country." A president begins to look like the beleaguered "old woman who lived in a shoe" who does not know what to do with all of the units, all of their employees, and all of their efforts.

Organizations also run on routines. According to political scientist Graham Allison, "Routines allow large numbers of ordinary individuals to deal with numerous instances, day after day, without much thought."[23] After only one day in office, Carter received the National Security Council's memo on shoe imports. The NSC staff, some of whom were career employees, had procedures to analyze problems and convey information to whoever was president. Routines of a different sort initiated U.S. involvement in the Diem coup. Wheels whirling in the State Department set in motion the American response when Kennedy was in Hyannis Port, Secretary of State Rusk was in New York, and Defense Secretary McNamara and CIA Director McCone were on vacation. Decentralization makes it difficult for an individual, even the head of the institution, to be singled out in decision making.

Ambiguous Decision Processes. Internal plurality expands as numerous decision processes are established among an organization's many units. Decentralization means that coordination often is lacking and that one part of the institution may not know what another is doing. The result is unclear approaches to decision making that may vary sharply from one situation to another. But despite the ambiguity, decisions are made. There are four types of ambiguity: informational, goal, operational, and participatory.

Informational ambiguity occurs when White House decision makers do not have complete information about situations in the environments. The Carter administration gave little attention to how the shoe import decision would affect other trade arrangements. The Kennedy people, including Ambassador Lodge, were always at least partly in the dark about the plans of the Vietnamese generals.

Goal ambiguity arises when people in the presidential institution do not know what they want or have several conflicting goals. It arises from disagreements about how to proceed. Battle lines within the Carter White House blurred the identity of the problem. Was it too many foreign shoes? the high price of shoes? the stagnation of American industries? the need to safeguard friendly foreign trade relations? Decision makers in the White House prevented Carter from simply implementing his campaign pledge for free trade. An especially clear-cut instance of goal ambiguity was the Kennedy administration's "have your cake and eat it too" position with respect to Diem. On several occasions, the official U.S. position on the Diem coup was to help only if the coup succeeded or to engage in covert efforts to "identify and build contacts with possible alternative leadership" but not actively to encourage the coup.

Operational ambiguity occurs when White House decision makers are unclear about who is in charge of the operation and how all efforts fit together. Whether the Office of Special Trade Representative or the Economic Policy Group was in charge of Carter's shoe import policy was muddled, yet it was clear that the Domestic Policy Group was *not* in on the action even though it had information about orderly marketing agreements that would have expedited a decision. The shoe import issue was framed as an economic and trade issue, not as a domestic issue. In the Kennedy operation, the relations between political and military units were unclear. Although General Harkins, U.S. commander in Vietnam, was consulted, the military's views were never fully incorporated into the decision-making process. The State Department, rather than the Pentagon, served as the primary information conduit because the Diem problem was perceived as a political problem. As a result, the military ramifications of the political decision were left largely unexamined. In some instances, operational ambiguity excludes certain units from decision making because of the way the problem is framed, even though the excluded units may have relevant expertise.

Participatory ambiguity arises when participants are not clear about who will join in the decision at what time and for how long. People's limited awareness of how the presidential institution operates prompts fluid participation. Carter's domestic staff could have played a major role in the shoe import decision but did not. Participation in the Diem decision also was fluid. Although the State Department initiated the proceedings, the national security adviser, CIA director, members of the National Security Council, and several experts on Vietnam entered and exited the decision process.

External Plurality

Two manifestations of external plurality—policy complexity and political fragmentation—connect the presidency to its environment. External plurality from policy complexity is evident in the many facets of the policy issue at hand (the "what" question). External plurality arises from political fragmentation when the various actors in the political system confront presidents' decisions and make it difficult for the president to get what he wants (the "will" question).

Policy Complexity. The single executive image calls for presidential decisions on a mass of issues, events, and conditions in the policy environment. The result is policy complexity in the plural presidency. Policy complexity stems from the number of policy proposals the presidency makes across issues, events, and conditions and from the conflicts among proposals.

Both the shoe import decision and the Diem coup decision reveal this complexity. The debate over import quotas intertwined domestic policy, economic policy, and foreign policy. A decision to help the shoe industry could have been a decision to harm friendly ties with other nations, anger consumers, and boost inflation. Domestic, foreign, and economic units in the White House were involved in the debate. The inability of the Kennedy people to decide what their options were after the first coup attempt revealed the complexity of the Diem affair. Fact-finding missions became substitutes for policy. In addition, Kennedy and Carter were busy making dozens of other decisions while the Diem coup and shoe import issue loomed.

Political Fragmentation. *Political fragmentation* refers to the dispersion of power throughout American society and government, rather than its concentration in the hands of a few. The dispersion results in two sorts of political fragmentation that further intensify the external plurality: group fragmentation and government fragmentation. Group fragmentation arises from the plethora of social, economic, and political groups (or fragments) in the United States and from the conflicts within and among them. These politically interested groups buffet the plural presidency. They identify policy problems and push for specific solutions. Various presidential offices recognize the importance of various groups and propose numerous policy initiatives, keeping the needs of "their" groups in mind. They also balance group demands with opinions from the larger public.

Group fragmentation confronted the Carter decision makers. Carter's shoe import decision was made within the White House, but the White House doors were always open. Pressure from interests outside the government—the AFL-CIO, the American Footwear Industries Association, the Volume Retailers Association—matched pressure from government departments outside the White House. In many ways, the Economic Policy Group encapsulated the fragmentation within the government. The interests of the State Department were not those of the Commerce Department; nor were the Commerce Department's interests those of the Labor Department. Yet the Economic Policy Group housed all. Carter's decision to adopt orderly marketing agreements was a compromise designed to upset as few groups as possible.

Government fragmentation occurs because so many institutions of government divide and share power. It reflects the constitutional framers' scheme of separation of powers, checks and balances, and federalism. The framers did not make life easy for presidents. Each fragment—the courts, the Congress, the executive departments and agencies, and state and local governments—competes with the presidency for policy success and public attention. Fragmented government presents the presidency with two alternate courses of action. One is a response to the overlap between the branches of government and to the system of checks and balances. The other is a response to the branches' separation from one another. In instances of overlap, the presidency must take into account the preferences of the other branches and develop strategies accordingly. In instances where one branch is separated from another, the presidency can proceed independently. Government fragmentation allowed the Kennedy decision to go forward without legislative intrusion. Congress did not fully know of Kennedy administration involvement in the Diem coup until the publication of the *Pentagon Papers,* a secret documentary history of the Vietnam War, leaked in 1973. Instead of dealing with the American Congress, the Kennedy people obliged the desires of South Vietnamese generals who pushed the United States along a rutted road to Saigon. Decentralized organization, ambiguous decision processes, policy complexity, and political fragmentation—make it difficult for a president to control the activities of the presidency's many offices and people. Presidents use the plural presidency to keep the demands of the single executive image in control. But presidents often find that the plural presidency itself is out of control.

PRESIDENTS' IMMEDIATE ADVISERS

Presidents work with a small group—no more than two dozen advisers. These immediate advisers, like the president they serve, work within the confines of the plural presidency. As Figure 7.1 (page 197) shows, their circle operates within the larger concentric circle of the plural presidency; it is not separate from that larger circle. Presidents use their immediate advisers to run interference for them in the plural presidency. The top aides winnow information and policy proposals received from the various offices of the institution and filter them, along with their own views, to the president. But the advisers do not work outside of the plural presidency; indeed, many of them head the very offices of the plural presidency.

Research on presidential decision making often focuses on the president's immediate advisers and the interpersonal networks within the group. Such attention to the president's immediate advisers, however, is misleading for two reasons. First, there is no *one* group of immediate advisers. Many groups form for particular policies and on specific occasions. Nixon and Kissinger constituted the "group" who planned the secret bombing of Cambodia. Kennedy and fourteen top advisers planned the American response to the Cuban missile crisis. But only in the most general sense did Kennedy make his Diem coup decision with a group of immediate advisers. Although one can identify such a group, each member had such institutional baggage that the intimacy of the group seems lost. Furthermore, there were actually several groups that shifted in composition as people attended and failed to attend key meetings and as plans shifted from the State Department to the National Security Council and back again. Carter's shoe import decision involved no small group of top advisers. Many people in many units helped make the decision. Some people do have much greater contact with a president than others: Sherman Adams with Eisenhower, H. R. Haldeman with Nixon, John Sununu with Bush. Yet the greater the demands on the institution, the more likely are others to join these top people in making presidential decisions.

Second, there are two key dimensions to understanding the dynamics among presidents and their advisers: access to presidents and competition among advisers. Presidents grant, restrict, and deny access to advisers. The advisers are socially bound by a common goal: to serve the chief executive. Each shares a personal commitment to an individual and not necessarily to the Constitution, the government, or the American people. The primary qualifications for the advisers' jobs are loyalty and dependability.

Cohesiveness may develop, accentuated by the similar backgrounds of many of the advisers. They are typically people the president has worked with before—during the campaign, in a previous office, or as a friend. They are most often white middle-aged professional men with middle to upper incomes and good educations. They often spend considerable time together as they map presidential strategies.

Yet cohesiveness does not fully describe the top advisers' interactions. White House advisers are not merely servants of the president. They are competitors with one another. Advisers often are hired because they are good at something others are not. Conflict is inevitable; sometimes it is encouraged. They jockey for access, representing different units with different outlooks both in and out of the White House. As the Kennedy example makes clear, key advisers are not found only within the White House. They include relevant department secretaries and agency heads who protect their own constituencies and viewpoints. Instead of being a tightly knit group that loyally follows presidential wishes, they are a loosely arrayed collection of individuals. Advisers develop contacts with people outside the White House—members of Congress, reporters, bureaucrats—to secure their positions inside the White House. During final negotiations on the Clear Air Act of 1990, William Reilly, head of the Environmental Protection Agency, leaked the contents of proposals on acid rain to environmental groups in order to prevent Bush's chief of staff John Sununu from derailing the plan.[24] Staff members work on behalf of presidents but also on behalf of themselves and their units. The combination of access and competition makes presidents' top advisers much less unified and much more a part of the plural presidency than one might imagine.

Access to the President

"Power in Washington is measured by a stern gauge: The direct proportion of access to the President, for the asset of the realm is information that flows only from the President," wrote Jack Valenti, a close adviser to President Johnson. "If you were to fluoroscope the brain and conscience of any top official within the government," he continued, "you would be able to chart the flight of agony caused by lost intimacy with the President, or derail of access to him."[25] Two questions can be raised about presidential access. How do advisers get access? Loyalty is one of the principal mechanisms by which advisers attempt to secure access. And what are the consequences of a president's access to a small group of top advisers? The president and this small group may become isolated from other individuals and other political goings-on.

Loyalty in Practice. Loyalty is in the eye of the beholder: the president. For instance, in September 1972, John Dean, Nixon's White House counsel, was brought into the inner circle of Nixon, White House Chief of Staff H. R. Haldeman, and chief domestic adviser John Ehrlichman. Dean quickly demonstrated his loyalty by practicing the value most admired by the group: toughness. Nixon wrote to Haldeman that Dean "had the kind of steel and really mean instinct that we needed."[26] But in March 1973, as the Watergate conspiracy began to unravel, Dean went to federal prosecutors to tell what he knew of the cover-up. Haldeman observed, "Dean shifted roles from one of the protectors of the President to the protector of himself."[27] In Nixon's mind, Dean was disloyal; he was shunned from the inner circle and asked to resign. Nixon told Ehrlichman, "You certainly can't risk his bouncing around here, playing his little game, tip-toeing through the files gathering ammunition."[28]

Advisers often demonstrate their loyalty by heartily agreeing with presidents, flattering them, or sheltering them from bad news. Woodrow Wilson's lone top aide, Colonel Edward House, admitted that he constantly praised the president. Once he told Wilson that he was the "one hope left to this torn and distracted world. Without your leadership, God alone knows how long we will wander in the darkness."[29] Henry Kissinger used flattery constantly in his dealings with Richard Nixon. At his first formal White House reception, Kissinger instinctively began to exalt the president, prompting Mrs. Nixon to lean over to her husband and ask, "Haven't you seen through him yet?"[30] Moreover, Gerald Ford remarked:

Few people, with the possible exception of his wife, will ever tell a President that he is a fool. There's a majesty to the office that inhibits even your closest friends from saying what is really on their minds. They won't tell you that you just made a lousy speech or bungled a chance to get your point across. . . . You can tell them you want the blunt truth; you can leave instructions on every bulletin board, but the guarded responses you get never vary.[31]

Isolation. Top advisers' deference and loyalty to the president may isolate these White House decision makers from outside political realities. Together the president and his top advisers may establish a way of looking at things that overlooks contradictory information and fails to acknowledge other viewpoints. Irving Janis observed that the isolation may prompt *groupthink,* or excessive cohesiveness in a group whose members like each other too much and think too much alike.[32] Janis discussed three symptoms of groupthink—each one a product of excessive cohesiveness:

1. The group overestimates its ability to succeed. It is overly optimistic and willing to take extreme risks. It believes it is inherently correct and morally right.

2. Close-mindedness plagues the group. It discounts the validity of outside information and stereotypes its opponents.

3. The group pressures its members toward uniformity. Deviance and opposition to the group's course are censored.

Excessive cohesiveness prevents the group from thoroughly researching a problem and making a realistic appraisal of alternative courses of action. The group fails to examine the risks of the option chosen and does not develop contingency plans. As a result, it blindly chooses a policy option that is doomed to failure. Janis observed groupthink during the Truman administration's decision to invade North Korea, Kennedy's handling of the Bay of Pigs invasion, Johnson's escalation of the Vietnam War, and Nixon's cover-up following the Watergate break-in.

Janis's analysis, however, is incomplete. Much of the evidence presented for groupthink is missing the importance of the presidential institution. The Truman, Kennedy, Johnson, and even Nixon decisions are better understood as instances of institution-work rather than as groupthink. Janis painted Nixon's Watergate decisions most starkly, as the private, personal exercises of an intensely cohesive group: a trio consisting of Haldeman, Ehrlichman, and Nixon— or a quartet if Dean is included.

The Watergate episode involved the cover-up of White House and Committee to Reelect the President (CRP; Nixon's re-election committee) involvement in the June 17, 1972, break-in of Democratic National Committee headquarters, located at the Watergate hotel and office complex in Washington, D.C. Two CRP employees, E. Howard Hunt and G. Gordon Liddy, both former White House staff members, supervised the break-in carried out by five others on the CRP payroll. Ehrlichman and Dean requested that hush money be given to and attorneys' fees be paid for Liddy, Hunt, and the five burglars so they would not reveal CRP involvement in the espionage. Nixon and Haldeman attempted to derail the FBI investigation of the break-in by suggesting that it would compromise secret CIA missions undertaken during the Bay of Pigs invasion. (Several of the burglars were expatriated Cubans.) Nixon, Haldeman, Ehrlichman, Dean, and John Mitchell (former attorney general and CRP chairman) imposed a "stonewall" strategy that denied the involvement of White House people in the break-in.[33]

Nixon's Watergate decisions, however, were not solely the result of conversations within the ingroup, as Janis proclaimed.[34] People at several levels of the White House staff, the Justice Department, the FBI, the CIA, and the Committee to Reelect participated in the planning of the break-in, in the cover-up, and in the disintegration of the cover-up. Many people out of the inner presidential loop had considerable influence on the decisions of the Nixon group. These second-level White House or CRP staff members—Jeb Magruder, Hugh Sloan, Gordon Strachan, Dwight Chapin, Alexander Butterfield, Frederick LaRue, L. Patrick Gray, and others—initially carried out plans to protect the stonewall. Later, each sought to protect himself from criminal prosecution. For instance, Hugh Sloan, treasurer for the Committee to Reelect and former White House aide, initially agreed to lie about the amount of money paid to Liddy for the Watergate job and related dirty tricks but then changed his mind. He resigned from his post rather than perjure himself before a grand jury investigating the break-in. Sloan's decision placed pressure on others, notably Magruder, campaign chief of staff and former White House aide.

The features that Janis pointed to—overestimation of success, close-mindedness, pressure toward uniformity—perhaps at work among Nixon, Haldeman, and Ehrlichman, were overwhelmed by the decentralized organization, ambiguous decision processes, policy complexity, and political fragmentation of the plural presidency. No matter how many instructions came from the top, the White House organization remained decentralized. The Nixon group never fully controlled the FBI even though the Nixon people relied on the bureau as a White House satellite. L. Patrick Gray, acting FBI director, zig-zagged between support and betrayal of the cover-up. Gray aided the cover-up several times by passing documents to John Dean and destroying other documents from Howard Hunt's White House safe. Later, however, Gray admitted these actions, revealed that Dean had lied about Hunt's connection to the White House, and told of others' illegal activities.

Ambiguity also vexed the Nixon White House. Immediately after the break-in the goal of the participants was unequivocal: to ensure Nixon's re-election. Yet within months, even before the election, participants' goals became increasingly ambiguous: to protect Nixon? to protect themselves? to tell the truth? The cover-up remained intact from June to October 1972. Between November 1972 and February 1973, it began to crumble; in March it collapsed. In March and April 1973, John Dean, James McCord (one of the burglars), and Jeb Magruder began to cooperate with Watergate prosecutors and discuss the involvement of numerous people. Participation was notably fluid. Many people were involved on many different levels undertaking many different tasks—political espionage, laundering campaign funds, paying hush money, masking the identities of the burglars, concealing the steps of White House aides. No matter how cohesive the Nixon advisory group was, it could not keep in line the "marginal" players or predict who might do what when the cover-up unraveled. There would be, as Nixon himself said, "minefields down the road."[35]

Nixon and Haldeman tried to use policy complexity to their advantage with their Bay of Pigs smoke screen. They sought to intertwine Cuba policy, CIA covert operations, and domestic surveillance in order to justify why the FBI should not investigate the break-in. But the Nixon group never adequately considered the government fragmentation that allowed the courts, Congress, and the press to investigate the matter in ways the White House could not direct.

Nixon attempted to hide behind claims of executive privilege, but this action made the members of the other institutions all the more suspicious.[36]

The isolation of presidents and their top advisers, then, should not be exaggerated. The decisions of even the most cohesive inner group cannot be divorced from the White House institution. Orders given from on high must be carried out below. When they are not, the cohesiveness of the inner group may be shattered. Disclosures by Dean, Magruder, and others forced Nixon to fire long-time aides and friends Haldeman and Ehrlichman. Nixon scrawled a note to himself on April 15, 1973, "I'm not going to die for Ehrlichman."[37] The group disintegrated from without.

Competitive Advisers

As much as loyalty regulates access to presidents, competition among advisers also directs presidents' decisions. The level of competition is affected by issue networks and influence networks.[38]

Issue Networks. Issue networks are groups of like-minded people who share the same issue preferences. John Kessel interviewed top aides in the Nixon, Carter, and Reagan White Houses. In the Carter White House, he found four different issue networks: (1) a liberal group; (2) a moderate group; (3) a hybrid group that was liberal on civil rights and ranged from conservative to moderate on the economy, from moderate to liberal on social welfare; and (4) a final "group" of individuals who could not be classified with the others. Such divergence could have contributed to the range of opinions on shoe import quotas. By contrast, Reagan's immediate advisers made up a single-issue network: a large group of conservatives committed to Reagan's social and economic conservatism.

Issue networks have important implications for White House decisions. The large degree of disagreement among the members of the Carter issue networks stirred competition over policy directions, making a coherent policy difficult. During Reagan's first term, when the White House was strongly unified on the desire to cut taxes and the budget, competitiveness over policy goals was minimal. The Nixon staff's issue networks were most cohesive in economic policy and civil rights. Table 7.1 depicts the differences among Nixon's, Carter's, and Reagan's immediate advisers.

Influence Networks. Another way to judge the competitiveness among presidents' top advisers is to examine the influence they have with one another and with the president. This internal influence derives primarily from respect and expertise. For instance, John Kessel found that in the Carter White House, staffers acknowledged the expertise of National Security Adviser Zbigniew Brzezinski but few respected him. During Reagan's first term, Chief of Staff James Baker

Table 7.1 Ideological Closeness of Three White House Staffs

Policy area	Nixon	Carter	Reagan
International involvement	3.4	4.1	2.7
Economic management	2.0	3.1	1.3
Social welfare	3.3	3.6	1.9
Civil liberties	2.2	5.1	1.4
Agriculture	2.8	4.0	2.1

Note: Median issue positions were based on scores ranging from 1.0 (conservative position) to 7.0 (liberal position). Results were obtained from interviews of Nixon's domestic policy council. Carter's senior staff members serving from 1977 to 1980, and Reagan's senior staff members serving between 1981 and 1983.

Source: Adapted from John H. Kessel, "The Structure of the Reagan White House," *American Journal of Political Science* 28 (May 1984): 234. Used by permission of the author and the University of Texas Press.

was most respected among the Reagan aides, and David Stockman, director of the Office of Management and Budget, was considered best informed. Table 7.2 provides the details of Kessel's findings.

External influence also is important. In competition with other advisers, aides claim outside political clout to add weight to their arguments. Defense Secretary Caspar Weinberger knew this in a showdown over the defense budget with OMB Director David Stockman in August 1981—an encounter that Stockman likened to the gunfight at the OK Corral.[39] Stockman discovered that a mistake had been made in the calculation of Defense Department budget figures

Table 7.2 Influence Exerted by White House Aides, Carter and Reagan

Unit	Carter head	Overall influence score	Reagan head	Influence score
National Security Council	Brzezinski	136	Clark	268[1]
Legislative Liaison	Moore	15[1]	Duberstein	125
Domestic Policy Staff/OPD	Eizenstat	343	Harper	169
OMB	McIntyre	90	Stockman	262[1]
Council of Economic Advisers	Schultze	102	Weidenbaum	1
Press Office	Powell	251	Gergen	84
Public Liaison	Wexler	138	Dole	0

1. Estimated values. Questions on influence were not asked of the individual, and so scores are based on the answers of others.

Note: Influence evaluated in answers to questions regarding the respect, expertise, position, and sanctions that individuals have in the eyes of other staff. Drawn from interviews of Carter's senior staff members who served from 1977 to 1980 and Reagan's senior staff members who served between 1981 and 1983.

Source: Adapted from John H. Kessel, "The Structure of the Reagan White House," *American Journal of Political Science* 28 (May 1984): 250. Used by permission of the author and the University of Texas Press.

in early February. Because the wrong base figures had been used, the five-year defense budget totaled $1.46 trillion—a 10 percent increase in real growth rather than the 5 percent increase on which Reagan had campaigned (real growth is the amount of money available after the effects of inflation have been removed). Stockman recognized that a huge budget deficit, not the balanced budget Reagan hoped to achieve, would result. Weinberger, a former OMB director under Nixon who had earned the nickname "Cap the Knife," refused to cut the Defense Department budget as much as Stockman thought it should be cut, and he had the collective support of the Defense Department, the separate support of the Army, Navy, Air Force, and Marines, and the backing of large defense industries.

In a meeting with Reagan and Stockman, Weinberger proposed an $8 billion reduction. Stockman wanted at least $23 billion cut. Reagan scribbled out three figures for three years. "How about $2, $5, and $6 [billion] over three years?" he inquired. "That would give us $13 billion in savings." Weinberger replied, "If that's your decision, sir, we'll find some way to manage."[40]

James Baker said of Weinberger, "He doesn't even think he's part of the administration."[41] It was to Weinberger's advantage to think that way. Obviously an aide cannot be too freewheeling or too independent because the doors to the Oval Office may swing shut. There is, however, a fair amount of latitude. The president's immediate advisers are creatures of the institution within which they work. Caspar Weinberger's ability to maintain hefty Defense Department budgets was less the result of his own ingenuity than a reflection of his institutional role as secretary of defense. Weinberger played two very different roles, depending on the units he served in the institution and the changing environments within which he acted. In 1981, Cap the Knife was long gone.

PRESIDENTS AND THEIR PERSONALITIES

People often assume that one of the most important ingredients, if not the most important ingredient, in presidents' decisions is their personalities. People find it intriguing to "psychoanalyze" presidents and love to gossip about their personal quirks: Truman's temper, Johnson's gruffness, Nixon's trickery, Reagan's friendliness. The single executive image writes much of this temptation into the body politic. The image commands that presidents act alone and thus makes presidents' personal styles important. When an office is held by one individual, it is tempting to think of the individual's personality (the innermost circle on Figure 7.1) as the key to his or her decisions. Yet presidents, like their advisers, are institutional creatures. Many times, they act in ways that do not reflect who they are or their dominant personality traits.

Dimensions of Personality

Political scientist James David Barber is the leading proponent of the importance of personality in presidential decision making. He argues that a president's (or anyone's) personality is largely determined by "character," the way in which he generally orients himself toward life.[42] Character develops in childhood as the individual interacts with parents, siblings, other relatives, and friends. There are two dimensions to character: activity and affect. *Activity* involves the level of energy the individual invests in life. How active is the individual? How readily does he participate? How often does he take the initiative? Activity can be arrayed along a continuum ranging from active to passive. According to Barber, Jimmy Carter relished being personally involved in White House decisions. He himself worked on the White House swimming pool schedule. Calvin Coolidge, in contrast, took two-hour naps in the afternoon after getting twelve hours of sleep at night. Carter would be considered active, Coolidge passive.

Affect, the second dimension, involves how the president feels about life. Does he enjoy life? Does he like himself and others around him? Is he happy about his job, his friends, his personal life? The affect dimension ranges from positive to negative. Jimmy Carter, after being in office ten months, was happy with his job and realistic about his accomplishments. He observed:

I am at ease. When we have difficulties, I don't withdraw. I am not paranoid. I recognize that some of the controversy and difficulties and failures are because of the ambitious nature of some of our undertakings. There has never been an evening when I went to bed that I didn't look forward to the next day.[43]

By contrast, two weeks after Richard Nixon's resignation from office, he remarked to one of his former staffers:

You see, don't you, you've got to be tough. You can't break, my boy, even when you know there's nothing left. You can't admit, even to yourself, that it is gone. Now, some people we both know think that you go stand in the middle of the bullring and cry, "mea culpa, mea culpa," while the crowd is hissing and booing and spitting on you. But a man doesn't cry. . . . I don't cry. You don't cry.[44]

Carter's outlook would be considered positive, Nixon's decidedly negative.

Barber maintains that the combination of the two dimensions results in four personality types: active-positive, passive-positive, active-negative, passive-negative (see Figure 7.2):

> *Active-Positive:* Congruence between action and affect exists. The individual has high self-esteem, optimism, and confidence, enjoys work, and is successful in relation to the environment. The person is adaptive.

Affect	Activity	
	Active	**Passive**
Positive	*Active-Positive* Franklin Roosevelt Harry Truman John Kennedy Gerald Ford Jimmy Carter George Bush	*Passive-Positive* William Taft Warren Harding Ronald Reagan
Negative	*Active-Negative* Woodrow Wilson Herbert Hoover Lyndon Johnson Richard Nixon	*Passive-Negative* Calvin Coolidge Dwight Eisenhower

Figure 7.2   Personality Types of Recent Presidents

[*Source:* Adapted from James David Barber, *The Presidential Character,* 4th ed. (Englewood Cliffs, N.J.: Prentice-Hall, 1992). Used by permission of the author.]

Active-Negative: A contradiction between intense effort and low personal reward occurs. The individual has low self-esteem, pessimism, and an aggressive stance toward the environment. The person attempts to be very active to compensate for internal feelings of inadequacy. The person is compulsive.

Passive-Positive: The individual seeks affection, wants to be liked, goes along with what others want rather than taking the initiative. He has low self-esteem, for which he tries to compensate by being agreeable and superficially optimistic. The person is compliant.

Passive-Negative: The person's effort is dictated by a sense of duty rather than enjoyment of the task. He emphasizes principles and procedures, gives service to compensate for low self-esteem, and avoids conflict. He reacts rather than initiates. The person is withdrawn.

Barber envisions the four categories as tendencies in personalities not as wooden boxes into which the presidents are entombed. He does believe, however, that each president is predominantly one type. Barber maintains that active-positive people—Franklin Roosevelt, Truman, Kennedy, Ford, Carter, and Bush—are best suited to be president. They are self-confident, open to new experiences, and willing to admit their mistakes. They are flexible and meet challenges with pragmatism and compromise. Barber asserts that passive-positive presidents, such as Reagan, and passive-negative presidents, such as Eisenhower, are much less likely to make bold efforts and instead react to the efforts of others. Active-negative individuals—Wilson, Hoover, Johnson, Nixon—Barber believes, are doomed to cause major policy fiascoes. Driven to succeed at all costs, they become increasingly rigid and cannot extricate themselves when a challenge turns into a crisis. Wilson's fight for the League of Nations, Hoover's response to the Great Depression, Johnson's escalation in Vietnam, and Nixon's cover-up of Watergate are stories of tragic figures who, according to Barber, should never have been president.

Pitfalls of Personality Studies

Barber and other personality analysts face two pitfalls: (1) questions of interpretation and (2) reductionism—attributing all outcomes to a single cause.

Questions of Interpretation. An episode of a popular 1970s British television show, "Monty Python's Flying Circus," played with the mystery that clings to personality. In a cartoon, a winged angel attempts to uncover why Leonardo's Mona Lisa smiles in her soft, whimsical way. The angel flies around Mona and with a paint brush carefully draws perforation lines at the top of the lady's head. The angel proceeds to open her head as if it were the lid to a cigarette box. To the angel's astonishment, out fly several colorful butterflies. The angel's technique, no matter how seductive, is unavailable to human beings. People never can be sure what is going on in someone's head. The person herself may not have it figured out. Analysts must rely on their own interpretations. The story told about personality is only as good as the interpretation used to tell it.

Because there are no universal standards of evidence and inference in personality studies, no interpretation can be confirmed. Interpretations of presidents' personalities vary. For instance, Fred Greenstein disputes Barber's characterization of Eisenhower as passive. According to Greenstein, Eisenhower intentionally appeared reticent in public so he could avoid pressure from reporters and politicians. Instead, he worked energetically behind the scenes.[45]

Barber's categorizations of Carter and Kennedy also are open to question. Despite Carter's positive outlook quoted above, many of those who worked around him commented on his compulsive work habits and moralistic stands. Such comments might suggest that he was more negative than positive. To confuse matters still more, in the shoe import decision, Carter exhibits neither a compulsive approach (with his finger in the decision-making process at every step) nor a moralistic stand. Which piece of evidence does the analyst weigh most heavily? Barber also types Kennedy as an active-positive. Yet it is unclear how Kennedy's energetic enthusiasm for life guided decisions about the Diem coup.

Even if there is solid agreement that a president is properly typed, there is no agreement about what effect personality has. No one personality type seems to be immune from making "bad" decisions or presiding over "bad" times. During the term of active-positive George Bush, the nation's economy registered its worst performance of the entire post–World War II period.[46] Although Barber concludes that active-negative types are most prone to mistakes, active-positive John Kennedy made what is typically considered a "big" mistake during the invasion of Cuba at the Bay of Pigs, and active-positive Gerald Ford was resoundingly criticized for his pardon of Richard Nixon.

Nor does one personality type have a corner on "good" decisions. George Washington, one of Barber's passive-negatives, was father of his country. Active-negative Lyndon Johnson, mired in Vietnam, made major strides in civil rights as part of his Great Society programs. Richard Nixon's first-term accomplishments—initiatives with China and the Soviet Union, winding down the Vietnam War, and proposals to revise the social welfare system—gave no hint of the tunnel of ruin that the active-negative Nixon would enter in his second term.

Reductionism.   Personality studies also fall prey to reductionism. Reductionist explanations suggest that one factor predicts a series of results. When someone explains that an action or event occurred "because she is a woman" or "because he is black" or "because of his childhood," one should suspect a reductionist argument. In personality studies, reductionism occurs when personality is assumed to be the most important cause of an event or action. This simplification is particularly alluring in studies of the presidency. Because one person supposedly is in charge, an analysis that *reduces* an explanation of a decision to personality is easily made. Yet typing Franklin Roosevelt and Gerald Ford as active-positive provides little information about the kinds of administrations the two ran, the staffs they employed, the policy preferences they held, or the decisions they made. Such reductions fail to consider elements other than personality in decision making: (1) aspects of a person's outlook, such as ideology or political skills, that are less directly tied to personality and (2) the institution and environment in which the person acts.

Ideological beliefs, more than personality foibles, may have dictated Herbert Hoover's response to the Great Depression. Hoover genuinely believed that relief programs would permanently harm the free enterprise system and were outside the proper scope of government. After Congress proposed a bill for $60 million of direct relief for farmers, Hoover responded that "prosperity cannot be restored by raids on the public treasury."[47] Although Barber typed Lyndon Johnson as active-negative, Johnson displayed dynamic political skills in his relations with Congress. Many members of Congress observed the friendly, caring Johnson who knew how to make people feel special.

Finally, the presidential environment, the plural presidency, and the president's immediate advisers make it difficult for presidents' innermost strengths and foibles to dictate presidential decisions. This is *not* to say that personality differences are of no import. This *is* to say that those differences are not as crucial as people would suspect.

In this regard, one may wonder what to make of Janis and Barber. Janis suggests that groupthink triggered such fiascoes as Watergate, Vietnam, and the Bay of Pigs invasion. Barber maintains that presidents' personalities were the causes. Personalities and group dynamics certainly entered into the decisions that produced these events, and one would not wish to remove their importance. Yet Janis and Barber oversimplify presidential decision making. Other institutional and environmental factors act on the personalities and the groups. As the foregoing discussion of Watergate suggests, Nixon's personality and his inner circle were confounded by people in diverse organizational units only nominally controlled by Nixon and the ingroup. Powerful political fragments in the form of the courts and Congress also tripped Nixon and his immediate advisers. Indeed, these environmental concerns bring into question Barber's passive categorization. In modern times it may be difficult for any individual to remain passive in the presidency. Passive-positive Ronald Reagan looked especially active during his first year in office as he pushed bold tax and budget initiatives through Congress. The single executive image builds in demands that presidents be involved in "everything." This suggests that all presidents will be active, regardless of their personalities.

In the "valley of decision," to use Theodore Sorensen's phrase, there are nearly sixteen hundred people who daily help the president make decisions and who make decisions for the president. Carter and Kennedy were surrounded by advisers, and their advisers had advisers. All these people reached out to departments, agencies, and groups across Washington and the world for options that the presidents considered. Contrary to impressions given by the single executive image, the internal feelings of one person and even his efforts with top advisers are only two features of the valley's vast terrain.

CONCLUSION

People are often fooled by what they know. People know, or at least think they know, something about presidents. Much of the election campaign is spent conveying candidates' images—their personal characteristics and backgrounds. Once elected, presidents face the media's "body watch," which displays their talents, moods, failures, and triumphs. People know the image of a single executive in charge of the government. People also may know something about the key people who work for presidents. A bounty of speculations and news reports follow any infighting among presidents' top aides. When Nancy Reagan attempted to oust Donald Regan as White House chief of staff for his handling of the Iran-contra scandal, people knew. When John Sununu, Bush's first chief of staff, was criticized for making personal trips by plane to his dentist and to stamp auctions at government expense, people knew. What people are unlikely to know or think about is the institution within which presidents and their aides work. Not knowing much about it, they are likely to presume the plural presidency is unimportant.

Yet expectations drawn from the single executive image demand that presidents develop this plural institution. When no one person can do everything that the image requires but everything must be done, the plural presidency takes over. A president is not always a necessary or sufficient condition for presidential decisions. The plural presidency makes numerous nondecisions—decisions not to act or not to pass information on to a president. In these instances, the president is neither necessary nor sufficient. There are decisions for which the president is necessary. The Carter shoe import decision and the Kennedy Diem coup decisions are examples. Yet the presence of Carter and Kennedy was not a sufficient condition for these White House decisions. No one, not even the president, can be singled out as the principal decision maker in the plural presidency. ■

F U R T H E R   R E A D I N G

On the Diem assassination, see: *Pentagon Papers* (New York: Bantam Books, 1971); David Halberstam, *The Best and the Brightest* (Greenwich, Conn.: Fawcett, 1969). On presidents' immediate advisers, see: Irving Janis, *Groupthink*, 2d ed. (Boston: Houghton Mifflin, 1982); John Kessel, "The Structure of the Carter White House," *American Journal of Political Science* 27 (August 1983): 431–463; John Kessel, "The Structure of the Reagan White House," *American Journal of Political Science* 28 (May 1984): 231–258; David Stockman, *The Triumph of Politics* (New York: Avon, 1986); Fred Greenstein, *The Hidden-Hand Presidency: Eisenhower as Leader* (New York: Basic Books, 1982); Seymour Hersh, *The Price of Power: Kissinger in the Nixon White House* (New York: Summit Books, 1983). On Watergate, see: *Presidential Transcripts* (New York: Dell Book, 1974); Staff of the *New York Times*, *The Watergate Hearings* (New York: Bantam Books, 1973); Bob Woodward and Carl Bernstein, *The Final Days* (New York: Avon, 1976); H. R. Haldeman, *The Ends of Power* (New York: Dell, 1978). On personality, see: James David Barber, *The Presidential Character*, 4th ed. (Englewood Cliffs, N.J.: Prentice-Hall, 1992); Alexander George and Juliette George, *Woodrow Wilson and Colonel House* (New York: Dover, 1964).

NOTES

1. Theodore Sorensen, *Decision-Making in the White House* (New York: Columbia University Press, 1963), 42.

2. Robert DiClerico, *The American President*, 3d ed. (Englewood Cliffs, N.J. 1990), 247–251.

3. Presidents continue to be concerned about shoes. President Reagan vetoed two bills that would have restricted shoe imports in 1985 and 1988, fearing retaliation by the shoe-importing nations.

4. "Lodge's Last Talk with Diem," Document 59, November 1, 1963, *Pentagon Papers* (New York: Bantam Books, 1971), 232.

5. *Pentagon Papers*, 162.

6. "Washington Message to Lodge on Need to Remove Nhus," Document 35, August 24, 1963, ibid., 194–195.

7. Ibid., 170.

8. Ibid., 171.

9. "Lodge Cable to Secretary Rusk on U.S. Policy Toward a Coup," Document 39, August 29, 1963, ibid., 197.

10. "Rusk Cable to Lodge on View of National Security Council," Document 40, August 29, 1963, ibid., 199.

11. *Pentagon Papers*, 173.

12. Ibid., 175.

13. "McNamara-Taylor Report on Mission to South Vietnam," Document 47, October 2, 1963, ibid., 211–212.

14. *Pentagon Papers*, 176.

15. "Kennedy Position on Coup Plot," Document 50, October 5, 1963, ibid., 215–216.

16. "Lodge Message to Bundy on Dealings with Generals," Document 52, October 25, 1963, ibid., 218.

17. "Harkins Message to Taylor Voicing Doubts on Plot," Document 54, October 30, 1963, ibid., 221.

18. "Lodge Response to Bundy on Letting Coup Plan Proceed," Document 57, October 30, 1963, ibid., 226–227.

19. "Further Bundy Instruction to Lodge on Contingency Plans," Document 58, October 30, 1963, ibid., 230.

20. *Pentagon Papers*, 189.

21. Alfred de Grazia, "The Myth of the President," in *The Presidency*, ed. A. Wildavsky (Boston: Little, Brown, 1969), 66, original emphasis.

22. Hugh Heclo, "The Changing Office," in *Politics and the Oval Office*, ed. A. Meltsner (San Francisco: Institute for Contemporary Studies, 1982), 162.

23. Graham Allison, *Essence of Decision: Explaining the Cuban Missile Crisis* (Boston: Little, Brown, 1971), 89.

24. Michael Weisskopf, "With Pen, Bush to Seal Administration Split on Clean Air Act," *Washington Post*, November 15, 1990, A23.

25. Jack Valenti, *A Very Human President* (New York: Norton, 1975), 66.

26. Richard Nixon, *RN: The Memoirs of Richard Nixon* (New York: Grosset and Dunlap, 1978), 682.

27. H. R. Haldeman, *The Ends of Power* (New York: Dell, 1978), 317.

28. Ibid., 334.

29. Cited in Robert DiClerico, *The American President*, 2d ed. (Englewood Cliffs, N.J.: Prentice-Hall, 1983), 221.

30. Seymour Hersh, *The Price of Power: Kissinger in the Nixon White House* (New York: Summit Books, 1983), 109.

31. Gerald Ford, *A Time to Heal: An Autobiography of Gerald R. Ford* (New York: Harper and Row, 1979), 147.

32. Irving Janis, *Groupthink*, 2d ed. (Boston: Houghton Mifflin, 1982).

33. Staff of the *New York Times*, *The Watergate Hearings* (New York: Bantam Books, 1973).

34. Janis, 215.

35. Meeting: Nixon, Dean, and Haldeman, March 21, 1973, 10:12–11:55 A.M. *The Presidential Transcripts* (New York: Dell, 1974), 120.

36. Bob Woodward and Carl Bernstein, *The Final Days* (New York: Avon, 1976).

37. U.S. House, Committee on the Judiciary, *Statement of Information on the Impeachment of Richard Nixon*, 5 vols., Vol. 4, Part 2, Exhibit 51.2. (Washington, D.C.: U.S. Government Printing Office.)

38. This typology modifies John Kessel, "The Structure of the Carter White House," *American Journal of Political Science* 27 (August 1983): 431–463, and John Kessel, "The Structure of the Reagan White House," *American Journal of Political Science* 28 (May 1984): 231–258.

39. David Stockman, *The Triumph of Politics* (New York: Avon, 1986), 306.

40. Ibid., 321.

41. Ibid., 322.

42. James David Barber, *The Presidential Character*, 4th ed. (Englewood Cliffs, N.J.: Prentice-Hall), 1992.

43. Quoted in *New York Times*, October 23, 1977, 36.

44. Quote from former White House aide Kenneth Clawson cited in *Washington Post*, August 9, 1979, D3.

45. Fred Greenstein, *The Hidden-Hand Presidency: Eisenhower as Leader* (New York: Basic Books, 1982).

46. *Arizona Daily Star*, April 21, 1992, 6.

47. Barber, 21.

CHAPTER 8

The Presidential Organization

O n a warm spring day in 1979, eight White House offices put the finishing touches on a presidential event. Jimmy Carter stood smiling at a group of small business owners in the White House Rose Garden. He applauded a guest who had invested his own money in a new business to make air filters. Carter, seemingly inspired by the garden setting, hailed the man's project: "now this originally tiny, new flower in the free enterprise garden of the United States has become a flourishing garden."[1]

The gathering lasted ten minutes, but it was several weeks in the making. The chief of staff's office placed a deputy assistant in charge of the event as project director. The Domestic Policy Staff sent to the speechwriters a list of "talking points" about American small businesses. The Press Office posted the event on its schedule for reporters; the press secretary announced it at his briefing. The Appointments Staff timed the event so reporters could meet their deadlines. The Office of Congresssional Relations apprised members of Congress about the ceremony, especially those from the home state of the businessman Carter would congratulate. The Photo Office sent White House photographers to capture the scene, and the staff secretary's office arranged for President Carter to sign souvenir photos for the several hundred people in attendance.[2]

On the surface, this is a routine, successful presidential appearance. It conveys the uniqueness, importance, power, and visibility of the single executive image. The president, as the only representative of the people, warmly meets ordinary citizens. The Rose Garden setting reinforces the uniqueness and importance of the presidency to small entrepreneurs invited to the president's house. Presidential activism is in evidence. The single executive image claims that presidents have the power to act in the national interest, so long as their actions do not violate the Constitution or federal laws (see Chapter 3). This activism extends presidential policy interests to all issues.

Carter thus becomes an expert on air filters and small businesses. He uses his visibility from the image to highlight small business issues to the press in a way that no other political figure can.

Beneath the surface, the event reveals the decentralized organization of the plural presidency. It addresses the "who" of decision making. Who makes the decisions, and in what ways are the participants linked to one another? Separate offices handle the press, the Congress, the policy, and the guests. Although there is some coordination from the top, most of the units go about their business independently. As outlined in Chapter 7, decentralization creates one form of internal plurality within the presidential institution (the other is ambiguous decision making, discussed in Chapter 9). The decentralized organization is characterized by a diversity of units, the diffusion of power across them, and a limited degree of top-down control. The single executive image spurs the organization and its decentralization. The more the image requires of presidents, the more presidents require of the organization.

A DECENTRALIZED ORGANIZATION

This chapter examines the decentralized organization of the plural presidency. *An organization* is a relatively complex set of offices, units, or staffs that carry out a set of functions. The functions are explicitly separated from one another, so that the offices are not interchangeable. Instead, there is a division of labor whereby each office carries out a particular function (or set of functions) and does not become involved in other functions. *Decentralization* is the distribution of power among various offices or individuals in roughly equal fashion. The result is limited coordination from the top. A *decentralized organization*, then, is a complex set of offices, units, or staffs, each confined to a specific jurisdiction, the complexity and size of which make it difficult to organize hierarchically—from top to bottom.

The U.S. Congress is a decentralized organization. Individual members develop power bases as the chairs or ranking members of the nearly 300 committees and subcommittees that carry out the work of Congress. A budget of over $1.8 billion and 25,000 staff members— some based in the committees, others based in the members' personal offices—increase the decentralization. This wide dispersal of power maddens the party leadership—the Speaker of the House and the majority and minority leaders of both houses—who find it difficult to dictate outcomes.

The American presidency also is a decentralized organization, comprising some 42 units and 1,600 people. It is decentralized because the single executive image requires presidents to accommodate so many policy areas, group demands, and actions of other branches. The units have jurisdiction over a particular policy area (foreign, military, domestic, economic), administrative task (budgeting, personnel, legislative proposals), or target of presidential influence (including the press, interest groups, and the public at large). The core of the organization is called the "Executive Office of the President" (EOP). The Executive Office of the President is merely a label. It is not one office with staff and coordinating functions. It is the umbrella name given to 19 units, including the White House Office, the National Security Council, the Office of Management and Budget, the Council of Economic Advisers, and the Office of Special Trade Representative (see Table 8.1). The White House Office is the core of the core. Like "Executive Office of the President," "White House Office" is just a label. The White House Office consists of 23 other offices that are deemed closest to the president, including the Office of Legislative Affairs, the Press Office, and the Office of the Chief of Staff (see Table 8.2). Each of these offices is as autonomous and as important as the offices in the larger Executive Office of the President. There are really 42 different offices within the Executive Office of the President.[3]

Because power is decentralized, it is difficult for the president or his senior staff to achieve coordination from the top. The presidential organization is not as large or as complex as that of Congress. Yet presidents, like the party leaders of Congress, cannot effectively monitor or even establish the direction for all the work that is done.

Table 8.1 Exective Office of the President

White House Office
Office of Administration
Council of Economic Advisers
Council on Environmental Quality
Domestic Policy Council
National Critical Materials Council
National Security Council
Central Intelligence Agency
National Space Council
Office of Management and Budget
Office of Federal Procurement Policy
Office of National Drug Control Policy
Office of Policy Development
Office of Policy Planning
Regulatory Information Service Center
Office of Science and Technology Policy
Office of U.S. Trade Representation
Office of the Vice President
Office of Domestic Policy and Council on Competiveness[1]

1. In the Office of the Vice President
Source: 1991/2 Federal Staff Directory (Mt. Vernon, Va.: Staff Directories, Ltd, 1991), vii–36. Used by permission.

Table 8.2   Units of the White House Office

Office of the Chief of Staff
Office of the Staff Secretary
Office of National Security Affairs
Office of the Counsel
Office of Communications
Office of Speechwriting
Office of Research
Office of Public Liaison
Office of Media Affairs
Office of Media Relations
Office of Public Affairs
Press Secretary
Office of Legislative Affairs
Office of Management and Administration
Office of Intergovernmental Affairs
Office of Economic and Domestic Policy
Office of National Service
Office of Special Activities and Initiatives (Advance Office)
Office of Political Affairs
Office of the Cabinet Secretary
Presidential Personnel Office
White House Military Office
Office of the First Lady

Source: 1991/2 Federal Staff Directory (Mt. Vernon, Va.: Staff Directories, Ltd, 1991), vii–36. Used by permission.

Alfred de Grazia observed:

On a normal issue that comes before the "President" some dozens of people are involved. It might be presumptuous to say that more of a collectivity is engaged than when the same type of issue would come before the Congress; but it would be equally presumptuous to say that fewer persons were taken up with the matter.[4]

This chapter maps four aspects of the decentralized organization of the plural presidency: (1) its size, (2) patterns of specialization, (3) the role of generalists, and (4) presidents' efforts at coordination.

PLAY BY NUMBERS

Organizational size is not accidental. It results from the problems an organization addresses. The great demands placed on the presidency from the single executive image increase its size. For most of its early history, the presidency was the president. There was no presidential organization. The U.S. government itself was small, and presidents were not active policymakers (see Chapter 2). The single executive image and the notion of presidential activism were missing. George

Washington had one secretary, his nephew Lawrence Lewis, whom Washington paid out of his own pocket. Thomas Jefferson had two aides—a personal secretary and a messenger—both of whom Jefferson also paid from personal funds. The White House had more servants than the president had staff. Andrew Jackson was the first president to enjoy a secretary paid at government expense. Major Andrew Jackson Donelson, Mrs. Jackson's nephew and a clerk of the General Land Office, was "detailed," that is assigned, to the White House as President Jackson's private secretary. In 1833, Congress for the first time designated a presidential clerk, rather than having one borrowed from elsewhere in the government, but the person only signed land patents. Some twenty-five years later, in 1857, Congress established funds for presidents' "official households," consisting of a personal secretary, messenger, and steward to supervise the mansion. Presidents managed with these three people until 1900, when Congress authorized funds for thirty additional White House aides on a total budget of $48,540. Congress added four extra top aides in the 1920s, bringing the total to thirty-seven. White House employees (including gardeners and cooks) numbered just over one hundred. The turn of the century was also a turning point of sorts for American presidents. Theodore Roosevelt was the first president to have a full-fledged "staff."[5]

Organizing the Presidency

An executive staff, however, is not an executive organization. Until the Great Depression, the immediate staff totaled fifty members. The depression immensely expanded demands for government and presidential activism and thus enlarged the scope of the single executive image (see Chapter 3). The president was increasingly looked on as the one person who could get the country out of the crisis. Franklin Roosevelt observed:

Last spring when I went to Washington, there were many people who came forward with the thought, verbally expressed, that the Government should take over all the troubles of the country, that we could, well as we used to say in the old days, 'Let George do it,' and I began to think sometimes that my first name was George.[6]

Roosevelt appointed the Brownlow Committee on Administrative Management to examine executive staffing needs. The committee strongly espoused the notion of executive activism: "the American Executive must be regarded as one of the very greatest contributions by our Nation to the development of modern democracy." It concluded that "the President needs help. His immediate staff assistance is entirely inadequate."[7] It urged the establishment of a separate presidential organization.

Congress gave Roosevelt the authority to deal with his staffing

Table 8.3 Growth of the White House Staff from Coolidge to Bush

President	Executive Office of the President	White House Office	Bureau of Budget/ OMB Staff
Roosevelt, I	103	47	—
Roosevelt, II	371	50	130
Roosevelt, III	121,318	51	467
Truman, I	78,389	188	602
Truman, II	1,269	256	513
Eisenhower, I	1,229	295	436
Eisenhower, II	2,357	408	438
Kennedy	2,058	422	497
Johnson	3,839	304	575
Nixon, I	5,227	478	644
Nixon, II	5,277	563	663
Ford	1,905	583	712
Carter	1,758	412	641
Reagan, I	1,624	380	626
Reagan, II	1,548	365	554
Bush[1]	1,656	380	560

1. 1989–1990.

Note: Entries are the average number of full-time employees for each term.

Source: For Coolidge, Hoover, and Roosevelt through 1940, U.S. Executive Office of the President, *Budget of the United States* (1924–1940). For all others, U.S. Department of Commerce, *Statistical Abstract of the United States* (1933–1990).

needs in the Reorganization Act of 1939. That summer Roosevelt created the Executive Office of the President. He dramatically increased the size of the presidential staff sixfold, from 105 to 631. Table 8.3 depicts this growth under Roosevelt and later presidents.[8] Originally, the EOP consisted of six offices, each with a set jurisdiction. Members of the president's immediate staff, still numbering around fifty, were organized in the White House Office. The Bureau of the Budget was brought from the Treasury Department to the White House to centralize more fully the budget process. The bureau mushroomed from 100 staff members in 1939 to 453 by 1943. It was revamped and renamed the Office of Management and Budget in 1970. Roosevelt established three other units: the National Resources Planning Board, the Liaison Office for Personnel Management, and the Office of Government Reports. In 1940 he installed the Office for Emergency Management as part of the direction of defense agencies during World War II, and by 1943, at the height of the war, it totaled nearly 200,000 people. "George" was not alone.

After World War II, the presidential organization grew along three paths: (1) presidents' desires to engage in policymaking, (2) Congress's desire for greater presidential involvement in policymaking, and (3) presidents' desires to have more control over policy implementation. This growth reflected modern presidential activism as an element of the single executive image and resulted in greater de-centralization within the plural presidency. Truman embarked on the first path, pursuing a series of postwar policy interests in the form of annual legislative programs. These, he felt, required an increase in his immediate staff. He dismantled the huge wartime Office of Emergency Management but simultaneously expanded the White House Office nearly fourfold, from 61 people in 1946 to 293 people in 1947. This was the largest percentage increase in growth ever in the White House Office.

Congress, seeing advantages to presidential activism, developed the second path. Several units of the Executive Office of the President were actually the creation of Congress, which desired greater policy coordination. In the Employment Act of 1946, Congress gave presidents the responsibility to "use all practicable means . . . to promote maximum employment, production, and purchasing power."[9] Congress created the Council of Economic Advisers (CEA) to advise presidents on measures that would ease inflation and unemployment. Presidents soon added a staff to the CEA. The CEA and its staff have remained roughly the same size since their founding (37 people in 1949, 27 in 1990), although there were several small increases during the Johnson and Nixon administrations. The National Security Act of 1947 gave presidents the responsibility for coordinating national defense and foreign policy. It also gave them the help of a committee of advisers—the National Security Council (NSC). The NSC itself has remained small, usually with fewer than 10 members. The NSC staff, however, has increased in size, peaking at 190 members during the Reagan administration (70 permanent members and roughly 100 "detailed" from other agencies, primarily the Pentagon.)[10] The number did not fall in the wake of the Iran-contra debacle.[11]

Presidents have resisted some congressional efforts. In 1970 Congress mandated that presidents more actively protect the nation's natural environment. It established the Council on Environmental Quality as a unit in the Executive Office of the President to aid presidents in meeting this responsibility. President Nixon resisted the creation of the unit although he later claimed it as one of his administration's accomplishments. A decade later, President Reagan attempted to dismantle the council by curtailing its staff and funds. Reagan reduced the staff size from 49 to 11 and hoped to eventually "zero-out" the agency by transferring remaining employees elsewhere. In the fiscal 1981 budget, Reagan ordered funds for the Council on Environmental Quality rescinded (that is, not spent). A tug-of-war ensued between the Congress, which had voted the money, and the president, who was unwilling to spend all of it. Pressure from Congress and citizens' groups secured the council's survival, although Reagan succeeded in cutting its operation. Upon taking office, the Bush administration somewhat revived the council: its staff grew slightly to 17, and its budget increased by 20 percent.

On the third path, presidents have sought to supervise the implementation of policy by directing executive departments and agencies from the White House. Eisenhower dramatically increased the size of the EOP and the White House Office to handle such supervision. The greatest post–World War II expansion of the EOP occurred in 1958, when personnel more than doubled from 1,218 to 2,660. Johnson sought to centralize the administration of the Great Society in the EOP and increased its total staff from 2,849 to 4,683 in one year, from 1965 to 1966. President Nixon attempted to control the executive branch directly from the White House Office, which more than doubled in size from 311 staff members in 1970 to 660 members in 1971. This relative increase was second only to the Truman expansion between 1946 and 1947. In addition, the absolute size of the White House Office was at its largest ever in 1971, and the total of 660 staffers has not been exceeded. Although other presidents have not increased staff size so sharply, they nonetheless attempt to draw the reins of government as close as possible to the White House.

Presidential Dollars

The size and durability of an organization can be judged by the amount of money it spends. Budgets are devices of self-justification and self-perpetuation. Organizations obtain importance and ensure longevity in direct proportion to the size of their budgets. Viewed in budgetary terms, the growth of the Executive Office of the President has been extraordinary. EOP staff size grew only 41 percent in the period since 1949. EOP expenditures, expressed in current dollars (which include the effects of inflation), have increased nearly thirteen times over the same years. Calculated in constant dollars, with the effects of inflation removed, the EOP budget posted an astronomical 200 percent increase. The budget increases of two units—the White House Office and the Office of Management and Budget—account for most of this growth. Figure 8.1 maps the budget growth of the Executive Office of the President.

Presidential Cuts

Many presidents have announced their intentions to end the waste of a swollen federal bureaucracy. Yet only a few have applied this bold declaration to their own portion of the puffed-up beast. Kennedy cut the budgets of the National Security Council and some lesser EOP units to streamline the organization that had developed during Eisenhower's tenure. The budgets of the White House Office, the Office of Management and Budget, and the Council of Economic Advisers did not suffer but instead increased during the Kennedy years. Ford was the only president to reduce the staff of the EOP in the postwar period. In Watergate's aftermath, he decreased the EOP by more than half, from 5,751 in 1974 to 1,910 in 1975. Yet Ford did not reduce the size of the White House Office or the Office of Management and Budget, both of which increased slightly over their counterparts in the Nixon administration. Nor were Ford's staff cutbacks matched by budget cuts. Ford actually spent more money in 1975 than Nixon did in 1974. Although Reagan pledged a smaller White House apparatus, his EOP budget was barely less than Carter's with inflation taken into account. Like brittle elastic, the size of the presidential organization is easily stretched but difficult to snap back.

The Paradoxes of Size

The growth of the presidential organization reveals the many hands of the presidency. This plurality defines a ring of three paradoxes. The first paradox is that presidents do not fully control the size and shape of their own organization. One would think that presidents

Figure 8.1 Expansion of Key White House Units, by President (in thousands of constant 1967 dollars)

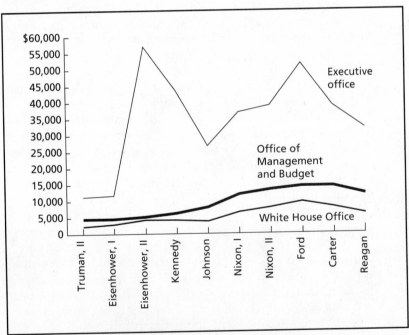

The Office of Management and Budget and the White House Office have grown steadily since Truman. Much greater growth has occurred in the budget of the Executive Office of the President. [*Source:* Gary King and Lyn Ragsdale, *The Elusive Executive* (Washington, D.C.: CQ Press, 1988), 216. Copyright © 1988. Used by permission of CQ Press.]

have considerable discretion in setting up this organization, and in a certain way they do. Presidents consistently add offices to show new commitments to policy matters or subtract units to show how their approaches differ from those of their predecessors. Within the Executive Office of the President, some units last a few years and then are forgotten—for example, the National Council on Marine Resources and Engineering Development, the Federal Property Council, and the Committee for Congested Production Areas. Yet many units have considerable longevity. The failed reorganization attempts of Carter and Reagan, as well as the more successful efforts of Kennedy and Ford, reveal that presidents find the core of the presidential organization difficult to reshape. President Reagan's attempt to dismantle the Council on Environmental Quality also underscores the first paradox. So long as issues and interests remain salient, the units handling them are difficult to absorb or abandon. Internal pressures supplied by established procedures, entrenched budgets, and inertia also make the organization less episodic—changing from one incumbent to the next—than it might appear.

The Executive Office of the President reflects the first paradox in two different lights. First, presidents cannot use the EOP to manage the presidential organization, because, as noted above, it exists only on paper. Two Carter aides observed that the EOP "hardly seems to have been designed at all; it just grew. Even its name is deceptive: The EOP is not an executive office. Rather, it is a bloated and disorderly grab-bag of separate and mutually suspicious staffs, units, councils, boards, and groups with strikingly different histories, purposes, and problems."[12]

Second, the presidential organization is not confined strictly within the walls of the Executive Office of the President. Because the EOP has no walls, the boundaries of the presidential organization are slightly fuzzy. The organization also encompasses top cabinet secretaries, the Joint Chiefs of Staff, and the heads of key agencies such as the Central Intelligence Agency and the Environmental Protection Agency.

Presidents' lack of control over the EOP creates a paradox within a paradox: Presidents have enlarged the White House Office partly to bring some order to the decentralized Executive Office of the President. The result is a large, decentralized White House Office that is a set of 23 offices with 400 employees and a budget of over $25 million. The larger the units of the White House Office, the more difficulty presidents have in controlling them. As a result many presidents retreat to a small group of senior-level advisers for information and opinions. There advisers, however, must get their information from somewhere. This need raises the final paradox: the president's senior advisers rely on the very plural organization over which the president lacks control.

ISSUE SPECIALIZATION

The more responsibilities presidents undertake, the more specialized offices they need. Three types of specialization are found in the presidential organization: issue specialization, target specialization, and task specialization. This section discusses issue specialization, and the next two sections describe target and task specialization.

Key units in the Executive Office of the President handle issues divided among three broad policy domains: national security, the economy, and domestic affairs. These categories make life easier for everyone. They permit divisions of labor, the development of expertise, and ease of communication. Yet because each category is so encompassing, several units, each with a slightly different jurisdiction, have responsibility for a single domain. Too, some of the units are not directly within the Executive Office of the President but include departments and agencies of the larger bureaucracy. As units compete to assert their hold on a specialty, clashes arise. There also is some overlap across the three policy domains, and offices compete to exercise their expertise. Issue specialization thus reinforces the decentralization of the White House.

National Security Affairs

The single executive image requires presidents to ensure the peace and security of the United States. The presidential organization responds to this requirement. The National Security Council (NSC), the national security adviser, the NSC staff, the secretaries of state and defense and their assistant secretaries, the Joint Chiefs of Staff, and the director of the Central Intelligence Agency are presidents' national security experts. The list quickly betrays the decentralization of the White House even in a single issue area. Information does not come from one distinct voice. The National Security Council is composed of four statutory members: the president, the vice president, the secretary of state, and the secretary of defense. Presidents customarily invite the chairman of the Joint Chiefs of Staff, the director of the Central Intelligence Agency, the national security adviser, and several others to attend NSC meetings.

The role of the NSC in shaping foreign policy has been limited. Although Presidents Truman and Eisenhower vigorously used the council for advice and policymaking, presidents since Kennedy have felt that the group was too large. Presidents have preferred smaller groups of close advisers. Kennedy, for instance, employed a group known as the Executive Committee of the National Security Council, although even it numbered fourteen people. The NSC has become principally a symbolic assemblage that can be brought together to display unity and reason in times of crisis.

The NSC staff and the national security adviser have supplanted the National Security Council. Eisenhower originally developed the staff as an expert support group for the council, but its role rapidly changed. Kennedy attempted to move foreign policymaking into the White House and out of what he saw as the unimaginative and stagnant State Department. The NSC staff, trimmed in size, became a vital linchpin in forming White House policy. It developed its own intelligence capacity by receiving all cable traffic from the State Department, Defense Department, and CIA. Nixon expanded the NSC staff, which included permanent members and "detailees" from other agencies, primarily the Pentagon. The number rose to 120 at the end of the Carter administration and 190 during the Reagan years. The Reagan administration also brought the NSC staff into the computer age. The NSC installed $10 million worth of computer and communications equipment so that it could collect in one place all the government's foreign policy information from the State Department, Pentagon, CIA, and National Security Agency (which is involved in intercepting international communications). Complete information that the NSC alone controlled became an important source of bureaucratic power.[13]

National security advisers (formally known as "Assistants to the President for National Security Affairs") are in charge of the NSC staff and have become close presidential advisers and prominent public figures. When a reporter asked Kennedy about the rising influence of his national security adviser, McGeorge Bundy, the president replied, 'I shall continue to exercise some residual functions."[14] The advisers have vied with the secretary of state for the title of top foreign policy adviser. During the Nixon administration the competition was so fierce that National Security Adviser Henry Kissinger forced out Secretary of State William Rogers. In an unprecedented move, Kissinger then held both positions.

In direct response to the omnipotence of Kissinger, President Carter promised to restore the secretary of state to the position of undisputed spokesman on American foreign relations. Secretary of State Cyrus Vance met often with Carter and was instrumental in Carter's peace initiative with Israel and Egypt. Yet Carter's flamboyant national security adviser, Zbigniew Brzezinski, was not to be outdone. Like Kissinger, he realized that his proximity to the president and his smaller organizational baggage—a staff of 120 as compared to the secretary of state's department of 25,000—would permit him considerable flexibility. Carter conceded that "Zbigniew Brzezinski and his relatively small group of experts were not handicapped by the intertia of a tenured bureaucracy or the responsibility for implementing policies after they were evolved."[15]

The inevitable confrontation between Vance and Brzezinski occurred in 1980, when Brzezinski and other White House aides convinced Carter to go ahead with a risky helicopter rescue of the American hostages in Iran. Vance, who favored a diplomatic solution, was on vacation. Upon his return, with the decision already made, the secretary presented his objections, calling the decision "ill conceived." Vance resigned in opposition to the use of force because he felt that Carter had not adequately consulted the State Department or him.[16] Secretaries of state do not always lose to national security advisers, however. President Bush's national security adviser Brent Scowcroft has been much less visible than many of his predecessors and than Secretary of State James Baker.

The clash between the national security adviser and the secretary of state is not a clash between two people. It reveals a see-saw between two organizational approaches to foreign policy. The side represented by the secretary of state and the State Department pursues diplomatic solutions using regular channels that are likely to be at least somewhat public and time-consuming. The side represented by the national security adviser is more likely to favor secret missions using less well known channels. Presidents differ in the extent to which they wish to use the two approaches.

The Economic Domain

The single executive image makes presidents amateur economists. As the single most powerful individual in the government and the nation, the president is expected to stop any deterioration of the economy and develop clever plans for recovery. The presidential organization steps in to meet these expectations. The Office of Management and Budget, the Council of Economic Advisers, and the Treasury Department play distinct roles in offering presidents advice about economic affairs. The Office of Management and Budget (OMB) is in charge of federal spending figures (both appropriations and expenditures) and the never ending preparation of the budget. The Council of Economic Advisers (CEA) and its staff grew out of a need, left unfulfilled by OMB, for macroeconomic policies, distinct from budgetary requirements. The CEA has three main functions: (1) forecasting future economic growth; (2) preparing an annual economic report (required of the president by Congress) that states projections for economic growth, spending, and employment; and (3) making general analyses of economic issues. These three jobs make the CEA a purveyor of expert analysis rather than policy advice.[17] The Treasury Department is responsible for revenue estimates and currency issues. The three organizations again reveal the presidency's decentralization: they have different perspectives, different backgrounds, different sizes, and different areas of expertise that frequently do not mesh.

A fourth agency, the Federal Reserve Board (the Fed), further complicates matters. The Fed, which sets policies on the money supply and interest rates, is an independent agency established by Congress. Presidents only sporadically oversee the Fed through their power to appoint its members. The Fed's outlook may differ from the outlook of the other economic units, and the Fed may intrude on an already crowded presidential space in economic affairs.

Conflict within the economic domain surfaced in 1984 in a clash between Secretary of the Treasury Donald Regan, a former chief executive officer of Merrill Lynch, and Chairman of the Council of Economic Advisers Martin Feldstein, a former economics professor. Regan, the self-proclaimed spokesman for the Reagan administration on economic policy, vehemently objected to a CEA report calling for a tax increase to bring down the federal budget deficit, then approaching $200 billion. He snarled: "As far as I am concerned, you can throw it [the CEA economic report] away; I have 35 years of experience in the market. The CEA has none. . . . Experience in the marketplace is a lot more valuable than time spent in the library." Shortly thereafter, Feldstein resigned and returned to academia.[18]

Domestic Affairs

The single executive image pushes presidents to deal with domestic policy concerns, including health care, education, civil rights, welfare, and social security. Thus, a domestic policy apparatus exists within the organization to handle the workload. In 1970, Richard Nixon formalized the White House's domestic policy operation with the creation of the Domestic Council, which officially elevated domestic policy concerns to the level of national security. The Domestic Council, consisting of the president, the vice president, the director of the Office of Economic Opportunity (since dismantled), and all department heads except the secretaries of defense and treasury, served as the domestic counterpart to the National Security Council.

Parallels between the two units were evident. Although the Domestic Council was supposed to formulate and coordinate domestic policy decisions, its members were too many and its meetings were too unwieldy. The Domestic Council Staff, directed by senior White House aide John Ehrlichman, took its place. The Domestic Policy Staff has continued in each subsequent administration. Although its title has changed from the Domestic Policy Staff under Carter to Office of Policy Development under Reagan and Bush, its basic charge in developing domestic policy initiatives has remained constant.

The Office of Management and Budget (OMB) further clutters the domestic policy space by its efforts to coordinate domestic priorities within the budget. The secretaries of the domestic departments (all but State and Defense) also give presidents advice. Presidents' domestic apparatus also relies on members of Congress, organized groups, businesses, and citizen organizations as sources for ideas. According to Bradley Patterson, a former White House aide, this makes "policy orchestration difficult and White House leadership hard to maintain."[19]

TARGET SPECIALIZATION

Much of what a president does is to try to convince other political players that what he wants done is what everyone should want done. He may use the single executive image as a resource in framing the persuasion and speak of his power, uniqueness, importance, and visibility. But, as the Carter example mentioned above attests, presidential persuasion also requires an organization to get out the president's message. There are four key targets of presidential persuasion and four corresponding units, each within the White House Office, responsible for the persuasion: (1) the Office of Legislative Affairs targets Congress; (2) the White House Press Office targets the press; (3) the Office of Public Liaison targets organized groups; and (4) the Office of Communication targets the public. These units may engage in some policymaking decisions, but they principally present presidents' views to the outside world.

Legislative liaison efforts sell presidential proposals and positions to Congress. Herbert Hoover relied on one staffer to supervise communication with Congress. Harry Truman, who pursued annual legislative programs, assigned two junior presidential assistants as congressional messengers. Eisenhower formalized the liaison efforts in 1953 with the creation of the Office of Congressional Relations with a staff of six.[20] Liaison with Congress became a key function of the presidential organization that has never been abandoned. The staff's size and duties have increased consistently, and the office was recently renamed the Office of Legislative Affairs. (The office is discussed in greater detail in Chapter 14.)

The White House Press Office has greatly expanded since presidents assigned their chief secretary the task of dealing with the press. Not only is there an officially designated press secretary, a practice begun by Franklin Roosevelt, but a Press Office of more than forty people during the Bush years. The main stage of the White House Press Office is the press secretary's daily briefing of reporters (described in Chapter 6). The office also holds other briefings, arranges press travel and interviews, and posts schedules and announcements of White House activities available for coverage. A Media Liaison Office deals with the non–Washington-based media, including regional, ethnic, and other specialized print or broadcast outlets.[21]

President Ford introduced an Office of Public Liaison designed to promote contact with significant ethnic, racial, and religious groups (see Chapter 10). The Carter White House followed suit. It had special assistants for blacks, Hispanics, women, Jews, major unions, and business groups. The office handled information from the groups, requests for meetings and appearances with Carter, and, most important, appointments by group members to government posts. The "special interest" assistants competed with each other to gather nominations for group members. The Carter administration had a strong record of hiring women and minorities. The Public Liaison Office continued to carry out its communication efforts under Reagan and Bush, although during the Reagan administration its appointments function ended.[22] It nonetheless reflects the group diversity that the presidency attempts to accommodate.

The White House also targets the public as a whole. Appearances such as Carter's in the Rose Garden and others around the country are carefully timed and planned. The Office of Communication devises strategies for all the communications of presidents, White House advisers, department secretaries, and other members of the administration. The Office of Communication coordinates the logistics of these activities—combining the efforts of the Press Office, the speechwriters, and the public appearance schedulers—and their content so that the administration appears to speak in unison. The number of presidential speechwriters has become larger as the volume of presidential messages has become louder. Peggy Noonan, a speechwriter for President Reagan, recalled that she was in charge of the emotional, tearful speeches that Reagan delivered so well. Other writers were reponsible for more technical, policy-specific speeches.[23] Media advisers are also members of the public relations team that trains presidents to speak in front of the camera. Recently, the public relations team has included inhouse pollsters who find out what the public and specific segments of the public think.

TASK SPECIALIZATION

Imagine that you are president for a year. Congress sends you 927 bills that you must decide whether to sign into law. Add to that some 1,600 requests for legislation and appropriations from departments and agencies that you must review. You sign forty-one executive orders that have the same force as any law, but you issue them independently of any other branch of government. You also must make 41,852 appointments to positions in the government, 110 of which are high-level jobs.[24] You must handle them all in order to maintain your image as the single most important and powerful figure in the nation. What do you do? You certainly do not do all this work yourself. Nor is it likely that you and your top advisers can manage it and remain sane.

Presidents employ task specialization. Two key units within the White House—the Office of Administration and the Office of Management and Budget—are assigned certain high-volume activities to ease presidential workloads. More than the other units of the White House, these offices establish standard operating procedures to carry out their duties. The routines allow staff members to deal automatically with the large volume of decisions that are channeled regularly through their offices. Presidents become the end points of two main routines: personnel selection and central clearance.

Personnel

Since Truman, procedures for hiring EOP and other personnel have become formalized and consolidated in one office. Truman named an aide whose primary responsibility was to review candidates for appointive positions. Eisenhower felt that all the lower-level appointments were "a constant annoyance," according to his chief of staff Sherman Adams, of which "he wanted no part."[25] As a result, the Eisenhower administration named a personnel chief as overseer of appointments. He compiled rosters of vacant positions and lists of candidates to fill them.[26] A formal personnel office of some sixty people was established under President Nixon. It is currently called the Office of Administration and follows a routinized selection process. The office keeps track on computer of all upcoming and existing vacancies. It solicits names of potential appointees from the White House staff, relevant agencies or departments, members of Congress, and relevant interest groups. The office then checks the credentials of these people and sends a short list of two or three names to the president along with its own recommendation of one candidate. The office also coordinates the financial, computer, and general support services of the EOP.

Central Clearance

The Office of Management and Budget is the largest presidential unit. It has over 550 people and carries out much of the president's daily business that is not in the foreign policy domain. OMB has become a prime policymaking unit in the presidential organization. It establishes and coordinates domestic and economic priorities by acting as a clearinghouse for policy proposals to and from the White House. OMB has four different types of clearance procedures: (1) budget preparation, (2) legislative clearance, (3) the enrolled bill process, and (4) administrative clearance.

In budget preparation, OMB screens and coordinates the budget requests made by departments and agencies in the executive branch. In the legislative clearance process, it screens proposed legislation from departments and agencies of the executive branch and units within the Executive Office of the President. Once Congress passes a piece of legislation, OMB recommends to the president whether to sign or veto it. This is known as the enrolled bill process. Finally, OMB evaluates administrative regulations established by departments and agencies to ensure that they are consistent with presidential policy desires. This evaluation is a relatively recent innovation called administrative clearance.

Budget Preparation. At some times, participation in the budget process has been the OMB's most important role; at other times, its least important role. Rosy or gloomy economic pictures and presidents' own interests have directed the ebb and flow. Before the Bureau of the Budget existed, requests for money from all federal departments and agencies were delivered like loose scraps of paper to the secretary of the treasury, who bound them, with little alteration, into a book of estimates that was forwarded to Congress. Congress and President Harding, tired of the uncoordinated requests, passed the Budget and Accounting Act of 1921, which required that presidents organize a single federal budget. To help, Congress established the Bureau of the Budget in the Treasury Department to review all proposals for funds submitted by the rest of the government and "to assemble, correlate, revise, reduce, or increase the estimates of the several departments or establishments."[27] Agencies could no longer independently submit proposals; they first had to gain the approval of the Bureau of the Budget.

The bureau acted as a neutral, professional naysayer that sought to cut the budget and eliminate presumed waste wherever possible. One bureau report recommended that each government employee receive only one pencil at a time and be given a new one only when the old stub was turned in. The bureau practiced what it preached. Charles Dawes, its first director, wrote in his diary, "of the appropriations of $225,000 for the Bureau of the Budget, we only spent $120,313.54 in the year's work. We took our own medicine." Dawes's successor, General H. M. Lord, personally checked bureau employees' drawers for too much stationery, too many paper clips, and other government supplies. He also established the "Two-Percent Club" for those agencies who reduced their budgets by that amount and the "One-Percent Club" for those less ambitious.[28]

The budget-cutting role of the unit fell out of vogue during the Great Depression and World War II, when President Roosevelt and Congress placed great emphasis on expanding the government. Truman and Eisenhower, however, strongly believed in balanced budgets and used the bureau to get them. With the expansion of government programs under Kennedy and Johnson, the bureau's budget influence again ebbed. The bureau was reorganized as the Office of Management and Budget under Nixon in 1970. It became a political arm of presidents, designed to supervise the executive branch rather than act as a neutral agency. Presidents hoped to gain control of the departments by their nominal control of the budget. President Reagan capitalized on this shift by having OMB and its director David Stockman play a key role in enacting extensive budget and tax cuts in 1981. Ballooning deficits as a result of the mismatch of defense increases and tax cuts have made OMB ever more central to the budget and domestic policy processes. Since the business of government has become tied to lowering the deficit, or at least not adding to it, OMB's importance continues.

Although its political importance to presidents has shifted, the Office of Management and Budget has remained a vital procedural player in the budget process. OMB conducts spring planning review sessions in April through June to explore the funding implications of major issues and programs covered in the upcoming budget. It then sets guidelines for executive departments and agencies, which develop draft budgets and return them to OMB. The OMB staff analyzes the departments' proposed budgets and holds hearings. Agency-by-agency reviews follow in November, when the OMB director makes final recommendations to the president. OMB gives departments and agencies their "marks"—recommended budget levels. The president reviews OMB's work, and the White House staff may hear appeals from various agencies. In December, OMB prepares final budget documents for transmittal to Congress in February of the next year.

Legislative Clearance. The Office of Management and Budget acts as a clearinghouse for departments' and agencies' proposals for legislation. It determines whether a request is "in accordance with the President's program." OMB reviews draft legislation and grades it "in accordance," or "i/a," "consistent with," "no objection," or "reject." Well over twenty-five thousand executive branch requests move through the clearance system every two years.[29] Presidents almost always follow OMB's recommendations about whether to include departmental measures as part of their legislative programs. OMB also conducts a similar clearing process for proposed executive orders and prepares the final language of many of them.

Enrolled Bill Process. An enrolled bill is a bill that has passed both houses of Congress and awaits the president's signature. Since 1938, enrolled bills have detoured first to the Bureau of the Budget/Office of Management and Budget before reaching the president. The Legislative Reference Division of OMB evaluates each enrolled bill. It distributes copies of the bill to departments, agencies, and units in the Executive Office of the President that are affected by, or interested in, the legislation. It then requires that within forty-eight hours the agencies submit a recommendation for presidential action.[30] The Legislative Reference Division collates these recommendations and, in a cover letter, outlines what the bill is about, reviews the departments' and agencies' positions, and makes its own recommendation.

OMB holds considerable influence over the fate of enrolled bills. One study of the Nixon and Ford administrations found that when OMB and the lead agency concurred on the disposition of a bill, the president proceeded to adopt the OMB/agency recommendation 96 percent of the time. When OMB and the lead agency split (OMB approval of the bill/agency disapproval), the president went with the OMB recommendation on 95 percent of the bills.[31]

Administrative Clearance. OMB also monitors the implementation of legislation. Legislation that is approved by Congress and signed into law by the president exists only on paper. It is up to executive agencies and departments to interpret the new law and adopt rules and regulations to make the law work. Administrative rule making often is more critical to the meaning of the law than is the wording of the law itself. Presidents since Nixon have required agencies to conduct analyses of proposed regulations.

In 1981, Reagan adopted the most thoroughgoing form of administrative clearance, giving OMB the power to review and delay all agencies' proposed rules and regulations. The Office of Information and Regulatory Affairs in OMB has a staff of eighty members who screen annually some 2,400 rules and regulations. From 1981 to 1985, of the 12,233 rules OMB reviewed, 1,500 were changed after review and some 450 were returned for reconsideration.[32]

Each agency must provide a regulatory impact analysis (RIA) of final rules, justifying costs, perceived advantages, and possible alternatives. OMB determines from the RIAs whether the rules are consistent with OMB's own criteria. If they are not, OMB returns the rules to the agency for changes.[33]

The administrative clearance process has had the effect of decreasing the number of regulations drafted. Agencies fear that OMB will reject their rules, so they live without them. Administrative clearance, then, is a very powerful tool. OMB ensures that administrative regulations conform to presidents' general policy orientations. As a former staff member of the Environmental Protection Agency remarked, "You don't spend two years thinking about a regulation without thinking about whether OMB is going to shoot it down."[34]

OMB and the Plural Presidency. Budget preparation, legislative clearance, enrolled bill evaluations, and administrative clearance reveal the imprint of the presidency on the government and the imprint of OMB on the presidency. OMB houses specialized units, which daily practice set routines and procedures to process presidential business. Many OMB staff members are career employees who perform their tasks no matter who is president. Of course, presidents may set overall budget targets, ensure the content of a particular piece of proposed legislation, or decide to veto a controversial bill. But often they merely ratify the recommendations of OMB on proposed legislation, proposed executive orders, and enrolled bills. The OMB's administrative clearance procedures do not even involve the president, although they work on the chief executives' behalf. OMB procedures purposely remove presidents from, rather than involve them in, as much daily presidential business as possible.

WHITE HOUSE GENERALISTS

Organizations employ generalists—people with no limits to their jurisdiction—to monitor the "big picture." Presidents need generalists to direct the energy of the staff toward presidential goals and to act as a centripetal force to tie the specialized offices together. The presidential organization has three individuals or groups that could act as generalists: the vice president, the cabinet, and the presidents' immediate advisers. Presidents, however, have employed only the last group with any regularity. The vice president and the cabinet are more nearly satellites of the presidential organization than integral parts of it.

Vice Presidents

Examined objectively, the position of vice president would seem to be a perfect place from which presidents could cultivate "assistant presidents"—general advisers who serve as policymakers, political analysts, and administrative directors. Vice presidential candidates are presidents' own choices. The Constitution gives vice presidents nothing to do other than cast rare tie-breaking votes as presiding officers of the Senate. Vice presidents' days, then, are virtually wide open. Yet, among *all* vice presidents, only Walter Mondale, Carter's vice president, served as a respected adviser who saw Carter at regular weekly meetings, was privy to many sensitive decisions, and received copies of documents that went through the Oval Office. Although George Bush's role was not as central as Mondale's, Bush, as Ronald Reagan's vice president, played an active role by heading several presidential committees and being involved in some foreign policy discussions.

For a president, the political value of a vice president ends the moment the team is elected. Vice presidential candidates routinely are selected to "balance the ticket" rather than for their credentials as astute and experienced politicians. The balance is most often regional (Nixon, a Californian, ran with Eisenhower, a small-town midwesterner; Johnson, a rural Texan, ran with Kennedy, an urban easterner), but it also may be youth (Quayle) or gender (Ferraro). These balancing criteria mean that vice presidents may offer their presidents little once in office.

John Adams, the first vice president, summed up the fate of most of his successors: "I am nothing, but I may be everything." While they wait, vice presidents perform ceremonial and symbolic duties. They make good will tours, attend funerals of heads of state, make speeches, and do what presidents do not wish to do personally. Lyndon Johnson assigned Vice President Hubert Humphrey the task of explaining the Vietnam War in speeches throughout the country. Humphrey, who privately opposed the war, nonetheless went on the hustings to defend the Johnson policy. He said: "I did not become Vice President with President Johnson to cause him trouble. I feel a deep sense of loyalty and fidelity. I believe that if you can't have that, you have no right to accept the office."[35] As ceremonial and public tasks have increased, vice presidents' staffs have grown to sixty members and to a budget of some $2 million. Woodrow Wilson's comment of one hundred years ago is still apt today: "The chief embarrassment in discussing his office is, that in explaining how little there is to be said about it, one has evidently said all there is to say."[36]

The Cabinet

Every president since Lyndon Johnson has entered office promising to give his cabinet a true voice in running the government. Every president since Johnson has left office holding few cabinet meetings and drawing control tightly into the White House.

The cabinet is the collective body of department secretaries and some agency heads brought together to offer presidents advice.[37] Although each member is a specialist representing a specific policy jurisdiction, together, so the rationale goes, cabinet members reason as a general body to provide the best possible advice. Washington initiated the practice, and presidents throughout the nineteenth century relied on their cabinets as principal advisory bodies for both foreign and domestic affairs. The cabinet's role began to change during the twentieth century. As government grew, cabinet departments grew, directing the secretaries' attention more toward their respective departments and away from the president. Presidents themselves saw their personal staffs grow and began to seek their opinions. The White House staff soon outstripped most of the cabinet in access to presidents.

Recent presidents have found it neither productive nor comfortable to meet with cabinets as a whole, let alone rely on their collective judgments. Richard Nixon, who sat through many cabinet sessions as vice president under Eisenhower, observed:

most of them were unnecessary and boring. On the few issues that cut across all departments . . . group discussions would sometimes be informative. But the day had long since passed when it was useful to take an hour and a half to have the Secretary of Defense and Secretary of State discuss the Secretary of Transportation's new highway proposal.[38]

Kennedy echoed Nixon's remarks: "Cabinet meetings are simply useless. Why should the Postmaster General sit there and listen to a discussion of the problems of Laos?"[39] Today, cabinet meetings have been reduced to media events that show presidents seeking broad-ranging advice about key issues or sudden crises.

There are at least three reasons for the absence of the cabinet as a unit of organizational or political importance. First, presidents select cabinet members just as they select vice presidential candidates—for political purposes. The cabinet makes a president's first statement about how he will bring a cross-section of Americans into his administration. It is customary today to have a woman, a black, a Hispanic, a westerner, and a southerner fill cabinet slots. Cabinets reflect major sections and sectors of the country. Presidents often do not know these appointees, nor do presidents know whether they will be able to work with them.

Second, the cabinet is a body of unequals. Cabinet members differ according to their own credentials, past ties to presidents, and, most of all, the status of their departments. Inner and outer cabinets can be distinguished. Inner cabinet members include the secretaries of state, defense, and treasury and the attorney general. These cabinet members act as general counselors because their departments have broad-ranging missions and multiple interests that cut across various policy areas. The other domestic policy departments constitute the outer cabinet. Their secretaries are chosen to represent interests in transportation, housing, labor, energy, health, and so on. They are advocates for their departments and clients rather than ecumenical counselors.[40]

Third, the most important reason for the failure of presidents to use the cabinet as a generalist group is the role of members of the cabinet as individuals. Members of the cabinet have two jobs: (1) they serve as heads of executive departments, and (2) they serve as presidential advisers. Department heads, even within the inner cabinet, are advocates for their own departments' outlooks. They stake out organizational turf that is departmental rather than presidential in focus. As presidential advisers, cabinet members recognize that they can have far greater impact in personal meetings with the president than in large group meetings with a dozen or more other people present. The cabinet, then, is one of the few organizations of government for which the whole is *less* than the sum of its parts.

Presidents' Immediate Advisers

The president's immediate advisers—in particular, the chief of staff—are principal coordinators who ensure, according to Donald Rumsfeld, Ford's chief of staff, "an orderly flow of work, meetings, paper, appointments, thought, and action that satisfies the President and serves the President."[41] These top advisers include the chief of staff, national security adviser, director of the Office of Management and Budget, assistant for domestic affairs, press secretary, communications adviser, counsel to the president, and several other assistants. They number no more than two dozen people and often fewer. Presidents always have relied on small groups of people who they hope will be loyal advisers. These people are commonly long-time friends or trusted campaign workers. People nicknamed Kennedy's immediate advisers, who included Kenneth O'Donnell, Lawrence O'Brien, and Robert Kennedy, the "Irish mafia." Carter was identified with the "Georgia mafia": Bert Lance, Charles Kirbo, Jody Powell, and Hamilton Jordan. Bush brought to the White House top campaign strategists John Sununu and James Baker (the latter had been a top adviser to President Reagan). John Ehrlichman, a top Nixon aide, pointed to the one factor that all senior appointments have in common: "The President's confidence is the only qualification for working in the White House."[42]

Nevertheless, that lone qualification leaves many White House staff members ill prepared for the governing responsibilities they undertake. A White House staffer observed, "The virtues needed in the crucible of a campaign—are almost the opposite of the preparation needed for life within the White House."[43] The campaign simplifies issues and heightens the differences between sides, but the White House depends on accurate information that takes into account the many positions of any one issue multiplied by several hundred issues. The immediate advisers act as intermediaries between presidents and other people within the Executive Office of the President and between other politicians and leaders both in and out of Washington. They are policymakers, gatekeepers, and coordinators. Often they give presidents their own views on policy matters. Even if they do not, the gates they leave open or shut may have a great deal to do with the direction policy takes.

COORDINATION

Presidents have employed three methods of coordination for the presidential organization: (1) competitive, (2) collegial, and (3) hierarchical (see Figure 8.2).[44] The advantages and disadvantages of each are outlined in Table 8.4. Ironically, their attempts largely corral the top advisers, rather than steer the Executive Office of the President below.

Franklin Roosevelt preferred a *competitive* approach. He acted as his own chief of staff and assigned tasks to staff members who reported directly to him. He had no chain of command; all his key staffers had access to him. To avoid isolation and maximize information, he often gave the same assignment to more than one aide. "There is something to be said for having a little conflict between agencies," Roosevelt commented. "A little rivalry is stimulating, you know. It keeps everybody going to prove that he is a better fellow than the next man. It keeps them honest too."[45]

A more common approach among presidents is the *collegial*

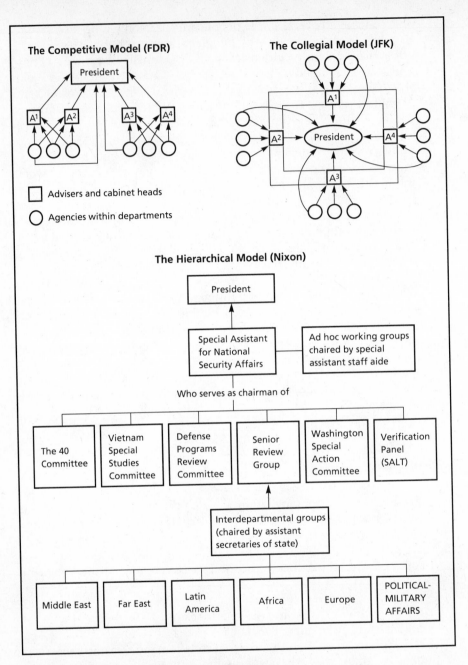

Figure 8.2 Methods of Presidential Coordination

In the *competitive* approach, the president acts as his own chief of staff and assigns several staffers to a single task. They compete to achieve the best results. In the *collegial* approach, the president also serves as his own chief of staff, but he assigns staffers separate tasks. Staff members share information and ideas to achieve the best results. In the *hierarchical* approach, the president uses a chief of staff who directs the flow of information to and from the president. Staff members are organized in a top-down chain of command to achieve the best results. [*Source:* Alexander L. George, *Presidential Decision Making in Foreign Policy: The Effective Use of Information and Advice* (Boulder, Colo.: Westview Press, 1980), 150, 156, 158. Copyright © 1980 by Westview Press. Reprinted by permission.]

Table 8.4 Presidential Administrative Models

Benefits	Costs
Hierarchical approach	
Orderly decision process enforces more thorough analysis.	The hierarchy which screens information may also distort it. Tendency of the screening process to wash out or distort political pressures and public sentiments.
Conserves the decision maker's time and attention for the big decision. Emphasizes the optimal.	Tendency to respond slowly or inappropriately in crisis.
Competitive approach	
Places the decision maker in the mainstream of the information network. Tends to generate solutions that are politically feasible and bureaucratically doable.	Places large demands on decision maker's time and attention. Exposes decision maker to partial or biased information. Decision process may overly sacrifice optimality for doability.
Generates creative ideas, partially as a result of the "stimulus" of competition, but also because this unstructured kind of information network is more open to ideas from the outside.	Tendency to aggravate staff competition with the risk that aides may pursue their own interests at the expense of the decision maker.
	Wear and tear on aides fosters attrition and high turnover.
Collegial approach	
Seeks to achieve both optimally and doability. Involves the decision maker in the information network but somewhat eases the demands upon him by stressing teamwork over competition.	Places substantial demands on the decision maker's time and attention. Requires unusual interpersonal skill in dealing with subordinates, mediating differences, and maintaining teamwork among colleagues.
	Risk that "teamwork" will degenerate into a closed system of mutual support.

Source: Richard T. Johnson, *Managing the White House* (New York: Harper and Row, 1974), 238. Copyright © 1974 by Richard Tanner Johnson. Reprinted by permission of HarperCollins Publishers.

method. It can be described as a wheel, with the president as the hub and his senior staff members as the spokes. All senior staff members have direct access to the president, who, as in the competitive approach, acts as his own chief of staff. Kennedy, Johnson, Ford, and Carter adopted this approach, although Ford and Carter eventually abandoned it. The collegial approach builds a team of equals who bring different points of view together and work toward consensus. The approach, however, may overwhelm presidents with too much information and too many decisions. The right hand may not know what the left hand is doing.

In the post-Watergate era, both Ford and Carter pledged "open"

Oval Offices and began their administrations with nine people reporting directly to them. Ford bogged down in the collegiality after several months. He named Donald Rumsfeld "staff coordinator" rather than giving him the more imperial title "chief of staff." Rumsfeld's successor, Richard Cheney, was reminded of the collegial approach at a White House staff party. He received a bicycle wheel mounted on a board with each of its spokes mangled and tangled. A plaque below read: "The spokes of the wheel: a rare form of management artistry as conceived by Don Rumsfeld and modified by Dick Cheney." Cheney left the wheel and a note on his desk as a gift to incoming Carter adviser Hamilton Jordan. The note read, "Dear Ham. Beware the spokes of the wheel."[46]

Carter, like Caesar, did not heed the warning. Carter began his term as his own chief of staff. Soon, though, he felt overwhelmed by the minutiae he often received. In addition, problems of coordination abounded. Carter and his chief foreign policy advisers, Zbigniew Brzezinski (national security adviser) and Cyrus Vance (secretary of state), decided to move toward a joint communiqué with the Soviet Union on resumption of Geneva talks on the Middle East. The Soviet Union then would play an active role in the region. The trio consulted no domestic advisers and did not foresee the outcries from American Jews when the idea was announced. Stuart Eizenstadt, Carter's domestic policy chief, wrote to his boss in December 1977:

I continue to believe that our most serious structural problem is the lack of internal White House coordination. There is no mechanism by which, on a regular basis, we can find out what the other is doing that may have impact on an area in which we are working . . . no one has been given the directive to sort out the various priorities of our work, to coordinate our work and make sure it is all going in the same direction, before it all pours in to you.[47]

Carter switched to a more hierarchical approach, making Hamilton Jordan his chief of staff.

A chain of command among senior staff members distinguishes the *hierarchical* method. The scheme involves one or more of presidents' top aides serving as chief(s) of staff. All information to and from the president runs through these chiefs. Eisenhower, Ford, Carter, and Bush used a single chief of staff. Sherman Adams, Eisenhower's chief of staff, approved all communication going to the president. If the letters "OK SA" did not appear on documents, they never appeared on Eisenhower's desk. In Adams's words, the chief of staff "would boil down, simplify, and expedite the urgent business that had to be brought to [the President's] personal attention and to keep as much work of secondary importance as possible off his desk."[48] The joke in Washington was "What would happen if Adams died and Eisenhower became president?"

Nixon and Reagan modified the hierarchy to allow multiple chiefs. Nixon had two gatekeepers, H. R. Haldeman and John Ehrlichman. Haldeman was officially designated chief of staff; Ehrlichman was head of domestic policy. But both restricted access to Nixon, and the three jointly planned political strategies and policy moves. In his first term, Reagan relied on a threesome: James Baker (chief of staff), Michael Deaver (media events), and Edwin Meese (policymaking). Together the three presented Reagan with a single option, which Reagan would accept, modify, or reject. In Reagan's second term, he abandoned the triumvirate for a single chief of staff—Donald Regan.

The hierarchical approach has advantages and disadvantages. In theory it provides presidents with options based on thorough analysis and frees them from constant staff interruptions, but it also can isolate them. Many chiefs of staff have been portrayed as demonic Rasputins who clutch power by denying others access to the president. The president becomes the weary, disarmed Czar Nicholas on the eve of the Russian Revolution.

There is, however, a growing consensus among White House staff members that neither the competitive nor the collegial approach works well any longer. In Richard Cheney's words, "Somebody has to be in charge."[49] The hierarchical approach permits the chief of staff to perform three roles: information broker, lightning rod, and personnel manager. Each role is difficult for presidents to perform themselves and impossible for presidents to do without.

As *information broker*, the chief of staff must "staff out" all issues so that all relevant sides return to the president. The chief then must coordinate and distill these many sides so the president has a manageable profile of options from which to decide or a single option that he may modify.

As *lightning rod*, the chief of staff takes the blame for unpopular administration decisions so that the president can appear statesmanlike. In the Bush White House, a good-cop, bad-cop routine became a staple, with John Sununu, first chief of staff, playing the heavy and taking the heat for the kind, gentle Bush. H. R. Haldeman summed up the dynamic: "Every President needs his s.o.b. and I'm Nixon's."[50]

As *personnel manager*, the chief of staff negotiates with cabinet officers and strokes the egos of key officials. Richard Cheney recalled that at least once a month he would get a phone call, "and it would be a situation in which Pat Moynihan [Ambassador to the United Nations] was calling threatening to resign or Henry Kissinger [Secretary of State] was threatening to resign because they didn't like each other."[51]

It should be kept in mind that there are limits to the reach of the hierarchy. Staff coordination is most successful at the very top. Below this level, the decentralization of the larger presidential organization prevails. Presidents, even with their chiefs of staff, control and coordinate only so much of the presidency.

CONCLUSION

The presidential organization is a quasi-personal, quasi-formal organization. In 1939, when Franklin Roosevelt established the Executive Office of the President, the White House organization was designed to be a personal organization—one that could be shaped and re-shaped by each president. Today, the personal organization is in constant motion. The people within it change frequently. Their stay is typically less than two years. At the end of each president's term, there is a mass exodus of people who clean out their drawers and their filing cabinets. Yet the White House organization also is a continuing formal enterprise. Bradley Patterson observes that there is "a set of elemental White House functions that cannot be severed from the presidency, nor can they be implanted elsewhere."[52]

The continuity of the White House organization results from a size, structure, and set of procedures that are difficult to dismantle, even though a large proportion of personnel within the organization come and go with each president. Perhaps nothing better underscores the continuity of the organization than a story about Nixon's last day in office. On the afternoon that Richard Nixon was to resign, a congressional staffer called the White House and asked if several minor pieces of legislation were "in accordance with the president's program."[53] There was no president, nor was there a presidential program on that afternoon, but the presidential organization remained intact and continued to operate as if that day was like any other.

Both the personal and the formal aspects of the organization identify the plural nature of the presidency—the way in which its units and people work in various uncoordinated, often conflicting ways. Size contributes to the plurality. Although presidents put their own people in various positions, there are simply too many people in too many well-established offices to act in a comprehensive, directed way. Specialization contributes to the plurality. Units and individuals carve out for themselves arenas of work that others are not supposed to touch. The Office of Management and Budget's central clearance procedures contribute to the plurality. OMB procedures that apply to a vast number of budget proposals, to proposed legislation, to final legislation, and to administrative regulations remove the president further and further from "his organization." Generalists survive the plurality but frequently have difficulty succeeding in it.

The decentralized organization poses a keen dilemma for presidents. Although the single executive image prompts presidents to seek singular control of information and policy decisions, they are forced to work through a collective apparatus. The pastiche of staffs, interests, and loyalties often makes it difficult for presidents to gain either the information or the control they seek. Presidents do not control the collective organization, although the collectivity controls many of their decisions. Although presidents are said to have "administrations," the organization of the presidency increases the independence and decreases the interdependence of "the president" and his "administration." This independence is embroidered into the plural presidency. ■

FURTHER READING

On the size of the Executive Office of the President, see: Gary King and Lyn Ragsdale, *The Elusive Executive* (Washington, D.C.: CQ Press, 1988); *1991/92 Federal Staff Directory* (Mt. Vernon, Va.: Staff Directories, Ltd., 1991). On the development and current organization of the Executive Office of the President, see: Harold Relyea, "Growth and Development of the President's Office," in *The American Presidency: A Policy Perspective from Readings and Documents,* ed. D. Kozak and K. Ciboski (Chicago: Nelson, Hall, 1985), 105–143; Bradley Patterson, Jr., *The Ring of Power* (New York: Basic Books, 1988). On the Office of Management and Budget, see: Larry Berman, *The Office of Management and Budget and the Presidency,, 1921–1979* (Princeton, N.J.: Princeton University Press, 1979). On White House chiefs of staff, see: Samuel Kernell and Samuel Popkin, eds. *Chief of Staff* (Berkeley: University of California Press, 1986).

N O T E S

1. *Weekly Compilation of Presidential Documents,* May 16, 1979 (Washington, D.C.: U.S. Government Printing Office, 1979), 820.
2. Michael Grossman and Martha Kumar, *Portraying the President* (Baltimore: Johns Hopkins University Press, 1981), 124–125.
3. The total is 42 not 43 because the White House Office is not counted as a unit.
4. Alfred de Grazia, "The Myth of the President," in *The Presidency,* ed. A. Wildavsky (Boston: Little, Brown, 1969), 50.
5. The figures for this paragraph are drawn from Harold Relyea, "Growth and Development of the President's Office," in *The American Presidency: A Policy Perspective from Readings and Documents,* ed. D. Kozak and K. Ciboski (Chicago: Nelson, Hall, 1985), 107–110.
6. Quoted in Arthur Tourtellot, *The Presidents on the Presidency* (New York: Doubleday, 1964), 369.
7. *Report of the President's Committee on Administrative Management* (Washington, D.C.: U.S. Government Printing Office, 1937), 5.
8. The figures on staff size and budgets discussed below are found in Gary King and Lyn Ragsdale, *The Elusive Executive* (Washington, D.C.: Congressional Quarterly Press, 1988), 205–216.

9. 60 U.S. Statute 24, February, 20, 1946.

10. Bradley Patterson, Jr., *The Ring of Power* (New York: Basic Books, 1988), 339.

11. Jane Mayer and Doyle McManus, *Landslide: The Unmaking of the President, 1984–1988* (Boston: Houghton Mifflin, 1988), 62. These authors list the size of the staff in 1985 as 186.

12. Ben Heineman, Jr., and Curtis Hessler, *Memorandum for the President* (New York: Random House, 1980), 176–177.

13. Mayer and McManus, 61.

14. Quoted in William Bundy, "The National Security Process, Plus Ça Change . . . ?" *International Security* 7 (Winter 1982–1983): 94–109.

15. Jimmy Carter, *Keeping Faith* (New York: Bantam Books, 1982), 53.

16. Tom Wicker, "A Tale of Two Silences," *New York Times*, May 4, 1980, E23.

17. Roger Porter, "The President and Economic Policy: Problems, Patterns, and Alternatives," in *The Illusion of Presidential Government*, ed. H. Heclo and L. Salamon (Boulder, Colo.: Westview Press, 1981), 209.

18. Quoted in James Conaway, "Goodbye, Marty," *Washington Post National Weekly Edition*, June 11, 1984, 21.

19. Patterson, 86.

20. Stephen Wayne, *The Legislative Presidency* (New York: Harper and Row, 1978), 141–142.

21. Grossman and Kumar, 89.

22. King and Ragsdale, 202.

23. Peggy Noonan, *Exit Laughing* (New York: Random House, 1989).

24. These figures are based on Ronald Reagan's workload in 1984 as drawn from King and Ragsdale.

25. Sherman Adams, *First Hand Report: The Story of the Eisenhower Administration* (New York: Harper, 1961), 57.

26. G. Calvin MacKenzie, *The Politics of Presidential Appointments* (New York: Free Press, 1981), 18–19.

27. Larry Berman, *The Office of Management and Budget and the Presidency, 1921–1979* (Princeton, N.J.: Princeton University Press, 1979), 4.

28. Ibid., 7.

29. Paul Light, *The President's Agenda* (Baltimore: Johns Hopkins University Press, 1982), 4.

30. Berman, 10.

31. Stephen Wayne, Richard Cole, and James Hyde, "Advising the President on Enrolled Legislation: Patterns of Executive Influence," *Political Science Quarterly* 94 (Summer 1979): 303–317.

32. Joseph Cooper and William West, "Presidential Power and Republican Government: The Theory and Practice of OMB Review of Agency Rules," *Journal of Politics* 50 (November 1988).

33. Ibid., 864–895. See also William West and Joseph Cooper, "The Rise of Administrative Clearance," in *The Presidency and Public Policy Making*, ed. G. Edwards, S. Shull, and N. Thomas (Pittsburgh: University of Pittsburgh Press, 1985), 192–214.

34. Quoted in Cooper and West, 876–877,

35. Adams and Humphrey quoted in Barbara Hinckley, *Problems of the Presidency* (Glenview, Ill.: Scott, Foresman, 1985), 101, 103.

36. Woodrow Wilson, *Congressional Government* (Gloucester, Mass.: Peter Smith, 1973), 162; first published in 1885.

37. Richard Fenno, *The President's Cabinet* (New York: Vintage Books, 1959).

38. Richard Nixon, *RN: The Memoirs of Richard Nixon* (New York: Grosset and Dunlap, 1978), 338.

39. Arthur Schlesinger, Jr., *A Thousand Days* (Greenwich, Conn.: Fawcett Books, 1967), 632.

40. Thomas Cronin, *The State of the Presidency*, 2d ed. (Boston: Little, Brown, 1980), 274–278.

41. Quoted from an interview with Patterson, 303.

42. John Ehrlichman interviewed by James Pfiffner, *The Strategic Presidency* (Chicago: Dorsey Press, 1988), 21.

43. Quoted in ibid., 21.

44. This scheme is adapted from Richard Johnson, "Presidential Style," in *Perspectives on the Presidency*, ed. A. Wildavsky (Boston: Little, Brown, 1975), 262–300.

45. Arthur Schlesinger, Jr., *The Coming of the New Deal* (Boston: Houghton Mifflin, 1959), 535.

46. Quoted in Pfiffner, 29.

47. Quoted in Patterson, 302.

48. Adams, 57.

49. Interview by Pfiffner, 29.

50. Quoted in R. W. Apple, Jr., "Haldeman the Fierce, Haldeman the Faithful, Haldeman the Fallen," *New York Times Magazine*, May 6, 1973.

51. Richard Cheney, "Twenty-five Years," in *Chief of Staff*, ed. S. Kernell and S. Popkin (Berkeley: University of California Press, 1986), 62.

52. Patterson, 85.

53. Hugh Heclo, "Introduction: The Presidential Illusion," in Heclo and L. Salamon, 3.

CHAPTER 9

Presidential Ambiguity

P resident Richard Nixon loved to contemplate tough decisions in the Lincoln sitting room, an intimate, informal parlor off the Lincoln bedroom upstairs at the White House. Nixon would build a fire, have his Irish setter King Timahoe by his side, and relax in a heavy leather wingback chair. Even in the summertime, Nixon would have his fire. He instructed the White House staff to turn up the air conditioning so Washington's sultry heat would not destroy the reflective mood. Nixon would spend hours staring intently at the fire's hue and body.

The single executive image promotes this view of presidents making the tough choices alone. But the image also presumes that a comprehensive, step-by-step decision process precedes presidents' efforts in the friendless cloister. In this view, the members of the president's staff follow a rational model of decision making. They explore all options, measure the costs and benefits of each, and select the option with the highest benefits and lowest costs. They then meticulously brief the president on their recommendation. The president's claim of power and importance from the single executive image presupposes that he has sufficient resources of staff, information, time, and ingenuity to apply this rational approach. Kennedy aide Theodore Sorensen described the rational ideal:

> first: agreement on the facts;
> second: agreement on the overall policy objective;
> third: a precise definition of the problem;
> fourth: a canvassing of all possible solutions, with all their shades and variations;
> fifth: a list of all the possible consequences that would flow from each solution;
> sixth: a recommendation and final choice of one alternative;
> seventh: the communication of that selection; and
> eighth: provision for its execution.[1]

Such a rational approach rarely, if ever, occurs in presidential (or any other) decision making. Using the single executive image, presidents claim that they are in charge of the government. This claim lands them in the midst of a maelstrom of decisions on policy issues, some of which may involve other institutions and the demands of organized group interests. The decentralized organization of the plural presidency steps in to develop policy proposals; devise plans to see the proposals through Congress, the executive branch, and the courts; and sell the proposals to attentive and not-so-attentive segments of the American public. Yet, the decentralized organization makes thousands of decisions annually in a less than fully informed and coordinated way. The diffused arrangement of offices and officers of the institution impedes the gathering of information. Lack of time may block attention to detail. Even with a strong chief of staff, coordinating the efforts of all of the offices and officers is difficult. The single executive image's edifice of a secluded president assisted by his efficient and omniscient staff crumbles in the day-to-day workings of the presidential organization.

This chapter addresses the "how" of presidential decision making—the way the presidential organization makes decisions. Within the decentralized organization, ambiguous decision processes displace rationality. Presidents and their staffs make decisions *in spite of not fully knowing* what is going on, what they want, how to get what they want, or who should be involved. The size of the decentralized organization promotes ambiguity. Because there are so many hands within the organization, some hands do not know what other hands are doing. Specialization also promotes ambiguity. Despite the division of labor, there is overlap among various offices' jurisdictions. Several specialties may clash or several offices may compete to dominate a particular specialty. These skirmishes result in ambiguity about what direction the institution should take, how things should be handled, and who should handle what. The president's top aides, who act as generalists, cannot dispel the ambiguity. Often they are too busy competing with each other for the president's attention to devote any time to coordination. Internal plurality in the presidency thus arises from the decentralized organization itself and from the ambiguous decision processes within it. The business of making decisions in the plural presidency is anything but business as usual.

FOUR TYPES OF AMBIGUITY

In place of the rational plan outlined by Sorensen, presidential decision making can be boiled down to four distinct but interrelated processes:

1. Information gathering on problems and solutions

2. Goal seeking about what should be accomplished

3. Coordination within the institution to accomplish the goals

4. Determining who will play the decision game

Ambiguity clouds each of those processes. Presidential decision makers cannot gather all the information they need to address problems and solutions. The absence of information or the presence of sketchy information produces *informational ambiguity*. Presidential decision makers are never crystal clear about the goals they are seeking. They may establish multiple goals or may not know what they hope to accomplish. This confusion fosters *goal ambiguity*. The coordination within the institution needed to accomplish goals is often lacking. Offices within the organization pursue independent directions. When it is unclear how the offices handling a decision will work together, the result is *operational ambiguity*. Decision makers can never be sure who will be involved in making a particular decision. For many White House decisions, there are no hard and fast rules about which offices have jurisdiction over a specific matter and which will remain on the sidelines. *Participatory ambiguity* arises.

Informational Ambiguity

The rational model suggests that decision makers should gather all relevant information when making decisions. Information gathering in the plural presidency, however, is complicated and anything but comprehensive. Recall from Chapter 7 that presidential decision makers pay heed to three environments: policy, interinstitutional, and group. In the *policy* environment, decisions pertain to events, conditions, and issues in the foreign, military, economic, and domestic arenas. In the *interinstitutional* environment, the conflicts, confusions, and cooperation among various institutions of government—Congress, the courts, executive departments and agencies, state and local governments—are salient. In the *group* environment, an array of organized interests—business lobbies, consumer and environmental groups, labor organizations, among others—make demands on the government. Presidential decision makers take into account each of these environments and their overlap. Yet they can hope to gather information on only a small portion of each. Some stones are always left unturned.

Late in 1989, the Bush administration prepared to announce American policy on global warming.[2] Informational ambiguity dogged Bush officials in their attempt to gather evidence on global warming. Global warming is a rise in Earth's temperature that occurs when chemical gases emitted into the atmosphere deplete the protective ozone layer. With the ozone layer diminished, more light penetrates to the Earth's surface, causing temperatures to rise. White House officials found an abundance of research on global warming but no agreement among scientists about the severity of the problem and its causes. The Bush administration knew that Congress too had been gathering information on global warming, some of which contradicted that of the White House. In addition, there was a split between businesses, which said that cries about ozone depletion were premature, and environmental groups, which said that the extent of depletion had actually been underestimated. Informational ambiguity thus arose from the policy, interinstitutional, and group environments.

Goal Ambiguity

The rational approach states that decision makers should have explicitly stated goals and know the relative importance of each. Within the plural presidency, however, informational ambiguity hampers such pristine goal seeking. It becomes difficult for decision makers to develop clear priorities when they have less-than-solid information about what is going on. Moreover, the decentralized organization of the White House exacerbates this goal ambiguity. Multiple offices have difficulty establishing a common set of goals. The units may disagree over what conditions are serious problems. They may identify several policy options, all good, that conflict. They may outline several policy options, all bad, that may be all that are available. Within units, conflicts may arise about which goals to pursue.

Five top Bush officials, each representing a different White House unit or executive department, asserted different goals on global warming. Energy Secretary James Watkins and Environmental Protection Agency chief William Reilly felt that the evidence on global warming was strong enough to warrant a firm American policy stand. Secretary of State James Baker, knowing that all other major Western nations attending the conference would advocate a tough attack on global warming, recognized the adverse diplomatic consequences of a soft stand by the United States. The president's science adviser, Dr. D. Allan Bromley, who chaired the Domestic Policy Staff working group on climate change, was doubtful about the extent of the greenhouse effect. He was influenced by Chief of Staff John Sununu, who was openly skeptical about the scientific evidence on global warming and hesitant to advance a policy that would cut the use of fossil fuels and thereby cost Americans jobs: "If you're going to make a trillion-dollar decision, if you're going to make a decision that's going to affect a million jobs, you ought to make it on the basis of what you know and not on the basis of what your emotions may lead you to feel."[3] The mix of these goals and their incompatibility fostered goal ambiguity.

Goals can be looked on as two-sided. One side identifies a problem to alleviate, say, global warming. The other side offers a program to remedy the problem, say, the elimination of chlorofluorocarbons (known to deplete the ozone). Intuitively, splitting the two sides may seem difficult, but politically it happens often. The Bush advisers tried to determine the status of global warming as a problem, completely independent of programs to alleviate the problem. Because of the complexity of the environment and uncertainty about how to proceed, different decision makers may work on the two sides separately. Uncertainty also prevents White House decision makers from calculating which condition in the environment is the "worst" problem. Instead, decision makers usually assess problems in relative terms.[4] They make simple calculations about whether a condition has worsened over a given time period or whether it looks worse than it did under a predecessor. Having made these calculations, decision makers see no necessary reason to examine the other side of the goal—namely, the program. The White House may announce that the nation's rising murder rate is an outrage but utter no word about how to lower it.

Uncertainty also prevents White House decision makers from determining which course of action is the "best" choice—the one solution that fully alleviates the problem. Instead, they "satisfice"—they accept satisfactory rather than optimal solutions. Decision makers' interests determine what is satisfactory. President Bush's interests in global warming were to safeguard his image as the "environmental president" (a characterization he had given himself during the 1988 election campaign) and to protect businesses that were opposed to paying for environmental changes. Thus, a satisfactory solution for Bush was to say something about global warming (to polish the image) but to do little about global warming (to protect businesses). When interests determine satisfaction, flipping the coin to the other side—the problem—is not necessary. The White House may announce a program to offer equipment and training money to police departments—when the crime rate is steady.

Operational Ambiguity

When decision making is rational, decision processes within an organization are coordinated and known to everyone. The decentralized organization and goal ambiguity of the plural presidency are barriers to such exactness. Instead, they produce operational ambiguity. The institution faces a dilemma of coordination. Units within the White House define problems and offer solutions without being fully aware of their own actions or others' actions. There is no White House operations manual. Trial and error often substitutes for coordination in linking units' efforts.

The Bush advisers fashioned the president's global warming policy by one well-tested political procedure: a fight. The Environmental Protection Agency, the Energy Department, and the science adviser's office shared jurisdiction over the policy. Sununu claimed superjurisdiction over all Bush decisions. Within the free-for-all of a decentralized organization, it becomes difficult to set up coordination mechanisms.

Participatory Ambiguity

The rational model indicates that only individuals with full knowledge of problems and solutions will make the final decisions. Operational ambiguity within and across offices gives rise to participatory ambiguity. No one is fully certain who will participate in decisions, who will bring problems and solutions together, and how much time can be devoted to decision making. Cohen, March, and Olsen write that "participants vary in the amount of time and effort they devote to different domains; involvement varies from one time to another."[5] Participatory and operational ambiguity are intertwined. Both depend on who formulates the question, who presents the alternatives, and how they are discussed. Who sets what policy is determined in an ad hoc fashion, depending on who participates when.

If Sununu had stayed out of the negotiations on global warming policy, Bromley might have been outvoted by the others. The original text of Bush's speech advocated tough policies to "cut off the added use of coal, oil and natural gas." This Sununu vetoed. Reilly, Watkins, and Baker fought back against Sununu's efforts to vitiate the text still more. In February 1990, President Bush announced U.S. policy on global warming, calling for economic and environmental concerns to be balanced: "our policies must be consistent with economic growth."[6]

In May 1992, Bush reaffirmed this policy at the United Nations' Earth Summit in Rio de Janeiro.[7] The decision to attend the Rio Conference (which was to put into effect a worldwide environmental plan) followed months of fractious debate within the administration, similar in tone to the debate two years before but with different players. Bush's conservative advisers and economic experts, including Richard Darman, director of the Office of Management and Budget, and Vice President Dan Quayle, opposed the trip. His campaign manager, Robert Teeter, National Security Adviser Brent Scowcroft, Environmental Protection Agency chief William Reilly, and senior officials at the State Department favored the move and carried the day—Bush would attend the conference.[8]

But this was only the first round of the debate. In Rio, Reilly, as the head of the American delegation, attempted to work out a compromise on one of the conference treaties so that the United States would support it. Vice President Quayle's office, strongly opposed to the treaty, leaked Reilly's memo about the specifics of the compromise. Word came from the White House that "We'll just have to give him more guidance" so that Reilly would understand that no compromise was desired.[9] Later, Reilly commented that his position at the conference had been so undermined that it was like doing a bungee jump and having someone cut the cord. The example demonstrates the extent of participatory ambiguity within the decentralized organization, even on a single policy matter. Players may gain the upper hand at one time but not again, depending on who else is in the game.

THE PRESIDENTIAL GARBAGE CAN

Although limited information, fuzzy goals, little coordination, and splintered participation replace intelligibility and simplicity in decision making, the presidential organization continues to make decisions at a frenetic pace. A question then arises, how do presidential decision makers working within a decentralized organization in which ambiguity is rampant still get done the job demanded by the single executive image? The answer is that they use what has been called the "garbage can" approach to decision making.[10] Problems, solutions, and political considerations are tossed into the can with no attention to order or orderliness. The garbage can model removes the most fundamental step in the rational model: people recognizing problems before seeking solutions. Without this logic, there are no longer neat, orderly stages beginning with the facts known about a problem and ending with a decision about how to solve the problem. Political scientist John Kingdon observes that recognizing problems and developing solutions are "different processes, they do not necessarily follow one another through time in any regular pattern.[11] The garbage can approach thus separates problems from solutions: problems are not necessarily identified before solutions are sought.

How are problems and solutions eventually linked? Political considerations tend to bring them together. President Bush attempted to pursue two solutions, incompatible at least on their face, to the problem of global warming. He sought to promote economic growth and protect the environment. Political strategy transcended the incompatibility between the environment and the economy. Bush wished to promote himself as the "environmental president" in the 1992 campaign and at the same time hoped to shore up his position with businesses, many of which were strong contributors to his election campaign. Thus, there are three types of "garbage" in the presidential garbage can: problems, policies (or solutions), and politics.

What Is the Problem?

Problems are distinct from conditions. People face all sorts of conditions every day: disease, addiction, dilapidated housing, unsatisfying jobs, bad weather. Conditions become problems only when people believe that something should be done about them. Critics charged that the Bush administration treated global warming as a condition, not as a problem to be dealt with quickly. A government official remarked:

We live with these social problems for a while, and then we finally decide that if we're serious about them we should do [something about] it. The problem doesn't have to get any worse or any better. It doesn't have to be some major change in the problem. Take poverty. Poverty didn't get any worse. Lyndon Johnson just decided to undertake this war on poverty. Why one moment seems better than another I don't know.[12]

The plural presidency's decentralized organization is designed to handle an array of problems. So "choosing the problems is the easiest part of the process," observed a White House aide. "There is relatively little conflict: the President and staff develop a consensus on the most valuable issues. We all have goals which lead us toward given issues. The trouble comes when you have to talk about specific solutions."[13] Table 9.1 lists the most important domestic problems identified by aides to Presidents Kennedy through Carter, as presented in research by political scientist Paul Light.

Three types of incentives work to identify conditions as major problems: (1) electoral, (2) programmatic, and (3) historical (see Table 9.2). Conditions often are "upgraded" to problems during a president's election campaign. George Bush announced during the 1988 campaign that America's education system had become a major problem, although the deteriorating condition of education had been apparent for some time. Problems also may be attractive foci of future

Table 9.1 Percentage of Domestic Programs by Issue Area, from Kennedy to Carter

Program	Kennedy/ Johnson	Johnson	Nixon, I	Nixon, II	Ford	Carter
Agriculture	4	2	3	0	0	2
Civil rights	7	4	3	0	0	0
Consumer affairs	4	10	5	4	0	10
Crime	4	9	13	4	19	0
Education	19	13	8	4	0	4
Energy	0	0	0	40	31	24
Government affairs	4	10	18	8	6	15
Health[1]	9	8	13	12	12	13
Labor/employment	19	5	5	0	6	9
Natural resources	13	17	18	20	6	7
Transportation	4	7	8	0	0	5
Urban affairs/welfare	17	18	10	8	19	11

1. Includes medical education—for example, nurses' training, medical school construction.
Source: OMB Legislative Reference Division clearance record in Paul Light, *The President's Agenda* (Baltimore/London: The Johns Hopkins University Press, 1991), 85. Used by permission.

Table 9.2 Benefits Sought in Domestic Programs (percentage)

President	Benefit		
	Electoral[1]	Historical[2]	Programmatic[3]
Kennedy	54	25	42
Johnson	44	37	52
Nixon	70	43	22
Ford	60	22	44
Carter	57	23	39

1. Programs intended to aid in the president's re-election efforts.
2. Programs intended to influence the way future historians will view the current president and presidency.
3. Programs that especially accord with the president's ideological orientation or personal beliefs.

Note: A total of 126 White House staff members were asked to name the benefits they hoped for in the selection of the top domestic programs of their respective administrations. Only the first two programs for each presidency were pursued. The percentages for each administration total more than one hundred because respondents could give more than one reply.

Source: Paul Light, *The President's Agenda* (Baltimore/London: The Johns Hopkins University Press, 1991), 72. Used by permission.

campaigns. As a Nixon campaign aide said, "Every President has to be reelected. That becomes the primary motive for decisions."[14]

Presidents and their administrations also identify certain problems with an eye toward good public policy. They have certain social concerns they wish to address. Lyndon Johnson, speaking of his Great Society measures, recalled his early career as a schoolteacher in the poor, drought-stricken hill country of Texas: "Somehow you never forget what poverty and hatred can do when you see its scars on the hopeful face of a young child."[15]

Finally, presidents identify problems that, if solved, will earn them their place in history. Presidents wish to be remembered for diplomatic breakthroughs with China (Nixon) and in the Middle East (Carter), for healing the nation (Ford), for revamping the economy (Reagan), and for pushing for civil rights (Johnson). As one Nixon aide recalled, "When public opinion polls go sour and Congress slows down, the President can always fall back on history. President Nixon spent a great deal of time wondering how his decisions would fare in twenty or thirty years."[16]

Events and conditions alone do not define problems. Since White House decision makers face informational ambiguity within the plural presidency, no objective indicators reveal when conditions need to be thought of as problems. Decision makers remain uncertain about the full details of conditions. There is, then, an interpretive, inherently political element to the definition of a problem. In identifying problems, presidential decision makers define other, possibly pressing conditions as "nonproblems," even though what is not addressed may be at least as critical as what is addressed. There were multiple signs about the weaknesses of the savings and loans during the 1980s, but the condition was not treated as a problem. Goal ambiguity also accompanies problem definition. People are uncertain how problems will overlap and whether they will create other, unintended problems. The Johnson administration's decision to tackle two problems simultaneously—poverty and war in Vietnam created a third problem—high inflation.

What Is the Solution?

Q: Did you ever fight over the agenda?

A: When didn't we fight? The hostilities usually came to a head over the State of the Union Address. We'd fight over the major programs and the laundry lists. We'd argue over the position of our pet projects and the President's emphasis. We'd fight over paragraphs, sentences, words, and even punctuation. I finally bought one of those pop-psychology marriage manuals to see if there wasn't some way to bring the staffs together.

Q: Did it work?

A: Hell no. You can't save a marriage like that.[17]

The single executive image demands that presidents not only address an array of national problems but use the importance, power, uniqueness, and visibility of their office to offer an assortment of solutions. Identifying solutions, however, is difficult for two reasons. First, the decentralization of the plural presidency makes it difficult to assert priorities. Although the offices of the presidency are designated to handle a variety of problems, how they prioritize solutions is another matter. Uncertainty prevails about where resources should be committed and who should benefit. Table 9.3 lists presidents' most important domestic programs as perceived by their staffs. Although there is considerable agreement about staff members on *the* most significant program, there is much less consensus on the others.

Second, the presidential environment creates further problems in establishing priorities. Establishing solutions is a matter of political importance in which other institutions and various organized groups have a stake. Solutions set up the political game of who calls the shots. Those who control the solutions, more than those who identify the problems, shape the direction of government and society. As political scientist E. E. Schattschneider wrote, "The definition of the alternatives is the supreme instrument of power."[18] Jimmy Carter learned that lesson in 1978, when organized labor pressured him to pursue a national health insurance plan. In 1977, the Carter people anticipated that a plan for comprehensive, universal insurance would die in Congress. They decided to shelve it, but labor leaders of the United Auto Workers and the AFL-CIO pushed Carter to present a bill. They, not Carter, succeeded in defining the alternatives. The

Table 9.3 President's Most Important Domestic Programs

President	Program	Percentage of staff mentioning program
Kennedy	Aid to education	91
	Medicare	77
	Unemployment	45
	Area development	18
	Civil rights	18
Johnson	Poverty	86
	Civil rights	79
	Medicare	64
	Aid to education	32
	Model cities	29
	Wilderness preservation	11
	Environmental protection	4
Nixon	Welfare reform	75
	Revenue sharing	65
	Crime	40
	Energy	35
	Environmental protection	15
Ford	Energy	79
	Inflation	50
	Regulatory reform	8
Carter	Energy	84
	Inflation	63
	Welfare reform	59
	Hospital cost containment	28
	Economic stimulus	19
	Reorganization	9

Note: Paul Light asked 126 White House staff members to name the most important domestic programs of their respective administrations. Respondents could give more than one reply.

Source: Paul Light, *The President's Agenda* (Baltimore/London: The Johns Hopkins University Press, 1991), 70. Used by permission.

Carter people had correctly assessed the political situation—the bill got nowhere—but being right was little substitute for being able to control the plan offered to Congress.

The first step in identifying solutions is to decide whether something should be done at all. A Carter staff member remarked, "Believe it or not, it is a legitimate solution to do nothing. To demand that Presidents always come up with detailed programs creates an overload."[19] Presidential decision makers assess whether it is wise to push a solution. How difficult will it be to get the solution through Congress or the bureaucracy? Will the public approve? Are foreign leaders convinced? Kennedy chose to do nothing about civil rights in 1961, his first year in office. During the election campaign, he had discussed it as a major national problem, yet the Kennedy administration recognized that he had been elected by the narrowest of margins and did not have enough clout to antagonize southern Democrats. Only when civil unrest broke out in Mississippi and Alabama did the Kennedy administration act.

Presidents do offer many solutions throughout their terms. The single executive image demands that presidents take bold initiatives across many policy areas. The question presidents face is the proper type of solution, both in substance and in form. Substance has to do with the dimensions and details of the plan. In early 1977, before labor's intervention, the Carter administration decided to pursue hospital cost containment in lieu of national health insurance. A Carter aide observed, "We felt that cost containment had to come first—the government couldn't undertake financing for health insurance if the costs continued to rise at 14 percent per year."[20] Later, as noted above, labor pushed the Carter people to change the substance of their solution to national insurance.

Solutions may take several political forms. Programs do not merely have substantive merit and costs; they also have political price tags. The White House often decides between legislative and administrative forms of action. It may be able to afford a solution in one form but not in another. Presidents may issue executive orders as simple, direct routes that avoid congressional controversy. In 1948, President Truman issued an executive order desegregating the armed forces, because he knew such desegregation would stumble in Congress. Presidents may seek to reorganize the government to draw control closer to the White House. President Nixon's executive order to revamp the Bureau of the Budget into the Office of Management and Budget in 1970 sought in part to achieve greater White House control of the executive bureaucracy.

The administrative route, however, is often not suitable for major initiatives. Avoidance of normal legislative channels weakens presidents' credibility and makes them look either hapless or imperial. When working with Congress, presidents and their staffs wonder whether to submit proposals or wait to veto competing efforts. They also must decide between new programs, which reflect a departure from current policy, and modifications of existing programs. And they must choose the size and cost of the program—the magnitude of the commitment they propose to Congress. Lyndon Johnson proposed a multi-billion-dollar commitment to education in the boom years of the 1960s. A quarter century later, with budget deficits soaring, George Bush promised education reform with a much smaller price tag. Questions about the form of a solution intertwine the administration's goals—how important is education—with substantive costs—what will be the drain on the budget—and political costs—how much time and energy is the president willing to spend.

Among all the solutions that presidents propose, they assert priorities—what they really want, as distinct from what they would like to get. There is considerable pressure from both inside and outside the White House for the administration to devise a list of urgent items. Members of Congress want to know which measures they can leave behind or delay. Much of the infighting within the presidential organization occurs in establishing these priorities.

In 1976, President Ford proposed a massive $100 billion "energy corporation" that would distribute funds for traditional and alternative energy sources. The administration supported in principle an energy development fund, but various program staffs and energy agencies opposed it. Vice President Nelson Rockefeller's office, which had originated the idea, was its lone strong backer. A Ford legislative liaison recalled, "Even before Ford gave the go-ahead, there was tremendous antagonism within the staff. One person really supported it: Rockefeller . . . There wasn't anyone in favor of the proposal outside of the VP's [Vice President's] office. After Ford gave the go-ahead, there was absolute indifference. No one would push the bill."[21] The energy corporation was a Ford solution, but it was not a Ford priority. Informational ambiguity in combination with goal ambiguity fostered the infighting. Staff members lacked sufficient information about the energy problem to identify the "best" solution—the one that would alleviate the problem and also create the greatest political benefits for the administration.

Finally, the White House pays passing attention to the feasibility or effectiveness of solutions. One might assume that the *first* question presidential decision makers ask is whether a program will work. Yet commonly this is the *last* inquiry presidents and their staffs make. Goal ambiguity stalls attention to the consequences of decisions. Because White House decision makers satisfice, they assume that choices that are "good enough" will work "well enough." Moreover, because the decision makers face a vast array of decisions, each of which they make quickly and incompletely, they are not likely to look backward or forward. "The staff naturally assumed that most of the programs will work as intended," a Johnson aide remarked. An Office of Management and Budget staff member explained:

The people in the White House are there for such a short time. The pressure is on making some impact and getting some programs passed. There is not enough time or reward in thinking carefully about effectiveness and implementation. The emphasis is really on quantity, not quality. The President could never be reelected on the effectiveness theme. "We didn't do much, but it is all working very well." Do you think the President could win on that?"[22]

What Are the Politics?

Problems and policies can proceed relatively independently of each other. One does not require the other. Chronic government problems—energy consumption, drug use, crime, budget deficits, welfare and medical costs—are viewed as intractable. Even if policies are proposed, they may have only a marginal effect on the problems. Programs also may be proposed when no specific problem is on the horizon. Technological advances offer capabilities to act even if there is no problem. As part of the "space race" with the Soviet Union, the Kennedy, Johnson, and Nixon administrations pledged a commitment to manned space flights to the moon. Not having an outpost on the moon was a "problem" once conducting lunar landings became technologically feasible. Politics brings problems and policies together. The essence of politics is the search for a viable coalition. The goal is not the policy itself; the goal is to ensure agreement. To build this coalition, presidential decision makers engage in political bargaining—a give-and-take to reach consensus on a policy choice. The bargaining takes place within the White House and between the White House and other institutions and interested groups.

Inside Bargains   Internal conflict is a way of life in any organization, including the White House, where there are multiple competing goals and multiple competing units. "Everyone was identified by their office or department," according to a Johnson staff member, who continued:

All the advice was colored by who belonged to what office and by who belonged to whom. The amount of power each one carried had an important effect on their weight with the President. One assistant would say that he had three departments and the policy staff behind him; another might argue that he had the House and Senate public welfare committees backing him. It was like a war game—each group moving their pieces around the board.[23]

Bargaining is a way out of operational and participatory ambiguity. The plural presidency has no well-established operational procedures for decision making. Coordination across several offices is difficult because each office has its own goals and relations with the president. In the absence of clear-cut procedures and neatly defined jurisdictions, who shows up and how people bargain become important. Because bargaining depends on the political influence and skills of the bargainers, agreements can be struck even if the players are not fully aware of how their unit works with other units. Bargains also tolerate ambiguous participation. No matter who plays in any one round, a bargain can be concocted with that group of players. If the participants change in the next round, the newly constituted group can construct another bargain. Bargaining helps to reach an agreement that satisfies as many of the goals for as many of the participants as possible. Bargaining does not "resolve" conflict to the extent that everyone shifts opinion and agrees on one common goal.

People retain their original goals, and considerable latent conflict about goals exists. Nevertheless, the organization moves along because a compromise has been reached. As one Kennedy aide summed up: "Most of the time we just worked things out. Sometimes we would go out for dinner or lunch and hammer out some kind of compromise."[24]

President Kennedy's decision to increase American advisers in Vietnam from 685 to 16,000 in 1961 exemplifies the politics of the garbage can approach. The plural presidency housed two camps. The *military* camp favored the immediate introduction of 8,000 combat troops and estimated that the maximum U.S. forces required could reach but would not exceed 205,000 men. This camp included General Maxwell Taylor, the president's personal military adviser, Secretary of Defense Robert McNamara, and National Security Adviser Walt Rostow.

The *cautious* camp did not wish to widen the American mission. Secretary of State Dean Rusk questioned how so few men could have a "decisive influence" and felt that America's prestige might be committed too deeply to "a losing horse."[25] George Ball, an under secretary of state who had worked closely with the French during their Indochina war, knew of "the false optimism of the generals, the resiliency and relentlessness of the Vietminh [communist independence forces], their capacity to exploit nationalism and to mire down a Western nation, the poisonous domestic effect."[26] The president himself worried that the introduction of combat forces would be just the beginning.

To bridge the two views, McNamara and Rusk submitted a recommendation to Kennedy calling for an increase in U.S. military advisers to 16,000, rather than the introduction of combat forces. Kennedy readily accepted the compromise without a larger discussion of the U.S. role in Vietnam. Kennedy felt he had held the line against combat troops. Yet, by dramatically increasing the American presence—of any kind—he made pulling out more difficult in every way. Soon after taking office, Johnson decided that combat troops were needed to protect the growing number of advisers. The politics of the Kennedy decision focused on satisfying the differing camps, not on analyzing the consequences of the policy. The test of a "good" policy, then, is not whether it is the most appropriate means to deal with a problem but whether various officials and offices agree with it.

Outside Bargains and Political Windows. Politics also colors the plural presidency's relations with other political institutions and with a multitude of organized groups. Events outside the White House make it possible for certain problems and solutions to be fused at some times but not at others. These opportunities are called "political windows." In space exploration, "window" denotes the time frame for launch or re-entry of the space vehicle. If a window is missed because of bad weather or technical failures, the spacecraft must wait for another suitable window to open. Political windows too are time frames for launching programs.[27] At certain times, the White House works effectively with other institutions and groups to open a political window and offer a policy solution. At other times, relations break down and the window remains shut.

In 1965, the lingering trauma of President Kennedy's death, an influx of new Democrats to Congress, and the legislative skills of President Johnson combined to open a political window through which the problems of poverty and health care were joined with the solutions of the War on Poverty programs, Medicare, and Medicaid. Without the change in the political picture, the problems would have remained on the streets and the programs on the drawing board. The Johnson administration capitalized on reinvigorated relations with Congress to open the window.

Similarly, the Carter administration pledged to deregulate various industries, believing that deregulation would permit the expansion of services at a lower cost. Carter's people chose the airlines over trucking as their priority problem, not because they had better solutions for airlines than for trucks but because they recognized that they could more successfully bargain with interested groups and other institutions. Moreover, with several key sponsors on Capitol Hill, airline deregulation had the best chance of passage in Congress. The Civil Aeronautics Board, the prime regulatory agency, supported the move. And the airline industry itself was not steadfastly opposed. By contrast, truckers and teamsters ardently opposed deregulation, and the Interstate Commerce Commission, responsible for the trucking industry, was slow to act, although some deregulation of trucking eventually took place.[28]

Political windows open, but they also close for a variety of reasons.[29] Feeling that decisions have addressed a problem adequately, presidents may move on to other items. When President Bush entered office, it appeared that the Reagan defense increases had been more than sufficient to address the problem of military weakness perceived in the early 1980s. Events also may shut a window. Fast changes in eastern Europe lessened the perceived military threat against America. A political window may close if efforts to address a problem fail. When the Carter administration was unable to pass either a hospital cost containment bill or a national health insurance plan, it became difficult to renew congressional interest in health care. Key group players may leave and close the window behind them. In 1990, several groups of elderly citizens abandoned their support of catastrophic health insurance and saw the existing law repealed.

PRESIDENTIAL TIME

Windows open, and hence problems, policies, and politics come together more easily at some times during presidents' terms than at others. Presidents have four years—1,461 days—to make their marks in office. Yet presidential time runs both slower and faster than the normal sixty-minute clock. There are two types of presidential time: organizational time and political time. Both types cause political windows to open with differing degrees of ease at various times throughout the term.

Organizational Time

The single executive image creates the impression that the presidency, relative to Congress, is an office of speed and dispatch. Yet the plural presidency, like the Congress, has a well-developed organization through which decisions are channeled. Organizational time ticks slowly. Many sources gather and sift information on behalf of presidents. There is ample opportunity for deliberation and delay as issues, options, and decisions stall, sputter, and move through the decentralized channels. Organizational time is at its slowest earliest in the term, when staff members are just beginning to understand their jobs, how to evaluate information, and the jurisdictions and routines of the various White House units. At this time, operational ambiguity is highest. Organizational time may speed up, and operational ambiguity may lessen as the term progresses. Jurisdictional lines are less blurred, staff members develop routines, and presidents devise coordinating mechanisms. Presidents commonly assign personnel, notably chiefs of staff, to highly visible superordinate positions to order the fray below. Political windows open or close most easily when presidents have the luxury to follow the organizational time clock. If events force presidents to act more quickly than the organization runs, the resulting decision may be inappropriate.

Eisenhower's decision in 1954 not to intervene militarily on behalf of the French in the Indochina war was made on organizational time.[30] When the communists surrounded the French garrison of Dien Bien Phu, Paris asked Washington for large amounts of aid, including money, materiel, and men. After eight years of conflict, the French feared that the loss of the garrison would mean the loss of the war. From January until May 1954, the French crisis was discussed at regular meetings of the National Security Council (NSC), two of NSC's subsidiary boards, the Joint Chiefs of Staff, and the policy planning staffs of the departments of State and Defense. In addition, Eisenhower formed a separate group known as the Special Committee to develop a complete area plan for Indochina. Within this committee, a "working group" also was formed.

Throughout February and March 1954, fighting at Dien Bien Phu worsened. The Special Committee, the working group, and the NSC concentrated on two options. First, reports from the Special Committee and the planning board of the National Security Council called for unilateral American intervention. Second, the working group proposed a multilateral effort, called United Action, which would involve the United States, Great Britain, and France. Negotiations with the British proceeded during April.

Dien Bien Phu fell on May 7, 1954. Eisenhower decided that unilateral action by the United States would lead only to a prolonged American commitment. He realized, as did one of his admirals, that there was no such thing as "partial involvement. One cannot go over Niagara Falls in a barrel only slightly."[31] The administration still pursued United Action. British Prime Minister Winston Churchill, however, was skeptical because he believed that Eisenhower was attempting to use the British as a patsy for a misguided American policy.[32] Churchill thought that Eisenhower was seeking the involvement of the British in order to spread blame if United Action failed. The British refused to participate in United Action. Few people realize that if Churchill had been receptive, American involvement in Vietnam would have started in 1954 rather than several years later.

The timing of real-world events and the timing of the Eisenhower deliberations coincided. The Eisenhower administration enjoyed the luxury of time because Dien Bien Phu did not fall overnight. As a result, the foreign policy organization could slowly and deliberately gather information and apply expertise to the French crisis. Although operational ambiguity existed among the several committees and staff groups, organizational time prevented the ambiguity from dominating the decision process. The search process allowed decision makers to define unilateral and multilateral options, and it gave Eisenhower the opportunity to keep the Indochinese window closed for the time being.

Political Time

The plural presidency also runs on political time—a highly compressed four-year cycle geared toward the next election. In contrast, many Washington politicians—those elected, those hired, and those appointed—have long time frames for action. Their clocks tick slowly. They have their careers—at least a decade but most likely two—to finish what they start. Even many members of Congress, who must look toward the next election, enjoy safe seats, which assure their political longevity. Most people in Washington come to stay. Presidents, however, come and go.

The Constitution commands that presidents serve only two terms, and political troubles often ensure that they do not want to serve longer, even if they could. Their political clock ticks fast and loud. Presidents attempt to produce major results quickly to ensure re-election and live up to the single executive image. Presidents' political time is like the White Rabbit's time in *Alice in Wonderland:* presidents are always in a hurry and often inevitably late. As one White House aide described it, "You should subtract one year for the reelection campaign, another six months for the midterms, six months for the start-up, six months for the closing, and another month or two for an occasional vacation. That leaves you with a two-year presidential term."[33]

Political time pushes the presidency to try to open political windows early in the term. Presidents announce policy priorities within the first several months in order to capitalize on their honeymoons. Presidents recognize that the longer they are in office, the more their influence will erode and the more likely they are to make decisions that will antagonize members of Congress and different groups in the country. In the course of the term, it becomes increasingly difficult to bring policy solutions and problems together successfully. The political windows all too often stick shut. Lyndon Johnson put it this way: "You've got to give it all you can that first year. Doesn't matter what kind of majority you come in with. You've got just one year when they treat you right and before they start worrying about themselves."[34]

Presidents on Time

Although organizational and political time run at opposite speeds, they are closely linked in two ways. First, political time helps create the slow organizational time of the plural presidency. Political time forces presidents to act in a hurry and to always act, and it creates the need for a large presidential organization to carry on the action. In such a compressed time span, it is impossible for presidents and a few close advisers to develop agenda items, see them through Congress, and have the executive branch implement them. It is infeasible for presidents and their immediate circles to steer foreign and military policy without intelligence information that they are ill equipped to gather. Limited political time forces presidents to draw on their presidential organization to accomplish what they want. The organization, however, operates on its own slow time schedule. Its pace of operation can be a decided constraint on opening political windows and achieving presidential victories.

Second, the joining of organizational and political time creates a dilemma for presidents. When is the "best time" to bring problems and solutions together? The political time clock says that the best time for presidents to open windows is early in their term. The organizational time clock acknowledges that presidents may wish to open windows early in the term but warns that the organization may not be ready then.

The Nixon administration recognized that organizational time lags behind political time. Nixon staffers spent a great deal of organizational time developing a thorough welfare reform plan; meanwhile, political time was ticking away. Delaying the announcement gave opponents a better opportunity to organize their attack, and the plan bogged down in congressional committee.[35] By contrast, in the early days of the New Deal, Roosevelt knew that the emergency called for quick action and announced that problems would be solved even before detailed plans were available. Back then, the White House was less well equipped to present a developed set of plans than it is today. Roosevelt recognized the importance of moving in political time. He presented to Congress legislation in its barest outline; the details of programs would be worked out later.

Because politics is the key to bringing together policies and problems, presidents and their staffs commonly agree that political time takes precedence over organizational time. They allow the organization to catch up with the demands in the political arena. Political time allows presidents to use the single executive image as a key resource. The "best time" for economic or domestic initiatives is early in the term, when the power, visibility, importance, and uniqueness of the image has not been tarnished by the wrong action or by no action. Presidents submit most of their legislative proposals to Congress in the first year and many of them within the first months of their term.[36] They also follow political time in leading the country through a foreign policy crisis, taking dramatic action soon after the crisis unfolds. The emphasis on political time provides presidents with more opportunities to open more windows.

THE GARBAGE CAN AT WORK

The plural presidency uses the garbage can approach to make policy decisions. In one instance, the garbage can approach directed President Truman's decision to invade North Korea. The *problem* Truman faced was Chinese intervention in the war. The president disregarded Chinese rumblings that the U.S. crossing into North Korea would be considered an act of aggression against China. The Chinese made several public statements and communicated privately through the Indian ambassador to China and other neutral channels in Moscow, Stockholm, and London. Intelligence reports also spotted Chinese troops in North Korea. But Truman and his advisers ignored all warnings. American officials discounted the veracity of the messengers. Truman felt that the Indian ambassador "had in the past played the game of the Chinese Communists . . . so his statement could not be taken as an impartial observer."[37] Secretary of State Dean Acheson observed that when Chou En-Lai, China's premier and foreign minister who was second in command to Mao, had informed the Indian ambassador, he had not made "an authoritative statement of policy."[38] It was all a "bluff" or attempts at "blackmail."[39] Informational ambiguity abounded in the clash between what the Truman administration was told and what it believed.

The *policy* Truman proposed was to order American troops to invade North Korea. General Douglas MacArthur crossed the thirty-eighth parallel in October 1950. His forces swiftly captured the North Korean capital, Pyongyang, and drove toward the Yalu River boundary with China. There in November he met a quarter million Chinese troops, who pushed the Americans back below the thirty-eighth parallel and took Seoul, the South Korean capital. Only a major counteroffensive launched by General Matthew Ridgway re-established the thirty-eighth parallel as the geographic boundary between north and south.

General Omar Bradley, head of the Joint Chiefs of Staff, summed up the gap between the problem and the policy by noting that America was "in the wrong war, at the wrong place, at the wrong time, and with the wrong enemy."[40] *Politics* was responsible for the gap. American officials viewed the Korean War as an ideological confrontation between democracy and communism (see Chapter 10). This perspective distorted and blocked reality. Truman officials could not trust the messengers because they were communists. Nor could Truman's advisers believe that the Chinese would advance an offensive against the greatest power of the free world. General MacArthur convinced Truman that he could take North Korea in a matter of months. Domestic politics also dogged Truman. The Republican leadership taunted Truman that failure to go north would be evidence of "appeasement." Midterm congressional elections were only two months away. The political climate and the taste of military victory moved Truman past containment into terrain heretofore charted only by the rhetoric of his Senate Republican enemies—the "liberation" of North Korea. The garbage can approach is apparent because politics, not the problem, dictated the policy's adoption; the problem, unresolved, dictated the policy's failure.

Garbage cans do not necessarily mean that decisions will backfire. During the 1960 campaign, Kennedy pledged in a speech in West Virginia to push for a redevelopment act for depressed areas of the country. The *problem* was areas of the country with chronically high unemployment rates, weak industrial bases, and low mobility of residents. The *policy* granted federal assistance in the form of loans and the construction of public facilities in rural and urban areas with high unemployment and low incomes. *Politics* was key to the passage of the Area Redevelopment Act in May 1961, the first major legislative victory of the Kennedy administration. Senator Paul Douglas of Illinois had introduced an almost identical bill in Congress six times during the 1950s. Twice the bill had died in committee, twice on the floor, and twice Eisenhower had vetoed it. Politics, not the merits of the policy, won the fight (as it had stalled the fight in the 1950s). Only when the Kennedy administration, following political time, made an all-out effort early in its term did the political window open and the legislation pass.[41]

CONCLUSION

The single executive image dictates that the president, as *the* one person in charge of the government, identify scores of pressing national problems and offer equal numbers of vigorous solutions. It portrays presidents and their staffs as fully rational decision makers who know the worst problems and offer the best solutions. The public imagery can give presidents quick and easy victories. They can highlight the problems in a major national address as millions listen. They can tout their accomplishments in State of the Union messages as a captive Congress looks on.

The single executive image belies the internal plurality of the presidency that exists in two distinct but interconnected ways. First, the internal plurality rests on the decentralized organization. The plurality is found in the sheer number of units and their diffusion of power within the organization. Second, how the units make decisions adds to the internal plurality. The plurality is found in multiple levels of ambiguity about what information is needed, what priorities should be set, how offices in the organization will coordinate to obtain these goals, and who participates.

The garbage can symbolizes the ambiguous decision processes by which the presidency sorts through the mass of work generated by the image. Politics works to fashion a connection between problems and policies, because decisions must be made even when presidential decision makers are unsure how the choices should be made. The decision makers often resolve the uncertainty through a series of bargains within the institution and other institutions and groups. The plural presidency's ambiguous decision processes, coupled with its decentralized organization, mean that presidents and their staffs always make decisions in a dark cluttered room. ■

F U R T H E R   R E A D I N G

On rational decision making, see: Graham Allison, *The Essence of Decision: Explaining the Cuban Missile Crisis* (Boston: Little, Brown, 1971). On ambiguous decision processes, see Charles Lindblom, "The Science of 'Muddling Through,' " *Public Administration Review* 14 (Spring, 1959): 79–88; On the garbage can model, see: Michael Cohen, James March, and Johan Olsen, "A Garbage Can Model of Organizational Choice," *Administrative Science Quarterly* 17 (March 1972): 1–25; John Kingdon, *Agendas, Alternatives, and Public*

Policies (Boston: Little, Brown, 1984); Paul Light, *The President's Agenda* (Baltimore: Johns Hopkins University Press, 1982). On Eisenhower and Vietnam, see: David Halberstam, *The Best and the Brightest* (Greenwich, Conn.: Fawcett, 1969); John Burke and Fred Greenstein, *How Presidents Test Reality* (New York: Russell Sage Foundation, 1989). On Truman and Korea, see: Harry S Truman, *Memoirs* (Garden City, N.J.: Doubleday, 1953); Dean Acheson, *Present at the Creation* (New York: Norton, 1969).

N O T E S

1. Theodore Sorensen, *Decision-Making in the White House* (New York: Columbia University Press, 1963), 18–19.
2. "Watkins Defends Policy on Warming," *New York Times*, February 9, 1990, A11; "The White House Effect," *The Economist*, February 3, 1990, 28–29; "He's Against Acid Rain; He's Also the Enemy Say Many Environmentalists; He's John Sununu," *Wall Street Journal*, March 2, 1990, A12.
3. "The White House Effect," 28.
4. Charles E. Lindblom, "The Science of 'Muddling Through,' " *Public Administration Review* 14 (Spring 1959): 79–88.
5. Michael Cohen, James March, and Johan Olsen, "A Garbage Can Model of Organizational Choice," *Administrative Science Quarterly* 17 (March 1972): 1.
6. "Watkins Defends Policy on Global Warming," A11.
7. *Arizona Daily Star*, April 23, 1992, 12.
8. "Bush to Attend Environmental Talks in Brazil," *Arizona Daily Star*, May 7, 1992, A1, A2.
9. "The Grinch of Rio," *Newsweek*, June 15, 1992, 31.
10. Cohen, March, and Olsen.
11. John Kingdon, *Agendas, Alternatives, and Public Policies* (Boston: Little Brown, 1984), 83.
12. Quoted ibid., 115.
13. Paul Light, *The President's Agenda* (Baltimore: Johns Hopkins University Press, 1982), 70.
14. Quoted ibid., 72.
15. State of the Union Message, *Public Papers of the Presidents: Lyndon B. Johnson, 1965* (Washington, D.C.: U.S. Government Printing Office, 1966).
16. Quoted in Light, 66.
17. Remarks of a White House aide quoted ibid., 1.
18. E.E. Schattschneider, *The Semi-Sovereign People* (New York: Holt, Rinehart and Winston, 1960), 68.
19. Quoted ibid., 106.
20. Quoted ibid., 74.

21. Quoted ibid., 154.

22. Quoted ibid., 145.

23. Quoted ibid., 188.

24. Quoted ibid., 175.

25. *Pentagon Papers* (New York: Bantam Books, 1971), 102.

26. David Halberstam, *The Best and the Brightest* (Greenwich, Conn.: Fawcett, 1969), 215.

27. John Kingdon refers to the windows as "policy windows," but because the emphasis here is on how politics opens and closes the windows, I refer to them as "political windows."

28. Kingdon, 175.

29. Ibid., 177.

30. For full details on this decision, see John Burke and Fred Greenstein, *How Presidents Test Reality* (New York: Russell Sage Foundation, 1989); and Halberstam, 169–180.

31. Howard Jones, *The Course of American Diplomacy* (New York: Franklin Watts, 1985), 461.

32. Burke and Greenstein, 80.

33. Light, 17.

34. As told by Harry McPherson, *A Political Education* (Boston: Little, Brown, 1972), 268.

35. Light, 43.

36. Ibid., 42, 45.

37. Harry S Truman, *Memoirs* (Garden City, N.J.: Doubleday, 1953), 362.

38. Dean Acheson, *Present at the Creation* (New York: Norton, 1969), 452.

39. Irving Janis, *Groupthink*, 2d ed. (Boston: Houghton Mifflin, 1982), 56.

40. Quoted ibid., 53.

41. Robert J. Spitzer, *The Presidency and Public Policy* (University, Ala.: University of Alabama Press, 1983), 76–80.

THE PLURAL PRESIDENCY: THE DECISIONS MADE

The decentralized organization of the presidency and the ambiguous decision processes that it adopts are not accidents. They result from the demands that the single executive image places on presidents. As the single most powerful, unique, important, and visible individual in the nation, presidents act on an intricate, ever changing, and vast policy environment. Presidents have established and expanded the organization in order to accommodate the intricacy of the presidential environment, which is characterized by policy complexity and political fragmentation. Presidents make numerous policy initiatives across a wide range of issues, including foreign aid to Russia, small business initiatives, and the cost of government paperwork. Part III examines the complexity of foreign policy (Chapter 10), economic policy (Chapter 11), and domestic policy (Chapter 12). Chapter 12 also considers the political fragmentation that confronts presidents especially in domestic policy.

Presidents' conduct of foreign policy relies on four policy tools: nuclear deterrence, covert action, diplomacy, and, primarily, conventional military action. Presidents have fought two kinds of conventional battles: (1) limited wars that involve large troop commitments but are designed to achieve political ends rather than all-out military victories and (2) emergency interventions, which involve a small troop commitment and are characterized by quick, overwhelming U.S. victories.

Presidents do not have economic policies; they have political policies about the economy. Thus, they do not often make decisions in the ways economists would prefer for the long-run stability of the economy. Instead, they propose budgets and tax cuts that are expedient in the political short run. Presidents' own policies add to the complexity of the economic policy area.

Presidents' efforts at domestic policy involve civil rights, social welfare, and business regulations. Within the domestic policy arena, presidents encounter political fragmentation of two types: government and group. The constitutional system of separation of powers and checks and balances creates numerous centers of power in American government. Presidents must wrestle with the Congress, the bureaucracy, and the courts to get what they want in domestic policy. In addition, group interests drive many domestic policy choices. Presidents propose domestic policies that they feel they can sell to the other branches of government and to the host of groups with access to the government. Thus, policy complexity and political fragmentation add to the plural nature of the presidency. ■

CHAPTER 10

Foreign Policy Complexity

N othing better underscores the policy complexity of the American presidency than the dramatic events that swept through eastern Europe in a single year, from February 1989 to February 1990. When George Bush took his oath of office in January 1989, the world looked almost black and white. Hugh Sidey observed that "[Bush] could look around at a tidy club of democratic, market-oriented friends staring across a wall at a bunch of backyard bullies. The wall fell down, the bullies were chased off, and now everybody wants into George's club."[1] By the time Bush delivered his State of the Union message in February 1990, the familiar faces and the familiar cold war games the club had loved to play had all but vanished:

> Hungary, February 11, 1989: The Hungarian Communist party approves the creation of a multiparty system.
> Soviet Union, March 26: Boris Yeltsin, former populist party boss, wins an at-large seat representing Moscow in the Soviet Parliament.
> Hungary, Mary 2: The government orders dismantled the fence along the Austrian border. Hungary becomes the first eastern European country to reopen a border with western Europe.
> Poland, June 4: Candidates affiliated with Solidarity, the national labor union outlawed for seven years, sweep Polish parliamentary elections. "Our defeat is total," General Wojciech Jaruzelski, Polish Communist party leader, tells party officials.[2]
> Poland, August 24: Solidarity government installed.
> Hungary, September 13: With Hungarian borders open, thousands of vacationing East Germans flee to the West.
> East Germany, November 9: East Germany opens the Berlin Wall. All travel and emigration restrictions are lifted.

Hungary, November 26: A national referendum determines that the next president will be chosen by parliament after free parliamentary elections in 1990.

Romania, December 25: President Nicolae Ceauşescu is executed.

Czechoslovakia, December 29: Playwright Vaclav Havel, a dissident and former political prisoner, is elected president.

Soviet Union, February 5, 1990: Mikhail Gorbachev pushes a plan through the Soviet Communist party's Central Committee to have the party surrender its monopoly on power.

The single executive image assures Americans that presidents, as the most powerful, important, visible, and unique national figures, will direct the country when jarring events such as those in eastern Europe occur. The four foundations of the single executive image—constitutional power, elections, symbolism, and the media—permit presidents a large, often unfettered, role in foreign policy decisions. Presidential activism presumes that presidents have the constitutional power to act on behalf of the nation in times of global uncertainty, so long as they do not violate the Constitution or federal laws. Presidential candidates frequently campaign on platforms of peace, international stability, and American military might. The symbolism of the office makes presidents the symbol of the nation to the world. The media highlight the drama of the president as warrior and diplomat.

The image further mandates that presidents take positions on almost every issue conceivable in foreign relations—drug trafficking, import quotas, military aid, global warming, espionage, nuclear weaponry, and the collapse of communism, to name a few. Even when presidents have little or no control over events, such as those in eastern Europe, the image nevertheless requires that they become involved. For instance, after the assassination of President Ceauşescu of Romania, President Bush announced U.S. recognition of "the new legitimate government of Romania" even though no authority was in full control anywhere in the country. Indeed, the image requires presidents' efforts, not only in foreign affairs but also in economic and domestic matters.

The single executive image, then, helps create the policy complexity of the institution. Policy complexity emerges from the number and breadth of policies the presidency develops and the overlaps and inconsistencies among them. The policy complexity is not only in the presidential environment but in the decisions that presidents make. As noted in Chapter 7, policy complexity is one manifestation of external plurality in the presidency (political fragmentation, another sign of external plurality, is covered in Chapter 12). The single executive image requires presidents to take charge of a chaotic, unpredictable environment. The ingredients of this environment become a part of the plural presidency itself as it makes the decisions that the single executive image requests of presidents.

Presidents alone or with their immediate advisers cannot keep track of the complexity. Thus, presidents rely on the decentralized organization of the plural presidency to develop what amounts to thousands of policy positions. In effect, Bush served as a spokesperson for the plural presidency in the announcement on Romania. Negotiations among American diplomats in Romania, the State Department, and the national security adviser led to the recognition decision. Often because of the number of units involved and clashes among them and across policy issues, ambiguous decision processes prevail. Decisions are often made without adequate information about the issues, about the goals sought in handling the issues, or about ways of achieving the goals.

This chapter and the next two chapters discuss the substance of presidential decisions—the "what" of presidential decision making. This chapter examines the complexity of foreign policy in three parts: (1) the policy domain—a set of policy issues with similar content, (2) the policy track—an ideological direction which establishes acceptable policies, and (3) policy instruments—methods that are used to implement the acceptable policies. Chapter 11 employs the same framework to discuss economic policy and Chapter 12 explores domestic policy.

THE FOREIGN POLICY DOMAIN

Within the presidential environment are multiple policy domains. In each domain are events, conditions, and political actors relevant to a set of issues that the single executive image directs presidents to handle. Three important policy domains are foreign and military affairs, the economy, and domestic matters. These broad categories are something of an analytic convenience, for within each domain are a multiplicity of issues that may overlap across categories. For example, debate has swirled around a U.S.-Mexico trade agreement proposed in 1990. Although this proposal was on its face a foreign trade matter, it raised economic issues about the relocation of American industries to Mexico and domestic issues about the benefits received by border states relative to the rest of the country. Policy domains are not sturdy boxes with the flaps tightly sealed. Each is like a cluttered attic stuffed with belongings long since out of their boxes.

Nonetheless, the three domains are politically relevant. They reflect the way the White House organization handles policy issues. There are special offices for foreign and military policy: the National

Security Council, the national security adviser, the secretaries of state and defense, the director of the Central Intelligence Agency, and the Joint Chiefs of Staff. There are separate offices for economic policy: the Council of Economic Advisers, the Office of Special Trade Representative, the Office of Management and Budget, and the secretary of the Treasury. There are separate offices for domestic policy: OMB, the Domestic Policy Council, and various domestic cabinet secretaries.

The foreign policy domain can be described as a system of "polycentrism." There are many centers of power; no one country completely dominates military, economic, and diplomatic relations among countries. Today the United States is the leading military force in the world. The republics of the former Soviet Union, at least in the near term, have turned inward to experiment with capitalism and democracy. Other countries—Japan and Germany—rival the United States as world economic powers. In addition, the United Nations has begun to organize many worldwide diplomatic efforts with the involvement of numerous countries. Polycentrism gives nations that are not military or economic powers considerable room to maneuver. The June 1992 United Nations Conference on the Environment (known as the Rio Summit) vividly revealed the polycentrism. Poor countries of the Southern Hemisphere bargained for and received pledges of aid from much wealthier nations of the North to protect species and plant life and boost their economies without ruining their environments. While Japan and the European Community pledged support for these efforts, the United States stood as the "odd man out," refusing to sign several of the treaties. The greater the polycentrism, the greater is the complexity that American presidents face in foreign affairs.

This polycentrism is new. Presidents from Truman through Reagan faced a foreign policy domain that was more nearly a hybrid "bipolycentric system."[3] Such a system involved bipolarity (formed by two military superpowers) and polycentrism (multiple nonmilitary power centers). After World War II, the military and nuclear superiority of two rivals—the United States and the Soviet Union—created a bipolar, "us-against-them" system. But polycentrism also existed. Each superpower had links with secondary powers aligned with the other superpower: the United States courted Romania before the fall of Ceauşescu; the Soviet Union directed overtures to France and Ireland. Secondary powers also developed fluid diplomatic and economic arrangements outside the bipolarity. The European Community and the Organization of Petroleum Exporting Countries (OPEC) became counterweights to the superpowers. This bipolycentrism ended with the collapse of the Soviet Union and changes in eastern Europe.

THE FOREIGN POLICY TRACK

Within the foreign policy domain, boundaries are established for acceptable policies, which are called *policy tracks*. The layout of the track reflects the values, interests, and goals of the country. Policy tracks are slow-changing, ideological directions that steer presidents' courses through the policy domain. Foreign policy tracks rest on precedents established by past presidents, Congresses, and foreign leaders; on past and current world situations; and on the views of the American public about the U.S. role in the world.

Should the United States be an isolate nation with little interest in world affairs? Should the United States be a global military, economic, and diplomatic power setting the tone for world events? Or should the United States be something in between? A policy track offers guidelines to a president about how a domain should be handled, what the government's involvement should be, and, perhaps most tellingly, what the government's roles should *not* be. Since World War II, American presidents have followed two foreign policy tracks: anticommunist globalism (Truman through Reagan) and global democracy (Bush and future presidents).

Anticommunist Globalism

A single, straight track charted the foreign and military policies of presidents from Truman through Reagan: *anticommunist globalism*. At its simplest, the policy track meant that America should protect the world from communism. This track grew out of the belief, firmly held by most Americans, that the United States was the best example of democracy in the world and should therefore protect and promote democracy across the globe. To achieve this goal, the United States embarked on military and financial support of various nations perceived to be in the clutches of communism.

The Truman Doctrine. In 1947 President Truman warned that "totalitarian regimes imposed upon free peoples, by direct or indirect aggression, undermine the foundations of international peace and hence the security of the United States."[4] In a single sentence, Truman alerted the world to the three aspects of America's global anticommunist policy track. Complexity was not merely part of the policy environment but was written into the policy itself. The policy focused on (1) "free peoples," including people living in authoritarian regimes that nonetheless could be distinguished from communist totalitarian regimes; (2) "indirect aggression," which could occur anywhere and at any time; and (3) "international peace," which was deemed essential to the security of the United States. No policy could have been more global.

President Truman proclaimed, "I believe that it must be the policy of the United States to support free peoples who are resisting attempted subjugation by armed minorities or by outside pressures."[5] The principal target of what became known as the Truman Doctrine was the Soviet Union. The Truman Doctrine urged a policy of *"containment."* George Kennan, director of the State Department's policy planning staff, who coined the term, called for "a long-term, patient but firm and vigilant containment of Russian expansive tendencies."[6] Truman's shorthand definition was "I'm tired of babying the Soviets."[7] Communism itself, whether Soviet backed or not, also had to be contained. The world was no longer engaged in a hot war in which people died and buildings burned. Instead, a cold war of threats, limited actions, verbal confrontations, and brinkmanship punctuated with stalemates, truces, and negotiations took hold.

The Truman Doctrine added to presidential policy complexity in three ways. First, the communist threat was perceived to take many forms and be geographically boundless. Although Truman's immediate concern in announcing the doctrine was a feared Soviet expansion toward Greece and Turkey, the threat was seen as insidious: if one country was threatened, it seemed likely that all countries in the region would fall, one by one. "Like apples in a barrel infected by one rotten one," wrote Truman's secretary of state Dean Acheson, "the corruption of Greece would infect Iran and all [countries] to the east. It would also carry infection to Africa through Asia Minor and Egypt, and to Europe through Italy, and France."[8] Later, the metaphor would change and Acheson's "apples" would become "dominoes," but the logic would hold. Eisenhower spoke of the domino theory or "the 'falling domino' principle. You have a row of dominoes set up, you knock over the first one, and what will happen to the last one is the certainty that it will go over very quickly."[9]

Second, the communist threat was also believed to be permanent. Though able to be contained, it would not go away. Finally, the threat was ultimately a perceived threat. American presidents judged whether a particular situation was indeed a threat to world peace and thus to American security. To be sure, some very real threats existed, as during the Cuban missile crisis. In other cases, however, such as instability in the Dominican Republic in 1965 and in Grenada in 1983, the military threat was less clear. In some instances, such as in Czechoslovakia in 1958 and Berlin in 1961, the threats seemed clear but the presidents looked the other way. Political interests often made a threat look more or less glaring than it may have been.

The Truman Doctrine established an almost endless one-track railroad that successive presidents steadfastly followed. Political scientist Cecil Crabb states that "The Truman Doctrine was the integrating principle of American postwar diplomacy toward the Soviet Union, toward Western Europe, toward the Middle East, toward the Third World, and toward almost every other major challenge confronting the United States in foreign affairs."[10] Although the policy of anticommunist globalism began with American financial aid to Greece and Turkey to prevent communist takeovers, the primary approach soon became military. The United States used force or the threat of force to protect imperiled countries. There were some policy variations from one president to the next, but the similarities far outweighed the differences. Presidents after Truman remained steadfastly on the track, though each attempted to leave his own mark.

Eisenhower and Massive Nuclear Retaliation. Eisenhower added a new twist to Truman's containment policy. The United States warned that it would use massive nuclear retaliation in response to aggressive actions by the Soviet Union. According to John Foster Dulles, Eisenhower's secretary of state, the policy of massive retaliation transformed an "awesome nuclear capability from an instrument of last resort to one of first resort."[11]

This nuclear brinkmanship, however, stumbled on two problems in the foreign policy environment. First, the Soviets caught up with the United States in the growing nuclear arms race. Second, world trouble spots did not cooperate with Eisenhower and Dulles. Brandishing atomic weapons, especially in the face of potential Soviet retaliation, was not an appropriate strategy for dealing with localized problems. Eisenhower himself recognized the limitations of the policy of massive nuclear retaliation in his second term. "Destruction is not a good police force," he declared. "You don't throw hand grenades . . . to police the streets so that people won't be molested by thugs."[12]

Although the policy faded, the general strategy of containment remained. The threat of communism became the leitmotif for a series of episodes, including the possibility of communist takeovers in Iran and Guatemala; communist resistance to the French in Indochina (Laos, Cambodia, Vietnam); a threatened communist Chinese invasion of Taiwan; Soviet squashing of rebellion in Hungary; instability in Lebanon; the establishment of a communist regime in Cuba; and trouble at the Suez crisis (which Dulles later acknowledged was not communist inspired).

Kennedy and Flexible Response. Kennedy embroidered on Eisenhower's policy by announcing a program of "flexible response" as part of his domestic and foreign policy initiatives called the New Frontier. Kennedy asserted: "We must be able to respond with discrimination and speed, to any problem at any spot on the globe at any moment's notice."[13] The United States would continue to build its nuclear stockpile but would also assert conventional military superiority. America should be capable of fighting "2½ wars" simultaneously: a conventional war in Europe against the Soviet Union, a Southeast Asian war, and a lesser involvement (a half war) elsewhere.[14] Although the full 2½-war strategy was never implemented because of its cost, in the first ten months of 1961 the defense budget dramatically increased by $6 billion. The flexibility extended to negotiations with the Soviets. While America's nuclear stockpile grew, the Nuclear Test Ban Treaty, the first arms limitation agreement between the Americans and the Soviets, was signed in August 1963.[15] The New Frontier, however, was not that new. Kennedy, like Eisenhower and Truman before him, saw the U.S. mission as "Pax Americana" (U.S.-imposed worldwide peace). Kennedy's policies were a reaffirmation of the sense of mission of Dean Acheson and of the rigidity of John Foster Dulles.

Nixon and Détente. Nixon, seeking to move beyond the cold war phase of anticommunist globalism, pursued a policy of détente—the easing of tensions between the United States and the communist world. Nixon favored détente because of the realization, drawn from the seeming endlessness of the Vietnam War, that the United States could no longer police the entire world. In addition, détente recognized the Soviet Union's parity with the United States in nuclear weaponry. Détente, then, was a corrective to the protracted military and diplomatic interventions of the United States from the end of World War II to the end of the Vietnam War.[16]

Nixon heralded new superpower cooperation by traveling to the Soviet Union for a major summit at which the two countries signed the first Strategic Arms Limitation Talks (SALT) agreement. This treaty limited the growth of the two nations' nuclear arsenals and placed caps on the numbers of missile launchers. Nixon also opened relations with the People's Republic of China, visiting Beijing in February 1972. Nevertheless, the easing of tensions mandated by detente was somewhat ambiguous. Skepticism and military competitiveness still marked American policy. Nixon pursued a "1½-wars" defense establishment in place of Kennedy's 2½-wars profile.[17]

Jimmy Carter and Human Rights. Although Jimmy Carter initially downplayed the Soviet threat, he nonetheless drew attention to U.S.-Soviet differences by a tough policy on human rights. He accused the Soviets of numerous human rights violations against Jews and other Soviet citizens. After the Soviet invasion of Afghanistan, the Carter administration returned to a harder line. The Soviet action reminded many of its assaults on Hungary, Czechoslovakia, and Poland some thirty years before. Since the Soviets had not changed, U.S. policy would not change. Carter also announced his variation of the Truman Doctrine, known as the "Carter Doctrine," toward the Persian Gulf: "An attempt by any outside force to gain control of the Persian Gulf region will be regarded as an assault on the vital interests of America and such an assault will be repelled by any means necessary, including military force."[18]

Ronald Reagan and the Evil Empire. Ronald Reagan, calling the Soviet Union the "evil empire," revealed how little America's foreign policy had varied since Harry Truman. In an early press conference, Reagan warned that the Soviets were "prepared to commit any crime, to lie, to cheat," and were responsible for "all the unrest going on. If they weren't engaged in this game of dominoes," Reagan believed, "there wouldn't be any hot spots in the world."[19] Reagan adopted a get-tough policy with a major defense build-up. When Reagan entered office in 1981, defense spending stood at $157 billion; by 1988, it had risen to $300 billion. The Reagan administration also introduced new defenses in space: the Strategic Defense Initiative, quickly nicknamed Star Wars.

From the cold war to Star Wars—the slogans had changed, but the direction of the foreign policy track had not. Reagan used his unyielding posture to negotiate an arms control treaty with the Soviets that called for (among other things) the elimination of intermediate-range nuclear missiles in Europe, despite the fact that the Soviet Union had far more intermediate-range missiles in Europe than did the United States. In a spirit of glasnost—openness and good feelings toward other nations—Soviet president Mikhail Gorbachev signed the intermediate-range nuclear force (INF) treaty in Washington in December 1987.

Global Democracy

Changes in the Soviet Union and in eastern Europe suggest that after forty years the anticommunist globalism policy track has reached an end. The ideological confrontation between the United States and the Soviet Union has been silenced. The global threat to American prestige and security has diminished. With the former Soviet Union and eastern European nations attempting experiments in electoral democracy and plagued by internal economic and domestic strife, there appears to be little for the U.S. to contain.

These changes do not simplify presidents' conduct of foreign policy. In fact, they heighten rather than diminish policy complexity. Unfriendly relations offered both the United States and the Soviet Union a predictable, if not altogether comfortable, vision of the world. Many American politicians based their careers on a tough stance against communism and in favor of a strong military. Many Soviet politicians based their careers on opposition to capitalism and support of military might. Friendly relations between the United States and the republics of the former Soviet Union ended this predictability. Thus, Bush and future presidents will travel on a new track, although one that still has some familiar touches of Truman's well-worn line.

The new goal of American foreign policy may be called "global democracy." It is likely to blend the old with the new and involve (1) the language of democracy, (2) military answers to world problems, and (3) international economic competition.

The Language of Democracy. Presidents will be loath to lose the symbolic advantage offered by the "us against them" fears of the cold war. In the aftermath of the cold war, they lost a pivotal component of patriotism, defined by what America is *not*—namely, communist. For decades, presidents had been able to rally public support against the "red menace." The classic example was the rise in John Kennedy's popularity that occurred after the Bay of Pigs fiasco. The fact that the aim of the invasion of Cuba was to fight communism overshadowed the fact that the invasion failed. To replace the fear of communism, presidents will turn to the language of democracy. President Bush proclaimed about the Persian Gulf War, "We know why we're there. We are Americans: part of something larger than ourselves. For two centuries, we've done the hard work of freedom. And tonight, we lead the world in facing down a threat to decency and humanity."[20]

Because the "red menace" is no longer red nor menacing, the Truman Doctrine will be applied to other bullies on smaller playgrounds. "They" become dictators and tyrants. America will set an example for emerging democracies and help create democracies American-style. The Bush administration's 1989 invasion of Panama in the name of democracy and its definition of Iraq's 1990 invasion of Kuwait as a confrontation between American democracy and the dictatorship of the malevolent Iraqi leader Saddam Hussein, the "butcher of Baghdad," exemplified the post–cold war approach.

Military Solutions. Like anticommunist globalism, the policy of global democracy will rely on the military. America's status as a superpower clings to its military might. Military spending has declined, but gradually. The Bush administration asserted that continued vigilance is necessary to be able to quiet the always unstable Middle East, topple dictators, and attack drug lords.

Economic Competition. Global economics will compete with global defense as America's chief concern. The United States does not have the ability to dominate world markets in the way it has sought to dominate world security. The freshly configured European Community (including a united Germany), in which trade barriers were dismantled and currencies linked, will be a key force in the post–cold war world. Japan already dominates the United States in various trade sectors. Thus, international economic competition greatly adds to the complexity of foreign policy. The international economy, like the domestic economy, is notoriously difficult for presidents (or any other world politician) to predict or control.

FOREIGN POLICY INSTRUMENTS

The single executive image portrays presidents as the nation's warriors and peacemakers. As first discussed in Chapters 2 and 3, presidents engage in military actions without congressional permission in matters of war and claim to be the "sole organ" of foreign relations in matters of diplomacy. Presidents' ability to have relatively free rein in these areas helps define the specific techniques or policy instruments they have available to implement foreign policy tracks. The four principal foreign policy instruments that presidents have at their disposal are (1) conventional military action, (2) nuclear deterrence and threat, (3) diplomacy and foreign aid, and (4) covert action. Policy complexity is revealed by the different opportunities afforded presidents by these four instruments. Policy complexity is heightened by the number of offices within the plural presidency that handle foreign policy and their varied interests in each instrument.

Conventional Military Action

Presidents since Truman have relied most heavily on conventional military force. Both anticommunist globalism and global democracy are difficult to maintain solely through economic means. Under anticommunist globalism, America had only limited control over the economic aid it sent. It was not always clear on what the money was spent or whether the money had the right effect. Under global democracy, no one country will have control over competition and trade. Thus, the use of military force for political purposes becomes an attractive option. For example, in a twelve-year period, from 1974 to 1986, U.S. troops were committed on twenty-one occasions.[21] Since the onset of the Korean War, defense spending as a proportion of gross national product has never fallen below 5 percent. It reached its highest point in 1954 (12.1 percent) and its lowest in 1979 (5.0 percent). Even the proposed military cutbacks of the 1990s call for only modest 2 percent annual declines in purchasing power after inflation over five years from fiscal year 1990 to fiscal year 1995.[22] Since World War II, presidents have adopted two chief devices in the exercise of conventional military force: limited war and emergency intervention (see also Chapter 3).

Limited War. Presidents contrast limited war with total or world war. "By fighting a limited war in Korea," Truman announced, "we have prevented aggression from succeeding, and bringing on a general war."[23] A limited war is restricted in its goals and means and lacks formal declaration. The war is fought in one country or one region. It is couched as a defensive action to protect the area rather than as an offensive action to conquer the enemy. Limited war was a principal tool of anticommunist globalism, as witnessed in America's involvement in the Korean and Vietnam wars. It also is a key instrument of global democracy, as evidenced by the Persian Gulf War. Because of its defensive, seemingly restricted nature, limited war allows presidents to portray themselves as national war heroes and thus to enliven the single executive image without risking global annihilation. Yet five features of limited war reveal its complexity:

1. Limited war emerges as part of an unlimited ideological clash between freedom and tyranny.

2. Limited war evokes the image of the prestige and security of the United States.

3. Limited wars are difficult to limit militarily.

4. Limited wars are difficult, if not impossible, to win.

5. Limited wars have strong domestic political and economic repercussions.

An Ideological Clash. As an instrument of anticommunist globalism, limited war was used by presidents in the ideological clash between democracy and totalitarianism. As an instrument of global democracy, limited war is used by presidents in a clash that is broader—between democracy and dictatorship. The simplistic (not simple) outlook that arises from both anticommunist globalism and global democracy ignores the possibilities of local independence movements, complex regional loyalties, rebellions, and civil strife. It instead assumes that the actions are part of a calculated conspiracy or the irrational acts of a dictator.

The Korean War was only incidentally fought about Korea. Korea was a proxy battleground for a large, deep U.S.-Soviet clash. Truman told the country:

It it your liberty and mine which is involved. What is at stake is the free way of life—the right to worship as we please, the right to express our opinions, the right to raise our children in our own way, the right to choose our jobs, the right to plan our future and to live without fear. All these are bound up in the present action of the United Nations to put down aggression in Korea.[24]

Equally, the Vietnam War was only incidentally about Vietnam. President Johnson asserted: "We fight because we must fight if we are to live in a world where every country can shape its own destiny. And only in such a world will our own freedom be finally secure."[25] If Johnson's audience had been blindfolded and Johnson's Texas drawl disguised, his listeners might have thought they were hearing Harry Truman's words of fifteen years earlier: "What is at stake is the free way of life." Similarly, President Bush categorically told reporters: "I view very seriously our determination to reverse out this aggression. . . . This will not stand. This will not stand, this aggression against Kuwait."[26]

The belief in the ideological confrontation between good and evil often hinders political decision makers from recognizing faulty premises about a war. This failure adds policy complexity of presidents' own making as they stick to their beliefs and miss signals and the significance of key events. One example of firmly held yet faulty beliefs held by three American presidents and shaping their views of Indochina was the domino theory: if one country falls to the communists, all countries in the region will also fall.

Eisenhower expressed the theory most clearly in discussing the security of Laos: "The fall of Laos to Communism would mean the subsequent fall—like a tumbling row of dominoes—of its still-free neighbors, Cambodia and South Vietnam and, in all probability, Thailand and Burma. Such a chain of events would open the way to Communist seizure of all Southeast Asia."[27] Kennedy included Japan, the Philippines, and India among the dominoes.[28] Johnson's belief in the domino theory was even more sweeping. As vice president, he returned from a fact-finding journey to Asia, convinced that if Vietnam got away, the United States would have to "surrender the Pacific . . . throw in the towel in the area and pull back our defenses to San Francisco and a 'Fortress America concept.'"[29] Yet throughout the entire period from Eisenhower to Johnson, various military intelligence reports found it likely that the fall of one country would lead to the fall of only one or two neighboring countries, not all the nations of the region.[30] At the end of the Vietnam War in 1975, two "dominoes"—Cambodia and Laos—did fall, but not as part of any unified action, and no other nations in Southeast Asia were lost to communism.

American Prestige. The ideological confrontation establishes a symbolic measure of national security and national prestige. Any conflict, whether between nations or within a nation, no matter how remote from the United States, can be construed as a threat to American security or prestige. To be sure, not all conflicts everywhere receive U.S. attention. Presidents have largely stayed away from conflicts in Africa, seeing few American economic or political interests in that continent. Presidents also avoided much involvement when the Soviets strengthened their hold on eastern Europe in the 1950s and 1960s. Using military force against Soviet troops in Czechoslovakia in 1958 and in response to the construction of the Berlin Wall in 1961 would have played dangerously with the bipolarity of the international system at the time. Such force would have tried to push the Soviets around in their own backyards. Eisenhower, Kennedy, and their advisers felt such action would open western Europe to retaliation from the Soviets.

Two areas of the world, however, have long held American interests: Southeast Asia, because of U.S. fears of domination by both the (former) Soviet Union and China, and the Middle East, because of its large oil reserves. Prior to the North Korean invasion, the Truman administration had deemed Korea less than vital to American national security.[31] Yet, when the North Koreans crossed the thirty-eighth parallel (the line dividing North from South), Secretary of State Dean Acheson told the country: "To back away from this challenge would be highly destructive of the power and the prestige of the United States."[32] Truman observed that "the Korean situation [was] vital as a symbol of the strength and determination of the West."[33] The symbolism of American prestige and security also became tightly wrapped around Vietnam. The United States backed into the Korean War as a test of American will. It could not back out of Vietnam because is was a similar crucible. Kennedy, as a senator, had maintained:

Vietnam represents a test of American responsibility and determination in Asia. If we are not the parents of little Vietnam, then surely we are the godparents. We presided at its birth, we gave assistance to its life, we have helped to shape its future. . . . This is our offspring—we cannot abandon it, we cannot ignore its needs. And if it falls victim to any of the perils that threaten its existence—communism, political anarchy, poverty and the rest—then the United States, with some justification, will be held responsible and our prestige in Asia will sink to a new low.[34]

And President Johnson made clear:

Around the globe, from Berlin to Thailand, are people whose well-being rests, in part, on the belief that they can count on us if they are attacked. To leave Vietnam to its fate would shake the confidence of all these people in the value of an American commitment and in the value of America's word.[35]

Similarly, in the Middle East, President Bush pronounced, "We're in the gulf because the world must not and cannot reward aggression. And we're there because our vital interests are at stake. And we're in the gulf because of the brutality of Saddam Hussein."[36] The Bush administration touted "a new world order where diverse nations are drawn together in common cause to achieve the universal aspirations of mankind—peace and security, freedom and the rule of law."[37] Yet despite the international coalition touted by the United States, the Persian Gulf War was from the outset America's war—in troops, money, planning, and prestige. The prestige of the United Nations or any other member nation was not at stake like that of the United States. Bush asserted, "When we win, and we will, we will have taught a dangerous dictator, and any tyrant tempted to follow in his footsteps, that the U.S. has a new credibility, and that what we say goes, and that there is no place for lawless aggression in the Persian Gulf."[38] The posture of "Pax Americana" seemed as vivid with Bush as it had with Kennedy and Johnson in very different eras and very different wars.

The symbolism has another consequence. Presidents typically are the officials who define how conflicts threaten national security. Presidents are so closely tied to issues of national security that their personal prestige becomes attached to national prestige. Although limited wars are difficult to win, the symbolism makes them equally distasteful for presidents to lose. Any such loss would shatter the image of a single powerful executive leading the nation in war. Fear of defeat may have been one factor in Truman's decision to widen the Korean War by crossing into North Korea. Eisenhower, Kennedy, and Johnson never seriously considered withdrawal from Indochina. Each was apprehensive that withdrawal would be construed as an American defeat. Johnson lamented, "I knew that if I ran out . . . I'd be the first American President to put my tail between my legs and run out because I didn't have the courage to stand up and support a treaty and support the policy of two other Presidents."[39] The Bush administration's prime strategy in the Persian Gulf War was to so overwhelm the enemy with troops, tanks, and missiles at the outset that the defeat of the allied forces would be impossible.

Unlimited Limited Wars. The most pressing issue surrounding limited war is how limited is limited. Indeed, can a war really be limited? The Korean War was intended to be limited in territory, troop commitments, the use of nuclear weapons, and time, but each one of the limits was either bent or broken:

Territory: Truman stressed in his initial nationwide address on the war in June 1950 that the U.S. sought only to "help the Republic of Korea repel the attack and help restore peace and security in that area."[40] Yet by November he had approved an American invasion of North Korea.

Troops: On June 27, 1950, Truman committed air and sea forces to aid South Korea. On June 29, he committed ground troops; on June 30, more ground troops were ordered. By September, four American divisions were in Korea—twice what General Douglas MacArthur, head of the United Nations forces, had requested.

Weapons: "Why don't we issue an ultimatum, make all-out war, drop the atomic bomb?" Truman rhetorically asked the American people. "The whole purpose of what we are doing is to prevent World War III. Starting a war is not the way to make peace. . . . Starting an atomic war is totally unthinkable for rational men."[41] Still, both Truman and Eisenhower on several occasions threatened the use of nuclear bombs to gain a truce.

Time: After crossing into North Korea, General MacArthur proclaimed that the "boys will be home by Christmas" of 1950. The war ended in 1953.

The incrementalism of the Vietnam War was far more striking than that of Korea. It is difficult to date the beginning of the war. It grew out of a gradually increasing commitment that sometimes looked like military and economic aid and at other times looked like war. Most of the war was a paradoxical "escalating military stalemate," according to James McNaughton, assistant secretary of state under Johnson.[42] The escalation began with secret CIA missions and small numbers of American advisers under Eisenhower, each of which was increased under Kennedy. The Johnson administration slowly and ineluctably moved from one level of limited war to a wider level and then a wider level still. Serious worries about going too far, too fast, accompanied each move upward, dampening the full progress of expansion. Johnson expanded Kennedy's covert effort by U.S. and South Vietnamese forces inside North Vietnam and Laos. The Johnson people implemented retaliatory bombing raids against North Vietnamese actions. In February 1965, these retaliatory raids gave way to full-fledged bombing known as Operation Rolling Thunder. James McNaughton commented that this operation involved a gradual increase in air strikes to "give the impression of a steady deliberate approach . . . designed to give the United States the option at any time to proceed or not, to escalate or not and to quicken the pace or not."[43] President Johnson and Secretary of Defense Robert McNamara personally selected the bombing sites one at a time and rejected any regular multiweek schedule.[44] As the bombing increased, ground troops were needed to protect the air bases. When it became apparent that bombing would not work quickly enough, the ground troops were given combat roles. Ever widening combat required more and more ground troops and continued bombing missions. American forces totaled 27,000 in mid-1965, 235,000 by early 1966, and 486,000 by the end of 1967.

But, with each increase, conflict brewed within the administration. The Joint Chiefs of Staff favored full-scale mobilization on the ground and in the air. Others in the administration, many from the State Department and National Security Council, and later Secretary of Defense McNamara, called for a less dramatic course. Johnson typically chose a position somewhere in between and felt he was pursuing a policy of moderation. The administration split wide open in 1968 when the Joint Chiefs pushed for full-fledged escalation and others, including a panel of foreign policy elder statesmen, called for de-escalation. On the last day of March, Johnson, compromising to the end, announced in a nationwide address a bombing halt, a token troop increase, and his plan not to run for re-election.

Conscious of the failures in Korea and especially in Vietnam, the Bush administration planned a different form of escalation in the sands of Saudi Arabia. Although the troop increases were incremental, the time frame within which troops were dispatched was extremely compressed—a matter of months, not years. On August 7, 1990, after Iraq stormed Kuwait, President Bush dispatched 50,000 U.S. forces to Saudi Arabia to protect it from an invasion by Iraq. By

August 22, 40,000 reserves were called up. In mid-October, U.S. forces in the Persian Gulf numbered 200,000. Over 400,000 troops were in place by early 1991. Then the war started. In contrast to the incremental shifts in Korea and Vietnam, one of the largest parts of the escalation in the Persian Gulf War took place before the war began. Less than a week into the war, the Pentagon announced that it had increased the troop ceiling to 560,000 people. President Bush and Colin Powell, chair of the Joint Chiefs of Staff, frequently commented that the war would not be "another Vietnam." The war ended in March 1991 when American forces reclaimed Kuwait.

Winning Limited War. Can a limited war be won? The Korean War ended at the same place it had started: the thirty-eighth parallel. There was no victory in the conflict. An uneasy stalemate left Korea divided. Similarly, peace negotiations ended American involvement in the Vietnam War in January 1973 with a cease-fire in place after most American troops had been withdrawn by the Nixon administration over a period of four years. The cease-fire left matters even worse in South Vietnam than in Korea. Thousands of North Vietnamese troops remained inside South Vietnam. South Vietnam fought for two more years until Saigon was overrun by North Vietnamese soldiers in May 1975. The Persian Gulf War ended without a full-scale invasion of Iraq, the capture of its capital Baghdad, or the deposing of its president, Saddam Hussein. Limited war introduces the notion that force *short of total military victory* can be used to obtain political objectives.

Limited Wars at Home. Limited wars are never limited to a theater of military conflict. They are enlarged by domestic politics and economics. In fact, in some instances they are more important for domestic political purposes than for foreign policy objectives. The aim of the Korean War was not simply to show the Communists U.S. will; it was also to show the Republicans Democrat Harry Truman's will. Congressional Republicans accused the administration of being "soft on communism." They demanded the invasion of North Korea and China and the use of atomic bombs to show that "appeasement" of communism was not the administration's true motive. Truman's decision to press into North Korea and his threatened use of nuclear weaponry grew out of this heavily charged partisan climate. Critics accused Bush of running from pressing domestic problems to the Persian Gulf.

American public opinion reflects an ambivalence about limited war. Two factors initially spur high support. First, people believe that a limited war will be short. One of the reasons for waging limited war is that the public is more likely to support such a conflict than to support a larger, longer war. In July 1950, only 14 percent of the American public expected the Korean War to last more than one year.

Second, people support a limited war because they view it as an ideological confrontation between freedom and tyranny. Defending the South Koreans was as incidental to Americans' support of the Korean War as it was to Truman's pursuit of it. In a Minnesota public opinion survey in August 1950, those who approved of Truman sending military forces to Korea were asked "Why?" Fifty-four percent said in order to "stop Russia and the Reds"; 17 percent felt Americans were "serving our own interests"; and 10 percent remarked that "oppressed people needed help." None of the respondents specifically mentioned a commitment to South Korea.[45] Support for the war in Iraq was at 75 percent throughout January 1991; many people feared Saddam Hussein was a latter-day Hitler.[46]

Limited war looks suspiciously limitless in its effect on the national economy. Because the war is supposedly limited, little initially may be cut out of the domestic budget to compensate for the bulging military budget.[47] Inflationary strains typically result. The Korean War had especially profound effects on the American economy. By the end of 1951, total requests for defense spending topped $74 billion. Arms expenditures reached 67 percent of the budget in 1952. Prices rose dramatically, at a rate of 25 percent a year; shortages mounted; and wage and price controls were imposed. Strains on the economy during Vietnam disrupted Johnson's other war—on poverty. In 1991, the combination of the Persian Gulf War and the soaring budget deficit reduced the American domestic agenda to a "minimalist approach."[48]

The Blood and Treasure of Limited War. The Korean War, Vietnam War, and Persian Gulf War were limited wars: they were geographically bounded, and, despite threats to the contrary, nuclear weapons were not used. Yet they were limited in peculiar ways. They were deadly and costly. The United States lost 34,000 lives and spent $15 billion in Korea. Fifty-seven thousand Americans died in Vietnam, and over $150 billion was spent. America spent $1 billion a day to fight in the Persian Gulf. Limited war is a far-reaching and complex element of presidents' foreign policy. The Korean War extended American security interests in such a way that America could and would fight in any obscure area of the globe. As James Nathan and James Oliver write, "although the arena was peripheral, the United States, it was believed, must respond in order to establish a reputation for action that would deter probes at the center."[49] In the future, threats to the periphery would be America's chief concern; force, short of total victory or all-out war, would be America's chief technique.

The Vietnam War represented both the nadir and the culmination of the Truman Doctrine. There is an impression, at once blurred yet magnified by two and one-half decades, that Lyndon Johnson broke with the past and rushed headlong into a decision to commit large numbers of ground troops to Vietnam. It is tempting to portray Johnson as the scapegoat for Vietnam. But Johnson's actions reflected the complexity of limited war as a policy instrument. He followed clear precedents from his predecessors. In addition, large pieces of the Vietnam puzzle had been cut out in Korea: an ideological crusade against communism and the desire for a victory that had eluded America in Korea.

Johnson's actions also laid bare the flaws of limited war vis-à-vis the foreign policy environment. The Vietnam War smashed the illusion of America as self-proclaimed world peacekeeper and the illusion that peacekeepers do not lose wars. It revealed how American prestige can blind policymakers to the internal politics of the country at war. It disproved the domino theory. It exposed the limitless nature of limited war, in which there are no rules about the size of the commitment or the length of the involvement.

The Persian Gulf War represents the return to favor of limited war. The Bush administration pursued a limited war that ended quickly with American prestige intact and military superiority heralded. It permitted the president to bask for a time in the image of a fearless, victorious hero. Although the outcome of the Persian Gulf War heightened this element of single executive image, Bush began to be criticized for diplomatic policy decisions made before the war that may have encouraged Iraq's aggression and for decisions made after the war not to deal more uncompromisingly with Hussein. Policy complexity thus remains a watchword for this and other limited wars.

Emergency Interventions. Presidents have offered emergency intervention, in effect symbolic war, as a substitute for limited war. This is a quick, vivid show of American military power in a small, nonstrategic country. The war is symbolic because it serves as a flexing of American military might but offers little chance that the United States will lose. Emergency interventions last no more than a few months; the number of troops is strictly limited; the president typically commits himself in advance to a timetable for the removal of troops. The Dominican Republic in 1965, the *Mayaguez* in 1975, Lebanon and Grenada in 1983, and Panama in 1989 are contemporary episodes of emergency intervention.

Emergency interventions arose in the aftermath of Vietnam. These encounters allow presidents to take advantage of the first two features of limited war while removing the drawbacks of the other three. Presidents assume none of the costs but all of the advantages of limited war. The five features of emergency interventions are as follow:

1. Emergency interventions involve an ideological clash between freedom and tyranny.

2. Emergency interventions evoke the image of the prestige and the security of the United States.

3. Emergency interventions are strictly limited militarily.

4. Emergency interventions are always won.

5. Emergency interventions have no strong domestic political or economic repercussions.

The ideological clash between good and evil remains intact. Even in the new era in which communism is no longer the glaring evil, other evils—drug barons, terrorists, lone dictators—are substituted. America's prestige can be dramatically placed on the line without any risk. The intervention is confined to a few months and a few troops. The intervention is not a war, so it has none of the economic effects of limited war. Because of its short duration, it gains public support and the president's own popularity receives a short-term boost. The "war" is always won. Presidents, Congress, and the public find these symbolic wars much safer than limited wars.

Gerald Ford offered the world a symbolic war barely one month after the fall of Vietnam. Ford took advantage of an incident involving an American merchant vessel, *Mayaguez*, which was seized by Cambodian patrol boats in May 1975 for violating Cambodia's territorial waters. Unaware that the Cambodian captors had already freed the thirty-nine American crew members, Ford ordered marines to an island off the Cambodian coast where the crew was supposedly held. U.S. Navy warships sank three Cambodian gunboats; fighter planes bombed an air base and oil depot. Forty-one Americans died. Ford proclaimed that he had saved the ship and the crew, but more importantly he had saved sagging American credibility both at home and abroad. Despite the loss of lives and the Keystone Cops rescue of sailors who were already freed, the American public resoundingly supported the Ford's action.

Ronald Reagan took similar actions in Grenada. On October 25, 1983, Reagan ordered 7,300 marines to take over the island to protect the lives of 1,000 Americans, mostly students, purportedly in danger from Grenada's anti-American, Marxist regime with ties to Cuba. Eighteen U.S. soldiers were killed and 115 wounded. By December 2, all combat troops were removed.[50]

On December 20, 1989, 13,000 troops joined 13,000 others already stationed in Panama to help depose President Manuel Noriega. President Bush, buoyantly announcing the capture of Noriega on January 3, 1990, remarked, "I ordered U.S. troops to Panama with four objectives: to safeguard the lives of American citizens, to help restore democracy, to protect the integrity of the Panama Canal treaties, and to bring General Manuel Noriega to justice. All of these objectives have now been achieved."[51] In less than two weeks, the symbolic war in Panama had been won.

Thus, emergency interventions offer presidents the opportunity to tout the single executive image—they are successful warriors who have upheld the causes of freedom and democracy with little bloodshed and in short order. Emergency interventions also minimize policy complexity. Presidents have a narrowly defined military objective and a short time frame within to achieve the objective. The manageability of emergency interventions, however, should not disguise the presence of other ingredients of the plural presidency. The decentralized organization of the White House and its ambiguous decision processes do not vanish. Prior to the Panama invasion, in October 1989, the United States chose not to support a coup attempt against Noriega that failed. The administration handled the coup attempt, according to Colin Campbell, "in an ad hoc manner, uninformed by overarching strategy and unaided by a systematic consultative process."[52] The president did not convene a meeting of national security advisers but instead made the decision through phone calls and informal gatherings. Thus, even when policy complexity is diminished, other elements of the plural presidency still affect presidential decisions.

Nuclear Deterrence

Presidents have used the threat of nuclear force, like the threat or actual use of conventional force, for political purposes in the international arena. Before the nuclear age, weapons were largely seen as the direct means to short-range military ends—winning a battle, holding a line of defense, establishing a foothold. Atomic weapons became instruments of diplomatic bargaining as much as, if not more than, instruments of warfare. Truman called the strategy "winning through intimidation."[53]

Presidents' primary approach on the anticommunist globalism track was deterrence. The United States developed a "second-strike capability"; that is, the nation had enough nuclear weapons to withstand an initial enemy nuclear attack so as to be able to respond with a devastating second attack of its own. The second-strike capability guaranteed "mutual assured destruction" (MAD); that is, each side had the ability to annihilate the other side. A direct nuclear attack by the enemy would result in immediate retaliation by the United States. Deterrence arises out of the belief that neither side wishes to ensure its own destruction. The MAD strategy, observed Harold Brown, President Carter's secretary of defense, "tells the world that no potential adversary of the United States could ever conclude that the fruits of his aggression would be worth his own costs."[54]

The nuclear option added to the complexity of presidents' foreign policy choices under anticommunist globalism. Uncertainty about its use and its risks prevailed. This complexity was at odds with the single executive image, which announces that presidents have the sole authority to "push the button" and commence nuclear war. The impression drawn from the single executive image, however, is not fully realistic. Presidents must depend on the military for assessments of when a nuclear attack on the United States is likely and what the effects of the U.S. launching of a nuclear attack of its own would be. Presidents must rely on career diplomats to deal with the technical questions that arise in arms control talks. They must rely further on military experts to tell them which weapons systems stay, which go, and which new ones should be developed.

On the global democracy track, the attractiveness of nuclear deterrence as a diplomatic device has been reduced by the lessening of tension between the United States and the former Soviet Union. In June 1992, President Bush and Russian president Boris Yeltsin signed an agreement that called for steep reductions in the number of intercontinental ballistic missile warheads (ICBMs) and submarine-launched missiles. The U.S. made fewer concessions than the Russians, who abandoned the long-standing Soviet insistence on nuclear parity between the two countries.

Diplomacy

Although the single executive image proclaims that the president is the "sole organ of foreign relations" for the United States, American diplomacy is anything but a singular operation. Presidents rely on connections between the State Department and the National Security Council in much of their diplomatic efforts. Presidents try hard to put a presidential stamp on American diplomacy, but much of it involves ongoing efforts that the State Department monitors no matter who is president. As an example, many diplomatic efforts are codified in international agreements—executive agreements that presidents may enter into on their own—and treaties that require Senate approval. Much of the negotiation for these agreements is handled within the State Department and involves the White House only late in the process.

International agreements are most prevalent in four areas: defense, trade, foreign economic aid, and domestic problems of the nation involved. Table 10.1 presents a look at U.S. international agreements by region and type of policy. Presidents since Truman, especially Republicans, have entered into numerous defense agreements. During the Nixon and Ford years, major Middle East arms deals were concluded with Israel, Jordan, Egypt, Iran, and Saudi Arabia. Reagan renewed them. Trade also is an important subject of diplomacy, especially between the United States and its neighbors, Mexico and Canada, and between the United States and western Europe and Japan. Foreign economic aid has been a modest, declining aspect of U.S. international agreements. Congress has asked tough questions about the ability of foreign aid programs to achieve

Table 10.1 U.S. International Agreements by Region and Policy Type, 1949–1983

	Foreign Trade, Diplomacy	Foreign Aid	Defense	Social Welfare/ Civil Rights	Government Economic Management	Natural Resources/ Environment	Agriculture	Ceremonial/ Cultural	Number of Agreements	Percentage of Total Agreements
Western Europe/Britain	197	40	514	163	202	428	225	15	1,784	20.8
Eastern Europe	75	10	13	18	26	43	82	28	295	3.4
Africa	24	62	53	65	68	58	211	19	544	6.3
Asia	302	83	323	162	163	240	576	19	1,868	21.7
Middle East	60	104	117	157	82	129	272	15	936	10.9
Central America	174	91	268	321	111	250	385	7	1,607	18.7
Canada	20	0	92	12	16	141	17	0	298	3.5
U.S.S.R.	31	0	20	7	3	24	42	9	136	1.6
Mexico	40	5	14	108	32	100	30	4	333	3.9
Multilateral	200	18	66	70	97	218	112	8	789	9.2
Number of agreements	1,123	413	1,480	1,083	800	1,631	1,952	108	8,590	

Note: Includes treaties, executive agreements, protocols, and conventions.

Source: Gary King and Lyn Ragsdale, *The Elusive Executive* (Washington, D.C.: CQ Press, 1988), Table 3-6, p. 150. Copyright © 1988. Used by permission of CQ Press. Coded and calculated from U.S. Department of State, *Treaties and Other International Agreements* (1950–1980) for 1949–1980; for 1981–1983, *Current Treaty Index* (1984).

desired ends. By far the largest number of U.S. international agreements pertains to domestic matters within the recipient country—agriculture, natural resources, social welfare, government management. These agreements predominate in U.S. responses to third-world nations. Most of the agreement partners have republican forms of government, but a fair proportion are authoritarian regimes, as shown in Table 10.2. Presidents and the State Department back such regimes because they are leery of changes in the foreign policy arena.[55]

Diplomacy is likely to be a much more important policy instrument for presidents on the global democracy track. With emphasis on the global economy increasing, presidents will find that they must negotiate on matters that the nations of the world hold in common: trade, energy, and the environment. Each area is immensely complex, involving not black and white issues of good and evil but distinctly gray issues of competition, dwindling resources, and sophisticated technologies.

Modern presidents have been actively involved in trade policy since the Reciprocal Trade Act of 1934, which authorized the president to negotiate reciprocal tariff reductions of up to 50 percent. It also gave presidents the authority to automatically extend those reductions to other countries by granting them "most favored nation" status. Presidential action on trade was expanded still further in 1948 when twenty-three countries including the United States drew up the General Agreement on Tariffs and Trade (GATT). President Truman did not submit GATT to Congress but instead committed the U.S. to it under his own authority. The Reciprocal Trade Act gave presidents responsibility for *bilateral* trade negotiations, but GATT gave presidents responsibility for *multilateral* trade negotiations.

GATT's main purpose has been trade liberalization. There have been eight rounds of talks, which have cut tariffs from 40 percent in 1948 to 4.7 percent today.[56] The talks are complex in and of themselves, going on for years at a time and dealing with such issues as the manipulation of technical standards, subsidies, government procurement, import licenses, rules on the origins of goods, restrictions on inward investment that interfere with trade, and protection of intellectual property.[57] But their complexity is heightened because many trade issues blur with domestic issues. The most recent round of GATT talks, known as the Uruguay Round, has focused on farm trade, which is as much a domestic issue as a trade issue.

The Rio Summit, mentioned at the beginning of this chapter, dealt with many issues pertaining to the environment and energy. The United States found it difficult to get its views across at the summit, let alone get its way. The environment and energy are also domestic as well as foreign policy issues, and because they are, Congress enters the scene, increasing the complexity still more. Presidents may wish to present themselves as the sole organ of foreign

Table 10.2 U.S. International Agreements by Regime Type, 1949–1983

President	Republican	Totalitarian	Military Authoritarian	Nonmilitary Authoritarian	Colonial	Multiple Regimes	Total
Truman	53.9%	1.8%	5.3%	30.9%	0.3%	7.9%	848
Eisenhower, I	49.0	2.3	5.9	33.0	0.2	9.4	962
Eisenhower, II	53.1	3.9	4.7	28.4	1.0	8.9	958
Kennedy	47.7	3.7	6.3	32.6	0.6	9.1	831
Johnson	44.0	7.0	7.2	27.4	0.8	11.3	915
Nixon, I	35.8	9.7	10.5	31.9	1.3	13.1	381
Nixon, II	34.4	15.7	6.0	29.4	0.5	10.7	776
Ford	35.6	7.5	11.9	33.9	0.1	8.1	1,169
Carter	38.8	8.6	9.9	33.4	1.3	6.6	638
Reagan	45.5	8.2	11.9	26.6			

Note: International agreements include treaties and executive agreements. *Republican regimes* are legislatures with two or more active political parties. *Totalitarian states* are one-party communist or socialist republics. *Military authoritarian regimes* are those led by military officers. *Nonmilitary authoritarian states* include monarchies, dictatorships, and states controlled by other autocratic elites. *Colonial regimes* are possessions of other nations. *Multiple regimes* refers to multilateral agreements signed by the United States and at least one country.

Source: Adapted from Gary King and Lyn Ragsdale, *The Elusive Executive* (Washington, D.C.: CQ Press, 1988), Table 3.9, pp. 156–159. Copyright © 1988. Used by permission of CQ Press. Coded and calculated from U.S. Department of State, *Treaties and Other International Agreements* (1950–1980) for 1949–1980; for 1981–1983, *Current Treaty Index* (1984).

relations, but playing this role becomes ever tougher in a world economy that the United States does not control.

Covert Action

The single executive image may predispose Americans to think that presidents would not use covert action, that the people's representative would not keep secrets from the people. Presidents, however, use covert action to achieve political objectives within the international arena and then go to great lengths to hide behind the image, denying their use of covert action and covering their tracks to make the denials plausible. An opposing image also prevails—an image of the Central Intelligence Agency as a behemoth that launches missions on its own, without presidential knowledge, direction, or approval. Neither image is correct. Presidents use two types of covert action: secret military operations, often part of a larger war effort, and covert political operations, in which they directly request CIA efforts to topple a government or create unrest in a country. Presidents and other government officials often have perceived covert action as the easiest solution—faster than diplomacy, less conspicuous and costly than a military effort, and, in the presence of "plausible deniability," less risky than both to public prestige if the plot does not work out.

Secret Military Operations.   Presidents engage in secret military operations typically to throw off guard the enemy, the world community, or the American public and Congress. Eisenhower, Kennedy, and Johnson all engaged in significant secret military efforts in Vietnam, Cambodia, and Laos. Eisenhower and Kennedy did so to avoid the impression that they had expressly violated the Geneva accords that arranged an armistice in Indochina after World War II. Johnson and Nixon hid troop movements and bombing raids to avoid large antiwar demonstrations and to avoid disrupting the public's support for the Vietnam War.

During 1969 and early 1970, Nixon also conducted secret bombing missions over Cambodia and Laos. To throw off track most American diplomats and military officers, Nixon sent a cable to U.S. ambassador to South Vietnam Ellsworth Bunker stating that no bombing of Cambodia would take place. At the same time, he directed General Creighton Abrams, commander of American forces in Vietnam, to prepare for the bombings. Air Force pilots involved in the missions were told they were dropping bombs on targets inside South Vietnam, as computerized radar stations guided the planes to their real targets over Cambodia.[58]

Other secret missions have been carried out to surprise the enemy. These have included Ford's rescue of the *Mayaguez*, Carter's aborted helicopter rescue of American hostages in Iran, and Reagan's initial order to invade Grenada.

Covert Political Operations.   Presidents engage in covert political operations for three broad reasons: (1) to fight tyranny, (2) to protect the economic interests of the nation, (3) for political convenience.

Covert action to fight tyranny is easy for presidents to defend under the rationale that the ends justify the means. Keeping the free world free is an extraordinary task that warrants extraordinary efforts. Because presidents cannot face the diplomatic and political costs of overt intervention, they often do covertly what they would not do otherwise. The Kennedy administration adopted a multifaceted program to eliminate the communist regime of Castro in Cuba. The plans included the Bay of Pigs invasion, Operation Mongoose (paramilitary activities, sabotage, and political propaganda to disrupt the Cuban government), and several assassination plots against Castro, which Lyndon Johnson called "Murder, Inc., in the Caribbean" when he learned about them upon taking office.[59] President Ford offered covert aid to two of the three contending factions in the Angolan civil war when the Soviet Union funded the third, communist faction. The CIA did not actively intervene but sent over $31 million in military hardware, transportation, and cash payments.[60]

Presidents also order covert action to protect the economic security of the nation. Presidents have defined "economic interests" very broadly to include the profits of a large fruit company and a multinational communications firm. In 1953, Eisenhower and the British favored the removal of Iran's premier Mohammed Mossadegh in favor of Shah Mohammed Riza Pahlavi, who was in exile. They believed that the shah would permit freer Western access to oil.[61] Kermit Roosevelt (Theodore Roosevelt's grandson), the primary CIA agent in the Middle East, worked to topple Mossadegh with Eisenhower's knowledge. After the shah was reinstated, Iran received $45 million in economic assistance from the United States. Five major American oil companies—New Jersey Standard, Mobil, Texaco, Gulf, and Standard Oil of California—received 40 percent of a new international consortium set up to exploit Iranian oil and avoid lower world oil prices.[62]

In the same year, Eisenhower asked his ambassador to Guatemala to direct the overthrow of the Guatemalan government of Jocobo Arbenz Guzmán. Arbenz advocated agrarian reforms and threatened the political and economic power of United Fruit Company, a large American company that owned hundreds of square miles of banana acreage. The ambassador said of Arbenz, "It seemed to me that the man thought like a Communist and talked like a Communist, and if not actually one, would do until one came along."[63] After several weeks of fighting and uncertainty, the CIA's handpicked coup leader arrived in the ambassador's private plane to assume power and maintain United Fruit's control of Guatemala.[64]

Under the direction of several presidents, the CIA spent as much as a billion dollars from 1958 to 1973 to prevent a communist government in Chile. During much of the period, the CIA's efforts, which included bribes, propaganda, and campaign funds for a centrist party, seemed to work. Their enemy, Marxist-socialist Salvador Allende, ran for the Chilean presidency in 1958 and 1964 and twice lost. But in 1970 Allende was elected president. With Allende in Chile and Castro in Cuba, Nixon remarked that "what you will have in effect in Latin America is a red sandwich, and eventually it will all be red." Nixon's domino theory logic masked a larger fear that Allende would nationalize the many American businesses that had subsidiaries in Chile, including International Telephone and Telegraph and the Anaconda and Kennecott copper companies. Nixon secretly informed Richard Helms, director of the CIA, "that an Allende regime in Chile would not be acceptable to the United States and instructed the CIA to play a direct role in organizing a military coup d'état in Chile to prevent Allende's accession to the Presidency."[65] Allende was killed in a bloody coup led by General Augusto Pinochet in September 1973.

Finally, presidents may order covert action for the sake of political convenience. The Kennedy administration's involvement in the Diem coup (discussed in Chapter 7) shows how presidents enter into the internal political manueverings of a country to make a situation more to the liking of the United States. Aides to Henry Kissinger, President Nixon's national security adviser and secretary of state, remember discussing the killing of Nguyen Van Thieu, South Vietnam's president, who was dragging his feet at the Paris peace talks. The idea, though not carried out, was not considered inappropriate.[66]

CONCLUSION

Presidents use the single executive image as a key resource in foreign affairs. They exercise their own presidential war-making power to order troops around the world. They act as the "sole organ of foreign relations" on behalf of the United States. Presidents devote much of their personal time and energy to foreign affairs because they have such sweeping unilateral authority. They can direct the nation to a single international goal. They typically command considerable public support for their international efforts. They also can use the image to assert the credibility of the United States to other nations.

Yet, in acting as the single executive in charge of the nation's foreign policy, presidents face a dizzying, messy conglomeration of international problems, the values and interests that define acceptable solutions, and the intricacies of the policies themselves. Presidents face three kinds of policy complexity. Uncertainty shapes the foreign policy domain. "When the president talks about 'Who is the enemy?' these days," observed Bush spokesman Marlin Fitzwater, referring to events in eastern Europe, "he says it's unpredictability and instability."[67] Fitzwater's comments could easily be applied to any world situation. On any one issue, presidents must attend to diverse people, events, and conditions. Indeed, there is no such thing as a single issue. Each issue is really a bundle of problems, many of which are tied to still other problems, each of which affects various people.

What is even more difficult to grasp is how policies carry their own complexity. All presidents ride on a policy track in an attempt to transform environmental uncertainty into predictability. Yet the ideological beliefs of American "good guys" against communist or dictatorial "bad guys," upon which anticommunist globalism and global democracy are based, actually stir greater complexity. The beliefs may act as blinders to existing conditions. In effect, presidents attempt to make the environment fit the policy rather than the policy fit the environment.

Policy instruments shake up still more complexity. Presidents use familiar techniques that pose problems for all users. Presidents typically do not choose just one of the four approaches—military action, nuclear deterrence, diplomacy, or covert action—and leave the other three on the shelf. Instead, they use various combinations of the four at all times to handle various problems in myriad areas of the globe. Nixon, for instance, during an ongoing limited war threatened to use nuclear force in Vietnam while conducting secret bombing missions against Cambodia in an effort to bring North Vietnam to peace talks. Nixon also started negotiations with the Chinese, began Strategic Arms Limitation Talks (SALT) with the Soviets, and pushed efforts in Chile, the Middle East, and elsewhere. The three kinds of policy complexity become written into the patterns of the plural presidency.

The decentralized organization and ambiguous decision processes of the plural presidency also magnify policy complexity. Presidents' foreign policy apparatus is broad and diffuse. It includes a multiplicity of advisers from units with different outlooks and expertise: the national security adviser, the National Security Council and its staff, the secretary of defense, the secretary of state, the Joint Chiefs of Staff, the director of the Central Intelligence Agency. These people and units often have a say about the decisions presidents make, and institutional ambiguity confounds what they have to say. It is never fully clear who will participate and how vigorously in any one decision. The White House decision makers also hold multiple conflicting goals about each of the policy instruments—when to use them and in what combination.

National Security Adviser Zbigniew Brzezinski depicted the intertwining of policy complexity, decentralized organization, and institutional ambiguity in the Carter administration in late 1978, when, he recalled, signals about the stability of the government of the shah of Iran were missed:

Our decision making circuits were heavily overloaded. The fall of 1978 was the time of the Camp David process and its aftermath. This was also the time of the stepped-up SALT negotiations, and during the critical December days we would literally rush from one meeting, in which the most complex positions on telemetry encryption or cruise missile definition would be hammered out, to another meeting on the fate of Iran. The fall . . . was also the period of the critical phase in the secret U.S.-Chinese negotiations. . . . In addition, the crisis in Nicaragua was beginning to preoccupy and absorb us. Finally, Cy Vance was heavily involved in key negotiations abroad, notably in the Middle East, while for Harold Brown this was the period of most difficult battles with the President over the defense budget. . . . It was unfortunately not a time in which undivided attention could be focused easily and early on what became a fatal strategic and political turning point.[68]

Unfolding events, the perspectives of other world politicians, competing advisers, ideological beliefs, multiple techniques, and the president direct U.S. foreign policy. Presidents can use the single executive image to portray themselves as premier foreign policy decision makers, but the complexity, decentralization, and ambiguity of the plural presidency bump them lower on the list. ■

F U R T H E R   R E A D I N G

On polycentrism and bipolycentrism, see: John Spanier, *Games Nations Play*, 5th ed. (New York: Holt, Rinehart and Winston, 1984). On American foreign policy, see: Charles Kegley and Eugene Wittkopf, *American Foreign Policy: Pattern and Process*, 2d ed. (New York: St. Martin's Press, 1982); Howard Jones, *The Course of American Diplomacy* (New York: Franklin Watts, 1985); James Nathan and James Oliver, *United States Foreign Policy and World Order*, 4th ed. (Boston: Little, Brown, 1989). On presidents and foreign policy, see: Cecil Crabb and Kevin Mulcahy, *American National Security: A Presidential Perspective* (Pacific Grove, Calif.: Brooks/Cole, 1991); Cecil Crabb and Pat Holt, *An Invitation to Struggle: Congress, the President, and Foreign Policy*, 3d ed. (Washington, D.C.: CQ Press, 1989). On limited wars, see: Harry S Truman, *Memoirs* (Garden City, N.J.: Doubleday, 1953); John Burke and Fred Greenstein, *How Presidents Test Reality* (New York: Russell Sage Foundation, 1989); John Mueller, *War Presidents, and Public Opinion* (New York: Wiley, 1973); *Pentagon Papers* (New York: Bantam Books, 1971); Bob Woodward, *The Commanders* (New York: Simon and Schuster, 1991). On covert action, see: Seymour Hersh, *The Price of Power: Kissinger in the Nixon White House* (New York: Summit Books, 1983); John Orman, *Presidential Secrecy and Deception* (Westport, Conn.: Greenwood Press, 1980).

NOTES

1. Hugh Sidey, "Freedom's Multi-Ring Circus," *Time*, January 8, 1990, 50.

2. Quotation is from "Days of the Whirlwind," *Newsweek*, December 25, 1989, 26–33.

3. John Spanier, *Games Nations Play*, 5th ed. (New York: Holt, Rinehart, and Winston, 1984), 260–288.

4. "Special Message to the Congress on Greece and Turkey," March 12, 1947, *Public Papers of the Presidents: Harry S Truman, 1947* (Washington, D.C.: U.S. Government Printing Office, 1949), 178.

5. Ibid.

6. George Kennan ("X"), "The Sources of Soviet Conduct," *Foreign Affairs* 25 (July 1947): 566–582.

7. Quoted in Cecil Crabb, *The Doctrines of American Foreign Policy* (Baton Rouge: Louisiana State University Press, 1982), 119.

8. Dean Acheson, *Present at the Creation: My Years in the State Department* (New York: Norton, 1969), 219.

9. News Conference, April 7, 1954, *Public Papers of the Presidents: Dwight Eisenhower, 1954* (Washington, D.C.: U.S. Government Printing Office, 1955), 382–383.

10. Crabb, 139.

11. Quoted in Townsend Hoopes, *The Devil and John Foster Dulles* (Boston: Little, Brown, 1973), 127.

12. Howard Jones, *The Course of American Diplomacy* (New York: Franklin Watts, 1985), 477.

13. "Annual Message to the Congress on the State of the Union," January 30, 1961, *Public Papers of the Presidents: John F. Kennedy, 1961* (Washington, D.C.: U.S. Government Printing Office, 1962), 23–24.

14. Charles Kegley and Eugene Wittkopf, *American Foreign Policy Pattern and Process*, 2d ed. (New York: St. Martin's Press, 1982), 103.

15. Although the Nuclear Test Ban Treaty did not limit underground tests because of opposition to on-site inspections, it ended the testing of nuclear bombs under water, in the atmosphere, and in outer space.

16. Cecil Crabb and Kevin Mulcahy, *American National Security: A Presidential Perspective* (Pacific Grove, Calif.: Brooks/Cole, 1991), 135–150.

17. Kegley and Wittkopf, 104.

18. "State of the Union Message," January 23, 1980, *Public Papers of the Presidents: Jimmy Carter, 1980–1981*, Bk. 1 (Washington, D.C.: U.S. Government Printing Office, 1981), 197.

19. Quoted in Jones, 592.

20. "Text of the State of the Union Address," *Washington Post*, January 29, 1991, A14.

21. Daniel P. Franklin, "War Powers in the Modern Context," *Congress and the Presidency* 16 (Spring 1987): 80.

22. "Measuring the Size of the Pie," *Congressional Quarterly Weekly Report*, June 23, 1990, 1975.

23. "Radio Report to the American People on Korea and on U.S. Policy in the Far East," April 11, 1951, *Public Papers of the Presidents: Harry S Truman, 1951* (Washington, D.C.: U.S. Government Printing Office, 1953), 225–226.

24. "Radio and Television Report to the American People on the Situation in Korea," September 1, 1950, *Public Papers of the Presidents: Harry S Truman, 1950* (Washington, D.C.: U.S. Government Printing Office, 1952), 610.

25. "Address at Johns Hopkins University: 'Peace Without Conquest,'" April 7, 1965, *Public Papers of the Presidents: Lyndon Johnson, 1965*, Bk. 1 (Washington, D.C.: U.S. Government Printing Office, 1966), 394.

26. Bob Woodward, *The Commanders*, (New York: Simon and Schuster, 1991), 260.

27. Quoted in Jones, 502.

28. Quoted in James Nathan and James Oliver, *United States Foreign Policy and World Order* (Boston: Little, Brown, 1981), 322.

29. "Report by Vice President Johnson on His Visit to Asian Countries," May 23, 1961, *Pentagon Papers* (New York: Bantam Books, 1971), 128–129.

30. John Burke and Fred Greenstein, *How Presidents Test Reality* (New York: Russell Sage Foundation, 1989), 141–142.

31. See Merle Miller, *Plain Speaking: An Oral Biography of Harry Truman* (New York: Berkeley, Medallion, 1974), 286–287; and John Mueller, *Wars, Presidents, and Public Opinion* (New York: Wiley, 1973), 24.

32. Acheson, 405.

33. Harry S Truman, *Memoirs* (Garden City, N.J.: Doubleday, 1953), 339.

34. Quoted in Nathan and Oliver, 322.

35. "Address at Johns Hopkins University," 395.

36. Transcript of News Conference of November 30, 1990, *Congressional Quarterly Weekly Report*, December 5, 1990, 4010.

37. "Text of the State of the Union Address," A14.

38. "Bush: Iraq Won't Decide Timing of Ground War," *Washington Post*, February 2, 1991, A1.

39. Quoted in Burke and Greenstein, 191.

40. "Radio and Television Address to the American People on the Situation in Korea," July 19, 1950, *Public Papers of the Presidents: Harry S Truman, 1950* (Washington, D.C.: U.S. Government Printing Office, 1952), 538.

41. "The President's Farewell Address to the American People," January 15, 1953, *Public Papers of the Presidents: Harry S Truman, 1953* (Washington, D.C.: U.S. Government Printing Office, 1954), 1197.

42. "Further McNaughton Memo on Factors in Bombing Decision," January 19, 1966, *Pentagon Papers*, 492.

43. "McNaughton's November Draft on Vietnam Aims and Choices," November 6, 1964, *Pentagon Papers* (New York: Bantam Books, 1971), 366.

44. *Pentagon Papers*, 397–398.

45. Mueller, 48.

46. *Washington Post*, January 29, 1991, A4.

47. This was particularly true during Vietnam. It was less the case during Korea because the Truman administration, with World War II in mind, immediately operated as a war-time economy.

48. John Yang, "Bush's Modest Domestic Proposals Contrast with Expansive World Role," *Washington Post*, January 30, 1991, A12.

49. Nathan and Oliver, 158.

50. *Congressional Quarterly Almanac, 1983* (Washington, D.C.: Congressional Quarterly, 1984), 39:135.

51. "U.S. Reactions to Surrender of Panama's Noriega," *Congressional Quarterly Weekly Report*, January 6, 1990, 51.

52. Colin Campbell, "The 'Let's Deal' Presidency," in *The Bush Presidency: First Appraisals*, ed. Colin Campbell and Bert Rockman (Chatham, N.J.: Chatham House, 1991), 207.

53. Quoted in Kegley and Wittkopf, 86.

54. Quoted ibid., 92.

55. Gary King and Lyn Ragsdale, *The Elusive Executive* (Washington, D.C.: Congressional Quarterly Press, 1988), Chap. 3.

56. Cecil Crabb and Pat Holt, *Invitation to Struggle*, 3d ed. (Washington, D.C.: Congressional Quarterly Press, 1989), Chap. 7; and "Poor Odds, High Stakes," *The Economist*, June 27, 1992, 77.

57. "Poor Odds, High Stakes," 77.

58. Seymour Hersh, *The Price of Power: Kissinger in the Nixon White House* (New York: Summit Books, 1983), 61.

59. John Orman, *Presidential Secrecy and Deception* (Westport, Conn.: Greenwood Press, 1980), 80.

60. Ibid., 152–155.

61. Nathan and Oliver, 186–188.

62. Nathan and Oliver, 187–188.

63. Testimony before U.S. Congress, House Select Committee on Communist Aggression, Hearings before the Subcommittee on Latin America, 83rd Cong., 2d sess., 1954, 24–26.

64. Nathan and Oliver, 188–190.

65. "Covert Action in Chile, 1969–1973," Staff Report of the Select Committee to Study Governmental Operation with Respect to Intelligence Activities, U.S. Senate, December 18, 1974, 94th Cong., 1st sess. (Senator Frank Church, Chair), 23.

66. Seymour Hersh, 275.

67. Quoted in "The Last Picture Show," *Time*, June 11, 1990, 14–15.

68. Zbigniew Brzezinski, *Power and Principle: Memoirs of a National Security Adviser, 1977–1981* (New York: Farrar, Straus, and Giroux, 1983), 358.

CHAPTER 11

Presidential
Economics

G eorge Bush stepped from the dense, heavy August heat into the feigned crisp air of the New Orleans Convention Center. He buoyantly raced to the podium to deliver his acceptance speech for the 1988 Republican nomination for president. Midway through the speech, the crowd went wild when Bush chanted: "Read my lips, NO NEW TAXES." The no-tax pledge was one Bush had made before and would utter almost daily during the 1988 presidential campaign. Yet the message stated in this way seemed to make more sense than it had before. It sounded better to the ear, like the coolness of the air-conditioned hall felt on the skin. The words were categorical, absolute, short, to the point, and they left no room for discussion. They were words of the single executive image as exploited by the Bush campaign. They seemed to promise an easy, direct solution to an immensely complex problem. A lone individual would hold the line against tax increases in spite of the largest deficit in American history. An overwhelming number of Americans agreed with Bush's no-tax plan.

By May 1990, the policy complexity of the plural presidency caught up with the rhetoric of the single executive. During his first year in office, Bush unfailingly held to his no-tax pledge, though many people in Washington felt he was whistling past a graveyard as the deficit continued to mount. Nor were there any "easy" solutions. Bush and his economic advisers knew that only 23 percent of the budget could really be cut. The rest involved relatively "uncontrollable outlays" that could not be scaled back. These included entitlement programs—programs in which individuals are entitled to participate if they meet a certain criterion of age, income, or family status (Social Security, Medicare, Medicaid, welfare, and food stamps are examples). They also included programs, such as farm price supports, that could not be tampered with for fear of major political fallout. And the interest on the deficit itself had to be paid, no matter what. The Bush administration offered little in the way of budget cuts or program eliminations because they would disrupt Bush's campaign pledge of a "kinder and gentler" America.

Bush also faced ornery members of Congress, a majority of whom knew taxes had to be raised but were unwilling to take the first step. "We are going to leap off the cliff hand in hand as I have always said," remarked Speaker of the House Thomas Foley (D-Wash).[1] Bush called for an economic summit with members of Congress to work on the budget and said that there would be "no preconditions." Democratic congressional leaders took these as code words meaning that Bush would entertain the idea of new taxes. White House spokesman Marlin Fitzwater reiterated the president's words. But, later, John Sununu, White House chief of staff, and Vice President Dan Quayle asserted that nothing had changed; the sacrosanct pledge was still untouched.

In a news conference on May 26, Bush seemed to sit gingerly on a picket fence, straddling between his old no-tax promise and his new words about no preconditions. In answer to questions about taxes, he stated, "Things are complicated out there on this subject, and we're trying hard to get a budget agreement, and that's the way it is, and we'll see how we go."[2] The single executive image and the plural presidency struggled.

Nearly a month went by before Bush vaulted from the fence. In a written statement rather than a public announcement, he observed tersely that "the size of the deficit problem and the need for a [budget] package that can be enacted require all of the following: entitlement and mandatory program reform; tax revenue increases; growth incentives; discretionary spending reductions; orderly reductions in defense expenditures; and budget process reform."[3] "Tax revenue increases" became a measure of the plural presidency's attack on the no-new-tax pledge of the single executive image. Budget choices could not be reduced to a slogan, nor could a single individual control their outcome. The White House acknowledged the complexity of the economic environment within which it worked and the economic policies it was about to support.

Five months followed of rampant haranguing within Congress and of epidemic indecision at the White House about a tradeoff between higher taxes for the wealthy and lower capital gains taxes. The government, out of money, actually shut down for a day. In late October 1990, the 1990 budget reconciliation act passed, which called for a five-year, $493 billion package of spending limits and tax increases on luxury goods, cigarettes, liquor, gasoline, and the incomes of the very wealthy.[4]

Campaigning for re-election in 1992, Bush declared that breaking the no-tax pledge was the worst mistake of his presidency. People, he said, felt they could not trust the president's word. Bush had carefully used the single executive image to his advantage throughout the 1988 campaign and during his first two years in office. But during the remaining two years, the policy complexity of the plural presidency blew up the advantage offered by the image.

Bush's dilemma was not unusual. Modern presidents since Franklin Roosevelt have portrayed themselves as budding economists. They invoke the single executive image to make promises of prosperity for everyone. They also claim credit for the bulge in people's pocketbooks in good times and point blame at Congress when money gets tight. They recognize that economic good news may boost their popularity and their re-election chances. Yet the very pledges the president makes as the one person in charge bring into play the policy complexity of the plural presidency. Presidents' budget requests for spending programs and tax adjustments extend their responsibility to literally every program in every policy area of the government. The plural presidency encompasses an intricate array of issue areas and fosters presidential proposals for defense, drugs, foreign aid, space exploration, veterans' benefits, roads, and things more readily recognized as relevant to economics—employment, incomes, taxes, deficits.

Presidents besides Bush have found themselves in hot economic water attempting to promote the single executive image. Ronald Reagan pledged to lower taxes, cut the budget, and increase defense in the simple, straightforward manner that Bush would use when he promised not to raise taxes. In Reagan's first term, this pledge worked for him politically. The slogans, however, masked the incongruity of the tax-budget-defense triad, which led to the ballooning budget deficit with which Bush was saddled. By Reagan's second term, criticisms of his policies mounted. In 1971, Richard Nixon ordered a wage and price freeze with little thought about what would happen once the controls were ended. What happened? Prices rose like steam escaping from a boiling kettle. In 1974, Gerald Ford introduced a program called "Whip Inflation Now" and proudly wore a "WIN" button in his lapel. But the plan was disparaged for being too simplistic. Later in the 1970s, Jimmy Carter advocated wage and price guidelines, but they never got off the ground because memories of the Nixon cauldron lingered.

This chapter presents the story of presidents coping with economic problems. The words "coping with economic problems" are chosen with care, because presidents do not make economic policy. What is generally considered to be economic policy is not based on economics, is not policy, and is not made.

Presidents do not have economic policies; they have only political policies. At the root of presidents' economic choices are political calculations about what businesses, labor unions, other organizations, and consumers expect and will accept as solutions to economic woes and how the choices will affect presidents' political fortunes. The normative question "What should the president do about the economy" collapses into the pragmatic political question "What can the president do to benefit from the economy?" Presidents often embrace politically attractive courses even when the economic reasoning is dubious.

Nor is there one central economic policy. The president proposes one of many competing and potentially contradictory political policies about the economy. Presidents have little opportunity to act autonomously in economic affairs. Congress fields the Congressional Budget Office (CBO), which draws up the congressional version of the federal budget. The House and Senate Budget Committees, the House and Senate Appropriation Committees, the House Ways and Means Committee, the Senate Finance Committee, the Joint Committee on Taxation, and the Joint Economic Committee are involved. The Federal Reserve Board, the government's central bank, acts independently of both the executive and the legislature to set the floors and ceilings for the nation's interest rates. Every federal department and agency takes part in the budget process. States and municipalities often contact these federal units to make sure they will receive a portion of the federal pie. Three units in the White House also bear some responsibility for economic affairs. The Council of Economic Advisers (CEA) deals with macroeconomic forecasts and trends (unemployment and inflation). The Office of Management and Budget (OMB) prepares the federal budget on behalf of the president. The Treasury Department is especially concerned with taxation, debt financing, and international economic decisions. In short, the American system has no central capacity to direct economic decisions.

U.S. economic policy is not made. The economy often dictates the choices of government decision makers. Businesses, labor unions, consumers, importers, world events, war, and the weather affect the direction of the economy. In 1990, when President Saddam Hussein ordered Iraq's invasion of neighboring Kuwait, U.S. gasoline prices went up a nickel overnight and a dime in a week. People lamented the absence of an American energy policy, but there was little to do but pay the new price.

This chapter explores the anarchy of American economic affairs and the disorder and confusion of government efforts to shape them. The policy complexity of the plural presidency is examined in four parts: (1) the policy domain, (2) the policy track, (3) policy instruments, and (4) the budget process.

THE ECONOMIC POLICY DOMAIN

Modern presidents face an economic domain that can most aptly be called the "international political market." It comprises three distinguishable but overlapping aspects: (1) the market aspect: the U.S. economy; (2) the political aspect: the federal budget; and (3) the international aspect: the world economy. Figure 11.1 depicts the gross national product (GNP) of the United States, adjusted for inflation. GNP is the measure of the total goods and services produced in the economy as a whole. American GNP has grown steadily and dramatically since the 1930s. The growth has increased the economic complexity that presidents must take into account. The size of the federal budget can be seen as a percentage of GNP in Figure 11.2, which provides an indication of how much of the economy is the government. Figure 11.3 shows imports to and exports from the United States. The balance of trade is an indicator of the American economy's dependence on foreign markets, foreign products, and foreign investments.

The key feature of the international political market is the interdependence of its members. The United States, like most other nations, no longer has a national economy that starts and stops at the country's borders. The U.S. economy is the largest in the world; the U.S. federal budget is the largest in the world. Partly as a consequence of both factors, the American economy has come to have large stakes in foreign economies, and foreign economies have enlarged their

Figure 11.1 GNP Adjusted for Inflation

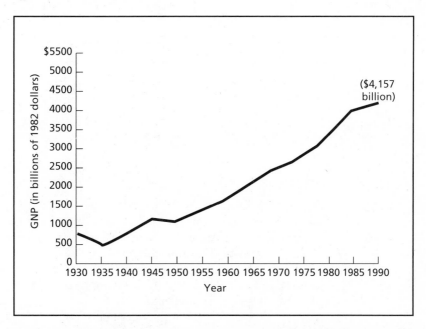

American GNP, the measure of total goods and services produced in the economy as a whole, has grown over seven and a half times since the 1930s. [*Sources: Statistical Abstract of the United States, 1991* (Washington, D.C.: U.S. Government Printing Office, 1991; U.S. Dept. of Commerce, *Survey of Current Business,* May 1991 (Washington, D.C.: U.S. Government Printing Office, 1991), 8.]

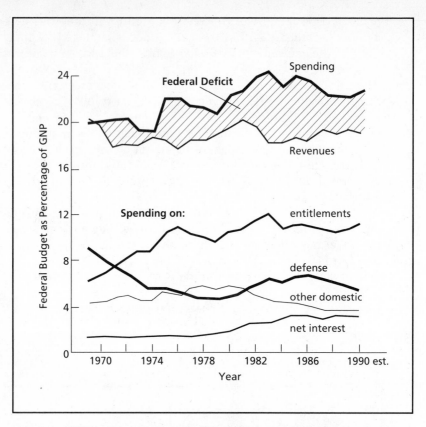

Figure 11.2   The Political Aspect: The Federal Budget as a Percentage of GNP

The top portion of the figure shows the overall increase in federal spending during the 1980s, even as revenues fell—resulting in a large federal deficit. The bottom part of the figure shows that most money in the federal budget is spent on entitlement programs such as Social Security. [*Source: The Economist,* June 23, 1990, 27; data from the Congressional Budget Office. © 1990 The Economist Newspaper Group, Inc. Reprinted with permission.]

stakes in the American economy. The American economy, once touted as self-sufficient, now imports heavily and has numerous direct investments abroad. Foreign capital arrives in the United States to help finance the growing federal budget deficit. The dollar is a pivotal international currency, although its market strength has eroded significantly since World War II. The complexity of the global market challenges American presidents.

Three months after the 1990 budget agreement passed, the budget deficit, fueled by a weakened economy, by war preparations in the Persian Gulf, and by higher oil prices, rose to $400 billion. "Congress just enacted the largest deficit reduction package in the nation's history and now we will be treated to the largest deficit in the nation's

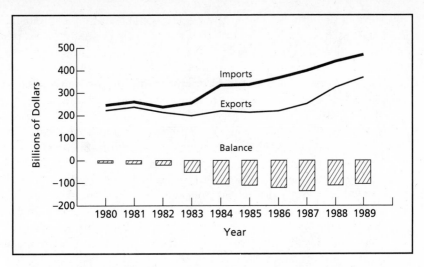

Figure 11.3   The International Aspect: U.S. Trade with the World, 1980–1989

The American trade deficit grew during the 1980s as fewer American goods were exported than were foreign goods imported. [*Source:* U.S. Department of Commerce, *U.S. Foreign Trade Highlights, 1989* (September 1990), 10.]

history," said Robert Reischauer, director of the Congressional Budget Office.[5] The unpredictability of the economic environment is one element of policy complexity. The plural presidency translates environmental factors into multiple conflicting priorities and the politics of "playing it by ear."

THE ECONOMIC POLICY TRACK

Presidents and other American politicians ride on a complicated economic track through the international political market. The twists and turns of the track exacerbate the policy complexity of the economic domain. The track has a firm, unshakable foundation: *free enterprise capitalism*. But the ties and fittings of *government intervention* have been added to this foundation. Logic might seem to dictate that government intervention should not be joined to a free enterprise foundation. But the American economic policy operates pragmatically, not logically, as a hybrid: *protective capitalism*. Capitalism predominates, but government protects citizens from its excesses.

Free Enterprise Capitalism

When Calvin Coolidge remarked that "the business of America is business," he spoke firmly about free enterprise capitalism as the foundation of the economic track. Americans, often without knowing why, uniformly believe in the benefits of laissez-faire capitalism. According to this nineteenth-century doctrine, usually translated to mean "leave it (the economy) alone," everyone should pursue his or her own personal financial interests. Private businesses should be "free" enterprises allowed to operate without government intervention. According to laissez-faire logic, an "invisible hand" ensures that the selfish pursuits of individuals and businesses actually promote the broad interests of society. The "invisible hand" is a clever metaphor for a very visible market factor: competition. Businesses seeking profits compete with one another and produce goods at an affordable price desired by consumers in the marketplace. Those who provide the best products at the best prices reap profits, and society benefits. In the United States, these economic beliefs are tied to important social values of freedom, individualism, security, and property, making them doubly powerful. The American dream is a dream about money and success.

Government Intervention

"Free enterprise" is an ideal type, a myth, that Americans believe in but that does not exist fully. Government intervention has long shaped the freedom of enterprise. In the early days of the republic, the government adopted land laws that permitted settlers to acquire cheap public land. Throughout the nineteenth century, protectionist trade laws aided growing manufacturing industries. Even after the "infant" industries were fully grown, high tariffs excluded foreign imports. At the century's end and after the turn of the century, the government imposed regulations on giant corporate monopolies known as "trusts." In the 1930s, the government interceded on behalf of people suffering from the Great Depression.

Sometimes the aim of government intervention was to make free enterprise freer. At other times, the intervention expressly restricted freedom. Nevertheless, Americans firmly maintain that they have a free enterprise system. And their belief may well be justified, given the relatively greater government intervention evident in other capitalist systems. Almost all other capitalist systems—for example, the planned economy in Japan and the large social welfare states in Europe—experience far more government activity than the United States. Yet despite these relative differences, Americans too rely heavily on government intervention in the economy. Capitalism and government intervention are now so closely joined that it is difficult to envision one without the other.

Protective Capitalism

The Great Depression of the 1930s permanently fused free enterprise capitalism and government intervention into protective capitalism.

More than at any time during the nineteenth century, the government entered the marketplace, and this time it did not leave. Instead, the government became the market's largest consumer and its largest producer. Before the economic collapse, federal spending had been modest; afterward, it soared. In 1929, federal expenditures were $3.3 billion; a decade later they had climbed to $8.9 billion, a 170 percent increase. Federal expenditure as a proportion of gross national product tripled from 3.2 percent in 1929 and to 9.7 percent in 1939.[6] Today it is 22 percent of GNP.

The most prominent legacy of the Great Depression and the New Deal was not the social welfare programs of Social Security, public assistance, and unemployment compensation, which became integral parts of American society, or the increasing regulation of American businesses, banks, farms, and factories. These were dramatic developments. But the most prominent legacy was the acceptance of the government's responsibility for a stable economy. Prior to the calamitous depression, government was expected to suffer inflationary spirals and economic downturns along with the rest of the nation. As a result of the Great Depression, government actively fashioned protective policies for economic growth and stability. Monetary policies (regulation of the money supply) and fiscal policies (government taxing and spending) were fashioned to achieve satisfactory levels of growth, inflation, and unemployment. Presidents have no direct control over monetary policy. They do, however, have some ability to steer fiscal policy.

Monetary Policy

Monetary policy is in the hands of an independent agency, the Federal Reserve Board. The Fed is the nation's central bank and regulator of all other banks. It protects economic stability by changing its discount rate, the interest rate it charges member banks to borrow money. The discount rate directs the nation's interest rates. When the economy slows, the Fed typically lowers its discount rate to ease credit. It also manages the nation's money supply through (1) the exchange of government securities (U.S. Treasury notes and bonds) on the open market and (2) changes in banks' cash reserve requirements—the money that banks must hold in reserve at regional Federal Reserve Banks. Herbert Stein, chair of the Council of Economic Advisers under Nixon, summed up relations between the White House and the Fed as

always rather touchy because of the Federal Reserve's independence and the feeling that we should not intrude in it. . . . I would not regard [the Federal Reserve] as part of the President's team. It certainly was not hostile—Arthur [Burns, then chair of the Federal Reserve] was not hostile. . . . But he didn't feel any obligation to us; he operated in a very independent way.[7]

This independence enlarges the economic policy complexity that presidents face and hampers their ability to manage it.

Fiscal Policy

The single executive image requires that presidents work to secure economic stability, and it ensures that presidents will be judged in office on how well the economy does. Presidents thus face a two-edged sword. When economic stability and prosperity prevail, presidents are typically judged with favor. When economic chaos comes, presidents are blamed for the bad times. To meet their obligations as the single executive, presidents have devised fiscal policies under the guise of protective capitalism. Yet protective capitalism has no agreed-upon standards for stability. Nor are there standards for the degree to which government should intervene to bring about stability. As a result, politicians and economists have some leeway to define acceptable routes for the economic policy track. Presidents have offered four: (1) balanced budgets, (2) Keynesian economics, (3) supply-side economics, and (4) deficit reduction.

Balanced Budgets. From the 1930s through the 1950s, presidents announced strong preferences for balanced budgets. The logic was that the balance itself afforded economic stability. This belief was based not on sophisticated economic theories but rather on intuitive ideas about family finances: "Never spend more than you earn." Franklin Roosevelt's experience typifies the politico-economic complexity facing presidents striving to balance the federal budget. Candidate Roosevelt campaigned hard in 1932 against Herbert Hoover, who had accepted several years of budget deficits to try to bail out the economy at the onset of the Great Depression. Throughout the 1930s, President Roosevelt maintained his preference for balanced budgets yet pursued a series of ad hoc economic recovery programs that yielded deficits. He did not, however, consciously create deficits to achieve economic recovery.

Truman and Eisenhower saw balanced budgets as the most desirable economic goal of the government. Truman wrote, "There is nothing sacred about the pay-as-you-go idea so far as I am concerned except that it represents the soundest principle of financing that I know."[8] Truman, however, did not always get what he wanted. Over his term, Congress appropriated $14.5 billion more than Truman requested.[9] The president and Congress did raise taxes in 1950 and 1951 to finance the Korean War. A small $2.2 billion deficit in 1950 and a $7.6 billion surplus in 1951 resulted. When Eisenhower left office in 1961, he took credit for three balanced budgets (1956, 1957, 1960) and two proposed balanced budgets. Through 1960, the rule of protective capitalism was that "the budget was to be balanced except in wartime (the old exception) and in depression (the new exception)."[10] Government's protective intervention in the economy was limited by budget constraints.

Keynesianism. The Kennedy administration effectively widened the protective capitalism track to invite more government involvement in the economy. It advocated that unbalanced, not balanced, budgets might foster economic stability under certain circumstances. The Kennedy people relied on John Maynard Keynes, an English economist writing in the 1930s, who proposed a demand-driven relationship between the government and the economy.

Keynes asserted that during bad economic times the government should intervene to "prime the pump" by means of "deficit spending"—spending more than it took in—to increase aggregate demand by consumers, businesses, and government for goods and services. As demand rose, the economy would be rejuvenated, and the "pump" would work on its own. Economists following Keynes based their calculations on a "full employment economy"—one operating at its peak potential. The government would spend as if the economy were at full employment in order to bring about full employment. Thus, the Keynesian approach posited a balanced economy, not a balanced budget.[11]

Keynesianism is as much a theory of politics as it is a theory of economics. In the hands of politicians, Keynes's ideas were at once simplified and made more absolute. Many politicians prized the heretofore unheard-of idea of a deliberately unbalanced budget. It allowed them to spend money without needing to raise taxes. Much of the money sponsored social welfare programs that were supposed to help the economy back to full employment. And because the goal was to deliver full employment, politicians could practice budget deficits but preach balanced budgets. A *New York Times* editorial on December 27, 1938, foretold the problems of Keynesian economics-turned-politics:

There is one objective standard that everyone understands clearly—Federal budgets "annually balanced." Once we depart from that, except under the sheerest necessity, we are adrift on the seas of confusion, for all sorts of ingenious reasons are invented for not going back, and the vested interest in keeping the new situation is enormous. . . . To enable a legislator to vote for appropriation bills and at the same time avoid voting for an increase in taxes is to provide him with the politician's paradise.[12]

Keynesian politics left several vital questions unanswered. First, no one knew what "full employment" was, although everyone knew that it did not require 100 percent of the work force to be employed. Kennedy inherited a mild economic slowdown in 1960 that put unemployment at 5.5 percent and pushed it to 6.7 percent by 1961. A debate ensued between Kennedy's White House economics team, which defined "full employment" as 4 percent unemployed (a figure used during the Eisenhower years), and Labor Department economists, who pushed for 3 percent unemployed as the goal.[13] Today, "full employment" typically is seen as 5 or 6 percent unemployed. Second, no one knew how much spending or how big a deficit was needed to achieve full employment. Walter Heller, Kennedy's chairman of the Council of Economic Advisers, referred to the process as "fine-tuning"—annually juggling the books on both the taxing and the spending sides to keep the economy stable or get the economy stable. Third, no one knew—and no one yet knows—how big a deficit was bad. Some economists argued that large deficits suppress economic growth. Others suggested that deficits are not deleterious so long as there is sufficient capital worldwide to fund them.

The Kennedy and Johnson years made modest deficits politically acceptable. Deficit spending became more nearly a catchall approach to add and improve domestic and military programs rather than a device to alleviate economic downturns.

During the 1970s, Keynesianism itself foundered. It posited an inverse relationship between inflation and unemployment, such that when inflation was high, unemployment would be low and vice versa. Yet the oil embargo of 1974 produced sharp increases in the prices of all petroleum products. These increases destabilized the economy as consumer spending slowed, forcing many firms to scale back production. The result was an unusual recession in which inflation and unemployment rose in tandem. (Typically, inflation slows in a recession.) The deficit grew but did little to bring the economy back to full employment. So-called stagflation continued through a second oil price shock in 1978.

Supply-Side Economics. The track zigzagged toward supply-side economics in 1981 with the inauguration of Ronald Reagan. Supply-side economics proposes tax cuts to spur an increase in the supply of goods (the production and sale of goods) and labor. Tax cuts are supposed to stimulate investments, which lead to a need for more labor to produce more goods. Supply-side economics maintains that greater production prompts greater corporate and individual income, which in turn increases tax revenues. Keynesian economics says that to combat inflation, demand must be dampened and taxes raised. Supply-side economics theorizes that to combat inflation, supply must be increased and taxes reduced. Keynesian economics maintains that federal spending or tax cuts will increase demand, bring about a full employment economy, and wipe away the deficit caused by the spending increases or tax cuts. Supply-side economics states that federal tax cuts will increase supply, bring about a "full production" economy, and wipe away the deficit caused by the tax cuts.

Reagan offered supply-side economics as part of a larger, essentially negative political message. "Reaganomics" called for less: less government spending, less deficit, a smaller money supply, and less government regulation, in addition to less taxation. Reaganomics proposed to narrow the government protection that Keynesianism had widened. The supply-side doctrine, however, did little to account for how lower taxes would fit with other parts of the economy that were not necessarily within the doctrine's reach. Lower taxes during a recession meant less revenue. Lower taxes tied to a budget with large defense increases and high uncontrollable expenditures meant high deficits. The theory did not foresee either result.

Deficit Reduction. With deficits ballooning, the protective capitalism track veered toward deficit reduction. According to the new economic thinking, economic stability hinged not on priming the pump but on shutting off the pump. The government has operated in the black only five times in the past forty-one years (1951, 1956, 1957, 1960, 1969).[14] Deficits during the 1960s were modest, averaging $5.0 billion from 1961 to 1967. A $25.2 billion deficit mounted in 1968. It was followed by the country's last surplus—$3.2 billion in 1969. Thereafter, "structural deficits"—the portion of the deficit due not to recession but to a basic imbalance in spending and revenues— emerged. A big jump in the deficit followed the first oil shock of 1974. The deficit increased tenfold from $6.1 billion in 1973 to $63.2 billion in 1974. It stayed high throughout the Carter years after the oil shock of 1978. The average annual deficit from 1977 to 1980 was $58 billion. In 1981, the deficit almost doubled from the previous year to $128 billion. In 1982, it nearly doubled again to $208 billion (see Figure 11.4).

Despite statements from the Reagan White House that budget deficit reductions were a high priority, it was Congress, not the president, that initiated the movement toward deficit reduction. In 1985, Congress passed the Gramm-Rudman-Hollings Balanced Budget and Emergency Deficit Control Act.[15] Gramm-Rudman-Hollings mandated that the budget deficit be lowered to specific levels each year until the budget was balanced. If Congress and the president could not meet the specified deficit level in a given year, then across-the-board budget cuts would be carried out. As Senator Rudman observed, the bill was "a bad idea whose time has come."[16]

Since Gramm-Rudman, questions of total spending and total borrowing have dominated fiscal policy discussions. The 1990 budget reconciliation act, discussed at the beginning of the chapter, replaced Gramm-Rudman. It is a two-part White House–Congress plan to live within spending limits rather than practice deficit reductions. First, entitlement programs are handled on a pay-as-you-go basis: increases in the programs can be implemented only when there is money to pay for them. Second, caps are established in three remaining budget areas: defense, domestic, and international policy. The 1990 act erects budgetary walls to separate the three areas. Spending increases in

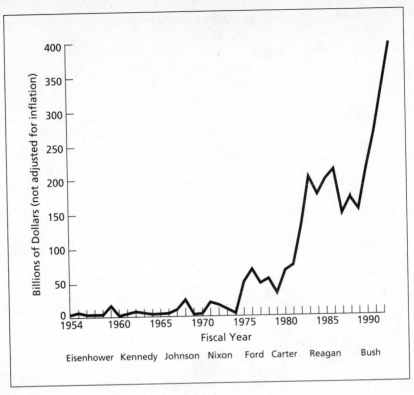

Figure 11.4 The Budget Deficit, 1954–1992

In 1981 the deficit almost doubled from the previous year and has risen uncontrolla-
bly since. [*Source: Congressional Quarterly Weekly Report,* November 26, 1988, 3379; updated
from *Congressional Quarterly Weekly Report,* May 9, 1992, 1235. Used by permission.]

Note: The government ran a surplus in 1956, 1957, 1960, and 1969. The figure for 1992
($399.7 billion) is an estimate.

one area can be compensated for *only* by equal decreases in the same
area, not by decreases in one of the other two areas. For instance,
any increases in some part of the domestic budget (say, education)
must be offset by decreases in some other part of the domestic budget
(say, crime control).

The budgetary walls were erected primarily because the defense
budget has been shrinking and the savings from the defense area are
to be used to help pay off the deficit. Without the budgetary walls,
it would be all too tempting for the president and Congress to use
the defense savings to increase funding of an existing domestic program or begin funding a new domestic program. If spending is not
kept within the caps, the 1990 budget law is supposed to trigger
spending cuts in the area that has exceeded the cap.

Balanced budgets, Keynesianism, supply-side economics, and
deficit reduction all maintain protective capitalism. Each includes the

government as an integral part of the free market. Even supply-side economics, which touted less government involvement in the economy, used government to bring the reduction about. The complexity of the economic policy track is revealed in the number of ways government can provide economic stability.

ECONOMIC POLICY INSTRUMENTS

Presidents' economic policy instruments are blunt tools—clubs where scalpels might be preferred. Just as there are no agreed-upon standards for economic stability, the instruments employed to bring about stability are inexact. Moreover, politics gets in the way of clarifying what, if any, economic effects they have. Presidents like to claim popular victories with techniques of dubious economic value. Presidents have adopted three specific instruments to keep the nation on the protective capitalism track: (1) adjusting taxes, typically downward; (2) adjusting spending, typically upward; and (3) wage and price controls.

Tax Politics

Presidents since Truman have offered tax cuts as the primary instrument of protective capitalism. Tax cuts offer presidents a ready tool to advance the single executive image. Presidents typically propose the cuts as swift, short-term economic solutions that give taxpayers and businesses an immediate benefit. Yet tax cuts are ultimately an uneasy blend of clear political advantages for the presidents and other politicians who offer them and unclear economic effects for the consumers and corporations that receive them. Policy complexity is reflected in tax cuts, for political gains often supersede economic merit.

Table 11.1 summarizes presidents' tax proposals and congressional enactments from Truman to Reagan. As the table shows, presidents and Congress jockey over taxes, compounding the complexity of this instrument. Presidents almost never get what they ask for. They also are faced with Congress introducing its own initiatives without a prior proposal from the White House. For instance, Truman and Eisenhower reluctantly introduced tax cuts in 1948 and 1954 to stave off larger cuts desired, and ultimately enacted, by Congress. Kennedy fully embraced this instrument in 1962 as a Keynesian measure. Although the budget was in deficit, Kennedy economists defended the tax cut as a means to bring the economy up to full employment and, they argued, achieve a balanced budget. It was the largest proposed tax cut in American history up to that time. It reduced individual income tax rates across the board, including a drop in rates for those in the highest bracket from 91 percent to 70 percent.

Table 11.1 Presidential Tax Proposals and Congressional Enactments, 1948–1990 (in billions of 1982 dollars)

Year	Presidential proposal		Congressional enactment		Difference	
	First year[1]	Fully effective[2]	First year[1]	Fully effective[2]	First year[1]	Fully effective[2]
1948	−3.2	—	−4.8	—	−1.6	—
1950	5.5	—	8.8	—	3.3	—
1951	10.0	—	5.7	—	−4.3	—
1954	−1.3	—	−1.4	—	0.1	—
1964	−6.3	−10.3	−7.7	−11.5	−1.4	−1.2
1968	7.4	—	10.9	—	3.5	—
1969	*	—	−2.5	—	−2.5	—
1971	−12.9	−9.3	−11.4	−10.0	1.5	−0.7
1975	−16.0	—	−22.8	—	−6.8	—
1976	*	—	−15.7	−6.2	−15.7	−6.2
1977	−13.8	−15.7	−17.7	−13.8	3.9	−1.9
1978	−24.5	−34.9	−18.7	−34.1	5.8	0.8
1980	*	—	3.6	—	3.6	—
1981	−56.6	−129.8	−37.7	−150.0	18.9	−20.2
1982	*	—	18.0	51.8	18.0	51.8
1984	*	—	10.6	22.5	10.6	22.5
1985	*	—	—	—	—	—
1986	11.5	−11.5	11.5	−15.1	0	−3.6
1987	6.1	—	9.4	15.8	3.3	9.7
1988	*	—	.4	—	.4	—
1989	5.3	—	5.6	5.1	.3	−.2
1990	8.9	20.4	15.6	26.6	6.7	6.2

*No presidential proposal.
1. Expected revenue change first full year after law is passed.
2. Expected revenue change first full year after law is fully effective, if different from first column.

Source: Paul Peterson, "The New Politics of Deficits," in *The New Direction in American Politics,* ed. J. Chubb and P. Peterson (Washington, D.C.: Brookings Institution, 1985), 381. Copyright © 1985. Used by permission of the Brookings Institution. Updated (for 1985–1990) by the author from Louis Talley, "Taxes: Significant Federal Tax Acts, 1954–1989," *CRS Report for Congress* (Washington, D.C.: Congressional Research Service, 1990), 4–5; and *Congressional Quarterly Weekly Report,* June 29, 1985, 1260; July 27, 1985, 1470; January 1, 1987, 46–47; and November 25, 1989, 3224–3225.

Corporate taxes also were reduced. Lowering tax revenues rather than increasing spending programs lent a somewhat "conservative" tinge to Kennedy's version of Keynes.

The Kennedy tax cut shows the tension between the economic and political aspects of this instrument and the policy complexity that results. Kennedy announced his proposal late in 1962. Congress debated the measure in 1963, when the economy was already recovering. It still had not acted on the bill when Kennedy was assassinated in November 1963. The new Johnson administration and Congress agreed in 1964 on a cut deeper than Kennedy originally had requested. When the cuts went into effect in stages in 1964 and 1965, the recovery was stronger still. Total spending, real output, and employment rose after the tax cut; but they had been rising before the cut. The Federal Reserve Board had eased interest rates and thereby increased the money supply in 1961, so it was difficult to discern what was the principal cause of expansion—the tax cut, the expansion of the money supply, or something else. Herbert Stein remarks, "The trend in thinking since the 1964 tax cut has been to emphasize the monetary contribution, and particularly to emphasize that the effect of [a] tax cut is likely to be quite temporary."[17]

Although it was unclear whether the tax cut had the desired economic effect, there was no question that it had the desired political effect. The Johnson administration hailed tax cuts as chief devices of "fine-tuning." It felt that continuous manipulation of tax rates would keep the economy at full employment without inflation. Presidents Nixon, Ford, and Carter fine-tuned the economy with cuts in 1971, 1975, 1977, and 1978. Congress fine-tuned still more in 1969 and 1976.

Reagan ended the rationale of fine-tuning but not the practice of tax cuts. In Reagan's move to supply-side economics, tax rates, which were previously cut to increase demand, were drastically reduced to spur supply. Reagan secured congressional passage of a $162 billion tax reduction, the largest in history, dramatically larger than the Kennedy cut, with the top income tax rate slashed from 70 percent to 50 percent. Yet the economic results intended by the Reagan tax cut, like those intended by the Kennedy cut, were not necessarily the results achieved.

The tax cut went into effect as the deepest recession of the postwar period brewed in 1981. However, the Federal Reserve Board kept interest rates high to combat rising inflation, a seemingly intractable problem of the late 1970s. The Fed's stance may have stalled any stimulative effect of the tax cut. In addition, the recession consumed the tax revenue boon that the cut had been expected to generate. The decline in tax revenue, the increased spending desired by the Reagan administration for defense, and fewer spending cuts than the administration desired in other parts of the budget worked together to produce a nearly $200 billion deficit. Inflation, however, did drop and stayed down for the remainder of the 1980s. Tax reform in 1986 reduced the tax rate still more. The top income tax rate dropped from 50 percent to 28 percent. All the while, the deficit continued to mount. Despite the ambiguous economic consequences of the 1981 and 1986 tax cuts, the political benefits for Reagan were apparent. Although Reagan's popularity dropped as unemployment rose in 1981 and 1982, a full-scale recovery was under way by the 1984 election. Looking forward to re-election, Reagan could ask people whether they were better off in 1984 than they had been four years earlier without fearing the answer.

In the span of just over two decades, tax rates for the highest income bracket dropped from 91 percent to 28 percent. Tax cuts, however, are the "easy" half of presidents' fiscal policy. How willing are presidents to adopt the "hard" part of fiscal tax policy—a tax increase that will pull the economy away from inflationary strains or reduce the deficit? For the most part, presidents have agreed to tax increases only in exchange for economic incentives they desire. President Johnson resisted a tax increase until 1968 when, no longer running for re-election, he acquiesced to a Vietnam tax surcharge passed by Congress. Nixon sought the continuation of the surcharge in exchange for congressionally sponsored income tax reduction and repeal of investment tax credits in 1969. But two years later Nixon changed course, asking for a large income tax reduction and the return of the investment tax credit. During the post–oil embargo recession in 1974, Ford proposed a tax increase in October designed to pay for antirecessionary plans that included improved unemployment compensation and aid to the housing industry. Yet a tax cut for business also accompanied the increase. The increase was abandoned completely in 1975 in favor of a temporary tax cut to give the economy a shot in the arm. Congress sent to President Reagan moderate increases in excise taxes in 1982 and 1984 in response to ever growing budget deficits. President Bush reluctantly agreed to assorted tax increases in 1990, as noted above.

One might think that presidents, acting under the single executive image, would bite the bullet and insist on tax increases to improve the economy. Typically, however, they try to avoid such political pain. The single executive image is ultimately a political image, not an economic theory. For instance, in 1992, Congress and President Bush repealed luxury taxes on yachts and expensive motorboats passed in 1990, bowing to pressure from boat builders who argued that the tax was forcing layoffs and bankruptcies.

Spending Politics

Presidents also have adopted spending programs as instruments of protective capitalism. Some of these efforts are Keynesian-like "pump priming" measures designed to spend the economy back to health. Franklin Roosevelt was not a Keynesian, but he spent like one. The New Deal programs that Roosevelt proposed and Congress passed were designed to alleviate the effects of the devastating economic crisis. The major programs included Social Security benefits for the elderly, unemployment compensation for idled workers, and welfare payments to poor, aged, and disabled persons and families with dependent children. Most spending programs since the New Deal have not waited for the economy to go sour. The New Deal programs were continued after the depression regardless of economic upswings and downturns. Presidents from Kennedy to Carter, who have all been Keynesians of various stripes, rarely used pump priming rationales when introducing their spending programs. They invoked instead the image of a single executive announcing programs that the country needs.

Spending Proposals. Presidents encounter three problems in proposing spending programs: (1) getting the money they ask for from Congress; (2) paying for the immediate costs of the program; and (3) estimating the programs' long-run costs. Lyndon Johnson's War on Poverty offers a good example of all three.

During 1965 and 1966, Johnson proposed and secured passage of several major social welfare programs: Medicare (medical care for the elderly); Medicaid (medical care for the poor); food stamps (vouchers for low-income families to purchase groceries); educational assistance programs, including Head Start for poor preschoolers; local employment training programs; an urban renewal program; and legal services for the poor. Johnson received from Congress over $10 billion less than he had requested for nondefense expenditures. Table 11.2 shows that this shortfall was not unusual. It depicts the differences

Table 11.2 Differences in Appropriations Proposed by President and Passed by Congress, 1947–1988 (in billions of 1982 dollars)

President	Average annual difference[1]		
	Defense	Nondefense	Total[2]
Harry Truman (1947–1953)	17.5	−3.1	14.5
Dwight Eisenhower (1954–1957)	−4.6	−0.3	−5.3
Dwight Eisenhower (1958–1961)	−1.0	0.1	−1.0
John Kennedy/Lyndon Johnson (1962–1965)	−2.4	−7.4	−9.3
Lyndon Johnson (1966–1969)	1.0	−10.4	−10.9
Richard Nixon (1970–1973)	−16.0	2.5	−12.8
Richard Nixon/Gerald Ford (1974–1977)	−9.2	25.4	15.8
Jimmy Carter (1978–1981)	9.8	−32.3	−21.6
Ronald Reagan (1982–1984)	8.9	5.6	16.4
Ronald Reagan (1985–1988)	2.7	19.1	21.9
Average			
Republican administrations	−3.2	3.1	5.8
Democratic administrations	7.8	−11.7	−3.4
All years	0.7	−0.1	1.1

1. Positive numbers indicate Congress authorized more than the president requested, and negative numbers indicate the reverse.
2. Includes defense, nondefense, and interest payments.

Source: Paul Peterson, "The New Politics of Deficits," in *The New Direction in American Politics,* ed. J. Chubb and P. Peterson (Washington, D.C.: Brookings Institution, 1985), 375. Copyright © 1985. Used by permission of the Brookings Institution. Updated by the author.

between presidents' proposed spending totals and the amounts actually appropriated by Congress. Only Eisenhower during his second term got what he wanted, almost. Congress has raised or lowered the requests of all other presidents since Truman.

The Johnson administration had only a rough idea about what the poverty programs would cost. It gambled that immediate funding would come from the "growth dividend" that supposedly had resulted from the Kennedy tax cut. But the success of the tax cut and the Fed's expansionary monetary policy were short-lived. Inflation began to heat up by mid-1965 and worsened as U.S. involvement in the Vietnam War deepened. As the inflation rate rose, the cost of the War on Poverty and the Vietnam War escalated. The Johnson administration wished to avoid a debate in Congress over cutting either the War on Poverty programs or the Vietnam War expenditures. Ultimately, the country did "afford" both the wars through continued deficits and because of inflation itself, which increased tax revenues by pushing people into higher tax brackets.

The Johnson administration and its successors had to estimate the social programs' long-term growth and budget for the new entitlements of Medicare, Medicaid, and food stamps. Entitlement programs automatically authorize, or entitle, individuals who meet certain eligibility requirements to receive benefits. For instance, all one has to do in order to be entitled to Medicare payments is be 65 years old. Funds must be paid out to those who qualify, regardless of what the government may be able to afford in a given year. Estimating the costs of entitlements means estimating the strength of the economy and the size of the benefit population over time. Budgeting is thrown out of whack if either is miscalculated.

Johnson faced growing costs from a big, old entitlement program, Social Security, as many more people reached retirement age. The number of recipients increased over 40 percent between 1965 and 1974, and their benefits rose by 20 percent. R. Kent Weaver remarks that "these increases were made through ad hoc legislative increases until 1972, when social security payments were increased 20 percent (beginning in 1974) and indexed to the consumer price index by a formula that inadvertently overcompensated for inflation."[18] Johnson also faced the growth of the brand-new entitlement programs: chiefly Medicare, Medicaid, and food stamps. The administration greatly underestimated the growth of these programs, especially Medicare.

Shown in Figure 11.5, the old and new entitlement programs became known as "uncontrollables." Short of cutting, eliminating, or capping the program, funding, at whatever level was necessary to meet the demand of qualified applicants, had to continue. The uncontrollability of the programs also had a political cast. Many entitlement programs, especially those for the elderly, became popular middle-class programs supported by a well-organized, politically active clientele. Between 1965 and 1970, these "uncontrollables" grew by some

$43 billion. Between 1975 and 1980, they grew by $56 billion; between 1980 and 1985, by another $56 billion.[19] In 1981, when the Reagan administration proposed large budget cuts, including Social Security, such a furor erupted that Reagan quickly promised that Social Security would be left untouched. Social programs now join wartime and depression as an exception to the balanced-budget rule. The fiscal and political uncontrollability of this exception heightens the policy complexity within the plural presidency.

Spending Curbs. Presidents also advocate spending cuts. Cuts are typically offered as measures of immediate cost savings or as a matter

Figure 11.5 Entitlement Payments for Individuals as a Percentage of Gross National Product, Fiscal Years, 1965–1990

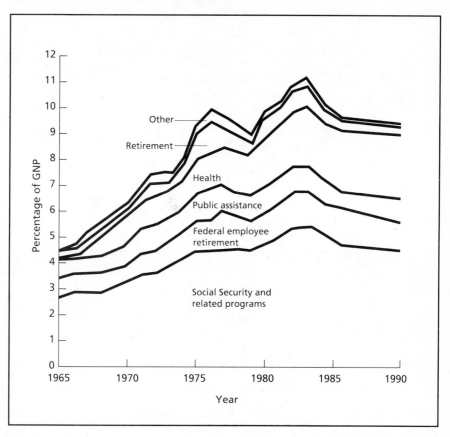

Entitlement programs grew sharply in the 1980s, untouched by the Reagan budget cuts. [*Source:* R. Kent Weaver, "Controlling Entitlements," in *The New Direction in American Politics,* ed. J. Chubb and P. Peterson (Washington, D.C.: Brookings Institution, 1985). Copyright © 1985. Used by permission of the Brookings Institution. Updated by the author from *Historical Tables, Budget of the United States Government, Fiscal Year 1990* (Washington, D.C.: U.S. Government Printing Office, 1989). Data from 1989 and 1990 are estimates.]

of ideology—frugality is good. The Reagan administration offered the most thoroughgoing attempt at reducing spending *qua* spending. From 1981 to 1988 there were significant decreases in government expenditures in certain areas: energy, education, the environment, revenue sharing, and community and regional development. But the austerity did not include defense, Social Security, Medicare and other health-related programs, agriculture, law enforcement, and commerce.[20] Many of the cuts from the early Reagan years have already been eroded.

Presidents also have used impoundment—temporarily or permanently withholding the spending of funds that Congress has appropriated. The practice dates back to Thomas Jefferson, who refused to spend money appropriated for gunboats on the Mississippi River because the purchase of the Louisiana Territory from France made them unnecessary. Presidents from Franklin Roosevelt through Kennedy used impoundment mainly to curb military programs. Johnson and Nixon broadened the scope of this policy tool to target domestic appropriations on the grounds of fighting inflation. Nixon's use of impoundment was the most controversial. He expanded it in three directions not taken by his predecessors. First, he impounded $18 billion, more money than any other president. Second, he sought to eliminate programs that he opposed by withholding all funds appropriated to them. Other presidents had only temporarily held up funds. Third, he claimed a "constitutional right for a President of the United States to impound funds" to prevent an inflationary spiral. Several of Nixon's impoundments were held unconstitutional by the Supreme Court.[21]

Congress responded with the passage of the Budget and Impoundment Control Act of 1974, which significantly curtailed the president's discretionary impoundment power. The act specifies two types of impoundments: "deferrals" postpone the spending of appropriated funds; "rescissions" withhold funds altogether. Deferrals can remain in effect until the end of a fiscal year unless disapproved by either house of Congress. Rescissions, however, cease after forty-five days unless approved by both houses of Congress. Since the passage of the act, presidents, especially Reagan, have temporarily rescinded millions of dollars of funds.[22]

Wage and Price Politics

Taxing and spending policies are indirect means of controlling the economy. They rest on hopes that businesses, unions, and consumers will do what the policies assume they will do. They also rest on a political exchange between the president and Congress. Each must convince the other that the changes in taxes and spending are politically the right changes. Wage and price mechanisms, by contrast, are direct means of controlling the economy. They are known as "incomes policies" because they directly affect the incomes of individuals and businesses. Presidents have both more and less latitude vis-à-vis Congress with wage and price policy. They can propose wage and price controls by issuing executive orders, which do not require congressional approval. Yet incomes policies are viewed as extraordinary measures that tamper with the very foundation of the track. Although such policies were used several times during the two world wars, wage and price controls have been instituted only once since then. In 1971, the Nixon administration imposed ninety-day controls in an effort to bring down inflation and inflationary expectations that had mounted during the Vietnam War.

Nixon's decision revealed the single executive image and the plural presidency at work. Herbert Stein, then chair of the Council of Economic Advisers, recalled that in a weekend meeting at the presidential retreat Camp David, most of the time was spent working on the announcement of the plan, not on the plan itself. Initially, Nixon was reluctant to make the speech on a Sunday, fearing that he would anger a large part of the viewing public by pre-empting "Bonanza," a favorite Sunday-night western. Others argued with the president that the impact of the announcement would be best if it were made before the financial markets opened on Monday morning. Nixon traded western fans for Wall Street financiers and agreed to make the Sunday speech. The announcement was kept completely secret to heighten the speech's drama and the vividness of the single executive image.

Although announcing the policy was easy, policy complexity within the plural presidency soon surrounded its implementation. The Office of Management and Budget and the Council of Economic Advisers had done some contingency planning for the operation of a control system, but the details of such a system were not worked out until later. "More important," explained Stein, "there was little consideration of what would happen after the freeze, which obviously could not last for long."[23] Unable to fully come to grips with the policy complexity, the administration chose to play it by ear during the freeze and in the post-freeze period.

THE BUDGET PROCESS

Presidents' main economic policy instruments of taxing and spending proposals ultimately depend on the budget. Budgeting goes to the very heart of government—how large it should be; the part it will play in citizens' lives; the commitments that should be made to defense, welfare, and other domestic and foreign priorities; and who should pay for programs. The most that presidents can hope for is that they can in some way modify the big budget picture, the budget's overall direction.

There is no one document that is *the* U.S. budget. Presidents annually present to Congress a hefty volume entitled "Budget of the United States," but it is only a list of presidential preferences—the administration's wish list, so to speak. No one expects the president's budget to pass, least of all the president. For instance, critics announced that Ronald Reagan's fiscal 1987 budget was "DOA" (dead on arrival) the day it was sent to Capitol Hill. Most presidents' influence emerges from battles at the margins with Congress over tax rates and spending priorities (among defense, social welfare, and other domestic programs).

On paper, the budget process has the appearance of rationality. Tables 11.3 and 11.4 spell out the presidential and congressional roles in the budget process. There are two neatly drawn timetables that assign specific dates to numerous steps. The process is thorough; it takes over a year to complete. It seeks input from numerous sources within the government. The input is checked, rechecked, and collated in the Office of Management and Budget. The Congressional Budget Office recreates much of the work of OMB to form its own

Table 11.3 Executive Branch Budget Timetable

Timing	Action to Be Completed
April–June	Conduct spring planning review to establish presidential policy for the upcoming budget
July–August	OMB provides agencies with policy guidance for the upcoming budget
September 1	Agencies subject to executive branch review submit initial budget request materials
September–January	OMB and the president review agency budget requests and prepare the budget documents
October 15	Independent agencies not subject to executive branch review submit initial budget request materials
November–December	Legislative branch and the judiciary submit initial budget request materials
December	Cabinet officers' and agency appeals to the president
1st Monday in February[1]	President's budget submitted to the Congress
January–February	OMB sends allowance letters to agencies
July 15	President submits mid-session updates of the budget estimates

1. This was previously done 15 days after the Congress convened in January, then on January 3, and now, after the passage of the Omnibus Budget Reconciliation Act of 1990, no later than the first Monday in February, which by 1990 had become the traditional release date.

Source: OMB Circular No. A-11

Table 11.4 Congressional Budget Timetable

Timing	Action to Be Completed
5 days before budget release	CBO's sequester preview report
1st Monday in February	Deadline for president to submit budget and revise GRH targets and caps
February 15	CBO's annual report to budget committees
Within 6 weeks of budget release	Standing committees submit views and estimates to budget committees
April 1	Budget committees report budget resolution
April 15	Congress completes budget resolution. If not, chairman of House Budget Committee files 302(a) allocations;[1] House Ways and Means Committee is free to proceed with pay-as-you-go allocations[2]
May 15	Appropriations bills may be considered in House
June 10	House Appropriations Committee reports last bill
End of previous session to June 30	If an appropriation bill violates caps, OMB sequesters 15 days after enactment
June 30	House completes action on annual appropriations bills
July 15	President submits midsession review
August 10	President's notification on military personnel exemption
August 15	CBO's sequester update report
August 20	OMB's sequester update report (with adjustments to caps and GRH targets)
October 1	Fiscal year begins
10 days after end of session	CBO's final sequester report
15 days after end of session	OMB's final sequester report (with adjustments to caps and GRH targets)
30 days after end of session	General Accounting Office's compliance report

1. Budget Act. Overall allocations of outlays, budget authority entitlements, and credit among House committees.
2. Legislation providing the offset (the pay) to be reported before legislation providing new entitlement spending (the go) could be reported.
Source: Senate Budget Committee.

independent assessments. Resolutions are passed as guidelines to work within. Reconciliation of all funding levels is reached, and the budget is put into place. The appearance of rationality, however, is deceiving. The process is thorough, but it is also confusing, fragmented, and decentralized. It is neither a presidential nor a congressional process. It reflects direction from the president, Congress, the bureaucracy, organized groups, unorganized interests, and ordinary citizens. The budget is an amorphous document that never really exists in one place, nor is it passed at one time.

The Presidential Phase

The most significant problem of the presidential budget process is uncontrollability. Presidents face two uncontrollable aspects of the budget: a large portion of the substance of the budget and the budget process itself. Presidents and other budget makers have very little room to maneuver. Forty-three percent of the fiscal 1993 budget was allocated to entitlement programs for individuals. These monies must be spent. Interest on the national debt accounts for another 15 percent of the budget that must be funded. There are also commitments to ongoing projects, such as the building of new weapon systems, ships, and aircraft, which would be difficult and inefficient to stop in progress. There are also payments for agricultural commodities and government support programs that must be made. Consequently, the controllable part of the budget amounts to roughly 23 percent of the total.

The political uncontrollability is evident each spring when the Office of Management and Budget initiates the executive budget process. OMB, the presidency's chief budget agency, has a staff of over six hundred. OMB reviews the administration's programmatic priorities for the coming year and addresses how they will be funded. It then sends broad economic guidelines to all departments and agencies, which must respond with their initial projections of funds needed for the next fiscal year. OMB collates this information and makes recommendations to the president. Working with the president and other economic advisers, OMB devises more precise guidelines. By the summer, departments and agencies prepare their budgets based on these guidelines. They submit their formal budgets to OMB in the fall. OMB conducts hearings and agency-by-agency reviews. OMB then transmits its recommendations to the president in December. Some political negotiations enter this phase as department and agency heads attempt to plead their case before the president or presidential advisers. OMB prepares the final budget document for delivery to Congress in February.

Presidents typically have very little to do with the presidential budget process. To be sure, presidents may enter the process at the beginning by providing overall guidelines for spending. They may enter it again at the end, trying to accommodate the needs of department heads annoyed by OMB's recommendations. But, by and large, the Office of Management and Budget dominates the presidential budget process.

The budget process clearly reflects three central aspects of the plural presidency. First, the budget itself is an example of policy complexity. The document contains thousands of pages and literally millions of line items, most of which presidents know little about. Second, the budget process is handled by OMB within the decentralized organization of the White House. The president is usually one step removed from the process. Third, the process is fraught with ambiguity. Indeed, ambiguous decision processes define presidential budgeting. What information is needed, what goals are important, how the budget process will operate, and who will participate are often unclear. The OMB often does not know what departments and agencies are up to. Departments and agencies are openly suspicious of OMB. Although presidents boldly proclaiming priorities for a new year may use the single executive image to great effect when they present their budgets to Congress, the plural presidency dictates the form that the budget takes.

The Congressional Phase

Presidential budgeting is only the first round. Although the president's presentation of the annual budget makes the White House a focal point of the budget process, focus does not imply control. The Constitution expressly makes Congress the appropriator of funds. "No money shall be drawn from the Treasury, but in consequence of Appropriations made by law," proclaims Article I. The presidential process is complex, but the congressional process is arcane. Prior to the Budget and Impoundment Control Act of 1974, the government's fiscal year began July 1. The date was switched to October, and Congress gave itself three extra months to accomplish its budgeting.

Four different types of committee are involved in congressional budgeting. First, *authorization* committees, such as the Energy and Commerce Committee, the Judiciary Committee, and the Agriculture Committee, pass substantive legislation on specific issues and authorize spending to enable the legislation. Although these committees authorize how much money they would like to see spent on a program, they cannot actually appropriate the funds.

Second, the House and Senate *appropriation* committees decide which programs that have been authorized will be funded and for how much. They present not one but thirteen separate appropriation bills for various aspects of the budget.[24] Each bill is brought to the floor for a vote at a different time. The appropriation committees say how much will be spent on government programs, but they do not raise the money needed to be spent.

Third, *tax* committees—the House Ways and Means Committee and the Senate Finance Committee—consider all proposals for taxes and other receipts in the budget.

Fourth, in the Budget and Impoundment Control Act of 1974, Congress added *budget* committees. Aided by the Congressional Budget Office, they are supposed to oversee a comprehensive congressional budget. The budget committees have had great difficulty looking after the whole budget. The Ways and Means Committee and

Appropriation Committee in the House are two of the most prestigious committees in Congress, and they dislike what they perceive to be the meddling of the budget committees. Territorial battles among the committees, then, are common.

The budget committees attempt to direct the process through the device of budget resolutions. They draft a budget resolution that is intended to set targets for the tax and appropriations committees. Congress is supposed to agree to this resolution by April 15. The authorization and appropriation committees then go about their business.

Beginning in 1980, Congress also provided for "reconciliation." Spending and taxing are reconciled to the preset budget totals. President Reagan used the reconciliation device with considerable success in 1981. The White House established budget targets and packaged more than two hundred programs into a single bill to minimize changes that might have occurred in dozens of separate votes.[25]

Even with reconciliation, chaos can and typically does occur. Wary of the Reagan-type control of *its* budget process, Congress now insists on far greater input into reconciliation. Congress has begun to construct the binding reconciliation at the last minute, just before the fiscal year is to start in October. Instead of reconciliation being the first thing accomplished in the budget process, it is now tacked on at the end. It no longer drives the process forward but instead follows it. This gives members of Congress greater opportunity to see that their top spending priorities are in place, regardless of whether these items form a coherent budget package. Indeed, in the frantic 1990 budget negotiations, agreement was reached only after the fiscal year had started and several stopgap spending bills had been passed.

Budgeting today is not merely part of the government's work; it consumes the government's work. Budgeting and the politics that envelops it have become an inconvenient, ugly proxy for governing. With abandon, White House officials, members of Congress, department and agency heads, organizations, and citizens bargain with each other for what they want. Bills are passed; dollars are assigned to the bills. This budgetary politics, in which all players are out for themselves, pushes off the real decisions of who shall pay, who shall receive, and how much they shall get. Those are the hard choices of governing, from which many people may have to sacrifice, not the easy choices of politics from which everyone gets something. When politics so consumes governing that hard decisions about what must be given up and about how much money should be raised are never made, then structural deficits result. When governing is attempted through budgeting, then budget resolutions, automatic spending cuts, spending caps, and pay-as-you-go schemes enforce "decisions" that the politicians have been unwilling to make. Governing approaches stalemate while politics goes on as a free-for-all.

CONCLUSION

It seems hard to believe that there was ever a time (1969) that the federal budget was balanced. Growing deficits have become heated campaign issues. Presidential candidates attack the incumbent of the other party for "fiscal irresponsibility" and "bankrupting future generations." They cry of waste, fraud, and extravagance. Simple homilies compare family finances with national finances: the American family should never spend more than it earns, nor should the American government. Candidates invoke the single executive image to proclaim that they will turn things around.

Voters are ambivalent about federal money—spending it or cutting back. Consistent majorities in public opinion polls favor reducing federal spending. Americans believe that the government is too big and spends too much. Yet when asked where to cut, they point to foreign aid, space exploration, and welfare—not to the largest parts of the federal budget. In other areas, such as Social Security, medical care, and education, they think federal spending is about right or should be increased. In this atmosphere of ambivalence, the complexity of economic policy grows.

Americans' attitudes reflect the tensions within protective capitalism. Although people wish to restrict government's interference in "free" enterprise, they accept massive federal spending, especially on entitlements. Presidents as the single executives in charge of the economy must preach the contradictory gospels of government intervention and government restraint. Because those two approaches do not make sense together except in the minds of many Americans, policy complexity is a permanent part of presidential economics and the plural presidency. ■

F U R T H E R   R E A D I N G

On presidential economic policy, see Herbert Stein, *Presidential Economics: The Making of Economic Policy from Roosevelt to Reagan and Beyond*, 2d ed. (Washington, D.C.: American Enterprise Institute, 1988); Paul Peterson and Mark Rom, "Lower Taxes, More Spending, and Budget Deficits," in *The Reagan Legacy*, ed. C. Jones (Chatham, N.J.: Chatham House, 1988), 213–240; R. Kent Weaver, "Controlling Entitlements," in *The New Direction in American Politics*, ed. J. Chubb and P. Peterson (Washington, D.C.: Brookings Institution, 1985), 273–341; Paul Peterson, "The New Politics of Deficits," in *The New Direction in American Politics*, ed. J. Chubb and P. Peterson (Washington, D.C.: Brookings Institution, 1985), 365–397. On the budget process, see: Aaron Wildavsky, *New Politics of the Budgetary Process* (Glenview, Ill.: Scott, Foresman, 1988); Howard Schuman, *Politics and the Budget*, 3d ed. (Englewood Cliffs, N.J.: Prentice-Hall, 1992).

NOTES

1. "Putting the T Back in the Budget," *The Economist,* June 30, 1990, 27.

2. "Bush Defends China Decision in Meeting with Reporters," *Congressional Quarterly Weekly Report,* May 26, 1990, 1685.

3. "President's Budget Proposal Stirs Reaction on the Hill," *Congressional Quarterly Weekly Report,* June 30, 1990, 2094.

4. George Hager, "Parties Angle for Advantage as White House Falters," *Congressional Quarterly Weekly Report,* October 13, 1990, 3391–3399.

5. Quoted in Steven Mufson, "$50 Billion Added to Deficit Forecast," *Washington Post,* January 8, 1991, A1.

6. Aaron Wildavsky, *The New Politics of the Budgetary Process* (Glenview, Ill.: Scott, Foresman, 1988), 67.

7. Quoted in John Woolley, *Monetary Politics: The Federal Reserve and the Politics of Monetary Policy* (Cambridge, England: Cambridge University Press, 1984, 110–111.

8. Harry S Truman, *Memoirs: Years of Trial and Hope* (Garden City, N.Y.: Doubleday, 1953), 41.

9. Paul Peterson, "The New Politics of Deficits," in *The New Direction in American Politics,* ed. J. Chubb and P. Peterson (Washington, D.C.: Brookings Institution, 1985), 375.

10. Wildavsky, 71.

11. Ibid., 138.

12. Quoted ibid., 66–67.

13. Herbert Stein, *Presidential Economics: The Making of Economic Policy from Roosevelt to Reagan and Beyond,* 2d ed. (Washington, D.C.: American Enterprise Institute, 1988), 103.

14. Ibid., 287.

15. The act was named for its three sponsors: Republican senators Phil Gramm of Texas and Warren Rudman of New Hampshire and Democratic senator Ernest Hollings of South Carolina.

16. *Congressional Quarterly Weekly Report,* December 14, 1985, 2605.

17. Stein, 111.

18. R. Kent Weaver, "Controlling Entitlements," in Chubb and Peterson, 312.

19. Paul Peterson and Mark Rom, "Lower Taxes, More Spending, and Budget Deficits," in *The Reagan Legacy,* ed. C. Jones (Chatham, N.J.: Chatham House, 1988), 224.

20. Elizabeth Sanders, "The Presidency and the Bureaucratic State," in *The Presidency and the Political System,* ed. M. Nelson (Washington, D.C.: CQ Press, 1988), 410–412.

21. *Train* v. *New York,* 420 U.S. 35 (1975); *Missouri Highway Commission* v. *Volpe,* 479 F.2d 1099 (8th Cir. 1973).

22. Gary King and Lyn Ragsdale, *The Elusive Executive* (Washington, D.C.: CQ Press, 1988), 127, 180.

23. Stein, 177.

24. The thirteen budget categories are (1) Agriculture; (2) Commerce, Justice, State, Judiciary; (3) Defense; (4) District of Columbia; (5) Energy and Water Development; (6) Foreign Operations; (7) Interior; (8) Labor, Health and Human Services, Education; (9) Legislative Branch; (10) Military Construction; (11) Transportation; (12) Treasury, Postal Service, General Government; and (13) Veterans Administration, Housing and Urban Development, Independent Agencies. See "Spending Allocations," *Congressional Quarterly Weekly Report* October 13, 1990, 3403.

25. Allen Schick, "How the Budget Was Won and Lost," in *President and Congress: Assessing Reagan's First Year*, ed. N. Ornstein (Washington, D.C.: American Enterprise Institute, 1982), 26.

CHAPTER 12

Policies and Political Fragments at Home

On May 9, 1992, an 81-second videotape touched off 72 hours of rioting in Los Angeles. The tape recorded four white police officers repeatedly beating and kicking a black suspect, Rodney King; a jury acquitted them on charges of using excessive force. George Bush went on nationwide television deploring the violence and ordering federal troops to the area. Yet, he stressed, he was genuinely "stunned" by the verdict, and the next day the Justice Department announced that it would seek federal charges against the police officers. Three days later, Bush and Democratic congressional leaders agreed on an outline for an urban aid bill designed to help rebuild riot-torn Los Angeles and prevent violence in other cities. Over a month later, both houses passed and Bush signed a $1.1 billion emergency aid bill to deliver business loans and summer jobs to Los Angeles and disaster relief to Chicago (to help clean up after river water flooded the downtown area).

In July, Congress and Bush also pressed forward on a second bill designed to keep Democrats and Republicans happy. It included $2.5 billion to create enterprise zones—the economic resuscitation of blighted areas through tax incentives. Originally, the plan had called only for urban enterprise zones to help rebuild inner cities. Although this version was supported by Housing and Urban Development Secretary Jack Kemp, it was opposed by White House staff members who felt that too many big-city Democratic mayors would be helped by the economic incentives package. Conservative Republicans in Congress insisted that rural areas could also benefit from enterprise zones. In addition, the White House and congressional Democrats reached a compromise on another $2.5 billion for an assortment of measures, including crime prevention (advocated by the White House) and job training, education, health care, and community development initiatives (backed by the Democrats).[1]

At first glance, the catalog of urban aid proposals might appear to lack internal coherence. Yet an unspoken, powerful ideology was entrenched in the aid bills and in Bush's initial response to the riots. Indeed, the ideology is so internalized and all-inclusive in American politics that it often goes unrecognized as an ideology, yet it is as dogmatic as Marxism and as intolerant of other ideas. The ideology— conservative liberalism—permits the positive involvement of government in society but in discrete rather than comprehensive ways. The second aid package was a careful balancing act between liberal and conservative programs: urban versus rural enterprise zones; crime control versus jobs, education, and health. Bush's televised speech reflected the same balance: government intervention to end the violence tempered by concern for Rodney King's civil rights. The practice of conservative liberalism in domestic affairs brings together in the plural presidency the policy complexity and political fragmentation that presidents encounter in their efforts to live up to the image of a single executive who can solve the nation's pressing domestic problems.

This chapter has five major sections. The first describes an overcrowded domestic domain that makes it difficult, though not impossible, for presidents to successfully propose major innovations. The second explains how this overcrowding arises in part from conservative liberalism, the main domestic policy track. The third and fourth sections examine two consequences of conservative liberalism: group fragmentation and government fragmentation and their interconnections. The fifth section considers how conservative liberalism, group fragmentation, and government fragmentation produce the policy instruments that presidents use to conduct domestic policy.

THE DOMESTIC DOMAIN

Presidents today face a domestic domain characterized by policy congestion. There are laws on the books and new policies are being proposed to deal with virtually every conceivable problem. Although existing laws cover all problems, new policy proposals also seek to cover (in presumably new ways) all problems. Many of the laws and proposals overlap, and some contradict each other. Policy congestion enveloped the two urban aid bills in 1992. The bills not only covered an array of solutions to the problems of the inner cities but also collided with other measures for the poor on Capitol Hill: energy assistance for low-income families, additional funding for Head Start, elementary education programs for disadvantaged areas, and immunization, to name only a few. Perhaps the biggest collision was with the $400 billion budget deficit. As a result, only $500 million would be allotted for the second urban aid bill in 1993; the remaining $2 billion allocated for 1994–1997 would have to come from cuts in other programs.

Policy congestion causes numerous policy proposals to collide and often causes presidents and other politicians to carve up issue areas into ever smaller parts in order to successfully negotiate the congestion. This approach allows new policies to be adopted despite the congestion of existing programs. When the government originally addresses an issue, its involvement can be broad and innovative. The longer the government is involved and the more policies the government offers in a particular area, the more likely are policies in various areas to affect each other and the greater is the policy congestion. The greater the policy congestion, the smaller are the questions addressed in the future. For example, in 1956, Eisenhower and Congress approved an interstate highway program to build a network of roads from coast to coast. Thirty-five years later, Bush introduced a highway plan calling not for new highways but for repairs, carpool lanes, toll booths on the interstates, and high-tech traffic warning signs.[2]

Within the congested policy arena, policy innovation is possible, especially when proposals attempt to alleviate the congestion itself. President Reagan's budget-cutting plans were initially successful in part because they promised to simplify and reduce government and thus lessen some of the congestion. Innovation is also possible in new areas of technological advancement, scientific discovery, or major societal changes. A technology that has not yet been invented or marketed, such as high-definition television, will open a new area of government activity. As more data become available on global warming, a path-breaking policy may emerge. With working mothers at record levels, a national day care policy may be proposed. For the most part, however, there are very few uncharted issues for government policymaking.

Policy congestion affects how problems are tackled. When laws are on the books, battle lines are drawn immediately around the issue of whether to change them. Sweeping reforms, if proposed, are not easy to adopt because they intrude on established practices; thus, policymakers resort to incremental adjustments at the margins of the current law. Because there are so many policies, many clashing with one another, institutions of government have a hard time anticipating the effects of the policies adopted. They constantly pass new laws to alleviate problems created by old laws, putting pressure on institutions to expand their organizational bases—to get more staff, more data, and more routines to handle the burgeoning workload.

The domestic policy domain is vast. It deals with problems of homelessness, housing, consumer protection, civil rights, crime, the environment, civil unrest, social welfare, agriculture, banking, education, wind, and rain. It offers a rude test of both the single executive image and the plural presidency. The single executive image assigns modern presidents the title of the nation's principal problem solver. Presidents typically introduce bold or at least new domestic plans in an effort to match the image, as Bush attempted to do with the two urban aid bills. Policy congestion does not prevent such presidential initiatives, but it assures that new plans are typically proposed in well-worn issue areas that have seen frequent battles among members of Congress, bureaucrats, interest groups, and presidents about what should be done. The idea of enterprise zones, for example, had been around since the beginning of the Reagan administration. As the single executive image demands more of presidents to offer initiatives, the plural presidency must juggle the interrelatedness, overlapping, and layering of issues. The minute problems and the overabundance of policies become glaring features of the policy complexity of the plural presidency.

THE DOMESTIC POLICY TRACK

Policy congestion results partly from the ideology that colors American domestic policies. Americans hold an absolute and all but irrational attachment to two kinds of liberalism—classical and modern—that combine to form conservative liberalism, which sets the domestic policy courses of presidents and other politicians. Conservative liberalism is an odd ideology because it grants citizens social freedoms but directs government to impose the values of a shifting majority. It is odd because it assumes government action to solve pressing social problems but is simultaneously skeptical that government should solve social problems. It is odder still because people are fooled into believing that there is no ideology at all behind many domestic policy decisions. Presidents attempt to stay on this track in announcing their domestic policies.

Classical Liberalism

Classical liberalism arose from the seventeenth-century English philosopher John Locke, who believed that government's duty is to protect citizens' lives, liberty, and property. In so doing, government's actions are strictly limited. Government exists to safeguard the rights and liberties of citizens, who are ultimately the best judges of their own interests. In the eighteenth and much of the nineteenth centuries, citizens guided by a faith in capitalism pursued individual enterprises as shopkeepers, traders, and farmers. Thus, government was restricted in scope and constrained in practice in order to ensure the maximum freedom of every citizen. The government abided by constitutional limits on public power, including the principle of majority rule, popular sovereignty, and separation of powers among lawmaking, law enforcement, and law interpretation.

In the United States, unlike many nations, there was no internal strife or rebellion about whether these principles were right. A wide spectrum of people agreed about the two fundamental strains of Lockean thought as they were handed down in America: democracy and free enterprise.[3] As discussed in Chapter 2, nineteenth-century presidents championed Locke. Their commitments to presidential restraint and governmental restraint rested on classical liberalism's notions of limited government and individualism.

Lockean logic did not give government much to do about domestic problems. Its role was narrow and largely negative. It engaged in a few activities (often referred to as "public goods") better carried out by one central public unit than by numerous private concerns (roads, post offices, schools, armed forces). But its primary function was to protect the people from themselves—to secure law and order, guard citizens' lives, and preserve property. Because Lockean liberalism was never questioned in America, it did not have to justify itself when competing ideologies cropped up from time to time. Nor did it grow as an ideology. It devolved into attempts at problem solving. Such pragmatism could take place only when people fundamentally believed in the same underlying principles. Even the most ideological issue of the nineteenth century—slavery—was handled by a series of compromises and accommodations until Lincoln's election.

By the turn of the twentieth century, classical liberalism looked inherently conservative—like a museum lady's perfume, fragrant but not the least bit seductive. When Locke wrote in England in 1690, liberal ideals were a major step away from hereditary monarchy; two hundred–odd years later in America, the ideals had barely changed at all. The conservative aspect of classical liberalism embraced notions of "small government" and laissez-faire economics, which advocated that people and businesses should run their own affairs.

The logic of the old liberalism, however, created pressures for a new kind of liberalism: liberal reform. Under classical liberalism, Americans distrusted government. So when large, corporate capitalism began to emerge and cause problems of monopolies, unfair labor practices, and strains on farmers and merchants, Americans blamed government. If government was to blame, then it should reform the problems. Modern liberalism thus interjected a positive and an active role for government. The government should intervene directly in society in order to redress the problems created by the excesses of classical liberalism. Under the doctrine of liberal reform, government should improve social conditions and the quality of people's lives. Modern liberalism's commitment to government originated from classical liberalism's distrust of government.

Modern Liberalism

Modern liberalism was shaped in the twentieth century in three waves by presidents who took the lead in espousing the philosophy.

Progressives Theodore Roosevelt and Woodrow Wilson were the first two presidents to advocate modern liberal beliefs. Government, they believed, should actively intervene to smooth the sharp edges of the economic system for small businesses and workers.[4] Developing one of the central components of the single executive image, Roosevelt and Wilson offered presidential activism tied to governmental activism (detailed in Chapter 3). They worked for antitrust laws; labor and occupational safety laws for adult and children workers; consumer laws for the inspection of foods, chemicals, and drugs; banking laws to establish the Federal Reserve System to regulate the nation's money supply; and laws to protect public lands. The Progressives maintained that government was the only device that could protect citizens from the excesses of growing industries and ameliorate the inequalities that resulted from truly "free" enterprise.

Franklin Roosevelt's New Deal dramatically expanded government involvement in public assistance to individuals, agricultural support, and commercial redirection. The government offered direct social welfare assistance to the aged, the disabled, the jobless, widows, and poor families with dependent children. It raised and stabilized farm prices and attempted to control farm production. It also offered protection for capitalism through support and supervision of banks, the stock market, and industry (through industry-wide codes for prices and labor in the National Industrial Recovery Act, later declared unconstitutional by the Supreme Court).

In the 1960s, the Great Society initiatives of Lyndon Johnson and Congress further enlarged the role of government. First, government was asked to make a strong commitment to the poor during good economic times. The New Deal had begged this question because it sought to help the poor in the midst of a devastating economic situation. The Great Society recognized the poor as a class and provided such assistance as medical care (Medicaid), food stamps, education, housing, and job training.

Second, the government broadened public assistance to a universal group—the elderly, a category in which nearly everyone would fall at some point. The New Deal's public assistance, including Social Security retirement benefits, was initially looked on as an exception in exceptional circumstances. Little thought was given to whether the social welfare programs would continue indefinitely once the economic emergency abated. During the 1950s, it became apparent that the programs were permanent. Although people worried that Republican Eisenhower might attempt to dismantle part of the system, he left matters alone. By the 1960s, Social Security retirement benefits in particular were a well-entrenched, highly popular, middle-class program. In 1965, the passage of Medicare—health care for all people over age 65—confirmed that public assistance to this universal group was not an extraordinary but a mandatory function of government.

Third, the government protected the civil rights of African Americans in an effort to enforce equality in education, employment, housing, and public facilities, including restaurants and hotels. Although civil rights efforts had been supported as early as the 1940s, nothing was more sweeping, before or since, than the Civil Rights Act of 1964. Government would protect, if not promote, the personal rights of all citizens. Modern liberalism called for "big government" that reshaped the resources and rights of society rather than merely protecting societal stability.

The Clash of Two Liberalisms

Classical liberalism was not abandoned in the rush to liberal reform. Indeed, the old liberalism held back its contemporary partner. The sphere of the state was extended, but distrust of it remained and free enterprise and rugged individualism stood. The end result was conservative liberalism. Although many critics considered the modern liberalism of the New Deal and the Great Society to be unbridled, it was not. Both programs deferred to classical liberalism. The New Deal's programs for farm subsidies and industry codes showed an intervention of government, but on behalf of free enterprise. The Great Society's War on Poverty was structured as a community action program involving private organizations, local public agencies, and local residents. The Johnson administration adopted the traditionally conservative viewpoint that Washington should not impose plans to eliminate poverty. Thus, modern liberalism continued to abide by classical beliefs in free enterprise, individualism, and limited government.

Conservative liberalism magnifies the complexity created by policy congestion within the domestic environment. It is not simply the vastness of the domain but the permissible policies for the domain that define domestic policy complexity. Conservative liberalism grants the permission: to achieve policy success, the presidency and other institutions must act within its policy strictures.

First, along the classical liberal rail, presidents find that they are inhibited, if not prohibited, from proposing comprehensive government action in certain areas, most especially areas in which the private (for-profit) sector has an immediate stake. This prohibition establishes certain "nonprograms" in domestic policy. For instance, President Ford's and more notably President Carter's proposals for a national energy policy were devoured by a well-established conservative-liberal "nonprogram": let the market decide. Presidents Reagan and Bush accommodated this nonprogram in their market-oriented energy plans. Likewise, presidents find "nonprograms" in areas where principles of individualism tell government to stay out. No president has proposed, nor is one likely to propose, a comprehensive public housing policy to provide adequate shelter for all citizens—homeless, poor, elderly, or young. Presidents also have a "nonprogram" for jobs. Conservative liberalism prohibits the view that the government should provide every able-bodied person a job. Individualism's notions of self-reliance countermand such possibilities.

Second, along the modern liberal rail, presidents encounter resistance to dismantling or cutting back certain existing government programs. President Reagan learned this in 1981 when he proposed to reduce Social Security retirement benefits. The Republican-controlled Senate passed a resolution (96 to 0) confirming a commitment to existing benefits, and Reagan quickly retreated. Under modern liberal logic, people have come to expect and approve of government intervention.

Finally, modern presidential programs reflect the tension between classical and modern liberalism. Richard Nixon's welfare reform program provides an apt example. Nixon announced in 1970 the Family Assistance Plan, which provided a guaranteed minimum income for every American family but also required the unemployed to take job training. According to the plan, it was the government's responsibility to place a floor under all people's incomes. The income floor was a modern liberal concept, expanding programs of the New Deal and the Great Society, which targeted only certain groups. Yet, in classic liberal fashion, the program hastened to remind people that it was their obligation to seek employment and end their reliance on government aid. An archetypical example of conservative liberalism, the plan simultaneously extended government aid to the poor and sought to limit it. Opposition to the program also reflected the boundaries within which conservative liberalism operates. The plan was killed in the Senate by an alliance of liberal members, who thought its support levels were too low and its job training requirements too strict, and conservative members, who felt that the government's role in society should not extend to guaranteeing people incomes.[5]

The presidency, then, must adapt to the inherent complexity of conservative liberalism in its policy proposals. No president will announce policies off the track—and succeed.

POLITICAL FRAGMENTATION

Conservative liberalism gives rise to another aspect of the plural presidency: political fragmentation. Political fragmentation results from the numerous demands placed on the presidency by organized groups, corporations, and attentive individuals and from the divisions of power across the several branches of government, including the presidency. The fragmentation is of two sorts: group and government.

Group Fragmentation

The two liberalisms help foster group fragmentation. Classical liberalism accepts groups because of its espousal of individual self-interests. The groupings, according to James Madison in *The Federalist*, No. 10, are "factions" that stem from differences of opinion based on attachments to different leaders and the possession of "different degrees and kinds of property."[6] They are a natural part of people's desire to pursue their own self-interest and the inevitable conflict that arises among these competing self-interests. French visitor Alexis de Tocqueville observed in 1835 that the groups "constitute, as it were, a separate nation in the midst of the nation, a government within the government."[7] Americans "of all ages, all conditions, and all dispositions," he observed, "constantly form associations. They have not only commercial and manufacturing companies in which all take part, but associations of a thousand other kinds, religious, moral, serious, futile, general or restricted, enormous or diminutive."[8]

Modern liberalism makes group preferences an integral part of governmental activism. Madison assigned what now seems a rather pejorative word, "faction," to groups, but modern liberals view groups in a more positive light. According to this school of thought, groups are ubiquitous; they emerge in every sector of society and if effectively organized have a positive influence on government. Individual citizens who lack the ability to directly influence government join groups that represent their interests in government. Scholars David Truman and Robert Dahl call the pervasiveness of groups "pluralism."[9] These writers run past Madison. They feel that government's role is to serve groups rather than check their unfavorable effects. They talk of "minorities rule," referring to numerous groups that affect politics (not exclusively ethnic or racial minorities). Government officials thus respond to a broad range of interests rather than to a handful of powerful people.

Conservative liberalism permits specific groups' preferences to tamp down bold, sweeping initiatives and court smaller more discrete ones. The groups prefer smaller initiatives because they allow groups to more easily get what they want. The small initiatives reinforce the requirements of the conservative side of liberalism. At the same time, the groups see the benefits of using government to meet their needs, thus preserving the modern side of liberalism. The resulting interest group politics has a centrifugal effect on domestic policy. Unique problems of specific groups are identified, but there is no general or overall plan for their solution. And modern liberalism requires government to be involved in all solutions. The more groups there are in American society, the more problems politicians, including presidents, are asked to address. Numerous groups, each with distinct claims, resources, and degrees of organization, add to the plurality of the presidency.

Interest Group Fragments.   Group fragmentation presents a dilemma for presidents. The single executive image explicitly maintains that presidents stand for all the people. But this very claim tempts groups to seek out presidents. Much of the work in the plural presidency involves meeting the goals of key groups and organizations. These groups, organized with money, offices, staffs, and memberships designed to obtain collective goals through the political process, are of two types: material and expressive.

Material Groups.   Material groups seek government policies favoring their own immediate economic interests. A corporation may desire a favorable change in the tax code. A farm association may request crop subsidies. A labor union may lobby for an increase in the minimum wage. Material groups operate through compromise and bargaining. They construct alliances among groups so that each will get some, if not all, of what it wants.

The most prominent material groups are business related. It would be very surprising if this prominence did not exist in a capitalist society that vigorously encourages "free enterprise." Charles Lindblom asserts that business people generally and corporate executives especially "take on a privileged role in government, that is, it seems reasonable to say, unmatched by any leadership group other than government officials themselves."[10] Woodrow Wilson put it more bluntly: "The masters of the Government of the United States are the combined capitalists and manufacturers of the United States."[11]

Businesses employ several approaches to their work in Washington. Corporations act on their own behalf. The number of business corporations operating offices in Washington increased from 50 in 1961 to over 600 by 1990.[12] "Peak associations" reinforce the work of individual corporations. These are organizations that seek to advance the general interests of business and industry, which often dovetail with the specific interests of corporations. The most prominent peak associations are the U.S. Chamber of Commerce, the National Association of Manufacturers, and the Business Roundtable. Peak associations mobilize most often when taxation or macroeconomic policies affect business interests. For example, they worked to defeat a consumer protection agency and labor law reform during the Carter administration. Trade associations, another element of the business connection to government, unite corporations in a single industry. Despite being competitors in the marketplace, companies with mutual interests in politics join together. Trade associations range from the large and influential American Bankers Association and National Association of Home Builders to the Association of Dressings and Sauces and the Bow Tie Manufacturers Association. The proportion of U.S. trade and professional associations headquartered in and around Washington increased from 19 percent in 1971 to 30 percent in 1982.[13]

Expressive Groups. As political scientist Robert Salisbury states, expressive groups are "formed around specific causes or categories of policy and mobiliz[e] support on the basis of appeals to the deeply felt value commitments of some segment of the public."[14] Motivated by an intense appeal to do what is "right," these groups oppose compromise. Their emotional politics contrasts sharply with the brokered politics of material groups. Expressive groups are often described as "single-issue" groups taking stands only on one issue—for example, the environment, abortion, pornography, taxes, hand guns, smoking, or drugs. They also differ from material groups in that they do not seek a selective benefit for only their membership or a specific population sector. Instead, they seek a universal benefit (as they define it) that will be shared by all citizens. Thus, if the National Taxpayers Union succeeds in achieving an across-the-board tax cut, all citizens, not just the union's members, will receive the benefit.

Salisbury comments that expressive groups do not have "political muscle in the usual sense, as measured by membership size, money, or even social status, although some are impressive in one or more of these respects."[15] Instead, they rely on three techniques.

First, expressive groups employ the media to sway public opinion. When the Exxon tanker *Valdez* spilled millions of gallons of oil off the coast of Alaska in 1989, pictures of dead birds and other wildlife thickly coated with black goo gave environmental groups considerable free ammunition to push for tanker restrictions and to criticize the Bush administration for not acting swiftly to sanction Exxon.

Second, expressive groups form political action committees (PACs) through which they disburse contributions and "independent expenditures" for and against presidential (and other) candidates. Independent expenditures are campaign monies that do not go to a candidate's campaign or a political party. Instead, the PAC spends the funds directly on television commercials and other advertisements to target the record of a candidate on an issue important to the group. During the 1988 presidential election campaign, the National Pro-Life Political Action Committee ran commercials against Michael Dukakis for his pro-choice stance on abortion.

Third, the expressive groups may organize political protests that involve many people who are not directly affiliated with the groups. Often political protests, whether peaceful or violent, are seen as spontaneous, disorganized, extreme, and deviant affairs. Yet protests most often are staged by organizations that meet, raise money, plot strategy, and plan the events. For instance, in the spring of 1990, the National Organization for Women and other women's groups called for a massive, nationwide demonstration in favor of abortion rights, and more than 1 million people rallied.

The Advocacy Explosion. The number of material and expressive organizations pursuing their interests in Washington has increased dramatically. The figures change so rapidly that they are difficult to keep up-to-date. From 1975 to 1990, the number of registered lobbyists increased from 3,400 to just under 9,000. In 1974, there were 608 political action committees, the campaign spending arms of organized groups. By 1990, there were well over 4,000.[16] Citizen and nonprofit groups also began to increase beginning in the 1960s, accounting for 15 percent of organizations with Washington offices by 1980.

The growing number of expressive groups adds to group fragmentation by disrupting the well-established bargaining channels within which material groups operate. In the "old days"—the 1950s—it was commonplace for a few organizations or, sometimes, only one organization to dominate a policy domain. The American Medical Association (AMA) all but governed health policy. The National Rifle Association so dominated firearms policy that no policy existed. As the twenty-first century approaches, substantially greater numbers of groups—both expressive and material—are attempting to secure their own policy interests. In health policy, the American Association of Retired Persons (AARP) competes with the AMA on medical care for the elderly. Numerous gun control groups lobby to promote a national waiting period for gun ownership. One-time near-monopolies of influence are being challenged by an accelerated process of interest fragmentation.

Presidential Interest Politics. Presidents must respond to a diverse and growing set of organized interests. Table 12.1 shows the importance of the White House to organized groups. Although groups are most likely to target Congress and executive agencies, 87 percent of organizations considered the (Reagan) White House an important target. This importance fosters the plurality of the presidency. Presidents recognize that groups focus on the legislative process, yet groups and presidents realize that by working together they may increase their leverage on the legislative process. Presidents forge relations with groups through election efforts, appointments, and policy proposals.

The presidency accommodates the preferences of the groups that were part of the president's winning electoral coalition and tries to ensure their support in the next election. Offices in the White House make presidential appointments based on interest group recommendations. Offices in the White House, notably the Office of Public

Table 12.1 Importance of Institutional Targets of Organizational Activity

Institution	Very Important	Somewhat Important	Not Too Important
Congress	89%	8%	2%
White House	55	32	12
Executive agencies	65	28	6
Courts	22	27	51

	Percent responding "Very Important"			
	Corporation	Trade Association	Union	Citizen Groups
Congress	94%	91%	95%	92%
White House	67	59	37	40
Executive agencies	68	82	58	40
Courts	18	21	28	28

Source: From *Organized Interests and American Democracy* by Kay Lehman Schlozman and John T. Tierney. Copyright © 1986 by Kay Lehman Schlozman and John T. Tierney. Reprinted by permission of HarperCollins Publishers.

Liaison and the Office of Policy Development (called the Domestic Policy Staff from Nixon through Carter), work closely with various groups to fashion policy proposals. Thus, interest group politics is used to simplify policy complexity: policy is decided by group preference.

Election Efforts.   One of the most heavily traveled pathways between groups and presidents is the electoral road. Presidential candidates attempt to forge winning coalitions of groups. Observers call these combinations of groups "presidential parties," as distinct from political parties.[17] Presidential parties are shifting groups of people who are supporters of a presidential candidate or of the president. Because political parties are relatively weak entities in America, presidential candidates and presidents, rather than ideologies or issues, serve as the focal point for presidential parties. For instance, a "Ronald Reagan presidential party" could be identified as early as 1964, when Reagan, not yet governor of California, campaigned actively for Barry Goldwater. The group grew in 1976, when Reagan challenged Ford for the Republican nomination for president. Presidential parties expand and contract as supporters of previous candidates and former presidents shift to new candidates. In 1980, the "Reagan party" solidified with a large group of Republicans, many of whom had been in the "Ford party" and the "Nixon party," and with working-class Democrats who felt uncomfortable in the "Carter party."

Often, presidential candidates urge material groups—including business people, professionals, farmers, and union workers—to become parts of their presidential parties. For instance, during the 1976 campaign, Carter won the strong endorsement of the National Education Association (NEA), a powerful teachers' organization, by promising that if elected he would sponsor the creation of a new federal Department of Education. He introduced the legislation soon after taking office and received the backing of the NEA in securing the bill's passage.

Presidential candidates also target groups whose members represent large demographic populations—for example, women, senior citizens, blacks, and Hispanics. During the 1960 election, John Kennedy made a strong appeal to the National Association for the Advancement of Colored People (NAACP) to express his concern about civil rights. Kennedy won 68 percent of the black vote, compared with 32 percent for Nixon.

Candidates also court expressive groups for their presidential parties. Ronald Reagan wooed anti-abortion activists in his 1980 election campaign, pledging to back an anti-abortion amendment to the Constitution if elected.

Presidential candidates not only seek electoral support from groups but also court their financial support. Presidential campaigns require vast sums of money to qualify for and to supplement federal campaign funds. The largest portions of these funds are obtained from wealthy individuals (many business people and professionals) and from organized interest groups, notably political action committees. Only those candidates who have the strong support of key interest groups are likely to win their party's nomination and the White House.

The White House tries to maintain these presidential parties once in office. A Reagan staff member who handled group liaison efforts observed, "The majority of groups I deal with happen to be part of the president's winning coalition. I want to make sure that those people who were with the president get things around here."[18] Contending with these ever changing presidential parties during an election and in preparation for re-election heightens the group fragmentation of the plural presidency.

Appointments. Presidents favor key groups with appointments to secure their continued support. President Carter appointed more women, African Americans, and Hispanics than any other modern president. Organizations working on behalf of those groups, however, complained about the appointments they did not receive rather than those Carter made. As a Domestic Policy Staff member observed, "the groups want 100 percent of what they want." Hispanic support for Carter illustrates the problem. A key Hispanic group gave the Carter transition team a list of a thousand names of candidates for appointment. Carter named forty-nine Hispanics to top posts and dozens of Hispanics to lower positions.[19] The appointments did little to secure the groups' electoral loyalty. Hispanics were overwhelmingly part of the "Carter presidential party" in 1976: 75 percent voted for Carter. But in 1980 many abandoned the party in favor of Reagan's presidential party, feeling that the economic problems that plagued the country during the Carter years had severely affected Hispanics. Only 54 percent of Hispanics voted for Carter in 1980.[20]

Groups may be angered if they are excluded from appointments. Feminist groups and Republican women were outraged when President Nixon said he had not appointed women to top positions in his administration because he had been unable to find any who were qualified. After more pressure from Republican congresswomen, the White House named several women to high-level positions.[21]

Policy Proposals. Presidents need groups and groups need presidents to get what each wants in legislative and administrative processes. Despite a large White House organization, presidents typically do not develop policy proposals inhouse. The White House lacks the time and in-depth expertise needed to develop the full details of a policy program. Groups often provide information and policy proposals to bring presidents' sometimes vaguely stated goals into concrete form.

During the Reagan administration, religious and conservative groups were instrumental in devising legislation for tuition tax credits for parents with children in private schools. Representatives of the groups, including ministers Jerry Falwell and Pat Robertson, were invited to the White House to help draft the legislation. "We spent from two in the afternoon to ten at night hammering legislation that would have the broadest support and meet the president's requirements for the bill," recalled a Reagan aide.[22] On another occasion, Anne Wexler, President Carter's chief group liaison, brought in representatives of the National Governors' Association, the Conference of Mayors, the National League of Cities, the NAACP, and the Urban League to work with the Domestic Policy Staff on urban legislation. "Every piece of that legislation," she observed "went through group scrutiny." When the draft bills were sent to Capitol Hill, members of Congress were told which groups were already supportive.[23]

Groups also offer presidents the necessary ingredients to build and hold coalitions on measures they both favor. White House staff members act as liaisons to organizations that share the president's goals. A skilled staff can tap this extramural influence to get a president's message out through nonpresidential channels. Many large organizations are expert at contacting their members on short notice through direct mail campaigns. According to one observer, "The Realtors can send out half a million Mailgrams within 24 hours. If they [the Realtors] have a hundred target congressmen, they can get out 100,000 Mailgrams targeted by district." Perhaps of greatest value, the message comes from a nongovernment source that the group members trust. The White House, then, can mobilize people without spending its own time and resources on the campaign. The group lobbying becomes an extension of White House lobbying. This can multiply the president's influence to the group's "memberships and through their memberships to the Congress."[24]

Too, presidents may provide groups with added visibility for their cause. When presidents speak on behalf of a group's position, the group receives a form of publicity that cannot be secured in other ways. Groups that were avidly working on a constitutional amendment to ban flag burnings were excited to have President Bush make several speeches on behalf of the cause. Although the measure failed in Congress, Bush's actions brought more pressure to bear on lawmakers than the groups alone could have mustered.

Groups' protests may derail presidents' policy efforts. They also rattle the foundation of presidents' claims that they are the leaders of all the people. President Kennedy tried to avoid focusing national attention on desegregation in the early months of his presidency. Despite campaign pledges in favor of civil rights, he feared angering white southern Democrats. His stance changed when white rioting erupted in Oxford, Mississippi, after James Meredith, an African American who met all academic entrance requirements, was denied admission to the University of Mississippi. Kennedy addressed the nation on September 30, 1961, to call for a return to law and order. As he spoke, the rioting continued and two people were killed. Kennedy's remarks were designed to appeal to both black and white audiences. Although Kennedy made no mention of civil rights in the speech, he chastised the mob but also praised the University of Mississippi, its football team, and local heroes of the Korean war.[25] Both blacks and whites faulted Kennedy's efforts.

The single executive image suggests that presidents act on behalf of all the people. Thus, presidents are under pressure to accommodate the disparate and often opposing groups that make up the people. The plural presidency attempts to accommodate these group demands. Various presidential offices recognize the importance of the groups and propose numerous policy initiatives with the groups in mind. Doing so, however, is often more difficult than it appears. The diverse groups may clash with one another over goals, methods, and outlooks. The resulting fragmentation is stamped onto the plural presidency.

Government Fragmentation

Conservative liberalism helps create government fragmentation. Separation of powers, checks and balances, and federalism carve up political power in the American government into numerous pieces. Classical liberalism's distrust of government and its acceptance of group interests mandated this fragmentation. "The constant aim," according to James Madison in *The Federalist*, No. 51, "is to divide and arrange the several offices in such a manner as that each may check the other" and "cure the mischiefs of factions."[26] Thus, as Richard Stout writes, "the Founders devised an extraordinary government—a political contraption that fragmented authority, counterbalanced one agency with another, and scattered vetoes all over the lot."[27]

The constitutional framers also designed government fragmentation as a key mechanism to control the ill effects of group fragmentation. Madison believed that it would be folly to control the causes of groups. To eliminate their differences—the causes of faction—would destroy basic political freedom. Instead, Madison argued, the effects, not the causes, of faction should be controlled. Madison believed that a republican form of government would provide the necessary restraints on factions' worst impulses. The size of the republic's territory would dilute clashes among competing interests across the country. Moreover, two features of the internal workings of the republican government were critical. First, if a faction consisted of less than a majority, the republican principle of "majority rule" practiced in the legislature would ameliorate the effects of that faction. Second, a representative government built on the twin scheme of separation of powers and checks and balances would prevent domination by any faction. A system of separate branches sharing power and keeping each other in check was devised partly to control groups' excessive tendencies.[28]

Madison's solution for the excesses of groups was a leap of faith. Jeffrey Berry observes that "the structure of American government has not, by itself, prevented some interests from gaining great advantage at the expense of others."[29] Majorities are notoriously unstable and transitory in a large republic with many group interests. Intense minorities can push majorities along and seek their acquiescence for the minority groups' favored policy choices. According to Robert Dahl, "In the sense in which Madison was concerned with the problem, majority rule is mostly a myth. . . . Instead, the more relevant question is the extent to which various minorities in a society will frustrate the ambitions of one another with the passive acquiescence or indifference of a majority of adults or voters."[30]

Classical liberalism establishes government fragmentation, and modern liberalism lives with it. Indeed, Madison underestimated two aspects of the connections between group fragmentation and government fragmentation. First, Madison failed to realize fully that groups could seek multiple avenues of influence within the separate houses of government and their many rooms. The constitutional arrangement accentuates rather than inhibits factions, especially those of a minority. An influential minority may advance its preference and veto the alternative favored by a majority or by a host of other minorities at any number of stages in the separated, checked, and balanced governmental process. Groups use government fragmentation to further their own interests rather than have the government's checks and balances cure the mischiefs of factions. For instance, numerous nationwide polls showed during the Reagan and Bush years that a majority of Americans supported a woman's choice to have an abortion. Numerous bills were passed in Congress attempting to uphold abortion. Yet groups opposed to abortion counted on Reagan and Bush to veto such bills. The difficulty of getting a two-thirds vote of both houses of Congress, constitutionally necessary to override the president's veto, ensured that the pro-life groups, as an influential minority, had great clout in the government relative to the majority of Americans.

Second, Madison failed to realize fully that the fragmentation of groups accelerates the fragmentation of government. Congressional committees and subcommittees, independent regulatory agencies, and presidential commissions and task forces reflect the increased workload of government and often the increasingly specialized interests of the body politic. Groups have lobbied for government programs, and the existence of government programs has led to the formation of groups to look out for the interests of the recipients of the programs or the people regulated by them. This fragmentation has reached the presidency. Offices in the White House now reflect group differences (the Office of Public Liaison) and regional and ethnic variations (the Office of Media Liaison, the personnel office). White House units, such as the Office of Legislative Affairs and the Office of Policy Development, also capitalize on groups' views to gain the upper hand in their dealings with other branches.

Presidents' Success in Fragmented Government

Group fragmentation and government fragmentation limit presidents' success in domestic policy. The pressures of the single executive image direct presidents to become involved in everything. With government fragmentation affecting "everything," directing the domestic agenda becomes difficult. The presidency pursues policies in an unlimited array of policy areas, and material and expressive groups pursue their specific policy interests. Congress, the courts, and the departments and agencies of the executive branch do likewise, with equal vigor. Group fragmentation and government fragmentation also increase policy congestion—the more players are involved in policymaking, the more likely are policies to multiply. Despite presidents' efforts to play central roles in the domestic domain, presidents ultimately must face the fact that Congress is better equipped than the White House to handle the policy congestion, conservative liberalism, and political fragmentation of the domestic domain. Slowness, caution, and resistance to change—the very features of Congress—characterize the domestic policy process.

First, Congress is better able to handle (and perpetuate) policy congestion. Its large staff and ongoing organization make addressing the breadth of the domestic arena relatively easy. Because its decentralization, especially in the committee system, elevates virtually every problem to the status of "priority," Congress actually creates much of the congestion. Second, conservative liberalism offers fewer dilemmas to Congress than to presidents. Congress's mechanisms of compromise and bargaining keep the legislative branch safely on the conservative liberal track. Third, Congress better accommodates group fragmentation. Presidents employ the presidency to carefully court groups, but Congress as a body has many more access points to groups—among its members and their staffs and among its committees and subcommittees and their staffs. Congressional access creates group congestion that may well rival policy congestion.

Finally, the domestic agenda is primarily legislative. Executive orders and administrative regulations are used, but most often in areas where legislation already is in place. Domestic policies have long histories in Congress that often go back years before a particular president takes office. An idea introduced and dismissed in one year may be taken seriously in the next, and a president may adopt it several years later. The saying "It is an idea whose time has come" usually means that there has been a long incubation process.[31] For instance, the idea behind food stamps originated during the New Deal but became dormant during World War II, when the economy rebounded. During the 1950s and early 1960s, Lenore Sullivan, a congresswoman from Missouri, introduced and reintroduced legislation for food stamps. Her efforts were met by claims that hunger was not a substantial problem in America or by halfhearted surplus commodities programs that distributed lard, rice, flour, butter, and cheese to the poor in amounts too small to ensure adequate nutrition. Then in 1964, with the support of the Johnson administration, the Food Stamp Act became law. It provides needy individuals and families with coupons that can be used to purchase food.

DOMESTIC POLICY INSTRUMENTS

Presidents have primarily adopted three domestic policy instruments—social insurance, social rights, and the collective good. Each instrument draws on the single executive image as presidents attempt to convey how their policies will best represent the public. Each also stays well on the conservative liberal track. To be sure, presidents differ from one another in the extent to which their policies are conservative or liberal. Among contemporary presidents, Republicans have been likely to propose policies with a conservative tilt, and Democrats have been likely to offer proposals of a more liberal nature. But, ultimately, the conservative liberal track makes liberal presidents conservative and conservative presidents liberal, for none of them can fall off the track if they wish to enjoy policy success.

Social Insurance

The government provides social insurance for businesses and individuals, in Theodore Lowi's words, by "attempting to eliminate risk or to reduce or share the costs of failure."[32] Social insurance is a liberal policy instrument because government takes an active role as insurer. It is a conservative policy instrument because it allows individuals, private corporations, and groups to do what they wish once the risk has been underwritten. It is conservative in another way as well, for there are elements of risk that the government refuses to underwrite, such as cradle-to-grave health insurance, because of its cost and its interference with private enterprise.

The term "social insurance" often applies only to social welfare programs for individuals, but the government actually insures against two types of risk: commercial risk and personal risk. Insurance for commercial risk protects businesses from failure and protects consumers against business failure. For instance, the government insures depositors against bank failures; it insures banks against defaulted student loans. The government paid out over $200 billion to pay off depositors and bail out failed savings and loans, which collapsed in record numbers beginning in the late 1980s. It also paid a record $200 million for student loan defaults between 1985 and 1990.

Insurance for individual risk protects people from personal hardship, including old age, disability, illness, joblessness, and poverty. People over age 65 receive monthly Social Security checks to insure against diminished income after retirement. But what the individuals do with the money is their own business. The government influences without directly intervening. "The government can manipulate [society]," says Theodore Lowi, "by manipulating the environment of conduct rather than having to attempt to control conduct itself."[33]

Presidents have actively provided both types of social insurance. Perhaps the most far-reaching form of commercial insurance that presidents have offered is to American farmers. Franklin Roosevelt introduced plans in 1935 and 1938 to insure farm prices and incomes. Today, agricultural policy remains within Roosevelt's framework. Like any good insurance policy, it establishes eligibility requirements for "policyholders." Farmers who wish to participate must agree to production controls—that is, they must plant less of a particular crop specified by the government. If they do participate, they are entitled to two forms of insurance: price supports and income subsidies. The government sets price supports—a minimum price for certain commodities—and pays farmers that price when the crop sells for less on the open market. The government also gives farmers direct income subsidies—cash payments that reimburse farmers for the cost of producing a crop when the cost is greater than the market price.

The most fully developed form of personal insurance is Social Security retirement benefits. The Social Security Act of 1935 established that retired employees over age 65 and the survivors of insured workers who die before age 65 (added in 1950s), regardless of need, would receive pensions from the government, raised through payroll taxes of working individuals. Presidents since Roosevelt have tampered with the key provisions of the Social Security Act only at their peril. The program has become a symbol of what government should do for its people.

Democrats and Republicans fight over who is more in favor of Social Security and who can best protect the elderly. In 1967, the Democrat-controlled Congress enacted a 13 percent across-the-board increase in Social Security benefits. As part of their campaign platform in 1968, Republicans proposed that Social Security retirement benefits automatically keep pace with inflation. Instead, in 1969 Democrats joined President Nixon and the Republicans to offer a 15 percent increase in benefits (5 percent more than Nixon's original request and more than the cost of living). Congress and the president approved a 10 percent increase in 1971 and a 20 percent increase in 1972 (both higher than the initial administration requests). Social Security benefits were then indexed to inflation, and cost-of-living adjustments (COLAs) became automatic as the Republican platform had proposed four years earlier. When Ronald Reagan proposed the end of COLAs in 1981, he received so much criticism that he soon abandoned the idea. Medicare, adopted in 1965 as compulsory insurance for certain hospital services for people over 65, also has been subject to political inflation. It is seen in tandem with Social Security as something the government should do for the elderly.

Social insurance policy thus advocates government intervention to promote the financial security of businesses and individuals. Though reflective of modern liberalism, social insurance continues to be limited by classical liberalism. In part the limitations are the result of philosophical beliefs about how far government should go. But the limitations also reflect political realities. Groups that are at high risk of financial ruin but do not represent a universal category of people and lack sufficient organization and clout to lobby for appropriate policies are the beneficiaries of more restrictive social insurance policies. For instance, Medicaid, enacted in 1966, insures medical care for the poor; this care is available not through government-sponsored health insurance like Medicare, but through a modest, federally assisted plan for state-run health programs.

Public assistance programs, commonly referred to as "welfare," have been similarly circumscribed. Welfare, as mandated under the

Social Security Act of 1935, provides payments to four groups of needy people: (1) the poor aged, (2) the poor disabled (who receive benefits beyond their normal Social Security payments), (3) the blind, and (4) dependent children of needy families. The fourth category of assistance, known as Aid to Families with Dependent Children (AFDC), is the largest public assistance program. It provides basic monthly cash assistance to poor families. There has been a long debate in American politics about welfare. The liberal view is that government should help those who cannot help themselves. The conservative view is that people should pull themselves up by their own bootstraps. Presidents' welfare policy proposals have typically fallen somewhere between these extremes. Presidents offer continued public assistance, but programs are designed to train people to get off the welfare rolls. Even President Reagan, who went farther than any other president in attempting to cut back on the welfare "safety net," only stabilized program expenditures at 1980 levels.[34]

Social Rights

Using the single executive image, presidents have advanced their role as leaders of the people by offering policies to protect the rights of racial and ethnic minorities, women, religious groups, and others. Presidents often seem uncomfortable as leaders on social rights issues. They implicitly recognize the political fallout they may experience because the policies, by definition, redistribute benefits from one group to another.[35]

Presidents since Franklin Roosevelt have been most involved in issues of racial discrimination. But many have been so in symbolic and hence politically safe rather than path-breaking ways. Roosevelt issued an executive order to establish nondiscriminatory employment in defense industries. By executive orders, Truman ended segregation of the armed forces in 1948 and promoted nondiscrimination in the awarding of government contracts, a policy Eisenhower continued. Kennedy belatedly issued a series of executive orders on civil rights as an alternative to honoring a campaign commitment to press for civil rights legislation.

The political climate changed in 1963 when Kennedy was forced to do battle with two powerful southern governors—Ross Barnett of Mississippi and George Wallace of Alabama—over court-ordered desegregation of state schools. No longer able to keep civil rights under wraps, Kennedy became convinced that he would lose the South in the 1964 election anyway and might as well seek civil rights legislation. On June 19, 1963, the Kennedy administration submitted to Congress a civil rights bill calling for an end to racial discrimination in public facilities and the desegregation of public education. After Kennedy's assassination, Johnson succeeded in pushing the bill through Congress in 1964. The act provided for an end to discrimination in public accommodations, such as hotels, restaurants, theaters, and commercial transportation. It outlawed discrimination in employment on the basis of race, sex, or ethnicity. This landmark legislation was followed by the Elementary and Secondary Education Act of 1965, which said that school boards would lose federal monies if they did not comply with desegregation plans; the Voting Rights Act of 1965, which called for national supervision of voter registration; and the Fair Housing Act of 1968, which banned discrimination in the rental and sale of most housing. Johnson issued a sweeping executive order that called for preferential hiring practices for minorities by government contractors—"affirmative action hiring."

That burst of civil rights legislation was followed by struggles joined by several Republican presidents over whether things were moving too far and too fast. Nixon pledged opposition to court-ordered busing as a means of desegregating schools. Reagan and Bush announced plans to dismantle affirmative action, which in their view had become a "quota system" preventing qualified whites from getting jobs. In 1990, Bush became the first president ever to veto a civil rights bill. He vetoed it because of the affirmative action language of the bill. Only after months of resistance did he sign the Civil Rights Act of 1991—when Democratic congressional leaders expressly included language stating that it was not a quota bill.

The Collective Good

Presidents introduce policies that involve government in the protection of the collective good. Omnibus policies are aimed at protecting the good of society by means of education, crime control, disaster relief, and quelling domestic violence. Individual sacrifice policies ask individuals to give up some personal benefit for the collective good. These policies are liberal because they acknowledge the role of government in securing the collective good. They are conservative in that they often let the marketplace decide what the collective good is.

A common omnibus policy consists of crime control proposals. Presidents Johnson, Nixon, Carter, Reagan, and Bush all advocated some type of anticrime plan during their terms. Presidential attention to crime control has also increased with greater concern about drugs and drug traffic. This is an easy collective-good policy for presidents to advocate. No one is in favor of crime. Presidents look as though they are boldly attacking a problem. Even if the problem never seems to go away, the single executive image is enlivened.

Policies that ask for individual sacrifice for the collective good are much more difficult to sell than omnibus policies for the collective good. Many people, including presidents, argue that chief executives are the only officials who can present tough choices to the American people. This may be true; but presidential calls for sacrifice do not ensure sacrifice, nor have many presidents been willing to fight overly hard for very many sacrifices. Often, they are inclined to offer laissez-faire policies that allow individuals and businesses to proceed with few restrictions. Environmental policies are key examples of collective-good issues. They ask people to change their lifestyles and ask industries to change the ways they do business.

Presidents have had mixed records on the environment. Richard Nixon established the Environmental Protection Agency (EPA) by executive order in 1970. EPA was charged with monitoring the environment and setting standards consistent with national environmental goals. The Clean Air Act of 1970 and the Federal Water Pollution Control Act of 1972, however, were primarily congressional (not presidential) initiatives. Indeed, the latter act was passed over the veto of Nixon, who objected to the cost of the legislation.

President Carter pushed for a strong clean air bill and clean water bill in 1977. President Reagan sought to push environmental policies toward laissez faire. Throughout his term he resisted tough enforcement of environmental standards as too heavy a regulatory burden on industries and other businesses, and he vetoed the Clean Water Act of 1987 (which became law after Congress overrode the veto). His administration slashed the EPA budget and sought to revoke several of the agency's rulings against polluters as too tough.

President Bush moved policies back slightly toward the collective-good end of the continuum by unveiling a clean air package in 1990 and touting himself as the "environmental president." The clean air legislation that passed Congress late in 1990 was a product of considerable congressional negotiation, but Bush's willingness to support such a measure, in contrast to Reagan's opposition, was critical to passage. Bush, however, was criticized in 1992 for returning to laissez-faire policies when he refused to support an international agreement that would have significantly reduced the risk of global warming, and when he approved the relaxation of numerous EPA guidelines on air quality, arguing that they were too burdensome on business.

Policies calling for individual sacrifice are inherently difficult for presidents to advance. These policies, more than others, infringe on the laissez-faire themes of conservative liberalism. The policies directly state that people should *not* protect their self-interests to advance the public interest. Moreover, such policies are successfully adopted only when sufficient numbers of self-interests are seen as protected within the public interest. Offering this protection is ultimately a matter of give-and-take among a host of interests, and give-and-take is often done best by Congress.

Of the three domestic policy instruments—social insurance, social rights, and the collective good—presidents are most likely to push social insurance and omnibus collective-good measures. When social insurance policy targets a universal group in the population, and when an omnibus measure attacks something to which everyone is opposed (such as crime) or supports something of which everyone is in favor (such as education), presidents can best balance the single executive image and the plural presidency. Presidents can claim convincingly that they are representatives of the people. In addition, they can handle the policy complexity and political fragmentation within the domestic arena by being able to propose something that may work or at least be popular among a host of groups.

CONCLUSION

Conservative liberalism, group fragmentation, and government fragmentation create the policy congestion of the domestic domain. Conservative liberalism places a premium on problem solving. Specific programs are established to solve specific problems within the narrow band of ideology. Interest group mobilization ensures that these programs are most likely to be discrete rather than sweeping. The fragmentation of government also makes small steps more likely than large reforms.

Presidents are faced with a dilemma. The single executive image tags them as the nation's top domestic problem solvers; yet, because there are so many problems, so many groups, and so many competing government institutions, success is never clear. The two Roosevelts, Woodrow Wilson, Lyndon Johnson, and Ronald Reagan claimed triumphant successes in domestic policy. But these are snapshot recollections; and the snapshots do not reveal the large, primarily congressional, effort that preceded and followed the presidential programs, the limited success of these presidents during their entire terms, and the problems that other presidents—Truman, Eisenhower, Kennedy, Nixon, Ford, Carter, and Bush, to name only the most recent—encountered.

To make matters rougher for presidents, the institution of the presidency not only accommodates domestic policy complexity and group and government fragmentation but also balances foreign and economic policy complexity. The policy complexity of the presidency is clear in each domain—foreign, economic, and domestic. It is absolutely glaring in the three domains together. Presidents must offer policies in a vast domestic domain on issues ranging from urban riots to hurricane relief. They also are busy presenting economic proposals that ask for everything from tax cuts on yachts to spending increases for child health care. In the foreign policy arena, they unilaterally move troops and engage in various diplomatic exercises that include boycotts of Serbia and trade talks with Japan. The breadth of these three domains, the interconnections among them, and the policies that presidents announce for them are the essence of the policy complexity of the plural presidency.

The complexity forces the presidency to fashion a decentralized White House organization that works within and across these three policy domains. The national security adviser, the National Security Council, the State Department, the Defense Department, the Joint Chiefs of Staff, and the Central Intelligence Agency handle foreign affairs. The Office of Management and Budget, the Council of Economic Advisers, and the Treasury Department cope with economic problems. The Office of Policy Development, the Office of Management and Budget, and the Office of Public Liaison deal with domestic issues. Each of the offices makes hundreds of decisions daily, many of which overlap, most of which the president knows little about.

Because of the vastness of the policy domains and the decentralization of the presidential organization, ambiguous decision-making processes arise. Ambiguity surrounds the information gathering of the organization, its goals, its operations, and who participates. Offices that work on foreign affairs may not have sufficient information on economic policy. Goals establishing priorities across foreign, domestic, and economic affairs may not be clear. Coordination is needed across the foreign-domestic-economic offices, but sufficient coordination may not be present. Often the operation of the White House is muddled and signals are mixed. Finally, with so many people fashioning policy across the policy domains, it is never clear who will participate and when.

The single executive image assures Americans that the president is the "sole organ" of the nation in foreign affairs, the person chiefly responsible for economic stability, and the nation's chief domestic problem solver. The decentralized organization of the plural presidency provides presidents an advantage by doing the presidents' work in the three policy domains. Without it, presidents would be unable to tout themselves as problem solvers of any kind. But the other three dimensions of the plural presidency also pose a disadvantage. Presidents ultimately may be dwarfed by the number of policy proposals they are expected to advance, by the ambiguous decision processes by which the proposals are made, and by the number of other players in groups and the government who have a stake in the proposals. Presidents must worry that the power of the single executive image does not dwindle as the plural presidency burgeons. ∎

F U R T H E R R E A D I N G

On conservative liberalism, see: Louis Hartz, *The Liberal Tradition in America* (New York: Harcourt Brace, 1955); Alexis de Tocqueville, *Democracy in America*, 2 vols. (New York: Vintage Books, 1945). On group fragmentation, see: Robert Dahl, *A Preface to Democratic Theory* (Chicago: University of Chicago Press, 1956); David Truman, *The Governmental Process* (New York: Knopf, 1951); Theodore Lowi, *The End of Liberalism*, 2d ed. (New York: Norton, 1979); Jeffrey Berry, *The Interest Group Society* (Boston: Little, Brown, 1984). On domestic policy, see: John Kingdon, *Agendas, Alternatives, and Public Policy* (Boston: Little, Brown, 1984); Theodore Lowi, *The End of Liberalism*, 2d ed. (New York: Norton, 1979); Steven Shull, *Domestic Policy Formation* (Westport, Conn.: Greenwood Press, 1983).

NOTES

1. See *Congressional Quarterly Weekly Report*, various issues from May 16, 1992, to July 11, 1992; and *Newsweek*, "Special Report: America on Trial," May 11, 1992.
2. Stephen Fehr, "Highway Plan Shifts Costs to States," *Washington Post*, February 14, 1991, A1, A6.
3. Louis Hartz, *The Liberal Tradition in America* (New York: Harcourt, Brace, 1955).
4. Ibid., 228.
5. Although Nixon did not get the Family Assistance Plan, he did succeed in a less spectacular yet fundamental reform: Supplemental Security Income, which combined Social Security programs for the elderly, the blind, and the disabled and gave them a minimum income as a matter of right. Under conservative liberalism, it was politically more acceptable to provide minimum incomes for these groups than for poor families who, by objective measures, were more in need of the money.
6. Alexander Hamilton, James Madison, and John Jay, *The Federalist Papers* (New York: Mentor, 1961), 78–79.
7. Alexis de Tocqueville, *Democracy in America*, 2 vols. (New York: Vintage Books, 1945), 1:199–200; first published in 1835.
8. Ibid., 2:114.
9. David Truman, *The Governmental Process* (New York: Knopf, 1951); and Robert Dahl, *A Preface to Democratic Theory* (Chicago: University of Chicago Press, 1956).
10. Charles E. Lindblom, *Politics and Markets* (New York: Basic Books, 1977), 172.
11. Quoted in Charles Beard and William Beard, *The American Leviathan* (New York: Macmillan, 1930), 252.
12. Robert Salisbury, "Interest Groups in Washington," in *The New American Political System*, 2d ed., ed. A. King (Washington, D.C.: American Enterprise Institute, 1990), 207.
13. Ibid., 204–205.
14. Robert Salisbury, "The Paradox of Interest Groups in Washington—More Groups, Less Clout," in *The New American Political System*, 2d ed., ed. A. King (Washington, D.C.: American Enterprise Institute, 1990), 210.
15. Ibid., 211.

16. Harold Stanley and Richard Niemi, *Vital Statistics on American Politics* (Washington, D.C.: CQ Press, 1988), 143.

17. John Kessel, *Presidential Campaign Politics* (Homewood, Ill.: Dorsey Press, 1980).

18. Quoted in Martha Kumar and Michael Grossman, "The Presidency and Interest Groups," in *The Presidency and the Political System*, ed. M. Nelson (Washington, D.C.: CQ Press, 1984), 304.

19. Gary King and Lyn Ragsdale, *The Elusive Executive* (Washington, D.C.: CQ Press, 1988), 236, Table 4.20.

20. Gerald Pomper, "The Presidential Election," in *The Election of 1980*, ed. G. Pomper (Chatham, N.J.: Chatham House, 1981), 72.

21. Jo Freeman, *The Politics of Women's Liberation* (New York: McKay, 1975), 205–207.

22. Quoted in Kumar and Grossman, 294–295.

23. Bradley Patterson, *The Ring of Power* (New York: Basic Books, 1988), 207.

24. Ibid., 201.

25. Theodore Windt, Jr., *Presidents and Protesters: Political Rhetoric of the 1960s* (Tuscaloosa: University of Alabama Press, 1990), 78–81.

26. Hamilton, Madison, and Jay, 322.

27. Richard Strout, "What the Founders Wrought," a review of *The Power to Lead*, by James MacGregor Burns, *New Republic*, April 9, 1984, 39–40.

28. The system of separate powers also was designed to keep in check the excesses of government itself.

29. Jeffrey Berry, *The Interest Group Society* (Boston: Little, Brown, 1984), 3.

30. Robert Dahl, *A Preface to Democratic Theory* (Chicago: University of Chicago Press, 1956), 133.

31. John Kingdon, *Agendas, Alternatives, and Public Policies* (Boston: Little, Brown, 1984).

32. Theodore Lowi, *The End of Liberalism*, 2d ed. (New York: Norton, 1979), 280.

33. Ibid., 289.

34. Paul Peterson and Mark Rom, "Lower Taxes, More Spending, and Budget Deficits," in *The Reagan Legacy*, ed. C. Jones (Chatham, N.J.: Chatham House, 1990), 227.

35. Lowi et al., 1961.

SINGLE IMAGE, PLURAL INSTITUTION

P residents employ the single executive image and the plural
presidency in their dealings with the other branches of government. The key currency of exchange the president has is
persuasion—the ability to influence others to do what the chief executive wants done. Presidents can use both the single executive
image and the plural presidency as mechanisms of persuasion vis-
à-vis the Congress (Chapter 13), the bureaucracy (Chapter 14), and
the courts (Chapter 15).

Presidents use the single executive image to offer presidential
programs—an annual list of legislative proposals of varying length
and complexity—for which presidents seek congressional support.
They proclaim that they are "chief legislators" who know best what
legislation Congress should pass. Ironically, the programs they offer are the products of the plural presidency. The president counts
on the presidency's decentralized organization to help piece together the legislation that will be sent to Capitol Hill. The organization copes with ambiguous decision making as dozens of proposals
are discussed and revised. Policy complexity emerges across the
many policy areas, and political fragmentation arises from the numerous groups that have stakes in the legislative proposals. Presidents try to use both the image and the institution to corral the 535
members of Congress, who, not surprisingly, see themselves as
chief legislators.

Presidents also attempt to act as chief executives in their relations with the bureaucracy. They use the single executive image to

claim that they are on top of the bureaucratic hierarchy and to announce plans to revamp the bureaucracy. In order to outline and attempt to implement reorganization plans, presidents employ the plural presidency to gain greater control over the unwieldy conglomeration of departments and agencies. As a result, the plural presidency itself becomes more and more of a bureaucracy.

Judicial interpretations and expansions of presidents' power enliven the single executive image. Often when presidents say they should have the power to do something that the Constitution does not expressly state, the courts have been willing to allow presidents such expanded power, as though the presidents themselves were on the bench. The plural presidency helps presidents make their many appointments to the federal judiciary. Presidents, using the presidency, attempt to influence the decisions of the judiciary through their selection of judges.

Thus, there is an interplay between the single executive image and the plural presidency. Presidents must use both to get what they want within the system of shared power provided by the Constitution. ■

In Congress Assembled

M ythology tells us that Saint George, the patron saint of England, was a dragon slayer whose quests were the subjects of several Renaissance and medieval paintings. The Renaissance paintings show a robust George in ornate armor, his muscular legs astride a majestic white stallion with flowing mane. His shiny lance, with intricately crafted handle, pokes at a scrawny, cowering dragon. The medieval canvases display a thin, forlorn man. He stands beside a small, swayback, brown horse whose legs are not proportionate to its body. Saint George's lance appears too heavy and tall for its user. Opposite the duo is an evil, grotesque crested dragon with wings and claws who spews fire from an elongated vermilion tongue.

The single executive image portrays presidents in their relations with Congress as the Renaissance Saint George—vigorous, husky, deft. They single-handedly present legislative initiatives and organize support for their passage. They threaten to use their veto and occasionally do use it, demonstrating the unilateral power of the executive office. They have a unique, important, and highly visible position in the congressional process.

The plural presidency reveals presidents in their relations with Congress as the medieval Saint George—weak, dazed, maladroit. The decentralized organization of the White House cannot control the even more decentralized organization of Congress. Ambiguous decision processes occur as numerous offices within the White House organization, from the Office of Legislative Affairs to the Press Office, have something to say about how to handle Congress. Responding to the policy complexity and the political fragmentation it incorporates, the plural presidency often sends multiple signals and a multitude of initiatives to Capitol Hill. It denies accountability for failed ventures and blames them on the legislative end of Pennsylvania Avenue.

Paintings, as artists and viewers will attest, depict slices of and slants on reality; they do not reproduce it. So it is with the single executive image and the plural presidency. The preceding chapters of this book have explained these two slices of the presidency from different angles. What has become clear is that *neither* the single executive image *nor* the plural presidency fully describes the presidency but *both* together do. Presidents work with the single executive image and the plural presidency, each of which offers resources and drawbacks. Thus, presidents are sometimes the medieval Saint George and sometimes the Renaissance Saint George.

This chapter discusses how presidents use both the single executive image and the institution of the plural presidency in their relations with Congress. The chapter is divided into six parts. The first provides an overview of presidential-congressional relations. Without an understanding of the constitutional and political foundations on which these relations rest, little can be said about how presidents work the single executive image and the plural presidency. The next two parts describe how presidents use the single executive image in their dealings with Congress through the presentation of a presidential program and the use of the veto. The fourth and fifth parts examine how the plural presidency dictates the agenda-setting process—that is, the development of the presidential program—and the agenda-selling process—that is, the effort to gain congressional approval. The final part of the chapter reviews factors influencing presidential success in Congress.

INSTITUTIONAL CONFLICT

John Rhodes, former minority leader of the House and Republican from Arizona, once remarked that "Congress loves to kick the President around regardless of who he is."[1] James Schlesinger, a cabinet secretary under two presidents, likened relations between the president and Congress to "permanent guerrilla warfare." Relations between presidents and Congress are based on conflict. The conflict stems from three factors:

The Constitution establishes much of the framework for dispute.[2] It provides that Congress is an equal, coordinate branch of government. Unlike parliamentary systems in which legislatures are executive driven, in the U.S. presidential system, Congress and the president take separate cars. The Constitution intended the legislative branch to be the premier branch by giving it the vital powers of the state: to declare war, maintain armed forces, tax, and spend. Although presidential influence on public affairs has grown since the Constitution was written, the legislative process still dominates American politics. While the legislative process may not be as visible a focal point for public and media attention as the presidency, many of Congress's decisions and nondecisions are more determinate of the government's course of action. When presidents profess to be the only elected officials who act on behalf of the entire nation, Congress can retort that it is the body that best acts on behalf of all the organized and unorganized groups in the nation.

The Constitution intensifies the conflict by providing for a bicameral legislature. Presidents must convince both the House and the Senate that their proposals merit passage. That the House, Senate, and presidents have separate electoral bases as specified in the Constitution makes matters worse. Presidents often have faced a Congress in which one or both houses are controlled by the opposite party. In seventeen of the forty-five Congresses from 1900 to 1992—for a total of thirty-four years—the majority party in one or both houses has been the party opposing the president.

Conflict also arises because Congress operates within time frames that differ from those of the presidency. The presidency, as discussed in Chapter 9, runs on *organizational* time—a moderately slow time in which the White House develops ways of gathering information and forming expertise, establishes internal procedures, and develops external ties—and on *political* time—a fast-paced, four-year cycle geared to the next election. Congress too runs on organizational and political time, but at a different pace from the presidency. Congress runs on slower organizational time and faster political time than the White House.

Within Congress there is considerable organizational continuity. Most members of Congress enjoy longevity in their jobs. The average length of service for a member of the House is twelve years; for a senator, ten years. Staff members also remain on Capitol Hill for long periods. The bargaining and coalition building that move Congress forward take a long time to develop. Nevertheless, members of Congress, especially in the House, are always running for re-election. Political time passes swiftly. Unlike the president, both houses face election cycles every two years, even though all members of the Senate are not up for re-election. The separate time cycles often put Congress out of sync with the presidency.

Conflict also arises because Congress has its own base of public support. Elections give members of Congress political bases, lodged in their district or state, independent of the president and party.[3] Although Congress as a body is often not well liked, individual members of Congress typically enjoy high popularity. Nor does their popularity, unlike the president's popularity, show signs of eroding over the course of their term. Many members actually become more popular the longer they are in office and thus may be insulated from presidential and party requests.

These differences in power base, time frame, and public support make conflict between Congress and presidents inevitable. Still, just as presidents need the media, presidents and Congress need each other. Constitutionally, presidents cannot successfully propose legislation unless Congress passes it, and Congress cannot legislate unless presidents sign the bills. The protracted organizational time frame of Congress makes dramatic initiatives from within the body unlikely. Presidents, as "outsiders," may be able to offer measures that move the body forward. Thus, the conflict is tempered by practicality. It is within this context of conflict and necessity that presidents bring the single executive image and the plural presidency to bear on the congressional process.

PRESIDENTIAL PROGRAMS

Presidents use the single executive image to announce legislative proposals. They may craft a media event to proclaim a single initiative. They may promote a host of ideas in their annual budget messages required by law. Presidents rely most often on packaging their priorities in State of the Union messages. Budget messages often are too complex and too often greeted with skepticism to achieve the sharp focus presidents want. Individual initiatives announced throughout the term may be lost in the congressional shuffle of policy debate. The ritual State of the Union message, however, gives presidents their best opportunity to appear as "chief legislators." Article II of the Constitution states: "He shall from time to time give to the Congress Information of the State of the Union, and recommend to their Consideration such Measures as he shall judge necessary and expedient."

Since Harry Truman, presidents have used State of the Union messages to capture congressional and national attention for packages of proposed legislation. They announce the president's program—an annual outline of major problems and what to do about them. The program brings the single executive image to life. It says that there is one person in charge, and it itemizes what he proposes to do about national issues. Presidents also use the opportunity to enumerate their achievements. This listing enlivens the image, showing that the program consists not merely of possible solutions but of actual results. Members of Congress are spectators for and not participants in the president's presentation. They stand when he enters the House chamber, and they interrupt his words with applause. Millions of citizens also listen to the speech, which the media cover live, pre-empting regular programming. Extensive media coverage before the speech is likely and after the speech is assured. A boost in the president's public approval ratings also is possible. The State of the Union Message grants a president considerable visibility, importance, and uniqueness as all eyes in the Congress and the country are on him. The Renaissance Saint George cannot be far away.

Types of Programs

Presidents' programs vary among three types: (1) the *grand simplification*, in which presidents concentrate on a few key programs; (2) *modest strides*, in which presidents announce multiple priorities but are not armed with shopping lists; and (3) the *encyclopedic design*, in which presidents proffer solutions to an entire range of problems. Of all presidents since Franklin Roosevelt, Ronald Reagan best mastered the grand simplification. He announced three major presidential priorities: tax and budget cuts and a defense build-up. They were structural issues that were comprehensive in their effects on American society. All other issues were in some way related to these three issues. The three constituted the administration's entire agenda for 1981. They also monopolized the congressional calendar. The grand simplification redirects the legislative process away from the many smaller issues that Congress deals with annually.

Richard Nixon's programs exemplified modest strides. Nixon outlined plans for welfare reform, revenue sharing with the states, and crime prevention. The programs were detailed attempts to deal with several national problems. Although Nixon's plans dealt with structural issues, they were not as fundamental or as integrated as Reagan's were. Gerald Ford's goals also were relatively modest. A Ford aide observed:

We couldn't label our program the great this or the new that. There wasn't enough there. We spent most of our time reviewing then-current federal programs and drafting modifications. Once the President imposed the no new spending rule, we turned toward 1977 as the first available opportunity. We all hoped that Mr. Ford could be elected, that we would have a chance to present a complete agenda at some point in the term.[4]

Many presidents at some point during their term have employed the encyclopedic approach. President Truman offered no fewer than twenty-one points of domestic legislation, ranging from agriculture to congressional salaries, in his message of 1945. Republican congressional members criticized Eisenhower when he did not immediately follow Truman's lead. "Don't expect us to start from scratch on what you people want," one Republican member of Congress told an Eisenhower staffer. "That's not the way we do things here."[5] Not to be outdone, in 1953 Eisenhower established an elaborate mechanism by which his encyclopedia was assembled. The Bureau of the Budget (now the Office of Management and Budget) requested in midyear that all agencies and departments submit a statement of their legislative priorities for the year. Sherman Adams, Eisenhower's chief of staff, and several aides spent two weeks in October going over the bureau's compilation. From that meeting and meetings between Eisenhower and cabinet members, they set forth the president's priorities in *every* major area of federal action. They presented a pared-down list of seven major topics to the cabinet in November and December. During the cabinet meetings, Eisenhower and cabinet members debated and modified some of the proposals. Members of Congress were then invited to the White House for a series of discussions on the measures before they were publicly announced in January in special messages to Congress on agriculture, labor law, Social Security, and foreign aid.[6]

Presidents employ the encyclopedic approach for several reasons. First, it meets the single executive image, which creates expectations that presidents can and should solve a long list of major problems. Second, the encyclopedia reflects the demands placed on the plural presidency by diverse groups, each seeking the resolution of various problems; it also reflects the complexity of the foreign, economic, and domestic policy domains. Too, the specialization of the many offices within the institution elbows presidents to deal with a litany of problems. Last, by using the encyclopedic approach, presidents speak to Congress in familiar terms, for Congress also approaches policy problems encyclopedically—handling long lists of both major and minor problems.

Although the single executive image pushes presidents toward the encyclopedia, the encyclopedia can weaken the single executive image as a resource. If presidents promise too many things and accomplish only a few of them, the image of a single executive in charge suffers. Kennedy offered twenty-five proposals in 1961 but could point to only a rural area redevelopment project as his main accomplishment. Critics began to suggest that the young, supposedly dynamic president was weak with Congress.

With contemporary Congresses, grand simplifications may offer presidents greater advantages than the heavy encyclopedias. The grand designs undercut the efforts of 535 policy entrepreneurs to identify key problems and offer innovative solutions. By addressing structural problems, a grand simplification defines by presidential fiat *the* most pressing of the nation's most pressing problems. It fits well with both the media's and the public's attention span. The media have clear "pegs" for their stories. The public need focus on only two or three items in order to be informed. The grand simplification offers an opportunity to strengthen the single executive image as a presidential resource.

Timing

The timing of a program's announcement is critical. Presidents can use the single executive image most dramatically if they "hit the ground running"—present major policy initiatives with great public fanfare in the first months of the first year of their term. "It's definitely a race," remarked a Carter aide. "The first months are the starting line. If you don't get off the blocks fast, you'll lose the race.

Congress will come in first."[7] The honeymoon with the press, the public, and Congress upon first taking office provides the president with the greatest opportunity to invoke successfully the single executive image. The inauguration lends greater visibility, uniqueness, and importance to the president than he is likely to experience during the remainder of the term. From this base, he can assert power to direct legislation. Congress often awaits these cyclical beginnings every four years as opportunities to move forward rather than be mired in the status quo.

Honeymoons, however, do not last. Presidents face a political "cycle of decreasing influence."[8] The longer presidents are around, the worse they do. This pattern holds not just in Congress but also in the public, the media, the executive branch, and even the White House staff itself. The longer the president waits, the more competition he encounters for scarce political space in the always crowded congressional agenda. Time also breeds opposition to any program. The earlier the president acts, the more likely he will be to build a coalition of support. Starting early also means having time to finish. The slow, cumbersome nature of the congressional process dictates that even legislation introduced in the early months of the term will still take a year or more to get through Congress. It will take another year or two for a program to be implemented. By then, presidents are already preparing for their re-election campaigns. In the words of a Kennedy adviser, "If you don't get going early, you'll be out of office before you get the program set."[9]

But hitting the ground running is neither easy nor fun. Presidents often stumble in their first months in office and delay taking aim at Congress. Presidents juggle political and organizational time in making their requests: they must act quickly to succeed in Congress, but the plural presidency may not be ready to go. The plural presidency, like any large institution, needs time to work properly. It may actually need more organizational time than most institutions because its flow of operation is disrupted every four to eight years by the arrival of a new president and new staff members. In addition, the single executive image pushes the plural presidency toward policy complexity. Presidents put on their agendas large, intricate problems—education, crime, health care, housing, welfare reform—that require large, intricate programs. The programs do not come prepackaged. A Carter staff member summed up the dilemma:

Even though we set the agenda early, we didn't have the proposal ready for several months. In part, it just took time for us to start moving. But primarily, the delays were from the nature of our agenda goals. We chose some very complicated issues. Welfare reform and energy tended to dominate both the presidential and staff time. They were highly technical issues and needed considerable work.[10]

Delay that may be unavoidable within the presidency will have unavoidable consequences once the programs move on to Capitol Hill. The Nixon administration faced great complexity in working out its welfare reform package, the Family Assistance Plan. When the plan arrived on Capitol Hill, opponents were waiting. A Nixon aide lamented, "We gave our opponents a great deal of time to fight the Family Assistance Plan. They had at least six months to prepare before the initial announcement. Then, because we were late, the program bogged down in committee. We gave them too many chances to hit us."[11]

Table 13.1 catalogs the number of domestic legislative requests that Presidents Kennedy, Johnson, Nixon, Ford, and Carter made

Table 13.1 Number of Presidential Requests of Congress in State of the Union Messages

	First-time requests	Repeat requests
Kennedy		
1961	25	0
1962	16	8
1963	6	12
Johnson, I		
1964	6	11
Johnson, II		
1965	34	4
1966	24	7
1967	19	8
1968	14	12
Nixon, I		
1969	17	0
1970	12	9
1971	8	12
1972	3	14
Nixon, II		
1973	20	3
1974	5	11
Ford		
1975	10	3
1976	6	7
Carter		
1977	21	0
1978	8	3
1979	8	5
1980	4	7

Source: OMB Legislative Reference Division clearance record in Paul Light, *The President's Agenda* (Baltimore/London: The Johns Hopkins University Press, 1991), 42. Used by permission.

Table 13.2 Requests for Legislation, First Year (percentage)

	January– March	April– June	July– September	October– December	Total
Kennedy 1961	76%	24%	0%	0%	100%
Johnson 1965	94	6	0	0	100
Nixon 1969	12	41	41	6	100
Nixon 1973	40	30	15	15	100
Carter 1977	33	57	10	0	100

Source: OMB Legislative Reference Division clearance record in Paul Light, *The President's Agenda* (Baltimore/London: The Johns Hopkins University Press, 1991), 45. Used by permission.

during their terms. The table shows that each president made more requests in his first year than later on. Table 13.2 indicates that all presidents acted during the first year but that Nixon and Carter waited longer than Kennedy and Johnson to unveil their requests. Ronald Reagan proceeded like Kennedy and Johnson; George Bush kept pace with Carter and Nixon.

There is another matter of timing that is also important: when to push a specific bill. Presidents must be wary of overloading the legislative process by attempting to push too many bills at once. Such overzealousness blurs the clarity of the image of a single executive calling the legislative shots. Lyndon Johnson remarked:

A measure must be sent to the Hill at exactly the right moment and that moment depends on three things: first, on the momentum; second, on the availability of sponsors in the right place at the right time; and, third, on the opportunities for neutralizing the opposition. Timing is essential. Momentum is not a mysterious mistress. It is a controllable fact of political life that depends on nothing more exotic than preparation.[12]

VETOES

Presidents assert the single executive image through the threat of vetoes and their actual use.[13] The veto is the one virtually unilateral power that presidents have in the congressional process. Woodrow Wilson observed that a president's "power of veto . . . is, of course, beyond all comparison, his most formidable prerogative."[14] According to the Constitution, a presidential veto automatically prevents a bill passed by both houses from becoming law unless two-thirds of both houses vote to override the veto. Getting two-thirds of all members of Congress to agree on a controversial action such as an override is a herculean task. Congress has overridden presidents' vetoes just over one hundred times in over two hundred years—a mere seven-tenths of 1 percent. This statistic applies only to regular vetoes. Congress cannot override "pocket vetoes"; it can only take the legislation up again in its next session.

Pocket vetoes occur when Congress adjourns before the elapse of the ten-day period that the Constitution gives presidents for making up their minds. During this period presidents may "pocket" (not sign) bills because Congress has adjourned, and there is really nothing that Congress can do in response. Presidents have employed the pocket veto almost as often as the regular veto. Between 1789 and 1992, presidents used the pocket veto on 1,055 bills and the regular veto on 1,454 bills. Actual vetoes are important in a president's legislative bag of tricks, and threats of a veto may be just as compelling. Because overrides are usually unsuccessful, presidents may exact compromises from Congress by threatening vetoes. Borrowing a phrase from another actor-politician, Clint Eastwood, President Reagan announced with great bravado in 1985 that any move by Congress to raise taxes "would make my day" and be met with a swift veto.[15] Table 13.3 summarizes the vetoes of presidents from Washington to Bush.

Nonetheless, presidents do encounter difficulties with vetoes. Strategically, vetoes are negative powers even though they are unilateral ones. Presidents stop what they do *not* want but do not get what they *do* want. Presidents since Grant have grumbled because they can veto only an entire bill. Unlike forty-three state governors, presidents do not have a line-item veto, which would permit them to reject specific provisions of legislation rather than the full bill. In the absence of a line-item veto, members of Congress on occasion delight in attempting to make bills veto-proof through nongermane amendments. They attach single items that a president wants to a larger bill that the president does not want. Presidents Reagan and Bush complained that this practice allows Congress to pass massive, unwarranted appropriation bills with no way for the president to fight back. For instance, in 1987 Congress passed the entire discretionary budget of the government in one omnibus bill. President Reagan had to accept the bill or force the cutoff of appropriations for the entire government. Reagan signed the bill.

Assessments of the line-item veto are mixed. Some argue that it would dangerously tip the legislative process in favor of presidents. Others conclude that Congress, following many state legislatures, would adopt ingenious methods to get around the line-item veto. "I really am afraid if we had line-item vetoes," predicted former Senate Majority Leader Howard Baker (R-Tenn.), "Congress would start sending [the President] appropriation bills with just one line."[16]

Table 13.3 Presidential Vetoes, 1789–1992

Years	President	Regular vetoes	Vetoes overridden	Pocket vetoes	Total vetoes
1789–1797	Washington	2	0	0	2
1797–1801	Adams	0	0	0	0
1801–1809	Jefferson	0	0	0	0
1809–1817	Madison	5	0	2	7
1817–1825	Monroe	1	0	0	1
1825–1829	J. Q. Adams	0	0	0	0
1829–1837	Jackson	5	0	7	12
1837–1841	Van Buren	0	0	1	1
1841–1841	Harrison	0	0	0	0
1841–1845	Tyler	6	1	4	10
1845–1849	Polk	2	0	1	3
1849–1850	Taylor	0	0	0	0
1850–1853	Fillmore	0	0	0	0
1853–1857	Pierce	9	5	0	9
1857–1861	Buchanan	4	0	3	7
1861–1865	Lincoln	2	0	5	7
1865–1869	A. Johnson	21	15	8	29
1869–1877	Grant	45	4	48	93
1877–1881	Hayes	12	1	1	13
1881–1881	Garfield	0	0	0	0
1881–1885	Arthur	4	1	8	12
1885–1889	Cleveland	304	2	110	414
1889–1893	Harrison	19	1	25	44
1893–1897	Cleveland	42	5	128	170
1897–1901	McKinley	6	0	36	42
1901–1909	T. Roosevelt	42	1	40	82
1909–1913	Taft	30	1	9	39
1913–1921	Wilson	33	6	11	44
1921–1923	Harding	5	0	1	6
1923–1929	Coolidge	20	4	30	50
1929–1933	Hoover	21	3	16	37
1933–1945	F. Roosevelt	372	9	263	635
1945–1953	Truman	180	12	70	250
1953–1961	Eisenhower	73	2	108	181
1961–1963	Kennedy	12	0	9	21
1963–1969	L. Johnson	16	0	14	30
1969–1974	Nixon	26	7	17	43
1974–1977	Ford	48	12	18	66
1977–1981	Carter	13	2	18	31
1981–1989	Reagan	37	9	39	76
1989–1992	Bush	37	1	5	35
Total		1,454	104	1,055	2,502

Source: For Washington to Ford: from *Presidential Vetoes, 1789–1976* (Washington, D.C.: U.S. Government Printing Office, 1978); for Carter and Reagan: from *Presidential Vetoes, 1977–1988* (Washington, D.C.: U.S. Government Printing Office, 1990); for Bush: *The Weekly Compilation of Presidential Documents,* various issues, and "Bush and Congress: Rising Feud Produced Legislative Deadlock," *New York Times,* August 9, 1992, A17.

AGENDA SETTING

There is more to presidents' programs and vetoes than the single executive image that meets the eye. Presidents' programs emerge from a complicated agenda-setting process that involves each element of the plural presidency. *Agenda-setting identifies a set of problems as priorities for solution.* The process selects certain issues as most pressing and most worthy of national attention, money, and action. According to political scientist John Kingdon, agendas are in part "the list of subjects to which government officials and those around them pay serious attention."[17] Complexity in the environment and in the policy itself accompanies the selection. For instance, with the Federal Deposit Insurance Corporation (FDIC) fund nearly out of money after a record number of bank failures, the Bush administration proposed an overhaul of the banking system. The policy environment was complex, involving such issues as international competition, risky loans, different treatment of large versus small banks, and the abuse of deposit insurance by pension funds. Complexity also characterized the policies the Bush administration announced: allowing banks to open interstate branches and to sell securities and insurance. The new policies reflected the inherent tension of protective capitalism. The measures insisted on government regulation but at the same time allowed banks to expand their services into new markets.

Political fragmentation makes priorities difficult to set, even before they are sent from the White House to Capitol Hill. Although people may think of the banking industry as a giant monolith, it is not. Community banks in rural areas and towns across the country deeply resented the Bush proposals to move banking away from Main Street and toward Broad Street. Small banks were not likely to take advantage of the opportunity to open branches in other states. Instead, they would watch while large out-of-state banks opened branches across the street from them. For months, during the preparation of the reforms, the American Bankers Association (big banks) and the International Bankers Association of America (small banks) attempted to advance their positions to the White House.

The decentralized organization of the White House structures the decisions. The banking reform plan was developed under the auspices of Secretary of the Treasury Nicholas Brady. Yet members of the Council of Economic Advisers, the staff of the Office of Management and Budget, and the Office of Policy Development inside the decentralized White House organization, as well as the Federal Reserve Board and the FDIC outside the White House, became involved in the efforts. Indeed, the plan was unveiled nearly two months late because of coordination problems between the Treasury Department and White House offices. In the meantime, the Federal Reserve, the FDIC, members of Congress, and the banks themselves offered reforms.

Ambiguity accompanies agenda setting. The plural presidency does not originate ideas for problems and programs; it typically filters them from elsewhere. As a result, ambiguity often arises about what information is needed to develop the programs adequately and what the goals of the programs are. A Kennedy aide observed: "The classic idea of the President as a competing source of programs is only partially correct. When you think about it, most of the programs originate in other institutions and in the public. The White House just isn't equipped to create many new ideas." A Nixon staff member agreed:

Most of our time was spent looking at proposals coming from the executive branch and Congress. I'd characterize the process as a funnel. We were quite prepared to winnow the incoming ideas, but I don't recall that we generated that much from inside. Our job was to select from the available proposals, not to be the starting point.[18]

The White House organization does not generate agenda ideas for two reasons: lack of time and lack of expertise.

The compressed political time frame in which the plural presidency operates makes it difficult to be original and tempting to borrow from others. A Nixon aide remarked: "We simply didn't have the time to search out new ideas. The fact that Congress was interested in a particular idea made it a logical candidate for discussion. If a congressional program existed that appealed to the President and had already been ironed out, why not take it?"[19] Presidents and their staffs have insufficient time to research issues fully and develop full-blown programs from scratch.

Congress and the executive bureaucracy are much better equipped to identify problems, all sorts of problems. Their organizational time is much slower than that of the presidency. They have the ability to study many problems over long periods of time. Congress and the bureaucracy also practice greater specialization than the White House, within jurisdictions in which staff members routinely delve into minutiae. A congressional subcommittee on sugar matches an Agriculture Department office on the same topic. Greater specialization means more expertise. Presidential decentralization, though extensive, cannot match this level of specialization.

The greater the familiarity with problems and the greater the number of people involved in an organization, the greater is the number of alternatives that will be developed to solve the problems. Presidents are most likely to find detailed, technical expertise in the bureaucracy. A Carter aide stated, "The executive branch has all the advantages . . . the information, the manpower, the congressional support, and the expertise."[20] From Congress, presidents will find "blended information"—a mix of the substantive (what is the problem like) and the political (are the vetoes there for a solution).[21] Bank reform was developed in the midst of preparations for and the fighting of the war with Iraq. At that time, Bush was paying only limited attention to domestic economic concerns, and the White House was relying heavily on experts in the Treasury Department.

AGENDA SELLING

Kingdon observes, "Setting the agenda and getting one's way are two very different things. The president may be able to dominate and even determine the policy agenda, but is unable to dominate the alternatives that are seriously considered, and is unable to determine the final outcome."[22] An agenda once set becomes a convenient target to attack. Members of Congress may indicate which parts they like and which they do not. The president's agenda also is a handy focus for the opposition party. Whatever the president proposes, the opposition party is likely to propose the opposite. So presidents employ the plural presidency not only to help set their agendas but also to help sell them to Congress.

Decentralized Persuasion

Presidents since Truman have relied heavily on three units within the decentralized White House to pursue their legislative agendas: the legislative liaison office, the Office of Policy Development (known as the Domestic Policy Staff from Nixon through Carter), and the Office of Management and Budget. Each acts as a liaison with Congress in different ways.

Legislative Liaison. Eisenhower formalized the Office of Congressional Relations in 1953 as the official White House liaison office with Capitol Hill. It has since been renamed the Office of Legislative Affairs. Pressure to develop their own legislative programs brought pressure on subsequent presidents to monitor the progress of their programs and other legislation through Congress. Rather than rely on their immediate staffs, presidents formalized and enlarged the Office of Legislative Affairs to include nearly fifty staff people. The liaison staff has four primary responsibilities: building cooperation with Congress, coordinating the administration's lobbying efforts, vote counting, and policy formulation.

First they cultivate positive, cooperative relations with members of Congress. "I never expected any member to commit political suicide in order to help the President, no matter how noble our case," said Larry O'Brien, head of the liaison office for Kennedy and Johnson. Johnson instructed his liaison staff: "The most important people you will talk to are senators and congressmen. You treat them as if they were President. Answer their calls immediately. Give them respect . . . they are your most important clients."[23]

Presidents Kennedy, Johnson, Nixon, Ford, Reagan, and Bush

organized their liaison offices around key blocs in Congress, based on combinations of geography, ideology, and party. The liaison office recognized the political fragments found in Congress. Some liaison staff members were assigned conservative Democrats; others courted their more liberal colleagues. Still other staffers were assigned to Republicans. Separate liaison teams handled the House and the Senate, thereby assisting presidents' coalition-building tasks because, as Eric Davis points out, "the form of organization was quite compatible with the building of majority coalitions by means of assembling groups of members."[24]

Carter initially reorganized the liaison office along issue lines. He felt members would support an issue on its merits and therefore would not have to be courted along other lines. When members of Congress made clear to Carter that he did not understand the factions and fragments within Congress that existed regardless of the merits of legislation, Carter switched to the other presidents' approach.

Second, the Office of Legislative Affairs coordinates the decentralized lobbying efforts of departments and agencies that have their own congressional liaison teams. Congressional liaison members meet weekly with the departments' legislative staff to ensure they work as a team. The White House liaisons often can count on the help of departmental lobbyists who are not directly involved in the subject matter of the bill but have strong ties to certain groups of members. If southern Democrats were wavering on a health bill, not only would a liaison be brought in from the Department of Health and Human Services, but Agriculture Department lobbyists who might be expected to have close ties with southern members could also be brought in.

Third, the Office of Legislative Affairs serves as a clearinghouse for "legislative intelligence"—for keeping track of head-count information on members' positions on specific measures and the favors that have been extended to members to secure their votes. Often the office provides this information to the party leadership to organize more support.

Finally, the Office of Legislative Affairs becomes involved in the formulation of policy. It accommodates the policy complexity of legislation in a manner different from that of other units in the White House. Its participation is not based on the substance of the issue. Liaison staffers claim no expertise on weapon systems or toxic waste. Instead, they comment on the strategic viability of a measure—that is, on how the policy initiative is packaged and sold, its chances for passage, and the key obstacles it must overcome.

Office of Policy Development and OMB. The legislative liaison office pays most attention to strategies for securing the agenda. The Office of Policy Development and the Office of Management and Budget coordinate the programmatic focus of the agenda. The Office of Policy

Development develops major presidential policy initiatives and closely examines individual proposals. OMB is charged with maintaining the integrity of the agenda as a package relative to the abundance of proposals floating through the Congress at any one time. OMB thus establishes the top priorities within the agendas—programs that are first among unequals.[25]

As an example, the Kennedy administration recognized that there was little chance that all twenty-five of its proposals would be passed by Congress in 1961. "There was no way we could get it all," one aide recalled. "Instead, we felt some pressure to tell Congress which items were most important, which ones had to pass, which ones the President felt he had to have. Even then, it didn't make much difference—we didn't get much anyway."[26] At the top of Kennedy's list were aid to education, Medicare, area redevelopment, manpower training, and youth unemployment. Bumped down were community health facilities, agriculture, water treatment, and food surplus distribution.

Presidents encounter difficulties if they do not establish such priorities. They strain the resources of the plural presidency and create obstacles in Congress. Using an encyclopedic design, Jimmy Carter asked Congress for ten major pieces of legislation on energy and for other legislation on government reorganization, hospital costs, and welfare reform. When the Domestic Policy Staff requested that Carter rank his main proposals to make the congressional work more manageable, Carter replied: "I have no preferences. My preference is to move ahead with everything at once."[27] Most of the proposals had to pass through the powerful House Ways and Means Committee, which determines the revenues for legislation. "We're talking about ten or so major things," commented Carter liaison chief Frank Moore, "and eight of them have to go through Ways and Means." The resulting logjam slowed the process and buried many of the proposals. Moore observed, "We overloaded the circuits and blew a fuse."[28]

Presidents as Lobbyists

Since Thomas Jefferson invited members of Congress over for dinner to discuss pending legislation, presidents have realized the advantages of personal persuasion in legislative affairs. Presidents can be their own best (or worst) liaison officers with congressional members. They use various mixes of accommodationist, combative, and detached legislative styles as events, bills, and members dictate.

Accommodationist Style. The accommodationist style requires the president to play the nice guy. He behaves like the benevolent head of a large political family and adopts a twofold strategy. Implementing the first part of the strategy, he keeps family members happy by doing them personal and political favors—making appearances at fund-raising dinners and campaign rallies, extending invitations to social gatherings, especially at the White House; making patronage appointments; naming post offices and other buildings after congressional members when doing so is at the president's discretion; and honoring members at birthdays or anniversaries.[29] As one member of Congress described it:

> Nobody but Lyndon Johnson would have helicoptered in to help me celebrate an anniversary in office—but he did. Nobody but Johnson would have remembered to write birthday greetings, to send pictures, to send invitations, in short, to do anything possible to help the most junior member of Congress feel recognized, wanted, cared for, and cared about.[30]

Although such things may sound trivial, they are both important and easy. Ronald Reagan skillfully practiced the accommodationist style. As president-elect, he went to Capitol Hill to discuss national priorities and the cabinet selection process with members of both parties. The gesture of the president going to Congress rather than asking members of Congress to come to the president was well received. A Reagan aide noted, "We had to lasso him to keep him off the Hill."[31]

Implementing the second part of the strategy, the accommodationist builds a coalition through bargaining and give-and-take. He attempts to get as many members of Congress involved in the proposal as possible, keeps tabs on support, and uses personal persuasion to convince members to join the coalition. Lyndon Johnson felt that the trick was to get members involved: "When people have a hand in shaping projects, these projects are more likely to be successful than the ones simply handed down from the top."[32]

Combative Style. Presidents who adopt a combative style play the heavy. Instead of keeping the political family happy, a combative president seeks to keep the family in line through the use of political muscle and sometimes dirty tricks. The combative president builds a coalition by threatening to withdraw support from a member's pet bill if the member does not support a presidential initiative. Although Lyndon Johnson often employed an accommodationist style, he also displayed a combative style—intimidating members to vote in a particular direction. Johnson once threatened to expose a member's mistress to the member's wife unless he voted with Johnson on a White House bill. Richard Nixon's relations with Congress grew combative, even bombastic, well before Watergate through the use of vetoes, impoundment of funds, and the withholding of information.

The combative president may attempt to take on Capitol Hill by attacking members' favorite projects. Jimmy Carter had campaigned to balance the budget and protect the environment. President Carter announced the elimination of nineteen water projects in his fiscal year 1978 budget. The effect in Congress was to anger members who saw the projects as vital to their states and to their own political interests. Other members worried that their own local projects might be next. The result, as Carter aide Bert Lance put it, was "100 percent alienation. . . . We alienated a large portion of the Congress: those who had projects and those who had hopes of projects."[33]

George Bush combined the accommodationist and combative styles in his dealing with lawmakers over the budget deficit in 1990. Before the beginning of the summer, Bush called for a bipartisan budget summit with congressional members in an attempt to work out a package on budget and deficit figures that would be acceptable to the White House and on Capitol Hill. Bush invited key members to a meeting in the Cabinet Room and listened intently to their proposals. By summer's end, a combative approach replaced Bush's accommodationist tack. He blasted Democratic members of Congress for foot dragging, overspending, and unreasonable partisan attacks.

Detached Style. When presidents adopt a detached style, they attempt to remove themselves from congressional liaison efforts as much as possible. Rather than keeping the family happy or keeping it in line, they leave the family alone, allowing Congress to go its own way. They minimize personal favors or contact with members. Their coalition-building effort relies most heavily on their formal congressional liaison staff.

Presidents most frequently invoke this style on bills they find only of marginal interest. They also may approach the passage of a bill hierarchically—sending a message to the congressional leadership in the expectation that the message will trickle down to the membership. Eisenhower did not wish to be heavily involved in the passage of legislation, although he kept in close contact with members, especially the Republican leaders. Nixon did not like face-to-face or telephone bargaining sessions with legislators to ask for votes.[34] President Carter initially adopted a detached style. He had campaigned as a Washington outsider, so he did not initially court members. Critics charged that President Bush took a similar hands-off approach to legislative priorities during the protracted Iraqi crisis.

PRESIDENTS' SUCCESS IN CONGRESS

A president may hit the ground running with grace and speed; he may present to Congress an elegantly simple agenda; he and his liaison team may court tirelessly each and every member of Congress. Still, success is not guaranteed. Among the factors that influence presidential success are the composition and the rules of Congress.

The Composition of Congress

One of the most important characteristics of Congress is party affiliation. A president is helped if he has a majority of members in both houses from his party, although such a majority in no way ensures the success of the presidential cause.

From 1989 through 1992, George Bush had fewer members of Congress from his party than any president since Truman. In his first year in office, he also had the lowest rate of agreement with Congress of any president in the first year. The rate of agreement dropped even lower in the following two years. In contrast, by most accounts Lyndon Johnson was one of the most effective presidents in legislative affairs. Because of his long years as majority leader in the Senate and his tutelage by friend and fellow Texan House Speaker Sam Rayburn, Johnson knew when to send up a bill, whose arm to twist, and how hard to twist it. In 1965 and 1966, he saw pass numerous pieces of legislation that had languished under Kennedy. His good fortune was partly due to the influx of thirty-eight freshman Democrats elected in 1964, most of them eager to take part in the Great Society.[35] Still, raw party numbers are not determinative. Presidents with majorities in both houses often struggle to get what they want. Presidents without those majorities often claim victories. Party affiliation is an important feature of the U.S. Congress. It organizes the membership, the leadership, and the committees. However, in Congress, unlike in the legislatures of parliamentary systems, "party discipline" is neither a word uttered nor an activity practiced.

Ideology and constituency are two other important characteristics of Congress.[36] Liberals and conservatives often vote on opposite sides of issues, regardless of their party affiliations. Ronald Reagan was able to capitalize on this and forged a coalition of conservative Democrats, nicknamed the "boll weevils," and Republicans to push through the 1981 tax and budget cuts. Ultimately, however, the composition of Congress rests most firmly not on party or ideology but on constituency. Members of Congress owe their jobs to their states' or districts' voters, not to their party, to an ideological commitment, or to a president. Many members will vote on issues according to what they think their constituents would prefer. If the president happens to be on the same side, he may share in the victory.

The Rules of Congress

Formal and informal rules of Congress also influence presidential success. Congressional procedures are designed to kill bills rather than pass them. Because of the number of hoops that every bill must go through, many bills do not survive. John Kennedy described with some exasperation the hurdles and decision points through which bills must proceed:

It is very easy to defeat a bill in the Congress. It is much more difficult to pass one. To go through a subcommittee . . . and get a majority vote, the full committee and get a majority vote, go to the Rules Committee and get a rule, go to the Floor of the House and get a majority, start all over again in the Senate, subcommittee and full committee, and in the Senate there is unlimited debate, so you can never bring a matter to a vote if there is enough determination on the part of the opponents, even if they are a minority, to go through the Senate with the bill. And then unanimously get a conference between the House and Senate to adjust the bill, or if one member objects, to have it go back through the Rules Committee, back through the Congress, and have this done on a controversial piece of legislation where powerful groups are opposing it, that is an extremely difficult task.[37]

In addition, the informal rules such as those pertaining to seniority and specialization impede presidents' ability to guide a bill. Individual members become more powerful the longer they stay in the body. Seniority creates independent power bases for many members, even of the president's party.

The Numbers in Congress

Presidential success in Congress can be evaluated by examining the public stands that presidents take on numerous bills. The Office of Management and Budget routinely announces them, and *Congressional Quarterly Weekly Report,* a magazine that covers all aspects of Congress, records the number of times a majority of members concur with the president's position. Although many people discuss this as success, concurrence is a better term. The measure merely depicts the number of times the president and Congress agree on bills. It does not say anything about who influenced whom. Members of both parties will overwhelmingly support many roll-call votes regardless of whether the president has a position. Ideological, constituent, and even party interests may overlap with the president's position. Figure 13.1 presents concurrence rates for the whole body, and Table 13.4 breaks them down by party.

Research has drawn five conclusions about congressional concurrence with presidents. The first three conclusions can be discerned from Figure 13.1 and Table 13.4. First, as the figure and table show, there appears to be a fair amount of agreement between Congress and presidents, regardless of party. Second, party improves agreement. As can be surmised from the data, the size of the president's party in Congress affects concurrence. Moreover, presidents who have congressional majorities achieve higher levels of agreement than those who do not. Kennedy, Johnson, and Carter did better with Democrat-controlled Congresses than did Eisenhower, Nixon, Ford, Reagan, and Bush. Third, presidents do better early in their terms than they do later on. This is true no matter whose party controls Congress.[38]

A fourth conclusion (which cannot be discerned from the figure and table) is that presidents' popularity with the public increases concurrence.[39] The more popular a president is, the more likely is Congress to agree with presidential positions. Finally, research con-

Figure 13.1 **Presidential Success on Votes, 1953–1991**

Presidential success is typically highest at the beginning of a president's term. In the post–World War II period, Presidents Johnson and Reagan were the two most successful presidents in their first year after election (1965 and 1981, respectively). [*Source: Congressional Quarterly Almanac, 1991* (Washington, D.C.: Congressional Quarterly, 1992), 8-B. Used by permission.]

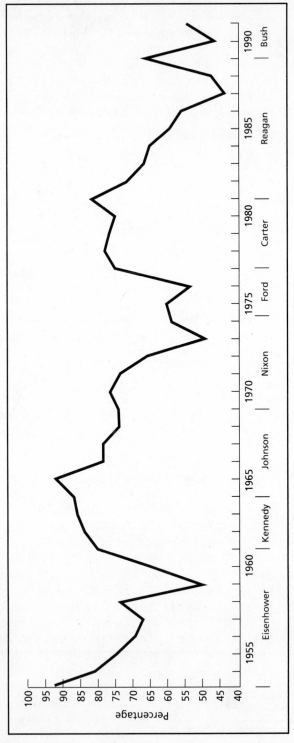

Note: Success is defined as a majority of both houses supporting the president's position on a bill.

Table 13.4 Presidential Support by Party, 1953–1986 (in percentages)*

Year	President's party	House		Senate	
		Democrats	Republicans	Democrats	Republicans
1953	R	45%	70%	42%	66%
1954	R	34	74	36	74
1955	R	42	52	37	70
1956	R	38	72	35	69
1957	R	48	52	44	69
1958	R	52	55	37	66
1959	R	34	72	28	73
1960	R	46	64	41	66
1961	D	73	26	68	31
1962	D	72	30	64	31
1963	D	75	21	63	37
1964	D	78	26	63	56
1965	D	75	24	64	44
1966	D	67	20	53	35
1967	D	70	28	56	42
1968	D	63	36	46	41
1969	R	48	57	42	65
1970	R	41	60	35	63
1971	R	41	71	33	65
1972	R	46	68	34	66
1973	R	31	65	24	64
1974	R	38	59	31	53
1975	R	37	68	36	67
1976	R	32	67	29	62
1977	D	61	32	62	39
1978	D	65	34	64	36
1979	D	64	26	67	39
1980	D	63	31	60	38
1981	R	39	72	33	81
1982	R	30	61	35	72
1983	R	28	71	39	73
1984	R	32	66	31	74
1985	R	28	68	27	76
1986	R	23	72	26	80

*On roll-call votes on which the winning side was supported by fewer than 80 percent of those voting.
R = Republican
D = Democrat
Source: George C. Edwards III, *At the Margins: Presidential Leadership of Congress* (New Haven: Yale University Press, 1989), table 3.1. Used by permission.

cludes that presidents' major national addresses boost concurrence. Presidents may invoke the single executive image through their addresses. Presidents suggest that the measures they seek from Congress are programs on behalf of the people. This suggestion gives rise to an intricate association among presidents' speeches, public popularity, and congressional concurrence. The speeches, as noted in Chapter 6, often increase public support. The public may be prompted to contact their congressional representatives in support of the presidential initiative. Members of Congress may be more favorably predisposed toward the presidential effort because of both the constituent pressure and the president's own lobbying.[40]

Research also has examined whether presidents are on the winning side more often on foreign policy votes than on domestic votes. According to the "two presidencies" thesis, presidents' success is higher in foreign affairs because members of Congress "rally around the flag." There has been a running debate for a quarter century about whether two presidencies—one in foreign and military affairs, the other in domestic affairs—actually exist.[41] Current empirical work finds little evidence of two presidencies when considering the major proposals that presidents from Eisenhower to Carter submitted to Congress. Overall, as seen in Table 13.5, there is little difference between foreign and domestic policy success for presidents' major proposals. Members of the opposition party treat presidents poorly on either set of issues.[42]

These statistical results, however, should not mask the fact that in their day-to-day actions presidents and Congress respond differently to each other in domestic and foreign affairs. Domestic affairs are more nearly the Congress's domain, for many of the issues are drawn from constituency interests and desires. Foreign affairs entail more unilateral actions of presidents—actions about which Congress may be able to ask questions only after the fact. These differences may not clearly show up in the votes taken on Capitol Hill, but they do define congressional-presidential relations.

Carter and Reagan

U.S. News and World Report conducted a survey of members of Congress in 1977 and found that only 7 percent rated President Carter as "very effective" with Congress. In 1981, the magazine found that 93 percent of the members felt President Reagan was very effective.[43] A comparison of Carter's and Reagan's uses of the single executive image and the plural presidency in their relations with Congress reveals why this huge disparity of opinion developed.

Two sharply contrasting images bracket the beginning and the end of the Carter presidency like book ends. The first image is of Carter, his wife, and daughter smiling and waving as they walked down Pennsylvania Avenue during the inaugural parade. Carter, try-

Table 13.5 Presidential Victories on Key Votes, 1957–1978

President	Years	Domestic issues			Foreign and defense issues		
		N	% Victories		N	% Victories	
Eisenhower	1957–1960	51	.608		17	.824	
Kennedy	1961–1963	47	.702		16	.688	
				.732			.736
Johnson	1964–1966	95	.853		17	.647	
Nixon	1969–1972	46	.652		18	.778	
Nixon	1973–1974	20	.500		7	.429	
Ford	1974–1976	27	.593	.565	13	.385	.600
Carter	1977–1978	22	.591		10	1.000	
President's party only							
Eisenhower	1957–1960	51	.863		17	.882	
Kennedy	1961–1963	47	.830		16	.983	
				.879			.853
Johnson	1964–1968	95	.926		17	.824	
Nixon	1969–1972	46	.848		18	.833	
Nixon	1973–1974	20	.950		7	1.000	
Ford	1974–1976	27	.852	.884	13	.692	.767
Carter	1977–1978	22	.864		10	.700	
Opposition party only							
Eisenhower	1957–1960	51	.412		17	.588	
Kennedy	1961–1963	47	.128		16	.250	
				.293			.382
Johnson	1964–1968	95	.337		17	.412	
Nixon	1969–1972	46	.239		18	.278	
Nixon	1973–1974	20	.300		7	.000	
Ford	1974–1976	27	.185	.217	13	.154	.167
Carter	1977–1978	22	.182		10	.300	

Source: Lee Sigelman. "A Reassessment of the Two Presidencies Thesis," *Journal of Politics* 41 (November 1979), 1201. Used by permission.

ing to keep his campaign promise to be the "People's President," left the trappings of power midway along the inaugural route. He stepped from the presidential limousine. He chose to wear not the traditional formal wear but an ordinary business suit that he had worn to his inaugural as governor of Georgia. In the early months of his term, he made a point to carry his own bags, he greeted the American public in a nationwide address seated before a fireplace in a worn-looking sweater, and he barred the playing of "Hail to the Chief" as too pretentious and regal. He would do things by himself, like a common person, and not in the way things had always been done in Washington.

Carter's down-home image, however, only partly matched the requirements of the single executive image. He gained visibility, but at the expense of uniqueness, importance, and power. As a result, his ability to push his legislative agenda was diminished. Carter's agenda was sweeping and comprehensive, but it too fell victim to a mismatch with the single executive image. He acknowledged the problems were long-range problems. He stated that presidents could not single-handedly fix them. Just as Carter's personal image was an outsider's image, so was his agenda an outsider's agenda, filled with issues that members of Congress did not like to hear about and positions that members did not like to take, such as a tax on gas-guzzling American cars, energy conservation, pollution controls on industry, and expensive health care reform. It was as though an angry but naive citizen had come to clean up Congress and the country.

In 1979, Carter talked of a national malaise that he had helped cause. The other book end was an image of Carter as incompetent and weak, someone who did not know how to call the shots. Carter became hostage to his failure to live up to the single executive image.

When Ronald Reagan took office, the limousine, "Hail to the Chief," and tuxedos were back and with them returned the uniqueness, importance, and power of the single executive. Most presidents are products of their immediate predecessors. They do what the previous president did not do; they do not do what the previous president did. The final image of the Carter presidency and the first image of the Reagan presidency were exact opposites. Reagan proclaimed that presidents could lead the country back to greatness. Reagan maintained that he would and could dismantle government. Reagan's agenda was sweeping and comprehensive. He proposed major budget cuts that affected the offerings of the entire government, excluding defense. He proposed tax cuts of an equally sweeping nature. It was a major agenda but with only three items (lowering taxes, cutting the budget, and increasing defense) seemed somehow manageable. Moreover, Reagan acted swiftly where Carter had been deliberative. In content, size, and timing, the Reagan agenda fit with the single executive image.

Carter's and Reagan's agendas were the products of the plural presidency. During the first months of Carter's term, proposals funneled in from all over the government, especially from Capitol Hill. The administration suffered from a backlog on Capitol Hill of Democratic legislation that had stalled during the Nixon and Ford years. The White House received eleven hundred letters from Democratic members in the first week requesting legislation, appointments, projects, and White House time. The administration supported eighty measures in the first year. The sheer volume posed problems for the Office of Management and Budget, which coordinated the initiatives. Some bills were hastily and poorly drafted. On some occasions, proposed legislation was already on the books. Carter officials axed items from their own proposals without telling Congress. Although the Carter White House faltered initially, improvements were made. The liaison staff was increased and reorganized to better meet the needs of members of Congress. Computers were introduced to track legislation, assess voting patterns, and process congressional mail. Nevertheless, the early reputation of White House ineptness and aloofness did not go away. By 1979, Carter had not been able to move any of his major legislative proposals through Congress. The body balkanized the energy package, abandoned hospital cost containment, restructured education initiatives, and fought over the Panama Canal treaty.[44]

In the Reagan case, several layers of the plural presidency pushed the legislative agenda. At the highest level, overall strategy was set by Reagan's top aides—James Baker (chief of staff), Edwin Meese (chief policy adviser), and Michael Deaver (chief media strategist)— and relevant cabinet officers. The Office of Management and Budget was responsible for the overall coordination of the proposals. It cleared the positions, programs, and testimony of all executive agencies before they went to Capitol Hill so as "not to divert congressional attention during major White House policy pushes."[45] More specifically, OMB and its director David Stockman coordinated the massive domestic budget cutting efforts of 1981. For the tax cut, the Treasury Department took the lead in calculating revenues, and OMB presented the policy.

In addition, several liaison offices conducted outreach measures to persuade, directly and indirectly, congressional members. The congressional liaison staff was in place well before Reagan was inaugurated. It not only shepherded legislation but handled a large volume of constituent casework forwarded from members of Congress. The Reagan White House also used the public liaison office to organize grass-roots support behind presidential programs that could be enlisted to persuade members of Congress. The public liaison office courted the support of over one thousand business groups and trade associations. It set up telephone banks before important presidential speeches to notify the groups of their content. It also arranged special prespeech briefings for the groups by Reagan or top aides. "Before the president goes on television, we first bring in our allies," commented a liaison officer. "He meets with them in private—several hundred at a time. He gives them an advance view of what he is going to do so that they can alert their allies to be prepared to go."[46] Members of Congress were flooded with phone calls soon after the Reagan speeches. The personnel office also was used to keep in close contact with members of Congress and arrange political appointments with their states in mind whenever possible.

Through these various components of the plural presidency, the Reagan administration was able to control the congressional agenda for 1981. Carter had mismanaged the resources of the single executive image and the plural presidency in the first year of his term. Reagan claimed both as key resources.

CONCLUSION

The single executive image and the plural presidency are at once resources for presidential action and constraints on presidential action in the legislative arena. For presidents, Congress is both the small, compliant Renaissance dragon and the menacing medieval monster. Congress defers to presidents' visions of the main legislative agenda. The presidential priorities indicate a direction for Congress to take (or to oppose). Congress is not good at agenda setting. The 535 members of the House and Senate have diverse and special interests. They are good at addressing problems; they are not good at separating big problems from small problems—subsidies for honeybee farmers and the MX missile are both important. Presidents and Congresses use the single executive image as a resource to focus national attention. The single executive image also can be a liability for presidents. They are blamed when Congress recasts and makes their priorities unrecognizable.

Congress finds it difficult to set aside the 535 diverse and special interests that compose it. Its prime vehicles for decisions are bargains and compromises that leave behind a single, pristine set of priorities. That is the nature of the medieval beast. At this point, the plural presidency takes over the joust. It employs a large-scale liaison effort to consummate the bargains and construct the compromises. The Office of Management and Budget coordinates the legislative efforts. Yet the plural presidency also acts as a constraint on presidents' actions. There are limits to the time and resources it can commit to any one legislative battle. Its own diversity and diffuseness may send mixed signals to Capitol Hill, just as muddled sounds are heard atop Capitol Hill. Overall, the single executive image and the plural presidency permit presidents to influence congressional decisions, but at the margins.[47] They are able to sway a relatively small set of votes that would have gone the other way. The framers' invention, which separates rather than joins the legislature and the executive and divides the legislature in two, prohibits presidents, no matter their resources, from doing more. ∎

FURTHER READING

On presidential-congressional relations, see: Louis Fisher, *The Politics of Shared Power: Congress and the Executive*, 2d ed. (Washington, D.C.: CQ Press, 1987); Michael Mezey, *Congress, the President, and Public Policy* (Boulder, Colo.: Westview Press, 1989); James Thurber, ed., *Divided Democracy: Cooperation and Conflict Between the President and Congress* (Washington, D.C.: CQ Press,

1991). On presidential vetoes, see: Gary Copeland, "When Congress and the President Collide: Why Presidents Veto Legislation," *Journal of Politics* 45 (August 1983): 696–710. On agenda setting, see: Paul Light, *The President's Agenda*, 2d ed. (Baltimore: Johns Hopkins University Press, 1989); John Kingdon, *Agendas, Alternatives, and Public Policies* (Boston: Little, Brown, 1984). On agenda selling, see: Stephen Wayne, *The Legislative Presidency* (New York: Harper and Row, 1978); Eric Davis, "Congressional Liaison: The People and the Institutions," in *Both Ends of the Avenue*, ed. A. King (Washington, D.C.: American Enterprise Institute, 1983), 59–95; James Pfiffner, *The Strategic Presidency* (Chicago: Dorsey Press, 1988). On presidential success in Congress, see: George C. Edwards III, *At the Margins: Presidential Leadership of Congress* (New Haven: Yale University Press, 1989); Jon Bond and Richard Fleischer, *The President in the Legislative Arena* (Chicago: University of Chicago Press, 1990); Steven Shull, ed., *The Two Presidencies* (Chicago: Nelson-Hall, 1991).

N O T E S

1. Quoted in Robert DiClerico, *The American President*, 2d ed. (Englewood Cliffs, N.J.: Prentice-Hall, 1983), 106.

2. See Louis Fisher, *The Politics of Shared Power: Congress and the Executive*, 2d ed. (Washington, D.C.: CQ Press), 1987.

3. See Richard Fenno, *Homestyle* (Boston: Little, Brown, 1978).

4. Quoted in Paul Light, *The President's Agenda* (Baltimore: Johns Hopkins University Press, 1982), 53.

5. Quoted in Richard Neustadt, "Presidency and Legislation: Planning the President's Program," *American Political Science Review* 49 (December 1955): 1015.

6. Ibid., 980.

7. Quoted in Light, 43.

8. Ibid., 36.

9. Quoted ibid., 43.

10. Quoted ibid., 49.

11. Quoted ibid., 43.

12. Quoted in Doris Kearns, *Lyndon Johnson and the American Dream* (New York: Harper and Row, 1976), 238.

13. See Gary Copeland, "When Congress and the President Collide: Why Presidents Veto Legislation," *Journal of Politics* 45 (August 1983): 696–710; and David Rohde and Dennis Simon, "Presidential Vetoes and Congressional Response," *American Journal of Political Science* 29 (May 1985): 397–427.

14. Woodrow Wilson, *Congressional Government* (Gloucester, Mass.: Peter Smith, 1973), 53.

15. Quoted in Norman Ornstein, "But Reagan Already Has Line-Item Veto Power," *Washington Post National Weekly Edition*, August 26, 1985.

16. Quoted in James Davis, *The American Presidency: A New Perspective* (New York: Harper and Row, 1987), 156.

17. John Kingdon, *Agendas, Alternatives, and Public Policies* (Boston: Little, Brown, 1984), 4.

18. Quoted in Light, 86.

19. Quoted ibid., 90.

20. Quoted ibid., 92.

21. Kingdon, 40.

22. Ibid., 26.

23. Quoted in Jack Valenti, *A Very Human President* (New York: Norton, 1975), 178.

24. Eric Davis, "Congressional Liaison: The People and the Institutions," in *Both Ends of the Avenue*, ed. A. King (Washington, D.C.: American Enterprise Institute, 1983), 75.

25. Light, 155.

26. Quoted ibid.

27. Quoted in James Pfiffner, *The Strategic Presidency* (Chicago: Dorsey Press, 1988), 146.

28. Quoted ibid., 145.

29. Stephen Wayne, *The Legislative Presidency* (New York: Harper and Row, 1978), 153–154.

30. Quoted in William Livingston et al., eds. *The Presidency and the Congress: A Shifting Balance of Power?* (Austin, Tex.: Lyndon B. Johnson School of Public Affairs, 1979), 311.

31. Quoted in Stephen Wayne, "Congressional Liaison in the Reagan White House: A Preliminary Assessment of the First Year," in *President and Congress*, ed. N. Ornstein (Washington, D.C.: American Enterprise Institute, 1982), 44–65.

32. Quoted in Kearns, 222.

33. Quoted in Pfiffner, 147.

34. Wayne, 160.

35. Joseph Cooper and Gary Bombardier, "Presidential Leadership and Party Success," *Journal of Politics* 30 (November 1968): 1012–1027.

36. See George C. Edwards III, *At the Margins: Presidential Leadership of Congress* (New Haven: Yale University Press, 1989).

37. *Public Papers of the Presidents: John F. Kennedy, 1963* (Washington, D.C.: U.S. Government Printing Office, 1964), 892, 894.

38. The first three points are made in Jon Bond and Richard Fleischer, *The President in the Legislative Arena* (Chicago: University of Chicago Press, 1990).

39. George Edwards, *Presidential Influence in Congress* (San Francisco: Freeman, 1980).

40. Lyn Ragsdale, "Presidents' Perpetual Campaign: Public Appearances from Truman to Reagan," mimeo, University of Arizona, 1992.

41. Steven Shull, ed., *The Two Presidencies* (Chicago: Nelson-Hall, 1991).

42. Aaron Wildavsky, "The Two Presidencies," in *The Presidency*, ed. A.

Wildavsky (Boston: Little, Brown, 1969), 230–243; and Lee Sigelman, "A Reassessment of the Two Presidencies Thesis," *Journal of Politics* 41 (November 1979): 1195–1205.

43. Courtney Sheldon, "How Reagan Rates with Congress," *U.S. News and World Report*, October 12, 1981, 27.

44. Wayne.

45. Ibid., 54.

46. Quoted ibid., 55.

47. Edwards.

CHAPTER 14

At the Top?

In the midst of preparations for a meeting with Latin American diplomats, Jimmy Carter discovered that a mouse had died inside an Oval Office wall. As the rancid odor intensified, the White House called the General Services Administration (GSA), which is responsible for the maintenance of federal buildings. The GSA refused to act because it recently had exterminated all the mice in the White House. The dead mouse obviously was an outside intruder and therefore the responsibility of the Interior Department, which is in charge of the White House grounds. A call placed to the Interior Department was similarly rebuked. The department was not responsible for a mouse now inside the White House; it handled outdoor problems only. An angry and frustrated Carter ordered officials from both agencies to the Oval Office, where he raved, "I can't even get a damn mouse out of my office!" A special joint task force was established to get rid of the wretched rodent.[1] Later Carter commented, "Before I became president, I realized and I was warned that dealing with the federal bureaucracy would be one of the worst problems I would have to face. It has been even worse than I had anticipated."[2]

The Constitution invests presidents as chief executives with the power to faithfully execute the laws, appoint department secretaries and other executive officials as specified by Congress, and request the opinions of department secretaries about subjects relating to their offices. The Constitution, however, waters down the presidential assignment by empowering Congress to create positions that can be "vested in the heads of department." Congress has used this power to give statutory authority to officials at or below cabinet rank, instead of presidents. It has allowed these officials wide latitude in drafting rules and regulations to enforce laws passed by Congress. Congress also creates independent agencies that presidents are not permitted to supervise directly. The term "chief executive," then, is a term of uncertain content. Presidents' relations with the bureaucracy depend less on constitutional law than on political strategies—of both presidents and bureaucrats.

Presidents have two interconnected strategies. They invoke the single executive image, which places them atop an imposing pyramid of departments, agencies, bureaus, commissions, and corporations. The image relies on official organization charts, such as the one shown in Table 14.1, as evidence that the presidents truly are *chief* executives. Charts depict a hierarchical arrangement in which the president is the "boss" of some 3 million people who work under him in an enormous apparatus variably called the executive branch, the bureaucracy, the executive bureaucracy, the government, and "they." The single executive image suggests that presidents are the only officials who can assert control over the operations of government.

The image allows presidents to capitalize on Americans' suspicions of bureaucratic authority. Presidents and presidential candidates make the bureaucracy a scapegoat for many of the ills of government and announce that they will attack it unreservedly. They criticize, as Nixon, Ford, Carter, and Reagan did, the executive branch for its red tape, excessive regulations, and monstrous growth. Reagan asserted in his Inaugural Address that "government is not the solution to our problem; government is the problem."[3] Presidents ardently contend that they can steady a ship they say is sinking. They will reduce its size, add new parts, dismantle wornout parts, streamline its design, or daringly propose a complete overhaul. The image of the bureaucracy as a sinister, overgrown leviathan becomes a vivid counter to the image of a single executive fighting back against, in the words of George Wallace, former governor of Alabama, "briefcase-toting, pointy headed bureaucrats."[4]

Presidents recognize that, despite the single executive image and the hierarchical organization charts, they are, according to Richard Rose, "apart from rather than a part of the executive branch of government."[5] Yet, because of the image and the charts, presidents seek to employ a second strategy: they attempt bureaucratic control using the plural presidency. They adapt the White House organization with tentacles that reach throughout the bureaucracy in an effort to make it run smoothly. They also enlarge the White House to take on more responsibilities that they hope to monitor directly.

Bureaucrats, however, have their own ideas about who controls them and the role presidents play in the government. Bureaucratic units exhibit a remarkable independence from each other and from the White House. It is not that they are out of control but rather that elements in American politics external to government guide them. The bureaucracy reflects three types of interests: (1) politically organized and active, (2) politically unorganized but active, and (3) politically unorganized and inactive. Fingers typically point to the impact of organized groups (such as the American Association of Retired Persons) on departments and agencies of the government (such as the Social Security Administration). These are only the most visible

Table 14.1: Executive Branch of the United States Government

THE PRESIDENT

Executive Office of the President

White House Office
Office of Management and Budget
Council of Economic Advisers
National Security Council
National Critical Materials Council
Office of Policy Development

Office of the United States Trade Representative
Council on Environmental Quality
Office of Science and Technology Policy
Office of Administration
Office of National Drug Control Policy
Office of the Vice President

THE VICE PRESIDENT

| DEPARTMENT OF AGRICULTURE | DEPARTMENT OF COMMERCE | DEPARTMENT OF DEFENSE | DEPARTMENT OF EDUCATION | DEPARTMENT OF ENERGY | DEPARTMENT OF HEALTH AND HUMAN SERVICES |

| DEPARTMENT OF HOUSING AND URBAN DEVELOPMENT | DEPARTMENT OF THE INTERIOR | DEPARTMENT OF JUSTICE | DEPARTMENT OF LABOR | DEPARTMENT OF STATE | DEPARTMENT OF TRANS- PORTATION | DEPARTMENT OF TREASURY | DEPARTMENT OF VETERANS AFFAIRS |

MAJOR INDEPENDENT AGENCIES, GOVERNMENT CORPORATIONS, AND OTHER ESTABLISHMENTS

Independent Regulatory Commissions and Boards

Board of Governors of the Federal Reserve System
Commodity Futures Trading Commission
Consumer Product Safety Commission
Equal Employment Opportunity Commission
Farm Credit Administration
Federal Communications Commission
Federal Election Commission
Federal Housing Finance Board
Federal Maritime Commission
Federal Trade Commission
Interstate Commerce Commission
Merit Systems Protection Board
National Labor Relations Board
Nuclear Regulatory Commission
Securities and Exchange Commission
U.S. International Trade Commission

Independent Executive Agencies

Central Intelligence Agency
Environmental Protection Agency
General Services Administration
National Aeronautics and Space Administration
Peace Corps
Office of Personnel Management
U.S. Arms Control and Disarmament Agency
U.S. Commission on Civil Rights
U.S. International Development Cooperation Agency

Government Corporations, Foundations, and Other

Administrative Conference of the U.S.
Appalachian Regional Commission
Corporation for Public Broadcasting
Export-Import Bank
Federal Deposit Insurance Corporation
National Credit Union Administration
National Railroad Passenger Corporation (AMTRAK)
National Science Foundation
Occupational Safety and Health Review Commission
Panama Canal Commission
Pension Benefits Guaranty Corporation
Postal Rate Commission
Resolution Funding Corporation
Resolution Trust Corporation
Smithsonian Institution
Tennessee Valley Authority
U.S. Postal Service

Source: U.S. Government Manual 1989–1990.

sets of external interests. Economic groups that are notorious for their lack of organization, such as American farmers and consumers, also have access to pieces of the bureaucracy (such as the Agriculture Department and the Food and Drug Administration). In addition, the needs of demographic groups whose daily lives depend on government programs, such as single mothers, the aged poor, and the unemployed, influence government (in the Health and Human Services Department and the Housing and Urban Development Department, for example). These people may not individually move the government, but their collective plights do. Bureaucrats within the agencies responsible for the programs feel strongly about helping their clients.

Those forms of input are types of representation not outlined in the formal demarcations of the Constitution or in the electoral system. Americans love to badmouth the bureaucracy, but they do so not fully recognizing the many ways in which they themselves use and influence it. The bureaucracy is a microcosm of American society, reflecting American values, conflicts, competing interests, apathy, and mobilization. The bureaucracy's principal strategy vis-à-vis presidents is to sustain these societal interests.

This chapter first explores the independence of the bureaucracy from the presidency and the dependence of the bureaucracy on societal interests. It next considers how presidents, using the single executive image, depict themselves as in charge of the bureaucracy. Finally, it details how presidents use the plural presidency to achieve some direction over the implementation of policy through the bureaucracy.

BUREAUCRATIC INDEPENDENCE

The executive branch slowly acquired its independence from the president. Throughout most of the nineteenth century, a partisan executive government tied the executive branch to presidents through party. Beginning in earnest with Andrew Jackson, presidents appointed numerous members of their own parties to positions throughout the government. Presidents practiced rotation in office—incoming chief executives swiftly replaced officials from the defeated party with appointees of their own party. George Washington, who objected to the increasingly partisan climate of the republic as he left office, nevertheless summed up what turned out to be the nineteenth-century approach. He wrote that it would be "a sort of political suicide" to appoint individuals not supportive of his Federalist party's goals.[6] The connection between executive employees and the chief executive, however, should not be exaggerated. Party, not the president, was the linchpin of the system. Presidents depended on state party officials and on members of Congress to supply them with names for the growing number of appointments. These party chiefs, whose political livelihood depended on the distribution of patronage, ensured that the appointees were more beholden to them than to the president.

The patronage approach declined with the Pendleton Act in 1883. The law was passed after a disappointed office seeker shot and killed President Garfield. It sought to replace the patronage system with a system of appointments of career civil servants, who would be chosen through examination, trained to be experts in a department, promoted on the basis of merit, and, barring gross misconduct, granted job security. Over the next several decades a second approach to presidential-bureaucratic relations emerged: neutral competence. A neutral pool of experts who served presidents of both parties emerged. It constituted a "permanent government," the units and employees of which were not beholden to presidents or to their political parties. According to Richard Nathan, "The essential point of the civil-service reform movement was that elected officials should make policy and that professionals in the career service should carry it out."[7]

Neutral competence has been more an ideal than a reality. The bureaucracy, aided by Congress, blurs the line between policymaking and policy execution: it makes policy as it executes it. Congress often writes general, vague legislation knowing that the details of the policy will be brought to life in bureaucratic regulations. Too, there is little that is neutral about bureaucratic practice. Although the civil service removes the executive branch from the caprice of partisan politics, the executive branch, like any other part of government, is a political entity with political interests. The bureaucracy makes many of its policy decisions in an effort to satisfy its clients: the Agriculture Department and farmers, the Veterans Affairs Department and veterans, the Labor Department and labor, the Nuclear Regulatory Commission and the operators of nuclear power plants, the Securities and Exchange Commission and Wall Street. Rather than neutral competence, a large part of the bureaucracy employs a strategy of clientele service. Though neutral with respect to partisan politics, bureaucratic units are partisans on behalf of their clients. This partisanship intensifies the independence of the executive branch from the chief executive. Neutral competence announces that the bureaucracy will not be beholden to the president; clientele service announces to whom the bureaucracy will be beholden.

Some departments, such as the State Department and the Justice Department, do not have readily identifiable clients that they serve; nonetheless, they develop outlooks and methods of operation that separate them from presidents. Departmental partisanship stands in place of clientele service. These departments do not like to be told by presidents what to do in their area of expertise.

Driven by a strategy of clientele service or by departmental partisanship, bureaucratic independence has developed along four dimensions: (1) outlook, (2) bureaucratic time, (3) bureaucratic space, and (4) bases of support.

Pluralist Versus Majoritarian Outlook

Different political outlooks separate presidents from the executive branch. Presidents uphold a majoritarian outlook on politics, suggesting that decisions are made by majority rule: one side wins; the other side loses; and the winning side holds a mandate to proceed. The majoritarian model is firmly grounded in presidents' election victories. They have been elected, however loosely through the halls of the electoral college, by a majority of voters. On this basis, presidents advance the single executive image, asserting mandates to govern on behalf of all the people. The majoritarian outlook suggests that the mandate is periodic. It is renewed or revised each election. The majoritarian approach further guides presidents' outlooks during their term of office in relations with Congress and with the public. Presidents work to convince a majority of the members of Congress and the public to support presidential initiatives.

By contrast, the executive bureaucracy operates from a pluralist outlook, which views all groups and interests within society as part of government. Thus, all sides are represented and no side ever truly wins or loses. Instead of majority rule, the bureaucracy bases its legitimacy at least partly on minorities' rule—the rule of clients. Presidents clash with the bureaucracy because they cannot apply a majoritarian model to a pluralist organization. On a key presidential measure, they cannot lobby for the support of a majority of bureaucrats, as they would lobby members of Congress, because majority rule is not one of the rules of the bureaucratic game.

Bureaucratic Time

Presidential time, as discussed in Chapter 9, moves at two speeds. Presidents' political time is compressed, intense, and episodic. Their organizational time is slower but still episodic, geared toward the next election. Bureaucratic time, in contrast, has no upcoming elections, no pressing deadlines. It is slow and continuous—for four reasons.

First, standard operating procedures of the various departments and agencies of the executive branch slow down the workings of government. These procedures establish guidelines or routines for executive officials to apply to numerous cases, and they ease everyday decision making. They are designed to coordinate the behavior of large numbers of people. An official who could devise a faster, easier way to proceed on a given case would have to follow the standard operating procedures anyway. For instance, the Internal Revenue Service has well-established procedures of notification, complaint, and appeal that are followed in tax review cases. Neither the tax examiner nor the individual taxpayer can propose skipping one of the steps, even if doing so would expedite the process.

Second, problems are viewed as so complex that individuals and agencies dismantle the problems into "quasi-independent parts" and deal with each part separately.[8] Because so many units are dealing in detail with so many subproblems, putting the pieces back together takes time.

Third, dismantling problems fragments power. The result is often organizational and policy overlap—several agencies are responsible for the same aspect of a program. As an example, ten different departments and agencies administer more than one hundred federal human services programs. The overlap slows down action.

Fourth, the executive branch is made up primarily of career civil servants whose average tenure is nearly two decades and who are difficult, if not impossible, to fire. The personal achievements of individuals within the executive branch are measured over lifetimes rather than over election times.

Bureaucratic Space

Bureaucratic space is vast and highly decentralized. Contrary to organization charts, bureaucratic space is shaped not like a pyramid but rather like an ample blanket. The federal government covers an ever increasing set of functions and handles each function in great detail. It is difficult to impose a hierarchy on such a vast array of functions. Many of them have no connection with each other; others of them overlap.

Bureaucratic space began to enlarge in the latter half of the nineteenth century, giving formal bureaucratic recognition to the protection of specific interests in an increasingly diverse economy. The Department of the Interior was created in 1849; the Agriculture Department was established in 1862 and made a cabinet position in 1889; the Justice Department was added in 1870. The growth dramatically continued at the turn of the century. Between 1901 and 1916, fifty-six agencies were added to the government. The Department of Commerce and Labor, established in 1903, was split into two departments by 1913. Other agencies, including the Department of Post Office, the Interstate Commerce Commission, the Reclamation Service, the Forest Service, the Food and Drug Administration, the Federal Reserve Board, and the Federal Trade Commission, came into being. The expansion continued during the New Deal and World War II. Although no new cabinet-level departments were added, key agencies such as the Securities and Exchange Commission, the National

Table 14.2 The Growth of Federal Civilian Employment

Year	Employees
1821	6,914
1831	11,491
1941	18,038
1851	26,274
1861	36,672
1871	51,020
1881	100,020
1891	157,442
1901	239,476
1911	395,905
1921	561,142
1931	609,746
1941	1,437,682
1951	2,482,666
1961	2,435,804
1971	2,794,787
1981	2,772,000
1991	3,596,000[1]

1. Estimate.
Source: 1821–1961: U.S. Bureau of the Census, *Historical Statistics of the United States* (Washington, D.C.: U.S. Government Printing Office, 1975), 1102–1103; 1971–present: various volumes from U.S. Bureau of the Census, *Statistical Abstract of the United States.*

Labor Relations Board, and the Federal Communications Commission were created. By 1948, 223 government organizations existed. The number peaked at 394 in 1973.[9]

The diversity of functions has precipitated a dramatic growth in the size of the federal work force, beginning in the later part of the nineteenth century, as seen in Table 14.2. The 51,020 civilian employees of the executive branch in 1871 tripled to 157,442 by 1891, doubled again to 239,476 by 1901, reached 395,905 by 1911, and by 1921 exceeded a half million.[10] The New Deal brought considerable expansion to the federal work force, which more than doubled in the decade from 1931 to 1941. Growth stabilized in the 1950s, when nearly 2.5 million people held federal jobs. Forty years later, in 1991, the figure had risen to just over 3.5 million employees. Of these people, 87 percent are employed outside Washington, D.C.[11] Estimates are that 28,000 employees have some policymaking responsibilities; of the 28,000, nearly 4,000 have considerable policymaking duties.

Presidents, in contrast, appoint a mere 2,000 executive branch officials. Size and function have created a bureaucratic omnipresence that minimizes presidential impact. Although it is commonplace to speak of "the executive branch," there actually are many executive branches. Four types of organization make up the bureaucracy: cabinet departments, independent agencies, independent regulatory commissions, and government corporations.

Cabinet Departments.   Departments are the largest units of the executive branch. The heads of departments constitute the president's cabinet. The current cabinet departments total fourteen: State, Defense, Treasury, Interior, Agriculture, Justice, Commerce, Labor, Health and Human Services, Housing and Urban Development, Transportation, Energy, Education, and Veterans Affairs. In addition, there are cabinet-level agencies, notably the Federal Bureau of Investigation and the Central Intelligence Agency, that lack formal department status but their directors are appointed by the president.

Formally, the departments are under the president, yet each is a separate bureaucracy made up of offices, agencies, bureaus, services, and divisions. Technically, the departments are arranged in a hierarchical fashion. An example demonstrates, however, that bureaucratic space is more decentralized than hierarchical. The director of the River and Trails Division within the National Park Service reports to the associate director for recreation resources, who, in turn, is responsible to the deputy director of the Park Service. The Park Service itself is under the assistant secretary of the interior for fish and wildlife and parks, who reports to the undersecretary of the interior, who is under the secretary of the interior. The secretary officially reports to the president. It is difficult to believe that the assistant secretary for fish and wildlife and parks knows much about what the River and Trails Division is doing. It is ludicrous to think that a president knows about (or is greatly concerned about) what the unit does. The more complex a hierarchy becomes, the more it collapses of its own weight into a decentralized organization with many access points, overlapping units, and little control from above.

Independent Agencies, Independent Regulatory Commissions, and Government Corporations.   There are some sixty agencies and commissions that are not part of the cabinet departments. Congress expressly established the units as independent of the president and attempted to free them from the general pressures of the political process and the partisan considerations that mold it. The independent agencies have grown on an ad hoc basis in attempts to solve discrete problems or set up specific programs. They include the National Aeronautics and Space Administration (NASA), the Peace Corps, and the Commission on Civil Rights.

Independent regulatory commissions, which include the Federal Reserve Board, the Federal Trade Commission, and the Interstate Commerce Commission, are "independent" because they, like independent agencies, are outside the regular departmental hierarchies. Presidents' formal authority over these units is limited to a highly restricted power of appointment. Congress establishes the terms of commission members, which are staggered, range from three to fourteen years, and rarely coincide with presidential terms. Members of the commissions can be removed only for cause. Congress also requires a partisan balance on many of the commissions. For instance, the Federal Communications Commission has seven members with staggered seven-year terms, and no more than four FCC members may be from one political party. Thus, when a new president takes office, he will find several positions on the commission occupied by individuals appointed by his predecessor.

The commissions are "regulatory" because they are specifically charged with establishing and administering regulations and adjudicating disputes that arise from these regulations for industries such as communications, transportation, banking, energy, and manufacturing.

There are also a small number of government-owned corporations, such as the U.S. Postal Service, AMTRAK, and the Corporation for Public Broadcasting, over which presidents have decidedly limited control.

The value of these agencies' independence has been questioned. Their insulation from the presidency results in a lack of policy coordination between the White House and the executive branch. Although they may be independent of the president and partisan pressures, critics contend that they often are not independent of the various industries and businesses they are assigned to regulate. Members of the agencies often are recruited from the industries themselves. This practice gives presidents ammunition to propose greater White House control.

Bases of Support

Bureaucrats have two sets of natural allies, in Congress and among their clients. Congressional committees and subcommittees share many of the same interests, clients, and jurisdictions as departments and agencies. Congressional committees combine the pluralist and majoritarian outlooks discussed above. The decisions of individual subcommittees, committees, and the House and Senate as bodies require that a majority be secured before legislation goes forward. The jurisdictions of the subcommittees and committees reflect a pluralist model in which all active substantive interests are accommodated (if not represented)—from sugar beet farmers to innner-city preschool teachers. Many congressional committees—such as the Agriculture Committee, the Banking Committee, and the Transportation Committee—like departments with similar jurisdictions, practice clientele service.

The clients of the bureaucracy define many of its interests and goals. People often argue that social service agencies are controlled by liberal Democrats who champion the values of the New Deal and the Great Society. In other agencies, such as the Agriculture Department or the Defense Department, there is said to be a more conservative message. This is only partly true. It is more accurate to say that many bureaucrats have a strong ideological commitment to client advocacy. They firmly believe in the severity of their clients' problems and in the programs in place to solve them, no matter what philosophical bent the programs may have. Client advocacy rather than liberalism or conservatism is the doctrine that directs much of the bureaucracy.

Until the 1980s, the prevailing view was that bureaucrats and their two sets of allies formed a series of "iron triangles" or "triple alliances": subgovernments consisting of an agency or bureau within the executive branch, a committee or subcommittee within Congress, and an organized interest group. The partners of the triads were thought to develop mutually beneficial arrangements to gain what they wanted in a particular policy area. They were most prevalent and influential in policy areas that were least visible and of least interest to most citizens. Organized groups passed information along to an executive agency, alerting the agency to a problem or the need for a program. The executive agency refined and added to this information. It developed a program submitted to the Office of Management and Budget to be included in the president's legislative program. Once the request arrived on Capitol Hill, the committee was favorably predisposed. Examples of iron triangles included farmers, the Agriculture Department, and the agriculture committees; weapons manufacturers, the Defense Department, and the armed services committees; and bankers, the Commerce Department, and the banking committees.

The changing character of Congress made it difficult for some of these relationships to be sustained. Congress has become a more individualistic institution in which members act as policy entrepreneurs outside the lines of the triangles. John Tierney and Kay Schlozman observe that "With the help of their larger and more expert staffs, these legislators pursue many different hobby horses on their own, developing new legislative initiatives, offering more floor amendments to bills of others, offering more amendments to bills from committees other than their own, and intervening in the processes of administrative policymaking."[12] Such entrepreneurship and the rise of large numbers of new citizens' groups and advocacy organizations has created large "issue networks" in the place of the iron triangles. These networks are connected through policy expertise rather than through the policy preferences or political stakes that welded together the triangles.

For years, tobacco growers and cigarette companies successfully prevented stringent antismoking and unfavorable tobacco policies with the support of the Agriculture Department and the House and Senate agriculture committees. Recently, consumer groups, health advocacy organizations, and the surgeon general have placed heavy pressure on the tobacco industry. The former iron triangle has become a much wider issue network of groups and government officials who wish to pursue policies different from those established by the triangle. This does not mean that the triangles do not exist within the networks; it means that they are not as dominant as they once were.

Neither the iron triangle nor the more fluid issue network is good news for presidents. Both essentially leave presidents on the outside looking in. The triangles are based on mutual self-preservation and on interests that presidents do not necessarily share. The policy expertise that drives the issue networks is not a White House forte. Although there is growing specialization within the White House, the resulting expertise is much less than the expertise of others in the thick of the network.

PRESIDENTIAL GOVERNMENT

Many presidents arrive in Washington armed with a belief, drawn from the single executive image, that they can recast the permanent government as presidential government. The single executive image defines presidential government, in Hugh Heclo's words, as "the idea that the president, backed by the people, is or can be in charge of governing the country."[13] Presidential government also implies a negative force—presidents crusade against bureaucratic red tape, waste, and delay. Presidents use each of the four foundations of the single executive image to make the claim. They assert national electoral mandates and translate them into a "superordinate responsibility over the machinery of government."[14] They combine their constitutional power to faithfully execute the laws with the cultural assumption of practical politics to announce varied administrative plans to revamp the bureaucracy. The media reinforce the idea of presidential government by simplifying the structure of government and portraying presidents at the top of a bureaucratic hierarchy. They devote considerable coverage early in the term to announcements of presidential appointees and stories of how they will "run" various departments and agencies.

Reorganization

Just as it has become expected that presidents propose legislative programs to deal with pressing national problems, presidents also regularly propose reorganization plans to correct bureaucratic exigencies. The reorganization plans are attempts to place presidential stamps on the permanent government. The efforts make presidents look like good managers who will bring greater coordination, accountability, and economy to the operations of the executive branch.

The key is "the look." Presidents recognize that reorganization plans display symbols of efficiency, simplicity, thrift, and size, even if they do not necessarily embody these qualities. The symbolism provides presidents with political influence with the public, if not with the bureaucracy. Americans would love to have someone straighten out the bureaucracy, but they recognize that such an accomplishment is unlikely. Presidents thus may gain public influence from exercising the imagery and are not likely to lose much.

Presidential reorganization efforts began in 1939 when Congress authorized presidents to propose such plans that would take effect in sixty days unless vetoed by both houses of Congress (later changed to either house). Between 1939 and 1973, presidents submitted 105 reorganization plans to Congress, which disapproved only 23. Congress, however, let lapse presidential reorganization authority in 1973 in the midst of Watergate battles. President Carter requested and received new authority in 1977. Congress renewed the power in 1984, though requiring a joint resolution for a plan to take effect. Presidents announce reorganization plans with great fanfare at the beginning of a term, and with diminishing enthusiasm later.

Presidents' reorganization efforts fall into three categories: modest changes, grand plans, and redirections.

Modest Changes. Of the three types of reorganization efforts, modest changes are the easiest (though not foolproof) actions. They offer the best match between the image of the single executive saying that something should be done and actually bringing the request to fruition. However, what may appear as a simple addition (or subtraction) is never simple.

Because of the labyrinth of the federal government, additions cannot be devised from scratch. They typically involve the transfer or consolidation of previously existing agencies into a new agency. Jimmy Carter proposed and Congress approved the creation of a new Department of Energy, but the "creation" involved the consolidation of three units already in operation: the Federal Power Commission, the Energy Research and Development Administration, and the Federal Energy Administration. Carter's "addition" raised few questions because the existing agencies were new and temporary and the deepening energy crisis called for a coordinated approach.

Efforts that disturb entrenched organizations stir up trouble. Once agencies are created and jurisdictions fixed, various interests in the agency, on Capitol Hill, and among organized interests have a stake in maintaining the organizational status quo. Lyndon Johnson proposed a new Department of Transportation that would combine several existing agencies, including the Maritime Administration, responsible for shipping. The shipping industry and longshoremen, not often on the same side of an issue, vigorously opposed the move. They felt it might compromise or destroy their relationships with the Maritime Administration. They also worried about the agency competing for resources with other units under the Transportation Department canopy. The House Committee on Merchant Marine and Fisheries, which was responsible for oversight of the Maritime Administration, also objected. The move would take the unit out of the committee's jurisdiction and effectively put the committee out of business. Staff members of the Maritime Administration complained, fearing their jobs might be lost or redefined. Congress did approve the new Transportation Department but left the Maritime Administration where it was.[15]

It is harder still to abolish agencies, as Reagan learned when he tried to fulfill his pledge to get rid of the Department of Education and the Department of Energy, created during the Carter administration. The imagery of swift, specific changes to the government is tempting, but opposition is often intense.

Grand Plans. Presidents offer ambitious grand plans to revamp the structure of government to meet the nation's long-term goals. A grand plan is an assertion that the president will fix not just a single problem of government but many problems associated with bureaucratic inertia.

Richard Nixon proposed a complete streamlining of government. He advocated retaining four core departments—Justice, Defense, State, and Treasury—and combining all others into four "superdepartments" for natural resources, human resources, economic development, and community development. Congress failed to implement Nixon's plan. For a time, Nixon attempted to circumvent Congress by designating four cabinet secretaries as "super-secretaries" who would coordinate policy in the four broad areas.

President Carter secured passage of the Civil Service Reform Act of 1978. The reform was designed to offer presidents some flexibility in the assignment of high-level administrators. It created the Senior Executive Service (SES) of eight thousand people, of whom 10 percent can be the president's own political appointees and the remainder are career civil servants. The career officials can be transferred within an agency (but not to another agency) if they do not carry out presidential interests. The reform afforded Carter the advantage of the single executive image successfully molding the bureaucracy, and it had a substantive impact. Elizabeth Sanders commented that "the SES is a particularly valuable resource for presidents who, on taking office, confront a bureaucracy staffed by ideologically unsympathetic upper-level bureaucrats."[16]

Redirections. Another way to bend the government to the president's will is to announce broad changes in the size and scope of government services. Viewed through the lens of the single executive image, redirections suggest that presidents not only control the government but can modify it to their own design.

Franklin Roosevelt dramatically increased the size of the bureaucracy in his first term, setting up agencies, some authorized by Congress, others initiated by executive orders, which were to combat the depression: the National Recovery Administration, the Civilian Conservation Corps, the Federal Emergency Relief Administration, and the Works Progress Administration. During World War II, the bureaucracy also grew as Roosevelt established the War Production Board and the Office of Price Administration. There were limits to these Rooseveltian expansions. Each of the new government units disappeared once the economic and military emergencies were over.

Ronald Reagan attempted a major retrenchment of government size, beginning with budget cuts in 1981. Table 14.3 shows that Reagan's efforts to shrink the welfare state while simultaneously enlarging defense worked. From 1981 to 1988, total government expenditures grew significantly—by 21.7 percent. Within this overall growth, social programs (except Social Security) declined, and all nondefense programs barely kept pace with inflation.[17] Moreover, Reagan sought to devolve federal responsibilities to state and local governments by consolidating various grants-in-aid programs.

It is unclear how long the Reagan legacy will last. Though bold in imagery, it is problematic politics. Many interests were disrupted by such redirection, and since 1989 spending on social programs and education has increased.

Reorganization plans give the impression that presidents can convert the permanent government into presidential government. They may offer a successful way for presidents to appeal to Americans' frustrations and suspicions about "pointy headed bureaucrats." But although reorganization may play well in Peoria, its reception in Washington is more chilly. The unwieldy bureaucracy is not easily reorganized. Many presidential changes leave the bureaucracy looking pretty much as it did before. Presidents, then, turn to the plural presidency in efforts to influence the bureaucracy. Reorganization plans offer presidents the opportunity to say that they are saving taxpayers' money, shaking up the bureaucracy, and showing a strong commitment to a particular public policy area. However, they do not give presidents the ability to direct, control, or even influence the bureaucracy. Much like an elephant hit by a pebble, it lumbers on, not knowing of the assault.

THE PLURAL PRESIDENCY AND RESPONSIVE COMPETENCE

Presidents employ the plural presidency to blur the distinction between policymaking and policy execution in favor of the White House. The bureaucracy often succeeds in both making and execut-

Table 14.3 Federal Budget Outlays, by Function, 1940–1996 (in billions)

Function	1940	1950	1960	1970	1975	1980	1985	1990	1991 est.	1996 est.
National defense	$1.7	$13.7	$48.1	$81.7	$86.5	$134.0	$252.7	$299.3	$289.9	$293.2
Human resources	4.1	14.2	26.2	75.3	173.2	313.4	471.8	619.3	692.1	956.8
Education, training, employment, and social services	2.0	0.2	1.0	8.6	16.0	31.8	29.3	38.5	42.8	40.9
Health	0.1	0.3	0.8	5.9	12.9	23.2	33.5	57.7	71.2	125.2
Income security	1.5	4.1	7.4	15.6	50.2	86.5	128.2	147.3	173.2	223.7
Social Security and Medicare[1]	0.0	0.8	11.6	36.5	77.5	150.6	254.4	346.7	373.4	531.2
Veterans' benefits and services	0.6	8.8	5.4	8.7	16.6	21.2	26.3	29.1	31.5	35.7
Physical resources	2.3	3.7	8.0	15.6	35.4	66.0	56.8	124.6	180.1	38.0
Commerce and housing credit[1]	0.6	1.0	1.6	2.1	9.9	9.4	4.2	67.1	119.5	−26.8
Community, regional development	0.3	0.0	0.2	2.4	4.3	11.3	7.7	8.5	7.7	5.4
Energy	0.1	0.3	0.5	1.0	2.9	10.2	5.7	2.4	2.6	3.4
Natural resources and environment	1.0	1.3	1.6	3.1	7.3	13.9	13.4	17.1	18.8	18.9
Transportation	0.4	1.0	4.1	7.0	10.9	21.3	25.8	29.5	31.5	37.1
Net interest[1]	0.9	4.8	6.9	14.4	23.2	52.5	129.4	184.2	197.0	211.0
Other functions[2]	0.8	8.0	7.8	17.3	27.5	45.0	68.2	60.9	80.5	86.6
Administration of justice	0.1	0.2	0.4	1.0	3.0	4.6	6.3	10.0	12.6	17.1
Agriculture	0.4	2.0	2.6	5.2	3.0	8.8	25.6	12.0	15.9	12.6
General government	0.3	1.0	1.2	2.3	10.4	13.0	11.6	10.7	11.2	14.2
General science, space, technology	0.0	0.1	0.6	4.5	4.0	5.8	8.6	14.4	15.8	23.9
International affairs	0.1	4.7	3.0	4.3	7.1	12.7	16.2	13.8	17.0	18.6
Undistributed offsetting receipts[1]	−0.3	−1.8	−4.8	−8.6	−13.6	−19.9	−32.7	−36.6	−39.1	−44.9
Total outlays	9.5	42.6	92.2	195.6	332.3	590.9	946.3	1,251.7	1,409.6	1,540.8

1. Includes both on- and off-budget amounts.
2. Includes other outlays not shown separately.

Note: Amounts in current dollars. For 1940–1975, ending June 30. Beginning 1980, ending September 30.

Source: Harold Stanley and Richard Nieimi, *Vital Statistics on American Politics*, 3d ed. (Washington, D.C.: CQ Press, 1992), 416. Used by permission.

ing policy, but the White House attempts to take charge of execution through a strategy of responsive competence. It strives to make the executive branch responsive to the policy goals of the chief executive. Presidents have adopted two approaches to responsive competence. The first formally centralizes policy implementation in the White House rather than having it devolve to various departments and agencies. The second makes the bureaucracy politically responsive to the White House.[18]

White House Centralization

Presidents attempt to centralize the implementation of policy in the White House. Rather than entrusting a department with the policy, the White House itself takes charge of the operation. As an example, the Johnson administration desired to exercise White House control over many Great Society programs, fearing that if it did not, the programs would be misdirected and misplaced in the bureaucracy. The Economic Opportunity Act of 1964 created a series of community action programs, including college work-study, summer employment for high school and college students, small business loans, VISTA (a domestic version of the Peace Corps), Head Start (an educational enrichment program for poor preschoolers), and legal services for the poor. The act also established a new agency to fight the War on Poverty—the Office of Economic Opportunity (OEO). OEO was specifically placed in the Executive Office of the President, rather than created as an independent agency or housed in the Department of Health, Education, and Welfare (where it was moved in the Nixon years).

This centralization effort gave Johnson numerous advantages. A new unit gave the White House the chance to move quickly, move in the directions it wanted to go, hire the "right" people, put sufficient resources into the office, and control the multitude of programs from one place. OEO, however, faced three challenges. First, it had to adopt routines for much of the mechanics of government—how to distribute funds, train employees both in the White House and in regional offices, buy supplies. These nuts-and-bolts decisions were fundamental to the operating of the office. Second, complex decisions had to be made about standards for program eligibility, guidelines for generating community involvement, and compliance requirements. With a new agency, many of these efforts resulted from trial and error. Third, OEO faced high expectations that it could achieve results, fast. But the very nature of the implementation strategy— White House control over community programs—made the going rough.

Other presidents have attempted to centralize more policy activities within the White House and have experienced problems similar to Johnson's. Nixon also invoked an administrative strategy designed to gain White House control of government. Nixon White House members shared long-standing antibureaucratic views in the country and especially in the Republican party, which saw big government as the enemy. They felt the enemy had become especially menacing during the Kennedy-Johnson years as program after program was implemented and the federal budget grew. One Nixon aide remarked that the "White House [was] surrounded" by these powerful liberal program interests entrenched from eight years of Democrat administrations.

The Nixon staff had good reason to worry about moving its new, more conservative and decentralized plans through the bureaucracy. A survey of career bureaucrats in domestic policy agencies taken at the time confirmed the Nixon staff's suspicions. Of the career bureaucrats, 47 percent said they were Democrats, 36 percent indicated they were Independents with no clear partisan leanings, and only 17 percent reported they were Republicans. The career bureaucrats also were asked about the future direction of the government. Their responses did not bode well for the Republican White House. Of the career officials, 32 percent favored much greater provision of social services, 22 percent preferred some additional services, 25 percent desired the present balance, 12 percent supported less government involvement, and 10 percent approved of much less government service.[19] The Nixon response was to expand the White House Office. Nixon increased the size of the White House Office more than any other president—doubling it between 1970 and 1971 from 311 to 660 people. Later, he offered his plan for new "superdepartments." Because there would be only four of them, he believed that the White House could monitor them directly. Nixon's initiatives, however, were largely stillborn. As noted above, Congress rejected the superdepartments, and Nixon's attention soon was turned from administration to Watergate.

The principal advantage of the centralization strategy becomes its central disadvantage. Presidents attempt to control more and more programs from the Executive Office of the President. Trade, space exploration, the environment, drugs, energy, and consumer affairs all have been brought into the White House, even though each policy is also housed elsewhere in the bureaucracy. The result is that the more people who are brought into the White House organization, the more like a small bureaucracy the White House becomes. The enlarged staff insulates presidents from the very things they wish to control. There is little personal contact between presidents and the average staffer and more specialization so staff members have little personal contact with each other. In short, the efforts make the plural presidency more plural. The organization becomes larger and more decentralized. Its decision-making processes become more ambiguous as it takes on responsibility for more aspects of government. Policy complexity and political fragmentation increase. Hence, it becomes more difficult for the president to maintain some sort of hierarchical control over the White House itself, let alone centralized control of the bureaucracy.

Politicizing the Bureaucracy

Presidents use the plural presidency to politicize the bureaucracy in two ways. The White House (1) places political appointees in key positions throughout the executive branch and (2) enforces political rules by which the branch must play. Presidents use the White House personnel office to screen political executives appointed to the bureaucracy. Political executives are officials at the undersecretary or assistant secretary level at the top of various departments and agencies. They typically are chosen on the basis of partisan, personal, or ideological loyalties or some combination of the three to ensure faithfulness to the White House.

These appointments are designed to offset the problem of "going native," which often occurs in departments and agencies. Political appointees are hired by the president to convey the presidential viewpoint to a department. If they gradually begin to adopt the departmental viewpoint, they are said to be "going native." Cabinet secretaries, assistant secretaries, and other political appointees come to rely on officials within the career bureaucracy for information and advice. Over their time in office, political executives may develop strong ties to their department while their commitment to the president fades.

A keen example of the "going native" syndrome occurred in 1971 during the India-Pakistan War. Secretary of State William Rogers, a long-time friend of President Nixon, announced State Department support for India. Meanwhile, the White House backed Pakistan. Charging that India was the aggressor, Nixon ordered the State Department to cut off all foreign military aid to India. Secretary Rogers refused. The State Department proclaimed that there was no evidence of Indian aggression. Nixon next ordered that all foreign economic aid to India be stopped. Rogers replied that a similar step should then be taken against Pakistan. Nixon finally called Rogers to the White House to inform him that although he could disagree about the policy, he had no right to disobey a presidential order. "The result," observed Henry Kissinger, who was then national security adviser, "was a bureaucratic stalemate in which White House and State Department representatives dealt with each other as competing sovereign entities, not members of the same team."[20] Immediately after the 1972 election, Nixon announced that Kissinger would serve as both national security adviser and secretary of state to (among other things) prevent this kind of State Department intransigence.

Presidents have periodically replaced political executives to guard against the "going native" problem. Nixon, at the start of his second term, asked for the resignation of some two thousand political appointees, including those at the deputy and assistant secretary level. The most important positions were filled by some eighty-four people from the bloated White House staff and the Committee to Reelect the President. These individuals were chosen for their personal loyalty to Nixon. It was felt that they could best monitor the activities of the bureaucracy from within. It is unclear what effect the new appointments had because Watergate clouded the rest of Nixon's term.

Ronald Reagan took a somewhat similar approach, which can be judged more clearly. Rather than being based on personal or partisan loyalty, the Reagan appointments were made with ideology as the chief criterion. Reagan remarked, "For the first time in half a century, we've developed a whole new cadre of young conservatives in government." Some succeeded in placing a conservative stamp on certain departments. The Justice Department's stands on pornography and civil rights took notable turns to the right. Conservative appointees had more difficulty changing the direction of the Department of Health and Human Services, whose career civil servants were suppporters of the programs Reagan wished cut. Internal department fights on abortion policy found no clear victor. Several ardent pro-life people appointed by Reagan to the department "got eaten alive by the technically more competent people who were buried in the Civil Service" and left. In addition, many other loyalists began to leave government after short stints for higher-paying jobs on the outside. They acknowledged that they were ideologically committed but not committed to public service.[21] Indeed, the average stay of political executives is twenty-two months, much shorter than civil servants' tenure of twenty-odd years. Differences in outlook and longevity limit the impact that political executives have on the career bureaucrats and create, in Hugh Heclo's words, "a government of strangers."[22]

Presidents use the central clearance procedures of the Office of Management and Budget (OMB) to rein in the bureaucracy. As described in Chapter 8, OMB screens the legislative proposals of the departments and agencies to determine whether they are "in accordance" with the president's program. OMB similarly evaluates budget requests and drafts of executive orders. OMB also requires departments and agencies to justify their rules and regulations before they are implemented. This administrative clearance, begun during the Nixon administration and drastically expanded under Carter and Reagan, may become a good substitute for adding departmental personnel of the president's liking. As stated in Carter's executive order, the clearance is comprehensive, directing departments to undertake "a careful examination of alternative approaches, . . . an analysis of the economic consequences of each, . . . and a detailed explanation of the reasons for choosing one alternative over the others."[23] It also has the potential for sharply politicizing the decisions of the bureaucracy. For instance, OMB blocked agency reports that were unfavorable to the Bush administration and forced a government scientist to soften his predictions on global warming to match the Bush administration stance.[24]

CONCLUSION

Presidents face a tough task in acting on the relevant units within the executive branch to implement a program approved by the Congress and signed into law. The law is likely to provide only the most general outline of the program that Congress and the president want. Presidents make their jobs more difficult by devoting less attention to implementation than to the creation of policy. Many programs are not presidents' priorities, so how the programs turn out is of limited importance to them. Presidents also recognize that implementation is time-consuming and the results are often slow in emerging. There is, then, less political benefit for presidents to tout how well a program is working than in proclaiming the creation of a new program.

In these haphazard relations with the bureaucracy, presidents use the single executive image and the plural presidency as resources; but the resources have built-in limits. The single executive image allows presidents to claim they are in charge of the government and to achieve some substantive reorganization victories. Richard Nathan observes that the most profound consequences of reorganization lie not in the "engineered realm of efficiency, simplicity, size, and cost" but rather in "political influence, policy emphasis, and communication of governmental intentions."[25]

The image, however, creates problems. Presidents most often dance on the tip of an iceberg in their reform efforts. The efforts that can be successfully implemented, such as the creation of a new department or the abolition of an agency or two, do not radically change the size and scope of government. More sweeping efforts, however, are difficult to implement—and, if implemented, difficult to sustain. Harold Barger argues:

By emphasizing the failures and shortcomings of the Executive Branch and by promising to correct the situation, each new president ironically becomes part of a problem he cannot solve. After raising public expectations that once and for all the government will suddenly start to function effectively and fairly, it is only a matter of time before the president himself becomes identified as responsible for its failure. This is because many Americans begin to believe that he is genuinely in control of its operations.[26]

The plural presidency similarly offers presidents advantages laced with drawbacks. Presidents have begun to rely on the plural presidency to regulate the regulations of the bureaucracy. The Office of Management and Budget's review of federal regulations allows presidents to place their own political stamp on the bulky paperwork of the executive branch. The policy complexity of the plural presidency commands the policy complexity of the bureaucracy. However, presidents' use of the White House as a command post for the government may have more negative consequences for presidents than positive influence on the bureaucracy. By enlarging the executive office to control the bureaucracy, presidents create their own mini-bureaucracies with all the attendant problems of control and organization.

"I thought I was the president," lamented Harry Truman, "but when it comes to these bureaucrats, I can't do a damn thing." Truman, it seems, was both right and wrong. Presidents are not *chief* executives to whom the bureaucracy is held accountable, but they are *political* executives with resources to pester it. ■

FURTHER READING

On presidential-bureaucratic relations, see: Richard Nathan, *The Administrative Presidency* (New York: Wiley, 1983). Joel Aberbach and Bert Rockman, "Clashing Beliefs Within the Executive Branch: The Nixon Administration Bureaucracy," *American Political Science Review* 70 (June 1976): 456–468. On presidential reorganization efforts, see: Elizabeth Sanders, "The Presidency and the Bureaucratic State," in *The Presidency and the Political System*, 3d ed., ed. M. Nelson (Washington, D.C.: CQ Press, 1990). On White House centralization and politicizing the bureaucracy, see: Terry Moe, "The Political Presidency," in *The New Direction in American Politics*, ed. J. Chubb and P. Peterson (Washington, D.C.: Brookings Institution, 1985), 235–272; Hugh Heclo, *A Government of Strangers* (Washington, D.C.: Brookings Institution, 1977).

NOTES

1. Hedrick Smith, "Problems of a Problem Solver," *New York Times Magazine*, January 8, 1978, 31–32.
2. Quoted in George Edwards III and Stephen Wayne, *Presidential Leadership*, 2d ed. (New York: St. Martin's Press, 1990), 251.
3. Inaugural Address, January 23, 1981, *Public Papers of the Presidents: Ronald Reagan, 1981* (Washington, D.C.: U.S. Government Printing Office, 1982), 2.
4. Quoted in Harold Barger, *The Impossible Presidency: Illusions and Realities of Executive Power* (Glenview, Ill.: Scott, Foresman, 1984), 152.

5. Richard Rose, *The Postmodern President* (Chatham, N.J.: Chatham House, 1988), 162.

6. John Fitzpatrick, ed., *Writings of George Washington* (Washington, D.C.: U.S. Government Printing Office, 1940), 315.

7. Richard Nathan, *The Administrative Presidency* (New York: Wiley, 1983), 6.

8. Graham Allison, *Essence of Decision: Explaining the Cuban Missile Crisis* (Boston: Little, Brown, 1971), 71.

9. Figures cited in Benjamin Page and Mark Petracca, *The American Presidency* (New York: McGraw-Hill, 1983), 202.

10. U.S. Bureau of the Census, *Historical Statistics of the United States: Colonial Times to 1970* (Washington, D.C.: U.S. Government Printing Office, 1975), 1102–1103.

11. *Statistical Abstract of the United States, 1990–1991* (Washington, D.C.: U.S. Government Printing Office, 1992).

12. John Tierney and Kay Schlozman, "Congress and Organized Interests," in *Congressional Politics*, ed. C. Deering (Chicago: Dorsey Press, 1988), 214.

13. Hugh Heclo, "Introduction: The Presidential Illusion," in *The Illusion of Presidential Government*, ed. H. Heclo and L. Salomon (Boulder, Colo.: Westview Press, 1981), 1.

14. Ibid.

15. Joseph Califano, *A Presidential Nation* (New York: Norton, 1975), 29.

16. Elizabeth Sanders, "The Presidency and the Bureaucratic State," in *The Presidency and the Political System*, 3d ed., ed. M. Nelson (Washington, D.C.: CQ Press, 1990), 424.

17. Ibid., 410.

18. Terry Moe, "The Political Presidency," in *The New Direction in American Politics*, ed. J. Chubb and P. Peterson (Washington, D.C.: Brookings Institution, 1985), 235–272.

19. Joel Aberbach and Bert Rockman, "Clashing Beliefs Within the Executive Branch: The Nixon Administration Bureaucracy," *American Political Science Review* 70 (June 1976): 459, 461.

20. Henry Kissinger, *The White House Years* (Boston: Little, Brown, 1979), 885.

21. "Influence of Sub-Cabinet Conservatives Is Mixed," *New York Times*, July 6, 1983, 10.

22. Hugh Heclo, *A Government of Strangers* (Washington, D.C.: Brookings Institution, 1977).

23. Executive Order 12044 of Jimmy Carter, quoted in Sanders, 417.

24. Sanders, 419.

25. Nathan, 7.

26. Barger, 152.

CHAPTER 15

Presidents in Court

Wednesday, July 24, 1974, 11:00 A.M.

Leon Jaworski, a Houston trial lawyer and now special prosecutor investigating the Watergate cover-up, pushed his way through a crowd of anxious reporters, photographers, and spectators as he entered the courtroom of the United States Supreme Court. Jaworski took his place at the table reserved for the government, confident that the Court had favorably decided his case against President Richard Nixon. The white-haired, soft-spoken Jaworski sought to secure the release of sixty-four tapes of White House conversations. Transcripts of some of the conversations, edited and issued by the White House, revealed the president and other White House officials discussing such matters as hush money for the Watergate burglars and impeding the FBI's investigation of the break-in at Democratic National Headquarters. On March 1, a federal grand jury had returned indictments against former Attorney General John Mitchell and six others on charges of obstruction of justice and conspiracy. Nixon had been named an unindicted co-conspirator. Jaworski sought the tapes as evidence in the trial of those indicted.

The president's lawyers claimed "executive privilege" in their refusal to turn over the tapes to Judge John Sirica of the U.S. district court. Past presidents had developed the doctrine that their conversations with advisers were confidential and not subject to examination, typically by Congress. Most often they had asserted executive privilege on the grounds of national security—the enemy should not know the president's plans. Always the confidentiality was confined to advice on the performance of official duties. Nixon, however, argued for a blanket policy of executive privilege, such that all conversations between a president and his advisers would be protected in all circumstances. The doctrine would be applied not just to Congress but also to judicial proceedings. It would apply to political conversations, in addition to those of an official nature. Jaworski responded that the president had no such general executive privilege. The Supreme Court had never decided a case on executive privilege, so no one knew whether the doctrine in any form was constitutional.

The court marshal suddenly announced: "The Honorable Chief Justice and the Associate Justices of the Supreme Court of the United States." Chief Justice Warren Burger took his seat in the center of the dais and slowly began to read the court's decision in *U.S.* v. *Nixon.* Jaworski realized that the Court had decided unanimously in his favor. The president would be ordered to release the tapes.[1]

Jaworski listened as Burger acknowledged that the doctrine of executive privilege was constitutional in matters of national security. Burger spoke of a "valid need for the protection of communications between high government officials and those who advise them in the performance of their manifold duties . . . a need to protect military, diplomatic, or sensitive national security secrets." The Court emphatically rejected, however, President Nixon's claim of a blanket executive privilege to protect the tapes. The president could not make "a generalized claim of the public interest in confidentiality of nonmilitary and nondiplomatic discussions."[2]

Nixon, vacationing in San Clemente, California, exploded when White House Chief of Staff Alexander Haig told him of the decision. He railed against three justices whom he had appointed but who had not supported him. Nixon fumed to Haig that he might not comply with the unanimous decision. Instead, he would burn the tapes and resign.[3] Haig and White House lawyers contended that Nixon would have to comply. At 4 P.M., in the Mai Tai Room of San Clemente's Surf and Sand Motel, Nixon's press secretary Ronald Zeigler informed the press that Nixon would abide by the Supreme Court's ruling.[4]

The Supreme Court's decision in *U.S.* v. *Nixon* provides a good, if unusual, example of presidents' relations with the Supreme Court. Although the Court denied Nixon's specific claim, it firmly endorsed the general principle of executive privilege. The case reveals two approaches the Court has taken to the presidency. The Court rebukes an individual president's claim of sweeping executive power, yet it greatly expands the powers of the presidency. The Court has on several other key occasions rejected a president's specific assertion of power. In some instances, as in the Nixon case, it has acted in an immediate and dramatic fashion to disapprove a president's actions. In other instances, the Court has acted more gingerly—after a crisis has passed. In general, the Court has taken a stand against presidential excesses when it believes a claim of presidential power unduly infringes on judicial or legislative power.

Although the decision shows how the Supreme Court restricts an individual president, it also demonstrates the Court's general willingness to expand presidential power. Indeed, the predominant pattern in the twentieth century is for the Supreme Court to add powers to the presidency. It has broadly defined not just executive privilege but the president's power in foreign affairs, law enforcement, and the removal of executive officials. It has protected the integrity of the presidential veto from congressional encroachments. The Court has sidestepped major debates on the president's power in war. It has allowed Congress relatively free rein in delegating power to the executive. In adding to these presidential powers, the Court often has adopted the executive's own constitutional interpretations.

On balance, the Court ratifies more often than it rejects presidents' claims about their own powers. The justices allow presidents to define their own powers, and they restrain presidents only under unusual circumstances. In so doing, the Supreme Court provides a good deal of the groundwork for the single executive image. Presidential-judicial relations help create the notion that there is in charge of the government one executive whom the Supreme Court, at least in part, has empowered.

October 29, 1987, 12:00 noon

One week after the acrid Senate defeat of his Supreme Court nominee Judge Robert H. Bork, President Ronald Reagan strode into the East Room of the White House with his new nominee, Federal Appeals Court Judge Douglas Ginsburg. Reagan had met Ginsburg for the first time half an hour before he presented him to reporters. During the preceding week, top White House officials debated who Bork's substitute would be. Attorney General Edwin Meese campaigned for Ginsburg, who Meese believed would vigorously uphold the conservative cause on the Court. White House Chief of Staff Howard Baker preferred a more moderate, mainstream conservative, Judge Anthony Kennedy. Baker saw Kennedy as a more conciliatory choice after the bitter Bork confrontation.

Kennedy was the front-runner as both men were interviewed at the Justice Department. After three evening sessions, however, Meese sought to torpedo Kennedy's nomination and Baker's accommodationist strategy. Meese called conservative activists, asking them to deluge the White House with messages of support for Ginsburg. William French Smith, former attorney general and long-time Reagan friend, called the president to back Ginsburg minutes before Reagan was to meet with Baker and Meese to make the final decision. Not only did Meese want the more conservative candidate to avenge the Bork defeat in the Senate, but he also wished to outmuscle Baker. According to a senior Reagan aide, Meese had "decided to make Baker a loser in this process—no matter what."[5] Reagan decided to go with Ginsburg.[6]

Nine days later, Ginsburg withdrew his nomination. Conservative senators abandoned the judge after his admission that he had smoked marijuana as a college student and law professor. Within the administration, Education Secretary William Bennett, a vocal conservative, volunteered before Reagan to get Ginsburg to quit. The president consented, saying, "Do what you think best." Bennett promptly called Ginsburg and advised him to bow out. A Meese aide then called on Ginsburg and received his official promise to withdraw. Reagan turned to Judge Kennedy, Baker's choice, whom the Senate ultimately confirmed.[7]

The Ginsburg nomination and its subsequent withdrawal indicate how active the plural presidency is in presidential decisions about the judiciary. Many of these decisions involve nominations to the courts. The Constitution provides that the president, with the advice and consent of the Senate, appoints federal judges, including the justices of the Supreme Court. Unlike Bork and Ginsburg, most nominees are swiftly confirmed by the Senate. Indeed, Bork and Ginsburg were only the fifth and sixth nominees in the twentieth century to face Senate challenges. Although the public impression often is that the president takes great interest in these nominations, the private machinations suggest that presidents rely on and may suffer from the complexities of the plural presidency in making their selections to the judiciary, even to the high court. Policy complexity, decentralized organization, ambiguous decision making, and group diversity cloud the clarity of presidents' control over their judicial nominations.

This chapter examines the relations between presidents and the courts, especially the U.S. Supreme Court. The first section explores the devices the Supreme Court has adopted to protect the independence of the judiciary from the other two branches. The second and third sections examine the courts' impact on the presidency and how they have helped advance the image of a single executive in charge of the government. The second section demonstrates how the courts have expanded presidential power; the third section discusses those instances in which presidential power has been constrained. The final section considers the effect of the plural presidency on the courts.

JUDICIAL INDEPENDENCE

The Constitution vests the judicial power of the United States in one Supreme Court and in such lower courts as the Congress may establish. The Congress has provided for two sets of lower courts: ninety-five U.S. district courts, where litigation begins, and thirteen U.S. courts of appeals, or circuit courts, which review cases from the district courts and from some federal agencies. There is thus a three-tier federal system consisting of district courts, appeals courts, and the Supreme Court.

In a system of separate powers checked and balanced, the most vital yet most precarious quality of the federal judiciary is its independence—independence from encroachment by Congress and by the president. Without such independence, the federal judiciary would be unable to play an effective role in saying what the law is and in attempting to enforce its view on the other two branches. Alexander Hamilton observed in *The Federalist,* No. 78, that the judiciary "has no influence over either the sword or the purse; no direction either of the strength or of the wealth of the society, and can take no active resolution whatever. It may truly be said to have neither FORCE nor WILL but merely judgment."[8] The Constitution seeks to protect the independence of the judiciary by granting federal judges tenure for life, subject to good behavior, and by forbidding that their salaries be reduced during their term in office. The Supreme Court has established three foundations that more thoroughly define judicial independence: judicial review, the doctrine of political questions, and public respect for the judiciary.

Judicial Review

The Constitution is silent on the most important ingredient of the judiciary's independence: judicial review. Judicial review is the power of the judiciary to declare unconstitutional, and therefore void, the actions of Congress, the president, the states, and other government officials. Although judicial review is not written into the Constitution, many framers saw it as one part of the checks and balances of the new government. In 1803, the Supreme Court first held a federal statute unconstitutional in *Marbury* v. *Madison.* Chief Justice John Marshall declared that "The Constitution is superior to any ordinary act of the legislature" and "a law repugnant to the Constitution is void." He asserted that "It is emphatically the province of the judicial department to say what the law is."[9] The following year, the Court declared a presidential order unconstitutional for the first time. Four years earlier, in 1799, John Adams had sent written instructions to U.S. naval commanders to seize vessels trading with French ports during a war with France. The Court found that Adams's actions conflicted with an existing statute, which took precedence.[10]

Full acceptance of Marshall's view of the Supreme Court as the final arbiter of the Constitution did not happen overnight. Presidents Jefferson, Jackson, and Lincoln advocated a doctrine of coordinate review, a direct rebuttal to judicial review. Each believed that the executive, legislative, and judicial branches all had authority to determine questions of constitutionality. In the view of these three presidents, the Supreme Court was not the final arbiter of the Constitution but merely one of three arbiters of the document. Jefferson complained of "crafty chief judge" Marshall's "twistifications of the law" as the Court held unconstitutional a Jefferson order in 1808 and four other actions by Madison in 1809 and 1810.[11]

Jackson's veto of the recharter of the Bank of the United States in 1832 illustrates the doctrine of coordinate review. On two previous occasions Congress had passed legislation authorizing the bank and thereby assuming its constitutionality. The Supreme Court, in *McCulloch* v. *Maryland* (1819), concurred that Congress had the power to charter the bank.[12] Nevertheless, Jackson claimed, the presidency, Congress, and the Court "must each for itself be guided by its opinion of the Constitution." Judicial review, Jackson opined, was "a dangerous source of authority."[13] Despite Jackson's argument, the Supreme Court has claimed successfully the final authority to interpret constitutional provisions. Legal scholar Alexander Bickel wrote of judicial review: "It is hallowed. It is revered. If it had a physical presence, like the Alamo or Gettysburg, it would be a tourist attraction."[14]

Political Questions

The Supreme Court has been able to serve as the final constitutional arbiter because, citing the doctrine of political questions, it refuses to act on the constitutionality of numerous decisions made by Congress and the president. The Court accepts as final and binding on the judiciary the decisions of one or both of the "political" branches of the government—the president or Congress. The justices are not elected; but when they engage in judicial review, they are challenging the actions of duly elected officials. Consequently, to avoid a confrontation with the president or Congress, the Court often rules that a particular issue is a "political question"—that is, a question that is out of its domain and that should be decided by elected officials.

Although judicial review makes the Supreme Court the final arbiter of the Constitution generally, the doctrine of political questions defines a large category of issues to which the Court refuses to apply judicial review. One of the earliest applications of the doctrine of political questions occurred in 1804 in a dispute over whether land belonged to Spain or the United States. The Court observed: "A question like this, respecting the boundaries of nations, is as has been truly said, more a political than a legal question."[15] The political questions doctrine effectively allows the executive and the legislature to practice coordinate review in key areas such as diplomacy, war, and legislative delegation of power to the executive. The doctrine is a form of self-imposed restraint to maintain the integrity of judicial review and the legitimacy and independence of the judiciary.

Public Respect

Precisely because the Supreme Court is not a political body—not elected by the people—it enjoys the respect of the people. It is seen as above politics, even though many people may recognize it as a policymaking institution. Despite its lack of coercive enforcement mechanisms, such as the sword or purse, its decisions are generally obeyed. The Court's ability to command rests not on money or might but rather on something much more ephemeral: legitimacy. All the courts stand as symbols for the entire legal order and the rule of law: the notion that people are not above the law but rather are subject to it. The courts are viewed as the upholders of the rule of law. They also are seen as having some legal expertise.

People have somewhat greater confidence in the Supreme Court than in Congress or the presidency. On average from 1966 to 1984, 21 percent of the public had the highest confidence in the White House, 18 percent in Congress, and 32 percent in the Supreme Court.[16] Although 32 percent is not overwhelming, the Court does fare better than the other two branches.

This residuum of public esteem, along with the doctrines of judicial review and political questions, gives the courts latitude to monitor and define the powers of the other branches. These three factors do not make the Supreme Court—or the judicial branch generally—supreme over the president or Congress. But they assure that the courts are not markedly inferior to the other branches.

JUDICIAL EXPANSION OF PRESIDENTIAL POWER

Throughout its history, the Supreme Court has done far more to expand than to restrict presidential power. The vagueness found in much of the Constitution about the executive has enabled not just presidents but also the Court to interpret powers broadly. The Court, like contemporary presidents, has embraced presidential activism (discussed in Chapters 2 and 3). The approach calls on presidents to do whatever is necessary in the best interest of the nation, *unless* there is a specific prohibition in the Constitution or the laws. Much of the argument the Court supplies in favor of expanded presidential power comes under the guise of separation of powers. The Court believes that the president and Congress, as co-equal branches, should have fairly free rein to carry out and define their own powers. The Court has helped presidents develop activism in four areas: foreign relations, military affairs, executive actions, and legislative delegation. In doing so, it has enlivened the image of a powerful single executive acting on behalf of the entire nation. What the president says he can do as a lone, powerful official often becomes what the judges say he can do.

Foreign Relations

The most clear-cut area of judicial concurrence with executive efforts is in foreign affairs. In 1936 in *U.S.* v. *Curtiss-Wright Export Corporation*, the Supreme Court resoundingly ratified the sole-organ doctrine—the view that the president alone speaks on behalf of the nation in foreign relations. According to the Court, power over the direction of foreign affairs is exclusively presidential:

In this vast realm with its important, complicated, delicate and manifold problems, the President alone has the power to speak or listen as a representative of the nation. He makes the treaties with the advice and consent of the Senate; but he alone negotiates. Into the field of negotiation the Senate cannot intrude; and Congress itself is powerless to invade it. . . .

It is important to bear in mind that we are here dealing not alone with an authority vested in the President by an exertion of legislative power, but with such an authority plus the very delicate, plenary and exclusive power of the President as *the sole organ of the federal government in the field of international relations*—a power which does not require as a basis for its exercise an act of Congress, but which, of course, like every other governmental power, must be exercised in subordination to the applicable provisions of the Constitution.[17]

Thus, the Court said that the president could act even without congressional delegation of authority. It affirmed in foreign policy an inherent, independent presidential power on which presidents have claimed, under the single executive image, to be the single most powerful official in the nation.

Subsequently, the courts have relied on the sole-organ doctrine to give presidents broad discretion in making treaties and executive agreements (the latter are international agreements, entered into by presidents, that do not require Senate approval). The District of Columbia Court of Appeals refused to require House consent for President Carter to implement treaties conveying U.S. property—the Panama Canal—to Panama.[18] Similarly, the Supreme Court in *Goldwater* v. *Carter* (1979) refused to require Carter to obtain Senate approval in order to terminate a defense treaty with Taiwan.[19] The Supreme Court has consistently validated executive agreements as binding and having the same force in law as treaties. In *Dames and Moore* v. *Regan* (1981), the Court unanimously upheld an executive agreement between the Carter administration and Iran that arranged for the release of U.S. hostages in exchange for freeing Iranian assets in the United States.[20] The Court found that Congress had delegated to the president certain economic powers over time and that Congress had implicitly ratified the president's actions by its failure to question the president's use of these powers. In 1948 the Court summed up its use of the political questions doctrine in foreign affairs:

the very nature of executive decisions as to foreign policy is political, not judicial. Such decisions are wholly confided by our Constitution on the political departments of the government, Executive and Legislative. They are delicate, complex, and involve large elements of prophecy. They are and should be undertaken only by those directly responsible to the people whose welfare they advance or imperil. They are decisions of a kind for which the Judiciary has neither aptitude, facilities nor responsibility and which has long been held to belong in the domain of political power not subject to judicial intrusion or inquiry.[21]

Military Affairs

The Supreme Court also has accepted presidential activism in times of war. During the Civil War, the Court upheld Lincoln's blockade of southern ports in April 1861 when Congress was not in session. The Court agreed with Lincoln that it was up to the president to act "without waiting for any special legislative authority," including a formal declaration of war.[22] Congress later ratified Lincoln's action, so it was not necessary for the Court to examine the constitutional basis of the president's action. Yet the Court nonetheless did so, approving the blockade as an exercise of presidential power alone.

The Court has studiously refused to take up the issue of presidents' power to send troops without first seeking a declaration of war or some other form of congressional authorization. This reticence has allowed presidents to act as a singularly powerful executive who can unilaterally make war. Generally, the Court has invoked the political questions doctrine to let Congress and the president fight this political battle themselves.[23]

The passage of the War Powers Resolution of 1973 over President Nixon's veto has done little to encourage the courts to leave the sidelines in this congressional-executive skirmish. The War Powers Resolution requires presidents to inform Congress whenever they commit troops to hostilities or order troops to an area where hostilities are "imminent." The courts have dismissed congressional challenges, based on the War Powers Resolution, to Reagan's decision to send military personnel to El Salvador to help train its armed forces,[24] to Reagan's order of the American invasion of Grenada,[25] and to Bush's initial troop commitment in the Persian Gulf.[26]

The courts' refusal to step into this "dread field" is not as adamant as it might appear.[27] The lower courts have been willing to treat disputes over war powers as justiciable—that is, as judicial matters rather than political questions. In the Grenada case, the court of appeals dismissed the congressional suit because the case was moot inasmuch as the invasion of Grenada had ended by the time the suit reached the court. The court did not dismiss the case because presidential war making was beyond judicial scrutiny.

The Supreme Court also has allowed presidents leeway in dealing with domestic problems associated with war. Perhaps the most infamous example is the Court's approval of Japanese internment camps established by President Franklin Roosevelt. After the Japanese attack on Pearl Harbor on December 7, 1941, Roosevelt was under severe pressure to remove Japanese Americans from the West Coast out of fear that their presence might facilitate a Japanese invasion of the North American mainland. In February 1942 Roosevelt signed an executive order that ordered the removal of citizens of Japanese ancestry to special "relocation camps" in western states farther inland. The following month, Congress passed a resolution in support of the president's executive order. Over 112,000 people, including 70,000 American citizens, were moved from their homes and jobs and detained for the duration of the war in ten camps where curfews and other restrictions were imposed. In 1943, a unanimous Court upheld the curfews in *Hirabayaski* v. *United States*.[28] In the following year, the Court confronted the issue of the relocation camps itself, which it had avoided in *Hirabayaski*. It again upheld the president's order and the congressional resolution in *Korematsu* v. *United States*.[29] Only after the relocation centers were being disbanded did the Court hold it unlawful to detain a loyal American citizen of Japanese ancestry (*Ex parte Endo*, 1944).[30]

Executive Actions

The Supreme Court has broadly construed the meaning of the president's "executive" activities in two key areas: law enforcement to ensure domestic stability and the removal of executive officials.

Domestic Stability. The Court defined the president's efforts as chief executive to ensure domestic stability in three post–Civil War cases. In *Mississippi* v. *Johnson* (1867), the state of Mississippi sought to stop President Andrew Johnson's enforcement of several Reconstruction acts that Mississippi contended were unconstitutional. The Court rejected Mississippi's claim that the president's actions were ministerial and lacking discretion. Instead, the Court held that the president's duty to see the laws faithfully executed was "purely executive and political," and the Court "forbid judicial interference with the exercise of Executive discretion."[31] In short, the president was immune from judicial direction in carrying out his official duties to faithfully execute the laws.

In the second case, *In re Neagle* (1890), the Court ruled that the president has an inherent power to defend the "peace of the United States" even though there was no statutory basis for action.[32] The Court decided the third case, *In re Debs* (1895), on similar grounds.[33] It found that although President Cleveland had no statutory authorization to seek an injunction against Eugene Debs in a national railroad strike, the strike affected the public interest and thus the president, acting through the U.S. attorney, had inherent authority to seek a judicial remedy to correct the situation.

Executive Appointments. The Court has worked to clarify the president's power in the appointment and removal of executive officers. After numerous congressional attempts to limit presidential removals during the nineteenth century, the Court in 1926 struck down a congressional provision that specified the grounds on which the president could remove postmasters. The Court held in *Myers* v. *United States* that the president could remove all executive officers—not just postmasters—for any reason or for no reason.[34] In 1935, in *Humphrey's Executor* v. *United States*, the Court qualified this global power for appointments to agencies, such as the Federal Trade Commission, that exercise "quasi-judicial" or "quasi-legislative" functions.[35]

Legislative Delegation

A dramatic expansion of presidential power has come from Congress. The legislature delegates to the executive powers that it might otherwise exercise on its own. By the strict logic of separation of powers, the only power Congress possesses to delegate is "legislative power." Yet logic prevents the legislature from delegating this power. Similarly, by the logic of separation of powers, the executive cannot receive or exercise anything but executive power. Both Congress and the president, however, have deftly avoided these untidy implications of the separation of powers. Congress has delegated power to the president in two ways. First, Congress specifies that a law goes into effect when the president determines an event has occurred or a set of conditions has been met. Second, Congress gives the president authority to make regulations, executive orders, or proclamations to carry out the substance of legislation. Together these two avenues of delegation have given presidents considerable leeway to expand presidential activism and hence enliven the single executive image.

Generally, the Supreme Court has been more than willing to permit those two transfers of power. The earliest case involved delegation of the first sort in *U.S.* v. *Brig Aurora*, which arose out of the Non-Intercourse Act of 1809.[36] The act forbid trade with France and Great Britain by authorizing the president to suspend its provisions when in his judgment certain events had taken place and to revive the restrictions when other events had occurred. The Court upheld the delegation, claiming that Congress should have the right to exercise such discretion. Thereafter, the Court expanded the second type of delegation. The Court's typical view is summarized in a 1904 case, *Butterfield* v. *Stanahan*, in which the justices examined a law calling for the regulation of imported teas, which required the executive to fix uniform standards for the products. Justice Edward D. White, delivering the opinion of the Court, wrote:

Congress legislated on the subjects as far as was reasonably practicable, and from the necessities of the case was compelled to leave to executive officials the duty of bringing about the result pointed out by the statute. To deny the power of Congress to delegate such a duty would, in effect, amount but to declaring that the plenary power vested in Congress to regulate foreign commerce could not be efficaciously exercised.[37]

In short, the Court typically acquiesces to Congress's decision about whether it is necessary to delegate its authority.

In attempts to control the power it has delegated to the executive, Congress has fashioned the "legislative veto." By means of this device Congress may disapprove of executive orders or regulations designed to enforce legislation. In the most typical instance, Congress requires that the proposed executive action lie before Congress for a specified period of time. If, during the time period, either house disapproves the measure, it is void.

The Supreme Court held the legislative veto unconstitutional in *U.S. Immigration and Naturalization Service* v. *Chadha* in 1983. It stated that such a legislative veto nullified the proper constitutional procedures of a presidential veto and override and thereby violated separation of powers.[38] Similarly, the Court negated a portion of the Balanced Budget and Emergency Control Act of 1985 (the Gramm-Rudman-Hollings Act). The act required the comptroller general to report his estimates of the budget deficit and necessary spending cuts to the president. If Congress failed to act, the president was required to do so. The Court objected to what it saw as a legislative officer reporting to and ultimately directing the president. Even though the president appointed the comptroller general, the person could be removed only by both the president and the Senate. "To permit an officer controlled by Congress to execute the laws," the Court declared in *Bowsher* v. *Synar* (1986), "would be, in essence, to permit a congressional veto."[39]

Supreme Court rulings against the legislative veto have done little, however, to eliminate them as statutory and informal devices. In the year immediately following the *Chadha* case, Congress placed fifty-three legislative vetoes into bills that President Reagan signed. In addition, it has become a frequently invoked informal device whereby committees permit an executive agency to do something so long as the agency seeks committee approval first. This practice usually gives the agency what it wants—flexibility—and the committee what it wants—control.[40] So the Court's restriction has been less than meets the eye.

The Court and the Single Executive Image

In the areas of foreign relations, military affairs, executive action, and legislative delegation, the Supreme Court has provided three types of sweeping statements about presidents' powers. One declares that the president acts alone. The Court's pronouncements on the sole-organ doctrine, the commander-in-chief clause, and executive action against domestic insurrection all place the president singularly in charge. A second statement provides that presidents have inherent executive powers. Again in foreign, military, and executive action, the Court holds that there is an unspecified executive power that is not limited to the language of the Constitution or the law. It has allowed presidents to fill in the blank. A final statement proclaims that presidents have broad discretion in exercising power. Notably in the area of legislative delegation, the Court permits the president virtually free rein once Congress has delegated the authority. Each statement is a loud and clear message about the single executive image. The Supreme Court offers a constitutional rationale for the president's efforts to act powerfully and autonomously.

COURT REBUFFS OF PRESIDENTIAL ACTION

Does the Supreme Court exercise any effective check on the president? The Court generally upholds presidential action but has taken presidents to task in three areas: military affairs, domestic executive action, and legislative delegation of power. Table 15.1 summarizes all Supreme Court rulings against presidents from 1789 to 1984. In

Table 15.1 Supreme Court Rulings Against Presidents, 1789–1984

President	Number of decisions
Jefferson	2
Madison	3
Monroe	1
Tyler	1
Fillmore	1
Lincoln	5
A. Johnson	2
Hayes	1
Garfield	0
Arthur	2
Cleveland	1
Wilson	2
Harding	2
Coolidge	3
Hoover	1
F. D. Roosevelt	8
Truman	3
Eisenhower	3
L. Johnson	2
Nixon	25
Ford	3
Carter	2
Reagan	0
	Total 73

Source: Michael A. Genovese, *The Supreme Court, the Constitution and Presidential Power* (Lanham, Md.: University Press of America, 1980), 264. Used by permission.

only seventy-three instances have presidents been rebuffed by the Court.

Military Affairs

The Court's efforts to constrain presidential action in wartime have been limited to the home front. President Lincoln suspended the writ of habeas corpus along military lines between New York and Washington. The writ requires the government to make known the charges against an individual being detained or imprisoned. In 1861, the military arrested Merryman, a prominent citizen of Baltimore, for aiding the enemy and imprisoned him at Fort McHenry. He obtained a writ of habeas corpus from Chief Justice Roger Taney, who claimed that under the Constitution only Congress could suspend the writ. According to Taney, writing an opinion from the circuit bench in *Ex parte Merryman,* the president's only power was to "take care that [the laws] be faithfully carried into execution as they are expounded and adjudged by the co-ordinate branch of the government to which that duty is assigned by the Constitution"—namely, the judiciary.[41]

Lincoln responded like Jackson with the doctrine of coordinate review. He maintained that "the executive was not subordinate to the judicial power, but was one of the three coordinate departments of government." Indeed, the executive was "the most active of all," "the most constantly in action," and "while the other departments were sworn to support the Constitution, the president was sworn to preserve, protect, and defend it."[42] Ignoring the Court, Lincoln proclaimed a far more sweeping suspension of the writ than the Court had just struck down. Congress did not authorize a suspension of the writ until March 1863. Lincoln's actions reveal limits to the Court's ability to enforce its way on an unwilling branch. In a showdown between a president exercising the power of the sword and a court determined to block its exercise, the president decidedly has the upper hand.

The Court faced similar issues in 1864 on the question of whether, as commander in chief, the president had the authority to establish special military tribunals across the country to try suspected spies. Lambdin P. Milligan was tried, convicted, and sentenced to be hanged as a spy by a military commander in Indianapolis. The Court declared in *Ex parte Milligan* that the president's power during war was not absolute. Martial law could not be declared in areas remote from actual warfare. Martial law, the Court observed, "could never exist where the Courts are open" but had to be "confined to the locality of the actual war."[43] The Court thus challenged Lincoln's actions after the war was over and Lincoln himself had been shot dead. The precedent stands for future presidents, but it has not been raised again.

In 1952, the Court ruled that the Truman administration lacked the authority to take over the nation's steel mills to avert a steelworkers strike during the Korean War. In seizing the mills, Truman relied on the doctrine of inherent powers, drawing on the commander-in-chief and the "take care that the law be faithfully executed" clauses of the Constitution. Truman said, "The President of the United States has very great inherent powers to meet great national emergencies." "I feel sure," Truman told a press conference , "that the Constitution does not require me to endanger our national safety by letting all the steel mills shut down."[44] The Court disagreed by a 6 to 3 vote, but with seven separate opinions.

The Court rejected the president's claim of inherent power in *Youngstown Sheet and Tube Co.* v. *Sawyer.* Justice Hugo L. Black, writing the opinion of the Court, argued that Truman's actions constituted a de facto statute and the Constitution did not provide presidents such lawmaking power.[45] Four of the six justices in the majority concluded that existing congressional guidelines pre-empted Truman's specific action. They emphasized that Congress had expressly rejected seizure as a method of settling labor disputes when it passed the Taft-Hartley Act. In addition, the Congress also had provided for limited seizure of private property in the Selective Service Act of 1948, though Truman chose not to act on this ground. The other two justices in the majority (Justices Black and William O. Douglas) wrote that the president had no power to seize private property even in an emergency.

The Court was most caustic about the view that the commander-in-chief clause conferred domestic powers on presidents. Justice Black wrote solemnly, "We cannot with faithfulness to our constitutional system hold that the commander-in-chief has the ultimate power as such to take possession of private property in order to keep labor disputes from stopping production. This is a job for the Nation's lawmakers, not for its military authorities."[46] Justice Robert H. Jackson, concurring in a separate opinion, said that the commander-in-chief clause did not permit the president to become "commander-in-chief of the country, its industries, and its inhabitants. . . . No doctrine [is] more sinister and alarming than that a president whose conduct of foreign affairs is so largely uncontrolled, and often even unknown, can vastly enlarge his mastery over the internal affairs of the country."[47]

Domestic Executive Action

The Supreme Court perhaps has been most willing to restrict presidential claims of unbridled law enforcement. Not only did the Court narrow President Nixon's claim of unlimited executive privilege in *U.S.* v. *Nixon*, but it also has restricted presidential attempts to seek injunctions, wiretaps, and the impoundment of funds.

Injunctions and Wiretaps. The Court has narrowed the president's claim of inherent power to seek injunctions without statutory authorization. In *New York Times* v. *United States,* the Court rejected the Nixon administration's claim that the president had an inherent constitutional authority to "protect the nation against publication of information whose disclosure would endanger the national security."[48] The case arose after the *New York Times* published a purloined copy of an official, secret Defense Department account of the Vietnam War—the *Pentagon Papers.* The Court held that the president's attempt at "prior restraint" (censorship before publication) violated constitutional protections of freedom of speech. Likewise in *U.S.* v. *U.S. District Court for the Eastern District of Michigan,* the Court decided that warrantless electronic surveillance ordered by President Nixon of a person accused of bombing a CIA office in Ann Arbor, Michigan, violated the person's constitutional rights.[49]

Impoundment. Impoundment is a refusal to spend appropriated funds or a decision to defer temporarily the spending of such funds. President Nixon claimed "the constitutional right for a president of the United States to impound funds and that is not to spend money, when the spending of money would mean either increasing prices or increasing taxes for all the people." According to Nixon, the president's duty to faithfully execute the laws meant he should not spend appropriated funds that would create inflationary pressures. By Nixon's interpretation, the president faithfully executes the laws of Congress by not spending money that Congress appropriates. "That right," Nixon asserted "is absolutely clear."[50] The Court disagreed with Nixon, finding the right murky at best. In *Train* v. *City of New York* the Court decided that the president had no discretion to withhold the funds.[51] Subsequently, Congress passed the Budget and Impoundment Control Act of 1974, which gave Congress the ability to oversee presidential impoundments.

Legislative Delegation of Power

It took almost a century and a half before the Supreme Court found an instance in which the Congress delegated unconstitutionally the essence of its legislative power. The most serious effort the Court has ever made to affect presidential and congressional action was against New Deal legislation. By late 1936, the Court had declared unconstitutional nine of the sixteen laws that were at the heart of the New Deal. The Court ruled in two key cases, *Panama Refining Co.* v. *Ryan* and *Schechter Poultry Company* v. *United States,* both decided in 1935, that Congress had delegated too much power to the president without setting standards for how the president should enforce the legislation. Congress had authorized the president to prohibit the shipment in interstate commerce of "hot oil"—oil produced in excess of state production quotas. The statute was silent on the circumstances under which the president should exercise the power. This authorization, the Court said in the *Panama* decision, gave the president too much discretion.[52] In the *Schechter* case, the Court struck down the National Industrial Recovery Act, which delegated to the executive the power to formulate codes of fair competition for all industries. The Court again said that Congress had provided no standards for executive action, thus leaving the president with "virtually unfettered" discretion for "enacting laws for the government."[53]

Although at the time the *Panama* and *Schechter* cases placed the Court on a collision course with the president and Congress, in subsequent cases the Court upheld delegations of authority. As Edward Corwin notes, "Neither of these precedents materially influenced congressional policy even at the time, and both have been subsequently relegated by the Court to its increasingly crowded cabinet of judicial curiosities."[54] Since then the Court has only rarely discovered instances of improper delegation, and Congress has kept right on delegating power to the president on an even larger scale and at a faster pace than before. Today the Court often upholds such congressional standards as "the public interest" or the "public convenience, interest, or necessity" as sufficient to permit delegation of authority to the president.[55]

Holding Presidents Accountable

Cases in the areas of military power, executive action, and legislative delegation reveal the Supreme Court's attempt to place some restrictions on presidential discretion. Although the Court has acknowledged an inherent executive power, it sees a difference between an inherent power and an unlimited one. In its efforts to hold presidents accountable to the Constitution, the Court has in effect built a fence around the area in which presidents are allowed to roam. Nonetheless, the fenced-off area is vast, and the fence itself is one that presidents can jump over with relative ease. The Court today is not particularly worried about presidents acting on powers delegated by Congress. It views this issue as an ingredient of separation of powers to be decided by the two coordinate branches. The Court is more worried about protecting citizens' rights infringed by unilateral executive action.

Although nearly ninety years separated the Court's decisions on Lincoln's declarations of martial law and Truman's seizure of steel mills, the decisions held one strong point in common: the Court is willing to chastise the president's excessive use of domestic authority in wartime. It is not, however, likely to touch the president's authority to run the war itself. The Court has been most insistent on fighting presidents' infringement on the activities of the other branches— injunctions and wiretappings (infringement on the courts) and impoundment (infringement on Congress). However, presidents do not resort to these actions frequently; so the Court places some limits on presidents and their development of the single executive image, but the limits do not dramatically curb presidents or alter the configuration of the image.

PRESIDENTIAL INFLUENCE ON THE JUDICIARY

While the courts have helped establish the parameters of presidential activism and, hence, the single executive image, the plural presidency has influenced the operations of the judiciary in three ways: (1) influence over court dockets, (2) enforcement of judicial decisions, and (3) White House selection of judicial nominees.

Court Dockets

The plural presidency has some ability to influence what cases the courts hear through the Office of Solicitor General in the Justice Department. The solicitor general is a presidential appointee who supervises the litigation of the executive branch. Put simply, the solicitor general is the lawyer for the executive branch.

When the government is a party to a lawsuit, the solicitor general or another lawyer from the solicitor general's office represents the government in court. The office decides which of the cases lost by the government will be appealed to the next highest court, including the Supreme Court. Although the Supreme Court controls the cases it hears (in contrast to the appeals courts, which must take cases that are properly appealed to them), the Supreme Court is more likely to accept cases filed by the solicitor general's office than by any other party. In recent years, the federal government has been a party to about half of the cases heard before the federal courts of appeals and the Supreme Court.[56] It has had a high success rate in these cases. From 1970 to 1990, the United States won 64 percent of its cases before the Supreme Court.[57]

The solicitor general's office also participates in cases to which it is not directly a party. The solicitor general files *amicus curiae* (friend of the court) briefs supporting or opposing the positions of other parties before the Supreme Court. The use of these briefs has increased dramatically since World War II. The government has filed *amicus curiae* briefs on such matters as school busing to end racial segregation, school prayer, abortion, reapportionment, and job discrimination against women. The Court usually allows the solicitor general to file these briefs. Through its direct cases and its *amicus* briefs, then, the solicitor general's office has a good deal to say about setting the agenda for federal appeals courts and the Supreme Court.

The solicitor general's office has been able to develop a fairly close working relationship with the Supreme Court. The office regulating the number of cases that it brings before the bench. If the solicitor general files too many cases before the Court, the Court is likely to respond by denying some of the government's petitions to be heard, and the solicitor general then will cut back on petitions. If the rejection rate goes down, the solicitor general's office may increase activity.[58]

The solicitor general's office has more expertise in dealing with the Court than do other litigants. The office attempts to anticipate the reactions of the Court by deciding which cases to bring and which arguments to make. Many of the attorneys in the solicitor general's office know how individual justices will react to certain arguments and think they know how the justices might vote.[59] Historically, there has been an overlap between the ideological outlook of the solicitor general's office and that of the Court. The liberal Warren court worked with liberal solicitor generals; the conservative Burger and Rehnquist courts worked with conservative solicitor generals.

The solicitor general's office is a fairly independent part of the plural presidency, but it is not immune from influence from other parts of the decentralized organization, including the president. For instance, Truman and Eisenhower, presidential staff members, and the solicitor general kept in close contact. In several cases, the White House actively lobbied the solicitor general to take a particular case to court or handle a brief in a specific way.[60] Thus, through the solicitor general's office, the presidency has an avenue of influence to the courts, especially the Supreme Court.

Enforcement of Court Decisions

Courts, as Hamilton noted, have the power of neither the sword nor the purse. They are highly constrained in the ways they can enforce the decisions they hand down. Under the system of separation of power, the courts must depend on the executive for such enforcement. Typically, presidents have responded to support the courts or at least the rule of law. But the degree to which a particular court decision is enforced is determined within the plural presidency. When, for example, the Supreme Court issued a ruling in 1971 calling for court-ordered busing to achieve racial balance in schools, the Nixon administration took efforts to narrow the extent of busing. Various strategy sessions in the Justice Department and at the White House produced guidelines for busing. In another instance, the Reagan and Bush administrations placed administrative restrictions on women's rights to an abortion as defined by the Supreme Court in *Roe* v. *Wade* (1973). The Reagan administration banned members of the armed forces from abortions on military bases and also ended federal assistance for abortions for poor women. The Reagan administration policy on military bases was made in the plural presidency amid negotiations and debate among officials in the Justice Department, the Defense Department, the Office of Policy Development, and the White House chief of staff's office, all of which fashioned the eventual policy. Thus, the plural presidency has some degree of administrative discretion that it may use to aggressively enforce a court decision or more narrowly restrict its impact.

White House Selection of Judicial Nominees

When presidents leave office, their advisers, cabinet officers, and many ambassadors leave with them. But more than several hundred people stay behind—the federal court judges the presidents have appointed. Presidents often view judges as instruments of presidential power. Presidents select judges with the idea that they will be among the truly faithful, willing to uphold the presidents' own views of the Constitution and the role of government. They also hope that the judges' decisions will be part of the presidents' legacy, because for years to come the courts will reflect their administrations' overall legal philosophy.

The judiciary, however, like the presidency, is an institution with multiple layers and its own set of rules. It does not necessarily behave in the way presidents want. Too, the process of judicial appointment is controlled less by presidents than they might like. In the ninety-five federal district courts, there are 525 judges. The thirteen courts of appeals or circuit courts have a corps of 159 full-time judges. With fifty or more judicial vacancies to fill a year, presidents may see judges as vehicles for achieving key legal policy goals, but presidents increasingly find characteristics of the plural presidency complicating the appointment process. Especially relevant to judicial appointments are ambiguous decision making, group fragmentation, and the decentralized organization. Often nominees emerge from ambiguous decision-making processes within the decentralized organization of the White House. Groups from around the country may demand a significant say in whom presidents will appoint, especially to the Supreme Court. Rather than involving the president personally, the decision is likely to involve institutional machinations.

Supreme Court Nominees.   Since 1789, presidents have nominated 131 people to be Supreme Court justices. The Senate has confirmed the appointments of 110 justices or roughly 84 percent of the presidential nominees. Table 15.2 shows the nominations that ran into trouble during the Senate confirmation process. Rejection was higher in the nineteenth than in the twentieth century: the Senate rejected one out of three nominees in the earlier period; one of ten in the later. There is little way of telling how many appointments a president will be able to make, as shown in Table 15.3. Jimmy Carter made no appointment during his term—the only full-term president in history to be denied the chance. By contrast, William Howard Taft, also a

Table 15.2 Supreme Court Nominees with Senate Problems

President	Nominee	Action
Washington		
1793	William Paterson	Withdrawn
1795	John Rutledge	Rejected
Madison		
1811	Alexander Wolcott	Rejected
John Adams		
1828	John J. Critinden	Postponed
Jackson		
1835	Roger B. Taney	Postponed
Tyler		
1844	John C. Spencer	Rejected
1844	R. H. Walworth	Withdrawn
1844	Edward B. King	Withdrawn
1844	R. H. Walworth	Withdrawn
1845	John M. Read	Postponed
Polk		
1846	G. W. Woodward	Rejected
Fillmore		
1852	Edward A. Bradford	Postponed
1853	George E. Badger	Postponed
1853	William C. Micou	Postponed
Buchanan		
1861	Jeremiah S. Black	Rejected
A. Johnson		
1866	Henry Stanbery	Postponed
Grant		
1870	Ebenezer R. Hoar	Rejected
1874	George H. Williams	Withdrawn
1874	Caleb Cushing	Withdrawn
Hayes		
1881	Stanley Mattheys	Postponed
Cleveland		
1894	W. B. Hornblower	Rejected
1894	W. H. Peckham	Rejected
Hoover		
1930	John J. Parker	Rejected
L. Johnson		
1968	Abe Fortas[1]	Withdrawn
1968	Homer Thornberry	Withdrawn
Nixon		
1969	Clement F. Haynsworth	Rejected
1970	G. Harrold Carswell	Rejected
Reagan		
1987	Robert H. Bork	Rejected
1987	Douglas H. Ginsburg	Withdrawn

1. Associate justice nominated for chief justice.
Source: Gary King and Lyn Ragsdale, *The Elusive Executive* (Washington, D.C.: CQ Press, 1988), 233–234. Copyright © 1988. Used by permission of CQ Press.

Table 15.3 Number of Presidential Appointments of U.S. Supreme Court Justices Who Actually Served on the Court

President	Dates in office	Number of appointments
Washington	1789–1797	10
J. Adams	1797–1801	3
Jefferson	1801–1809	3
Madison	1809–1817	2
Monroe	1817–1825	1
J. Q. Adams	1825–1829	1
Jackson	1829–1837	6 (5)[1]
Van Buren	1837–1841	2 (3)[1]
W. H. Harrison	1841	0
Tyler	1841–1845	1
Polk	1845–1849	2
Taylor	1849–1850	0
Fillmore	1850–1853	1
Pierce	1853–1857	1
Buchanan	1857–1861	1
Lincoln	1861–1865	5
A. Johnson	1865–1869	0
Grant	1869–1877	4
Hayes	1877–1881	2
Garfield	1881	1
Arthur	1881–1885	2
Cleveland	1885–1889; 1893–1897	4[2]
B. Harrison	1889–1893	4
McKinley	1897–1901	1
T. Roosevelt	1901–1909	3
Taft	1909–1913	6
Wilson	1913–1921	3
Harding	1921–1923	4
Coolidge	1923–1929	1
Hoover	1929–1933	3
F. D. Roosevelt	1933–1945	9
Truman	1945–1953	4
Eisenhower	1953–1961	5
Kennedy	1961–1963	2
L. B. Johnson	1963–1969	2
Nixon	1969–1974	4
Ford	1974–1977	1
Carter	1977–1981	0
Reagan	1981–1989	4
Bush	1989–1993	2
		Total 110

1. Jackson had nominated Catron, but the latter was not confirmed until Van Buren had taken over.
2. Two in each of his two terms, which split by Harrison's single term.

Source: From *The Judicial Process: An Introductory Analysis of the Courts of the United States, England, and France,* "Fifth Edition," by Henry J. Abraham, 55. Copyright © 1962, 1968, 1975, 1980, 1986 by Henry J. Abraham. Reprinted by permission of Oxford University Press, Inc. Updated by the author.

one-term president, appointed six justices. Presidents average one appointment every twenty-two months.

Presidents have far greater control over selecting Supreme Court justices than they have over selecting lower court judges. Presidents are more likely to know their Supreme Court nominees personally or at least have some firsthand information about them. Franklin Roosevelt, Truman, Kennedy, and Johnson had personal associations with nearly every Supreme Court nominee they submitted to the Senate.[61] Nixon, Reagan, and Bush were more concerned with the ideological credentials of the candidates—desiring to place strict conservatives on the Court—and were less likely to know the nominees personally. Even when presidents do know their nominees, the plural presidency has a hand in the decision. The candidates face lengthy background checks, interviews, and analyses of their writings. Although most of these checks originate in the Justice Department, they often become decentralized across various White House offices, including the Office of the White House Chief Counsel (the White House lawyer), the White House personnel office, and in some cases the office of the chief of staff.

Often, as with the Ginsburg nomination, discussed at the beginning of the chapter, signals from within the administration about who should be nominated or how the nomination will play out in the Senate are ambiguous. In a political deal during the 1952 presidential campaign, Dwight Eisenhower promised the first opening on the Supreme Court to Governor Earl Warren for delivering California to the Republican ticket. The first opening turned out to be the chief justiceship, which Eisenhower did not wish to give to Warren. Debate ensued within the administration about how Warren could be placated and who else could be nominated as chief justice. After several sets of signals emanated from the White House, Warren pressured Eisenhower to honor the deal and Eisenhower capitulated. Later, Eisenhower expressed his displeasure at the liberal decisions of Warren and another one of his appointees, William Brennan. Asked whether he had ever made any mistakes as president, Eisenhower replied, "Yes, two, and they are both sitting on the Supreme Court."[62]

Presidents submit their candidates not only to the Senate for approval but in a significant sense to the legal community and to the public at large. In accommodating the group fragmentation of the plural presidency, presidents consider representational qualifications in making their Supreme Court nominations. This representation, which involves the extent to which a nominee can be identified with a significant portion of the American public, is both descriptive and doctrinal. Relevant attributes include political party, region of the country, religion, and ethnicity. Presidents consider political party an important qualification in part because it is a good indicator of how close a nominee's views will be to those of the president. Few cross-party nominations are made; they are made when the president feels that he would face difficulty in the Senate or seeks national unity.

Presidents, especially in the nineteenth century, sought sectional balance on the Supreme Court. Washington commented on his appointment of North Carolinian James Iredell to the Court in 1790 that no one from North Carolina had yet received a judicial appointment. Lincoln expressed dismay upon filling two "southern vacancies," created at the start of the Civil War, with northerners. Franklin Roosevelt told Wiley Rutledge of Iowa upon his nomination to the Court that "we had a number of candidates for the Court who were highly qualified, but they didn't have geography—you have that."[63]

A rise in religious, ethnic, and gender qualifications has accompanied the decline in sectionalism. Observers refer to a "Catholic seat," a "Jewish seat," a "black seat," and most recently a "woman's seat." Since William McKinley's appointment of Joseph McKenna in 1898, there has been a Roman Catholic sitting on the bench almost continuously. Woodrow Wilson appointed the first Jew to the Court—Louis Brandeis. His appointment in 1916 was followed by Benjamin Cardozo (Hoover, 1932), Felix Frankfurter (Roosevelt, 1938), Arthur Goldberg (Kennedy, 1963), and Abe Fortas (Johnson, 1965). Since then, however, no members of the Jewish faith have been appointed to the Court. Indeed, some observers commented that when President Reagan nominated the first woman to sit on the Supreme Court —Sandra Day O'Connor—a woman's seat replaced the Jewish seat. George Bush continued to reserve a seat for a black jurist when he nominated conservative Clarence Thomas to replace liberal civil rights advocate Justice Thurgood Marshall, the first African American appointed to the Supreme Court. Despite presidential attempts at diversity, most members of the Court are white, Anglo-Saxon, Protestant males from upper-middle-class backgrounds.

Representational qualifications also place the nominations of justices in the thick of group fragmentation. Organized campaigns, both for and against nominees, have preceded many appointments to the Court. Although the justiceships are appointive positions, many interest groups and active citizens work to elect or defeat the nominee. At the simplest level, letter-writing campaigns are orchestrated on behalf of many of the top names. A study of the appointment of Pierce Butler to the Supreme Court in 1922 revealed the names of some fifty people who wrote President Harding in support of the candidate during the forty-four days the seat was vacant.[64] Much more elaborate national campaigns for and against nominees have characterized several recent nominations.

Organizations attempt to influence the Senate confirmation process by publicly endorsing or rejecting the nominee, conducting letter-writing campaigns to pertinent senators, airing television commercials, and appearing as witnesses during the confirmation hearings. The National Association for the Advancement of Colored People (NAACP) and the National Organization for Women (NOW) led the opposition to President Reagan's ill-fated nomination of Robert Bork and President Bush's fiercely contested nomination of Clarence Thomas. Many other African American, women's, Hispanic, and labor organizations spoke out against the Thomas nomination, especially after charges of sexual harassment surfaced against the judge. Presidents must take into account this group diversity in developing their strategies to push a particular nominee.

Presidents have varied greatly in the extent to which they uphold doctrinal requirements for prospective justices. Some presidents have appeared to be completely disinterested in the differences between their own policy views and those of their nominees. Republican Herbert Hoover selected well-known liberal Democrat Benjamin Cardozo in 1932. At the other extreme, President Ulysses S. Grant selected two justices in order to influence the outcome of a case before the Court. In 1870, a divided Supreme Court handed down a decision prohibiting paper money as legal tender. Grant, who believed in paper money, chose his nominees accordingly. Once they were confirmed, he had the government ask the Court to reconsider the decision. It did so and reversed its earlier ruling.[65]

Generally, presidents are most likely to judge the policy stands of prospective justices under three conditions:

1. Controversy over important issues is highly salient among well-organized groups.

2. The president has stated a position on a salient issue.

3. The Supreme Court's position on an issue is uncertain or hostile.

Lincoln sought justices who were strongly pro-Union. Franklin Roosevelt anxiously placed trusted New Dealers on the Court to shift the balance away from justices who had overturned major New Deal legislation. Reagan, though reticent to confront Congress on the issue of abortion, applied a litmus test of opposition to abortion to his appointees to the Court.

Lower Court Judges. The decentralized organization of the plural presidency is most evident in presidents' appointment of lower court judges. Presidents do not know the qualifications of the great majority of serious candidates for lower federal judgeships, nor do they have time to find out. The backgrounds of district court judges and appeals court judges have been very similar under five presidents from Johnson to Reagan.[66] Although President Carter succeeded in appointing more blacks and women than other presidents, as Tables 15.4 and 15.5 show, in all other respects the Carter appointees looked much like each other and much like those of earlier presidents. Presi-

Table 15.4 Characteristics of District Court Appointees (percentage)

Characteristics	Johnson	Nixon	Ford	Carter	Reagan
Race					
White	93.4%	95.5%	88.5%	78.7%	93.0%
Black	4.1	3.4	5.8	13.9	0.8
Hispanic	2.5	1.1	1.9	6.9	5.4
Asian	—	—	3.9	0.5	0.8
Sex					
Male	98.4	99.4	98.1	85.6	90.7
Female	1.6	0.6	1.9	14.4	9.3
Religious background					
Protestant	58.2	73.2	73.1	60.4	61.2
Catholic	31.1	18.4	17.3	27.2	31.8
Jewish	10.7	8.4	9.6	12.4	6.9
Party					
Democratic	94.3	7.2	21.2	94.1	3.3
Republican	5.7	92.8	78.8	4.5	96.9
Independent	—	—	—	1.5	—
Law school education					
Public institution	40.2	41.9	44.2	50.5	34.1
Private (non-Ivy)	36.9	36.9	38.5	32.2	49.6
Ivy League	21.3	21.2	17.3	17.3	16.3
Experience					
Judicial	34.3	35.1	42.3	54.5	50.4
Prosecutorial	45.8	41.9	50.0	38.6	43.4
Neither	33.6	36.3	30.8	28.2	28.7
Occupation					
Politics/government	21.3	10.6	21.2	4.4	7.8
Judiciary	31.1	28.5	34.6	44.6	40.3
Law firm	44.3	58.2	44.3	47.7	52.0
Professor of law	3.3	2.8	—	3.0	2.3
Other	—	—	—	0.5	1.6
Total appointees	122	179	52	202	129

Source: Gary King and Lyn Ragsdale, *The Elusive Executive* (Washington, D.C.: CQ Press, 1988), 238. Adapted from Sheldon Goldman, "Reaganizing the Judiciary: The First Term Appointments," *Judicature* 68 (April–May 1985): 318–319. Copyright © 1988. Used by permission of CQ Press.

dents rely on the White House institution and the Justice Department to evaluate the candidates, make recommendations, and see that the eventual nominees are confirmed by the Senate. Of equal importance is the tradition of "senatorial courtesy," which especially influences the appointment of district court judges. Based on an informal reciprocal arrangement among senators, senatorial courtesy allows senators of the president's party from the state where the district court vacancy occurs to sponsor a candidate and to veto candidates they

Table 15.5 Characteristics of Circuit Court Appointees (percentage)

Characteristics	Johnson	Nixon	Ford	Carter	Reagan
Race					
White	95.0%	97.8%	100.0%	78.6%	93.5%
Black	5.0	—	—	16.1	3.2
Hispanic	—	—	—	3.6	3.2
Asian	—	2.2	—	1.8	—
Sex					
Male	97.5	100.0	100.0	80.4	96.8
Female	2.5	—	—	19.6	3.2
Religious background					
Protestant	60.0	75.6	58.3	60.7	67.7
Catholic	25.0	15.6	33.3	23.7	22.6
Jewish	15.7	8.9	8.3	16.1	9.7
Party					
Democratic	95.0	6.7	8.3	89.3	—
Republican	5.0	93.3	91.7	5.4	100.0
Independent	—	—	—	5.4	—
Law school education					
Public institution	40.0	37.8	50.0	39.3	29.0
Private (non-Ivy)	32.5	26.7	25.0	19.6	45.2
Ivy League	27.5	35.6	25.0	41.1	25.8
Experience					
Judicial	65.0	57.8	75.0	53.6	70.9
Prosecutorial	47.5	46.7	25.0	32.1	19.3
Neither	20.0	17.8	25.0	37.5	25.8
Occupation					
Politics/government	10.0	4.4	8.3	5.4	3.2
Judiciary	57.5	53.3	75.0	46.4	61.3
Law firm	30.0	35.5	16.6	32.3	19.4
Professor of law	—	6.7	—	14.3	16.1
Other	—	—	—	1.8	—
Total appointees	40	45	12	56	31

Source: Gary King and Lyn Ragsdale, *The Elusive Executive* (Washington, D.C.: CQ Press, 1988), 239. Adapted from Sheldon Goldman, "Reaganizing the Judiciary: The First Term Appointments," *Judicature* 68 (April–May 1985): 324–325. Copyright © 1988. Used by permission of CQ Press.

do not like. Other senators go along, knowing that they will have an appointment coming up at some point.

Presidents Carter and Reagan sought to alter the role of senators in the judicial selection process. Carter agreed that senators would continue to sponsor district court judges but decided that a special United States Circuit Judge Nominating Commission with thirteen panels (one for each circuit) would handle appellate court nominations. Each panel consisted of laypeople and lawyers who reviewed applications and interviewed possible nominees. They then recommended to Carter from three to five names.

Reagan abolished the commission and turned over the nomination process to a White House Judicial Selection Committee, which decided whom the president should nominate on the basis of recommendations from the Office of Legal Policy in the Justice Department.[67] The White House Selection Committee consisted of the attorney general, the deputy attorney general, the counsel to the president, several assistant attorneys general, and other White House advisers, including the chief of staff. This change institutionalized the appointment process in the White House. It not only afforded the Reagan White House a chance to screen for the policy and ideological beliefs of potential judges but also permitted greater ability to defend the White House against senatorial courtesy. The Selection Committee arranged for day-long interviews with Justice Department officials and placed the candidates' written record, including articles and opinions, into a computer data bank.[68] Although some people criticized the screening process as too heavily reliant on doctrinal qualifications rather than other qualifications, one administration official summed up the White House position: "A president who fails to scrutinize the legal philosophy of federal judicial nominees courts frustration of his own policy agenda."[69]

The White House Judicial Selection Committee fits a pattern within the plural presidency. The president's interest in judicial appointments brings them into the White House. However, the sheer volume of such appointments makes it difficult for the president to preside over the screening process. An office that allows greater control of appointments from the White House is set up, but there is no more control by the president (the new office is similar to the personnel office that handles other White House appointments). The Bush administration has kept the committee. Thus, a new organizational component is added to the plural presidency.

CONCLUSION

Justice Robert H. Jackson, in his concurring opinion in the *Youngstown* steel seizure case, provided a classic analysis of presidential power. Jackson distinguished among three levels of power. On the first level, the president acts in accordance with the expressed or implied authorization of Congress. Here, Jackson asserted, the president's "authority is at its maximum." When the executive and legislature act together, they should be accorded "the widest latitude of judicial interpretation." The second level is a "zone of twilight" where the president and Congress share authority or the distribution of authority is uncertain. On this level, "congressional inertia, indifference, or quiescence may sometimes, at least as a practical matter, enable, if not invite, measures of independent presidential responsibility." The judiciary's acceptance of these presidential actions depends on "the imperatives of the events and contemporary imponderables" rather than on abstract theories of law. In this zone, presidents exercise inherent executive power. On the third level, in which Jackson included *Youngstown*, the president undertakes measures "incompatible with the expressed or implied will of Congress." Here, said Jackson, the president's power was "at its lowest ebb."[70]

Jackson's comments summarize the Supreme Court's approach to presidential power. On the first two levels, the Court has helped craft a singularly powerful executive office. On the third level, the Court has defined some, though not many, things that are incompatible with the will of Congress. At all three levels, the Court has given great weight to presidents' own interpretations of their power. At these levels, too, the single executive image emerges. The Court's acknowledgment of lone action, inherent executive power, stewardship, and discretion helps give presidents the single executive image as a resource. Although in the day-to-day political decisions of presidents the Court may appear more remote from the presidency than does Congress or the bureaucracy, the Court has been instrumental in providing presidents the power to conduct these daily affairs with the other branches of government. The judiciary thus helps give presidents the single executive image as a resource. Presidents can further embolden the single executive image by means of the power granted in the Court's precedents.

The presidency influences the decisions of the judiciary through agenda setting, enforcement, and the selection of judges and justices. In those cases in which the administration wishes to take a firm stand, the president relies on the Office of the Solicitor General to know the mood of the court. The plural presidency also monitors court decisions and decides how much enforcement effort will be brought to bear. In their court nominations, presidents rely on the decentralized organization and its often ambiguous decision processes. The plural presidency has become increasingly sensitive to the demands of groups about who should be appointed. Ironically, the powers that the Supreme Court has acknowledged for presidents dictate that the plural presidency be in place. Presidents cannot without help conduct the affairs of state, enter wars, maintain domestic stability, seek the removal of executive officials, and issue orders under a delegation of power from Congress. The plural institution that assists presidents in working with the judiciary results from the expression of singular power that the Court has granted presidents. ■

FURTHER READING

On presidential-court relations, see: Glendon Schubert, *The Presidency in the Courts* (Minneapolis: University of Minnesota Press, 1957); Robert Scigliano, *The Supreme Court and the Presidency* (New York: Free Press, 1971); Michael Genovese, *The Supreme Court, the Constitution, and Presidential Power* (Lanham, Md.: University Press of America, 1980). On Supreme Court decisions on the presidency, see Johnny Killian, ed. *The Constitution of the United States of America* (Washington, D.C.: U.S. Government Printing Office, 1987). On presidential court appointments, see: Henry Abraham, *Justices and Presidents: A Political History of Appointments of the Supreme Court*, 2d ed. (New York: Oxford University Press, 1985); David Danelski, *A Supreme Court Justice Is Appointed* (New York: Random House, 1964); Sheldon Goldman, "Reaganizing the Judiciary: The First Term Appointments," *Judicature* 68 (April–May 1985): 313–329.

NOTES

1. Eight members of the Supreme Court heard the case. Justice William Rehnquist excused himself from the case because he had served as an assistant attorney general in the Nixon administration. The account of the Court's deliberations is found in Bob Woodward and Carl Bernstein, *The Final Days* (New York: Avon, 1976), 283–284.
2. *U.S.* v. *Nixon*, 418 U.S. 683 (1974).
3. Woodward and Bernstein, 287.
4. Ibid., 304–305.
5. "If at First You Don't Succeed, . . ." *Time*, November 9, 1987, 50.
6. "Spoiling for a Second Round," *Newsweek*, November 9, 1987, 42–46.
7. "Sins of the Past," *Time*, November 16, 1987, 18–20.
8. Alexander Hamilton, James Madison, and John Jay, *The Federalist Papers* (New York: Mentor, 1961), 465.
9. *Marbury* v. *Madison*, 1 Cranch 137, 177 (1803).
10. Glendon Schubert, *The Presidency in the Courts* (Minneapolis: University of Minnesota Press, 1957), 361.
11. The Jefferson quotation is found in Robert Scigliano, *The Supreme Court and the Presidency* (New York: Free Press, 1971), 24. Court decisions holding presidential actions unconstitutional are catalogued in Schubert, Appendix A, 361.
12. *McCulloch* vs. *Maryland*, 4 Wheaton (17 U.S.) 316 (1819).
13. James D. Richardson, ed., *Messages and Papers of the Presidents*, 20 vols. (New York: Bureau of National Literature, 1897), 3:1144–1145.
14. Quoted in Benjamin Page and Mark Petracca, *The American Presidency* (New York: McGraw-Hill, 1983), 280.

15. *Foster* v. *Neilson*, 2 Pet. 253 (1829).

16. Gary King and Lyn Ragsdale, *The Elusive Executive* (Washington, D.C.: CQ Press, 1988), 366–367.

17. *U.S.* v. *Curtiss-Wright Export Corporation*, 299 U.S. 304 (1936); emphasis added.

18. *Edwards* v. *Carter*, 580 F.2d. 1055 (C.A.D.C. 1978).

19. *Goldwater* v. *Carter*, 444 U.S. 996 (1979).

20. *Dames and Moore* v. *Regan*, 452 U.S. 654 (1981).

21. *Chicago & S. Air Lines* v. *Waterman S.S. Corp.*, 333 U.S. 103, 111 (1948).

22. *Prize Cases*, 2 Bl. (67 U.S.) 635, 668 (1863).

23. See *Holtzman* v. *Schlesinger* (1973).

24. *Crockett* v. *Reagan* (1982).

25. *Conyers* v. *Reagan* (1984).

26. *Dellums* v. *Bush* (1990).

27. Edward Corwin, *The President: Office and Powers* (New York: New York University Press, 1957), 16.

28. *Hirabayaski* v. *U.S.*, 320 U.S. 81 (1943).

29. *Korematsu* v. *U.S.*, 323 U.S. 214 (1944).

30. *Ex parte Endo*, 323 U.S. 283 (1944).

31. *Mississippi* v. *Johnson*, 4 Wall. (71 U.S.) 475, 499 (1867).

32. *In re Neagle*, 135 U.S. 1 (1890).

33. *In re Debs*, 158 U.S. 546 (1895).

34. *Myers* v. *U.S.*, 222 U.S. 52 (1926).

35. *Humphrey's Executor* v. *U.S.*, 295 U.S. 602 (1935), and *Wiener* v. *U.S.*, 357 U.S. 349 (1958). In using the terms "quasi-legislative" and "quasi-judicial," the Court means that independent regulatory agencies such as the Federal Trade Commission legislate in their ability to develop various regulations and they adjudicate by holding hearings for individuals and companies that have violated the regulations.

36. *U.S.* v. *Big Aurora*, Cranch 382 (1812).

37. *Butterfield* v. *Stanahan*, 192 U.S. 471 (1904) at 494.

38. *U.S. Immigration and Naturalization Service* v. *Chadha*, 103 U.S. 2764 (1983).

39. *Bowsher* v. *Synar*, 478 U.S. 714 (1986) at 726.

40. Louis Fisher, *The Politics of Shared Power* (Washington, D.C.: CQ Press, 1987), 94–104.

41. *Ex parte Merryman*, 17 Fed. Cas. 144, No. 9487 (1861). Taney heard Merryman's petition for a writ of habeas corpus sitting as a circuit court judge. Until 1891, Supreme Court justices "rode circuit": they toured the country making decisions as appeals court judges.

42. Quoted in Corwin, 145.

43. *Ex parte Milligan*, 4 Wall. (71 U.S.) 2 at 127 (1866).

44. *Public Papers of the Presidents: Harry S Truman, 1952–1953* (Washington, D.C.: U.S. Government Printing Office, 1955), 250–251, 273, 290–291, 293–294, 301.

45. *Youngstown Sheet and Tube Co.* v. *Sawyer*, 343 U.S. 579 (1952) at 587.

46. Ibid.

47. Ibid., at 591.

48. *New York Times* v. *United States*, 403 U.S. 713 (1971).

49. *U.S.* v. *U.S. District Court for the Eastern District of Michigan*, 407 U.S. 297 (1972).

50. Quoted in Larry Berman, *The New American Presidency* (Boston: Little, Brown, 1987), 85.

51. *Train* v. *City of New York*, 420 U.S. 35 (1975).

52. *Panama Refining Co.* v. *Ryan*, 293 U.S. 388 (1935).

53. *Schechter Poultry Company* v. *U.S.*, 295 U.S. 495 at 541–542 (1935).

54. Corwin, 127.

55. Johnny Killian, ed., *The Constitution of the United States* (Washington, D.C.: U.S. Government Printing Office, 1987), 76.

56. George Edwards and Stephen Wayne, *Presidential Leadership*, 2d ed. (New York: St. Martin's Press, 1990), 334.

57. Scigliano, Chap. 6.

58. Ibid.

59. Ibid., 193.

60. Norman Thomas and Richard Watson, *The Politics of the Presidency*, 2d ed. (Washington, D.C.: CQ Press, 1986).

61. Scigliano, 95.

62. Quoted in Henry J. Abraham. *Justices and Presidents: A Political History of Appointments to the Supreme Court*, 2d ed. (New York: Oxford University Press, 1985), 263.

63. Scigliano, 111.

64. David Danelski, *A Supreme Court Justice Is Appointed* (New York: Random House, 1964), 156–158.

65. The first legal-tender decision was *Hepburn* v. *Griswold*, 8 Wall. 603 (1869); the second case was *Knox* v. *Lee*, 12 Wall. 457 (1870).

66. See Sheldon Goldman, "Reaganizing the Judiciary: The First Term Appointments," *Judicature* 68 (April–May 1985): 313–329.

67. David O'Brien, "The Reagan Judges: His Most Enduring Legacy," in *The Reagan Legacy*, ed. Charles O. Jones (Chatham, N.J.: Chatham House, 1988), 67–68.

68. Ibid., 68.

69. Quoted ibid., 69.

70. *Youngstown Sheet and Tube Co.* v. *Sawyer*.

16

Presidential Politics

A t war in 1991, George Bush seemed to move decisively and on his own schedule. He acted with clarity of purpose against Iraq and propelled victory by ultimatums and deadlines. He kept intact a coalition of nations jealously suspicious of one another. His public popularity soared to the highest levels ever recorded for an American president. Congress watched from the sidelines, afraid to challenge the conquering hero.

But, like a television image during a thunderstorm, the president who was so sharply focused during the war soon seemed to fade in and out. At peace, Bush failed to anticipate the scope of Iraq's postwar turmoil. Although the war had ended, a new struggle began between the Iraqi government and Kurdish rebels. The rebels had followed Bush's advice to attempt to overthrow Iraqi president Saddam Hussein. Their tattered efforts at resistance failed, and hundreds of thousands of Kurds fled into the mountains along Iraq's border with Turkey. World leaders pressured the Bush administration, which belatedly decided to intervene to guarantee the Kurds a safe harbor at the edge of perdition.

At home, economic problems continued. The White House offered no plan other than cajoling the Federal Reserve Board to reduce interest rates to solve rising unemployment and slow growth. The Treasury, the Federal Reserve Board, and the White House disagreed over steps to bolster a dangerously weakened banking system. Less than one month after the war ended, only 42 percent of the public felt that the country was moving in the right direction, and 63 percent disapproved of the way Bush was handling the economy.[1]

During the immediate postwar period, pundits wondered what had happened to George Bush. Had he lost his resolve? Had he retreated to reticence as a matter of political pragmatism? How could he be so skilled one minute and so diffident the next? Most analysts painted the shift as unique to Bush—his style and personality had led him, and the country, in another way.

Bush's handling of the war and the postwar period illuminates a much larger puzzle than that posed by this president's inner character or outward political style. The two central pieces of the puzzle are image and institution. How they sometimes interlock and how at other times they seem mismatched are the essence of presidential politics. The single executive image portrays the president as the one person in charge of the government. The plural institution is a large, diverse conglomerate of offices, procedures, and personnel handling an array of policy and political concerns often in ambiguous ways. Presidential politics is the way in which presidents attempt to influence others—whether nonchalant citizens or earnest politicians—that their decisions are the right decisions. Presidents rely on the two central features of their office—image and institution—to put together the deals, make the bargains, and persuade others of the soundness of the presidential course of action.

During the Persian Gulf War, Bush had the power to act because the image and institution worked together. Presidents at war enjoy the best opportunity to join image and institution. As commanders in chief, they come as close as possible to living up to the image of one person in charge. They give the orders and time the events. They typically enjoy an immense boost in public support, for the American people rally around presidents in war. Too, the institution may have sufficient autonomy to control the battlefield and manipulate the political playing field. This is not to say that presidents always enjoy the benefits of warriors. The dilemma of Lyndon Johnson in 1967 and 1968 attests to their limits.

Bush had hard luck on the postwar home front because features of the institution blurred the image of Bush as an effective policymaker. Presidents are trapped in large gray areas over which they have been given authority but lack control. In economic and domestic reforms, the single executive image can be presented, but the dynamics of the institution and the surrounding environment make it difficult to sustain. The differences between Bush at war and Bush at peace are endemic to presidential politics. All presidents fade in and out of focus. This chapter first reviews the highlights of the two central aspects of the office. Then it considers the nature of presidential politics that grows out of the image and institution.

THE SINGLE EXECUTIVE IMAGE

Claims of singularity let presidents open doors of power, uniqueness, importance, and visibility. The president is viewed as the single most powerful official in the government. He is touted as uniquely important—the only official elected by the entire nation. He is the most visible figure in the nation, if not the world. The image of one person in charge rests on four foundations: the Constitution, presidential elections, public attitudes, and the media.

The framers of the Constitution created a strong independent executive, but they did not intend to make the president uncommonly powerful. Nor did presidents of the nineteenth century view the office in such bright light. Changes at the beginning of the twentieth century, however, slowly fused presidential activism and governmental activism. Theodore Roosevelt and Woodrow Wilson insisted that the president could do whatever was in the best interest of the nation. At the same time, the government began to intervene in more and more aspects of society. The result was a powerful executive in an omnipresent government.

Modern presidents assert powers unmentioned in the Constitution. They exercise unilateral military power and have unequaled control over diplomacy. They claim a fiscal power to draw up an executive budget. They develop an agenda-setting power to submit full legislative programs to Congress. They establish a lawmaking power by issuing executive orders that often substitute for congressional legislation. Presidents are busier and have more constitutional power than the framers could have imagined.

Presidents use their election victories to justify their exercise of power. They proclaim that they have a mandate to exercise power on behalf of the people. Election campaigns also draw public attention to personal leadership. Candidates attempt to convey images and make promises as the "people's president." They pledge to rid the nation of all major ills, act as a moral hero, and inspire citizens to serve their country. The assurances reinforce the view that a single person, acting on behalf of the people, can successfully run the government.

Assumptions deeply ingrained in the American political culture fix eyes on the ability of one person to take charge. American individualism reinforces the importance of the independence, hard work, and solitary effort of one person. Pragmatism calls for quick, simple solutions to complex problems and relies on the president as the chief national problem solver. Americans see themselves as the "chosen people" who know democracy and freedom better than any other nation does. Presidents become the leaders of the chosen people. They also stand above political parties and organized interests. Based on these assumptions, presidents are symbols of the nation. The symbolism serves to personalize and simplify government. People view the government through presidents. The symbolism shapes people's expectations of how presidents should behave in office and their views of how successful presidents are in office.

The media of newspapers, magazines, radio, and especially television help people concentrate on presidents as the central focus of politics. Presidents are unquestionably the most visible politicians in the country. News organizations ensure that this visibility is self-fulfilling. They define anything and everything a president does as newsworthy. The White House press team does all it can to get out the president's story. The public is left little choice but to understand national events through the pivotal role of presidents.

Presidents can use the single executive image and its power, visibility, uniqueness, and importance to convince other politicians that what they propose is what the nation wants and needs. They gain leverage to advance plans to meet the concerns of the nation, as a unique democratic figure who knows best. President Bush told the American people about the Persian Gulf, "We know why we're there. We are Americans: part of something larger than ourselves. For two centuries, we've done the hard work of freedom. And tonight, we lead the world in facing down a threat to decency and humanity."[2]

THE PLURAL INSTITUTION

The single executive image places demands on presidents that they alone or with their top advisers cannot meet. Presidents supposedly in charge of the entire government require an elaborate, large, plural institution in order to match the imagery. One key indicator of the institution is that presidential decisions often are made with little personal involvement of the presidents. The institution has four salient features: policy complexity, political fragmentation, decentralized organization, and ambiguous decision making.

The single executive image pushes presidents to take care of policy problems in all areas of defense, foreign relations, the economy, and domestic affairs. The institution must accommodate the policy complexity within a policy area and across policy areas. In foreign policy, presidents rely most heavily on conventional military actions to police global democracy. Presidents order U.S. intervention in areas where democracy is being violated or where they feel democracy should be introduced. At the same time, presidents also practice efforts in nuclear deterrence, covert action, and diplomacy.

Presidents are sorely limited in their impact on the economy. The condition of the economy mostly hinges on national and international market factors and monetary policy over which presidents have little control. Presidents have offered tax cuts as their primary economic device. Although tax cuts often do not have the desired economic effect, they typically do have the desired political effect.

In the domestic arena, presidents confront both policy complexity and political fragmentation. Presidents offer domestic initiatives, typically in well-worn issue areas that have seen frequent activity from members of Congress, bureaucrats, the courts, and diverse interest groups. Both government and group fragmentation hamper presidents' plans to advance a domestic agenda. Each type of policy carries with it its own complexity; all the policy types together magnify complexity.

Presidents devise an elaborate, decentralized organization to accommodate policy complexity and political fragmentation. Some forty-two offices and sixteen hundred people compose the White House. It is arranged along policy lines with units in place for all major policy areas. It also is arranged to target specific political groups, including Congress, the press, and interest groups. One core of the organization is the Office of Management and Budget, which carries out much of the president's daily business, including agencies' budget and legislative requests, administrative regulations, and bills passed by Congress.

The organization practices ambiguous decision making. Decisions are made using a garbage can approach in which problems are not necessarily identified before solutions are sought. White House participants strike political bargains that bring problems and solutions together.

The single executive image creates demands that foster a complex plural institution. With its decentralized organization, ambiguous decision making, complex policies, and political fragmentation, the institution wears down the clarity of the image. Presidents can say they are in charge, but the very institution that backs them up stands as testimony that they often are not.

Several months after the end of the Persian Gulf War, reports surfaced that President Bush was out of touch with the inner workings of his own White House. A war of offices, personalities, and ideology had erupted among Bush's economic advisers about what economic plan to set forth, leaving Wall Street and the business community angry and confused. Cabinet secretaries nearly unanimously called for the ouster of Chief of Staff John Sununu, who was increasingly viewed as insensitive and power driven. Meanwhile, Sununu attempted to maneuver past Brent Scowcroft, Bush's national security adviser, on decisions regarding a pending trip to Asia. And Boyden Gray, chief counsel to the president (the White House lawyer), angered cabinet members and key Republicans with his handling of the 1991 Civil Rights Act.[3] In the balance between the image and the institution lies the nature of presidential politics.

PRESIDENTIAL POLITICS

To effectively marshal the image and institution, American presidents follow eight strategies. The first three advance the imagery. The remaining five draw on institutional arrangements. If presidents do not follow these strategies, their ability to influence others—their ability to win the political game—is severely diminished.

The Power of Image

1. Create the Proper Candidate "Feel."   Presidents are judged by what they say and how they say it long before they are elected. For many presidents, the images they project and the promises they make as candidates define their terms in office. The campaign eschews complexity and rationality in candidates' messages in favor of simplicity and emotion. Candidates recognize that their audience is typically looking the other way. American citizens, consumed with work, families, friends, sports, and entertainment, only occasionally glance over their shoulders at the political arena. To capture these wandering gazes, successful presidential candidates tell a simple story, one anchored in emotion, not in fact. In it, they single-handedly offer an end to all major national problems, whether the woes be a declining national image abroad or a rising budget deficit at home. There is always a happy ending. The storytellers present themselves on an emotional level. They create a dramatic persona who upholds basic American values of strength, greatness, independence, and patriotism. Whether the candidate does in fact have any or all of these qualities is obscured. As political scientist Bruce Miroff observed, "What matters is that he is presented as having these qualities, in magnitudes far beyond what ordinary citizens can imagine themselves to possess."[4]

Unsuccessful candidates' plots are more complicated and matter-of-fact. Their tales recount long-term solutions or hard choices. Statements about tax increases, sacrifices in living standards, and intractable social problems are inelegantly choreographed. The losers present themselves as mortals who do not know all the answers. Their candidacies gain no clear popular sympathy. The emotional and symbolic bond between candidate and electorate is missing, as is victory at the polls.

Every four years, Americans renew their impressions of the single executive image. They do not like tough talk, even though they declare that they do. They do not like bad news, even though they say they can take it. Voters wistfully prefer a bright picture of the future told by a personable, self-assured talker. Elections tightly weave the single executive image into the fabric of the American body politic. Political victory is the reward for a good campaign story.

2. Dominate the Public Space.   Public familiarity with presidents to the diminishment of other politicians and institutions continues after the election. Cultural assumptions focus on heroic problem solvers. The mass media give presidents more coverage than they give all other public figures. Presidents also dominate the public space through the use of "spectacles." According to Bruce Miroff:

A spectacle is a kind of symbolic event, one in which particular details stand for broader and deeper meanings. What differentiates spectacle from other kinds of symbolic events is the centrality of character and action. A spectacle presents intriguing and often dominating characters not in static poses but through actions that establish their public identities.[5]

Consider the differences between professional boxing and professional wrestling. Boxing is a true contest requiring skill and endurance. The outcome of a match is unknown before the match takes place. Millions of dollars a year are bet on who will win. The result of a professional wrestling match, by contrast, is preordained. There is no need to bet. The good guy gets knocked around by his evil opponent but finally triumphs. Wrestling is an example of spectacle. Presidents are sometimes like boxers and at other times like wrestlers. In some cases, presidents are spirited, heavyweight fighters slugging it out with other politicians, most likely members of Congress, bureaucrats, judges, or journalists. Who will win is not clearly known. But in a growing number of cases, presidents are involved in spectacles akin to professional wrestling matches. They portray themselves as a larger-than-life protagonist who, in Miroff's words, "engages in emblematic bouts with immoral or dangerous adversaries."[6]

Spectacles become the pictures that typify presidencies. Although people focus on the presidency more than on other aspects of government, their attention to the presidency is decidedly narrow. They recall the most visible incidents of a president's term—the spectacles—while many other details of the administration dim. The spectacles may depict failures or successes. People recall Jimmy Carter's Iranian hostage crisis as a spectacle of failure. Carter's campaign image of a gentle, moral, and open man who was a smart manager gave way to the image of a hapless, weak, inept figure. The spectacle of the aborted marine rescue of the hostages encapsulated Carter's public profile. It reminded people that Carter lacked some key qualities of the single executive image.

People recall Ronald Reagan's invasion of Grenada as a spectacle of success. The president acted single-handedly against, in his words, "a brutal group of leftist thugs." The good guys and the bad guys were clearly labeled, and within a span of hours the good guys won. Reagan proclaimed, "Our days of weakness are over. Our military forces are back on their feet and standing tall."[7] The spectacle depicted the president as a decisive, tough, and courageous leader of an equally bold nation. Indeed, the most striking spectacles are presidents at war. They create a man-on-horseback illusion. The presidency's growth in wartime is largely psychological, not administrative or military. Spectacles create the standards of the single executive image from which presidents lose or gain political advantages.

3. Plan Grand Simplifications in Legislative Affairs. If presidents cannot take the nation to war, they can bring it a comprehensive yet simple package of legislation designed to cure national ills. These spectacles may not be as riveting as battlefield encounters, but they offer other advantages. The stakes are not as high, and success may be more easily claimed. Presidents achieve their greatest success by offering sweeping reforms. These provide the best opportunity to break down coalitions in Congress that may resist change and to take Congress away from what it does best—acting on a series of small changes in discrete policy areas.

In legislative affairs, the types of programs that presidents offer may reflect a direct link between the president and the people. Solutions often become simplified, personalized, and short-term, by-passing far-reaching entanglements and avoiding complex situational factors. Congress, also heavily reliant on constituent support, has, according to political scientist David Mayhew, a "penchant for the blunt simple action—the national debt limit, the minimum wage, the price rollback, the 10 percent across-the-board budget slash, the amendment cutting off aid to Communist countries."[8] The close affiliation of both institutions with the public leads to "the ability of mass publics to prescribe means as well as ends" in policymaking.[9] The public, fed by media demands, often looks for quick action and immediate results and gets them. Presidents may gain immediate power in the public arena from these policies. In the short term, such policies reflect the image of singularity. They thereby reinforce most citizens' overly simplified view of the presidency and may be tickets to re-election.

Modern presidents' primary resource is their ability to use these three strategies to capture public attention and support. The political advantage they gain from the feel of the campaign, spectacles, and grand legislative designs is not immediately a result of their own actions. Instead, it depends on the public's reaction. Using each strategy, presidents offer distracted citizens a form of symbolic reassurance that someone is in charge. They gain power only to the extent that the public feels this reassurance. Presidents rely, in effect, on other people's money. In their negotiations with other politicians, they capitalize on public sentiment to get what they want. When public sentiment turns against them, as the gap between their actions and the expectations fostered by the single executive image widens, their political advantage diminishes.

The unique role that presidents have acquired from the power of imagery rests on "passive democracy." It is *democratic* in the sense that there is an ongoing, always updated referendum or plebiscite by the public on a president's success in office. Public opinion results are announced and a president's fortunes are analyzed according to the good or bad news. It is *passive* because the referendum typically requires little effort by individuals to answer how they feel about the president's performance. Too, public attitudes often are examined secondhand through viewpoints of journalists and their interpretation of polls.

Passive democracy is a contradiction in terms. Notions of democracy usually require some form of activity by the citizenry. Yet, whether a logical contradiction or not, it is a political reality that gives presidents the mainstay of their power. "Public sentiment is everything," said Abraham Lincoln. "With public sentiment nothing can fail, without it nothing can succeed."[10] With popular belief in the single executive image and the incumbent president's ability to live up to the image come public sentiment. George Bush's popularity was the highest of any president since Truman immediately after the Persian Gulf War, when people believed that Bush was living up to the single executive image. His popularity plummeted to among the lowest of any president since Truman one year later, when people no longer felt that Bush looked so singularly in control.

Institutional Politics

Institutional politics says that presidents use the office, not the image, to influence others. Institutional politics is decidedly more complex than the politics of the image. It has no set rules. Presidents acquire a political advantage from taking charge of the institution and its relations with other institutions. Yet, oddly enough, presidents do not automatically lose the advantage when they claim that they are not in charge or that things have gotten out of hand. Presidents must employ institutional strategies that facilitate positive public sentiment. But they also must adopt strategies that directly satisfy politicians who are not so easily plied with presidential spectacles. These politicians require material benefits in order for presidents to get what they want.

4. Act Fast. Presidents must move their legislative agendas quickly. Timing is critical in any institution. The White House runs on two clocks: (1) organizational time—the internal time of meetings, memos, and deadlines; and (2) the much faster political time—the external time of deals, coalitions, and re-election. Acting fast allows presidents to speed up organizational time so it is in sync with political time. Fact action on the grand simplification reduces policy complexity and decision ambiguity. Because the agenda touches on only a few dramatic issues, there can be sufficient opportunity for the organization to accommodate the agenda in a unified rather than disparate fashion. The fast pace allows the White House greater control over the outcome of legislation and takes advantage of the honeymoon early in the term. It may pressure members of Congress to support the president's plan.

To move quickly, the president-elect must plan and set priorities with his transition team. He also must hire experts with considerable substantive background and political skill on the subjects at hand. Doing these things will give him an advantage with Congress—the presidential institution operates on the same time as the single executive image, and the president is then able to hit the ground running after the inauguration.

5. *Organize with a Single Chief of Staff.* One of the predominant lessons for presidents since the creation of the Executive Office of the President is the value of a single chief of staff to control the machinations of the White House organization. The chief of staff lends order to the plural presidency. Although no person can control the plural presidency, a single chief of staff enables presidents to have better control of their portion of the presidency. Because the presidency is both a personal and an institutional office, the chief of staff becomes a bridge between the two aspects. There is then no benefit in the rhetoric of cabinet government or in a collegial staff organization that supposedly gives the best minds free rein.

6. *Avoid Philosophical Blinders in Policy.* Presidents are to some degree locked into decisions by the policy tracks on which the nation rides. Global democracy in foreign and military affairs, protective capitalism in economic affairs, and conservative liberalism in domestic affairs give presidents their directions. The ideological directions can create blinders that hamper innovation and place pressure on presidents to act like their predecessors. Yet presidents must be willing to read history and recognize the mistakes of the past. In its involvement in Iraq, the Bush administration kept the nation on a foreign policy path similar to the path on which it had been for forty years, but it went to great lengths to avoid recreating the disasters of Vietnam. Presidents must recognize the policy complexity that lies beneath what may appear to be a simple, straight policy track.

7. *Do Not Run Against the Bureaucracy or Congress.* Presidents and presidential candidates love to criticize the government. They suggest that the bureaucracy is strangling citizens with red tape. They announce that Congress looks out for special interests that contradict the will of the people. Such public rhetoric, however, may come to haunt presidents' relations with the bureaucracy and with Congress. If presidents constantly rail against the bureaucracy, bureaucrats are unlikely to be responsive to presidential interests. If they blame Congress for the nation's direction, members will be less likely to support the president's program. Presidents must develop effective relations with both branches. Presidents must control not only the plural institution but its relations with other institutions.

8. *Be Able to Explain What You Have Done.* Presidents must be able to explain a particular decision or event in such a way that institutional goings-on match public expectations defined by the single executive image. Most often, presidents strive to present a united front among all leading officials in the administration on a policy decision. Presidents attempt to keep people's eyes focused on themselves and on a tightly knit staff. They hide the complexity and disparateness of the institution.

During the Persian Gulf War, President Bush and his team of military and diplomatic advisers appeared to stand and speak in unison on all issues of the war—when to start, when to stop, how many people to use. After the war, it became clear that there was less unity than had been portrayed. Colin Powell, chair of the Joint Chiefs of Staff, had wanted the president to continue economic sanctions. The president and others vetoed this option as politically too slow. The army commander in the field, General Norman Schwarzkopf, wanted to continue the mission all the way to Baghdad to topple Iraqi leader Saddam Hussein. Bush and others decided to stop the mission once the main Iraqi army units had been crushed inside the border.[11] Nonetheless, the public explanation was one of unity and agreement.

If presidents do something wrong, unethical, or inept, they must be able to provide a plausible explanation for what has happened. The most frequent explanation is to blame others—advisers and offices of the plural presidency from which the president appears distant. Presidents suggest that they are engulfed in an impossible organization and are unable to control those within it. The classic distinction is between Reagan's explanation of the Iran-contra affair and Nixon's explanation of Watergate. Reagan recaptured his popularity and retained his office because he explained away his own involvement in the diversion of monies from the Iranian arms sales to the Nicaraguan contra rebels. Reagan invoked an explanation that the president simply could not control all of the officials involved. Richard Nixon was never fully able to do so. He tried in vain to craft a series of explanations that said he had the right to withhold evidence "as president" and "in the interest of national security." Such explanations left Nixon open to charges of aggrandizement and complicity. For Nixon, the single executive image collapsed from the weight of the plural presidency. For Reagan, the plural presidency propped up the image.

The ability of presidents to deny responsibility poses a contradiction to democracy, passive or otherwise. When presidents offer explanations that are plausible but false, accountability and democratic responsiveness are lost. Moreover, the American citizenry loses control of the presidency as it follows its own course, and responsibility for that course vanishes internally. Indeed, Hamilton commented that "the plurality of the executive tends to deprive the people of the two greatest securities they can have for the faithful exercise of any delegated power, first the restraints of public opinion, which lose their efficacy" because of the number of people involved and uncertainty of who is to blame, and second, the opportunity to discover not only who is involved but what the nature of the misconduct is "in order either to [secure] their removal from office or to [administer] their actual punishment in cases which admit of it."[12] Plausible explanations are an important tool of institutional politics, but they also can be an ominous aspect of the links from institutional to image politics.

CONCLUSION

Writers on the presidency have invested considerable energy in labeling presidents and presidencies. Their central focus has been power. Do presidents have too much, too little, or an appropriate amount of power? Taking their cues from political scientist Richard Neustadt's pivotal work, writers have concentrated on how a president exercises power within a context of mutual bargaining—give-and-take—with members of Congress, bureaucrats, world leaders, organized groups, staff members, the press, governors, the American public, and others.[13] Some presidents have been characterized as effectively powerful, others as too powerful, and still others as not powerful enough.

Beginning with Franklin Roosevelt and continuing through John Kennedy, writers portrayed an impressive office at the center of government from which presidents could and should do all that was necessary to provide for the best interests of the nation.[14] Presidents were seen as aggressively but appropriately using power. Works written during the Johnson and Nixon years pointed to an "imperial presidency" in which presidents aggrandized power at the expense of the public good and the Constitution.[15] Discussion of an impossible or "no-win" presidency followed during the Ford and Carter administrations.[16] According to this analysis, presidents were expected but unable to cope with national problems, hampered by unrealistic public expectations, and hemmed in by a recalcitrant Congress and an entrenched bureaucracy. The view of the presidency as an impressive office has returned to fashion as writers cite Reagan's public and legislative skills and Bush's military prowess.[17]

The labels "impressive," "imperial," and "impossible" have been used to provide general characterizations of successive occupants of the Oval Office. Presidential power, as it has been conceived, depends on its use by individual presidents. Thus, the debate about whether presidents have too much, too little, or adequate power awaits new incumbents to ride familiar swings on the old pendulum. Yet, in the sequential comparison of presidents, a satisfactory cumulative explanation of the office has not emerged. The writers have overlooked the fact that the office is at once impressive, imperial, and impossible. Presidents' power is a matter of politics. Presidential politics rests not merely on the mutual bargaining of presidents with other politicians. It depends on the single executive image and the plural presidency as sources of power—sources of presidents' bargaining advantages. People's comments that "The president is powerful" or "The president is weak" or "The president is power hungry" make sense only when the intermeshing of the image and the institution is understood.

Richard Nixon is typecast as an imperial president. During Watergate he acted outside the bounds of democratic responsiveness required by the single executive image. Offices and advisers in the White House conspired to throw investigators off the trail and deny wrongdoing. Yet Nixon also acted as an impressive chief executive as he negotiated new diplomatic relations with the People's Republic of China. His deeds matched the demands of the single executive image for swift, dramatic personal action by the president. Within the presidential institution, top officials in the State Department, Defense Department, Central Intelligence Agency, and National Security Council acted in concert. The appearance of singular presidential action was matched by united institutional machinations. Too, Nixon appeared mired in an impossible presidency in his efforts to impose wage and price controls. Public expectations from the single executive image suggested that the president should have been able to control the economy swiftly. Yet the complexity of the economy and debates between the Council of Economic Advisers and the Office of Wage and Price Stability gave Nixon more than he had bargained for. The policy complexity and decentralized organization of the institution stalled the wage-price policy and blurred Nixon's image as a decisive policymaker. Nixon's impressive, impossible, and imperial presidency stemmed from the match and the mismatch of the single executive image and the plural presidency.

As Bush pursued his fourth year in office, the president's environmental advisers feuded over the stance Bush should take at a major United Nations summit on the environment in Rio de Janeiro. Cabinet officials and White House staffers joined in accusing Bush's new chief of staff, Samuel Skinner, who had replaced fired John Sununu, of indecision and an inability to prioritize. Deputy Chief of Staff W. Henson Moore was blamed for everything Skinner was not. The administration mounted only halfhearted efforts to secure its plans to reform education, urban ills, and trade. Bush's popularity tumbled to 37 percent.[18] Presidential politics continued as usual. ∎

FURTHER READING

On presidential spectacles, see: Bruce Miroff, "The Presidency and the Public: Leadership as Spectacle," in *The Presidency and the Political System*, 3d ed., ed. M. Nelson. (Washington, D.C.: CQ Press, 1990). On presidential power, see: Richard Neustadt, *Presidential Power* (New York: Wiley, 1960); Clinton Rossiter, *The American President* (New York: Mentor Books, 1960); Arthur Schlesinger, Jr., *The Imperial Presidency* (Boston: Houghton Mifflin, 1973).

N O T E S

1. *Washington Post*, April 12, 1991, A4.

2. "Text of the State of the Union Address," *Washington Post*, January 29, 1991, A14.

3. "The Man Called 'Nunu,'" *Newsweek*, December 2, 1991, 30–31.

4. Bruce Miroff, "The Presidency and the Public: Leadership as Spectacle," in *The Presidency and the Political System*, 3d ed., ed. Michael Nelson (Washington, D.C.: CQ Press, 1990), 293.

5. Ibid., 290.

6. Ibid., 291.

7. "Farewell Grenada," *Time*, December 26, 1983.

8. David Mayhew, *Congress: The Electoral Connection* (New Haven: Yale University Press, 1974), 138.

9. Ibid., 139.

10. Quoted in George Edwards and Stephen Wayne, *Presidential Leadership*, 2d ed. (New York: St. Martin's Press, 1990), 90.

11. Bob Woodward, *The Commanders* (New York: Simon and Schuster, 1991).

12. Alexander Hamilton, James Madison, and John Jay, *The Federalist Papers* (New York: Mentor Books, 1961), 428–429.

13. Richard Neustadt, *Presidential Power* (New York: Wiley, 1960).

14. In addition to Neustadt, see Clinton Rossiter, *The American President* (New York: Mentor Books, 1960); James MacGregor Burns, *The Deadlock of Democracy* (Englewood Cliffs, N.J.: Prentice-Hall, 1963); and James MacGregor Burns, *Presidential Government: The Crucible of Leadership* (Boston: Houghton Mifflin, 1966).

15. See Arthur Schlesinger, Jr., *The Imperial Presidency* (Boston: Houghton Mifflin, 1973); Richard Nathan, *The Plot That Failed: Nixon and the Administrative Presidency* (New York: Wiley, 1975); and Joseph Califano, *A Presidential Nation* (New York: Norton, 1975).

16. See Paul Light, *The President's Agenda* (Baltimore: Johns Hopkins University Press, 1982); Hugh Heclo and Lester Salomon, eds., *The Illusion of Presidential Government* (Boulder, Colo.: Westview Press, 1981); and Thomas Cronin, *The State of the Presidency*, 2d ed. (Boston: Little, Brown, 1980).

17. See Fred Greenstein, ed., *The Reagan Presidency: An Early Assessment* (Baltimore: Johns Hopkins University Press, 1983); Norman Ornstein, ed., *President and Congress: Assessing Reagan's First Year* (Washington, D.C.: American Enterprise Institute, 1982); and Richard Rose, *George Bush as a Postmodern President* (Strathclyde, Scotland: Centre for the Study of Public Policy, 1991).

18. "Bush: The White House Blame Game," *Newsweek*, June 22, 1992, 33–34.

The Constitution of the United States of America*

Preamble

We the people of the United States, in order to form a more perfect union, establish justice, insure domestic tranquility, provide for the common defense, promote the general welfare, and secure the blessings of liberty to ourselves and our posterity, do ordain and establish this Constitution for the United States of America.

Article I

Section 1 All legislative powers herein granted shall be vested in a Congress of the United States, which shall consist of a Senate and a House of Representatives.

Section 2 The House of Representatives shall be composed of members chosen every second year by the people of the several States, and the electors in each State shall have the qualifications requisite for electors of the most numerous branch of the State Legislature.

No person shall be a Representative who shall not have attained to the age of twenty-five years, and been seven years a citizen of the United States, and who shall not, when elected, be an inhabitant of that State in which he shall be chosen.

Representatives and direct taxes shall be apportioned among the several States which may be included within this Union, according to their respective numbers, *which shall be determined by adding to the whole number of free persons, including those bound to service for a term of years and excluding Indians not taxed, three-fifths of all other persons.* The actual enumeration shall be made within three years after the first meeting of the Congress of the United States, and within every subsequent term of ten years, in such manner as they shall by law direct. The number of Representatives shall not exceed one for every thirty thousand, but each State shall have at least one Representative; *and until such enumeration shall be made, the State of New Hampshire shall be entitled to choose three, Massachusetts eight, Rhode Island and Providence Plantations one, Connecticut five, New York six, New Jersey four, Pennsylvania eight, Delaware one, Maryland six, Virginia ten, North Carolina five, South Carolina five, and Georgia three.*

When vacancies happen in the representation from any State, the Executive authority thereof shall issue writs of election to fill such vacancies.

The House of Representatives shall choose their Speaker and other officers; and shall have the sole power of impeachment.

---

*Passages no longer in effect are printed in italic type.

Section 3   The Senate of the United States shall be composed of two Senators from each State, *chosen by the legislature thereof*, for six years; and each Senator shall have one vote.

Immediately after they shall be assembled in consequence of the first election, they shall be divided as equally as may be into three classes. The seats of the Senators of the first class shall be vacated at the expiration of the second year, of the second class at the expiration of the fourth year, and of the third class at the expiration of the sixth year, so that one-third may be chosen every second year; and if vacancies happen by resignation or otherwise, during the recess of the legislature of any State, the Executive thereof may make temporary appointments until the next meeting of the legislature, which shall then fill such vacancies.

No person shall be a Senator who shall not have attained to the age of thirty years, and been nine years a citizen of the United States, and who shall not, when elected, be an inhabitant of that State for which he shall be chosen.

The Vice-President of the United States shall be President of the Senate, but shall have no vote, unless they be equally divided.

The Senate shall choose their other officers, and also a President *pro tempore*, in the absence of the Vice-President, or when he shall exercise the office of President of the United States.

The Senate shall have the sole power to try all impeachments. When sitting for that purpose, they shall be on oath or affirmation. When the President of the United States is tried, the Chief Justice shall preside: and no person shall be convicted without the concurrence of two-thirds of the members present.

Judgment in cases of impeachment shall not extend further than to removal from the office, and disqualification to hold and enjoy any office of honor, trust or profit under the United States: but the party convicted shall nevertheless be liable and subject to indictment, trial, judgment and punishment, according to law.

Section 4   The times, places and manner of holding elections for Senators and Representatives shall be prescribed in each State by the legislature thereof; but the Congress may at any time by law make or alter such regulations, except as to the places of choosing Senators.

The Congress shall assemble at least once in every year, and such meeting *shall be on the first Monday in December, unless they shall by law appoint a different day.*

Section 5   Each house shall be the judge of the elections, returns and qualifications of its own members, and a majority of each shall constitute a quorum to do business; but a smaller number may adjourn from day to day, and may be authorized to compel the attendance of absent members, in such manner, and under such penalties, as each house may provide.

Each house may determine the rules of its proceedings, punish its members for disorderly behavior, and with the concurrence of two-thirds, expel a member.

Each house shall keep a journal of its proceedings, and from time to time publish the same, excepting such parts as may in their judgment require secrecy; and the yeas and nays of the members of either house on any question shall, at the desire of one-fifth of those present, be entered on the journal.

Neither house, during the session of Congress, shall, without the consent of the other, adjourn for more than three days, nor to any other place than that in which the two houses shall be sitting.

Section 6 The Senators and Representatives shall receive a compensation for their services, to be ascertained by law and paid out of the treasury of the United States. They shall in all cases except treason, felony and breach of the peace, be privileged from arrest during their attendance at the session of their respective houses, and in going to and returning from the same; and for any speech or debate in either house, they shall not be questioned in any other place.

No Senator or Representative shall, during the time for which he was elected, be appointed to any civil office under the authority of the United States, which shall have been created, or the emoluments whereof shall have been increased, during such time; and no person holding any office under the United States shall be a member of either house during his continuance in office.

Section 7 All bills for raising revenue shall originate in the House of Representatives; but the Senate may propose or concur with amendments as on other bills.

Every bill which shall have passed the House of Representatives and the Senate, shall, before it become a law, be presented to the President of the United States; if he approve he shall sign it, but if not he shall return it with objections to that house in which it originated, who shall enter the objections at large on their journal, and proceed to reconsider it. If after such reconsideration two-thirds of that house shall agree to pass the bill, it shall be sent, together with the objections, to the other house, by which it shall likewise be reconsidered, and, if approved by two-thirds of that house, it shall become a law. But in all such cases the votes of both houses shall be determined by yeas and nays, and the names of the persons voting for and against the bill shall be entered on the journal of each house respectively. If any bill shall not be returned by the President within ten days (Sundays excepted) after it shall have been presented to him, the same shall be a law, in like manner as if he had signed it, unless the Congress by their adjournment prevent its return, in which case it shall not be a law.

Every order, resolution, or vote to which the concurrence of the Senate and House of Representatives may be necessary (except on a question of adjournment) shall be presented to the President of the United States; and before the same shall take effect, shall be approved by him, or being disapproved by him, shall be repassed by two-thirds of the Senate and House of Representatives, according to the rules and limitations prescribed in the case of a bill.

Section 8 The Congress shall have power

To lay and collect taxes, duties, imposts, and excises, to pay the debts and provide for the common defense and general welfare of the United States; but all duties, imposts and excises shall be uniform throughout the United States;

To borrow money on the credit of the United States;

To regulate commerce with foreign nations, and among the several States, and with the Indian tribes;

To establish an uniform rule of naturalization, and uniform laws on the subject of bankruptcies throughout the United States;

To coin money, regulate the value thereof, and of foreign coin, and fix the standard of weights and measures;

To provide for the punishment of counterfeiting the securities and current coin of the United States;

To establish post offices and post roads;

To promote the progress of science and useful arts by securing for limited times to authors and inventors the exclusive right to their respective writings and discoveries;

To constitute tribunals inferior to the Supreme Court;

To define and punish piracies and felonies committed on the high seas and offenses against the law of nations;

To declare war, grant letters of marque and reprisal, and make rules concerning captures on land and water;

To raise and support armies, but no appropriation of money to that use shall be for a longer term than two years;

To provide and maintain a navy;

To make rules for the government and regulation of the land and naval forces;

To provide for calling forth the militia to execute the laws of the Union, suppress insurrections, and repel invasions;

To provide for organizing, arming, and disciplining the militia, and for governing such part of them as may be employed in the service of the United States, reserving to the States respectively the appointment of the officers, and the authority of training the militia according to the discipline prescribed by Congress;

To exercise exclusive legislation in all cases whatsoever, over such district (not exceeding ten miles square) as may, by cession of particular States, and the acceptance of Congress, become the seat of government of the United States, and to exercise like authority over all places purchased by the consent of the legislature of the State, in which the same shall be, for erection of forts, magazines, arsenals, dockyards, and other needful buildings; and

To make all laws which shall be necessary and proper for carrying into execution the foregoing powers, and all other powers vested by this Constitution in the government of the United States, or in any department or officer thereof.

Section 9 *The migration or importation of such persons as any of the States now existing shall think proper to admit shall not be prohibited by the Congress prior to the year 1808; but a tax or duty may be imposed on such importation, not exceeding $10 for each person.*

The privilege of the writ of habeas corpus shall not be suspended, unless when in cases of rebellion or invasion the public safety may require it.

No bill of attainder or ex post facto law shall be passed.

No capitation, or other direct, tax shall be laid, unless in proportion to the census or enumeration herein before directed to be taken.

No tax or duty shall be laid on articles exported from any State.

No preference shall be given by any regulation of commerce or revenue to the ports of one State over those of another; nor shall vessels bound to, or from, one State, be obliged to enter, clear, or pay duties in another.

No money shall be drawn from the treasury, but in consequence of appropriations made by law; and a regular statement and account of the receipts and expenditures of all public money shall be published from time to time.

No title of nobility shall be granted by the United States: and no person holding any office or profit or trust under them, shall, without the consent of the Congress, accept of any present, emolument, office, or title, of any kind whatever, from any king, prince, or foreign state.

Section 10 No State shall enter into any treaty, alliance, or confederation; grant letters of marque and reprisal; coin money; emit bills of credit; make anything but gold and silver coin a tender in payment of debts; pass any bill of attainder, ex post facto law, or law impairing the obligation of contracts, or grant any title of nobility.

No State shall, without the consent of Congress, lay any imposts or duties on imports or exports, except what may be absolutely necessary for executing its inspection laws: and the net produce of all duties and imposts, laid by any State on imports or exports, shall be for the use of the treasury of the United States; and all such laws shall be subject to the revision and control of the Congress.

No State shall, without the consent of Congress, lay any duty of tonnage, keep troops or ships of war in time of peace, enter into any agreement or compact with another State, or with a foreign power, or engage in war, unless actually invaded, or in such imminent danger as will not admit of delay.

Article II

Section 1 The executive power shall be vested in a President of the United States of America. He shall hold his office during the term of four years, and, together with the Vice-President, chosen for the same term, be elected as follows:

Each State shall appoint, in such manner as the legislature thereof may direct, a number of electors, equal to the whole number of Senators and Representatives to which the State may be entitled in the Congress; but no Senator or Representative, or person holding an office of trust or profit under the United States, shall be appointed an elector.

The electors shall meet in their respective States, and vote by ballot for two persons, of whom one at least shall not be an inhabitant of the same State with themselves. And they shall make a list of all the persons voted for, and of the number of votes for each: which list they shall sign and certify, and transmit sealed to the seat of government of the United States, directed to the President of the Senate. The President of the Senate shall, in the presence of the Senate and House of Representatives, open all the certificates, and the votes shall then be counted. The person having the greatest number of votes shall be the President, if such number be a majority of the whole number of electors appointed; and if there be more than one who have such majority, and have an equal number of votes, then the House of Representatives shall immediately choose by ballot one of them for President; and if no person have a majority, then from the five highest on the list said house shall in like manner choose the President. But in choosing the President the votes shall be taken by States, the representation from each State having one vote; a quorum for this purpose shall consist of a member or members from two-thirds of the States, and a majority of all the States shall be necessary to a choice. In every case, after the choice of the President, the person having the greatest number of votes of the electors shall be the Vice-President. But if there should remain two or more who have equal votes, the Senate shall choose from them by ballot the Vice-President.

The Congress may determine the time of choosing the electors and the day on which they shall give their votes; which day shall be the same throughout the United States.

No person except a natural-born citizen, *or a citizen of the United States at the time of the adoption of this Constitution,* shall be eligible to the office of President; neither shall any person be eligible to that office who shall not have attained to the age of thirty-five years, and been fourteen years a resident within the United States.

In cases of the removal of the President from office or of his death, resignation, or inability to discharge the powers and duties of the said office, the same shall devolve on the Vice-President, and the Congress may by law provide for the case of removal, death, resignation, or inability, both of the President and Vice-President, declaring what officer shall then act as President, and such officer shall act accordingly, until the disability be removed, or a President shall be elected.

The President shall, at stated times, receive for his services a compensation, which shall neither be increased nor diminished during the period for which he shall have been elected, and he shall not receive within that period any other emolument from the United States, or any of them.

Before he enter on the execution of his office, he shall take the following oath or affirmation: "I do solemnly swear (or affirm) that I will faithfully execute the office of the President of the United States, and will to the best of my ability preserve, protect and defend the Constitution of the United States."

Section 2   The President shall be commander in chief of the army and navy of the United States, and of the militia of the several States, when called into the actual service of the United States; he may require the opinion, in writing, of the principal officer in each of the executive departments, upon any subject relating to the duties of their respective offices, and he shall have power to grant reprieves and pardons for offenses against the United States, except in cases of impeachment.

He shall have power, by and with the advice and consent of the Senate, to make treaties, provided two-thirds of the Senators present concur; and he shall nominate, and by and with the advice and consent of the Senate, shall appoint ambassadors, other public ministers and consuls, judges of the Supreme court, and all other officers of the United States, whose appointments are not herein otherwise provided for, and which shall be established by law: but Congress may by law vest the appointment of such inferior officers, as they think proper, in the President alone, in the courts of law, or in the heads of departments.

The President shall have power to fill up all vacancies that may happen during the recess of the Senate, by granting commissions which shall expire at the end of their next session.

Section 3   He shall from time to time give to the Congress information of the state of the Union, and recommend to their consideration such measures as he shall judge necessary and expedient; he may, on extraordinary occasions, convene both houses, or either of them, and in case of disagreement between them, with respect to the time of adjournment, he may adjourn them to such time as he shall think proper; he shall receive ambassadors and other public ministers; he shall take care that the laws be faithfully executed, and shall commission all the officers of the United States.

Section 4 The President, Vice-President and all civil officers of the United States shall be removed from office on impeachment for, and on conviction of, treason, bribery, or other high crimes and misdemeanors.

Article III

Section 1 The judicial power of the United States shall be vested in one Supreme Court, and in such inferior courts as the Congress may from time to time ordain and establish. The judges, both of the Supreme and inferior courts, shall hold their offices during good behavior, and shall, at stated times, receive for their services a compensation which shall not be diminished during their continuance in office.

Section 2 The judicial power shall extend to all cases, in law and equity, arising under this Constitution, the laws of the United States, and treaties made, or which shall be made, under their authority; to all cases affecting ambassadors, other public ministers and consuls; to all cases of admiralty and maritime jurisdiction; to controversies to which the United States shall be a party; to controversies between two or more States; *between a State and citizens of another State;* between citizens of different States; between citizens of the same State claiming lands under grants of different States, and between a State, or the citizens thereof, and foreign states, citizens or subjects.

In all cases affecting ambassadors, other public ministers and consuls, and those in which a State shall be party, the Supreme Court shall have original jurisdiction. In all the other cases before mentioned, the Supreme Court shall have appellate jurisdiction, both as to law and fact, with such exceptions, and under such regulations, as the Congress shall make.

The trial of all crimes, except in cases of impeachment, shall be by jury; and such trial shall be held in the state where said crimes shall have been committed; but when not committed within any State, the trial shall be at such place or places as the Congress may by law have directed.

Section 3 Treason against the United States shall consist only in levying war against them, or in adhering to their enemies, giving them aid and comfort. No person shall be convicted of treason unless on the testimony of two witnesses to the same overt act, or on confession in open court.

The Congress shall have power to declare the punishment of treason, but no attainder of treason shall work corruption of blood, or forfeiture except during the life of the person attained.

Article IV

Section 1 Full faith and credit shall be given in each State to the public acts, records, and judicial proceedings of every other State. And the Congress may by general laws prescribe the manner in which such acts, records, and proceedings shall be proved, and the effect thereof.

Section 2   The citizens of each State shall be entitled to all privileges and immunities of citizens in the several States.

A person charged in any State with treason, felony, or other crime, who shall flee from justice, and be found in another State, shall on demand of the executive authority of the State from which he fled, be delivered up, to be removed to the State having jurisdiction of the crime.

No person held to service or labor in one State, under the laws thereof, escaping into another, shall, in consequence of any law or regulation therein, be discharged from such service or labor, but shall be delivered up on claim of the party to whom such service or labor may be due.

Section 3   New States may be admitted by the Congress into this Union; but no new State shall be formed or erected within the jurisdiction of any other State; nor any state be formed by the junction of two or more States, or parts of States, without the consent of the legislatures of the States concerned as well as of the Congress.

The Congress shall have power to dispose of and make all needful rules and regulations respecting the territory or other property belonging to the United States; and nothing in this Constitution shall be so construed as to prejudice any claims of the United States, or of any particular State.

Section 4   The United States shall guarantee to every State in this Union a republican form of government, and shall protect each of them against invasion; and on application of the legislature, or of the executive (when the legislature cannot be convened), against domestic violence.

Article V

The Congress, whenever two-thirds of both houses shall deem it necessary, shall propose amendments to this Constitution, or, on the application of the legislatures of two-thirds of the several States, shall call a convention for proposing amendments, which, in either case, shall be valid to all intents and purposes, as part of this Constitution, when ratified by the legislatures of three-fourths of the several States, or by conventions in three-fourths thereof, as the one or the other mode of ratification may be proposed by the Congress; provided *that no amendments which may be made prior to the year one thousand eight hundred and eight shall in any manner affect the first and fourth clauses in the ninth section of the first article;* and that no State, without its consent, shall be deprived of its equal suffrage in the Senate.

Article VI

All debts contracted and engagements entered into, before the adoption of this Constitution, shall be as valid against the United States under this Constitution, as under the Confederation.

This Constitution, and the laws of the United States which shall be made in pursuance thereof; and all treaties made, or which shall be made, under the authority of the United States, shall be the supreme law of the land; and the judges in every State shall be bound thereby, anything in the Constitution or laws of any State to the contrary notwithstanding.

The Senators and Representatives before mentioned, and the members of the several State legislatures, and all executive and judicial officers, both of the United States and of the several States, shall be bound by oath or affirmation to support this Constitution; but no religious test shall ever be required as a qualification to any office or public trust under the United States.

Article VII

The ratification of the conventions of nine States shall be sufficient for the establishment of this Constitution between the States so ratifying the same.

Done in Convention by the unanimous consent of the States present, the seventeenth day of September in the year of our Lord one thousand seven hundred and eighty-seven and of the Independence of the United States of America the twelfth. In witness whereof we have hereunto subscribed our names.

GEORGE WASHINGTON
and thirty-seven others

Amendments to the Constitution*

Amendment I

Congress shall make no law respecting an establishment of religion, or prohibiting the free exercise thereof; or abridging the freedom of speech, or of the press; or the right of the people peaceably to assemble, and to petition the government for a redress of grievances.

Amendment II

A well-regulated militia being necessary to the security of a free State, the right of the people to keep and bear arms shall not be infringed.

Amendment III

No soldier shall, in time of peace, be quartered in any house without the consent of the owner, nor in time of war, but in a manner to be prescribed by law.

Amendment IV

The right of the people to be secure in their persons, houses, papers, and effects, against unreasonable searches and seizures, shall not be violated, and no warrants shall issue but upon probable cause, supported by oath or affirmation, and particularly describing the place to be searched, and the persons or things to be seized.

---

*The first ten amendments (the Bill of Rights) were adopted in 1791.

Amendment V

No person shall be held to answer for a capital, or otherwise infamous crime, unless on a presentment or indictment of a grand jury, except in cases arising in the land or naval forces, or in the militia, when in actual service in time of war or public danger; nor shall any person be subject for the same offense to be twice put in jeopardy of life or limb; nor shall be compelled in any criminal case to be a witness against himself, nor be deprived of life, liberty, or property, without due process of law; nor shall private property be taken for public use without just compensation.

Amendment VI

In all criminal prosecutions, the accused shall enjoy the right to a speedy and public trial, by an impartial jury of the State and district wherein the crime shall have been committed, which district shall have been previously ascertained by law, and to be informed of the nature and cause of the accusation; to be confronted with the witnesses against him; to have compulsory process for obtaining witnesses in his favor, and to have the assistance of counsel for his defense.

Amendment VII

In suits at common law, where the value in controversy shall exceed twenty dollars, the right of trial by jury shall be preserved, and no fact tried by a jury shall be otherwise reexamined in any court of the United States, than according to the rules of the common law.

Amendment VIII

Excessive bail shall not be required, nor excessive fines imposed, nor cruel and unusual punishments inflicted.

Amendment IX

The enumeration in the Constitution, of certain rights, shall not be construed to deny or disparage others retained by the people.

Amendment X

The powers not delegated to the United States by the Constitution, nor prohibited by it to the States, are reserved to the states respectively, or to the people.

Amendment XI
[Adopted 1798]

The judicial power of the United States shall not be construed to extend to any suit in law or equity, commenced or prosecuted against one of the United States by citizens of another state, or by citizens or subjects of any foreign state.

Amendment XII
[Adopted 1804]

The electors shall meet in their respective States, and vote by ballot for President and Vice-President, one of whom, at least, shall not be an inhabitant of the same State with themselves; they shall name in their ballots the person voted for as President, and in distinct ballots the person voted for as Vice-President, and they shall make distinct lists of all persons voted for as President, and of all persons voted for as Vice-President, and of the number of votes for each, which lists they shall sign and certify, and transmit sealed to the seat of government of the United States, directed to the President of the Senate; the President of the Senate shall, in the presence of the Senate and House of representatives, open all the certificates and the votes shall then be counted; the person having the greatest number of votes for President shall be the President, if such number be a majority of the whole number of electors appointed; and if no person have such majority, then from the persons having the highest numbers not exceeding three on the list of those voted for as President, the House of Representatives shall choose immediately, by ballot, the President. But in choosing the President, the votes shall be taken by States, the representation from each State having one vote; a quorum for this purpose shall consist of a member or members from two-thirds of the States, and a majority of all the States shall be necessary to a choice. And if the House of Representatives shall not choose a President whenever the right of choice shall devolve upon them, before *the fourth day of March* next following, then the Vice-President shall act as President, as in the case of the death or other constitutional disability of the President.

The person having the greatest number of votes as Vice-President shall be the Vice-President, if such number be a majority of the whole number of electors appointed; and if no person have a majority, then from the two highest numbers on the list the Senate shall choose the Vice-President; a quorum for the purpose shall consist of two-thirds of the whole number of Senators, and a majority of the whole number shall be necessary to a choice. But no person constitutionally ineligible to the office of President shall be eligible to that of Vice-President of the United States.

Amendment XIII
[Adopted 1865]

Section 1 Neither slavery nor involuntary servitude, except as a punishment for crime whereof the party shall have been duly convicted, shall exist within the United States, or any place subject to their jurisdiction.

Section 2 Congress shall have power to enforce this article by appropriate legislation.

Amendment XIV
[Adopted 1868]

Section 1 All persons born or naturalized in the United States, and subject to the jurisdiction thereof, are citizens of the United States and of the State wherein they reside. No State shall make or enforce any law which shall abridge the privileges or immunities of citizens of the United States; nor shall any State deprive any person of life, liberty, or property, without due process of law; nor deny to any person within its jurisdiction the equal protection of the laws.

Section 2 Representatives shall be apportioned among the several States according to their respective numbers, counting the whole number of persons in each State, excluding Indians not taxed. But when the right to vote at any election for the choice of Electors for President and Vice-President of the United States, Representatives in Congress, the executive and judicial officers of a State, or the members of the legislature thereof, is denied to any of the male inhabitants of such State, being twenty-one years of age and citizens of the United States, or in any way abridged, except for participation in rebellion, or other crime, the basis of representation therein shall be reduced in the proportion which the number of such male citizens shall bear to the whole number of male citizens twenty-one years of age in such State.

Section 3 No person shall be a Senator or Representative in Congress, or Elector of President and Vice-President, or hold any office, civil or military, under the United States, or under any State, who, having previously taken an oath, as a member of Congress, or as an officer of the United States, or as a member of any State legislature, or as an executive or judicial officer of any State, to support the Constitution of the United States, shall have engaged in insurrection or rebellion against the same, or given aid or comfort to the enemies thereof. Congress may, by a vote of two-thirds of each house, remove such disability.

Section 4 The validity of the public debt of the United States, authorized by law, including debts incurred for payment of pensions and bounties for services in suppressing insurrection or rebellion, shall not be questioned. But neither the United States nor any State shall assume or pay any debt or obligation incurred in aid of insurrection or rebellion against the United States, or any claim for the loss of emancipation of any slave; but all such debts, obligations, and claims shall be held illegal and void.

Section 5 The Congress shall have power to enforce, by appropriate legislation, the provisions of this article.

Amendment XV
[Adopted 1870]

Section 1 The right of citizens of the United States to vote shall not be denied or abridged by the United States or by any State on account of race, color, or previous condition of servitude.

Section 2 The Congress shall have power to enforce this article by appropriate legislation.

Amendment XVI
[Adopted 1913]

The Congress shall have power to lay and collect taxes on incomes, from whatever source derived, without apportionment among the several States, and without regard to any census or enumeration.

Amendment XVII
[Adopted 1913]

Section 1   The Senate of the United States shall be composed of two Senators from each State, elected by the people thereof, for six years; and each Senator shall have one vote. The electors in each State shall have the qualifications requisite for electors of [voters for] the most numerous branch of the State legislatures.

Section 2   When vacancies happen in the representation of any State in the Senate, the executive authority of such State shall issue writs of election to fill such vacancies: Provided, that the Legislature of any State may empower the executive thereof to make temporary appointments until the people fill the vacancies by election as the Legislature may direct.

Section 3   This amendment shall not be so construed as to affect the election or term of any Senator chosen before it becomes valid as part of the Constitution.

Amendment XVIII
[Adopted 1919; repealed 1933]

Section 1   After one year from the ratification of this article the manufacture, sale or transportation of intoxicating liquors within, the importation thereof into, or the exportation thereof from the United States and all territory subject to the jurisdiction thereof, for beverage purposes, is hereby prohibited.

Section 2   The Congress and the several States shall have concurrent power to enforce this article by appropriate legislation.

Section 3   This article shall be inoperative unless it shall have been ratified as an amendment to the Constitution by the legislatures of the several States, as provided by the Constitution, within seven years from the date of the submission thereof to the States by the Congress.

Amendment XIX
[Adopted 1920]

Section 1   The right of citizens of the United States to vote shall not be denied or abridged by the United States or by any State on account of sex.

Section 2   The Congress shall have power to enforce this article by appropriate legislation.

Amendment XX
[Adopted 1933]

Section 1   The terms of the President and Vice-President shall end at noon on the 20th day of January, and the terms of Senators and Representatives at noon on the 3d day of January, of the years in which such terms would have ended if this article had not been ratified; and the terms of their successors shall then begin.

Section 2   The Congress shall assemble at least once in every year, and such meetings shall begin at noon on the 3d day of January, unless they shall by law appoint a different day.

Section 3 If, at the time fixed for the beginning of the term of the President, the President-elect shall have died, the Vice-President-elect shall become President. If a President shall not have been chosen before the time fixed for the beginning of his term, or if the President-elect shall have failed to qualify, then the Vice-President-elect shall act as President until a President shall have qualified; and the Congress may by law provide for the case wherein neither a President-elect nor a Vice-President-elect shall have qualified, declaring who shall then act as President, or the manner in which one who is to act shall be selected, and such persons shall act accordingly until a President or Vice-President shall have qualified.

Section 4 The Congress may by law provide for the case of the death of any of the persons from whom the House of Representatives may choose a President whenever the right of choice shall have devolved upon them, and for the case of the death of any of the persons from whom the Senate may choose a Vice-President whenever the right of choice shall have devolved upon them.

Section 5 Sections 1 and 2 shall take effect on the 15th day of October following the ratification of this article.

Section 6 This article shall be inoperative unless it shall have been ratified as an amendment to the Constitution by the Legislatures of three-fourths of the several States within seven years from the date of its submission.

Amendment XXI
[Adopted 1933]

Section 1 The eighteenth article of amendment to the Constitution of the United States is hereby repealed.

Section 2 The transportation or importation into any State, Territory, or Possession of the United States for delivery or use therein of intoxicating liquors, in violation of the laws thereof, is hereby prohibited.

Section 3 This article shall be inoperative unless it shall have been ratified as an amendment to the Constitution by conventions in the several States, as provided in the Constitution, within seven years from the date of submission thereof to the States by the Congress.

Amendment XXII
[Adopted 1951]

Section 1 No person shall be elected to the office of President more than twice, and no person who has held the office of President, or acted as President, for more than two years of a term to which some other person was elected President shall be elected to the office of President more than once. But this article shall not apply to any person holding the office of President when this article was proposed by the Congress, and shall not prevent any person who may be holding the office of President, or acting as President, during the term within which this article becomes operative from holding the office of President or acting as President during the remainder of such term.

Section 2   This article shall be inoperative unless it shall have been ratified as an amendment to the Constitution by the legislatures of three-fourths of the several States within seven years from the date of its submission to the States by the Congress.

Amendment XXIII
[Adopted 1961]

Section 1   The District constituting the seat of Government of the United States shall appoint in such manner as the Congress may direct:

A number of electors of President and Vice-President equal to the whole number of Senators and Representatives in Congress to which the District would be entitled if it were a State, but in no event more than the least populous State; they shall be in addition to those appointed by the States, but they shall be considered for the purposes of the election of President and Vice-President, to be electors appointed by a State; and they shall meet in the District and perform such duties as provided by the twelfth article of amendment.

Section 2   The Congress shall have the power to enforce this article by appropriate legislation.

Amendment XXIV
[Adopted 1964]

Section 1   The right of citizens of the United States to vote in any primary or other election for President or Vice-President, for electors for President or Vice-President, or for Senator or Representative in Congress, shall not be denied or abridged by the United States or any State by reason of failure to pay any poll tax or other tax.

Section 2   The Congress shall have the power to enforce this article by appropriate legislation.

Amendment XXV
[Adopted 1967]

Section 1   In case of the removal of the President from office or of his death or resignation, the Vice-President shall become President.

Section 2   Whenever there is a vacancy in the office of the Vice-President, the President shall nominate a Vice-President who shall take office upon confirmation by a majority vote of both Houses of Congress.

Section 3   Whenever the President transmits to the President pro tempore of the Senate and the speaker of the House of Representatives his written declaration that he is unable to discharge the powers and duties of his office, and until he transmits to them a written declaration to the contrary, such powers and duties shall be discharged by the Vice-President as Acting President.

Section 4   Whenever the Vice-President and a majority of either the principal officers of the executive departments or of such other body as Congress may by law provide, transmit to the President pro tempore of the Senate and the Speaker of the House of Representatives their written declaration that the President is unable to discharge the powers and duties of his office, the Vice-President shall immediately assume the powers and duties of the office as Acting President.

Thereafter, when the President transmits to the President pro tempore of the Senate and the Speaker of the House of Representatives his written declaration that no inability exists, he shall resume the powers and duties of his office unless the Vice-President and a majority of either the principal officers of the executive department(s) or of such other body as Congress may by law provide, transmit within four days to the President pro tempore of the Senate and the Speaker of the House of Representatives their written declaration that the President is unable to discharge the powers and duties of his office. Thereupon Congress shall decide the issue, assembling within forty-eight hours for that purpose if not in session. If the Congress, within twenty-one days after receipt of the latter written declaration, or, if Congress is not in session, within twenty-one days after Congress is required to assemble, determines by two-thirds vote of both Houses that the President is unable to discharge the powers and duties of his office, the Vice-President shall continue to discharge the same as Acting President; otherwise, the President shall resume the powers and duties of his office.

Amendment XXVI
[Adopted 1971]

Section 1   The right of citizens of the United States, who are eighteen years of age or older, to vote shall not be denied or abridged by the United States or by any State on account of age.

Section 2   The Congress shall have power to enforce this article by appropriate legislation.

Amendment XXVII
[Adopted 1992]

No law, varying the compensation for the services of the Senators and Representatives shall take effect, until an election of Representatives shall have intervened.

Presidents and Vice Presidents of the United States

President and political party	Born	Died	President's term of service	Vice president	Vice president's term of service
George Washington (F)	1732	1799	April 30, 1789–March 4, 1973	John Adams	April 30, 1789–March 4, 1793
George Washington (F)			March 4, 1793–March 4, 1797	John Adams	March 4, 1793–March 4, 1797
John Adams (F)	1735	1826	March 4, 1797–March 4, 1801	Thomas Jefferson	March 4, 1797–March 4, 1801
Thomas Jefferson (DR)	1743	1826	March 4, 1801–March 4, 1805	Aaron Burr	March 4, 1801–March 4, 1805
Thomas Jefferson (DR)			March 4, 1805–March 4, 1809	George Clinton	March 4, 1805–March 4, 1809
James Madison (DR)	1751	1836	March 4, 1809–March 4, 1813	George Clinton[a]	March 4, 1809–April 12, 1812
James Madison (DR)			March 4, 1813–March 4, 1817	Elbridge Gerry[a]	March 4, 1813–Nov. 23, 1814
James Monroe (DR)	1758	1831	March 4, 1817–March 4, 1821	Daniel D. Tompkins	March 4, 1817–March 4, 1821
James Monroe (DR)			March 4, 1821–March 4, 1825	Daniel D. Tompkins	March 4, 1821–March 4, 1825
John Q. Adams (DR)	1767	1848	March 4, 1825–March 4, 1829	John C. Calhoun	March 4, 1825–March 4, 1829
Andrew Jackson (DR)	1767	1845	March 4, 1829–March 4, 1833	John C. Calhoun[b]	March 4, 1829–Dec. 28, 1832
Andrew Jackson (D)			March 4, 1833–March 4, 1837	Martin Van Buren	March 4, 1833–March 4, 1837
Martin Van Buren (D)	1782	1862	March 4, 1837–March 4, 1841	Richard M. Johnson	March 4, 1837–March 4, 1841
W. H. Harrison[a] (W)	1773	1841	March 4, 1841–April 4, 1841	John Tyler[c]	March 4, 1841–April 6, 1841
John Tyler (W)	1790	1862	April 6, 1841–March 4, 1845		
James K. Polk (D)	1795	1849	March 4, 1845–March 4, 1849	George M. Dallas	March 4, 1845–March 4, 1849
Zachary Taylor[a] (W)	1784	1850	March 4, 1849–July 9, 1850	Millard Fillmore[c]	March 4, 1849–July 10, 1850
Millard Fillmore (W)	1800	1874	July 10, 1850–March 4, 1853		
Franklin Pierce (D)	1804	1869	March 4, 1853–March 4, 1857	William R. King[a]	March 24, 1853–April 18, 1853
James Buchanan (D)	1791	1868	March 4, 1857–March 4, 1861	John C. Breckinridge	March 4, 1857–March 4, 1861
Abraham Lincoln (R)	1809	1865	March 4, 1861–March 4, 1865	Hannibal Hamlin	March 4, 1861–March 4, 1865

Presidents and Vice Presidents of the United States
(Continued)

President and political party	Born	Died	President's term of service	Vice president	Vice president's term of service
Abraham Lincoln[a] (R)	1808	1875	March 4, 1865–April 15, 1865	Andrew Johnson[c]	March 4, 1865–April 15, 1865
Andrew Johnson (R)	1822	1885	April 15, 1865–March 4, 1869		
Ulysses S. Grant (R)	1822	1885	March 4, 1869–March 4, 1873	Schuyler Colfax	March 4, 1869–March 4, 1873
Ulysses S. Grant (R)			March 4, 1873–March 4, 1877	Henry Wilson[a]	March 4, 1873–Nov. 22, 1875
Rutherford B. Hayes (R)	1822	1893	March 4, 1877–March 4, 1881	William A. Wheeler	March 4, 1877–March 4, 1881
James A. Garfield[a] (R)	1831	1881	March 4, 1881–Sept. 19, 1881	Chester A. Arthur[c]	March 4, 1881–Sept. 20, 1881
Chester A. Arthur (R)	1830	1886	Sept. 20, 1881–March 4, 1885		
Grover Cleveland (D)	1837	1908	March 4, 1885–March 4, 1889	Thomas A. Hendricks[a]	March 4, 1885–Nov. 25, 1885
Benjamin Harrison (R)	1833	1901	March 4, 1889–March 4, 1893	Levi P. Morton	March 4, 1889–March 4, 1893
Grover Cleveland (D)	1837	1908	March 4, 1893–March 4, 1897	Adlai E. Stevenson	March 4, 1893–March 4, 1897
William McKinley (R)	1843	1901	March 4, 1897–March 4, 1901	Garret A. Hobart[a]	March 4, 1897–Nov. 21, 1899
William McKinley[a] (R)			March 4, 1901–Sept. 14, 1901	Theodore Roosevelt[c]	March 4, 1901–Sept. 14, 1901
Theodore Roosevelt (R)	1858	1919	Sept. 14, 1901–March 4, 1905		
Theodore Roosevelt (R)			March 4, 1905–March 4, 1909	Charles W. Fairbanks	March 4, 1905–March 4, 1909
William H. Taft (R)	1857	1930	March 4, 1909–March 4, 1913	James S. Sherman[a]	March 4, 1909–Oct. 30, 1912
Woodrow Wilson (D)	1856	1924	March 4, 1913–March 4, 1917	Thomas R. Marshall	March 4, 1913–March 4, 1917
Woodrow Wilson (D)			March 4, 1917–March 4, 1921	Thomas R. Marshall	March 4, 1917–March 4, 1921
Warren G. Harding[a] (R)	1865	1923	March 4, 1921–Aug. 2, 1923	Calvin Coolidge[c]	March 4, 1921–Aug. 3, 1923
Calvin Coolidge (R)	1872	1933	Aug. 3, 1923–March 4, 1925		
Calvin Coolidge (R)			March 4, 1925–March 4, 1929	Charles G. Dawes	March 4, 1925–March 4, 1929

President	Born	Died	Term	Vice President	Term
Herbert Hoover (R)	1874	1964	March 4, 1929–March 4, 1933	Charles Curtis	March 4, 1929–March 4, 1933
Franklin D. Roosevelt (D)	1882	1945	March 4, 1933–Jan. 20, 1937	John N. Garner	March 4, 1933–Jan. 20, 1937
Franklin D. Roosevelt (D)			Jan. 20, 1937–Jan. 20, 1941	John N. Garner	Jan. 20, 1937–Jan. 20, 1941
Franklin D. Roosevelt (D)			Jan. 20, 1941–Jan. 20, 1945	Henry A. Wallace	Jan. 20, 1941–Jan. 20, 1945
Franklin D. Roosevelt[a] (D)			Jan. 20, 1945–April 12, 1945	Harry S Truman[c]	Jan. 20, 1945–April 12, 1945
Harry S Truman (D)	1884	1972	April 12, 1945–Jan. 20, 1949		
Harry S Truman (D)			Jan. 20, 1949–Jan. 20, 1953	Alben W. Barkley	Jan. 20, 1949–Jan. 20, 1953
Dwight D. Eisenhower (R)	1890	1969	Jan. 20, 1953–Jan. 20, 1957	Richard Nixon	Jan. 20, 1953–Jan. 20, 1957
Dwight D. Eisenhower (R)			Jan. 20, 1957–Jan. 20, 1961	Richard Nixon	Jan. 20, 1957–Jan. 20, 1961
John F. Kennedy[a] (D)	1917	1963	Jan. 20, 1961–Nov. 22, 1963	Lyndon B. Johnson[c]	Jan. 20, 1961–Nov. 22, 1963
Lyndon B. Johnson (D)	1908	1973	Nov. 22, 1963–Jan. 20, 1965		
Lyndon B. Johnson (D)			Jan. 20, 1965–Jan. 20, 1969	Hubert H. Humphrey	Jan. 20, 1965–Jan. 20, 1969
Richard Nixon (R)	1913		Jan. 20, 1969–Jan. 20, 1973	Spiro T. Agnew	Jan. 20, 1969–Jan. 20, 1973
Richard Nixon[b] (R)			Jan. 20, 1973–Aug. 9, 1974	Spiro T. Agnew[b]	Jan. 20, 1973–Oct. 10, 1973
				Gerald R. Ford[c]	Dec. 6, 1973–Aug. 9, 1974
Gerald R. Ford (R)	1913		Aug. 9, 1974–Jan. 20, 1977	Nelson A. Rockefeller	Dec. 19, 1974–Jan. 20, 1977
Jimmy Carter (D)	1924		Jan. 20, 1977–Jan. 20, 1981	Walter F. Mondale	Jan. 20, 1977–Jan. 20, 1981
Ronald Reagan (R)	1911		Jan. 20, 1981–Jan. 20, 1985	George Bush	Jan. 20, 1981–Jan. 20, 1985
Ronald Reagan (R)			Jan. 20, 1985–Jan. 20, 1989	George Bush	Jan. 20, 1985–Jan. 20, 1989
George Bush (R)	1924		Jan. 20, 1989–Jan. 20, 1993	Dan Quayle	Jan. 20, 1989–Jan. 20, 1993
Bill Clinton (D)	1946		Jan. 20, 1993–	Al Gore	Jan. 20, 1993–

Note: D—Democrat; DR—Democratic-Republican; F—Federalist; R—Republican; W—Whig.
a. Died in office.
b. Resigned.
c. Succeeded to the presidency.

Source: Sidney Milkis and Michael Nelson, *The American Presidency* (Washington, D.C.: CQ Press, 1990), 401–403. Copyright © 1990. Data from *Presidential Elections Since 1789*, 4th ed. (Washington, D.C.: Congressional Quarterly, 1987), 4; Daniel C. Diller, "Biographies of the Vice Presidents," in *Guide to the Presidency*, ed. Michael Nelson (Washington, D.C.: Congressional Quarterly, 1989), 1319–1346. Used by permission of CQ Press.

Political Parties in Congress and the Presidency

Year	Presidential candidate		Congress	House			Senate		
	Winner	Loser		Majority	Opposition	Other	Majority	Opposition	Other
1789–1791	F (Washington)	F (Adams)	1st	Ad-38	Op-26	—	Ad-17	Op-9	—
1791–1793	F (Washington)	—	2nd	F-37	DR-33	—	F-16	DR-13	—
1793–1795	F (Washington)	F (Adams)	3rd	DR-57	F-48	—	F-17	DR-13	—
1795–1797	F (Washington)	—	4th	F-54	DR-52	—	F-19	DR-13	—
1797–1799	F (J. Adams)	DR (Jefferson)	5th	F-58	DR-48	—	F-20	DR-12	—
1799–1801	F (J. Adams)	—	6th	F-64	DR-42	—	F-19	DR-13	—
1801–1803	DR (Jefferson)	F (Adams)	7th	DR-69	F-36	—	DR-18	F-13	—
1803–1805	DR (Jefferson)	—	8th	DR-102	F-39	—	DR-25	F-9	—
1805–1807	DR (Jefferson)	F (Pinckney)	9th	DR-116	F-25	—	DR-27	F-7	—
1807–1809	DR (Jefferson)	—	10th	DR-118	F-24	—	DR-28	F-6	—
1809–1811	DR (Madison)	F (Pinckney)	11th	DR-94	F-48	—	DR-28	F-6	—
1811–1813	DR (Madison)	—	12th	DR-108	F-36	—	DR-30	F-6	—
1813–1815	DR (Madison)	F, I, DR (Clinton)	13th	DR-112	F-68	—	DR-27	F-9	—
1815–1817	DR (Madison)	—	14th	DR-117	F-65	—	DR-25	F-11	—
1817–1819	DR (Monroe)	F (King)	15th	DR-141	F-42	—	DR-34	F-10	—
1819–1821	DR (Monroe)	—	16th	DR-156	F-27	—	DR-35	F-7	—
1821–1823	DR (Monroe)	I, DR (Adams)	17th	DR-158	F-25	—	DR-44	F-4	—
1823–1825	DR (Monroe)	—	18th	DR-187	F-26	—	DR-44	F-4	—
1825–1827	C (J. Q. Adams)	DR (Jackson)	19th	Ad-105	J-97	—	Ad-26	J-20	—
1827–1829	C (J. Q. Adams)	—	20th	J-119	Ad-94	—	J-28	Ad-20	—
1829–1831	D (Jackson)	NR (Adams)	21st	D-139	NR-74	—	D-26	NR-22	—
1831–1833	D (Jackson)	—	22nd	D-141	NR-58	14	D-25	NR-21	2
1833–1835	D (Jackson)	NR (Clay)	23rd	D-147	AM-53	60	D-20	NR-20	8
1835–1837	D (Jackson)	—	24th	D-145	W-98	—	D-27	W-25	—
1837–1839	D (Van Buren)	W (Harrison)	25th	D-108	W-107	24	D-30	W-18	—
1839–1841	D (Van Buren)	—	26th	D-124	W-118	—	D-28	W-22	—
1841–1843	W (Tyler)[a]	D (Van Buren)	27th	W-133	D-102	6	W-28	D-22	2

Years	President	Opponent	Congress	House Majority	House Minority	House Other	Senate Majority	Senate Minority	Senate Other
1843–1845	W (Tyler)	—	28th	D-142	W-79	1	W-28	D-25	1
1845–1847	D (Polk)	W (Clay)	29th	D-143	W-77	6	D-31	W-25	—
1847–1849	D (Polk)	—	30th	W-115	D-108	4	D-36	W-21	1
1849–1851	W (Fillmore)	D (Cass)	31st	D-112	W-109	9	D-35	W-25	2
1851–1853	W (Fillmore)	—	32nd	D-140	W-88	5	D-35	W-24	3
1853–1855	D (Pierce)	W (Scott)	33rd	D-159	W-71	4	D-38	W-22	2
1855–1857	D (Pierce)	—	34th	R-108	D-83	43	D-40	R-15	5
1857–1859	D (Buchanan)	R (Fremont)	35th	D-118	R-92	26	D-36	R-20	8
1859–1861	D (Buchanan)	—	36th	R-114	D-92	31	D-36	R-26	4
1861–1863	R (Lincoln)	SD (Breckinridge)	37th	R-105	D-43	30	R-31	D-10	8
1863–1865	R (Lincoln)	—	38th	R-102	D-75	9	R-36	D-9	5
1865–1867	R (A. Johnson)[b]	D (McClellan)	39th	U-149	D-42	—	U-42	D-10	—
1867–1869	R (A. Johnson)	—	40th	R-143	D-49	—	R-42	D-11	—
1869–1871	R (Grant)	D (Seymour)	41st	R-149	D-63	—	R-56	D-11	—
1871–1873	R (Grant)	—	42nd	R-134	D-104	5	R-52	D-17	5
1873–1875	R (Grant)	D, LR (Greeley)	43rd	R-194	D-92	14	R-49	D-19	—
1875–1877	R (Hayes)	—	44th	D-169	R-109	14	R-45	D-29	2
1877–1879	R (Hayes)	D (Tilden)	45th	D-153	R-140	—	R-39	D-36	1
1879–1881	R (Arthur)[c]	—	46th	D-149	R-130	14	D-42	R-33	1
1881–1883	R (Arthur)	D (Hancock)	47th	R-147	D-135	11	R-37	D-37	1
1883–1885	R (Arthur)	—	48th	D-197	R-118·	10	R-38	D-36	2
1885–1887	D (Cleveland)	R (Blaine)	49th	D-183	R-140	2	R-43	D-34	—
1887–1889	D (Cleveland)	—	50th	D-169	R-152	4	R-39	D-37	—
1889–1891	R (B. Harrison)	D (Cleveland)	51st	R-166	D-159	—	R-39	D-37	—
1891–1893	R (B. Harrison)	—	52nd	D-235	R-88	9	R-47	D-39	2
1893–1895	D (Cleveland)	R (Harrison)	53rd	D-218	R-127	11	D-44	R-38	3
1895–1987	D (Cleveland)	—	54th	R-244	D-105	7	R-43	D-39	6
1897–1899	R (McKinley)	D, P (Bryan)	55th	R-204	D-113	40	R-47	D-34	7
1899–1901	R (McKinley)	—	56th	R-185	D-163	9	R-53	R-26	8
1901–1903	R (T. Roosevelt)[d]	D (Bryan)	57th	R-197	D-151	9	R-55	D-31	4
1903–1905	R (T. Roosevelt)	—	58th	R-208	D-178	—	R-57	D-33	—

Political Parties in Congress and the Presidency
(Continued)

Year	Presidential candidate		Congress	House			Senate		
	Winner	Loser		Majority	Opposition	Other	Majority	Opposition	Other
1905–1907	R (T. Roosevelt)	D (Parker)	59th	R-250	D-136	—	R-57	D-33	—
1907–1909	R (T. Roosevelt)	—	60th	R-222	D-164	—	R-61	D-31	—
1909–1911	R (Taft)	D (Bryan)	61st	R-219	D-172	—	R-61	D-32	—
1911–1913	R (Taft)	—	62nd	D-228	R-161	1	R-51	D-41	—
1913–1915	D (Wilson)	PR (Roosevelt)	63rd	D-291	R-127	17	D-51	R-44	1
1915–1917	D (Wilson)	—	64th	D-230	R-196	9	D-56	R-40	—
1917–1919	D (Wilson)	R (Hughes)	65th	D-216	R-210	6	D-53	R-42	—
1919–1921	D (Wilson)	—	66th	R-240	D-190	3	R-49	D-47	—
1921–1923	R (Harding)	D (Cox)	67th	R-301	D-131	1	R-59	D-37	—
1923–1925	R (Coolidge)	—	68th	R-225	D-205	5	R-51	D-43	2
1925–1927	R (Coolidge)	D (Davis)	69th	R-247	D-183	4	R-56	D-39	1
1927–1929	R (Coolidge)	—	70th	R-237	D-195	3	R-49	D-46	1
1929–1931	R (Hoover)	D (Smith)	71st	R-267	D-167	1	R-56	D-39	1
1931–1933	R (Hoover)	—	72nd	D-220	R-214	1	R-48	D-47	1
1933–1934	D (F. Roosevelt)	R (Hoover)	73rd	D-310	R-117	5	D-60	R-35	1
1935–1936	D (F. Roosevelt)	—	74th	D-319	R-103	10	D-69	R-25	2
1937–1938	D (F. Roosevelt)	R (Landon)	75th	D-331	R-89	13	D-76	R-16	4
1939–1940	D (F. Roosevelt)	—	76th	D-261	R-164	4	D-69	R-23	4
1941–1942	D (F. Roosevelt)	R (Willkie)	77th	D-268	R-162	5	D-66	R-28	2
1943–1944	D (F. Roosevelt)	—	78th	D-218	R-208	4	D-58	R-37	1
1945–1946	D (Truman)e	R (Dewey)	79th	D-242	R-190	2	D-56	R-38	1
1947–1948	D (Truman)	—	80th	R-245	D-188	1	R-51	D-45	—
1949–1950	D (Truman)	R (Dewey)	81st	D-263	R-171	1	D-54	R-42	—

Years	President	Opposition candidate	House			Senate		
1951–1952	D (Truman)	—	82nd	D-234	R-199	1	D-49	R-47	—
1953–1954	R (Eisenhower)	D (Stevenson)	83rd	R-221	D-211	1	R-48	D-47	1
1955–1956	R (Eisenhower)	—	84th	D-232	R-203	—	D-48	R-47	1
1957–1958	R (Eisenhower)	D (Stevenson)	85th	D-233	R-200	—	D-49	R-47	—
1959–1960	R (Eisenhower)	—	86th	D-283	R-153	f	D-64	R-34	—
1961–1962	D (Kennedy)	R (Nixon)	87th	D-263	R-174	—	D-65	R-35	—
1963–1964	D (L. Johnson)g	—	88th	D-258	R-177	—	D-67	R-33	—
1965–1966	D (L. Johnson)	R (Goldwater)	89th	D-295	R-140	—	D-68	R-32	—
1967–1968	D (L. Johnson)	—	90th	D-246	R-187	—	D-64	R-36	—
1969–1970	R (Nixon)	D (Humphrey)	91st	D-245	R-189	—	D-57	R-43	—
1971–1972	R (Nixon)	—	92nd	D-254	R-180	1	D-54	R-44	2
1973–1974	R (Nixon)	D (McGovern)	93rd	D-239	R-192	1	D-56	R-42	2
1975–1976	R (Ford)	—	94th	D-291	R-144	—	D-60	R-37	2
1977–1978	D (Carter)	R (Ford)	95th	D-292	R-143	—	D-61	R-38	1
1979–1980	D (Carter)	—	96th	D-276	R-157	—	D-58	R-41	—
1981–1982	R (Reagan)	D (Carter)	97th	D-243	R-192	—	R-53	D-46	1
1983–1984	R (Reagan)	—	98th	D-269	R-165	—	R-54	D-46	—
1985–1986	R (Reagan)	D (Mondale)	99th	D-252	R-182	—	R-53	D-47	—
1987–1988	R (Bush)	—	100th	D-259	R-176	—	D-55	R-45	—
1989–1990	R (Bush)	D (Dukakis)	101st	D-260	R-175	—	D-55	R-45	—
1991–1992	R (Bush)	—	102nd	D-267	R-167	—	D-56	R-44	—

Note: Ad = Administration. AM = Anti-Masonic. C = Coalition. D = Democratic. DR = Democratic-Republican. F = Federalist. I = Independent. J = Jacksonian. L = Liberal Republican. NR = National Republican. Op = Opposition. P = Populist. PR = Progressive. R = Republican. U = Unionist. W = Whig.

[a] And W (W. Harrison).
[b] And R (Lincoln).
[c] And R (Garfield).
[d] And R (McKinley).
[e] And D (F. Roosevelt).
[f] Excludes Hawaii; two senators (one Republican, one Democrat) and one representative (Democrat) seated in August.
[g] And D (Kennedy).

Source: Gary King and Lyn Ragsdale, *The Elusive Executive* (Washington, D.C.: CQ Press, 1988), 426–429. Copyright © 1988. Used by permission of CQ Press.

INDEX

Aaron, Daniel, 87n
AARP. *See* American Association of Retired Persons
Aberbach, Joel, 425n
Abortion rights, 352, 353; executive orders and, 75
Abraham, Henry J., 447n, 457n
Accommodationist persuasion style, 387–388
Acheson, Dean, 271, 275n, 283, 308n
Active presidents. *See* Activism; Presidential activism
Activism: governmental, 32–33; presidential, 31–32. *See also* Governmental activism; Presidential activism
Activist government, restrained president within, 47–50
Adams, John, 38, 39, 94, 111, 240, 430
Adams, John Quincy, 42, 44, 57n, 58n, 95, 111, 119
Adams, Sherman, 204, 236, 246, 250n, 376
Administrative clearance, 239
Advisers: plural presidency and, 85. *See also* Presidential advisers
Advocacy groups, 353
AFDC. *See* Aid to Families with Dependent Children
Affirmative action, 75
African Americans: civil rights of, 348
Agencies, 405 (table): abolishing, 416; creating, 415–416; growth of, 409–411; independent, 411. *See also* agencies by name; Regulatory agencies
Agenda selling, 385–389
Agenda setting, 383–385; after Civil War, 51–52; Congressional dominance over, 43; government, presidential activism and, 63; by Jackson, 45–46; Jefferson and, 40–41; plural presidency and, 396–397; presidential precedents and, 35; Roosevelt, Franklin, and, 71–72; veto power as, 45–46; Washington and, 37–38
Aid to Families with Dependent Children (AFDC), 363
Allison, Graham, 8, 23n, 200, 218n, 425n
Almond, Gabriel, 152n
Ambiguous decision making, 6–7, 17–18, 85, 199–200, 201–202, 252–273, 384
American Association of Retired Persons (AARP), 353, 403
Amicus curiae briefs, 443

Anderson, John, 93
Angola, covert political operations in, 304
Anticommunist globalism, 282–286, 288; ideological clash and, 289–290
Anti-Masons, political conventions and, 95
Apple, R. W., Jr., 251n
Appointments: executive, 435–436; political, 421–423; presidential, 355–356
Appropriations: Congressional committees, 337; president versus Congress, 329 (table)
Area Redevelopment Act (1961), 272
Arthur, Chester, 53–54
Attack politics, 111–112; 114–116
Atwater, Lee, 114

Bailey, Harry, Jr., 59n
Baker, Howard, 257, 381, 428
Baker, James, 209–210, 211, 232, 243, 247, 255, 397
Balanced budgets, 320–321
Ball, George, 192, 266
Barber, James David, 88n, 153n, 212, 213–214, 216, 219n
Bargaining, 265–267
Barger, Harold, 423, 424n
Basler, R.P., 89n
Bay of Pigs, 149, 287, 304
Beard, Charles, 368n
Beard, William, 368n
Behavior, presidential, 138–140
Bennett, William, 428–429
Berman, Larry, 89n, 250n, 457n
Bernstein, Carl, 184n, 219n, 455n
Berry, Jeffrey, 358, 369n
Binkley, Wilfred, 59n
Bipolycentrism, 281
Biskupic, Joan, 89n
Blau, Joseph, 153n
Boland Amendment, 10, 15–16
Bombardier, Gary, 400n
Bond, Jon, 400n
Bork, Robert H., 428
Bowsher v. *Synar*, 437
Braestrup, Peter, 183n
Briefings, White House, 170–171
Brodie, Fawn, 125n
Brody, Richard, 153n
Brown, Stuart, 58n
Brzezinski, Zbigniew, 190, 231, 246, 306–307; influence networks and, 209

Buchanan, James, 49–50, 95
Budget, Bureau of the, 85, 227, 228 (fig.), 316 (fig.), 320–321, 333–338, 339, 418 (table)
Budget and Accounting Act (1921), 237
Budget and Impoundment Control Act (1974), 73–74, 332, 337, 441
Budget committees, in Congress, 337–338
Budget control, presidential, 73–74
Budget deficit, 316–317, 323–324; rise in, 324 (fig.). *See also* Deficit
Budget reconciliation act (1990), 312
Bundy, McGeorge, 194, 231
Bundy, William, 250n
Bureaucracy, 5, 402–406; agencies and, 411; cabinet departments, 411; government corporations, 412; independence of, 406–414; independent regulatory commissions, 411–412; Johnson, Lyndon, and, 419; neutral competency of, 407; Nixon and, 419–420; OMB and, 422–423; pluralist vs. majoritarian outlook of, 408; policy execution and, 417–419; president and, 467; reorganization of, 423–424; size of, 409–412; space and, 409–412; time and, 408–409. *See also* Presidential organization
Bureaucrats, support bases, 412–414
Bureau of the Budget, 225; enrolled bill process, 238
Bureaus. *See* bureaus by name
Burke, John, 275n, 309n
Burns, James MacGregor, 369n, 471n
Burr, Aaron, nomination of, 94
Bush, George, 11, 124n, 213, 215; abortion rights and, 359; advisers of, 204, 205, 243; affirmative action and, 364; banking industry and, 383, 385; campaigns of, 103, 123; Congress and, 390; and crime control, 364; domestic programs of, 344; Dukakis and, 114–116; and Eastern Europe, 278–279; economic policy of, 311–313; education and, 263–264; and election of 1992, 91, 116–117; electoral college and, 118, 121; enforcement of court decisions by, 444; environment and, 254–261, 365; executive orders and, 75; expectations of, 142; health of, 162; honeymoon phase of, 146; ICBM reductions and, 299; image of, 109; and King, Rodney, 342; legislative requests of, 380; logic of pragmatism and, 131–132; as media creation, 155; and Middle East, 291, 292; as national symbol, 138; news management by, 172–173; nonpartisanship of, 134; organization coordination by, 246; Panama intervention by, 9, 82, 187, 297, 298; and Persian Gulf War, 287, 289, 293–294, 434, 458–459, 461, 462, 468; political window and, 267; popularity of, 149–150, 466; and presidential

behavior, 139; and presidential politics, 458–459; press antagonism and, 159; and Reagan Democrats, 105; status of, 470; Supreme Court nominations of, 449; tax increases and, 328; war-making powers of, 80–81
Business: material groups and, 351; money, success, and, 318
Busing, 444
Butterfield, Alexander, 207
Butterfield v. *Stanahan*, 436

Cabinet, 241–242; shadow, 91
Cable News Network (CNN), 168
Caddell, Patrick, 110, 114, 126n
Calhoun, John C., 42, 43, 45
Califano, Joseph, 425n, 471n
Cambodia, 290; secret military efforts in, 303
Campaigns. *See* Presidential campaigns
Campbell, Angus, 125n
Camp David process, 307
Candidates. *See* Presidential elections
Cannon, Carl, 125n
Capitalism, 318; free enterprise, 317–318; laissez-faire, 318; protective, 318–319
Carter, Jimmy, 9, 89n, 153n, 250n; advisers of, 243; appointments by, 355–356; bureaucracy and, 402; campaign of, 103; effectiveness with Congress and, 394–397; and crime control, 364; decision making by, 189–191, 196; diplomatic powers of, 89n; disillusionment phase and, 147; domestic programs of, 233, 262 (table); economic policy of, 313; electoral college and, 122; environmental record of, 365; EOP and, 229; forgiveness phase and, 147–148; government reorganization by, 415, 416; and human rights, 285; Iranian hostages and, 82, 162, 306–307, 464; issue networks and, 209; and judicial selection process, 452–453; legislative agenda of, 73, 380, 387; media events and, 159; and Middle East, 260; and national health insurance, 261–262, 263; as national symbol, 138; organization coordination by, 245–246; peak associations and, 351; personality of, 212, 213, 214; persuasion and, 234, 388–389; political window of, 267; popularity of, compared with Reagan, 148 (fig.); presidential debates and, 113; program timing of, 377–378; public expectations of, 140–141; secretary of state and, 231; secret military operations of, 303; shoe import decision, 204; speeches of, 175; spending politics and, 329; Supreme Court and, 433; and Supreme Court nominations, 445; symbolism and, 136; tax cuts and, 327; war-making powers of, 80

Carter Doctrine, 285
Casey, William, 10, 13
Cassidy, John, 126n
Caucus system. *See* Congressional caucus system; Political conventions
CBO. *See* Congressional Budget Office
CEA. *See* Council of Economic Advisers
Central Intelligence Agency (CIA), 10, 17, 303; and Allende government in Chile, 305; cowboys and, 14; and Iran premier removal, 304; and Vietnam War, 293
Centralization, of White House, 419–421
Chambers, William, 124n
Character, presidential, 212
Checks and balances, 8, 429–430
Cheney, Richard, 156, 246, 247, 251n
Chief executive: president's efforts as, 435; Washington's definition of, 37
Chief legislator: president as, 370, 375
Chief of staff, 246–247, 467
Chile, 305
China, Nixon and, 260
Chosen people: Americans as, 132–133; presidential speeches and, 175
Chou En-Lai, 271
Christian, George, 184n
Chubb, J., 329n, 331n, 340n, 425n
Churchill, Winston, 269
CIA. *See* Central Intelligence Agency
Ciboski, K., 249n
Circuit court appointees, 452 (table)
Civil rights, 363–364; executive orders on, 74; government protection of, 348; Johnson and, 260; Kennedy and, 357; organizations, 8
Civil Rights Act: 1866, 51; 1964, 348; 1990, 8; 1991, 364, 462
Civil service, 407
Civil service commission, 53
Civil Service Reform Act (1978), 416
Civil War, 50–51; presidential restraint after, 51–56
Classical liberalism, government fragmentation and, 358
Clawson, Kenneth, 219n
Clay, Henry, 42, 43, 56, 58n, 95, 119
Clean Air Act: 1970, 365; 1990, 205
Clean Water Act (1987), 365
Cleveland, Grover, 52, 54, 119, 435
Clientele service: Congressional, 412–414; of government departments, 407–408
Clinton, Bill, 91, 124n; campaign of, 103, 104; and election of 1992, 116–117; electoral college and, 121
Coalitions, group support and, 356–357
Cobb, Roger, 152n
Cohen, Michael, 257, 274n
COLAs. *See* Cost-of-living adjustments
Cole, Richard, 250n
Collegial organization coordination, 243–246, 244 (fig.), 245 (table)

Colson, Charles, 219n
Combative persuasion style, 388–389
Combs, James, 183n
Commander in chief, 40, 56,78. *See also* War
Committees, and Congressional budgeting, 337
Committee to Reelect the President (CRP), 207
Communication, White House Office of, 166, 234
Communism, Truman Doctrine and, 282–284
Community action programs, 419
Competition, among presidential advisers, 209–211
Competitive organization coordination, 243, 244 (fig.), 245 (table)
Conaway, James, 250n
Congress, 372–401; activism of, 55; agenda setting by, 43; agreement with presidents, 391–394, 392 (fig.), 393 (table), 395 (table); appropriations and, 329 (table); and budget process, 73–74, 335 (table), 337–338; bureaucratic support by, 412–414; committees in, 42; constitutional relationship of executive with, 29–30; and courts, 429; as decentralized organization, 221; declaration of war by, 40; economic policy and, 314; expansion of presidential activities by, 226; institutional conflict and, 373–375; Jackson vs., 46; legislative liaison and, 385–386; members as presidential nominees, 94; party composition of, 389–390; party control and presidential success, 391, 393 (table); power of, 42; presidents and, 68, 73, 379 (table), 380 (table), 389–397, 436–437, 441–442, 465, 467; problem solving and, 384; Radical Republicans in, 51; rules of, 390–391; sectionalism and, 49–50; war-making role of, 80; and War of 1812, 43
Congressional activism, 51–54
Congressional Budget Office (CBO), 74, 314, 334–335
Congressional caucus system, 94–95
Congressional Relations, Office of, 220, 234, 385
Conservative liberalism: as ideology, 343; and policy congestion, 348–349; political fragmentation and, 349–360
Constitution: bureaucracy and, 402, 406; checks and balances in, 429–430; debates over executive and, 26–30; electoral college and, 118, 119; executive and, 24, 46, 50–51, 57n, 78, 86–87, 91, 460; and governmental fragmentation, 7, 358; judicial power and, 429–430; legislative power and, 29–30; president's role and, 24, 50–51, 78, 86–87, 91; and shared power system of, 371; Supreme

Court as arbiter of, 46; territorial expansion and, 39–40. *See also* Presidential activism; Washington, George
Containment, 283; nuclear retaliation, 284
Contras, 9–16
Conventional military action, as foreign policy instrument, 288–298
Conventions. *See* Political conventions
Coolidge, Calvin, 63, 66–68, 70, 88n, 168, 212, 317
Cooper, Joseph, 250n, 400n
Coordinate review doctrine, 430, 439
Copeland, Gary, 39n
Cornwell, Elmer, 67, 88n, 177, 184n
Corporations, government, 412
Corwin, Edward, 51, 57n, 442, 456n
Cost-of-living adjustments (COLAs), 362
Council of Economic Advisers (CEA), 226, 232, 314, 333
Council on Environmental Quality, 226
Court decisions, presidential enforcement of, 444–445
Courts: appointment to lower, 450–453; presidential influence on, 443–453; presidential nominations to, 445–453; presidents and, 426–457
Covert action, 303–305; political operations, 304–305
Crabbe, Cecil, 283, 308n
Crawford, William, 57n, 58n, 95; electoral college and, 119
Crime control proposals, 364
Cronin, Thomas, 152n, 251n, 471n
Crotty, William, 125n
CRP. *See* Committee to Reelect the President
Cuban missile crisis, 7–8, 204
Culture, and perceptions of presidency, 127–129
Cunningham, Noble, Jr., 124n
Current, Richard, 58n, 125n

Dahl, Robert, 350, 358, 368n, 369n
Dames and Moore v. *Regan*, 433
Danelski, David, 457n
Davis, Dwight, 185n
Davis, Eric, 400n
Davis, James, 124n, 400n
Davis, Richard, 112, 125n
Dean, John, 205–206, 207, 208
Deaver, Michael, 247, 397
Decentralized organization, 85, 199, 200–202, 248, 462; agenda setting and, 383; and policy complexity, 280; presidency as, 6; target specialization of, 234
Decentralized organization of the presidency, 221–223; generalists and, 240–243; presidential coordination and, 243–248; size of, 223–224; specialization patterns of, 230–239
Decentralized persuasion, 385–387

Decision making, 186–187, 188--219; ambiguity of, 6–7, 17–18, 252–273; circles of, 197, 197 (fig.); environments of, 254; out-of-the-ordinary decisions, 191–196; presidential personalities and, 211–216; rational model and, 252–253; routine, 189–191; solutions and, 261–264. *See also* Presidential decision making
Defense agreements, 299
Deferrals, 332
Deficit, 311, 316–317; interest on, 311–312; reduction in, 323–324; rise in, 324 (fig.); spending, 321; trade, 317 (fig.)
DeGrazia, Alfred, 23n, 196–198, 218n, 223, 249n
Democracy: antiparty, 133–134; global, 282, 286–287; passive, 465–466; rhetoric of, 92
Democratic National Committee, 101
Democratic party: allegiance to Ronald Reagan and, 105; liberalism of, 361; political conventions of, 95; and sectionalism, 49–50
Democratic-Republicans, 38, 40–41, 42; caucuses of, 58, 94; Democrats as faction of, 44; National Republicans as faction of, 44–45
Dennis, Jack, 22n, 153n
Departments, 407–411
Depression, 70–71; presidential activism during, 70–72
Détente, Nixon and, 285
Devine, Donald, 152n
Dewey, Thomas, 101, 119
DiClerico, Robert, 218n, 219n, 399n
Diem coup, 191–196, 198, 201–202, 305
Diplomacy, 61; and foreign policy, 299–303; and global democracy track, 301; presidential, 35–37, 39–40, 42, 44, 63, 76–78, 89n, 149
Discrimination, 75, 363–364
Disillusionment phase, of presidential popularity, 146–147
District courts, appointees to, 450–452, 451 (table)
Division of labor, in institutions, 4–5
Domestic affairs, and presidential organization, 233
Domestic Council, 233
Domestic domain, 280, 281, 342–369, 461
Domestic executive action, 440–443
Domestic legislative requests, 379–380, 379 (table), 380 (table)
Domestic policy, 278; agenda setting and, 37–38; Bush and, 458–459; executive action and, 37; fragmentation and, 359–360; Washington's precedents and, 37–39. *See also* Domestic domain
Domestic policy instruments, 360–366
Domestic Policy Office, 354
Domestic Policy Staff, 220, 233, 385

Domestic policy track: and classic liberalism, 345–346, 348–349; and modern liberalism, 346–349

Domestic programs, 260 (table); 262 (table)

Domestic stability, president's powers and, 435

Dominican Republic: emergency intervention in, 296; troops in, 136

Duong Van "Big" Minh, 195

Dowd, Maureen, 126n

Dual executive. *See* Plural presidency

Dukakis, Michael: campaign against Bush, 114–116; electoral vote and, 118; PACs and, 352; and Reagan Democrats, 105

Dulles, John Foster, 284

Eastern Europe (1989–1990), 278–279

Easton, David, 153n

Economic affairs, and presidential organization, 232–233

Economic aid, foreign, 299–301

Economic competition, and global democracy, 287

Economic Opportunity, Office of (OEO), 233, 419

Economic Opportunity Act (1964), 419

Economic policy, 276–277; of Bush, 311–312; domain of, 314–317; political policy as, 313–314

Economic policy instruments, 325–333

Economic policy track, 317–325; fiscal policy and, 320–325; free enterprise capitalism and, 317–318; government intervention and, 318; monetary policy and, 319–320; protective capitalism and, 318–319

Economic security, covert political operations and, 304

Economy: government responsibility for, 319; as policy domain, 280, 281; presidential impact on, 150, 461

Edelman, Murray, 153n, 157, 182n

Edwards, George C., III, 153n, 183n, 250n, 400n, 414n, 424n, 457n, 471n

Ehrlichman, John, 169, 172, 184n, 205, 207, 208, 233, 243, 247, 251n

Eisenhower, Dwight D., 213, 214; and balanced budgets, 320–321; executive orders and, 75; full employment and, 322; Indochina war and, 268–269; and interstate highway program, 344; and Iran covert political operations, 304; and Laos, 290; and massive nuclear retaliation, 284; nondiscrimination and, 363; organization coordination by, 246; popularity of, 143; press conferences of, 169; primary elections and, 96; program style of, 376–377; secret military operations of, 303; Social Security system

and, 347; Supreme Court nominations of, 448; tax cuts and, 325; television use by, 68

Eizenstadt, Stuart, 190, 246

Elder, Charles, 152n

Elderly, public assistance to, 347–348

Elections, 90–126; campaigns, 460; of 1828, 47; of 1832, 46, 47; of 1840, 47–48; of 1988, 114–116; of 1992, 116; general, 102–117; group efforts and, 354–355; primaries and, 98–102; reforms and, 47

Electoral college, 29, 91, 117–122; and popular election of electors, 47

Elementary and Secondary Education Act (1965), 364

El Salvador, Reagan and, 434

Emancipation Proclamation, 50

Emergency actions, of presidents, 50–51

Emergency interventions, 79, 81–83, 296–298

Emergency Management, Office for, 225, 226

Employment, federal civilian, 410 (table)

Employment Act (1946), 226

Enrolled bill process, 238–239

Entitlement programs, 311, 329–330, 331 (fig.)

Environment: Bush and, 470; groups concerned with, 352; presidential, 197 (fig.), 198–199; and public good, 365; quality of, 226; U.S. position and, 301–302

Environmental policy, 254–261

Environmental Protection Agency (EPA), 365

EOP. *See* Executive Office of the President

EPA. *See* Environmental Protection Agency

Europe, social welfare states in, 318

European Community, 281

Executive: appointments by, 435–436; constitution and, 26–30; constitutional provisions for, 29–30; as policymaker, 45. *See also* Presidency; President(s)

Executive action: government and presidential activism and, 63; Jackson and, 45; and post–Civil War presidents, 52–54; presidential precedents and, 35; states' rights and, 45; Supreme Court and, 435–436; Washington and, 37

Executive agencies, 413

Executive agreements: international, 76; presidential power and, 433; since Roosevelt, Franklin, 77 (table)

Executive branch, 5, 404–405 (table); budget timetable of, 334 (table)

Executive Office of the President (EOP), 221, 227–228, 229, 420; chief of staff and, 467; creation of, 225

Executive orders, 74–75; since Roosevelt, Franklin, 75 (table)

Gallup Poll, and presidential popularity, 243

Gans, Herbert, 183n

Garfield, James, 53, 54, 95, 103, 407

General Agreement on Tariffs and Trade (GATT), 301

General elections, 102–117; campaigns for, 102–104; as horse race, 112–113; image and, 108–112; and incumbent performance, 107–108; organization for, 103

George, Alexander L., 244n

Gerry, Elbridge, 58n

Gilbert, Clinton, 66, 88n

Ginsburg, Douglas, 428–429, 448

Global democracy, 282, 286–287, 288; economic competition and, 287; military solutions and, 287; nuclear deterrence and, 299

Global warming, policy ambiguity about, 254–261

GNP. See Gross national product

Goal ambiguity, 255–256

"Going native" problem, 421–422

Goldman, Peter, 126n

Goldman, Sheldon, 451n, 457n

Goldsmith, William, 57n

Goldwater, Barry, 89n, 111, 354

Goldwater v. *Carter*, 433

Gorbachev, Mikhail, 128, 286

Government: civil rights protection by, 348; departments of, 407–408; as employer, 62; expenditures of, 62; growth of bureaucracy, 409–411; growth of federal civilian employment, 410 (table); market regulation by, 61–62; public assistance of, 347–348; size of, 403

Governmental activism, 60–62; expansion of, 72–73; joined with presidential activism, 62–63; during New Deal, 72; and presidents as lawmakers, 69–73; theory of, 32

Governmental restraint theory, 33, 43

Governmental theories, 32–33

Government corporations, 412

Government fragmentation, 202–203, 357–359, 461–462

Government intervention: in economic affairs, 318; in foreign affairs, 33; social insurance and, 362; in society, 33

Graber, Doris, 158n, 162, 182n, 183n

Gramm, Phil, 340n

Gramm-Rudman-Hollings Balanced Budget and Emergency Deficit Control Act (1985), 323–324, 437

Grant, Ulysses S., 52, 53, 450

Grass-roots caucus/convention, 98

Gray, L. Patrick, 207, 208

Great Britain: elections in, 90, 91; monarchy in, 128; nominating system in, 94–95

Great Depression (1930s), 318–320

Great Society, 72, 347, 348, 349, 419

Greener, William, Jr., 166, 183n

Greenstein, Fred, 135, 153n, 184n, 214, 219n, 275n, 309n, 471n

Grenada, 147, 159, 296, 297, 303

Grossman, Michael, 154n, 157, 176, 177, 177n, 178n, 179, 180, 182n, 249n, 369n

Gross national product (GNP), 315; adjusted for inflation, 315 (fig.); entitlement payments and, 331 (fig.)

Group fragmentation, 202–203, 350–357, 461–462; and advocacy groups, 353; and appointments, 355–356; and election efforts, 354–355; of expressive groups, 352–353; of interest groups, 351–352; and policy proposals, 356–357; and presidential interest politics, 353–354; and White House institution, 8–9

Groups: advocacy, 353; expressive, 352–353; material, 351–352; and presidential interest politics, 353–357

Groupthink, 206–207, 216; Watergate and, 207–209

Growth dividend, 330

GSA. See General Services Administration

Guatemala: coup in, 199; U.S. role in removing Arbenz government, 304

Guthrie, K. Kendall, 185n

Hager, George, 340n

Halberstam, David, 275n

Haldeman, H.R., 204, 205, 207, 208, 219n, 246–247

Hamilton, Alexander, 30, 31–32, 36, 57n, 89n, 368n, 455n, 471n; courts and, 444; and executive role, 28; Federalists and, 38; governmental activism and, 56; judiciary and, 430; public opinion and, 468; strong government and, 39; war declaration and, 78

Harding, Warren, 1, 3, 63, 66, 70, 73, 168, 237

Harkins, Paul, 193, 194–195, 201

Harrison, Benjamin, 52, 54, 55, 119

Harrison, William Henry, 48, 55

Hart, Gary, 110

Hart, Roderick, 176, 184n

Hartz, Louis, 368n

Hayes, Rutherford B., 52, 53, 54, 55

Head Start, 329, 419

Heclo, Hugh, 61, 87n, 197, 218n, 250n, 251n, 414, 422, 425n, 471n

Heineman, Ben, Jr., 250n

Herdon, W. H., 89n

Hersh, Seymour, 183n, 219n

Hershey, Marjorie, 115–116, 126n

Hertsgaard, Mark, 183n

Hessler, Curtis, 250n

Hierarchical organization coordination, 246–247, 244 (fig.), 245 (table); chief of staff and, 246–247

Hierarchy, in decentralized organization, 200

Hinckley, Barbara, 88n, 152n, 184n, 251n
Hirabayaski v. *United States*, 435
Hirschfield, Robert, 57n
Hirsh, Herbert, 153n
Hodgers, A.G., 59n
Hodgson, Godfrey, 153n
Hofstadter, Richard, 87n
Hollings, Ernest, 340n
Honeymoon phase: of popularity, 143, 146; press relations during, 179–180; and program timing, 378
Hoopes, Townsend, 308n
Hoover, Herbert, 63, 66, 214, 215; activism of, 70–71; and balanced budget, 320; legislative liaison and, 234; pragmatic politics and, 132; press conferences of, 168; primary elections and, 96; radio use by, 67; Supreme Court nominations of, 449, 450
Horton, Willie, 115
House of Representatives, 42, 119, 337
Hughes-Ryan Amendment, 12
Human rights, Carter and, 285
Humphrey's Executor v. *United States*, 436
Humphrey, Hubert, 96–97, 104, 107, 119, 240
Hussein, Saddam, 168, 287, 291, 458, 468
Hyde, James, 250n
Hyperimagery, 110

Ideological clash, 289–290
Ideology: in Congress, 390; and domestic policy, 343; and personality types, 215
Image: and elections, 108–112; and passive democracy, 465–466; power of, 463–466; as simplification, 2; single presidency, 1–4. *See also* Single executive image
Imminent hostilities, 82–83
Impeachment, and Tyler, 48. *See also* Johnson, Andrew; Nixon, Richard
Imperial presidency, 469, 470
Imports and exports, presidential activism and, 40
Impoundment, 332, 441
Income: policies, 333; redistribution of, by taxation, 62
Incumbent, performance of, 107–108
Independent agencies, 411
Independent regulatory commissions, 411–412
Indian affairs, 61
India-Pakistan War (1971), 421
Individualism, 129–131; fallacy of symbol, 130
Indochina, war in, 268–269
Inflation, 327; and supply-side economics, 322. *See also* Economic policy
Influence networks, 209–211, 210 (table)
Information, vs. news, 163–165
Informational ambiguity, 201, 254–255
Information broker, chief of staff as, 247

INF treaty. *See* Intermediate-range nuclear force treaty
Inherent powers doctrine, 440, 441
Initiatives, and presidential popularity, 150–151
Injunctions, and presidential power, 441
In re Debs, 435
In re Neagle, 435
Institutional ambiguity, of presidency, 6–7
Institutional conflict, Congress, president, and, 373–375
Institutional features, of presidency, 188–189. *See also* Decision making; Plural presidency
Institutional politics, 466–469
Insurance, social, 361–363
Intercontinental ballistic missile warheads (ICBMs), 299
Interest groups, fragments of, 351–353
Interinstitutional environment, 198, 254
Intermediate-range nuclear force (INF) treaty, 286
Internal plurality, 199–202
International agreements, 299, 300 (table); by regime type (1949–1983), 302 (table)
International crises, and presidential popularity, 149
International political market, 314–317
International Trade Commission (ITC), 189
Interstate Commerce Act (1887), 52
Interstate highway program, 344
Intervention, in economic affairs, 318
Invisible hand, in economics, 318
Iran: Carter administration and, 306–307; coup in, 198; hostages and, 82, 162; secret military efforts in, 303; U.S. role in removing premier, 304
Iran-contra affair, 217; chronology of events in, 14 (table); explanation of, 468; and plural presidency, 4, 9–16
Iraq, 80. *See also* Hussein, Saddam; Persian Gulf War
Isolation, of president by advisers, 206–209
Israel, and Iran-contra affair, 11–12
Issue networks, 209, 210 (table)
Issue specialization, of presidential organization, 230–233

Jackson, Andrew, 44–47, 58n, 88n, 153n; agenda setting by, 45–46; attack politics and, 111; and Bank of the U.S., 430–431; and bureaucratic independence, 406; courts and, 430, 439; electoral college and, 119; and executive action, 45; national bank and, 45–46; nomination of, 95; presidential organization of, 224; public leadership of, 44; rating of, 143; and single executive image, 55; and states' rights, 45; veto power expansion by, 45–46

Jackson, Jesse, 115, 116
Jackson, John, 125n
Jackson, Robert H., 440, 453–454
Janis, Irving, 206–207, 208, 216, 219n, 275n
Japan, planned economy in, 318
Japanese, internment of, 434–435
Jaros, Dean, 153
Jay, John, 38, 89n, 368n, 455n, 471n
Jay Treaty, 36, 38
Jefferson, Thomas, 58n; activism as legacy of, 42; agenda setting by, 40–41; attack politics and, 111; courts and, 430; Democratic-Republicans and, 38; free press and, 159; as lobbyist, 387; nomination of, 94; presidential organization of, 224; public leadership and, 41; rating of, 143; and Washington's foreign affairs, 37
Johnson, Andrew, 51–55
Johnson, Loch, 88n
Johnson, Lyndon, 211, 214–215; advisers to, 205; attack politics and, 111; and budget deficits, 322; cabinet and, 241; civil rights and, 260, 363–364; Congress and, 390; and covert political operations, 304; and crime control, 364; domestic programs of, 262 (table); education and, 263; electoral college abolition and, 122; executive orders and, 75; foreign policy role of, 76; Great Society of, 347; groupthink and, 207; imperial presidency and, 469; legislature and, 72, 380, 385–386; news leaks and, 172; organization coordination by, 245; persuasion style of, 388; policy ambiguity and, 264; popularity of, 150; and presidential behavior, 139; public policy and, 260; secret military operations of, 303; speeches of, 175; Supreme court nominations of, 449; symbolism and, 136–137; taxes and, 327, 328; as vice president, 240; and Vietnam War, 79–80, 195, 289, 291, 292, 295–296; war-making powers of, 83; and War on Poverty, 329–330; and White House centralization, 419
Johnson, Richard T., 245n, 251n
Jones, Charles, 340n, 457n
Jones, Howard, 275n, 308n
Judicial review, 430–431
Judiciary: expansion of presidential power by, 432–438; independence of, 429–432; interpretations by, 371; presidential selection of nominees to, 445–453
Justice Department, 443

Kaid, Lynda, 185n
Kearns, Doris, 399n
Kegley, Charles, 308n
Kennan, George, 283, 308n

Kennedy, John F., 213, 214, 215; advisers and, 203, 204, 243; and Bay of Pigs, 287; budget cuts and, 227; cabinet and, 241; civil rights and, 262–263, 363–364; congressional rules and, 390–391; covert political operations of, 304; and Cuban missile crisis, 7–8, 204; decision making and, 188; Diem coup and, 191–196, 198, 201, 202, 305; domestic programs of, 262 (table); electoral college and, 121; emotional reactions to, 136; executive orders and, 75; and flexible response, 284–285; funds impoundment and, 332; group support and, 355, 357; groupthink and, 207; and ideological clash, 290; Keynesian economics and, 321–322; Khrushchev meeting and, 149; legislature and, 380, 385–386, 387; and national security adviser, 231; news stories and, 177; Nixon debate with, 108; nonpartisanship of, 134; organization coordination by, 245; political time and, 272, 273; popularity of, 150; presidential power and, 469; press and, 160, 169; primary elections and, 96; program timing of, 378; reorganization attempts of, 229; secret military operations of, 303; speeches of, 175; spending politics and, 329; staff internal conflict and, 266; Supreme Court nominations of, 449; tax cuts and, 325, 326–327; television use by, 68; and Vietnam War, 291, 293
Kennedy, Robert F., 96, 97, 243
Kernell, Samuel, 184n, 251n
Kessel, John, 209, 210, 219n, 369n
Ketcham, Ralph, 58n
Keynesianism, 321–322
Killian, Johnny, 89n, 457n
King, A., 368n
King, Gary, 89n, 152n, 171n, 184n, 228n, 249n, 250n, 340n, 369n, 446n, 451n, 456n
Kingdon, John, 274n, 275n, 369n, 383, 400n
Kissinger, Henry, 130, 152n, 204, 206, 231, 247, 421, 425n; briefings by, 171; leaks by, 171–172; Vietnam and, 305
Knight, Kathleen, 153n
Korean War, 79, 294; costs of, 295; as ideological clash, 272, 289; and presidential popularity, 150; Truman and, 271–272; as unlimited limited war, 292
Korematsu v. *United States*, 435
Kozak, D., 249n
Kumar, Martha, 154n, 157, 176, 177, 178n, 179, 180, 249n, 282n, 369n

La Follette, Robert, 93, 95–96,124n
Laissez-faire capitalism, 318
Laos: ideological clash and, 290; secret military efforts in, 303

Lawmaker, president as, 69–73
Leadership: moral, 133; precedents and, 35; public, 38–39; public expectations of, 141 (table), 141–143
League of Nations, 65
Lebanon, and emergency intervention, 296; marines in, 82, 83
Legal Policy, Office of, 453
Legal-tender decisions, 457n
Legislation: executive orders; civil rights, 363–364; New Deal, 71–72; OMB and, 238. See also Congress
Legislative Affairs, Office of, 234, 385, 386
Legislative agenda, presidential persuasion and, 385–387. See also Agenda setting
Legislative agenda-setting power: of Carter, 73; of Johnson, Lyndon, 72; of Kennedy, 72; of Nixon, 72; of Reagan, 72; of Roosevelt, Franklin, 72–73; of Truman, 72
Legislative delegation, of presidential power, 436–437
Legislative liaison, 234, 385–386, 397
Legislative power, 42. See also Congress
Legislative process. See Congress; Presidential activism; Presidential restraint
Legislative Reference Division, of OMB, 238
Legislative veto, 437
Levy, Leonard, 58n
Liaison Office for Personnel Management, 225
Liberalism: classical, 345–346, 348–349; modern, 346–349
Light, Paul, 154n, 250n, 262n, 274n, 379n, 399n, 471n
Limited war, 79–81, 288–289; costs of, 295–296; domestic uses of, 294–295; winning, 294
Lincoln, Abraham, 50–51; campaign costs of, 102; courts and, 430, 439; habeas corpus and, 439; martial law and, 442; public and, 151, 466; rating of, 143; war-making powers and, 83–84
Lindblom, Charles E., 274n, 351, 368n
Line-item veto, 381
Livingston, William, 400n
Lobbyist, president as, 387–389
Locke, John, 345–346
Lodge, Henry Cabot, 192, 195, 201
Lorant, Stefan, 59n
Lower courts, appointment to, 450–453
Lowi, Theodore, 361, 369n
Lukas, Anthony, 185n

MacArthur, Douglas, 150, 272, 292
MacKenzie, G. Calvin, 250n
Maclay, William, 57n
Madison, James, 29, 31–32, 42–43, 89n, 358, 368n, 455n, 471n; and executive action, 37; factions and, 350; and presidential restraint, 31; war-making powers of, 83
MAD strategy. See Mutual assured destruction strategy
Management and Budget, Office of. See OMB
Manheim, Jarol, 170n, 184n
Marbury v. Madison, 430
March, James, 23n, 257, 274n
Margolis, Lawrence, 88n
Market regulation, governmental, 61–62
Marshall, John, 36, 430
Marshall, Thomas, 124n
Martial law, 439
Martz, Larry, 126n
Mason, Edward C., 58n
Material groups, 351–352
Matusow, Barbara, 183n
Mayaguez, 9, 296, 297, 303
Mayer, Jane, 23n, 184n, 250n
Mayhew, David, 465, 471n
McCarthy, Eugene, 96
McClure, Robert, 125n
McCulloch v. Maryland, 45, 431
McDonald, Forest, 58n
McFarlane, Robert "Bud," 10, 13, 15. See also Iran-contra affair
McGinniss, Joe, 125n, 139, 153n
McGovern, George, 101; campaign costs of, 103
McGovern-Fraser Commission, nominating convention reforms and, 97–98
McKinley, William, 52, 55, 76, 449
McManus, Doyle, 23n, 184n, 250n
McNamara, Robert, 166, 193, 293
McPherson, Harry, 275n
Media: campaign coverage by, 112–113; Coolidge, and, 67; news-making and, 160–165; as news organization, 155; presidential, 155–185; presidential race coverage by, 91–92; Roosevelt, F., and, 68
Media Liaison Office, 165–166, 234
Media primary, 101–102
Medicaid, 329, 330
Medicare, 329, 330, 347, 362
Meese, Edwin, 247, 397, 428
Meltsner, A., 218n
Middle East: American prestige and, 290–291; Carter and, 260. See also Iran; Iraq
Military action: emergency interventions as, 296–298; as foreign policy instrument, 288–298
Military affairs: government and presidential activism and, 63; judicial expansion of presidential power in, 434–435; presidential activism in, 51; secret, 303. See also War
Military policy, 280–281. See also Foreign policy

Military power, unilateral presidential actions and, 79. *See also* War
Military strategies, 2
Military tribunals, presidential authority and, 439
Milkis, Sidney, 59n, 88n
Miller, Merle, 309n
Miller, William, 87n
Minorities rule, 350
Miroff, Bruce, 152n, 463, 464, 471n
Mississippi v. *Johnson*, 435
Mitchell, John, 207, 426
Moe, Terry, 425n
Mondale, Walter, 110, 121, 148, 190, 240
Monetary policy, 319–320
Monroe, James, 42, 44, 76
Monroe Doctrine, 44
Moral principles, presidential public appeals and, 64
Mueller, John, 153n, 309n
Mufson, Steven, 340n
Mulcahy, Kevin, 308n
Multilateral trade negotiations, 301
Murray, Robert, 88n
Mutual assured destruction (MAD) strategy, 298
Myers v. *United States*, 436

NAACP. *See* National Association for the Advancement of Colored People
Nathan, James, 295, 309n
Nathan, Richard, 407, 423, 425n, 471n
National agenda. *See* Policy agendas
National Association for the Advancement of Colored People (NAACP), Kennedy and, 355
National bank, 43, 44–46, 48
National Defense Council, 233
National Education Association (NEA), 355
National health insurance, 261–262
National Industrial Recovery Act, 347, 442
National Organization for Women, 353
National Republicans, 44–45, 46, 111
National Resources Planning Board, 225
National Security Act (1947), 226
National security adviser, 85, 230
National security affairs, presidential organization for, 230–232
National security and prestige, foreign policy and, 290–292
National Security Council (NSC), 10, 14, 85, 160, 192, 226, 230–231, 299; and Diem overthrow, 195
NATO. *See* North Atlantic Treaty Organization
NEA. *See* National Education Association
Nelson, Michael, 59n, 88n, 125n, 184n, 369n
Network television, 161–163
Neustadt, Richard, 151, 154n, 399n, 471n

Neutrality Act, 36
New Covenant, 117
New Deal, 71–72, 319, 328–329, 348, 349
New Federalism, 72
New Freedom, 65, 70
New Frontier, 72, 285
News: content of, 163–165; production of, 160–163; White House control of, 159
News conferences, televised, 68–69
News management, 165–173; daily White House story as, 176–181; leaks as, 171–172; presidential drama and, 173–176; press conferences, 168–170; results of, 172–173; story coordination as, 165–168; White House briefings and, 170–171
News media. *See* Media
News organizations, types of, 155–156
New York Times v. *United States*, 441
Ngo Dinh Diem, 191–196, 198, 201–202, 305
Nguyen Khanh, 195
Nguyen, Van Thieu, 305
Nhu (Vietnam), 191, 192
Niemi, Richard, 369n
Nimmo, Dan, 183n
Nixon, Richard, 207, 219n, 251n; administration leaks and, 171; advisers of, 204, 205–206; budget preparation and, 237; bureaucracy politicization of, 421–422; cabinet and, 241; campaign costs of, 103; campaign momentum of, 104; and Chile government overthrow, 305; China and, 163, 260; civil rights and, 364; communication strategy of, 166; courts and, 426–427, 440; and crime control, 364; defense agreements and, 299; and détente, 285; domestic policy operation and, 233; domestic programs of, 262 (table); economic policy of, 313; electoral college and, 119, 121; environmental record of, 365; expectations of, 142; foreign policy of, 76, 285, 306; funds impoundment and, 332; gatekeepers of, 246–247; government reorganization by, 416; group support and, 356; groupthink and, 207–209; honeymoon phase of, 146; image makers and, 108–109; impeachment and, 59n; imperial presidency and, 469, 470; impoundment and Supreme Court, 441; issue networks and, 209; Kissinger and, 130; legislative agenda setting of, 62; legislature and, 380, 385–386; OMB and, 263; organization coordination by, 246–247; personality of, 211, 212, 214, 215, 216; persuasion style of, 388; policy implementation by, 227; and presidential ambiguity, 151; presidential organization of, 248; press and, 159, 169–170; program style of, 376; program timing of, 379; scandal and, 150; secret military

Plural presidency, 4–9; agenda setting and, 396–397; bureaucracy and, 423–424; components of, 85; decentralized organization of, 367; decision making and, 186–187, 188–219, 276–277; and Diem overthrow, 195; external plurality and, 202–203; and foreign policy complexity, 306; four dimensions of, 16–18; and garbage can policymaking approach, 271–273; and group demands, 357; influence on court cases, 443; interest politics and, 353; internal plurality, 199–202; needs for, 84–85; Nixon and, 333; OMB and, 239; plausible deniability of, 18; and presidential activism, 84–85; presidential advisers and, 204–211; program ambiguity and, 384; and responsive competence, 417–423; secret policy operations and, 9–16; and single executive image, 19–20, 370–371, 461–462; and White House internal staff conflict, 265–266. *See also* Presidential decision making
Pocket vetoes, 381
Poindexter, John, 13, 23n. *See also* Iran-contra affair
Police actions, wars as, 78
Policy: agendas, 69–74; ambiguity, and global warming, 254–261; domestic, 342–369; economic, 311–341; public appeals for support of presidential, 68
Policy complexity, 16, 85, 278, 366–367; basis of, 279–280; foreign policy, 278–310; inconsistencies in, 7–8; Nixon and, 208–209; and plural presidency, 202; of presidency, 7–8
Policy decisions, approaches to, 271–273
Policy Development, Office of, 354, 385, 386–387
Policy environments, 198, 254
Policy initiatives, 276
Policy instruments, 306–307
Policymaker, president as, 131–132
Policymaking, perspective distortions and, 272. *See also* Iran-contra affair
Policy messages, media and, 157
Policy performance, expectations of, 140–141, 141 (table)
Policy planning, as news stories, 180
Policy proposals, 2, 7
Policy stands, and presidential appeals, 65
Policy tracks, 282; foreign policy, 282–287
Political action committees (PACs), 352
Political appointees, in bureaucracy, 421–423
Political campaigns. *See* Presidential campaigns
Political candidate, image of perfect, 110
Political conventions: brokered, 95–97;

grass-roots caucus and, 98; primary elections and, 98–102
Political culture, 127, 129–134, 152n
Political fragmentation, 17, 85, 202–203, 278, 279; conservative liberalism and, 349–360; domestic policy and, 359–360; government, 357–359; group fragmentation, 350–357; and legislative priorities, 383; and plural presidency, 202–203; of presidency, 8–9
Political operations, covert, 304–305
Political parties: attitudes toward, 92–93; as barriers to democracy, 92–93; and Congressional composition, 389–390, 391; decline of, 101–102; defections among identifiers, 106 (fig.); Democrats as faction of Democratic-Republicans, 44; development of, 42; early, 38; as factions, 92–93; identification with, 105–106, 125n; National Republicans and, 44–45; nominating convention reforms and, 97–102; presidential independence from, 133–134; presidential parties and, 354; sectionalism and, 49–50. *See also* Democratic-Republicans; Federalists; Whigs
Political policy, and economic policy, 277, 313–317
Political primaries. *See* Primary elections
Political symbols, 135–137
Political time, 269–270, 374
Political windows, 267
Politics: and domestic programs, 263; institutional, 466–469; of problems and policies, 264–267
Polk, James, 48–49, 81, 83
Pollard, James, 184n
Polls. *See* Public opinion polls
Polsby, Nelson, 101, 125n
Polycentrism, 281
Pomper, Gerald, 121, 126n, 369n
Popkin, S., 251n
Popularity. *See* Presidential popularity
Popular vote, 118–119
Porter, Roger, 250n
Powell, Jody, 181–182, 243
Power: decentralization of, 222; from election victories, 91; of executive, 27; governmental, 34–35; multiple theories of, 33–35; presidential, 31–32, 34–35; and single executive image, 2, 91
Power centers, international, 281
Power criterion, of single executive image, 26–56
Pragmatism, 131–132, 135
Precedents: of active and restrained presidents, 35–55; and agenda setting, 40–41; of Congressional power, 42; of Jefferson, 39–41; public leadership and, 41; war-making powers and, 40
Presidency: as decentralized organization, 221–223; disarray after Lincoln, 51–55;

and governmental theories, 32–33; imperial, 469, 470; institutional features of, 4–9, 188–189; personalization of, 64–69; power of, 1; of restraint, 26–59; and sectionalism, 49–50; single executive image of, 1–4. *See also* Electoral college; Plural presidency; Single executive image
President(s), 1–2; accountability of, 442–443; and budget process, 336–337; bureaucracy and, 402–425; Congressional concurrence with, 391–394, 392 (fig.), 393 (table), 395 (table); courts and, 426–457; creating power of image, 463–466; daily news story about, 176–181; diplomacy of, 76–78; drama as news management strategy, 173–176; and executive branch, 5; Executive Office of, 222, 222 (table); familiarity with, 2–3; ideal, 93, 102; as individual vs. image, 25; influence on judiciary, 443–453; inherent powers doctrine of, 440; isolation by advisers, 206–209; as lawmaker, 69–73, 74–75; legislative agendas of, 466–467; as lobbyist, 387–389; mediated intimacy via television, 68; personalities and, 196, 211–216; policy implementation by, 227; and policymaking/policy execution distinction, 417–419; policy proposals and group support, 356–357; popularity and Congressional success, 391; precedents of, 35–55; public appeals of, 64–66; public appearances by, 174 (fig.); as public celebrities, 69; public perceptions of, 127–153; relationships with key advisers, 196–198, 197 (fig.); as single executive image, 459–461; social insurance provided by, 361–363; speech themes of, 173–176; as spokesperson on foreign relations, 432–434; State of the Union message use by, 375; success in Congress of, 389–397; Supreme Court as check on, 438–443; Supreme Court nominations by, 445–450, 446 (table), 447 (table); time of voters' decisions for, 104 (table); unique position of, 3; vetoes by, 380–381, 382 (table); visibility of, 2. *See also* Executive; Plural Presidency; Presidential decision making; Single executive image
Presidential activism, 24, 60–61, 62–63, 60–87; and budget control, 73–74; after Civil War, 51–55; Constitution and, 86; during Depression, 70–72; in diplomacy, 36–37; and foreign policy, 279; and growth of presidential organization, 225–227; of Jackson, Andrew, 44–47; and Jefferson's public leadership, 41; joined with governmental activism, 62–63; and liberal reform, 347; of Lincoln, 50–51; Monroe and, 42; of Polk, 49; precedents of, 35–37; presidents

as lawmakers, 69–73; of Roosevelt, Franklin, 71–72; of Roosevelt, Theodore, 62–63; single executive image, plural presidency, and, 84–85; and Speaker of the House, 42; Supreme Court acceptance of, 434; theory of, 31–32; of Washington, 35–39; of Wilson, 62–63. *See also* Diplomacy; War
Presidential advisers, 204–211; access to president and, 205–209; cabinet as, 241–242; cohesiveness among, 205, 206–207; competition among, 209–211; immediate, 242–243; loyalty of, 205–206; and presidential personality, 216
Presidential ambiguity, 252–275; and garbage can approach to policy decisions, 271–273; goal ambiguity, 255–256; informational, 254–255; operational, 256–257; participatory, 257–261; politics of, 264–267; presidential time and, 268–271; solution to, 261–264
Presidential appointments, for group support, 355–356
Presidential campaigns, 102–104; Bush/Dukakis, 114–116; feel of, 114–117; money for, 102–103; organization and, 103; strategies of, 103–104; voters' perceptions of, 104–113
Presidential debates, televised, 113
Presidential decision making, 188–217; ambiguity of, 252–273; circles of, 197, 197 (fig.); foreign policy complexity and, 280; and presidents' personalities, 196; processes of, 253–261
Presidential economics, 311–341
Presidential elections, 90–126, 460, 463. *See also* Presidential nominations
Presidential environment, 197 (fig.), 198–199, 216
Presidential interest politics, 353–357
Presidential leadership, public opinion and, 38–39
Presidential nominations: brokered conventions, 95–97; phases to, 94–98
Presidential organization, 220–251; coordination of, 243–247, 244 (fig.), 245 (table); cuts in, 227–228; decentralized, 221–247; paradoxes about, 228–229; staff hiring and, 236
Presidential personalities, 211–216; character and, 213–214; dimensions of, 212–214; pitfalls of studies, 214–216
Presidential popularity, 143–151; blunders and, 149; diplomacy and, 149; disillusionment phase of, 146–147; economy and, 150; forgiveness phase of, 147–148; honeymoon phase of, 146; initiatives and, 150–151; international crises and, 149; presidents' initiatives and, 150–151; quiescence and, 149; rating of, 145 (fig.); scandal and, 150; ups and downs of, 148–151; waging war and, 149–150

Presidential power(s), 460–461; in emergencies, 50–51; judicial expansion of, 438; legislative delegation of, 441–442; means and, 34; Supreme Court and, 427–428; theories of, 31–32; war and, 40
Presidential-press symbiosis, 156–160, 176, 179, 181–182
Presidential programs: and Congress, 375–380; timing of, 377–380; types of, 376–377
Presidential ratings, 144 (fig.)
Presidential restraint: after Civil War, 51–55; of Coolidge, 66; and governmental activism, 47–50; of Harding, 66; of Hoover, 66; Jefferson and, 39–41; and patronage, 52–54; post-Civil War, 51–56; slavery and, 43; Taft, William Howard, and, 65–66; theory of, 31–32; of Whigs and Republicans, 49–50. *See also* Jefferson, Thomas
Presidential restraint theory, 31–32; policy agenda of Washington and, 37–38
Presidential time, 268–271; Nixon and, 270–271; organizational, 268–269; political, 269–270
Press: briefings, 166; conferences, 168–170, 170 (fig.), 171 (table). *See also* Media; Presidential-press symbiosis
Press secretaries, presidential, 156–157, 166
Price, and wage politics, 332–333
Primary elections, 91; candidate and, 98; emergent, 95–97; media, 97–98; money for, 100; and political conventions, 98–102; rise of presidential, 99 (table); television coverage of, 99–100; uncommitted delegates, 98
Pringle, Henry, 88n
Private sector, liberalism and, 348
Problem solving, president and, 131–132. *See also* Decision making
Progressives, 62, 69–70, 347
Protective capitalism, 318–319
Public appeals, for policy support, 68
Public appearances, and news management, 174 (fig.)
Public assistance, 347–348, 362–363
Public expectations, of president, 137–143
Public leadership: of Adams, John Quincy, 44; in early 20th century, 63–69; government and presidential activism and, 63; of Jackson, 44, 47; Jefferson and, 41; of Monroe, 44; of post-Civil War presidents, 54–55; presidential precedents and, 35; and presidential restraint, 66; radio politics ad, 66–68; Washington and, 38–39
Public Liaison, Office of, 8, 234, 235
Public opinion: polls, 101, 112; presidential influence on, 75; presidents as leaders of, 63–64; use of symbolism to manipulate, 137

Public relations, 467–468
Public spectacles, 463–464
Public support, president and, 38
Pump priming. *See* spending politics

Quasi-legislative/quasi-judicial agencies, 456n
Quiescence, 135–136, 149

Racial discrimination, 363–364
Racism, 152n
Radical Republicans, 51, 53
Radio politics, 66–68
Ragsdale, Lyn, 89n, 152n, 154n, 171n, 184n, 185n, 228n, 249n, 250n, 340n, 369n, 400n, 446n, 451n, 456n
Rather, Dan, 159, 162
Rational model of decision making, 252–253
Reagan, Ronald, 211, 212, 216, 218n, 250n; abortion rights and, 359; affirmative action dismantling and, 364; budget cuts and, 331, 332; bureaucracy politicization of, 422; COLAs and, 362; communication strategy of, 166–167; Congress and, 390, 394, 396, 397; and crime control, 364; defense agreements and, 299; disillusionment phase and, 147; economic policy of, 313; electoral college and, 121; and El Salvador, 434; enforcement of court decisions by, 444–445; and environmental quality, 226, 229, 365; and evil empire, 286; executive orders and, 75; foreign policy domain of, 281; forgiveness phase and, 147; government reorganization by, 416, 417; Grenada and, 82, 297, 464; groups supporting, 355, 356; image of, 109; influence networks and, 209–210; and Iran-contra affair, 9–16, 468; and judicial selection process, 452–453; Lebanon and, 82–83; legislature and, 380, 385–386; Libya raids and, 137; news and, 164, 172, 177; OMB and, 237, 239; organizational cuts of, 228; organization coordination by, 247; persuasion and, 235, 388; policy congestion and, 344; popularity of, 148 (fig.), 150; presidential interest politics and, 353; presidential party for, 354; press conferences of, 169–170; program style of, 376; public expectations of, 140–141; and Reagan Democrats, 105; scandal and, 150; secret military operations of, 303; social insurance cutbacks and, 363; Social Security benefit cutbacks and, 349; speeches of, 175; and supply-side economics, 322–323, 327; Supreme Court appointments of, 428–429; symbolism and, 157; tax cuts and, 327–328; television coverage of, 162; vetoes and, 381; war-making powers of, 80

Reaganomics, 72, 322–323
Reciprocal Trade Act (1934), 301
Reconciliation, and budget, 335, 338
Reconstruction, 51–55
Reductionism, and personality studies, 215–216
Reform, liberal, 346–348
Regan, Donald, 209, 217, 233
Regulation: agencies for, 70; governmental, 61–62; Roosevelt, Theodore, and, 65
Regulatory commissions, independent, 411–412
Rehnquist, William, 455n
Reilly, William, 205, 255, 257–258
Relyea, Harold, 249n
Reorganization Act (1939), 225
Reorganization plans, presidential, 414–415
Republican party, 49; conservatism of, 360–361; Lincoln and, 50; Radical Republicans, 51; western states and (1972–1988), 120 (fig.)
Rescissions, 332
Resolutions, as budget guidelines, 335
Responsibility, and plural presidency, 18, 19
Restraint. See Presidential restraint
Richardson, James D., 57n, 59n, 455n
Robertson, James, 152n
Robinson, Michael, 125n
Rockman, Bert, 425n
Roe v. Wade, presidential enforcement of, 444–445
Rohde, David, 399n
Rom, Mark, 340n, 369n
Roosevelt, Franklin D., 213, 215; as activist president, 71–72; budgets and, 237, 320; briefings of, 170; executive orders and, 74–75; foreign policy of, 76; funds impoundment and, 332; government reorganization by, 417; and Japanese internment, 434–435; and liberal reform, 347; organization coordination by, 243; persuasion and, 234; popularity of, 149; presidential organization of, 224–225; presidential power and, 469; presidential time and, 271; press conferences of, 169; program style of, 376; and public, 67–68; rating of, 143; social insurance and, 361–362, 363; spending politics and, 328–329; Supreme Court nominations of, 449; war powers of, 78–79; White House organization and, 248
Roosevelt, Theodore, 32, 57n, 62–65, 69–70, 76, 87n, 93, 142, 143, 168, 347, 460
Rose, Richard, 425n, 471n
Rubin, Richard, 88n, 125n, 184n
Rubner, Michael, 84, 89n
Rudman, Warren, 340n
Rust v. Sullivan, 75

Safire, William, 166, 183n
Salisbury, Robert, 352, 368n
Salomon, Lester, 87n, 250n, 251n , 425n, 471n
SALT. See Strategic Arms Limitation Talks
Sanders, Elizabeth, 340n, 416, 425n
Scandal, and presidential popularity, 150
Schattschneider, E.E., 261, 274n
Schechter Poultry Company v. United States, 441, 442
Schick, Allen, 341n
Schlesinger, Arthur, Jr., 58n, 251n, 471n
Schlozman, Kay, 354n, 425n
Schubert, Glendon, 455n
Scigliano, Robert, 455n
Secord, Richard, 10, 11, 12, 13. See also Iran-contra affair
Secret operations, Iran-contra affair and, 9–16
Sectionalism, 43; presidency and, 49–50; on Supreme Court, 449
Segregation, 75, 363
Selective Service Act (1948), 440
Senate: Supreme Court confirmations by, 449–450, 451–453; Finance Committee, 337–338; Supreme Court nominees and, 446 (table); treaty making and, 36
Senatorial courtesy, 451–452
Senior Executive Service (SES), 416
Separation of powers, 8
SES. See Senior Executive Service
Shadow cabinet, 91
Shafritz, Jay, 59n
Sheatsley, Paul, 153n
Sheehan, Margaret, 125n
Sheldon, Courtney, 401n
Sherman Anti-Trust Act (1890), 52
Shoe imports, 189–191, 218
Shull, Steven, 250n, 400n
Shultz, George, 11, 15, 159, 172
Shuman, Howard, 334n, 335n
Sidey, Hugh, 278, 308n
Sigel, Roberta, 22n
Sigelman, Lee, 153n, 401n
Simon, Dennis, 154n, 399n
Simplification, as political symbol, 135
Single executive image, 1–4, 24–25; bureaucracy and, 403, 423; Bush and, 311, 458–461; constitutional power and, 26–59; decision making and, 188–217; in diplomacy, 76–78; elections and, 91, 92–94; and foreign affairs, 305–307; and foreign policy complexity, 279; foundations of, 155–182; and group demands, 357; journalism and, 160–165; legislative proposals and, 375; media primary and, 102; Nixon and, 333; party seesaw and, 41; permanent emergence of, 63–87; and plural presidency, 19–20, 186–187, 370–371; and policy complexity, 366; power criterion and, 25–26, 84; president's personality and, 211; presidential

Territorial expansion, 49, 61
Tet offensive, 162
Thomas, Clarence, 449, 450
Thomas, Norman, 250n, 457n
Thompson, K., 23n, 89n
Tierney, John, 354n, 425n
Timing, of presidential programs, 377–380
Tocqueville, Alexis de, 350, 368n
Tonkin Gulf Resolution, 79–80, 81
Totalitarianism, 282–284
Tourtellot, Arthur, 249n
Tower Commission Report, 17, 23n
Trade: agreements, 299; associations, 351–
  352; deficit in, 317 (fig.); presidential
  decisions about, 189–191
Train v. *City of New York*, 441
Tran Van Dan, 194
Treasury Department, 232, 237
Treaties, 36, 39–40, 76–77, 433
Truman, David, 350, 368n
Truman, Harry S, 211, 213, 275n, 309n,
  340n; and balanced budgets, 320; bipolycentric system and, 281; and bureaucracy, 424; electoral votes and, 119;
  executive orders and, 75; foreign policy
  and, 76, 281; groupthink and, 207; and
  Korean war, 79, 271–272, 289, 292, 294;
  legislature and, 72, 234; limited war in,
  288; news stories and, 177; popularity
  of, 150; presidential organization of,
  226; press conferences of, 169; program
  style of, 376; segregation and, 363;
  speeches of, 175; staff growth and, 228;
  State of the Union message and, 375;
  steel mill seizure and, 440, 442; tax cuts
  and, 325; television use by, 68; War
  Powers Resolution and, 82
Truman Doctrine, 198, 282–284, 287, 295
Tulis, Jeffrey, 58n, 86, 88n
Tunstall, Jeremy, 183n
Turtellot, Arthur, 59n
Tyler, John, 48, 76

Ullmann, Owen, 183n
"Uncontrollables," spending programs as,
  330–331
Unilateral presidential action: as com-
  mander in chief, 56; in diplomacy, 77–
  78; of Lincoln, 51; precedent in treaty
  making, 37; war-making powers, 79
Uniqueness, and single executive image,
  2, 91
United Nations Conference on the Envi-
  ronment, 257, 281
United States Circuit Judge Nominating
  Commission, 452
Unlimited limited wars, 292–294
Urban problems, 329, 342–343
U.S. v. *Brig Aurora*, 436
U.S. v. *Curtiss-Wright Export Corporation*,
  76, 432–433
U.S. v. *Nixon*, 427, 440

U.S. v. *U.S. District Court for the Eastern
  District of Michigan*, 441
U.S. Immigration and Naturalization Service
  v. *Chadha*, 437

Valenti, Jack, 205, 219n, 400n
Van Buren, Martin, 47
Vance, Cyrus, 231–232, 246, 307
Verba, Sidney, 152n
Veto, 45–46, 52, 55–56, 380–381, 382
  (table)
Vice presidents, 240–241
Vietnam War, 79–80, 81, 291–294; costs
  of, 295–296; as ideological clash, 289;
  inflation and, 330; overthrow of Diem
  and, 191–196; and presidential popularity, 150; secret military efforts in, 303;
  television coverage of, 162; voters and,
  107
Vinegar, Richard, 185n
Visibility: mediated images and, 156; presidential, 156–160; of presidential candidates, 92; and single executive image,
  2, 91
Voters, 104–114

Wage and price politics, 332–333
Wallace, George, 93, 119, 121, 403
War: declared, 78; domestic problems
  associated with, 434–435; emergency
  intervention as, 81–83; Jefferson and,
  40; limited, 288–289; Lincoln's activism
  and, 50–51; at pleasure, 83–84; presidency after Jefferson and, 42–43; presidential activism during, 434–435; and
  presidential popularity, 150–151; presidential powers, 78–84; presidential
  precedents and, 35
Warner, Malcolm, 183n
War of 1812, 43
War on Poverty, 329–330, 348
War Powers Resolution (1973), 9, 80–83,
  434
Washington, George, 30, 215; as active
  president, 35–39; bureaucracy and, 406;
  Neutrality Proclamation of, 57; presiden-
  tial organization of, 224
Watergate conspiracy, 138, 206, 207–209,
  426
Watson, Richard, 457n
Wayne, Stephen, 125n, 250n, 400n, 424n,
  457n, 471n
Weaver, R. Kent, 331n, 340n
Webster, Carol, 153n
Weinberger, Caspar, 11, 15, 23n, 210–211
Weisman, Steven, 183n
Weisskopf, Michael, 218n
Welfare, 362–363
West, William, 250n
Western expansion, presidential restraint
  and, 43
Whigs, 41, 46–50, 95

White, Leonard, 58n
White House, 5–6; agenda setting and, 383; centralization of, 419–421; communication strategy of, 166–167; as decentralized organization, 367; decentralization and legislative agendas, 385–387; and Federal Reserve Board, 319–320; generalists in, 240–243; internal conflict of, 265–266; judicial nominees selection by, 445–453, 446 (table), 447 (table); news management by, 165–173, 176–181; office fragmentation in, 359; offices in, 5, 353–354; outside bargains, political windows, and, 266–267; personnel office of, 448; press relations with, 157–158. *See also* Presidential organization
White House aides, 210 (table). *See also* Presidential advisers
White House Chief Counsel, Office of, 448
White House Judicial Selection Committee, 453
White House Office: growth of, 227, 228 (fig.); enlargement of, 228–229

Wicker, Tom, 250n
Wildavsky, Aaron, 23n, 182n, 218n, 251n; 340n, 400n–401n
Williams, T. Harry, 58n, 125n
Wilson, Woodrow, 59n, 87n, 152n, 206, 214, 351, 399n; activism of, 62–63; diplomacy and, 76; and liberal reform, 347; presidency and, 460; and presidents as lawmakers, 70; press conferences of, 168; public appeals of, 64–65; rating of, 143; restraint of, 55; Supreme Court nominations of, 449; veto and, 380; vice president and, 241; war powers and, 78
Windt, Theodore, Jr., 369n
Wiretaps, and presidential power, 441
Wise, David, 183n
Wittkopf, Eugene, 308n
Woodward, Bob, 183n, 184n, 219n, 309n, 455n, 471n
Woolley, John, 340n
World War II, programs after, 72–73

Yeltsin, Boris, 299
Youngstown Sheet and Tube Co. v. Sawyer, 440, 453